California Real Estate Finance

NINTH EDITION

California
Real Estate
Finance

NINTH EDITION

Robert J. Bond, Ph.D.
Certified Financial Planner

John Fesler
Consultants West Financial Service, Inc.

Rick Boone
Orange Coast College, Costa Mesa
Investment Realtor®

United States

California Real Estate Finance, Ninth Edition
Robert J. Bond, John Fesler, and Rick Boone

Vice President/Editor-in-Chief: Dave Shaut

Acquisitions Editor: Sara Glassmeyer

Developmental Editor: Arlin Kauffman, LEAP Publishing

Editorial Assistant: Michelle Melfi

Senior Marketing and Sales Manager: Mark Linton

Senior Manufacturing Buyer: Charlene Taylor

Senior Art Director: Pamela Galbreath

Content Project Management: Pre-PressPMG

Production Service/Compositor: Pre-PressPMG

Copyeditor: Pre-PressPMG

Cover Designer: Jeff Bane, CMB Design, Ltd.

Cover Image: (top) Chris Rodenberg Photography; (center) Shutterstock/Michael Ransburg; (bottom) Shutterstock/Sklep Spozywczy

Permissions Acquisition Manager/Text: Mardell Glinkski-Schultz

Permissions Acquisition Manager/Photo: Deanna Ettinger

For product information and technology assistance, contact us at
OnCourse Learning & Sales Support, 1-855-733-7239.

For permission to use material from this text or product.

Library of Congress Control Number: 2010925129

ISBN-13: 978-0-538-79832-7

ISBN-10: 0-538-79832-7

OnCourse Learning
3100 Cumberland Blvd Suite 1450
Atlanta, GA 30339
USA

Printed in the United States of America
2 3 4 5 6 7 17 16 15

Brief Contents

Contents

8 QUALIFYING THE PROPERTY 196

9 QUALIFYING THE BORROWER 234

12 CONSTRUCTION LOANS 328

13 BASIC MATHEMATICS OF REAL ESTATE FINANCE 354

14 CREATIVE FINANCING APPROACHES 402

15 FINANCING SMALL INVESTMENT PROPERTIES 444

Preface

This ninth edition is prepared to not only refine the readers' understanding of the basic real estate lending practices, but deals with the enormous changes that have occurred in the financial arena during the past several years. The subprime mortgage days of "easy money" and flexible qualifying guidelines is presented as a backdrop to the continuing changes in rules and regulations designed to rein in the excesses of those heady days, when it seemed that "anyone could get a loan."

For the real estate novice, this edition resolves much of the mystery surrounding real estate financing and its terms and basic principles. For the more experienced, the increasingly complicated aspects of real estate lending and the new legislative mandates are made easier to understand. A plus for all readers is the detail given to the new developments in real estate financing that impact not only the real estate practitioner but every real estate buyer and seller.

NEW TO THIS EDITION

This edition is one of the most current and practical textbooks on real estate financing principles and practices in California. An alphabet of acronyms describes the numerous, newly legislated rules and regulations that touch practically every aspect of real estate financing. We have addressed the new regulations and discuss the positive and negative aspects of each. The Home Valuation Code of Conduct (HVCC), which we review in Chapter 8, is a good example of legislation passed to control perceived abuses in the appraisal process, but which has resulted in unintended consequences.

The Home Mortgage Disclosure Act (HMDA) is treated for the first time. Alternative mortgage instruments (AMIs) and other loan variations, hard money loans, new buyer qualification requirements, buyer and seller closing costs, and other topics are discussed to increase understanding of these financing principles.

Additional changes in this ninth edition include:

- Chapter 1: A discussion of what happened to create the financial problems of the last decade and a look ahead to the rules and regulations that will likely guide future financing.

- Chapter 2: A look at the growing role of government regulatory agencies and an expanded review of each agency's goals, rules, and oversight obligations.

- Chapter 3: An explanation of the Mortgage Loan Disclosure Act (MLDA) and a new Truth-in-Lending form which identifies new time frames for disclosure information and, in turn, impacts the time required to initiate the appraisal process. A detailed discussion of the new Mortgage Loan Disclosure Statement (MLDS), designed to provide more accurate disclosure information to borrowers. Also, an explanation and review of the new Fraud Enforcement Act (FERA) regarding its intention and likelihood of controlling fraudulent loan practices.

- Chapter 4: The introduction of the hybrid loan and an enhanced review of the positive and negative aspects of adjustable rate mortgage financing. A necessary look at all the aspects of the reverse mortgage (which is important, as its use by seniors continues to increase). A thorough explanation of the advantages of biweekly mortgages and how to establish them. Finally, a Case & Point discussion of the government's intervention to reduce foreclosures.

- Chapter 5: The modified role of real estate practitioners to keep up with lender policy changes. The emerging new rules around conventional financing result in new buyer qualification guidelines, changes in private mortgage insurance (PMI) coverage, and the revised use of buy-down loans. A detailed explanation of the Stimulus Bill as well as its affect on lending practices into the future.

- Chapter 6: A look at the new FHA rules, including what might be expected in 2010. The current and future role of government-sponsored entities (GSEs) and the continuing role of Fannie Mae and Freddie Mac.

- Chapter 7: Details of the new required Good Faith Estimate (GFE) form and its attempt to reign in abusive practices related to yield spread premium (YSP). A discussion of the positive and negative aspects of YSP along with an evaluation of the new form itself. The expectations for Fannie Mae and Freddie Mac going into the next year. Updated changes to Fannie Mae and Freddie Mac as they have adjusted to the new financial climate.

- Chapter 8: Full details of the Home Valuation Code of Conduct (HVCC) (its imposition has caused significant changes to the appraisal process). New suggestions to help real estate agents relate to appraisers in this changing environment.
- Chapter 9: An introduction of new risk-based qualification and pricing models and how borrowers are impacted by these more restrictive policies.
- Chapter 10: Introduction of the new Mortgage Disclosure Improvement Act (MDIA). An explanation of how borrowers are impacted by the increased emphasis on disclosure and the resulting increase in documentation.
- Chapter 11: Expanded information on short sales and foreclosures to reflect their increase during the last several years. An explanation of the government's efforts to restore the housing sector of the economic spectrum.

Although the revisions in the final chapters are less dramatic than those in the preceding chapters, the following information is introduced:

Chapter 9: The Case&Point looks at the real estate representative's need to function at his or her best ability in order to flourish in this more competitive environment.

Chapter 12: Mello-Roos Community Facilities Act and its impact on some home purchases.

Chapter 13: Introduction of the Qualifier Plus IIIx Calculator.

Chapter 14: The changes in secondary financing rules and their impact on selling options.

Chapter 15: The regulations now imposed because of the past use of "flips" by investors.

Global Changes: Vocabulary and terms surrounding real estate financing have grown with the alphabet soup of the new regulations. While the financial language can at first seem complicated, as you progress through the chapters, you will find that the text makes them easier to understand. The glossary will add to your understanding and is a great asset when you need to check the meaning of a word or term. Use of the online flashcards for electronic vocabulary review at www.cengage.com/realestate/bond is recommended.

Case & Point: Recognizing this as a unique period in real estate financing, nearly every chapter includes this feature, which provides insight into past and present financial developments.

With so much of our lives influenced by the Internet, readers will appreciate the numerous references to helpful websites sprinkled throughout the text. Although some Internet-related resources appear in some chapters, the new Appendix discusses specific uses and groups potential sites based on the information being researched. Over time, some sites are likely to become outdated and irrelevant, and some may try to "sell" products or services to the public. However, to the extent that they prove useful, they are included throughout the text and in the Appendix. It should be noted that the inclusion of firms promoting their lending policies and products on the Web is not meant to construe endorsement of the firms or their offerings.

Each chapter in the book is self-contained, allowing instructors to adapt the book to various course formats. Instructors and students alike will appreciate the multiple-choice questions and the questions for discussion—both designed for testing, learning, and review of the material covered in each chapter.

ACKNOWLEDGMENTS

Any book, in its final form, is the result of the time and talents of many individuals. While we cannot acknowledge all of the contributors, we are grateful for their review of information, their insights, and their suggestions—all of which have enhanced this edition. We hope that we have successfully included the information that they so generously provided.

We would also like to express our appreciation to those who served as reviewers and who provided insightful comments and valuable suggestions.

Robert Anderson
Los Angeles City College

Martin Welc
Saddleback College

About the Authors

Robert J. Bond is an alumnus of the College for Financial Planning. Prior to becoming a certified financial planner, he worked in a variety of fields related to finance, including banking, real estate brokerage, real estate consulting, and financial advising. Bob has taught at CSULA, UCLA, the American Institute for Continuing Education, and the College for Financial Planning. He spent 30 years teaching courses in finance, real estate, and investments at Los Angeles Valley College before his retirement. Past publications include *Getting Started in California Real Estate, California Real Estate Principles, Real Estate Practice, Real Estate Finance, Personal Finance*, and *The HP-12C in Action!* Bob was an editorial reviewer for the Real Estate Educators Association Journal and real estate columnist for the *Antelope Valley Press*. He is also an active member of the National Association of Real Estate Editors. Bob developed the telecourse and was the on-camera instructor and consultant for the educational series, *Real Estate and You*, produced through the Southern California Consortium for Instructional Television. He also wrote and produced videotapes for a variety of real estate continuing education courses, including creative financing, ethics, and other DRE-approved courses.

John Fesler was an Anthony Schools Instructor for the RE license exam prep for six years. He was also a weekend instructor at Hancock Community College for community subjects, including understanding your credit, preparing for a loan, and understanding investment properties. John was a California Association of REALTORS® (CAR) instructor authorized to teach the state-required ethics course. He was also the committee chairman for a local Real Estate Association Long-Range Planning Committee and Grievance Committee and served on the Professional Standards Committee. He has trained real estate licensees in understanding the FHA, in using the real estate calculator, and in financing. John is currently involved in the educational field as an instructor for real estate finance at College of the Redwoods, Eureka, CA, as well as the developer and author of the information found at the educational site www.humboldthomeloans.com.

Rick Boone teaches real estate classes part time at Orange Coast College, Costa Mesa, and continues working full time as an investment REALTOR®. Enjoying both industries, he is able to use real life situations and examples to further enhance students' understanding of classroom material. Rick also uses his experience to represent other part-time teachers at his district as a vice president of the teachers union and member of the negotiations team. Graduating with a BA from Biola University, La Mirada, CA, Rick believes that education is very important. He continues his own, currently pursuing an MBA at CSU Fullerton.

Authors' Note

The field of real estate financing, by its very nature, is a continuing work in progress and creates a constant challenge to remain current and up-to-date. The information contained herein will hopefully start you on a successful and satisfying journey into this exciting world and encourage your continuing search for the most recent changes. May you blossom as you travel over each page of this text and in your potential real estate career.

Dedication

Dennis McKenzie

The world of real estate lost a legend with the passing of Dennis McKenzie. Authoring many books that changed and shaped real estate education, Dennis was a well-recognized course author and instructor and the recipient of the CARET Teacher of the Year award. Dennis was the director of the College of the Redwoods' real estate curriculum and was a popular real estate course instructor.

We will miss Dennis' infectious enthusiasm, his inquisitive mind, and his inexhaustible energy. His contributions to California real estate education and to the overall real estate community will be long remembered.

Bob Bond
John Fesler
Rick Boone

California
Real Estate
Finance

NINTH EDITION

Chapter

1

PREVIEW

This chapter provides a short overview of real estate finance. After completing this chapter, you should be able to:

1. Describe current financing trends in the real estate market.
2. Trace the flow of money and credit into the mortgage market.
3. Discuss the role of the Federal Reserve System.
4. List five characteristics of the California mortgage market.
5. Explain and illustrate two basic types of promissory notes.
6. Describe the differences among a deed of trust, a mortgage, and an installment sales contract.

Introduction to Real Estate Finance

1.1 WELCOME TO THE REAL WORLD OF REAL ESTATE FINANCING

Great wealth has been created via investment in real estate. But real estate is expensive and few people ever accumulate sufficient savings to pay with cash alone. Most real estate transactions depend, therefore, on a buyer's ability to obtain financing. Without it, most people can't buy the real estate.

Even people who have sufficient funds rarely pay cash for real estate but elect to use "other people's money" in order to maximize the investment potential of their purchase. Income tax deductions and investment yields (as noted in a later chapter) also encourage purchasing with borrowed funds, called "leverage." Thus, whether by necessity or by choice, financing is essential for most real estate transactions.

A Bit of History

Historically, real estate financing had operated within a fairly established set of rules. The guidelines identified down payment, credit, income, and employment experience requirements. Qualifying ratios based upon a borrower's income compared to the monthly mortgage payments prevailed. Loan guideline flexibility was limited and potential buyers had to demonstrate an ability to "afford" the mortgage payments.

Then in 2000 lending regulations were relaxed in an effort to allow more borrowers to qualify to purchase a home. Investors wanted higher returns on their money and pressured banks to lend money. Increasing home values, coupled with the prevailing attitude that more people should be able to purchase a home, resulted in a

3

relaxation of qualifying requirements and buyers acquiring loans for which they could qualify but, as it turned out, could not afford. During the next few years, more and more lenient loan options were introduced. So-called "liar loans" were widely used to allow otherwise unqualified borrowers to purchase homes. This, in turn, fueled an explosion of home appreciation.

As home values grew, owners were encouraged to tap their growing equity and use the funds for consumer spending. Home-owners were besieged with offers to use their equity for everything from buying a vehicle to taking that dream vacation. Many accepted the fantasy that property values would continue to escalate and that "easy borrowing guidelines" would continue and prevail. Homeowners refinanced (some more than once), using their equity much like a never-ending line of credit.

The Ability to "Fog a Mirror" was Sufficient to Get a Loan

As is too often the case, a good idea becomes corrupted and abused. Thus was the case with the new loan options designed to help more people buy homes. As these loan options evolved, mortgage brokerage ads proclaimed that "anyone can obtain a loan." While not completely true, many of the new loan instruments were seen as requiring borrowers only to prove they were alive by "fogging a mirror."

Interest-only, stated income, 100 percent loans were introduced. Perhaps the most grievous of the new loan options was the negatively amortized adjustable rate mortgage, or Option ARM. These loans allowed a borrower to qualify and make initial monthly mortgage payments at a low 1 to 2 percent interest rate. The monthly payments in such loans were insufficient to pay even the interest due on the mortgage, resulting in the unpaid amount being added to the loan balance in what are called negatively amortized loans. We will discuss this in more detail in Chapter 4.

The Old Rules Return

In hindsight, it seemed inevitable that the uncontrolled escalation of home values accompanied by ever diminishing guidelines for loan qualification would come to an end. But, for many, it seemed their best option to obtain wealth was by buying a home and letting it appreciate exponentially over a short period of time.

As home values adjusted downward and the easy money loan options collapsed, borrowers found themselves with adjusted monthly payments beyond their capacity to pay. Many of the most creative loan instruments were suddenly characterized as "toxic" and homeowners found they owed more than their homes were now worth. A monetary crisis developed that became a worldwide phenomenon.

Investors became more cautious with a return to more historically sound home loan financing methods. As we examine the basic principles of real estate financing, we will explore its continuously changing landscape as well as the currently available real estate home loan programs. While the main emphasis will focus on financing residential real estate, Chapter 15 will discuss the financing of residential income properties.

Roller-Coaster Ride

Real estate in the form of land and improvements comprises a substantial amount of the total net worth of the United States. From 2000 to 2006, skyrocketing appreciation, accompanied by historically low interest rates, encouraged homeowners to tap their equity and use those funds for consumer spending. This in turn, helped fuel the economic growth of the United States from 2003 to 2006. In addition, the real estate industry is a major employer, providing billions of dollars in income for millions of American workers and investors. When mortgage funds are scarce, real estate activity and employment decline, and a general hardship is felt throughout the economy. Unfortunately, the housing cycle can be irregular and wild, with great booms followed by disastrous busts, as shown in Figure 1.1.

Several "boom times" in real estate occurred in the early 1960s, 1971–1973, 1975–1979, 1982–89, and the late 1990s to mid-2000s.

However, between these periods were some bad years—1966, 1969, 1974, 1980–1981—and a severe housing crash from 1990 to 1996 in many parts of California.

During 2006 and 2007, the robust real estate market began to unravel. The usual causes of a bust in the real estate market include high interest rates, government deficits, and better investment opportunities. But the turmoil in the mid-2000s was fueled by several years of greed throughout the finance system and a consistent relaxation of loan requirements, and resulted in a complete breakdown of our banking system and a worldwide economic crisis. (We will discuss the restoration of loan quality requirements and the creation of more stringent loan requirements in Chapters 5 and 9). The consequences of even more minor disruptions can cause what is known as

FIGURE 1.1 The roller-coaster ride of the housing market.

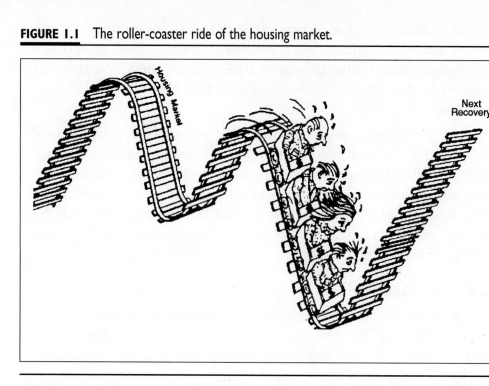

disintermediation, which is the sudden flow of funds out of thrift institutions (which grant real estate loans) into the general money market (where real estate loans are not common). By 2008, the excesses of the preceding years affected all aspects of the banking world and the lack of liquidity (the lack of funds for real estate loans) reached distressing proportions.

Such drying up of real estate funds wreaks havoc in the housing market. In short, real estate activity is directly tied to the availability and cost of mortgage funds and to the general state of the economy. As these two items shift up and down, so goes the real estate market.

Therefore, an agent's or an investor's success in real estate partially depends on a thorough understanding of trends in the mortgage market. The remainder of this book is devoted to an explanation of real estate finance, including a reduced range of creative and alternative financing techniques used in buying and selling real estate.

1.2 SHORT OVERVIEW OF THE MORTGAGE MARKET

Real estate financing usually requires the buyer to find a new loan at a lending institution, or occasionally the seller is asked to carry paper, or a combination of both. In all cases the interest rate and terms of real estate loans are dictated by the operations of the money and mortgage market. This section is a short primer on the operations of the mortgage market, stressing the functions of money and the role of the **Federal Reserve System**.

1.3 THE MEANING OF MONEY

Money has been defined in a variety of ways: a medium of exchange, a standard of value, a storehouse of value. In general, money is anything that people will accept in exchange for goods and services. Its value lies primarily in our confidence that other people will accept the money in exchange for their goods and services. Contrary to popular belief, money does not have to be a precious metal. Anything that is universally accepted by society can be used as money. Figure 1.2 outlines the many forms of money.

FIGURE 1.2   Money is …

Money is commonly considered to be:

1. Coins.
2. Paper currency.
3. Checking accounts, technically called demand deposits.
4. Negotiable orders of withdrawal accounts, or NOW for short.
5. Money market accounts issued by financial institutions.

Near money consists of assets that can be quickly converted to cash, such as:

1. Savings accounts, technically called time deposits.
2. U.S. government bonds.
3. Cash value of life insurance.
4. Preferred and common stocks on organized exchanges.
5. Money market mutual funds.

The following items operate like money but are forms of *credit*:

1. Personal credit cards ("electronic IOUs"). Not debit cards, which are merely a way to access funds in a checking account.
2. Bank-allowed overdrafts (ODs).
3. Credit reserves.
4. Home equity lines of credit.

Money and credit are frequently used interchangeably—but they are not the same. *Money* means currency and checking accounts, while *credit* consists of loan funds or savings that a saver or lender makes available to a borrower. Both money and credit can be used to purchase real property; that is why both terms are frequently used in the real estate business.

How Is Money Created?

Our money supply is usually thought to consist only of coins and paper currency issued by the government. But money is comprised of more than the "cash" that people have in their wallets and purses. Indeed, the bulk of what is called the money supply is in the form of checking accounts—that is, money that individuals and businesses have deposited into checking accounts, plus the money "created" by the banking system under what is called **fractional reserve banking**. This will be explained and illustrated shortly.

How Is Money Accumulated?

Money accumulates in many ways. The principal method is through savings—that is, spending less than one earns. Money is earned in one of four ways:

1. Wages, fees, and commissions in exchange for labor and services.
2. Interest and dividends in exchange for the use of capital.
3. Profits in exchange for management and entrepreneurship.
4. Rents in exchange for real and personal property usage.

To repeat, savings are accumulated funds not needed at the time that they are earned. Savings represent surplus money put aside for future use. There are many ways to save money, and where those savings will ultimately accumulate depends upon the needs, degrees of risk, and personal preferences of individuals. Although it is not necessary to explain the various methods of saving, it is important to recognize that the *ultimate source of funds for borrowing is savings*. In other words, one person's savings becomes another person's source for borrowing. If people spent all of their income, there would not be any funds for borrowing! The greater the rate of savings inflows, the greater the reservoir for borrowing.

At the beginning of 2009, the American savings rate had reduced to near zero. The loans made during the preceding several years through a lack of adequate qualifying standards were beginning to default. Homeowners had used their home equity as "piggy banks" or large checking accounts and found themselves largely overencumbered. The scene was set for what was to become known as a "financial melt-down".

The global economy expanded during this time and other countries sustained our borrowing appetite by loaning our nation money. That a borrower could be from one country and the saver or lender from another, was not uncommon before the "melt-down"; it was an extraordinary time of borrowing. In subsequent chapters we will discuss its effect on our financial industry.

1.4 THE FLOW OF MONEY AND CREDIT INTO THE MORTGAGE MARKET

If the source of all loans, including mortgage loans, is ultimately savings, how do savings via money and credit flow into the mortgage market? Stated differently, how does capital for real estate financing accumulate? This occurs through a process called the *circular flow of the economy.* Do not be troubled by this section, which appears to be heavy stuff! We have tried to simplify; if you are not comfortable with the basic economics, just read lightly and go on to the next section, which deals with the Federal Reserve. There we get into the nitty-gritty of how money is created to finance real estate transactions.

As noted in Figure 1.3, the production of goods and services requires that money be paid for the use of labor, raw materials, entrepreneurship, and capital. This money is called personal income, and all or some of it may be taxed, spent on goods and services, or saved. That which is saved is usually deposited in financial intermediaries, which, in turn, pump funds back into production.

FIGURE 1.3 Simplified circular flow of the economy, excluding the impact of foreign trade and savings entering the U.S. economy.

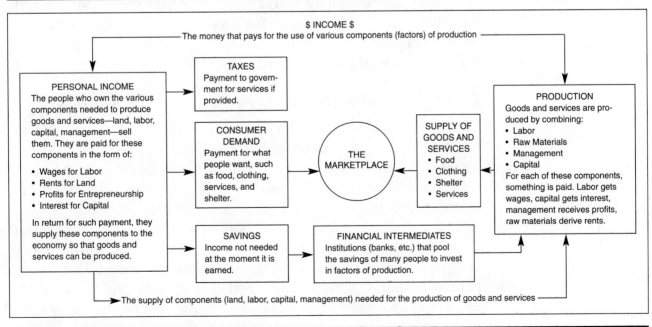

Figure 1.3 is a simplified model of how U.S. savings accumulate to become the reservoir for future loans. Carefully trace this circular flow until you understand that individuals "own" land, labor, capital, and entrepreneurship (the supply components), and that businesses need these supply components to produce. Thus, businesses "buy" land, labor, and capital from individuals, thereby giving individuals income in the form of wages, rents, interest, and profits. This personal income is then taxed, spent, or saved. That which is saved becomes capital for borrowing.

Intermediation of Savings

According to the circular flow of the economy, income that is not taxed away or consumed in the marketplace represents savings. Where these savings go depends largely on the kinds of returns desired by the saver. Many dollars flow into savings or commercial bank accounts, Certificates of Deposit (CDs), credit unions, life insurance premiums, and so on.

Savings or commercial banks, credit unions, life insurance companies, and other financial institutions are referred to as "intermediaries," since they are wedged between the saver and the ultimate investment outlet into which the money will be placed. Pooling the savings of many people is called **intermediation**, or acting as a "go-between" for saver-depositors and borrowers on home loans.

Many of the dollars saved through intermediaries are loaned to real estate buyers, builders, developers, and investors. This in turn stimulates the real estate market and generates income and profits for sellers, real estate agents, loan brokers, and lending institutions. At the same time, this process makes it possible for people to buy homes and investors to acquire income property.

Disintermediation of Savings

Where savers place their funds depends on convenience and on how much depositories or investment outlets are willing to pay in interest. It can be said that a bidding process takes place, with savings going to the highest bidder, commensurate with safety and other criteria laid out by the saver. Money may be deposited with virtually absolute safety, up to designated dollar amounts, in an insured savings account in a bank or other thrift institution. However, when opportunities for greater returns present themselves, people withdraw part or all of their deposits and seek higher returns elsewhere. Since banks and thrift institutions frequently place their funds into real estate loans, the withdrawal of deposits is referred to as disintermediation—that is, deposits are removed from the institutions that act as intermediaries. When such withdrawals occur on a massive scale, the impact on the real estate market can be drastic. If people suddenly withdraw their savings and buy government notes and money market funds, the supply of mortgage money declines and the real estate market can enter into a slump.

Reintermediation of Savings

When the flow of savings again returns to the thrift institutions that act as intermediaries for the placement of mortgage loans, this process is referred to as **reintermediation**. If yields on government bonds plunge or the stock market crashes, money may reenter banks and thrift institutions in search of safety. As money returns to thrift institutions, the funds available for real estate loans increase, interest rates soften, more buyers can qualify for loans, and the housing market begins to pick up.

Thus the processes of intermediation, disintermediation, and reintermediation all have a dramatic impact on the real estate market. To understand this process fully, we must examine the role of the Federal Reserve System and the U.S. Treasury.

1.5 FEDERAL CONTROL OF THE MONEY SUPPLY

Although some economists disagree, most believe that manipulating the supply and cost of money and credit helps to achieve economic balance. To this end, the Federal Reserve System and the U.S. Treasury are each involved in efforts to balance the national economy. Though not always successful, these agencies have a profound effect on the financing of real estate. In this section the Federal Reserve System and the U.S. Treasury are discussed in detail.

The Federal Reserve System (Monetary Policy)

The Federal Reserve System (often called the "Fed") is sometimes viewed as the "fourth branch" of the U.S. government. It is charged with maintaining sound credit conditions to help counteract inflation and deflation, to encourage high employment, and to safeguard the purchasing power of the dollar.

The Federal Reserve System contains 12 districts located throughout the United States. Each district is served by a regional Federal

Reserve Bank that is coordinated and directed by a seven-member board of governors appointed by the president. The Fed has control over all banks and thrift institutions.

The Fed performs numerous functions, including the issuance of currency. However, this section is concerned only with its ability to influence the money supply. After all, money is the key to real estate transactions without which real estate activities would come to a grinding halt. This ability to control the supply and cost of money and credit is referred to as **monetary policy**. The principal ways in which the Fed exerts its influence on the money supply are through **reserve requirements**, **open-market operations**, and **discount rates**.

Reserve Requirements

All banks and thrift institutions must set aside reserve funds in order to protect depositors. Even more important than the security, the Fed is able to manipulate the amount of money in circulation by adjusting the reserve rate up or down. For example, if the reserve requirement is 20 percent, banks would need $200 in reserves for every $1,000 of deposits. (In reality, reserve requirements vary with the size of the institution and form of account—the 20 percent used here is illustrative only.) Any money beyond the required reserves may be lent out at a ratio, in this case, of 5 to 1. In other words, the banks may then create $5 of credit for every excess reserve dollar.

To see how banks actually create money, let us return to our example of a $1,000 deposit. Assume that bank policy requires that 20 percent of each deposit in checking accounts must be kept as a reserve against withdrawals. The remaining 80 percent can be used to create a loan.

Now let us assume that $1,000 is deposited into Bank A. Bank A will put $200 in reserve and loan out $800 to Mr. X. Mr. X will take the $800 and spend it. The receiver of this money will probably deposit the funds into Bank B. Bank B now has an $800 deposit, of which $160—20 percent—is kept in reserve, and $640 is lent to Ms. Y. She spends the $640 and the receiver deposits the money into Bank C. Bank C now has a $640 deposit, of which $128 is kept in reserve and $512 is lent to others. In theory, this process continues until all funds are exhausted. Table 1.1 illustrates this process.

A single $1,000 deposit under a 20 percent reserve requirement can expand to become a $5,000 deposit, $4,000 of which is loaned

TABLE 1.1   How banks create money.

Banks	Deposits	Reserves (@20%)	Loans ("Debt Fiat")
Bank A	$1,000.00	$ 200.00	$ 800.00
Bank B	800.00	160.00	640.00
Bank C	640.00	128.00	512.00
Bank D	512.00	102.40	409.60
Bank E	409.60	81.92	327.68
Plus all others	1,638.40	327.68	1,310.72
Totals	$5,000.00	$1,000.00	$4,000.00

out. In essence, the banking system has created additional purchasing power through demand deposits. This has the same effect on spending as increasing the amount of coin and paper money.

In the real world, does this creation of bank money always occur at a constant, smooth rate? Not usually. Some banks differ in their reserve policy and each bank varies in the amount of loans available from each deposit. In addition, "leakage" occurs when people fail to deposit money in banks. Referring to Table 1.1, what would happen if the borrower of the $640 from Bank B buys merchandise and the store owners put the $640 under their mattress instead of depositing the money in Bank C?

Change in the Reserve Requirements

All banks that are members of the Federal Reserve System are required to keep a certain percentage of each deposit as reserves. These reserves are kept at the regional Federal Reserve Bank. If the Fed feels that **easy money** and credit are feeding inflation, it can raise the reserve requirements, which will force banks to restrict their lending, as money must be diverted from loans to cover the shortage in reserves. This action is designed to decrease the amount of money in circulation, drive up interest rates, and eventually lessen inflation by slowing down spending.

What will happen if the Fed decreases the reserve requirements? Will this increase or decrease the money supply? Will this raise or lower interest rates? Trace the steps that were outlined above to check your understanding.

Open-Market Operations

As part of its money-management tools, the Fed is allowed to buy and sell government securities, called *open-market* operations. Banks must buy them, but the public, consisting of private citizens and *financial institutions*, also may buy and sell government securities as a form of investment. When the Fed buys government securities from the public, the seller of these securities (the public) receives the Fed's check, which the seller then deposits in a local bank. The local bank forwards the check to the Fed for payment. When the Fed receives its own check, it increases the reserves of the local bank by the amount of that check. The local bank now has more reserves than are required and therefore can grant more loans. *Thus, when the Fed buys government securities from the public, it increases the money supply by increasing bank reserves, which, in turn, will support more loans.*

What happens to the money supply when the Fed sells government securities to the public? The money supply tightens up, which increases interest rates and discourages borrowing.

To review, let us trace what happens when the Fed sells government securities. When government securities are sold, the public purchases them by writing checks on their local bank. The Fed receives the buyer's check and subtracts it from the reserve account of the local bank. The local bank now has less in reserve and therefore must constrict its lending. *So when the Fed sells government securities, it decreases bank reserves, which, in turn, decreases the bank's ability to grant loans.*

Once again we notice that the ultimate effect is a change in the money supply by manipulating bank reserves. But the Fed still has another important tool—changes in the discount rate.

Discount Rates

Banks borrow from each other via the Federal Reserve Bank's lending facility known as the "discount window". Primary borrowing is usually for the purpose of avoiding having a bank's reserves dip below the required minimum. The rate charged for this overnight borrowing is called the *discount rate*. The term "banker's bank" is used to describe the relationship of the Federal Reserve Bank to a member bank. The discount rate is not to be confused with the so-called **prime rate** (rate given to a bank's most favored corporate borrowers) that is charged by commercial banks. The two are compared in Figure 1.4.

The higher the Fed's discount rate charged to the bank, the more likely a higher interest rate will be charged by the bank to the real estate borrower. A higher discount rate generally indicates a more restrictive monetary policy is being adopted . Over time, the discount rate tends to adjust fairly closely with other short-term interest rates. While a change in the discount rate can affect long-term

FIGURE 1.4 Discount rate versus prime rate.

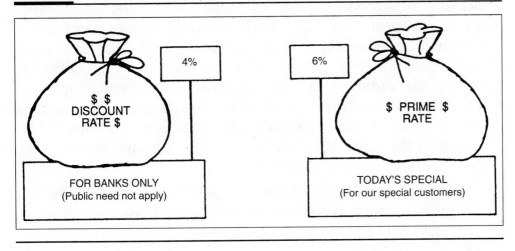

FIGURE 1.4 Discount rate versus prime rate.

home mortgages, it tends to most immediately affect short-term lending options. For this reason, consumers can be confused when a reduction in the discount rate does not immediately affect long-term mortgage rates.

Ultimately, an upward adjustment in the discount rate is likely to translate into higher home mortgage rates. Any increase in rates can have a dampening effect on potential buyers of real estate. Many prospective home buyers will simply postpone the purchase of a home, for example, in the hope that interest rates will soon come down.

The reverse is also true. The lower the discount rate, the lower the potential rate of interest charged by the bank to real estate borrowers. A greater demand for loans is expected to follow, and the number of real estate loans actually placed will increase.

Federal Funds Rate

Although not technically listed as a major tool of the Fed, the **federal funds rate** is one of the most closely watched indicators as to the current thinking of the Federal Reserve managers. What is the federal funds rate? When one bank is at a maximum loan-to-reserve requirement, it cannot grant additional loans to expand business until its reserves are increased. Or if the bank has granted too many loans relative to its existing reserves, it must, by law, either call in some loans or increase its reserves. One way to solve these problems is to borrow excess reserves from another bank that currently is not granting additional loans. The federal funds rate, then, is the rate of interest one bank charges another for the overnight use of excess reserves. This alternative source of temporary funds can be used instead of borrowing from the Federal Reserve noted above.

The Federal Reserve, in its efforts to fight inflation or recession, increases or decreases the money supply to keep the federal funds rate in a certain trading range. This will encourage one bank to borrow the excess reserves of another and use the reserves to grant more loans, which should expand the economy. If the Fed wishes to slow the economy, it may tighten up the money supply and force the federal funds rate to rise. This discourages one bank from borrowing excess reserves from another bank, thereby discouraging the granting of additional loans. This will tend to keep the economy from expanding.

It should be noted that during the 2009 banking crises, the lack of liquidity prevented banks from borrowing from each other. In turn, real estate financing tightened and fewer loans were made.

Summary of the Major Federal Reserve Tools[*]

Changes in the reserve requirements, open-market operations, and changes in the discount rate all help the Fed control the supply of bank money. Of these tools, the most commonly used is open-market operations. To increase the money supply, the Fed will either decrease the reserve requirement, buy government securities, decrease the discount rate, or use some combination of all three.

To decrease the money supply, the Fed will either increase the reserve requirement, sell government securities, increase the discount rate, or use some combination of all three. In addition, the Fed will keep a close eye on the federal funds rate and attempt to raise or lower this rate, depending on its economic goals.

The U.S. Treasury (Fiscal Policy)

Whereas the Federal Reserve Board determines monetary policy, the U.S. Treasury, under the direction of Congress and the president, acts as the nation's fiscal agent, managing the federal government's enormous debt. The government's spending and taxing policy is referred to as **fiscal policy**, in contrast to the monetary policy of the Fed. How much the federal government spends, and how much it takes in through taxation, will decidedly affect real estate financing. For example, if the U.S. Treasury decides to issue long-term debt instruments called treasury certificates, consisting of notes and bonds, to help finance government spending, more money is therefore siphoned off from mortgage investments. The impact is similar to the Fed's increasing the reserve requirement. Fewer homes

---

[*] *The Essentials of Real Estate Economics*, 5th ed., Dennis J. McKenzie and Richard Betts, Thomson South-Western, 2006, Mason, OH.

would be constructed and purchased because of the reduction in available capital. This is called the "crowding out" effect. The opposite, of course, is also true. If the government decides to curtail or reduce its spending, more money is made available for the capital markets, including the financing of real estate.

During the late 1990s and early 2000s, the "crowding out" effect had a minimal impact on housing because of the massive amount of U.S. government notes, bonds, mortgages, and other securities purchased by foreign countries and their citizens.

The Treasury is more than just the supplier of funds for federal spending. It has long been involved in the initial funding of new programs designed to bolster the economy. It helped establish the Federal National Mortgage Association (Fannie Mae), the Government National Mortgage Association (Ginnie Mae), the Federal Land Bank system, and other agencies that have played such important roles in real estate financing activities.

The Treasury led the way in 2008 with its promotion of the "Recovery Act," followed by the 2009 adoption of the "Make Home Affordable" program. Both were designed to assist a floundering real estate market and both received mixed reviews regarding how much help was actually provided.

Much more could be said about taxing policy, deficit spending, government intervention, and other interrelated topics. However, these are better left to a course in economics. Suffice it to say that when government spending exceeds revenue from taxation, deficit spending occurs, which leads the U.S. government to borrow more, driving up interest rates, which in turn tends to fan the flames of inflation. Inflation occurs when prices for goods and services increase, usually from too much money chasing too few goods. The net result of inflation can be a mixed blessing to real estate owners and licensees. Real estate values usually keep up with—and very often exceed—the rate of inflation. However, inflation drives up the cost of housing and interest rates, which can prevent some people from acquiring homes.

1.6 COST CHARACTERISTICS OF THE MORTGAGE MARKET

From a lender's point of view, cost, interest rates, and profits are the economic factors that drive the mortgage market. This section describes the underlying cost issues that influence the California loan market.

Cost of Mortgage Money

Many economic variables affect the price of money available for California real estate loans. International factors, such as an unfavorable trade balance, can have an impact on local lending. National factors, such as actions taken by the Federal Reserve Board and the U.S. Treasury, inflation, and business cycles, are even more important. Local factors that affect the cost of mortgage money include the level of employment, population trends, and the level of development in the community. Discussions of these larger issues are better left to economists. Closer to home, the institutional factors that affect the local cost of mortgage money include the following:

1. *Deposit cost.* This is the raw cost a lender must pay to attract depositors. The higher the interest rate paid on savings accounts, the higher the rate of interest the institution must charge for lending out mortgage money.

2. *Borrowing costs.* Many lenders need to tap the bond and other markets to obtain working capital. The costs of underwriting and floating a stock or bond offering will be passed on to the real estate borrower.

3. *Sales cost.* Promotional costs to attract borrowers, including advertising, loan solicitors, and so on, will be passed on in the form of higher interest rates.

4. *Administration.* Needless to say, there are overhead and administrative expenses in any business. Rent, utilities, management, maintenance, and other operating costs must be recouped and will affect the cost of borrowing.

5. *Reserves.* As pointed out earlier, reserves are required to be set aside by commercial banks and other institutional lenders. This presents an opportunity cost, the price of money that must sit idle and unproductive.

6. *Liquidity.* With the many past problems that have plagued institutional lenders, capital requirements and the need to liquidate assets are more critical than ever. This has to be factored into the cost of money for institutional lenders. The eventual lack of liquidity was largely viewed as the main culprit in the demise of subprime lenders.

7. *Profit.* Again, as with any enterprise, lenders are in the business of making a profit for their stockholders and for themselves.

The cost of a loan to a borrower is essentially the sum of these seven factors. An old rule of thumb that had long been followed by real estate lending institutions was that it took a spread of approximately 2 to 4 percent over the deposit interest rate paid to savers to break even before profit.

In the highly competitive California mortgage market, this spread had sometimes been squeezed down to only 2 percent or even less. Hence, if a bank was paying 4 percent interest to attract deposits, it had to receive 6 percent on its loans just to break even. Of course, there were some exceptions and variations in this rule, including the type of loan, term, points, and so on. However, it should be clear that, as in other types of businesses, the most efficient institution is likely to be the one that can make the most profit while lending at the lowest rate. Those that cannot compete because their costs exceed their income will fail. In short, it can be said that lending institutions, like retailers, try to buy money at wholesale (interest rate paid to depositors) and mark it up and sell it at retail (interest rate charged borrowers). During the housing crisis of 2009, the Fed reduced the cost of funds to lenders to nearly zero in an attempt to encourage home lending. While home mortgage interest rates did decline, lenders were able to achieve a 4 to 5 percent margin over their cost of the funds, resulting in substantial profits for financial institutions during this period of adjustment.

What Causes Mortgage Interest Rates to Change?

Underlying all interest rate changes for real estate loans are the market forces of supply and demand. After all, credit is a product that is bought and sold. Borrowers compete in the credit markets, just as buyers do for other goods and services. Specific forces influencing changes in mortgage interest rates include:

1. *Excessive government spending.* Government deficit spending tends to cause higher inflation and/or interest rates as the government drains away funds from the private sector or inks up the printing presses for more money.

2. *Large government borrowing amounts.* As the federal government increases its spending faster than its collection of tax revenues, it will, out of necessity (barring congressional approval of a raise in its debt ceiling), need to compete in the capital markets for money. Such competition invariably raises interest rates (this is the so-called crowding out effect).

3. *Inflation.* As a companion to excessive government spending and borrowing, inflation is an inevitable consequence that tends to cause increases in interest rates even with increases in the money supply. Monetarists hold that a rise in the supply of money may help lower interest rates, but only for a brief period. As the money

supply swells, so do expectations of rapid inflation. Thus, over the long run, lenders increase interest rates to protect or maintain their real profit margins against the expected increase in inflation.

4. *Supply*. As income increases, the money stock also increases, fueling economic expansion. If demand for loans does not keep pace, interest rates trend downward.

5. *Demand*. A strong demand for credit pushes interest rates upward. Even as the money supply continues to grow, the economy becomes overheated and competing borrowers (buyers of credit) bid up prices. As prices begin to climb, lenders naturally want higher interest rates to hedge against inflation.

6. *Federal Reserve actions*. (Review the discussion of the Federal Reserve in the previous section.) Figure 1.5 illustrates how the Fed attempts to balance the problem of high interest rates against excessive inflation rates.

"Tight" versus "Easy" Money

Tight money, a frequent expression among real estate practitioners, refers to restrictive money policies of the Federal Reserve System as it attempts to combat inflation by reducing the money supply. Any action to reduce the money supply will ordinarily cause interest rates to rise, unless of course the demand for funds is correspondingly reduced. On the other hand, when demand remains

FIGURE 1.5   Balancing the interest–inflation conflict.

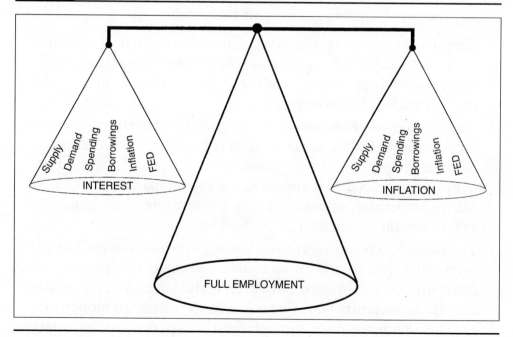

the same or actually increases, competition for the restricted supply of money climbs. Money invariably is taken out of thrift institutions for "greener pastures," those places where higher returns are paid for funds. This condition was referred to earlier as disintermediation.

Easy money, by contrast, is a relatively loose money policy of the Fed, which attempts to combat recession by increasing the supply of money in circulation. As money supplies increase, employment will normally increase, leading to increased income and, in theory, savings. As savings build up in the coffers of thrift institutions, interest rates move downward. With the return of funds to the thrift institutions—the major dispensers of mortgage funds—reintermediation is said to occur. Real estate activities usually pick up steam under easy money and low interest rate conditions.

The year 2009 may long be remembered as the year that these economic expectations somehow malfunctioned. In spite of massive infusions of funds to lending institutions, accompanied by historically low home mortgage rates, home values plunged and unemployment soared. The loss of lender liquidity along with tightening home mortgage qualifying guidelines reduced home sales. The loss of home values coupled with the increasing monthly payments of the previously acquired, unwise subprime mortgages resulted in record home foreclosures. While this near perfect storm of negative housing impacts was felt even more heavily in California than in other parts of the nation, optimism prevailed there that the housing market would recover and thrive.

The California Mortgage Market

California is unique in terms of the national mortgage market because of characteristics peculiar to this state.

1. *Large population and high demand.* California is the most populous state, continues to attract new residents, and has a high birth rate. State officials expect California's population to rise from nearly 37 million in 2009 to 60 million by 2050!

2. *Financial institutions.* California contains the largest number of banks and thrift institutions. Obviously, thrift institutions want to be where the greatest demand for real estate loans can be found. Californians have a greater choice of lenders than do residents of other states.

3. *Mortgage loan correspondents.* California has attracted many experienced and diversified mortgage loan correspondents (brokers) who represent out-of-state life insurance companies and

other institutional and noninstitutional lenders. This brings additional mortgage money to California.

4. *Title companies.* Title insurance originated in California and it continues to increase in volume. Escrow companies, too, are peculiar to this state, though the use of both title and escrow firms is spreading to other states. This easy, low-cost closing process attracts lenders and borrowers.

5. *Security.* The **deed of trust** is used almost exclusively, rather than the mortgage instrument, as the legal basis for securing real estate loans. This gives greater protection to lenders, because it allows a quick foreclosure process.

6. *Active secondary market.* This is where existing real estate loans are sold to U.S. and foreign purchasers. These secondary market sales bring fresh capital to the California real estate market.

7. *Diversification.* California's economy is one of the most diversified worldwide and is growing with a mix of ethnic and social diversity that is expected to continue creating new opportunities for housing and financing.

1.7 INSTRUMENTS OF REAL ESTATE FINANCE

The economic environment of the mortgage market establishes the trends for interest rates and financing terms, but the actual loan is created using a variety of financing instruments. This section introduces instruments of real estate finance, leaving specific details to later chapters.

Promissory Notes

When money is borrowed to purchase real estate, the borrower agrees to repay the loan by signing a *promissory note*, which outlines the terms of repayment and sets the due date. The promissory note is legal evidence that a debt is owed. The two most common types of promissory notes in general use are the **straight note** and the **installment note**.

The *straight note* is an *interest-only note*. Under a straight note, the borrower agrees to pay the interest periodically (usually monthly) and to pay the entire principal in a lump sum on the due date. For example, if you borrow $100,000 for five years at 8 percent interest rate, the monthly payments are $666.67 per month ($100,000 × 8% ÷ 12 months). The $666.67 payments cover just the monthly interest. Thus, five years hence, on the due date, you must pay back the entire $100,000 principal. In other words, your payments were only large enough to cover the monthly interest and did not reduce the $100,000 principal.

The second type of real estate *promissory note*, is the installment note. An installment note requires periodic payments that include both principal and interest. This reduction in principal is referred to as *amortization*. Suppose you borrowed $100,000 for 30 years at 8 percent interest, payable at $733.76 per month, including both principal and interest. At the end of 30 years you would find that the entire principal had been paid back. Each monthly payment of $733.76 not only included the monthly interest due but also reduced the $100,000 principal. An installment loan that includes both principal and interest in equal installment payments that self-liquidate the debt is called a fully **amortized loan**. Under such an amortized loan there is no **balloon payment** on the due date of the loan. The Civil Code defines a balloon payment as any payment on an amortized loan that is more than double the amount of a regular installment.

One variation of the installment note is to have monthly payments that are large enough to pay the monthly interest and reduce some of the principal, but the monthly principal portion is not sufficient to entirely liquidate the debt by the due date. Thus, on the due date the remaining unpaid principal must be paid in a balloon payment. For example, a $100,000, 30-year loan at 8 percent interest payable at $700 instead of $733.76 per month would require a balloon payment of $50,321.35 on the due date. Why? Because the $700 per month was enough to cover the monthly interest ($666.67), but not enough to cover the monthly interest plus all of the monthly principal, which would have taken $733.76 per month. Thus the unpaid balance over the 30-year life of the loan, $50,321.35, must be paid on the due date in the form of a balloon payment.

In the past, some borrowers signed negatively amortized promissory notes. Negatively amortized means that the loan payment does not even cover the monthly interest. Each month this shortage is added to the principal owed, resulting in an increased loan balance, which in turn incurs additional interest. This is the magic of compound interest in reverse, as it accumulates greater debt. As mentioned previously, a $100,000 loan at 8 percent payable interest only would result in a $666.67 monthly payment ($100,000 × 8% ÷ 12 months). If a borrower only paid $600 per month, the difference between an interest-only payment of $666.67 and the

$600 payment = $66.67. Each month, this $66.67 shortfall would be added to the $100,000 loan and begin to accrue interest. If this shortfall continued for 30 years, the borrower would still owe a balloon payment of $199,357.30 on top of paying $600 per month for 30 years! Total paid would be $600 × 360 payments (30 years × 12) = $216,000 + $199,357.30 balloon payment, for a grand total of $415,357.30 to pay off a $100,000 negative amortized loan during a 30-year period.

Variations on Fixed Interest Rate Notes

In recent years, lenders have introduced many variations of the standard promissory notes, with alphabet-soup-sounding names such as ARM, GPM, and so on. These are collectively called Alternative Mortgage Instruments, or AMIs for short. Chapter 4 is devoted to these loans.

Deed of Trust (Trust Deed)

To give added assurance that the promissory note will be paid when due, real estate lenders require security for the obligation. The most logical security is real estate currently owned or about to be acquired by the borrower. To secure an interest in the borrower's property, most lenders in California use a deed of trust (or trust deed).

A deed of trust is a three-party instrument between a borrower, called the **trustor**; a third party, called the trustee; and a lender, called the **beneficiary**. Under a deed of trust, the trustor deeds bare legal title to the trustee, who keeps the title as security until the promissory note is repaid. Once the debt is repaid, the beneficiary (lender) orders the trustee to reconvey the title to the trustor (borrower) using a deed of reconveyance. If the trustor should default on the loan, the beneficiary can order the trustee to hold a trustee's sale and sell the property to obtain the cash needed to pay the loan. Figure 1.6 illustrates how title is passed between a trustor and trustee in a deed of trust.

Frequently in other states, a mortgage is used instead of a deed of trust to secure a real estate loan. But in California, mortgages are rare—most lenders insist on deeds of trust instead. Why? Because in most cases, deeds of trust favor the lender over the borrower. If the borrower should default under a deed of trust, the lender can order the trustee to sell the property without a court proceeding, and it can be accomplished in approximately four months. Once the sale takes place, the borrower loses all rights to redeem the property.

Foreclosure under a mortgage usually requires a court proceeding and can take up to one year. After this foreclosure takes place,

FIGURE 1.6   The creation of a real estate debt and its payment, using a deed of trust.

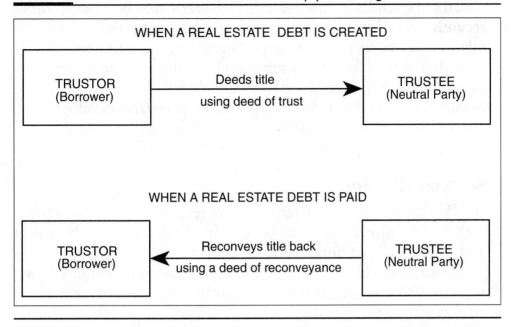

the borrower could have a one-year right of redemption. Most California real estate lenders therefore prefer to use deeds of trust rather than mortgages as security instruments because foreclosure is quicker, cheaper, and has no right of redemption after the sale.

Installment Sales Contracts

Another real estate financing instrument is an **installment sales contract** (agreement of sale). An installment sales contract is an agreement between the buyer and seller, where the buyer is given possession and use of the property and in exchange agrees to make regular payments to the seller. While the buyer has equitable title, legal title to the property remains with the seller until the terms of the contract are met, at which time the seller formally deeds the property to the buyer. In essence, under an installment sales contract, the seller (vendor) becomes the lender for the buyer (vendee). With the exception of Cal Vet Financing, made using the Contract for Sale (covered in detail in Chapter 6), lending institutions such as banks or thrift institutions are not needed in such a transaction.

The lack of a legal title poses some risks for the buyer. It is often several years between the time the buyer signs the installment sales contract and the time the seller delivers the deed. If the seller should die, become bankrupt, become incompetent, or encumber the title during this interim, the buyer could become involved in legal entanglements. In addition, if the seller under a contact of sale has an existing loan on the property, the use of this contract violates the lender's "due on sale" clause if one is present. More recently, foreclosure-help scams surfaced using the installment sale as a device to falsely promise financially strapped homeowners that they would be able to re-purchase their home when their financial condition improved. In light of these mostly negative possibilities, except for the special area of large land developments, the advantages that an installment sales contract may have had in the past seem to fade away in favor of the use of a deed of trust.

Special Clauses

In addition to repayment terms, many real estate financing instruments contain special clauses or loan conditions that the borrower and lender agree to honor. These clauses are known by such names as acceleration clause, alienation clause, escalation clause, prepayment penalty clause, interest change clause, and so on. These clauses will be examined in detail as we progress through the textbook and they are defined in the Glossary.

The Language of Real Estate Finance

By now you have discovered that the field of real estate finance has developed a language consisting of specific terms and concepts. As you read this textbook, try to learn the language and then use it in your real estate discussions. Refer to the Glossary from time to time to reacquaint yourself with words and terms that tend to lose their meaning when we don't use them on a regular basis. Learning the terms and concepts will help you communicate with inexperienced clients and friends who do not understand financial terms, as well as enable you to converse with real estate professionals.

1.8 THE FIVE-STEP FINANCING PROCESS

Borrowing money to purchase, exchange, refinance, construct, or make capital improvements to an existing home can be viewed as a **five-step financing process**:

1. *Application.* The loan process begins with the application filled in by the borrower, as detailed in Chapter 10. The form includes information on the applicant's financial condition, including the amount and consistency of income along with outstanding debts and expenses. The application also requests information concerning the property, including location, age, size of lot, and improvements. If the application is for a construction loan, details concerning the proposed improvements are required by lenders.

2. *Analysis/Processing.* After the completed application form is received, the lender reviews it to determine if the borrower and the property appear to meet the lender's standards. If the application was taken by an intermediary, such as mortgage broker, it is forwarded to the ultimate lender for analysis. If the applicant is acceptable, the lender presents the proposed financing terms to the borrower. The applicant may accept, reject, or attempt to negotiate with the lender to obtain more favorable terms. This topic is detailed in Chapters 8 and 9.

3. *Qualifying/Underwriting.* After an agreement is reached, loan documents are drawn, disclosure forms are prepared, and instructions for the escrow and title insurance companies are issued. Lenders establish processing patterns in accordance with their own policies and procedures. Much more is said about this step in Chapters 7 through 10.

4. *Funding/Closing.* After processing, the loan closing phase begins. This involves signing all loan papers and transferring the title. Practices vary within the state in the handling of the escrow. Closing is detailed in Chapter 10.

5. *Servicing.* This refers to loan collections and recordkeeping. It includes necessary follow-up to ensure that the property is maintained; that insurance, taxes, and other obligations are paid; and that delinquency is prevented in order to reduce the possibility of foreclosure. Some lenders do their own servicing, while others pay independent servicing companies fees for handling the paperwork. Chapters 10 and 11 deal with servicing and other post-closing issues.

SUMMARY

Real estate finance is the key factor in most real estate transactions. When mortgage funds are available, real estate sales take place. If mortgage money is scarce, activity in the real estate market declines.

Money is created by the banking system using fractional reserve banking, and this money is added to the supply of money issued by the U.S. government.

Money is earned through wages, interest, profits, and rents. Some of these earnings ultimately find their way into savings in banks and thrift institutions, which account for a sizable amount of the credit extended for real estate purchases and construction. When savings are withdrawn from these banks and thrift institutions and used elsewhere for higher returns, disintermediation occurs, which can result in a decline in the real estate market.

The Federal Reserve System (the Fed) is able to increase the supply of money by decreasing reserve requirements of member banks, buying government securities in the open market, decreasing its discount rate to borrowing banks, and other means. The Fed is able to decrease the availability of mortgage funds by increasing reserve requirements, selling government securities, increasing the discount rates, and other means.

The U.S. Treasury, as the fiscal agent of the federal government, also greatly affects the availability of real estate funds via its spending and taxing policies. When the government reduces its spending and borrowing, more money is available for real estate lending. And, conversely, when the government increases its spending and borrowing, less credit is pumped into real estate transactions.

The cost of mortgage money is affected by the price paid to attract deposits, lenders' borrowing costs, sales costs, administration, reserves, and profit goals. Interest rate fluctuations are largely influenced by government spending, government borrowing, inflation, and supply and demand.

The California market is unique in terms of the national mortgage market because of characteristics peculiar to this state. Among these are its large population, high demand, large amount of big institutional lenders, existence of many diversified mortgage loan correspondents, title insurance and escrow companies, and a very active secondary market.

Just like many other professionals, real estate lenders use tools or instruments to complete a task. In California, the major instruments of real estate finance are the promissory note, the deed of trust, and, to a lesser extent, the installment sales contract.

IMPORTANT TERMS AND CONCEPTS

Amortized loan	Federal Reserve System	Monetary policy
Balloon payment	Fiscal policy	Open-market operations
Beneficiary	Five-step financing process	Prime rate
Deed of trust (trust deed)		Reintermediation
Discount rate	Fractional reserve banking	Reserve requirements
Disintermediation	Installment note	Straight note
Easy money	Installment sales contract	Tight money
Federal funds rate	Intermediation	Trustor

REVIEWING YOUR UNDERSTANDING

Questions for Discussion

1. In addition to coins, what are the other two types of money? Do the terms credit and money mean the same?

2. "The source of all mortgage funds is ultimately savings." In your own words, explain this statement.

3. Explain how the Federal Reserve Board can increase or decrease the money supply using each of the following tools: reserve requirements, open-market activities, and discount rates.

4. How does an interest-only promissory note differ from an installment note?

5. Why are trust deeds used in California instead of mortgages?

6. How does an installment sales contract differ from a deed of trust as a security device for real estate financing?

7. Explain this statement: "Finance is the fuel that makes a real estate transaction run."

Multiple-Choice Questions

1. The real estate housing market can best be characterized as having
   a. a steady growth.
   b. a cyclical up-and-down movement.
   c. no influence in the general economy.
   d. none of the above.

2. According to the circular flow of the economy, when people supply the land, labor, and capital to business, the people receive in return
   a. goods and services.
   b. savings.
   c. income.
   d. taxes.

3. The chief requirement for acquiring most real estate is
   a. sufficient financing.
   b. high initial deposit.
   c. low down payment.
   d. income tax deductions.

4. An example of disintermediation is the flow of funds from
   a. money markets to thrift institutions.
   b. bond markets to mortgage markets.
   c. thrift institutions to money market funds.
   d. money markets to mortgage markets.

5. If the Federal Reserve Board wished to expand the money supply using open-market operations, it would
   a. cut federal taxes.
   b. increase government spending.
   c. sell government securities.
   d. buy government securities.

6. Which of the following statements is true?
   a. The prime rate is the same as the discount rate.
   b. A decrease in reserve requirements will tend to decrease the money supply.
   c. The California mortgage market usually has an oversupply of loanable funds.
   d. The federal funds rate is the interest one bank charges another for the use of overnight funds.

7. Leverage is best defined as
   a. potential income tax write-offs.
   b. the use of other people's money.
   c. the exchange of an existing home for a higher priced home.
   d. the exchange of a higher priced home for a lower priced dwelling.

8. On a deed of trust, the borrower is called the
   a. trustor.
   b. trustee.
   c. beneficiary.
   d. mortgagee.

9. When a borrower pays off a real estate loan, the trustee issues a
   a. deed of trust.
   b. trustee's deed.
   c. deed of repayment.
   d. deed of reconveyance.

10. A $100,000 loan at 8 percent interest, amortized for 30 years, all due and payable in 5 years, secured by a deed of trust, will involve
    a. periodic payments.
    b. a balloon payment.
    c. a lien on the borrower's title.
    d. all of the above.

11. If savers withdraw their funds from savings banks to buy corporate bonds, this is an example of
    a. mediation.
    b. intermediation.
    c. disintermediation.
    d. reintermediation.

12. The fiscal agent of the federal government is the
    a. U.S. Treasury.
    b. Federal Reserve System.
    c. commercial banking system.
    d. Federal Housing Finance Board.

13. The 100 percent interest-only loans were designed to entice home buyers to qualify based principally on their
    a. projected income.
    b. stated income, even if untrue.
    c. net worth.
    d. negatively amortized adjustable rate mortgage.

14. Qualifying a borrower takes place at what step in the financing process?
   a. analysis.
   b. application.
   c. servicing.
   d. closing.

15. All of the following can cause mortgage interest rates to rise except
   a. rapid inflation.
   b. excessive government borrowing.
   c. a large increase in the money supply.
   d. a large increase in the demand for loan funds.

16. What is sometimes called the "fourth branch" of government?
   a. U.S. Treasury.
   b. Federal Reserve System.
   c. Resolution Trust Corporation.
   d. U.S. Congress.

17. So-called liar loans became commonplace from about 2000 to 2007, which were characterized by
   a. relaxed lending regulations.
   b. home buyers qualifying without sufficient resources.
   c. an explosion in appreciation of housing.
   d. all of the above.

18. Loan collection and recordkeeping is referred to as loan
   a. processing.
   b. servicing.
   c. analysis.
   d. closing.

19. The lender in a deed of trust is called the
   a. trustor.
   b. vendor.
   c. trustee.
   d. beneficiary.

20. The party holding bare legal title under a trust deed is the
   a. beneficiary.
   b. trustor.
   c. title company.
   d. trustee.

CASE & POINT

What Happened and What Is Ahead

As home values accelerated in the early 2000s, homebuyers often felt that if they didn't buy then, they might not be able to purchase in the future. Buyers' ability to purchase was enhanced by the increasingly relaxed qualifying standards for real estate loans. Subprime lending practices created an environment wherein it seemed that anyone could qualify for a loan.

The available loan instruments during the height of the subprime lending craze included 100 percent financing, interest-only loans, adjustable rate mortgages with negatively amortized features, stated income loans ultimately known as "liar" loans, and a host of "easy-to-qualify" options. In spite of some critics, the rationale for these easy loan practices was to help people achieve the American dream of homeownership. For those few who worried about their ability to make the mortgage payments in the future, they were reassured that they could always sell at a profit as home values continued to climb.

The result of the easy money years was a record home foreclosure rate in 2008–2009. While many borrowers were approved for loans for which they ultimately found themselves unable to afford, two loan options created the majority of the foreclosure woes; Negam and "easy to qualify." As home values began to decline, those with 100 percent financing found they were trapped in their homes. Lack of equity disallowed refinancing to reduce their original high interest rate loans. And since borrowers were unable to sell their homes for what they owed, short-sale transactions became prevalent.

The negatively amortized adjustable rate mortgages (ARMs) began to adjust with payments often near doubling. Homeowners could not afford the increased payments and the fact that borrowers had often exaggerated their income to originally qualify meant that they were unable to refinance. The loss of home values further complicated any opportunity to refinance as well as prohibited the ability to sell. The dream of homeownership, based on the belief that home values would continue to climb unabated, collapsed.

At the same time, in response to previously over-easy loan practices, qualifying requirements tightened and the number of loan options reduced dramatically. Homeowners found fewer refinance options available and prospective home buyers found it increasingly difficult to qualify for a home purchase loan. Gone, probably forever, were the mirror loans, so called because it seemed that if borrowers could prove they were alive by fogging a mirror, they seemed eligible for a home loan. We returned to the more sane financing practice of having to prove one's ability to afford a mortgage. But, as is often the case when a market correction occurs, the pendulum swung from "anyone can get a loan" to very tight eligibility rules.

There was some incongruity in the finance world. The real estate sector of the economy was struggling. Many felt that the ability of buyers to purchase homes and of beleaguered home-owners to escape foreclosure and retain their homes were critical to any economic rebound. But the lending practices seemed to dampen the ability for a rebound. The home finance world was clearly in transition and seemed to evolve on a daily basis. But there were some good things happening:

Home value reductions made it more affordable for buyers to purchase.

Home values stabilized. Slowly, in parts of California, some appreciation began to occur.

- Interest rates remained historically low, encouraging buyers.
- Home purchases lost importance as purely an investment. Instead, the more old-fashioned purpose of having one's own place became the motivation for purchasing.

Among the continued evolution of the industry, we can anticipate:

- reduced future annual real estate appreciation rates.
- some expansion of loan options, stated income loans for self-employed borrowers being one of the first anticipated restored programs.
- guidelines for both realtors and loan sources to be adopted, revised and re-revised in attempts to curb excessive and abusive practices.
- interest rates to remain on the historically low side, although periods of inflation will naturally occur.
- added emphasis on professionalism for both realtors and lending practitioners.

Chapter

2

PREVIEW

An institutional lender, also known as a financial intermediary, is any depository that pools funds of clients and depositors and invests them in real estate loans. The lending policies of these institutions have a profound impact on the real estate market. In California, institutional lenders include savings banks (former savings and loan associations), commercial banks, and life insurance companies. They are differentiated from non-institutional lenders, such as individual or private lenders, in the following important ways:

- Institutional lenders are highly regulated and closely supervised by federal and state agencies, whereas private lenders are relatively free of regulations.

- Private lenders invest their own funds directly, or through mortgage brokers, into real estate loans, rather than through a financial intermediary.

- Regulated institutional lenders are not subject to usury laws and may charge any rate of interest. In contrast, many private lenders make "personal" loans that are subject to **usury laws**, which place legal limits on rates of interest. (See Chapter 3 for details.)

- Many institutional lenders qualify to make Department of Veterans Affairs (DVA) and Federal Housing Administration (FHA) loans.

- As described in Chapter 7, there is an active secondary market for institutional loans. The ability to sell loans to the secondary market drives prices and terms and maintains a supply of mortgage funds in the primary market.

Institutional Lenders

- Institutional lenders and federal regulations, in some cases, set private mortgage insurance (PMI) requirements, discussed in Chapter 5.

- Most conforming lenders offer **rate lock-in** periods, guaranteeing an agreed-upon interest rate in advance of closing. Lock periods typically vary from 14 to 60 days; however, more recently, lenders have restricted maximum lock periods to 30 or 40 days. Generally, the shorter the lock-in period, the lower the rate.

Figure 2.1 distinguishes three broad classifications of lenders: institutional, non-institutional, and private lenders. How these lenders fit into the mortgage market will be explained in this and upcoming chapters. In Figure 2.2, we show how savings become real estate loans.

FIGURE 2.1 Sources of money in the mortgage market.

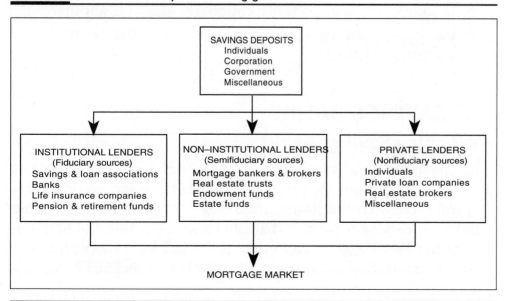

FIGURE 2.2   How savings become real estate loans.

After completing this chapter, you should be able to:

1. Demonstrate how savings deposits become real estate loans.
2. Differentiate institutional from non-institutional lenders.
3. List three types of institutional lenders and briefly explain the differences between them.
4. Discuss several of the trends facing institutional lenders.
5. Decide when to use one institutional lender over another.
6. List five regulatory agencies that supervise the operations of institutional lenders.

2.1 SAVINGS BANKS

What Is a Savings Bank?

In simple terms, a savings bank is a **financial intermediary** that accepts savings from the public and invests these savings principally in real estate trust deeds and mortgages. Previously called savings and loan associations, most changed their name after the S&L crisis of the 1980s. Often referred to as "thrift" institutions, the label "savings bank" has become a catch-all title that includes S&Ls and credit unions. Since deregulation in the 1980s, they offer services competitive with many commercial banks.

Savings banks may be either mutual or capital stock institutions. As a mutual institution, depositors and borrowers are given share certificates or receipts in return for deposits of money. This is why a deposit in a mutual thrift is often referred to as a *share liability* rather than a savings deposit. A capital stock institution, on the other hand, issues shares of stock to its investors, representing fractional shares of ownership of the institution.

A savings bank is also classified as either a state-chartered or federally chartered institution. A *state-chartered* thrift institution is licensed by the State of California and operates under the supervision of a state commissioner and, if insured, also under the **Federal Housing Finance Board**. By contrast, a *federally chartered* savings bank is licensed by the Federal Housing Finance Board and is readily identified by the word federal in its corporate title, such as Fidelity Federal Savings. To the saver or borrower, however, there is little difference between state and federal institutions, since the laws and regulations under which they operate are so similar. They have substantially "parallel authority," which means that home buyers can shop for loans almost anywhere.

Lending Characteristics of Savings Banks (Thrifts)

The chief lending characteristics of savings banks include the following:

- Government regulations require that a majority of their assets must be in real estate loans. Business and consumer loans are permitted to a limited extent, but pale when compared with loans secured by real property.

- Although loan-to-value (LTV) limits vary from bank to bank and depend on the availability of money in the marketplace, the current standard is a maximum 90 percent LTV. Starting in 2006, down payment requirements became less flexible; 100 percent LTV programs were the first to be eliminated, soon followed by 95 percent LTV loans. Exceptions continue to be government-backed loans, such as FHA and DVA. Most thrifts limit the maximum loan amount on a property to 1 percent of their total assets. Hence, larger thrifts are able to accommodate large loan requests more readily than smaller savings banks and may be more flexible on LTV limits.

- Most thrifts limit their loan due dates to 30 years, although 40-year loans are available in some cases. Fifteen-year loans are also available in the home financing market. In the past, when interest rates were on the rise, some banks offered shorter-than-normal due dates. A three-, five-, or seven-year due date would still have payments amortized over 30 years, but have a "balloon" payment due at the end of the term. A "rollover" loan would ignore the principal balance due and convert it to an adjustable rate for the remainder of the term.

- Interest rates in the past were highest among the institutional real estate lenders. This was due to the large demand for loans and to the higher risks associated with higher **loan-to-value ratios** (LTV). Currently, rates charged by commercial banks and savings banks are basically the same and most lenders have adopted "risk-based" pricing models (discussed in Chapter 9).

- Thrift banks' basic real estate lending is on single-family, owner-occupied dwellings. However, in a favorable market, thrifts will also finance mobile home loans, non-owner-occupied dwellings, apartments, and commercial and industrial properties.

- Combination loans may also be available. Referred to as "construction-to-permanent" loans, they combine construction (short-term financing) and **take-out loans** (long-term or permanent financing) into one loan with only one loan application and one closing. This is dealt with further in Chapter 14.

- Savings banks are permitted to make collateral loans secured by the borrower's savings accounts, savings certificates, bonds, existing secured notes, and certain other forms of readily liquid assets. These institutions started with "secured" credit cards to help restore the credit of their customers. This establishes a credit card limit that is secured with the consumer's savings account, limiting the bank's liability.

Trends in the Savings Bank Industry

Increased competition from commercial banks and mortgage companies, combined with imbalances between money-scarce and money-surplus areas that create demands for multiregional lending programs, have contributed to the loss of stature of savings banks (thrifts) as the principal source of home loans. Beginning in the mid 1990s, mortgage companies became more dominant in local home mortgage arenas and have remained so through the present.

2.2 COMMERCIAL BANKS

What Is a Commercial Bank?

A **commercial bank** is, as the name implies, a commercial institution that functions as a depository for funds and a place to borrow money. Commercial banks have two different forms of deposits: demand deposits and time deposits. The bulk of their funds are in demand deposits, which are deposits in business and personal checking accounts. Rarely are such funds used for long-term mortgage lending, due to the highly volatile nature of such funds—that is, they may be withdrawn on demand by the depositor and therefore cannot be depended on to remain in the account for very long. For this reason they are also referred to as transaction money or transaction accounts.

Finance companies, on the other hand, appeal to "hard to finance" borrowers and are generally characterized by higher interest rates accompanied by severe prepayment penalties. Concerns have been expressed that some borrowers find it difficult to extricate themselves from the loan process. Some finance companies do not report on-time payment records to credit repositories, providing no credit building option for borrowers.

Time deposits, or interest-bearing savings accounts, provide the bank with long-term funds that are invested into a variety of outlets, including real estate financing.

Commercial banks are always stock corporations that operate under a license or charter from either the state or the federal government. A state-chartered bank is licensed to do business by the California Department of Financial Institutions. A nationally chartered bank is given its license by the Comptroller of the Currency and is readily identifiable by the word *national* in its title, such as South Coast National Bank.

Lending Characteristics of Commercial Banks

Commercial banks may make any type of loan on virtually any type of reasonable collateral. Although their primary function is to make short-term business loans, California banks are aggressive in the home loan market. Commercial banks are also a primary source for short-term construction financing, noted more in Chapter 14.

Following the guidelines of the times, banks regularly made home loans up to 95 percent loan-to-value ratio, for as long as 30 years on single-family dwellings. Most banks required private mortgage insurance on loans whose ratio of loan-to-value was in excess of 80 percent.

The chief characteristics of bank real estate loans are the following:

- Active in the regular home loan market, commercial banks can make FHA and DVA loans with more liberal loan-to-value ratios and fewer limitations than imposed on nongovernmental or conventional loans.

- Construction loans are favored and have maturity dates generally of 24 months or less, though they may extend to 60 months. Many banks require a firm take-out agreement whereby a responsible, permanent investor—such as a savings bank or life insurance company—will extend long-term financing upon completion of construction.

- The property offered as collateral is usually in close proximity to the bank or one of its branches.

- Commercial banks are active seekers of home improvement and home equity loans, even though they constitute a junior lien against the property.

- Banks make **swing loans**, sometimes referred to as **bridge loans**, which are short-term **interim loans** used to bridge the time during which a property remains unsold. For example, if a homeowner purchases a replacement house before selling the first house, a swing loan provides the funds to fill the gap until the sale proceeds are available.

The lien may exist on both the "old" and the "new" homes. Swing/bridge loans may have monthly payments or may be set up to be paid in a single lump sum upon sale of the old home.

Trends in the Commercial Banking Industry

Recent developments in commercial banking that have or will have an impact on lending activities include:

1. *Larger banks.* By 2007, during the so-called subprime meltdown, acquisitions and mergers became common place. Big banks absorbed smaller ones or forced them out of business, resulting in fewer locally owned sources for consumers. While mergers were deemed necessary to keep entities from complete collapse, a new phrase became popular: they were "too big to be allowed to fail." This explains why some large institutions had to be infused with huge amounts of money. This will be addressed in subsequent chapters.

2. *Interstate banking.* Many banks have gone nationwide. Geographical restraints are largely ineffective because of interstate deposit-taking, automatic teller machines, and electronic banking

that knows no state borders. Acquisitions of failing banks by out-of-state banks continue throughout the nation.

3. *Longer maturities.* Despite reliance on demand deposits as their principal sources of capital, banks are allowing longer payoff terms. This is especially true when a bank is located in an area where there are few savings banks. In such situations, commercial banks are the only source of real estate loans and can exercise considerable control over loan rates, terms, and, in effect, even local building activity. Banks have become more influential in the housing market in recent years as they began selling loans into the Fannie Mae/Freddie Mac lending arena.

4. *Diversification.* The trend is to limit banks to underwrite commercial paper, mortgage-backed securities, municipal revenue bonds, and other financial undertakings. But the movement to allow banks to sell insurance and securities and/or to broker real estate transactions has effectively been derailed in the current economic climate, in which concerns have surfaced about how big institutions should be allowed to become.

5. *Electronic banking.* In recent times, many banks "without walls" have sprung up, effectively operating without physical branch locations. Virtual banks require no rent for brick and mortar, no tellers or even paper, and they never close. Depositors, borrowers, and investors can do virtually all their transactions on the Internet. Nonetheless, traditional banks have retained their customer base by moving their existing customers to lower-cost Web-based banking.

Battle for Depositors

Commercial banks and savings banks have traditionally been rivals for depositors. It used to be that savings banks, when they were S&Ls, were allowed to pay regular savings account customers a slightly higher interest rate than were commercial banks. On the other hand, only commercial banks were allowed to handle checking accounts.

Not so today! Current legislation (1) allows savings banks to handle checking (negotiable order of withdrawal, NOW for short) accounts and make a variety of personal consumer loans; (2) permits both commercial banks and savings banks to pay interest on checking accounts; and (3) eliminates the interest-rate differential between regular savings accounts in thrifts and in banks. As a result, the war for depositors continues to escalate. The impact of this legislation on the real estate market continues to be debated by housing experts, consumer groups, and the two industries (thrifts and commercial banks) themselves. There are pros and cons on both sides of the issue.

Community Reinvestment Act (CRA)

To guarantee fair lending practices, Congress passed the CRA, which requires all federally supervised financial institutions (thrifts, commercial banks, credit unions, etc.) to disclose lending data in their lobbies and elsewhere. Lenders are required to report data regarding the race, gender, income, and census tract of people to whom they make loans. Its stated purpose is "to assist in identifying discriminatory practices and enforcing antidiscrimination statutes." The CRA encourages lenders to offer mortgages for low- and moderately priced housing and meet other credit needs for low- and moderate-income families. The basic idea is that if an institution accepts deposits from a certain area, it should also offer loans in that area.

CRA ratings are made public for all banks and **thrift institutions**. The government grades each institution on how well it

- Knows the credit needs of its community
- Informs the community about its credit services
- Involves its directors in setting up and monitoring CRA programs
- Participates in government-insured, guaranteed, or subsidized loans
- Distributes credit applications, approvals, and rejections across geographic areas
- Offers a range of residential mortgages, housing rehabilitation loans, and small business loans

All of these criteria are designed to protect consumers against unlawful discrimination. A positive CRA rating is a prerequisite for institutions to open new branches and to engage in expansions, acquisitions, and mergers, since outside third parties can petition agencies to deny these activities to institutions with poor CRA grades.

Ironically, the desire to provide loans for as many borrowers as possible is now partially blamed for the subprime loan explosion and eventual housing problems that began to surface as early as 2007. The rise of the increasingly "easy to qualify" loan instruments of the early 2000s are now criticized as the major contributor to the housing crises that resulted in record foreclosures nationally and major financial problems globally.

Home Mortgage Disclosure Act (HMDA)

The CRA requirements include having lenders retain borrower information from which any discriminatory acts can be determined. The primary source of information for this enforcement is the information gathered via the Fannie Mae/Freddie Mac loan application (known as the 1003). The Information for Government Monitoring Purposes section of the 1003 seeks information regarding a borrower's ethnicity, race, and sex. This section is considered so important that if the borrower refuses or fails to provide the information, the lender is required to "note the information on the basis of visual observation or surname."

2.3 LIFE INSURANCE COMPANIES

Life insurance companies are another important source of real estate financing, particularly for commercial properties, such as shopping centers and office buildings. They are also a major source of credit for large apartment house projects, hotels and motels, industrial buildings, and regional shopping malls. Many people pay for life insurance, but not many claims are paid out at one time. So, the savings of life insurance companies can be substantial and available to lend out for added revenue. Of course, there must be a reserve account and the additional money has to be in a safe investment.

What Is a Life Insurance Company?

A **life insurance company** is a firm that specializes in the insuring of lives for specified amounts in exchange for specified premium payments. The premiums are invested until such time as funds are needed to pay claims or to establish reserves for losses. These premiums are invested in many outlets, including trust deeds and mortgage loans.

Life insurance companies are organized either as mutual companies owned by the policyholders (insureds) who share in the earnings through premium rebates, or as stock companies owned by the stock-holders who, as with any other corporation, are entitled to dividends on earnings. Regardless of whether stock or mutual, insurance companies are licensed by the state in which they are incorporated and/or where they have their principal offices. Each insurance company is governed by the state where it conducts business, and each state regulates the permitted types of loans, maximum loan-to-value ratios, and other conditions.

Lending Characteristics of Life Insurance Companies

In general, life insurance companies have the broadest lending powers of the **institutional lenders**. Their investment policies are flexible and cover a wide range of financing activities. The laws governing life insurance company activities vary from state to state. Under California laws and regulations, any company not incorporated within this state, but doing business here, is subject to the same restrictions that are placed upon California-based companies.

The chief lending characteristics of life insurance companies include the following:

- Loan-to-value ratios are apt to be on the cautious side, frequently less than 80 percent.

- Payback terms are long, usually 30-year amortizations, with occasional **lock-in clauses** that prevent a loan from being paid off before a specified date. For example, there might be a 10- or 15-year lock-in clause on a 30-year loan. The borrower would not be able to pay off the loan until after the lock-in date.

- Interest rates and other fees on conventional loans have traditionally been the lowest among the institutionals, though in recent times they have been steadily climbing.

- Insurance companies prefer to grant large real estate loans (in the millions) as opposed to smaller residential home loans. Many major commercial and industrial developments have insurance company take-out loans.

- Construction loans generally are not desired. Instead, life insurance companies will make the take-out, or permanent, loan after the structure has been completed according to plans and specifications.

- Loan **correspondents** are widely used as agents of insurance companies. Many life insurance companies will contract for such representation whenever they deem it profitable. In this way the insurance company is relieved of the burden of originating and processing loans, as well as some administrative and service functions. Correspondents are especially used in California, where there is a high demand for loans, but where few insurance companies are actually headquartered. Detailed information concerning lending authority for insurance companies is found in the California Insurance Code, especially in Section 1150.

Trends in the Life Insurance Industry

Trends that affect life insurance lending practices include the following:

1. *Equity conversion positions during inflationary periods.* Here the lender has the option to convert part of the mortgage into an equity position in the property: a shared investment. In short, the

lender has the right to convert a portion of the mortgage owed into a part of the ownership of the property at a later date.

2. *Upfront participations* (piece of the action). As a condition of granting a loan, an insurance company may require an upfront share of the income produced by the property to help increase the yield on the loan. Such sharing is called **equity participation**. Participation may also take the form of an "equity kicker" such that, instead of income, the lender takes a percentage ownership in the property. Increasingly, however, insurance companies are buying whole projects as sole owners. In periods of rapid inflation, when fixed interest rates become discouraging as investment funds become scarce, participations become an attractive supplement.

3. *Variable and fixed annuities.* As more people purchase insurance company annuity contracts, larger supplies of funds become available for reinvestment. Real estate loans are one way insurance companies reinvest annuity contributions.

4. *Holding companies and joint ventures.* Where state law does not prohibit the practice, a number of life insurance companies are purchased or reorganized under the umbrella of holding companies. In such instances, interrelated lending activities are made possible because other firms that may be joined together under the parent holding company include such entities as commercial banks, savings banks, and even development companies that furnish construction financing, permanent financing, and so forth.

A variation of this concept of pooling resources is through the media of joint ventures. Under such a venture, a life insurance company may provide the needed financing while a well-established developer will furnish the requisite know-how and co-develop a project.

2.4 MUTUAL SAVINGS BANKS

Mutual savings banks operate much like former savings and loan associations, but they exist chiefly in the northeastern United States. None exist in California, but it is important to consider them because of the large contribution they make in furnishing capital for residential loans via the secondary marketplace. **Mutual savings banks**, also called mutual thrifts, are not commercial banks. They are organized in substantially the same way regardless of the state in which they are chartered. They are banks for savings deposits that have no stockholders and are organized to pool the interests of those of moderate means. Managed by a board of trustees, directors, or managers, mutual savings banks distribute their earnings, after payment of necessary business expenses and taxes, to the depositors in the form of dividends, or the earnings are added to the bank's surplus or reserve funds.

Depending on state law, the maximum loan-to-value ratio varies from 50 to 90 percent, exclusive of government-backed loans. When money becomes tight and the yields on other investment outlets increase, mutual savings banks pull back on their real estate lending activities and expand their lending in non-real estate areas.

2.5 DEPOSITORY INSTITUTIONS AND MONETARY CONTROL ACT

The Monetary Control Act completely phased out restrictions on interest rates that lenders can pay depositors. As a result, new systems for raising, mobilizing, and investing money were developed. All of this was intended to increase the yields offered to savers and depositors based upon the terms of their checking and savings accounts. In deregulating financial institutions, we saw the homogenization of these institutions. It had become difficult to distinguish between savings banks (thrifts) and commercial banks; so close were their respective functions. Reserves were more or less uniform, consumer lending powers of every variety were ultimately granted, territorial lending restrictions were phased out, and restrictions against junior financing were lifted; a wave of new types of deposits and classes of savings accounts continued to emerge out of the deregulation process.

Additionally, the act expanded the lending authority of federal thrift institutions to allow investment in consumer loans, commercial paper, corporate debt securities, and junior trust deeds. It authorized these institutions to make acquisitions, development and construction loans, and removed the geographical lending restrictions along with certain dollar limitations on residential real estate loans.

By 2009, following what were viewed as lending abuses, the movement for greater monetary oversight grew.

2.6 PENSION AND RETIREMENT FUNDS

Potentially the largest sources of real estate financing continue to be public and private **pension fund**. There are hundreds of thousands of private pension funds and state, local, and federal pension funds nationwide, representing billions in assets. The Mortgage Bankers Association of America's projection that the growth of these funds would create an enormous amount of potential mortgage funds has remained mostly unfulfilled. The loss of equity of many funds in the late 2000s is likely to continue to impact the availability of these funds in the future.

Administration and Lending Policies of Pension and Trust Funds

Administrators of pension funds include trust departments of commercial banks and life insurance companies; trustees of unions; boards of trustees appointed by a governor or mayor, in the case of state and local government employees; and employers. Lending policies vary considerably from fund to fund, with no uniform administrative practices followed. Prudence, market conditions, size of the fund, philosophy of the administrators, and other factors dictate how the funds might best be invested at any given time. In California, the massive PERS (Public Employees Retirement System) has a very large home loan program as does the STRS (State Teachers Retirement System). As lenders increased their down payment requirements starting in mid 2008, these programs continued to offer employees 100 percent financing by allowing them to use 5 percent of their fund contributions for a down payment accompanied by a 95 percent LTV loan.

Individual Retirement Accounts (IRAs) and Keogh Plans

As private pension programs became more popular with liberalized tax-deferred contributions for Individual Retirement Accounts for employees, and allowances under the Keogh Plan for self-employed persons, substantially more of these dollars entered the capital markets. These funds were an important source of real estate financing on all levels.

For years, most pension funds had been invested in government securities and in corporate stocks and bonds. However, the rapid increase in the assets of pension funds and the desire to diversify these investments motivated some fund managers to look at real estate loans as an additional source of investment.

But as the subprime market flourished, the mostly conservative fund managers were reluctant to invest in what they viewed as risky mortgages. But since other sources of investment money were so plentiful, these funds were hardly missed.

2.7 GOVERNMENT REGULATORY AGENCIES

A variety of federal and state agencies govern activities and practices of institutional lenders. For real estate financing purposes, the most significant are briefly outlined below and discussed in greater depth in other chapters.

Massive changes in the regulatory structure at the federal level were instituted as a result of widespread failures of thrift institutions in the 1980s and early 1990s. A whole new alphabet soup of acronyms replaced many of the old, beginning with the law itself, the **Financial Institutions Reform, Recovery, and Enforcement Act (FIRREA).** Following the perceived excesses of the subprime lending practices, in 2009 additional regulatory oversight of many of the federal agencies created by FIRREA was recommended in an attempt to further protect and reassure consumers:

1. *Office of Thrift Supervision (OTS)*. This is a branch of the U.S. Treasury. It was created by FIRREA to replace the Federal Home Loan Bank Board as the chief regulator of all federal and many state-chartered thrift institutions, including savings banks and S&L associations.

2. *Savings Association Insurance Fund (SAIF)*. This agency was created by FIRREA to replace the Federal Savings and Loan Insurance Corporation (FSLIC), which became insolvent. SAIF collects insurance premiums on checking and savings deposits from all federally insured savings associations. It is managed by the *FDIC (Federal Deposit Insurance Corporation)*, but SAIF insurance premiums are kept separate from premiums paid by commercial and savings banks in a Bank Insurance Fund (BIF). In 2005, Congress merged the SAIF and BIF into one insurance fund called the Deposit Insurance Fund (DIF). At the same time, the federal deposit insurance level was increased from $100,000 to $250,000 on retirement accounts. The same law gave the FDIC the option to increase insurance ceilings on regular bank accounts from $100,000 using an inflation factor starting in 2010.

3. *Federal Deposit Insurance Corporation (FDIC)*. This familiar federal agency's main task is to promote public confidence in the financial systems of commercial and savings banks and is empowered to insure deposits only (not securities or mutual funds) up to designated amounts per account, presently $250,000 per depositor per bank. This increased amount of insurance will expire on December 31, 2013, and the level, except for some retirement accounts, will revert to $100,000. Guarding the public's deposits,

the FDIC's success is measured by the fact that since its initiation, no depositor has lost a single cent of insured funds via any bank failure. The FDIC's ability to reassure the public was clearly tested in 2009 with the collapse of one of the largest entities in California, Indy Mac Bank. Recognizing that customers' deposits were insured safely stopped what had begun to be a "run on the bank." The FDIC manages the Savings Association Insurance Fund as well as the Bank Insurance Fund.

4. *Federal Housing Finance Board (FHFB)*. This five-member Board oversees mortgage lending by the 12 regional Federal Home Loan Banks. Its mission is to support local, community-based financial institutions, facilitate access to credit, and insure that lenders carry out their housing and community development finance requirements. It is also responsible for providing statistical data to the housing industry. Under the "Housing and Economic Recovery Act of 2008 (HERA)," Government Sponsored Enterprises, known as GSEs, (discussed in Chapter 6) provide stability and liquidity in the mortgage market and support affordable housing.

5. *Federal Reserve Bank Board (FRBB)*. This agency oversees the Federal Reserve System, regulates activities of commercial banks, and regulates the flow of money and credit, as discussed in Chapter 1.

6. *Federal Home Loan Mortgage Corporation (FHLMC)*. Popularly called Freddie Mac, when coupled with the Federal National Mortgage Association (FNMA), known as Fannie Mae, both entities function as integral parts of a "secondary mortgage market" in which loans are purchased from participating lenders. The primary purpose of both entities is to ensure stability to the mortgage market by creating liquidity, accessibility, and affordability for residential mortgage financing. By 2008 the mortgage meltdown had affected both entities, and the Federal Housing Finance Agency was appointed conservator for FNMA when the U.S. Department of the Treasury was required to "loan" the agency $200 billion to enable it to continue to provide liquidity to the mortgage market (discussed more fully in Chapter 7).

7. *Office of Comptroller of the Currency (OCC)*. This agency is responsible for regulating and supervising nearly 1,600 national banks and 50 federal branches of foreign banks in the U.S., which account for nearly two-thirds of the total assets of all U.S. commercial banks (as of June 2009). One of the OCCs objectives is to ensure the safety and soundness of the national banking system. Additionally, while ensuring fair and equal access to financial

services for all segments of the community, it also promotes competition by encouraging banks to offer new products and services.

8. *California Department of Financial Institutions (DFI).* Under the jurisdiction of the California Business, Transportation, and Housing Agency and a cabinet-level post, the financial commissioner supervises all state-chartered banks. The DFI oversees the operation of approximately 700 state-licensed financial institutions, including about 200 state banks and 200 state credit unions, and is charged with maintaining the integrity of all financial services provided by this network of institutions. If insured, state institutions also operate under supervision of the FHFB.

2.8 TRADE ASSOCIATIONS

In addition to statutory regulatory agencies, a variety of **trade associations** help foster and promote the interests of member firms. Membership is strictly voluntary, but the benefits are great enough to provide broad appeal to lenders to join. It is axiomatic that where a community of interests exists, firms will band together in order to protect and enhance those interests.

Several important trade associations are the following:

1. *California League of Savings Institutions.* Headquartered in Los Angeles, this organization consists of both state and federally chartered California-based savings institutions. With 9 of the 10 largest S&Ls located in California in the early 1990s, the League wielded considerable influence. Following the S&L scandals, this influence diminished.

2. *Mortgage Bankers Association of America (MBA).* This trade association comprises the principal investors and lending interests in the mortgage banking field. Representing an industry that employs over 280,000 people pledged to extend affordable housing across the nation, the MBA promotes fair and ethical lending practices via a wide range of educational programs and publications. The organization and its members have extended their reach in recent years beyond just the urban mortgage field. Membership combines into one group all of the leading lenders in the mortgage industry and is a major influence in today's home mortgage arena.

3. *American Bankers Association (ABA).* Commercial banks throughout the nation, both federally and state chartered, may join this association. This voluntary organization provides valuable financial data to member banks, government agencies, economists and

researchers, and the public at large. The ABA also offers a broad educational program through the American Institute of Banking.

4. *National Association of Independent Mortgage Bankers (NAIMB)*. This association consists of many members whose banks are not part of a large bank chain. Many independent bankers hold membership in the ABA as well.

5. *Institute of Life Insurance.* This institute, located in New York, comprises the voluntary membership of most of the life insurance companies operating throughout the United States. Its *Life Insurance Fact Book* is published annually and is highly informative not only as to life insurance facts but also for those interested in real estate portfolios of member firms.

6. *National Association of Mortgage Brokers (NAMB).* This is the lobbying group for loan brokers nationwide. Members subscribe to a code of ethics and pledge to participate in lending practices that promote integrity, professionalism, and confidentiality. The mortgage broker industry is regulated by federal law as well as state laws and licensing boards. NAMB provides education and guidance to an industry that still provides over 50 percent of all residential loans originated in the U.S.

Finally, fueled by what some believed to be overzealous Congressional action, a national licensing program was inacted beginning 2010. A national registry was created and by the end of 2010 all loan originators will be required to take a national test after completing 20 hours of required education, provide credit information, submit fingerprints, and undergo a federal background check. Additionally, each state is charged with developing their own complimentary testing and qualifying program. Current licensees in California, considered one of the most difficult states in which to acquire a real estate license, will be required to complete both the national and state licensing procedures no later than September 2010 in order to continue to function as a loan originator.

SUMMARY

Savings banks (thrifts), commercial banks, and life insurance companies are major providers of real estate mortgage funds. Each operates according to statutory provisions of federal and state laws, by-laws of the individual institutional lender, and self-imposed policies, which vary according to market conditions. In general, savings banks offer the highest loan-to-value ratios in the area of conventional loans, and they specialize in the financing of residential properties.

Commercial banks historically favored commercial and industrial properties but recently have been more active in residential properties. Another major bank role is in short term construction financing, since banks are more prone to quick turnover of deposits held in the form of checking (or demand) accounts. Life insurance companies have the broadest lending powers of the institutional lenders but favor only prime properties and large loan packages. They deal through loan correspondents in areas where loan demand is high but where they have no offices.

Besides policing themselves through individual efforts, institutional lenders (institutionals) are subjected to rules and regulations by various government agencies and trade associations. Federally chartered savings banks are regulated by the Federal Housing Finance Board and the Savings Association Insurance Fund, while state-chartered savings banks are supervised by the California Banking Commissioner. Federally chartered commercial banks are governed by the Federal Reserve Board of Governors, the Comptroller of the Currency, and the Federal Deposit Insurance Corporation, while the California Department of Banking oversees state-chartered commercial banks.

IMPORTANT TERMS AND CONCEPTS

Bridge loan

Commercial bank

Correspondent

Equity participation

Federal Deposit Insurance Corporation (FDIC)

Federal Home Loan Mortgage Corporation (FHLMC)

Federal Housing Finance Board

Federal Reserve Bank Board (FRBB)

Financial Institutions Reform, Recovery, and Enforcement Act (FIRREA)

Financial intermediary

Home Mortgage Disclosure Act

Institutional lender

Interim loan

Life insurance company

Loan-to-value ratio

Lock-in clause

Mutual savings bank

Office of Thrift Supervision (OTS)

Pension fund

Rate lock

Savings Association Insurance Fund (SAIF)

Savings bank

Swing loan

Take-out loan

Thrift institution

Time deposit

Trade association

Usury

REVIEWING YOUR UNDERSTANDING

Questions for Discussion

1. Briefly explain the difference between a commercial bank and a savings bank (thrift).

2. List three lending characteristics for each of the following lending institutions:
   a. savings bank
   b. commercial bank
   c. life insurance company

3. Identify one trend affecting the lending policies for each one of the principal lending institutions operating in California.

4. What is the difference between a regulatory agency and a trade association?

Multiple-Choice Questions

1. Which of the following is not an institutional lender?
   a. mortgage company.
   b. commercial bank.
   c. savings bank.
   d. life insurance company.

2. The term "savings bank" includes
   a. thrift institutions.
   b. savings and loan associations.
   c. credit unions.
   d. each of the foregoing.

3. A checking account is also known as a
   a. time deposit.
   b. demand deposit.
   c. certificate of deposit.
   d. personal account.

4. The Bank Insurance Fund (BIF) merged with SAIF into a single insurance fund, the Deposit Insurance Fund (DIF), providing for up to
   a. $100,000 insurance of bank accounts.
   b. unlimited insurance for checking accounts.
   c. $250,000 insurance of bank accounts.
   d. any amount tied to inflation-indexed accounts.

5. The relatively sudden flow of funds out of thrift institutions into the stock market is called
   a. reverse annuity.
   b. disintermediation.
   c. reintermediation.
   d. variable annuity.

6. Easy-to-qualify loan instruments of the early 2000s
   a. have had no effect on housing inventory.
   b. resulted in reducing foreclosures.
   c. made homeownership impossible for millions of potential buyers.
   d. are criticized as the major contributor to the housing crisis.

7. Loans combining construction and permanent financing are commonly referred to as
   a. dual.
   b. take-out.
   c. all-inclusive.
   d. combination.

8. Which institutional lender favors very large commercial property loans?
   a. savings banks.
   b. credit unions.
   c. life insurance companies.
   d. savings and loan associations.

9. Passbook savings accounts are technically
   a. time deposits.
   b. demand deposits.
   c. commercial deposits.
   d. industrial deposits.

10. Regarding commercial banks
    a. acquisitions and mergers became unpopular after the subprime meltdown of 2007.
    b. small banks absorbed large banks in order to stay afloat.
    c. Large banks became too big to allow them to fail.
    d. regional and nationwide banks became more stable during 2007–2008.

11. In their efforts to raise money for mortgage lending, savings banks have turned to such devices as
    a. mortgage-backed bonds.
    b. disintermediation.
    c. unsecured personal loans.
    d. all of the above.

12. The bulk of funds held by commercial banks is in the form of
    a. certificates of deposit (CDs).
    b. cash.
    c. demand deposits.
    d. securities.

13. Some institutional lenders have a threshold that requires private mortgage insurance for loan-to-value ratios that exceed:
    a. 50 percent
    b. 80 percent
    c. 70 percent
    d. 60 percent

14. A loan provision that prevents an early payoff of a loan prior to a set date is called
    a. a prepayment clause.
    b. a lock-in clause.
    c. a subordination clause.
    d. an acceleration clause.

15. Freddie Mac was established to
    a. provide insurance for savings accounts.
    b. govern the operations of savings banks.
    c. create a secondary market for savings banks.
    d. regulate checking accounts for savings banks.

16. Finance companies
    a. appeal to hard-to-finance borrowers.
    b. are usually offered with no pre-payment penalty.
    c. are generally characterized by lower interest rates.
    d. make loans only if secured by personal property.

17. Insuring the deposits of commercial banks and savings banks is the
    a. Office of Thrift Supervision.
    b. Savings Association Fund.
    c. Federal Home Loan Mortgage Corporation.
    d. Federal Deposit Insurance Corporation.

18. When a lender takes an upfront share of the income produced by a property it is called
    a. equity participation.
    b. a roll-over provision.
    c. a shared investment.
    d. intermediary subordination.

19. Which federal law tracks the lending practices of banks and thrift institutions to ensure fair borrower treatment?
    a. Borrower's Rights Act.
    b. Home Fairness Act.
    c. Resolution Trust Act.
    d. Community Reinvestment Act.

20. Since the economic debacle of 2007, down payments for the purchase of a home are expected to become
    a. more flexible.
    b. less stringent.
    c. more receptive to buyers of high-priced homes.
    d. none of the above.

CASE & POINT

The Secure & Fair Enforcement for Mortgage Licensing Act of 2009 (SAFE)

Fueled by what some believed to be overzealous action, Congress enacted this Nationwide Mortgage Licensing System (NMLS) in 2009 in an attempt to create a minimum continuity and conformity regarding the licensing of mortgage originators across the country. It is designed to become the central repository of licensing information while state agencies (e.g., California Department of Real Estate) will remain the regulatory arm of the program. Every state was mandated to develop a mortgage-originator licensing process for participation in the NMLS no later than December 2010. But all mortgage loan originators had to initially register by January 31, 2010.

All mortgage loan originators will be required to take a national test after completing 20 hours of required pre-test education. Each originator must provide credit information, submit fingerprints and undergo a federal background check. Additionally, each state is charged with developing their own complimentary testing and qualifying program that is to encompass a minimum 8 hour annual Continuing Education requirement for the maintenance of a license. California licensees, will be required to complete both the national and state licensing procedures no later than September 2010 in order to continue to function as a mortgage loan originator.

California's current real estate licensing requirements are some of the most rigorous in the nation, already requiring the completion of 45 hours of continuing educational study every four years along with the submission for a fingerprinting background check. Nevertheless, California will now have to incorporate this new license endorsement requirement. As of February 2010, California had not yet developed its state testing element. In an effort to level the playing field among all originators, the new procedures will now include those mortgage lenders currently functioning under the Department of Corporations as well as those licensed via the California Department of Real Estate.

While recognizing the value of education, critics wonder how a national test can encompass the numerous details unique to each state's mortgage broker practices. Some believe that the new requirements will spawn a whole new industry for those offering the 20 hour educational course along with "crash course" test preparation training, including sample tests, all designed to help licensees pass the new test.

The background check, including credit history, is a concern for many current licensees. Many worry that the recent downturn in the economy may well have negatively affected their credit history. Although there have been assurances that the credit report alone will not endanger the loss of a license, mortgage brokers are understandably concerned that they could be deprived of a livelihood due to circumstances beyond their control.

Coupled with all the other newly adopted regulations (discussed in Case and Point presentations throughout this text), mortgage loan brokering has its challenges as we move into the next decade.

Chapter

3

PREVIEW

In Chapter 2, institutional lenders were described as real estate lenders whose activities are highly regulated by various state and federal agencies.

In this chapter, you will study non-institutional lenders—real estate lenders whose activities are not as strictly regulated as institutional lenders. Noninstitutional lenders include private parties, mortgage companies, syndicates, real estate investment trusts, pension and trust funds, endowment funds, and credit unions.

After completing this chapter, you should be able to:

1. List five major noninstitutional lenders.
2. Describe major provisions of the California Real Property Loan Law.
3. Discuss the role that mortgage correspondents, mortgage bankers, mortgage companies, and mortgage brokers play in real estate finance.
4. Discuss why pensions, trust funds, and credit unions are increasing in importance in the financing process.
5. Describe how and why the role of the real estate broker as a financial advisor is becoming increasingly challenging.

Noninstitutional Lenders and The California Real Property Loan Law

3.1 PRIVATE PARTY LENDERS

Although the term *private party lenders* in its broadest sense refers to virtually all nongovernment lenders, for our purpose, a **private lender** means a person who lends directly to another person. This narrow definition will help distinguish a private lender from the other forms of noninstitutional lenders discussed in this chapter.

Lack of Structure

There is no formal structure to the private lender industry. Individuals ordinarily do not operate in concert with one another. Private lenders have no association such as those found with other forms of lenders and are, at best, highly fragmented and scattered throughout California. An individual may, of course, form a partnership or a corporation, but these are mere business organizations designed to facilitate the operation of the individual's investments into real estate trust deeds or mortgage loans.

Unlike institutional lenders, private individuals have fewer laws and regulations that restrict their lending activities. There are no uniform policies; practices, procedures, and policies vary considerably from one private lender to another. However, individuals can be subject to the usury statutes that dictate the maximum interest rate that may be legally charged. Exemptions from the usury law are discussed later in this chapter. The benefit of using this type of loan is there might be more flexible standards or money available in a shorter period of time. A borrower might use this lender because he did not qualify for a more "standard" loan.

Types of Private Lenders

Direct Private Lenders

People invest in real estate loans for a variety of reasons, primarily because they are not satisfied with the returns paid on other forms of investments. This difficulty in finding safe investment options became particularly acute as the economy faltered in the late 2000s. The return on typical "safe" bank savings and CD accounts fell, in some cases, to under 2 percent, even if deposited for a three-year term. Despite the fact that these accounts were insured by the Federal Deposit Insurance Corporation up to a designated amount, depositors were dissatisfied with this low interest rate. In more normal times, the bank or thrift institution would have turned around and re-loaned the deposit money at a much higher rate of interest. In many instances, money became very scarce for those wanting to borrow. At the same time, real estate sales slowed, reducing a potential investment opportunity for those seeking a higher return. While making direct loans on real estate a private lender can eliminate the go-between broker. Caution must be exercised as the appraisal, loan screening, and other services provided by the intermediary are also eliminated. Thus, private lenders must perform these loan services themselves. On the plus side, however, where the risks are greater, the rewards for the private lender may also be greater in the form of higher interest rate yields.

Indirect Private Lenders

In order to obtain a higher interest rate or to overcome the loan screening burdens of direct lending, many private individuals place money through **mortgage brokers**. This is a symbiotic relationship in which investors rely upon a mortgage broker for expertise, while the broker assists borrowers who don't necessarily meet the qualifying guidelines of institutional lenders. The private lender's lack of knowledge and sophistication can be addressed at the same time that he or she is matched with a borrower who needs private money. The key for success is that the broker recommend "suitable" transactions, protecting both the investor and the prospective borrower. In short, the broker takes a borrower and a lender and puts them together, as seen in Figure 3.1. The broker's commission is usually paid for by the borrower.

Sellers as Private Lenders

In the process of selling their property, a seller sometimes becomes a lender. A buyer may not have enough cash for the down payment or may choose not to tie up his or her capital in equity. Hence the

FIGURE 3.1   The role of the mortgage broker.

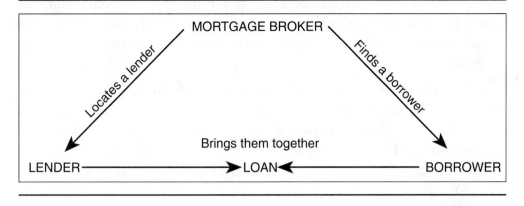

seller is placed in the position of either having to turn down the offer, renegotiate more favorable terms, or "carry back a loan." This is usually the difference between the down payment plus a new loan and the sales price. The vast majority of these seller carry back loans are in the form of a junior encumbrance, typically, a second trust deed. On some occasions they may be first loans, where a seller is willing to finance the entire transaction him- or herself, such as on a free and clear property (property free of any loans). In effect, sellers become lenders by financing part or all of their equity.

It should also be mentioned that seller carry back loans are exempt from usury laws; that is, sellers can charge any interest rate they wish, as noted later in this chapter.

NOTE: Logically, it was thought that seller financing would become more important as more stringent qualifying guidelines were adopted in the financing arena. For instance, it seemed to make sense that a borrower who had a 10 percent down payment with a seller willing to "carry 10 percent" as a second trust deed, allowing the institutional lender to make only an 80 percent loan-to-value ratio loan, would be acceptable to institutional lenders. But, lending practices in the late 2000s eliminated seller financing in such situations—resulting in a reduction of some real estate transactions—at a time when housing sales were declining. Fewer seller carry backs were also due to sellers not having enough equity in their property. With no equity, all the buyer's money would go toward paying off the existing loan.

Characteristics of Private Lenders

Private lenders generally have some common characteristics, regardless of whether the loan is made directly by the individual or indirectly through a loan broker. *The following information is predicated on a "typical" market operation. While the lending abuses of the early 2000s suspended some of the use of seller financing, the market functions in cycles and it is expected that seller financing will again be reinstated as a viable part of real estate financing options.*

- Private lenders are, for the most part, less formal and therefore make highly subjective loan decisions, especially when making a loan directly to a borrower. On the other hand, mortgage brokers who represent some private lenders are usually very sophisticated and provide guidelines and counseling for their investor clients.

- High interest rates are normally charged, due to the high risks involved. However, exceptions exist in seller carry back transactions where a relatively low rate may be acceptable due to offsetting benefits (i.e., higher price, shorter escrow, no other offers, etc.). To compensate for a 6 percent rate (for example), a seller might either increase the price of the property or be willing to settle for the lower rate when the rates quoted on new first loans are so low that buyers are unwilling to pay higher-than-market rates on the junior loan.

- Most private lenders operate in the second trust deed market. As pointed out previously, this is often created by the needs of the marketplace, when a seller carries back a second deed of trust in order to close the transaction. Frequently these second loans are thereafter sold to investors, usually at a discount, when the seller needs cash. Today's secondary market reluctance to purchase loans that include seller carry back loans has all but eliminated, at least temporarily, the use of such second trust deeds. Part of the mortgage broker's responsibility has been to "structure" the transaction and its terms depending upon whether the seller anticipates retaining or selling the note.

- Private lenders rarely make prime loans and almost never get involved in construction financing. (Prime loans are those that involve the least risk to lenders and are usually first liens.)

- Most loans are on single-family dwellings because this type of property is most familiar to the typical private investor, and also because the size of the loan is relatively modest.

- The vast majority of loans by private individuals are made within the local geographic areas.

- The term of a private loan is usually short—most commonly between two and five years—and often calls for a balloon payment. When institutional lenders accept secondary financing, they usually require specific note requirements, including a minimum term and sometimes a minimum interest rate, and the note must be structured accordingly.

- Monthly collections may be performed through a mortgage company or financial institution, though individual lenders may in some cases collect themselves. The setup and collection fees charged by commercial and savings banks are relatively small, since these institutions are interested in obtaining the customer's account. Some offer free collection service when the customer maintains a minimum balance in a savings or checking account.

- A large number of private party loans are seller carrybacks.

3.2 USURY LAW

Many states have passed laws establishing the maximum rate of interest that can be charged on various types of loans. Interest rates that exceed the maximum rate are considered usurious and therefore illegal. In some instances if a lender is found guilty of usury, the borrower would not have to pay any interest!

In California the maximum rate for loans secured by real property is the greater of 10 percent or 5 percent above the Federal Reserve Bank of San Francisco discount rate, unless the lender is exempt from the law. California regulations exempt from the usury law institutional lenders such as banks and their loan *correspondents*, thrift institutions, and life insurance companies. Also exempt from usury laws are noninstitutional lenders including *mortgage companies*, industrial loan companies, **credit unions**, personal property brokers, owners who carry back paper when they sell, and any transaction that uses a real estate broker. This law is almost primarily for direct private lenders. For example, real estate loans from regulated institutional lenders can be at any rate, whereas an actual direct, hard money real estate loan (not a seller carry back) from a private lender is not exempt, unless a real estate licensee is handling the transaction.

The pros and cons of usury laws are currently being debated. Proponents believe that usury laws protect consumers against certain greedy lenders, while opponents believe usury laws restrict the supply of loan funds and drive some borrowers to do business with illegal loan sharks. See Figure 3.2. The emergence of payday loans and subprime lending re-introduced the question of what is usurious in today's lending market.

FIGURE 3.2 A loan shark.

3.3 MORTGAGE COMPANIES

The terms **mortgage bankers**, **mortgage brokers**, and *mortgage companies* frequently are used interchangeably, but they are not the same. These entities are not thrift institutions, nor are they depository institutions, but they do assist by bringing the borrower together with a lender and charge a fee for this service.

Structure and Types of Mortgage Agencies

Mortgage bankers are generally incorporated businesses that can make loans with their own funds or through a line of credit. The mortgage banker originates, finances ("funds"), and closes loans secured by real estate and then resells them to various investors.

When a mortgage banking company represents a life insurance company, bank, thrift association, pension fund, or other lender, it is called a **mortgage correspondent**. It "corresponds" on behalf of its principals in dealing with prospective borrowers. The mortgage correspondent is paid a fee in exchange for originating, processing, closing, and frequently servicing loans. The mortgage company may be given exclusive territories, in which case the correspondent will be entitled to a fee, even if it had not actively solicited the loan; or it may be nonexclusive, in which case the correspondent can, in effect, be in competition with a lender that it represents. For instance, a lender may have a retail office providing loans with different rates and terms than the correspondent who is placing a loan with them on a wholesale basis. Whatever the type of arrangement, mortgage loan correspondents serve a very valuable function in real estate financing for lenders whose headquarters or principal offices are located great distances from the properties on which they make loans. Correspondents have been especially successful in the Far West, particularly in California.

Although most mortgage companies act as correspondents in investing others' funds, there are many firms that invest their own funds exclusively. Another category of mortgage lender is a hybrid, both investing money into real estate trust deeds and mortgages for others in an agency or fiduciary capacity and investing its own funds in the role of a principal.

Mortgage loan brokers are in the business of locating borrowers and lenders and arranging loans between them, and in the process they earn a commission or fee. As such, the loan broker takes no risk of loss. Another distinction between a mortgage banker and a mortgage (or loan) broker is that mortgage bankers frequently service the loans of the lenders that they represent, whereas mortgage brokers usually do not.

Lending Characteristics of Mortgage Companies

Mortgage companies that do not loan their own funds are restricted in their lending activities to the same restrictions that govern their principal(s). Thus, if a California mortgage loan representative or banker correspondent represents an eastern life insurance company, they have the same loan-to-value limitations placed on its loans as the insurance company has. This is easy to understand in that any representative is a mere agent and stands, therefore, in the shoes of its principal, the lender. Aside from the legal restrictions, the correspondent reflects the lending philosophy, policies, and practices of those lenders—whether giant institutions or individuals—that it represents. This applies to both construction and permanent loans.

In California, mortgage companies are licensed by either the Department of Corporations (DOC) or the Department of Real Estate and they are subject to lending and other general business regulations. There has long been a controversy over whether loan representatives of banks, who are generally licensed under the D.O.C., have an advantage in that they have functioned under less restrictive disclosure requirements than those with real estate licenses. The new Recovery Act of 2008 made some attempts to level the playing field by requiring consistent licensing laws to apply to all loan representatives. (This will be discussed more fully in the Case & Point in Chapter 5).

Mortgage companies may also engage in a number of related real estate activities. These include brokerage, development, construction, and property management. These activities are especially important as additional potential ways to create income when activity in the mortgage market slows down.

3.4 REAL PROPERTY LOAN LAW

Subprime Borrowers and Predatory Lending

The collapse of the subprime lending environment led to lots of finger-pointing regarding who was to blame for the excesses and abuses committed. Was it the loan programs developed and marketed by the major lenders or the loan officers' promotion of those products to consumers that were primarily responsible? What role did appraisers play in the constantly accelerating home values? Did consumers, anxious to buy a home at any price, play a part in the ultimate failure of subprime lending practices? While we continue to debate who or what to blame, the need for the Real Property Loan Law became very clear.

The original motivation for subprime loans to allow more buyers to purchase homes was laudable. The constant reduction in loan qualification requirements, however, resulted in too many people buying homes that they would soon discover they could not afford. **Subprime loans** were usually granted to homeowners with low credit scores who wished to purchase or refinance a home. Subprime loans were also granted to credit-damaged or lower-income borrowers. These loans were granted at higher interest rates and fees to reflect the additional risk incurred by the lender. Many of these loans had 2 or 3 year terms, promoted on the basis that the short term would allow the borrower to correct any credit blemishes and then be eligible for a refinance at better rates and terms, all with the anticipation that the market would continue in its never-ending incline. Too often, the borrower did not improve his or her credit record. Then, the market stopped its incline. Thus was born the practice of enticing subprime homeowners into a series of refinances in which their equity (if any) was stripped away by high fees and balloon payments that led to still-another larger refinance. This process was repeated until the homeowner's equity was totally depleted, often resulting in foreclosure.

Consumer advocates and various government agencies became increasingly concerned that some lenders had taken advantage of the situation by charging excessive interest and fees beyond a reasonable markup for the additional risk of granting loans to subprime borrowers. Numerous new regulations were adopted in 2009 in an effort to curb such excesses of "predatory lending."

Purpose of the Mortgage Loan Broker Law

As pointed out earlier, individuals may become indirect lenders by investing through an intermediary, called a mortgage broker. In California, this intermediary must be a licensed real estate broker, and is hence called a loan broker, and governed by Sections 10240 through 10248 of the California Business and Professions Code (B&P) (Article 7: Real Property Loans). This segment of the real estate law is popularly referred to as the "Mortgage Loan Broker Law" by real estate practitioners.

The purpose of the **Real Property Mortgage Loan Law** is to protect certain borrowers who acquire loans secured by real estate. The law requires that prospective borrowers be supplied with complete loan information. The broker must provide the applicant with a completed **Mortgage Loan Disclosure Statement** (MLDS) when the loan is initiated and prior to the borrower being obligated to proceed with the loan. The MLDS, coupled with the Truth-in-Lending (TIL) disclosure (more fully discussed in Chapter 10) provides a borrower with the details of the prospective loan. Rules have long required that these disclosures be provided to the borrower within three days of his or her submitting a loan application. The Mortgage Disclosure Improvement Act (MDIA) imposed additional disclosure rules, as described in the Case & Point in Chapter 10.

Which of the two MLDS disclosure forms (traditional or non-traditional) to be used depends upon whether the loan being sought is a fixed or adjustable rate, interest only, or other optional loan product. Because of the perceived abuses associated with past subprime lending, a separate non-traditional MLDS disclosure form is required with any loan other than a typical fixed rate option.

Figure 3.3 is a reproduction of the Traditional Mortgage Loan Disclosure Statement produced by the California Department of Real Estate. It contains information about estimated costs, expenses, and commissions to be paid by the applicant for the proposed loan. In another attempt to ensure that borrowers are aware of their loan terms and to avoid any last minute surprises regarding loan costs, new rules require that the initial disclosure be within a certain "tolerance" of the final costs and terms. In other words, the final annual percentage rate (APR) calculation (disclosed on the TIL) must be within one-eighth percent of the original calculation or a new disclosure must be provided, signed, and returned prior

FIGURE 3.3 Sample mortgage loan disclosure statement.

STATE OF CALIFORNIA
DEPARTMENT OF REAL ESTATE
Serving Californians Since 1917

MORTGAGE LOAN DISCLOSURE STATEMENT/GOOD FAITH ESTIMATE

RE 883 (Rev. 8/08)

Borrower's Name(s):_____

Real Property Collateral: The intended security for this proposed loan will be a Deed of Trust on (street address or legal description) _____

This joint Mortgage Loan Disclosure Statement/Good Faith Estimate is being provided by _____ ,
a real estate broker acting as a mortgage broker, pursuant to the Federal Real Estate Settlement Procedures Act (RESPA) if applicable and similar California law. In a transaction subject to RESPA, a lender will provide you with an additional Good Faith Estimate within three business days of the receipt of your loan application. You will also be informed of material changes before settlement/close of escrow. The name of the intended lender to whom your loan application will be delivered is:

☐ Unknown   ☐ _____ (Name of lender, if known)

GOOD FAITH ESTIMATE OF CLOSING COSTS

The information provided below reflects estimates of the charges you are likely to incur at the settlement of your loan. The fees, commissions, costs and expenses listed are estimates; the actual charges may be more or less. Your transaction may not involve a charge for every item listed and any additional items charged will be listed. The numbers listed beside the estimate generally correspond to the numbered lines contained in the HUD-1 Settlement Statement which you will receive at settlement if this transaction is subject to RESPA. The HUD-1 Settlement Statement contains the actual costs for the items paid at settlement. When this transaction is subject to RESPA, by signing page three of this form you are also acknowledging receipt of the HUD Guide to Settlement Costs.

HUD-1	Item	Paid to Others	Paid to Broker
800	*Items Payable in Connection with Loan*		
801	Lender's Loan Origination Fee	$_____	$_____
802	Lender's Loan Discount Fee	$_____	$_____
803	Appraisal Fee	$_____	$_____
804	Credit Report	$_____	$_____
805	Lender's Inspection Fee	$_____	$_____
808	Mortgage Broker Commission/Fee	$_____	$_____
809	Tax Service Fee	$_____	$_____
810	Processing Fee	$_____	$_____
811	Underwriting Fee	$_____	$_____
812	Wire Transfer Fee	$_____	$_____
		$_____	$_____
900	*Items Required by Lender to be Paid in Advance*		
901	Interest for ____ days at $_____ per day	$_____	$_____
902	Mortgage Insurance Premiums	$_____	$_____
903	Hazard Insurance Premiums	$_____	$_____
904	County Property Taxes	$_____	$_____
905	VA Funding Fee	$_____	$_____
		$_____	$_____
1000	*Reserves Deposited with Lender*		
1001	Hazard Insurance: ____ months at $_____ /mo.	$_____	$_____
1002	Mortgage Insurance: ____ months at $_____ /mo.	$_____	$_____
1004	Co. Property Taxes: ____ months at $_____ /mo.	$_____	$_____
		$_____	$_____
1100	*Title Charges*		
1101	Settlement or Closing/Escrow Fee	$_____	$_____
1105	Document Preparation Fee	$_____	$_____
1106	Notary Fee	$_____	$_____
1108	Title Insurance	$_____	$_____
		$_____	$_____
1200	*Government Recording and Transfer Charges*		
1201	Recording Fees	$_____	$_____
1202	City/County Tax/Stamps	$_____	$_____
		$_____	$_____
1300	*Additional Settlement Charges*		
1302	Pest Inspection	$_____	$_____
		$_____	$_____

Subtotals of Initial Fees, Commissions, Costs and Expenses $_____ $_____

Total of Initial Fees, Commissions, Costs and Expenses $_____

Compensation to Broker (Not Paid Out of Loan Proceeds):

Mortgage Broker Commission/Fee $_____

Any Additional Compensation from Lender ☐ No ☐ Yes $_____

(Approximate Yield Spread Premium or Other Rebate)

FIGURE 3.3   Sample mortgage loan disclosure statement. (continued)

ADDITIONAL REQUIRED CALIFORNIA DISCLOSURES

I.   Proposed Loan Amount: $ _____

    Initial Commissions, Fees, Costs and
        Expenses Summarized on Page 1: $ _____

    Payment of Other Obligations (List):
        Credit Life and/or Disability Insurance (see V below) $ _____

    _____ $ _____

    _____ $ _____

Subtotal of All Deductions: $ _____

Estimated Cash at Closing ☐ **To You** ☐ **That you must pay** $ _____

II. General Information About Loan

    1.   Proposed loan term   ☐ Years ☐ Months

☐ **FIXED RATE LOAN**	☐ **ADJUSTABLE RATE LOAN (EXAMPLE 6-MONTH ARM; 1-YEAR ARM)**
Fixed rate loan_____% payable at $_____ month	Proposed interest rate:____% Fully indexed rate _____% Proposed monthly payment $_____ Maximum interest rate _____% Interest rate can increase_____% each_____months Maximum loan payment can be $_____ after_____ months
☐ **INITIAL FIXED RATE LOAN(EXAMPLE 2/28; 3/1; 5/1)**	☐ **INITIAL ADJUSTABLE RATE LOAN (EXAMPLE LOW ENTRY RATE ARM)**

Proposed initial fixed interest rate:____%
Initial fixed interest rate in effect for____months
Proposed initial monthly payment $_____
Adjustable interest rate of _____% will begin after
    fixed rate period ends
Monthly payment can increase to $____after fixed rate period ends
Fully indexed rate____%
Maximum interest rate____%
Interest rate can increase _____% each _____ months
Maximum loan payment can be $_____ after_____months
	Proposed initial adjustable interest rate____%
	Initial interest rate in effect for____months
	Proposed monthly payment $_____
	Fully indexed rate_____%
	Maximum interest rate _____%
	Interest rate can increase_____% each _____months
	Monthly payment can increase to $____ after initial
	    adjustable rate period ends
	Maximum loan payment can be $_____ after _____ months

    2.   This loan is based on limited or no documentation of your income and/or assets and may have a higher interest rate, or more points or fees than other products requiring documentation: ☐ No ☐ Yes.

    3.   The loan is subject to a balloon payment: ☐ No ☐ Yes. If Yes, the following paragraph applies and a final balloon payment of $_____ will be due on ___/___/___ *[estimated date (month/day/year)]*.

    NOTICE TO BORROWER: IF YOU DO NOT HAVE THE FUNDS TO PAY THE BALLOON PAYMENT WHEN IT COMES DUE, YOU MAY HAVE TO OBTAIN A NEW LOAN AGAINST YOUR PROPERTY TO MAKE THE BALLOON PAYMENT. IN THAT CASE, YOU MAY AGAIN HAVE TO PAY COMMISSIONS, FEES, AND EXPENSES FOR THE ARRANGING OF THE NEW LOAN. IN ADDITION, IF YOU ARE UNABLE TO MAKE THE MONTHLY PAYMENTS OR THE BALLOON PAYMENT, YOU MAY LOSE THE PROPERTY AND ALL OF YOUR EQUITY THROUGH FORECLOSURE. KEEP THIS IN MIND IN DECIDING UPON THE AMOUNT AND TERMS OF THIS LOAN.

III. Prepayments: The proposed loan has the following prepayment provisions:

    ☐ No prepayment penalty (you will not be charged a penalty to pay off or refinance the loan before maturity)

    ☐ You will have to pay a prepayment penalty if the loan is paid off or refinanced in the first _____ years. The prepayment penalty could be as much as $_____. Any prepayment of principal in excess of 20% of the
        ☐ original loan balance or
        ☐ unpaid balance
    for the first _____ years will include a penalty not to exceed _____ months interest at the note interest rate but not more than the interest you would be charged if the loan were paid to maturity.

    ☐ Other – you will have to pay a prepayment penalty if the loan is paid off or refinanced in the first _____ years as follows:

    _____
    _____

IV. Taxes and Insurance:

    ☐ There will be an impound (escrow) account which will collect approximately $_____ a month in addition to your principal and interest payments for the payment of ☐ county property taxes*☐ hazard insurance ☐ mortgage insurance ☐ flood insurance ☐ other_____.

    ☐ If there is no impound (escrow) account or if your escrow (impound) account does not include one or more of the payments described above, you will have to plan for the payment of ☐county property taxes * ☐hazard insurance ☐ mortgage insurance ☐ flood insurance ☐ other_____ of approximately $_____ per year.

    In a purchase transaction, county property taxes are calculated based on the sales price of the property and may require the payment of an additional (supplemental) tax bill from the county tax authority by your lender (if escrowed) or you (if not escrowed).

V.   Credit Life and/or Disability Insurance: The purchase of credit life and/or disability insurance by a borrower is NOT required as a condition of making this proposed loan.

VI. Other Liens: Are there liens currently on this property for which the borrower is obligated? ☐ No ☐ Yes
    If Yes, describe below:

Lienholder's Name	*Amount Owing*	*Priority*
_____	_____	_____
_____	_____	_____
_____	_____	_____

FIGURE 3.3 Sample mortgage loan disclosure statement. (continued)

Liens that will remain or are anticipated on this property after the proposed loan for which you are applying is made or arranged (including the proposed loan for which you are applying):

Lienholder's Name	Amount Owing	Priority

NOTICE TO BORROWER: Be sure that you state the amount of all liens as accurately as possible. If you contract with the broker to arrange this loan, but it cannot be arranged because you did not state these liens correctly, you may be liable to pay commissions, costs, fees, and expenses even though you do not obtain the loan.

VII. Article 7 Compliance: If this proposed loan is secured by a first deed of trust in a principal amount of less than $30,000 or secured by a junior lien in a principal amount of less than $20,000, the undersigned licensee certifies that the loan will be made in compliance with Article 7 of Chapter 3 of the Real Estate Law.

    A. This loan ☐ may ☐ will ☐ will not be made wholly or in part from broker controlled funds as defined in Section 10241(j) of the Business and Professions Code.

    B. If the broker indicates in the above statement that the loan "may" be made out of broker-controlled funds, the broker must inform the borrower prior to the close of escrow if the funds to be received by the borrower are in fact broker-controlled funds.

VIII. NOTICE TO BORROWER: THIS IS NOT A LOAN COMMITMENT. Do not sign this statement until you have read and understood all of the information in it. All parts of this form must be completed before you sign it. Borrower hereby acknowledges the receipt of a copy of this statement.

Name of Broker	License #	Broker's Representative	License #

Broker's Address

Signature of Broker	Date	OR	Signature of Representative	Date

Borrower	Date	Borrower	Date

Department of Real Estate license information telephone number: (916) 227-0931, or check license status at www.dre.ca.gov

to the consummation of the loan. (Critics' comments regarding this new rule will be addressed in Chapter 10, when the TIL is discussed more fully.)

Exceptions to the Mortgage Loan Broker Law

It is easier to state which lenders and what transactions are not covered by the law than to list those that are covered. Exempt from the Real Property Loan Law are:

- Regulated institutional lenders.
- Purchase money transactions in which a seller, via his or her equity in the property, carries back a portion of the loan as part of the sale price. However, if a seller is in the business of carrying back loans in eight or more transactions per year, the Mortgage Loan Broker Law does apply.
- Loans secured by first trust deeds when the principal amount is $30,000 or more.
- Loans secured by junior trust deeds when the principal amount is $20,000 or more.

TABLE 3.1 Maximum commissions.

Type of Loan	PERCENTAGE COMMISSION			
	Less Than Two Years	Two Years but Less Than Three	Three Years and Over	Exempt Transactions
First trust deeds	5%	5%	10%	Loans of $30,000 and over
Junior trust deeds	5%	10%	15%	Loans of $20,000 and over

Maximum Commissions

The maximum commission rates mortgage loan brokers can charge are regulated by law, as shown in Table 3.1. As the table shows, the shorter the term of the loan, the less commission the broker may charge as a percentage of the face amount of the loan. On loans of $30,000 and over for first liens, and $20,000 for junior liens, the broker may charge as much as the borrower agrees to pay, sometimes referred to as "what the market will bear." This limitation on commissions and the difficulty in making sure that no violation of the law occurs is the main reason why lenders have "minimum" loan amount requirements. Even for loans covered by the law, competition frequently keeps the rates below the maximum allowed.

Other Costs and Expenses

Mortgage brokers are also limited as to the amount of costs and expenses, other than commissions, that they may charge a borrower under the Real Property Loan Law. These costs include fees for appraisal, escrow, title insurance, notary, recording, and credit investigation. Such costs and expenses may not exceed 5 percent of the amount of the loan. However, if 5 percent of the loan is less than $390, the broker may charge up to that amount, provided that the charges do not exceed actual costs and expenses paid, incurred, or reasonably earned by the broker. Regardless of the size of the loan, as long as it comes under the Real Property Loan Law, the borrower cannot be charged more than $750 for miscellaneous costs and expenses.

To simplify, the foregoing costs and expenses can be translated into chart form, as shown in Table 3.2.

TABLE 3.2   Maximum charges for other costs and expenses.

LOAN AMOUNT	Under $7,801	$7,801 to $13,999	$14,000 to $29,999	First Loans of $30,000 and over and Junior Loans of $20,000 and over
MAXIMUM CHARGES	$390	5% of loan	$700	No legal limitations
	—But not to exceed actual costs and expenses—			

As the table shows, the broker may charge as much as the borrower is willing to pay on first loans of $30,000 and above, or on junior loans of $20,000 and over. Again, competition plays a significant role in keeping down the costs and expenses.

Balloon Payments

As mentioned earlier, the term balloon payment describes the final payment owed when an amortized loan becomes due as an amount that is more than twice the amount of the smallest installment. Under the Real Property Loan Law, a balloon payment is prohibited if (1) the term of the loan is for six years or less, and (2) the loan is secured by the dwelling place of the borrower. Again, this provision does not apply to loans carried by sellers or loans made by regulated lenders. These particular balloon payment rules apply only if the loan is covered by the Real Property Loan Law.

Insurance

A borrower is not required to purchase credit life or disability insurance (except in Cal Vet Loans) as a condition of obtaining the loan. However, the lender can insist for self-protection and by the terms of the trust deed, that fire and hazard insurance be obtained on improved property until the loan has been repaid. If licensed to sell such insurance, the loan broker may also act as the insurance agent for the borrower, but borrowers are not obligated to purchase the coverage through the mortgage loan broker. They may purchase insurance from their own insurance agent and it is a good idea to "shop around" for the best rates.

Miscellaneous Provisions of the Mortgage Loan Broker Law

Mortgage brokers are prohibited from charging loan servicing or collection fees to be paid by the borrower. Late charges, if any, may not exceed $5 or 10 percent of the principal and interest part of an installment payment, whichever is greater. If the installment payment is made within 10 days of its due date, however, no late charge can be assessed.

3.5 SYNDICATIONS

Loosely defined, a **syndication** is a group of two or more people who combine their financial resources for the purpose of achieving specific investment objectives. Investment capital can be pooled or combined for the purpose of financing real estate transactions or for the purchase of real property. Syndicates may take the legal form of a limited partnership (accompanied by limited liability), which is the most favored in California; a general partnership; corporation; real estate investment trust; or a joint venture.

Syndicates are formed for a variety of reasons, including these:

1. *Improved purchasing power* obtained by combining the resources of many who could not afford to purchase individually, but through the principle of leverage could acquire a relatively high-priced property.

2. *Better bargaining power*, again due to the application of the principle of leverage (less down payment), wherein a larger capital base can command lower prices and allow larger purchases. In purchasing larger properties, lower operating expense ratios are usually present.

3. *Diversification*, which enables investors to spread their capital into different types of investments or different properties and, thereby, limits their loss exposure in any one investment.

4. *Professional management and administration* of the real estate portfolio in order to minimize costs and maximize the benefits. Professional services may be too costly for the average investor and disproportionate to capital investment. By pooling resources with others, however, a team of specialists, such as attorneys, appraisers, real estate brokers, accountants, and investment analysts can be more affordable.

Individuals may participate in a syndication and collectively invest in a wide variety of real estate ventures. There are basically three types of syndication: (1) equity syndicates, which purchase real estate; (2) mortgage (or debt) syndicates, which grant loans to others for the purchase of real property, creating creditor/debtor relationships; and (3) a hybrid of these two, combining both equity and debt.

3.6 REAL ESTATE INVESTMENT TRUSTS AND ENDOWMENT FUNDS

The **real estate investment trust (REIT)** is a creature of the federal tax law. It was created in 1960 with the goal of encouraging small investors to pool their resources with others in order to raise venture capital for real estate transactions. It has been called the 'mutual fund' of the real estate business. Just as mutual funds invest in a diversified portfolio of corporate stocks and bonds, REITs invest in a diversified portfolio of real estate and mortgage investments, using a large number of investors who combine their funds.

Types of REITs

As with syndications, there are three types of REITs:

1. *Equity trusts*—investors buy income-producing property and obtain their return from current rents, tax benefits, and capital gains.
2. *Mortgage trusts*—investors loan money secured by real estate and obtain their income from interest and loan fees.
3. *Hybrid trusts*, which are a combination of these two types.

To qualify as a trust, there are many tests that must be met. Two main requirements are that there must be at least 100 different shareholders, and that at least 95 percent of its taxable income must be distributed to the investors each year. This latter requirement is to avoid the double taxation aspect of some corporations. (Note: a corporation shields the investor, but double taxation occurs as the corporate income is taxed once and then again when profits are distributed to the individuals).

The legal ramifications of REITs are beyond the scope of this book; anyone interested in forming or participating in REITs should seek legal counsel.

REITs as a Source of Financing

The favorable income tax incentives of REITs attract funds from thousands of small investors, which, in turn, become an important source of real estate financing. REITs concentrate on income-producing properties, most often large commercial projects. REITs generally do not limit themselves to one area or type of loan, but diversify their holdings both as to type of property and geographical location.

Lending activities of REITs center primarily around land development and take-out loans for such projects as condominiums, office buildings, shopping centers, garden and high-rise apartment complexes, hotels and motels, industrial properties, warehouses, and major single-family subdivision developments.

The Ups and Downs of REITs

During the economic crisis of the 1970s, many REITs folded under the pressures of poor management, excessive speculation, withdrawal and cancellation of take-out commitments, termination of bank lines of credit, poor credit analysis, excess building in many parts of the country (particularly in the condominium market and in recreational projects), and sagging demand.

In the 1980s, to restore confidence in the REIT, concessions worked out between REITs and the banking and securities industries slowly revived their activity. This slow revival continued until the late 1990s, when a hot stock market put a damper on REITs. People were getting better returns in their own investments. By 2001, the stock market declined and some money began to flow back into REITs. Within a few years, REITs were once again booming. REITs remain volatile, subject to the whims of the real estate market. 2008, for instance, saw REITs gain popularity in the early months because commercial real estate was not as affected as residential property during that stage of the real estate market re-positioning. By mid-2009, however, REITs became less influential as the economic slowdown grew in intensity and especially affected the speculative nature of real estate.

Pension Funds

Pension funds collect monthly contributions from workers, and occasionally from the employer, and then invest the proceeds in an attempt to create a lump sum of money upon which the worker may draw upon at retirement age. Examples include the California State Teachers Retirement Fund and various union funds, such as the United Auto Workers. The bulk of pension funds are invested in traditional securities, such as stocks, bonds, and various government instruments and are normally not used to make a direct loan in the real estate market.

However, with the advent of mortgage-backed securities, pension funds are indirectly becoming a significant player in the real estate market through the purchase of existing real estate loans in the secondary market. When a pension fund buys an existing loan from a traditional real estate lender, it gives the said lender the funds to make another direct real estate loan to a new borrower. Although there have been cases in which pension funds were used directly to fund certain real estate projects, for the most part, pension funds enter real estate investment via the secondary market.

The promised high yields of what became known as real estate derivatives (mortgage loans divided and packaged for global sale) were irresistible, and both pension and endowment funds invested heavily. When the subprime meltdown and its accompanying collapse of the derivative market occurred, huge losses were absorbed by these funds.

For example, the California Public Employees' Retirement System (CalPERS) and the California State Teachers' Retirement System (CalSTRS) are two of the nation's largest pension funds. Both funds were invested in real estate securities and were significantly impacted by the downturn in real estate values. As the second largest public pension fund in the nation, with assets totaling just over 123.8 billion (as of July 2009), CalSTRS had over 12 percent of its fund invested in real estate securities. The real estate portfolio return for 2008–2009 declined 43 percent.

CalPERS' real estate investment portfolio (at the end of 2008) was 21.8 billion with a 2008 real estate portfolio return of minus 12.6 percent. This contrasted with a total fund performance for the year of minus 5.1 percent.

However, the developing a trend in which pension funds (especially CalSTRS and CalPERS in California) are used to help the contributor to the fund purchase a home under favorable loan terms were unaffected by the losses noted above. The popular low-down payment loan options continue to help their contributors acquire a home in California's high-priced housing market.

Endowment Funds

Endowment funds of colleges and universities, hospitals, cemeteries, charitable foundations, and other endowed institutions operate like pension funds. They receive their funds in the form of gifts and attempt to invest in "safe" mortgages that will offer high returns. Accordingly, they offer a good source of financing for commercial and industrial properties, and in sale-leaseback arrangements. Many commercial banks and mortgage companies handle investments for endowment funds which were also hard hit by the collapse of the real estate derivative market noted above.

3.7 CREDIT UNIONS AND FINANCE COMPANIES

A credit union is a mutual, voluntary, cooperative organization of people who agree to save their money together and to make loans to each other. Originally, credit unions were formed by members

FIGURE 3.4   The growing role of credit unions.

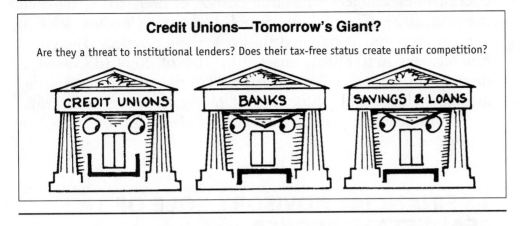

of a particular group, commonly by occupational or professional affiliation. Today, credit unions are formed without any occupational or professional affiliation. There are credit unions throughout the United States, representing many millions of members. Figure 3.4 discusses some impact of their growing role.

For the most part, credit union lending in real estate has been short term and locally focused. Attempts at long-term loans had been mostly few and experimental until recently. More long-term loans are now made and have mostly adopted typical conventional lending qualifying requirements. The credit union niche remains a shorter term loan, often with an adjustable rate but with more flexible guidelines for both the borrower and the property.

Finance Companies

Although involved chiefly in personal and consumer loans, **finance companies** (also known as credit companies or industrial banks), increased their participation in real estate lending as a precursor to subprime loans. These high-risk loans with high rates and short-term duration, were typically less than seven years, and were often secured by a combination of real and personal property.

Many of these loans were junior trust deeds. The typical borrower was one who did not qualify for a prime loan from a thrift institution or bank. But as the explosion of subprime loans expanded to a new group of "niche" lenders who made riskier loans with constantly diminishing qualifying guidelines, the influence of finance companies diminished. While continuing to provide financing to the riskiest of borrowers, even this group of borrowers was reduced as "pay day" loans (loans to be paid from a future pay check) grew in popularity. These loans were criticized for allowing borrowers to become trapped in the loan cycle of high interest rates and fees with little chance of ever paying off their debt. In 2009, Congress undertook the task of finding ways to reign in what were considered abusive lending practices. The Fraud Enforcement Act (FERA) enacted in May of 2009 (discussed in detail in the Case & Point in Chapter 14) targeted reduced documentation loans and falsification of mortgage-applicant information and documentation and did not address a growing problem with pay day loans.

3.8 FINANCIAL ADVISORY ROLE OF THE REAL ESTATE BROKER

The idea of a "one-stop shop" has been discussed for years. It has always been enticing to think that real estate agents could assist buyers, to whom they have just sold a home, to acquire both home insurance and home financing and collect additional compensation for their efforts. Plus, agents would retain control of the transaction and thereby assist their buyers through the entire process. The introduction of computerized loan origination programs re-fueled the discussion with many believing that real estate agents were in a prime position to fulfill the mortgage needs of their clients.

With full disclosure, real estate agents may collect a fee for this service. However, regulations mandate that an agent must perform actual services to legally collect a fee. Additionally, court cases have affirmed that collecting a referral fee carries with it a personal liability for providing accurate loan information that is compatible to the needs of the client. In spite of the temptations, many real estate brokers do not want to take the chance that agents would get into areas beyond their expertise and that inadvertent violation would occur.

Computerized Loan Origination

The advances in automated lending services by institutional lenders have had a dual affect on loan originations. While it made the preparation and submission process faster and easier, it also caused some mortgage originators to become less educated about loan requirements. It became easy to submit the loan to the automated program and let it determine if the borrower was qualified. The result was a substantial increase in what turned out to be less than qualified mortgage originators.

While a loan could be inserted into a desktop underwriting (DU) process, and the loan originator could acquire a loan approval, the loan still had to be submitted to an underwriter whose job it was to confirm all of the documentation. The old adage of "garbage in, garbage out" became prevalent as some computer approvals were obtained without obtaining the necessary documentation. When the final loan was submitted, too often underwriters required additional documentation or, in the worst cases, denied the loan.

As the subprime market faltered, qualifying guidelines tightened and available sources of loan funds were reduced, the computerized models were best accompanied by well-informed loan originators who could counsel potential borrowers and acquire the necessary documentation for the loan process. In an effort to avoid the subprime abuses of the past, new regulations proliferated and loan originations once more became an arena requiring considerable expertise.

Buyer-Borrowers Going Directly Online to Obtain a Real Estate Loan

As the market boomed, a surge of Internet use, coupled with heavy website advertising by lenders (like Lending Tree, Ditech, and Quicken Loans), encouraged many consumers to obtain real estate loans online. Some predicted that the trend would grow, eventually replacing the need for face-to-face interactions between borrower and lender. This cyberspace system was relatively short-lived as lenders chose mostly to work only with the well-qualified, also known as "A type," borrowers. In some cases, lenders used what were commonly called "come on quotes" with the only objective to get the loan application submitted. The anonymity of the Internet shielded these companies from disappointed "non A" type borrowers who where regularly denied loans. As the subprime market grew, these Web-lenders depended upon the fact that borrowers required little documentation for their loans. It was easy to put everyone into a subprime loan, whether or not it was the best loan option for them.

As the subprime market imploded, borrowers once again required the services of local loan originators to walk them through the maze of new qualifying requirements and help correct their credit blemishes. While by 2009 the influence of cyberspace underwriting had waned considerably, lending is cyclical and we may see a resurgence of Web-lending in the future.

SUMMARY

Noninstitutional lenders include private parties, mortgage companies, syndicates, a variety of funds, and credit unions. Compared with institutional lenders, there are fewer restrictions placed upon their lending activities.

Private lenders include direct private lenders, indirect private lenders, and sellers who carry back purchase money trust deeds. They deal primarily in junior loans of comparatively small amounts but as lending requirements tighten, private sources often gain in both popularity and use.

Mortgage bankers and mortgage companies are usually incorporated businesses that act as agents, or loan correspondents, for institutional lenders. As such, they are generally subject to the same laws and regulations as their principals. Many mortgage bankers also lend out their own funds, while mortgage brokers do not.

Under the Real Property Loan Law, mortgage loan brokers are limited as to the amount of costs, expenses, and commissions they may charge borrowers. These restrictions apply only to first loans of less than $30,000 and junior loans of less than $20,000.

Syndicates and real estate investment trusts each pool the funds of many people to invest in real estate and mortgages. In theory, they should be able to offer improved purchasing power, stronger bargaining positions, diversification, and professional management of their portfolios. But, to date, their success has been mixed.

Pension funds, trust funds, endowment funds, and credit unions are playing ever-expanding roles in financing real estate transactions, particularly where the traditional sources of financing are unwilling or unable to lend.

Computerization and rapidly expanding Internet use retain the potential to change the way real estate loans are analyzed and granted.

IMPORTANT TERMS AND CONCEPTS

Credit union

Endowment fund

Finance company

Mortgage banker

Mortgage brokers

Mortgage correspondent

Mortgage Loan Disclosure Statement

Private lenders

Real estate investment trust (REIT)

Real Property (Mortgage) Loan Law

Subprime loan

Syndication

REVIEWING YOUR UNDERSTANDING

Questions for Discussion

1. Differentiate between institutional and noninstitutional lenders.

2. What is the chief difference between direct private lenders and indirect private lenders?

3. How do sellers of real estate help finance the sale? To what extent are they governed by the usury law?

4. Who is exempt from the California Usury Law?

5. Distinguish among the following:
   a. mortgage banker
   b. mortgage company
   c. mortgage broker
   d. mortgage loan correspondent

6. What is a syndicate? How does it differ from a real estate investment trust?

Multiple-Choice Questions

1. The law specifically governing the amount of commissions loan brokers may earn is called the
   a. Real Estate Law.
   b. Real Property Loan Law.
   c. Mortgage Loan Disclosure Law.
   d. Real Property Securities Act.

2. The Real Property Loan Law is embodied in the
   a. Civil Code.
   b. Code of Civil Procedures.
   c. Real Estate Code.
   d. Business and Professions Code.

3. Exempt under the Real Property Loan Law are
   a. first trust deeds of under $30,000.
   b. second trust deeds of under $20,000.
   c. purchase money loans carried back by sellers.
   d. loans maturing in more than six years.

4. Regarding computerized loan originations, the advances in automated lending services by institutional lenders has had a profound effect by
   a. making the preparation and submission process slower and more complicated.
   b. causing some mortgage originators to become less educated about loan requirements.
   c. easing the qualifying of loan applicants.
   d. leading to more denials of loans even for well-qualified applicants.

5. Private lenders possess the following characteristics:
   a. they make highly subjective loan decisions.
   b. they charge lower interest rates on higher priced homes.
   c. they usually sell junior trust deed loans to financial institutions.
   d. they make loans usually secured by free and clear properties.

6. An owner of a small condominium lists the property for $400,000. After two months a broker submits an offer for $370,000 and the seller counters for $385,000, which the buyer accepts. The buyer's acceptance included a $2,000 deposit and the following terms: 10 percent down, a new first of $300,000, and the seller to carry back the difference. This seller carry back is an example of a/an:
   a. hard money loan.
   b. purchase money loan.
   c. installment sales contract.
   d. secondary market loan.

7. The original motivation for sub-prime loans was to
   a. allow more buyers to purchase homes.
   b. meet the requirements of the Federal Housing and Recovery Act.
   c. upgrade lending standards.
   d. assist the home building industry to improve their profit margins.

8. The most popular organizational form of real estate syndication in California is
   a. general partnership.
   b. living trust.
   c. limited partnership.
   d. real estate investment trust.

9. An organized group of people who agree to save their money and to make loans to one another is called a
   a. syndication.
   b. credit union.
   c. pension fund.
   d. trust fund.

10. As a rule, credit unions most often deal with which of the following types of loans?
    a. apartment property loans.
    b. short-term consumer loans.
    c. industrial property loans.
    d. commercial property loans.

11. What is popularly called the "mutual fund" of the real estate business?
    a. pension fund.
    b. credit union.
    c. syndication.
    d. real estate investment trust.

12. Under the Real Property Loan Law, before a loan can be made, a loan broker must provide the applicant with
    a. an escrow closing statement.
    b. a Mortgage Loan Disclosure Statement.
    c. an RESPA Disclosure Statement.
    d. a deposit receipt.

13. A balloon payment is
    a. the same as a lump sum payment due on a straight note at maturity.
    b. a term used to describe a pre-payment penalty.
    c. any payment made on a loan when the sales price has been inflated.
    d. any payment on a loan that is more than double the amount of the regular payment.

14. The Mortgage Loan Disclosure Statement (MLDS), coupled with the Truth-in-Lending Disclosure, provides a borrower with details of a prospective loan within how many days of submitting a loan application?
    a. 3
    b. 5
    c. 7
    d. 10

15. California law sets the usury maximum for certain limited types of loans secured by real property at
    a. 10 percent.
    b. the discount rate charged by the Fed.
    c. 10 percent, or 5 points above the current Fed discount rate, whichever is higher.
    d. 5 points above the prime rate.

16. Who is not exempt from California's usury law?
    a. private hard money lenders who make direct loans.
    b. commercial banks.
    c. transactions involving a real estate broker.
    d. a seller who carries back a loan on behalf of the buyer of an owner-occupied home.

17. The chief characteristic of private lenders is that they invest
    a. their own funds.
    b. in prime real estate loans.
    c. large sums of money in any one loan.
    d. primarily in commercial real estate properties.

18. The traditional Mortgage Loan Disclosure produced by the California Department of Real Estate requires that the annual percentage rate (APR) calculation must be within what percentage of the original calculation or a new disclosure must be provided before the loan can be consummated?
    a. one-eighth percent.
    b. one-quarter percent.
    c. one-half percent.
    d. none of these.

19. To prevent from being taxed on its income, an REIT must distribute annually at least what percent of its ordinary income to its shareholders?
    a. 100 percent
    b. 95 percent
    c. 90 percent
    d. 85 percent

20. Which of the following, using a line of credit, lends its "own" money?
    a. mortgage broker.
    b. mortgage banker.
    c. loan agent.
    d. real estate agent.

CASE & POINT

Yield-Spread Premiums: Good or Bad?

Mortgage brokers/lenders are usually paid for their efforts via an origination fee. This fee is disclosed on the HUD-1 Form along with identifying all of the costs associated with the acquisition of the loan. A yield spread premium (YSP) is a form of compensation received from a source lender/investor when the interest rate on the loan exceeds a lower rate for which the borrower qualifies, usually called the lender's par rate. It can also be used as an incentive for a broker to use a specific product or program. The YSP is not always disclosed on the HUD-1, as it is not a cost to the buyer. While YSP has been a part of lending for many years, it became an issue with the pricing of loans during the subprime lending explosion.

In a more normal lending environment, those who refinance home loans are sometimes encouraged to use YSP to pay their loan fee because of tax circumstances. But for most home buyers, paying an origination fee makes sense since it qualifies for a tax deduction in the year that it is paid on a purchase loan.

The complaint in recent years is that borrowers were enticed by offers of a "no-cost" mortgage, only to discover that they had agreed to pay an interest rate above the current market rate. In other words, there is no such loan as a no-cost option. A borrower paid the lender for his/her efforts in obtaining the loan funds either with an origination fee or a higher interest rate, which produces a yield spread premium, which was then paid to the originating lender.

Paying an interest rate above market rates to compensate a mortgage broker/lender is not necessarily a bad thing for the borrower, as it can reduce the upfront costs of the mortgage. Depending upon how long a borrower anticipates holding the mortgage, paying a higher interest rate could be more economical than paying high up-front fees.

Advocates insist that YSP, when used responsibly, can be a tool to assist borrowers, especially those short of cash. Critics, on the other hand, point to the fact that too often, borrowers can still be "sold" a higher rate loan for which the lender collects both an origination fee plus the YSP, which can still remain largely undisclosed.

Disclosure requirements have been updated and, in response to this past abuse, many lenders now limit the amount of service release that can be charged. The rationale of the past, in which brokers defended the payment of YSP on the grounds that they helped a person who would otherwise not been able to obtain financing acquire a loan, is no longer viable.

The motivation for the new Good Faith Estimate (GFE) form (see the Case & Point in Chapter 9) introduced in January 2010 was primarily to eliminate the ability of loan originators to obtain undisclosed YSP income. YSP must now be disclosed only as a credit to buyer costs and the GFE attempts to more clearly alert borrowers to the relationship of YSP to the acceptance of a higher interest rate. Whether the new form accomplishes its goals is likely to be debated for some time to come by various industry participants.

With the return to less exotic loan options accompanied by the new disclosure rules, the use of YSP will likely be used less frequently. But the question is still viable regarding whether YSP is good or bad, ethical or not, promotes unscrupulous pricing or is a real help to cash-strapped borrowers. It is important to determine for oneself the answers to the following:

1. Do the opportunities for YSP to assist borrowers outweigh the potential for abuse?
2. Will the new disclosure requirements be sufficient to curb the potential abuses of YSP use?
3. Can you think of an alternative that could provide help to borrowers while avoiding the potential for abuse that YSP affords?
4. Would the loan industry be better served with the elimination of the use of YSP? (This is under review by some financial regulators).

Chapter

4

PREVIEW

Adjustable rate mortgages (ARMs) and other alternative mortgage instruments are financing instruments that represent alternatives to the standard fixed rate, fully amortized loan program.

The past few years saw a dizzying choice of mortgages, both traditional and non-traditional, particularly with the ARM, each with an enormous number of variations, combinations, and permutations. With hundreds of different home loan products in the marketplace, buyers were presumably afforded opportunities to get mortgages that better fit their specific requirements. In retrospect, as the number of loan programs grew, so did the opportunities for unscrupulous lenders to "sell" loan options that resulted in the subprime meltdown of 2007–2009.

After completing this chapter, you should be able to:

1. Discuss why, under certain market conditions, the fixed rate mortgage is again popular with many lenders.
2. List and briefly describe the various types of alternative mortgage instruments.
3. Explain how negative amortization works.
4. Give reasons why balloon mortgages are not favored by consumers.

Note: You'll encounter some math in this chapter, but all problems have been completed for you and you can jump ahead to Chapter 13 to see how they are solved using two different calculators, the Calculated Industries Qualifier Plus IIIx, and the HP 12C.

Adjustable Rate and Other Alternative Mortgage Instruments

5. Demonstrate how a reverse annuity mortgage may be helpful for some older homeowners.

6. Compare the differences between 15-year loans and biweekly loan payments, and the payments on a standard 30-year loan.

4.1 OBJECTIVES AND RATIONALE

The principal objective of ARMs and other alternatives was initially to transfer some of the risk of continually rising inflation from the lender to the borrower, while at the same time tailoring loans more closely to the borrower's financial circumstances. In an effort to broaden the number of borrowers who could purchase a home, the loan options became more and more flexible. To remain competitive, many lenders who traditionally granted only standard fixed interest rate loans felt compelled to participate. The result was that ARM options literally exploded into use. The darling of the industry became the option arm (sometimes referred to as the "pick-a-pay" loan) which was negatively amortized. The interest-only and stated income qualifying options also expanded the use (or abuse) in the loan arena. In many cases, borrowers erroneously relied upon expected appreciation to bail them out of the accruing negative amortization and resulting increasing principal balance.

What was the driving force behind this change to ever more flexible loan programs? There was no single cause, but the most notable was a desire to expand homeownership to more borrowers, which the advent of mortgage-backed securities helped promote. There was a concern that the continued appreciation of home values would prohibit borrowers from ownership. There was also a false sense that these same appreciating home values would continue into the foreseeable future, accompanied by the failure to accept the reality that markets always adjust.

Purpose of Adjustable Rate and Other Alternative Loans

Adjustable rate financing has been available for years. The virtue of ARM loans varies depending upon whether they are viewed from the lender's or the borrower's perspective.

For many years, banks promoted mostly ARM loans. The ARM shields the bank from interest rate increases or decreases as borrowers shared in the risk of rate fluctuations, especially in a rising market. When the bank has to pay more, the borrower has to pay more. The inability of the banks to sell ARM loans to the secondary market (Fannie Mae and Freddie Mac, discussed in Chapter 7) prompted them to eventually offer fixed rate products.

ARM loans had a resurgence during the heyday of the subprime lending frenzy. But, following the 2008–2009 recession, ARM financing rapidly lost popularity. We should remember that this form of financing has a long history, and continues to be used substantially in Europe and other places. In California, the Cal-Vet loan program has been using adjustable rates since the program was initiated nearly 90 years ago. We will review Cal-Vet loans in Chapter 6, but it should be noted here that this program has had a very stable experience with adjustable rates.

Other reasons are proffered, some real and some mythical, as to why one might select an adjustable rate mortgage.

1. **The borrower can qualify for a larger loan amount:** While this may have been true several years ago, this may be more of a myth than a reality in today's ARM market. In the past, borrowers actually "qualified" at the low ARM start rate, which resulted in their being able to borrow more money and purchase a more expensive home. Most ARM products today, however, require a borrower to qualify at the "fully indexed rate" (i.e., the index plus the margin). The fully indexed rate is usually slightly lower than a comparable fixed rate but will hardly allow a borrower to qualify for much additional loan amount.

2. **When a borrower wants lower initial payments:** An ARM with a very low start rate accompanied by low monthly payments is more likely to have negative amortization than a higher start rate loan. These "negam" loans can result in an erosion of one's equity. Often called "pick-a-pay loans," the borrower is typically provided

the option each month to make either (1) the minimum payment, (2) a higher payment that will, at least, pay all the interest, or (3) a payment amount that will fully amortize the loan. While the initial payment amount may be predicated on the initial low interest rate, the loan accrues interest at the fully indexed rate (described above), resulting in unpaid interest having to be added to the loan balance. This is "negative amortization" or "deferred interest." (Negatively amortized loans are discussed in more detail on page 92.)

3. **When the borrower wants to make principal reduction payments:** As market conditions tightened in 2009, buyers were sometimes required to purchase a new home prior to selling a current residence. Looking to the future, for those wanting to make a significant principal reduction payment on their newly acquired loan, the "no-neg" ARM loan (without a prepayment penalty) was sometimes appropriate. The future payment would reduce the loan balance by the amount of the principal pay down reduction at the loan's next adjustment date.

Although used more sparingly now, adjustable rate mortgages remain available in today's mortgage marketplace. There are times when an ARM makes perfect sense. When acquiring such financing, a borrower must be certain to understand all of the characteristics of the selected loan. It is important to avoid surprises after the loan process has been completed and it is too late to make adjustments to the loan terms.

4.2 ADJUSTABLE RATE MORTGAGES (ARMs)

What Is an Adjustable Rate Loan?

The **adjustable rate mortgage (ARM)** is a flexible loan instrument, in which the interest rate and the monthly payments may be adjusted periodically to correspond with changes in a selected index. While ARM financing has, at least temporarily, lost some of its luster, these loans remain available and, as financing is cyclical, are likely to make a comeback sometime in the future.

Historically, adjustable rate mortgages have been made by mortgage companies, thrift institutions, and banks. The earliest adjustable terms were labeled variable rate mortgages (VRMs), variable interest rate loans (VIRs), and adjustable mortgage loans (AMLs). Although there may be some minor differences between these and today's ARMs, they basically work in the same way. For our purposes, ARM means any loan without a fixed interest rate during its term.

Some Things to Know About Adjustable Rate Mortgages

ARM loan popularity can most often be traced to the fact that it is usually offered at a lower initial interest rate than traditional fixed rate loans. To further encourage borrowers to use ARM loans, lenders may offer "teaser rates," which are abnormally low rates designed to attract borrowers. Once the loans are granted, the low teaser rate soon disappears and the usually higher ARM rates take effect. The low teaser rates of the past allowed some buyers to qualify for a loan that they would not have otherwise been able to obtain. When teaser rates adjusted and some borrowers began to experience difficulty with the increasing monthly payments, lenders made some changes. While still offering teaser rates in their advertising, lenders required borrowers to qualify at the more normal "fully indexed" ARM rate.

Although the terms of any loan may vary considerably from another, there are several common characteristics of practically any adjustable rate financing. The following is an attempt to help you understand the "language" of ARMs.

INTEREST RATE ADJUSTMENTS: Adjustments to the interest rate must reflect the movement of a single, specific, neutral index, subject to an rate adjustment limitations contained in the loan contract.

INDEX: Most common indexes are Treasury bills, Treasury securities, 11th District Cost of Funds, or LIBOR (London Interbank Offered Rate). Each index, while beyond the control of the lender, is an indicator of current economic conditions that guides lenders in their interest rate adjustments. While claims are made as to which index is the most stable under certain conditions, you can satisfy yourself by examining the recent history of each index over the past three years or so. These indexes have a public history and daily values that are easy to find in any Internet search engine.

MARGIN: The margin is the percentage amount added to the index at each adjustment period to determine the new interest rate to be paid by the borrower. Sometimes referred to as the "lender's profit," but more commonly known as the "differential" or "spread," the margin is established by individual lenders based on their estimated expenses and profit goals. While the margin in any given loan remains constant, in relation to the index, for the life of the loan, margins between lenders can and do vary.

PAYMENT ADJUSTMENTS: Another flexible feature of an ARM is that the monthly payment amount may be increased or decreased by the lender to reflect changes in the interest rate. The frequency with which such adjustments can occur is determined by the specific terms of the ARM loan acquired by the borrower and can be monthly, quarterly, biannually or annually.

THE CEILING RATE: Loans have two **cap** rates, a limitation on the amount by which the payment and/or the interest rate can change at any single adjustment and a life time cap. The most frequently used payment "ceiling rates" are: a.) 1 percent every six months or 2 percent per year maximum adjustment on interest rate at any one adjustment period; or b.) 7.5 percent adjustment on the payment rate at any one adjustment period.

The maximum rate change that may occur over the full life of the loan is generally between 4 and 6 percent, depending upon the initial start rate. Borrowers are cautioned against an overemphasis on this maximum interest rate since, in most instances, it depends on the stability of the index and market adjustments.

In those cases where a borrower accepts a payment cap, there can be a difference between the amount due and the amount actually paid. This difference is known as "deferred interest" or "negative amortization" and is added to the balance of the loan. This type of loan is described more fully on page 92.

NOTICE OF PAYMENT ADJUSTMENTS: The lender must usually send a notice of an adjustment to the payment amount in 30 days (but not more than 45 days) before it becomes effective. This notice will contain at least the date and amount of payment adjustment, change in index and interest rate, change in principal loan balance, and who to contact for further information and clarification.

PREPAYMENT PENALTY: Most ARMS may be prepaid in whole or in part without penalty at any time during the term of the loan. Of course, all terms of the loan are negotiable, so this could vary between lenders and will be noted on the good faith estimate.

ASSUMABILITY: Most ARM loans may be assumed without change in the loan terms by a "qualified" borrower acceptable to the lender. There is usually an assumption fee of approximately 1 percent based on the then remaining unpaid principal balance.

Even though they may be "less popular," there is a wide array of adjustable rate mortgages available in today's marketplace. When acquiring such financing, one must be certain the lender explains fully and in detail the loan characteristics of the selected loan.

A comprehensive list of questions that borrowers should ask when considering an ARM loan is located at the end of this section.

Negative Amortization and Adjustable Rate Mortgages

Negatively amortization loans become more popular during periods of high inflation, usually accompanied by rapid appreciation of home values. This was the exact economic atmosphere we experienced during the early 2000s. Rapid inflation can create a need to qualify a borrower at a low entry-level rate of interest, even though the payments may later increase via regular rate adjustments. The loan, particularly if negatively amortized, will require re-amortization over a shorter term of years.

With negatively amortized loans, the initial monthly payments will likely be inadequate to pay the interest, let alone provide for any principal reduction. Whatever the amount of the interest shortfall, it is added to the existing principal balance of the loan, and the following month, the process is repeated. Since the interest shortfall is always added to the principal balance existing at the time, the borrower ends up paying interest on interest, and the principal balance grows with compounding effect. Every month, the amount owed gets larger!

While these loans may be less popular than a few years ago when double digit appreciation was higher than any accrued negative amortization, this type of ARM "controls the loan's payments." As payments increase by a maximum of 7.5 percent each year, it could be a good fit for those who need to have a low monthly payment and wish to know the exact amount of each year's increase. These loans are more likely to have prepayment penalties assessed during the first three years of the loan. Depending upon the borrower's specific need for lower initial payments, the 30 year due in three-, five- or seven-year fixed rate (see page 98 for more details) might be an alternative to the ARM loan.

Point of Reference: All negatively amortized ARM loans contain a provision limiting the amount of deferred interest that can be added to the loan balance before the loan must be recast, amortizing the new balance over the remaining term of the loan. Most lenders have adopted the guideline that a loan must be recast when the negative amortization amount reaches 20 percent of the original loan amount. It is anticipated that, in most cases, this threshold will be reached in four to five years. The interest rate used to recast the loan is usually a fixed rate, often higher than the current ARM rate. The result is generally a higher monthly payment, many times creating a payment burden for the borrower.

Comparing ARMs to fixed rate loans can be confusing, so we've compiled a comprehensive list of questions that borrowers should ask when considering an ARM, located at the end of this section (page 104).

To summarize, two changes can take place in connection with an ARM: a change in the interest rate and a change in the monthly payment. One can occur without the other. If changes in the payments are not made concurrently to accommodate the higher interest rates, negative amortization can take place, resulting in a debt increase rather than a decrease. There has been a definite movement by lenders away from granting real estate loans with negative amortization. Borrowers were more interested in the fact that negam loans made qualifying for loans easier, based on the lower payments associated with negam financing. The fantasy that the massive appreciation in home values at the time would more than offset any loss of equity via the negative amortization proved to be very inaccurate.

Note: The "option arm" loan program that was so popular during the past several years has all but disappeared. While it provided three payment options to the borrower, the lowest payment option was the one most often selected. This was a negatively amortized payment plan that resulted in sizeable deferred interest being added to the loan balance each month. Borrowers often acquired 100 percent financing with this loan and worse still, qualified at the lowest payment amount. When real estate values adjusted downward, there was little if any equity contained in the property with which to allow refinancing. Coupled with the pending adjustment of the ARM portion of the loan to a much higher rate and accompanying payment, borrowers were squeezed and unable to either make the higher payments or sell their homes. The result was a sizeable increase in foreclosures and short sales. Many borrowers discovered that they had merely rented their homes for a few years before having to abandon them to the lending institutions via foreclosure. No wonder this financing option has virtually disappeared!

Disclosure Requirements for ARMs

The technical aspects of the features of ARM loans can be confusing to borrowers. Therefore, lenders who issue ARMs must comply with Regulation Z of the Federal Truth-in-Lending Law. Regulation Z requires lenders who offer ARMs to give each potential borrower certain specific information about ARM loans. The major disclosure items are

1. The index used, where the index is found, and a five-year history of the index.
2. How interest rates and margins interact to determine payments and what the current rates are.
3. If teaser rates are used, when they can change.
4. The interest and payment adjustment periods and how many days' warning *will be provided* before a change occurs.
5. Negative amortization features, if any.
6. Maximum caps on (1) the annual interest increase and (2) the total for the loan.

The lender may comply with Regulation Z by giving the potential borrower the *Consumer Handbook on Adjustable Rate Mortgages,* published by the Federal Reserve and the Federal Home Loan Bank Board. A new three-page Mortgage Loan Disclosure Statement (MLDS) has been developed to assure the full disclosure of any ARM loan. Finally, California lenders are required to have the borrower sign an adjustable rate loan rider to the promissory note (see Figure 4.1).

FIGURE 4.1   Sample adjustable rate loan rider.

ADJUSTABLE RATE LOAN RIDER
(CHANGE DATE LIMIT)

NOTICE: THIS DOCUMENT CONTAINS PROVISIONS FOR A VARIABLE INTEREST RATE. INCREASES IN THE INTEREST RATE WILL RESULT IN HIGHER PAYMENTS. DECREASES IN THE INTEREST RATE WILL RESULT IN LOWER PAYMENTS.

This Rider is made this . . . . day of . . . . , 19 . . . . , and is incorporated into and shall be deemed to amend and supplement the Mortgage, Deed of Trust, or Deed to Secure Debt (the "Security Instrument") of the same date given by the undersigned (the "Borrower") to secure Borrower's Note to . . . . SAVINGS & LOAN ASSOCIATION . . . . (the "Lender") of the same date (the "Note") and covering the property described in the Security Instrument and located at *(Property Address)* . . . .
. . . .

Modifications. In addition to the covenants and agreements made in the Security Instrument, Borrower and Lender further covenant and agree as follows:

A. INTEREST RATE AND MONTHLY PAYMENT CHANGES

The Note has an "Initial Interest Rate" of . . . . . . %. The Note interest rate may be increased or decreased on the . . . . . day of the month beginning on . . . . , 19 . . . . and on that day of the month every . . . . . months thereafter. Each date on which the rate of interest may change is called a "Change Date".

Changes in the interest rate are governed by changes in an interest rate index called the "Index".

(A)   The Index

Beginning with the first Change Date, the interest rate will be based on an Index. The "Index" is the "Monthly Weighted Average Cost of Funds Index for Eleventh District Savings Institutions" which is published monthly by the <u>Federal Home Loan Bank of San Francisco</u>. The most recent Index figure available as of the date 45 days before each Change Date is called the "Current Index".

If the Index is no longer available, the Lender will choose a new index which is based upon comparable information. The Lender will give notice of this choice.

(B)   Calculation of Changes

Before each Change Date, the Lender will calculate the new interest rate by adding . . . . basis points (. . . . . . %)(this amount is called "Margin") to the Current Index. The Lender will then round the result of this addition to the nearest one-eighth of one percentage point (0.125%). This rounded amount will be the new interest rate until the next Change Date, subject to the limitations set forth in Section (C) below.

Based on the new interest rate, the Lender will determine the amount of the monthly payment that would be sufficient to reamortize the loan based on the unpaid principal balance of the loan expected to be owed on the Change Date plus interest at the new rate which will result in substantially equal payments over the remaining term of the loan.

(C)   Limit on Interest Rate Changes

If the calculations set forth in Section (B) above result in a new interest rate of which is more than . . . . . higher or lower than the interest rate in effect immediately prior to the Change Date, the interest rate change will be limited to . . . . . . For the purpose of the first adjustment, the new interest will not be more than . . . . . higher or lower than . . . . %. Also, during the term of the loan the interest rate may never be higher than . . . . %, and may never be lower than . . . . %.

(D)   Effective Date of Changes

Each new interest rate will become effective on the next Change Date. If Borrower's monthly payment changes as a result of a change in the interest rate, Borrower's monthly payment will change as of the first monthly payment date after the Change Date as provided in the Note.

(E)   Notice to Borrower

The Lender will mail Borrower a notice by first class mail at least thirty and no more than forty-five days before each Change Date if the interest rate is to change. The notice will advise Borrower of:

    (i)   the new interest rate on Borrower's loan;
    (ii) the amount of Borrower's new monthly payment; and
    (iii) any additonal matters which the Lender is required to disclose.

B. LOAN CHARGES

It could be that the loan secured by the Security Instrument is subject to a law which sets maximum loan charges and that law is interpreted so that the interest or other loan charges collected or to be collected in connection with the loan would exceed permitted limits. If this is the case, then: (A) any such loan charge shall be reduced by the amount necessary to reduce the charge to the permitted limit; and (B) any sums already collected from Borrower which exceeded permitted limits will be refunded to Borrower. Lender may choose to make this refund by reducing the principal owed under the Note or by making a direct payment to Borrower.

ADJUSTABLE RATE LOAN RIDER—CALIFORNIA   LN 164 0289

FIGURE 4.1   Sample adjustable rate loan rider. (continued)

C. PRIOR LIENS

If Lender determines that all or any part of the sums secured by this Security Instrument are subject to a lien which has priority over this Security Instrument, Lender may send Borrower a notice identifying that lien. Borrower shall promptly act with regard to that lien as provided in paragraph 4 of the Security Instrument or shall promptly secure an agreement in a form satisfactory to Lender subordinating that lien to this Security Instrument.

D. TRANSFER OF THE PROPERTY

If there is a transfer of the Property subject to paragraph 17 of the Security Instrument, Lender may require (1) an increase in the current Note interest rate, or (2) an increase in (or removal of) the limit on the amount of any one interest rate change (if there is a limit), or (3) a change in the Base Index figure, or all of these, as a condition of Lender's waiving the option to accelerate provided in paragraph 17.

By signing this, Borrower agrees to all of the above.

.... (Seal)
—Borrower

.... (Seal)
—Borrower

STATE OF CALIFORNIA

COUNTY OF _____   } ss.

On _____, 20 _____, before me, the undersigned, a Notary Public in and for

said State, personally appeared _____

_____

personally known to me (or proved to me on the basis of satisfactory evidence) to be the person(s) whose name(s) _____

subscribed to the foregoing instrument and acknowledged that _____ executed the same.

WITNESS my hand and official seal.

(Reserved for offical seal)

_____
Notary Public in and for Said State

Advantages of an Adjustable Rate Mortgage to the Borrower

- Lower initial rates when compared with fixed rates (although the difference is slight unless the borrower elects to use a negatively amortized loan). Even then, depending upon the loan option, the fully indexed rate for qualifying purposes may not be much different than the fixed rate loan.

- Easier qualifying for home purchases (of reduced value, as borrowers are now required to qualify at fully indexed rates).

- Initial costs of the loan are usually smaller (although this would depend upon how we interpret "initial costs").

- Ability to qualify for a larger loan at the lower interest rate in some situations.

- Potential for lower payments as the index comes down.

- Generally easier assumability upon resale.
- No prepayment penalties. Although one can acquire an ARM without a prepay, in all but the "conforming ARMs" the borrower may end up paying a price, usually in the margin, which adds to the overall rate. Prepayment penalties are designated as either "soft" or "hard." Soft penalties allow the property to be sold without penalty but require that the penalty be paid if the property is refinanced within the noted time period. Hard penalties require the fee to be paid under all circumstances within the time frame. The kind of prepayment penalty and the time period for which the borrower is obligated are determined with the pricing/cost of the loan. For instance, a borrower selection of a soft prepay for a two-year period might cost an additional half point vs. a hard prepay for a two-year period at no additional cost.
- Lower interest charges during the early years. Given that the average life of a loan is only seven to eight years, the ARM may result in less interest paid than might occur with a fixed rate loan during the same period.
- Ability to make principal reduction payments. The ARM allows for principal payments that affect the monthly payment, whereas principal reduction payments with a fixed rate merely affect the term of the loan.
- A better investment may be made with an ARM. For every month your rate is lower than the fixed rate, you are saving money. If you save money for 20 months, as an example, and pay a comparative amount higher than the fixed rate you could have gotten for 16 months, your overall loan payments would still be less over the 36 month total period.

What Are Some Questions to Ask and Issues to Consider for Adjustable Rate Mortgages?

What is the beginning ("teaser") interest rate? What index is used?

What is the formula that is used to set the rate? What is the past performance of the index?

How much is the margin?

Is the beginning interest rate the sum of the index plus the margin? Is it fully indexed?

Do you qualify at the teaser rate or the fully indexed rate?

When can the first interest rate adjustment be made?

How often thereafter can the interest rate be adjusted?

By how much can the interest rate change at the time of adjustment?

Is there an interest rate cap for the life of the loan?

Is there an interest rate floor for the life of the loan?

Is the interest rate cap based on the starting interest rate or something else? When can the monthly payment first change?

How often thereafter can the monthly payment change?

What is the largest monthly payment that can be charged?

By how much can the monthly payment change? Is negative amortization involved?

Is there a limit on the amount of negative amortization?

If so, does the loan automatically recast?

Are changes in the monthly payments directly tied to interest rate changes? Can you lock in interest rates, margin, and monthly payments at application? What is the cost to originate the loan?

Is the loan assumable under the original terms?

Is the loan fully assumable, or does a new borrower have to qualify?

Can the loan be converted to a fixed rate loan?

How is the conversion rate determined?

If it can be converted, when? At what expense?

Note: The last five questions are related to assumability and conversion. Typically, a new borrower must "qualify" to assume the ARM loan and a fee is usually charged. The reality may be that after a couple of adjustments, and given the fact that the borrower must qualify, there is little incentive for said assumption when the new borrower could acquire a new adjustable loan at a lower rate. Depending upon the assumption fee charged, there could be some savings in the costs of acquiring the loan.

Disadvantages of an Adjustable Rate Mortgage to the Borrower

- Income may not increase proportionately with increases in payments.

- In a slow real estate market, the rate of appreciation may be less than the rate of increase in the interest rates; that is, the spread between the value of the property and the outstanding loan balance could shrink each year, rather than increase.

- In some cases, the prospect for negative amortization means that borrowers may owe more than they would net out of the resale proceeds if the property is sold in the early years.

- The risk of rising interest rates is borne partly by the borrower, since the risk of change in the cost of funds can be shifted entirely to the borrower, within maximum caps allowed over the life of the loan.

4.3 HYBRID LOAN OPTIONS

Several hybrid loan programs have been available over the years. All consist of some form of fixed rate and adjustable rate combination. The lending restraints initiated in 2008 and 2009 slowed the use of these loans, at least temporarily. But the loan industry is cyclical; while their influence has waned recently, we are likely to see a resurgence of these loans again in the future. There are many variations of hybrid loan options, with most of them beginning with an initial fixed rate term, then adjusting to an ARM for the remaining loan period. The following are brief highlights of the more popular options.

Fixed to ARM

This hybrid loan typically starts as a **fixed rate loan** for an established period of time (e.g., three, five or seven years) after which it converts or "rolls over" to an adjustable rate mortgage. In general, the shorter the fixed rate period the lower the initial rate. The popularity of these loans vary with the economic times. Depending upon the fixed rate term, the difference in rate between the hybrid loan and the current 30-year fixed loan can be significant. At other times, the spread between the two rates is insufficient to promote the convertible option. The eventual ARM loan typically adjusts on an annual basis with the adjustment terms identified at origination time. Sometimes referred to as a rollover loan, it is mostly used in a situation wherein a borrower expects to liquidate their home prior to the loan's conversion.

Two-Step Mortgage

While similar to the fixed to ARM convertible loan, the two-step loan allows the borrower to acquire a lower interest rate loan for an initial period (usually five or seven years), after which the loan changes to either another fixed rate or adjustable loan. When converted, a new fixed rate would be at the then prevailing rate. When converted to an ARM, the terms, including a lifetime interest rate ceiling, would have also been set at the origination.

ARM to Fixed

An ARM loan that has an option to convert to a fixed rate loan usually has more complicated rules regarding how and when such a conversion can occur. The time frame during which a conversion is allowed is called the "window period." The conversion terms are identified at the time the loan is created, but the most likely option allows an election on the loan's annual anniversary starting the 13th month through the 60th month or the second, third, fourth and fifth years of the loan. Since the conversion is limited to taking place only on the anniversary date each year, the timing could result in missing a lower rate that may have occurred outside the allowed time frame.

The usual reason for exercising a conversion option is the borrower's fear that the existing ARM rate is likely to exceed any converted fixed rate. Note that any conversion privilege will be to a fixed rate anywhere from .375 (3/8) percent to .5 (1/2) percent above the 60-day Freddie Mac rate at the time. The amortization period will be for the remaining term of the loan. The converted rate will likely be slightly above the prevailing fixed rate. There may also be a cost for exercising the conversion.

After what was deemed the start of a recession in 2007, by mid-2008, lenders were very reluctant to do any loans that suggested much creativity. This included most hybrid loan types.

The costs of conversion should also be investigated. Some lenders may not charge for converting but may have a higher conversion interest rate than other lenders. Certain lenders may charge half a point for converting but may have a lower conversion interest rate. These alternatives should be sought out while you are seeking your original loan. After the loan is funded, it is too late to change these terms.

4.4 BALLOON PAYMENT FIXED RATE LOANS

In a **balloon mortgage** the amortization period is 30 years, but the entire unpaid balance is due sooner, most often at the end of the fifth or seventh year. A payment that is more than double the amount of a regular installment is, by Civil Code definition, a balloon payment.

The balloon payment mortgage, although used to finance commercial properties, has not met with huge success in financing homes because of the balloon feature. Unless the note calls for a rollover, there is no assurance that the loan will be rewritten with a new rate at maturity. Thus balloon payment home loans are frequently seller carry back loans used during tight, or high-interest, mortgage markets.

Example: A balloon mortgage would work as follows: a $200,000 loan at 6 percent, amortized for 30 years but due in 5 years, will have monthly payments of principal and interest of $1,199.10. After 60 complete payments (five years × 12 payments per year), the remaining loan balance due and payable will be $186,108.71. (In Chapter 13, Real Estate Math, we will demonstrate how we calculated these numbers.)

The greatest problem confronting the borrower who uses a loan amortized in 30 years, but due in 5 or 7 years, is the inability to meet the balloon at maturity. (We'll discuss a variety of ways to help overcome this problem in Chapter 11). Even if the borrower is able to arrange new financing, whether with the same or different terms and lender, the borrower will likely be subject to new expenses, including an origination fee and other closing costs for the refinanced amount.

4.5 REVERSE ANNUITY MORTGAGE (RAM)

A **reverse annuity mortgage (RAM)** is a government-backed loan option for elderly home owners, 62 or older, who are "equity rich but cash poor." Under a reverse mortgage, a homeowner borrows against their equity, either in a lump sum or in monthly payments. The unique aspect of the loan is that the lender gets repaid only when the house is sold. The homeowner, in the meantime, has the option of remaining in the home until his/her death with no change in the loan terms. In some cases, this results in the lender losing money as the occupant lives longer than expected and has "drawn" more in cash than the actual value of their equity.

While these loans have been available for decades, relatively few people had taken advantage of them until the last few years. The popularity of the RAM has increased substantially and with the aging population growing rapidly, several million potential borrowers will be eligible for a reverse mortgage.

This program is for owner-occupied single-family dwellings, condos, one-to-four dwelling unit apartment buildings, and manufactured homes on separate lots. While these loans are ultimately sold to the secondary market, neither Fannie Mae nor FHA makes direct reverse loans. Instead, approved lenders make the loans with Fannie Mae and FHA backing.

In the past, the profile of a typical borrower was an individual in his/her mid-70s, living alone with no heirs and an income near the poverty level. In other words, the borrower was substantially poorer than other elderly households. A recent study of the program revealed a disturbing aspect: 60 percent of reverse mortgages were paid off for reasons other than the homeowner's death, the result of the homeowner forced to leave his or her home due to illness, the need for elder care, etc. The departure from the home often required a sale of the property, usually resulting in huge costs to the homeowner. Evidence is quite clear that a borrower who moves out of the home or sells it within a few years of acquiring the reverse mortgage will owe a substantial amount in fees and interest but is unlikely to have proportionately received much money via the cash advances.

The idea of being able to acquire a monthly stipend via borrowing against one's home equity, and without having to qualify for the mortgage, is enticing. The up-front fees paid to lenders that originate these loans can be substantial and profitable for the lender. Not only are there the typical mortgage closing costs but a "fee set-aside" is deducted to cover the "projected" costs of servicing the account. The final fee schedule can be quite steep and must be weighed against the time anticipated for the borrower to remain in the home.

As more people become eligible for this program and as the profitability for lenders remains high, there is an increased likelihood that more lenders will enter the reverse mortgage arena. This could result in some lenders being less concerned with what is best for the elderly client and more focused on the profit margin of making the loan. Unless the proliferation of lenders is coupled with reforms to protect the consumer, unwary seniors could be lured into inappropriate, unfavorable, or unnecessary reverse mortgages with little recourse against the originating lender.

It is clear that caution is advised and that a potential borrower needs to acquire competent, unbiased counseling regarding both the advantages and the many pitfalls of a reverse mortgage. Sometimes, after good counseling, it may be better to simply sell the home and use the equity in other ways. While a reverse mortgage may be just what some elderly homeowners need, it is not the answer for everyone.

The three main programs are:

1. *Home Equity Conversion Mortgage.* FHA loan limits apply; this is an ARM loan, usually tied to one-year T-bills with a certain cap above the starting interest rate. In spite of the fact that the loan amount with this option may be lower because FHA establishes maximum loan amounts on a county-by-county basis, this is the most frequently used program and is often perceived to offer the borrower the most protection.

2. *Home Keeper Program.* Fannie Mae loan limits apply; this is an ARM loan, usually tied to one-month CD rates with a certain cap above the starting interest rate.

3. *Conventional Programs.* Lenders offering RAM loans not backed by FHA insurance or Fannie Mae secondary mortgage require-ments can establish their own loan limits and other requirements. The result is that larger loan amounts are often available via this option.

Under all programs, the maximum LTV ratio is determined by a formula based on the borrower's age, interest rates, and appraisal and/or maximum loan, as often found using the annuity principle. Payment options for the borrower usually include:

1. *Term option.* Equal monthly payments for a fixed number of years.

2. *Tenure option.* Equal monthly payments for as long as the bor-rower occupies the home.

3. *Line of credit option.* Funds drawn as needed (including a lump sum) up to the maximum loan amount that is calculated based on among other things, the age of the borrower and the current interest rate. Caution must be exercised with this option, as the funds could be exhausted requiring a refinance (if the home value has appreciated) and bring another round of steep fees. If the home hasn't appreciated, disallowing any future funds and thereby eliminating the owner's ability to retain their home, a sale may have to occur and the owner could lose his/her property.

RAM Basics—FHA and Fannie Mae Programs

1. Borrower pays loan fees, closing costs, and a monthly servicing fee to issue the checks (approximately $30). In addition, under the FHA program, mortgage insurance premiums will be charged. Most of these fees can be financed as part of the loan, which also means less money in pocket.

2. The loan becomes due and payable upon death, on sale of the home, or if the borrower vacates the home for more than one

year (including time spent in a rest home). The amount due consists of all payments made to the borrower, plus accrued interest. However, the amount payable shall not exceed the value of the home, even if the total payments received, plus interest owed, are more than the value of the home. If the home appreciates above the payoff amount, the borrower, or his or her heirs, gets to keep the excess funds from the sale after paying off the loan and closing costs.

3. Because of past abuses, most reverse mortgage borrowers are required to attend an education session before a loan can be approved. This is designed to prevent relatives, so-called friends, or service providers such as home repair people from taking advantage of an elderly homeowner.

4. Fannie Mae's "Home Keeper for Home Purchase" program, uses a very large down payment combined with a reverse mortgage to acquire a home with no monthly payments. Although not as common as the other reverse mortgage programs where seniors stay in their existing home, this purchase program might be ideal for an older homeowner who wishes to move closer to relatives and loved ones.

5. Funds received are tax-free because they represent a loan that must ultimately be repaid. One drawback is the up-front fees, which can be easily twice the cost to secure a traditional purchase money mortgage.

These websites may be helpful as you seek additional information: www.reversemortgage.org, www.freedomfinancial.com, and www.FannieMae.com.

4.6 MISCELLANEOUS ALTERNATIVE PLANS

There are two other alternative mortgage programs that are frequently used. Because lending practices are forever changing, we can expect other creative options to be proposed in the future.

Fifteen-Year Mortgage

In an effort to build equity faster, to have a free and clear home sooner, and to obtain lower interest rates, borrowers can opt for a 15-year, as opposed to a 30-year, loan. Depending upon the market conditions, a borrower may acquire a lower interest rate, usually between one-quarter and one-half percent less than the 30-year loan. See the Example for interest rate comparisons.

Biweekly Loan Payments

You can reduce your loan term without having to make the higher monthly payments associated with the 15-year mortgage. Some lenders offer borrowers the option of a biweekly payment schedule instead of traditional monthly payments.

A **biweekly loan payment** is made every two weeks, resulting in 26 biweekly payments per year. This is the equivalent of making 13 monthly payments. A biweekly payment is merely one-half of a monthly payment paid every 14 days. The extra payments apply more money against the principal loan amount, thereby greatly reducing the time it takes to pay off the loan. More important to some borrowers may be the fact that they are paid on an every two-week basis and paying half the loan payment each pay period may be easier for personal budgeting purposes.

If you get paid monthly, you can also acquire the savings by paying a little extra with each monthly payment. This can be done by taking your normal monthly payment and dividing it by twelve. Add this 1/12 payment to your monthly payment to lower your principle balance faster.

How much faster is a loan paid off using biweekly instead of monthly payments? Depending upon the size of the loan and its terms, a rule of thumb is that it is approximately one-third faster—a traditional 30-year monthly amortized loan being paid off in about 21 years using biweekly payments.

Lenders will make these loans as long as they can sell them in the secondary market. Sometimes these loans are not popular to investors as servicing them is more time consuming and costly. Homeowners often receive notices from companies who will arrange such a payment plan. Be careful! In most cases, the lender and/or the company will charge $350 to $750 as a one-time fee to initiate the service. Plus, there is usually a monthly charge for maintaining the service. The process involves simply collecting the biweekly payments via an automatic deduction process from your checking account and then making the "one extra payment" for the borrower at the end of each year. With a bit of self discipline, a home owner can do it themselves.

Here is one way to do it: Deposit one-twelfth of the monthly payment into a savings account each month. In November, write a separate check for the "one extra payment" amount and send it to the lender with a note indicating that the payment is for "principal paydown only." This will enable a borrower to identify within 60 days (when the lender provides a year-end statement regarding loan balance, interest paid, etc.) that the lender has credited the account accurately. Some feel that this "one payment" method is better than a small additional monthly payment made to principal paydown (noted above) because accurate accounting with the lender is easier to track.

Example: A $100,000 fixed rate loan at 6 percent, amortized for 30 years, requires a monthly principal and interest payment of $599.55. The same $100,000 loan at 5 3/4 percent, amortized for 15 years, requires a monthly payment of $830.41.

$830.41	per month for 15 years at 5 3/4 percent
$599.55	per month for 30 years at 6 percent
$230.86	per month more for a 15-year than for a 30-year loan program

This 15-year loan is especially attractive to high-income borrowers who wish to have their homes paid off prior to retirement. For the interest-rate conscious borrower, the amount of interest that is saved can be substantial. Using the above data (but ignoring pennies), we have:

$115,838	interest payable over 30 years at 6 percent ($599.55/mo. × 360 pmts., less $100,000 loan amount)
49,474	interest payable over 15 years at 5 3/4 percent ($830.41/mo. × 180 pmts., less $100,000 loan amount)
$ 66,364	interest saved

(Mortgage amounts differ. To determine the savings obtained with a $300,000 loan, for instance, merely multiply the above numbers by three.)

Of course, no analysis of interest costs can be complete without comparing income tax consequences of one scheme over another, nor would we ignore the time value of money, but these aspects are well beyond the scope of this text.

(We'll see how biweekly loan payments are computed in Chapter 13.)

For many borrowers, this is a way to have a 30-year loan—with its smaller monthly payment and with just one voluntary extra principal and interest payment every year (or more often if it is affordable)—save on interest paid and shorten the loan term. And it's possible to do without being locked into the larger required payments, should they become burdensome. Of course, these prepayments can be accomplished only if they are not prohibited under the terms of the promissory note. If the borrower makes the 13th monthly payment, he/she must make sure the lender is aware of its purpose: principal reduction only.

Typical Questions

1. WILL IT WORK ON ANY LOAN OPTION? Absolutely! FHA, VA, and conventional loans, both fixed and adjustable rate mortgages, 30- or 15-year terms. This can benefit you by paying less interest over the life of the loan, regardless of the type of loan.

2. WHEN CAN ONE START? The sooner the better! Whether one has a brand new loan or has been making payments for months or years, money can be saved in the form of unpaid interest. It works for both new and existing loans.

3. HOW LONG DOES ONE HAVE TO PARTICIPATE TO MAKE IT WORTHWHILE? Money is saved the very first payment, but the longer one participates, the greater the savings in unpaid interest and the shorter the payoff term. It is advised that one retain his or her own record of extra payments and an analysis of the benefit via year-by-year savings. Here's an example of the possible savings on a $100,000 loan at eight percent interest:

Mortgage paid off:	30 years versus 21 years
Total interest paid:	$164,155 versus $106,748
Total interest saved:	$ 57,407

4. IF I DON'T PLAN TO STAY IN THE HOME FOR 30 YEARS, IS IT STILL A GOOD THING TO DO? It might be! An analysis of the current loan situation can identify the possible savings over the next several years and assist in your decision making. Generally, it is a good plan for practically everyone simply because it initiates a habit that saves money immediately and that hopefully would continue with any new mortgages acquired.

5. SHOULD THE PLAN ONLY BE USED WITH A PERSONAL RESIDENCE? The same kind of savings will occur with any mortgage, including mortgages on rental or commercial properties. It is best to analyze each mortgage separately to determine the savings that could occur. This plan could be particularly good for people hoping to retain and use rental

property for future income purposes by paying off the mortgage early.

6. IS THERE A BETTER ALTERNATIVE INVESTMENT? Depending upon the economy at the time, one may find another, more lucrative investment vehicle. One must always compare investment strategies based upon return on investment, risk, safety, etc.

4.7 EPILOGUE

We have discussed just a sampling of mortgage alternatives. The financial market's climate at any given time determines its acceptance of creative loan options. Following the 2007–2009 recession, there was a return to more standard loan products. This was clearly a reaction, some said an overreaction, to the extremely flexible loan options that characterized the subprime loan market. Under all market conditions, licensees must be cautious in recommending loan plans that may not be suitable for the client. As the foreclosure crises beginning in 2006 grew, buyers blamed everyone, including real estate licensees, for promoting loan options that proved unsustainable.

During this time of readjustment, one of the most condemned loan options was the Option ARM, a loan that allowed borrowers to pick how their monthly payments were calculated. Also called "pick-a-payment" or "cash flow ARM," monthly payments could be calculated as if the interest rate was only 1 or 2 percent, even though the market adjustable rate was 6 percent. The result is negative amortization, which is added to the principal balance and increases the amount of interest paid. Once the balance reaches 100 to 120 percent of the original loan, a payoff or recasting is required. Borrowers then faced rescheduled payments increased by 50 percent and more, contributing largely to the foreclosure woes of many.

The financing smorgasbord offered in the mortgage cafeteria should provide alternatives paired with individual needs and abilities to repay. The real estate broker today is expected to be knowledgeable about financing alternatives, which means continuous exposure to and understanding of new financing vehicles, techniques, and choices. But the real estate licensee is well advised to depend upon knowledgeable mortgage representatives to help their borrowers make final loan decisions.

SUMMARY

Beginning in 2002, financing of real estate underwent a revolution, as a host of innovative mortgages were created so that in theory, loans could be matched to the borrower instead of tying all borrowers to just one loan type.

In the past, loan applicants were concerned about how much they could borrow, at what interest rate and fees, and how much the monthly payments would be. The more savvy applicants might ask about prepayment penalties and loan assumability. As housing appreciation grew to double digits, the focus shifted to "how can I buy before I will no longer be able to afford anything"? Thus, more and more flexible loan options emerged in an effort to assure that practically everyone could enjoy the American dream of homeownership. Adjustable rate mortgages (ARMs), are loans whose interest rate moves up and down based upon a neutral index. These loans became increasingly popular from 2004–2006. Elements of the ARM include a neutral index that regularly adjusts and a margin that adds to that index adjustment. Adding these two elements total the borrower's interest rate. The maximum rate allowed over the term of the loan is the life cap (or ceiling) and there is an additional limitation, the payment cap, exercised at each loan adjustment period. Understanding the language of ARMs allows a borrower to discern if the loan will be a negatively amortized or a no-neg loan.

A hybrid loan allows the borrower to switch between an ARM and a fixed rate loan during a predetermined "window period." A balloon-type loan that is amortized for 30 years, with the entire unpaid balance due at the end of the fifth or seventh year, may be offered by some home lenders. A payment that is more than double the amount of a regular installment is, by Civil Code definition, a balloon payment.

A reverse annuity mortgage (RAM) allows homeowners, aged 62 or older to tap their owner-occupied home equity with no monthly repayments. In essence, the homeowner receives a monthly payment from the lender and does not need to pay the loan back until he or she moves out, sells, or dies. The home must be owned free and clear, or have a low-balance existing loan. Neither Fannie Mae nor FHA make direct reverse loans. Instead, approved lenders make the loans with Fannie Mae and FHA approval.

Other alternative loan packages include two-step mortgages, 15-year loans and biweekly payment plans. Since real estate and its financing are cyclical, it is likely that we will see the emergence of other creative loan options again in the future. Each of the alternative mortgage instruments discussed in this chapter is intended to answer borrowers' questions and to provide potential solutions to various borrowing needs. While there may not be a solution to every buyer's loan needs, these options do offer some alternatives to financing, without which the purchase of real estate could be severely limited.

IMPORTANT TERMS AND CONCEPTS

Adjustable rate mortgage (ARM)

Balloon payment

Biweekly loan payment

Cap

Fixed rate loan

Negative amortization

Reverse annuity mortgage (RAM)

REVIEWING YOUR UNDERSTANDING

Questions for Discussion

1. What are the key characteristics of ARM loans?

2. What is the main lender risk in granting loans amortized in 30 years, but due in 7 years?

3. List the main elements of a RAM loan.

Multiple-Choice Questions

1. The principal objective of an Adjustable Rate Mortgage (ARM) loan is to
   a. reduce the risk of foreclosure.
   b. limit mortgage choices during periods of tight money.
   c. establish predictable cash flow during erratic real estate markets.
   d. share the risks of rising interest rates between lender and borrower.

2. Under an ARM loan, the distance between the actual rate paid by the borrower and the index is called the
   a. adjustment.
   b. cap.
   c. term.
   d. margin.

3. The maximum interest rate that a lender can charge under an ARM is called the
   a. cap.
   b. margin.
   c. term.
   d. adjustment.

4. In an ARM loan, when the initial interest rate is abnormally low it is known as the _____ rate.
   a. index
   b. teaser
   c. capped
   d. basement

5. Reverse annuity mortgages are growing more popular with an aging population. Those who qualify
   a. must be over age 59.
   b. usually have very little equity in their homes.
   c. can borrow either in lump sum or in monthly payments.
   d. must remain in their home until sold.

6. The first month's interest on a $200,000 loan at 9 percent payable at $1,800 per month is:
   a. $1,800
   b. $1,600
   c. $1,500
   d. $1,300

7. The first month's negative amortization (shortfall) amount on a $200,000 loan at 9 percent payable at $1,300 per month is:
   a. $600
   b. $500
   c. $300
   d. $200

8. The reverse annuity mortgage (RAM) is especially designed for
   a. poor families.
   b. younger borrowers.
   c. older borrowers.
   d. those unable to meet balloon payments.

9. The loan plan that offers borrowers an adjustable interest rate with the right to switch to a fixed rate at a later date is the
   a. dual rate, variable rate mortgage.
   b. rollover mortgage.
   c. reverse annuity mortgage.
   d. pledged account mortgage.

10. Under a convertible loan, the time period when the borrower is allowed to switch from an ARM to fixed rate or vice versa is called the _____ period.
    a. shift
    b. crossover
    c. section
    d. window

11. An advantage of a 15-year mortgage over a 30-year loan is that
    a. borrowers can qualify with a smaller down payment.
    b. monthly payments are always lower than in the traditional 30-year loan.
    c. borrowers can usually secure a lower interest rate.
    d. borrowers build up equity faster, even with a much higher interest rate.

12. If a borrower is unable to meet a balloon payment, the borrower might arrange to
    a. obtain an extension of the loan with the existing lender.
    b. refinance the property.
    c. sell the property.
    d. all of the above.

13. One option under a RAM program, where the borrower is scheduled to receive monthly payments for a fixed number of years, is called
    a. tenure option.
    b. set option.
    c. term option.
    d. line of credit option.

14. Which of the following will trigger a demand for payoff for a borrower under a RAM loan?
    a. moving to a second home for six months
    b. staying in a rest home for more than one year
    c. taking in a roommate
    d. receiving a cash inheritance of more than $250,000

15. Adjustable rate mortgages
    a. represent alternatives to standard fixed rate, fully amortized mortgages.
    b. are available only for owner-occupied dwellings.
    c. are the preferred choice by most borrowers.
    d. transfer some of the risk of rising inflation from borrower to lender.

16. The reason why a home buyer may opt for an adjustable rate mortgage over a fixed rate mortgage containing a "teaser rate" is to
    a. reduce initial monthly payments.
    b. avoid late charges commonly associated with fixed rate loans.
    c. avoid negative amortization.
    d. avoid prepayment penalties.

17. A 15-year loan, as opposed to a 30-year loan, will
    a. have no impact on annual interest deductions for income tax purposes.
    b. result in slower equity buildup.
    c. create a faster equity in the property, all other things being equal.
    d. initially generate lower monthly payments.

18. A biweekly payment program requires the borrower to make _____ payments per year.
    a. 12
    b. 13
    c. 24
    d. 26

19. When compared with a 30-year loan, the 15-year loan is especially attractive for borrowers who desire to reduce their
    a. monthly installment.
    b. total interest payments.
    c. principal payments.
    d. mortgage insurance premiums.

20. ARM loans pose difficulties for prospective borrowers to understand due to each of the following, except
    a. its simplicity compared to fixed rate instruments.
    b. the relationship of an index to U.S. Treasury securities.
    c. the relationship of the index to the so-called margin.
    d. how interest rates are adjusted to reflect a particular index.

CASE & POINT

Government Intervention to Stem ARM Foreclosures (Or Why We Should Understand the Problem Before Trying to Solve It)

Very early in the subprime meltdown it was recognized that ARM financing was accounting for a disproportionate number of the growing foreclosures. Only later would it be identified that nearly 60 percent of the borrowers facing foreclosure had been eligible for a more stable loan option. Instead, they had opted for—or as some later complained been "sold"—an ARM product. The "option arm" with its very low start rate was very popular, in spite of its negatively amortized aspect. Many borrowers believed that our real estate market would only continue to appreciate. The rationale of the lenders was that they were helping buyers maximize their purchasing power. Buyers seemed eager to accept lower payments that allowed them to qualify for a larger loan amount and hence a more expensive home. As it turned out, buyers were "betting" that continued double digit appreciation would not only protect them from equity erosion from negative amortization but that there were huge profits to be gained as home values seemed to continue to explode. How wrong everyone was!

By January 2008, the rate of foreclosures was alarming. Borrowers who acquired loans starting in 2005 through June 30, 2007, experienced significant rate changes and projections were that millions more would soon be facing foreclosure. The Obama Administration quickly announced plans aimed at borrowers currently making on-time payments on loans still at their introductory rates but who were identified as unable to afford the soon-to-be adjusted rates and accompanying payments. The information was unfortunately vague as to the procedure for determining those who would not be able to afford payment adjustments. Plus, it seemed that those who had already missed payments, thereby signaling that they were unable to make their adjusted payments, were not eligible for this remedy. Ironically, many of the borrowers who were now ineligible for assistance had been advised by these same institutions that the only way to receive any help was to actually go into default and possible foreclosure. Having taken that advice, they now found that having missed payments made them ineligible under the new guidelines.

Government plans remained unclear while proposals were tweaked and revised in an effort to find something that might provide relief to a growing number of distressed homeowners. The process was complicated by the fact that the very institutions that had perpetrated the loan excesses were now being asked to "voluntarily" work to resolve the burgeoning foreclosure situation.

As is too often the case with new government plans, an overemphasis was placed on making sure that ineligible borrowers could not abuse the programs. In addition, the lenders were charged with voluntarily implementing the plans and continued to demonstrate a reluctance to really make them work. The result was constant revisions and relatively few borrowers ultimately acquiring assistance. The original anticipation that millions of homeowners would be helped proved to be overly optimistic.

As the eligibility criteria continued to develop, it became clear that the number of borrowers who were likely to meet the increasingly complicated rules would decline. New predictions estimated that no more than 100,000 to 600,000 would ultimately be assisted nationwide, far fewer than the millions projected when the proposals were first introduced.

During the first quarter of 2008, Washington legislators announced that they were planning to help all borrowers who were struggling with home payments—not just those facing potential foreclosure. No details were provided and, again, many believed that to be an empty promise. By the third quarter of 2009, the programs had been revised several times but still with little real assistance to the increasing number of struggling homeowners. Many began to see these efforts as merely bailout plans serving the banks and other investors to the detriment of the consumer who desperately required help. By the end of 2009, the housing market continued to struggle, and it was reported that 24 percent of mortgages nationally were either under water or in foreclosure. While some economists indicated that the worst of the recession was behind us, other pundits were predicting that by 2011, nearly 50 percent of mortgages would be under water or in foreclosure. It is safe to say that the housing difficulties are not over yet!

Chapter

5

PREVIEW

This chapter covers conventional loans, their advantages and disadvantages, and how to compare one lender with another. Buy-down loans are explained and several examples are given. The California Fair Lending Regulations are outlined and analyzed. This chapter concludes with a discussion of private mortgage insurance (PMI) companies.

After completing this chapter, you should be able to:

1. Define a conventional loan.
2. List several advantages and disadvantages of a conventional loan.
3. Describe what to look for when choosing a lender.
4. Demonstrate how the Community Home Buyers Program assists first-time buyers.
5. Give an example of a buy-down loan.
6. Outline the basic features of the California Financial Discrimination Act.
7. Explain how private mortgage insurance (PMI) works.

Conventional Loans

5.1 WHAT IS A CONVENTIONAL LOAN?

There are two major categories of loans. One is **government-backed loans,** which include the Federal Housing Administration (FHA), the U.S. Department of Veterans Affairs (DVA), the California Department of Veterans Affairs (Cal-Vet), and various other state, county, and city-backed subsidized home loan options, usually funded via bond issued programs. Any loan that is not a government-backed loan is called a **conventional loan**. The majority of loans originated on one-to-four-unit, residential properties are conventional loans.

Conventional versus Government-Backed Loans

Today, a buyer's ability to acquire financing must often be determined *before* the buyer starts looking for a home to purchase. Today's borrowers are challenged to determine what loan will best serve their home-buying need from a shrinking list of available options. Potential buyers need competent guidance when comparing loan types as well as identifying the option(s) for which they can actually qualify. The advantages and disadvantages of conventional loans versus government-backed loans are outlined below. Recognize that the differences between the two types of loans have diminished following the return to the less-flexible underwriting guidelines of conventional loans.

Advantages (Past and Present) of Conventional over Government-Backed Loans

1. *Conventional loans were generally able to be processed in less time.* Automated underwriting revolutionized the industry by reducing processing time frames for conventional loans. The government

agencies also streamlined their processing (via "direct endorsement" and "DVA automatic" underwriting, covered in Chapter 6), but the time frame for loan approvals still lagged compared to the conventional procedure.

Recent regulations, coupled with industry layoffs, have extended the time periods, making any difference between the processing time frames for conventional versus government loans much less obvious today. Whereas 30-day, and sometimes much shorter, loan approvals used to be fairly commonplace, borrowers must be more patient today with all loan options.

2. *Documentation.* Processing a conventional loan generally involves less paperwork. There may be fewer forms to complete, and the routine of processing can be more flexible. The subprime loan explosion resulted in a dramatic reduction in documentation, particularly with the "limited" or "no" doc loans. It was clear, following the collapse of the subprime programs, that lenders needed more borrower data with which to make informed decisions. Critics, however, believe that the pendulum has swung from requiring virtually no documentation to asking for way too much information. Advocates, on the other hand, insist that this documentation is necessary to ensure an acceptable, quality loan. We will review today's documentation requirements in Chapter 9.

3. *Loan amounts.* In theory, there is no legal limitation on conventional loan amounts when the loan-to-value (LTV) ratio is 80 percent or less. The majority of loans originated are sold into the secondary market (discussed in Chapter 7) and guidelines there are well established.

The FHA sets maximum loan amounts on a home loan depending on geographical location. The DVA has no dollar loan maximum, but individual lenders do limit veterans' loan amounts because the DVA guarantees only part of the loan. Cal-Vet's maximum loan on a single-family dwelling is limited and can vary from year to year. Dollar limits on government-backed loans will be covered in Chapter 6.

4. *Number of lenders.* If you apply for a DVA-guaranteed loan and the loan is rejected by the DVA, you have no alternative lender. There is only one U.S. Department of Veterans Affairs, just as there is only one FHA and one California Department of Veterans Affairs. In the past, if a loan was turned down by one conventional lender, there may have been another who could approve the loan due to differences in underwriting guidelines, providing a distinct advantage over government-type loans. Those options have mostly disappeared as qualifying requirements have toughened and fewer loan

programs have become available. When a loan is denied by one lender, the likelihood of approval elsewhere is now slim.

5. *Flexibility of portfolio lenders.* When a lender keeps a loan in-house, instead of reselling it in the secondary market, it is called a ***portfolio loan***. These loans became enormously popular during the subprime frenzy, requiring only minimum paperwork or documentation, as evidenced by their names: No Income-No Asset (NINA) documentation or a Stated Income-Stated Assets (SISA) loan. Initially, these loans required a larger down payment and relied heavily on a borrower's credit scores and the results of the property's appraisal. As more and more flexible guidelines were adopted, borrowers were judged almost exclusively on their credit scores. Hence, the term "mirror loans" was adopted referring to the fact that if one could prove they were alive by fogging up a mirror, they could most likely acquire financing. These loans were mostly ARMs, and eventually 100 percent of the purchase price of a home could be borrowed. Many portfolio lenders have ceased to exist and/or no longer offer such easy-to-get loans.

Disadvantages (Past and Present) of Conventional over Government-Backed Loans

1. *Higher down payments.* In certain price ranges, many buyers chose government-backed financing because the loans often require a smaller down payment than was available in conventional loans. In appropriate price ranges, DVA-backed loans do not require any down payment (although a lender may require one if the sales price is higher than the appraised value); FHA and Cal-Vet programs only require a small down payment. However, during the recent subprime frenzy, conventional real estate loans with no-to-low down payment were offered and, to a large extent, replaced the government-backed loans. The 97 percent Freddie Mac loan even became known as an FHA "look-alike" and the 100 percent loan option became increasingly popular. As financing is cyclical in nature, government loans are again in vogue.

2. *Prepayment penalties.* FHA, DVA, and Cal-Vet loans do not have a prepayment penalty. Fannie Mae and Freddie Mac loans typically do not include prepayment penalties. In contrast, most of the subprime ARM-type loans and many portfolio-type conventional loans did contain prepayment penalties.

Sources of Conventional Money

Determining where to acquire a loan can be confusing. The main sources of conventional money are mortgage bankers and mortgage companies, commercial banks, and savings banks. But which to choose?

Lenders who retain (portfolio) their loans, rather than selling them to Fannie Mae or Freddie Mac, can establish their own criteria for loan submissions. Other than having to adhere to basic state and federal regulations, these lenders have relative freedom in making loans. Often these are local lenders who are able to somewhat customize a loan to meet the specific needs of a local borrower. However, most lenders wish to resell their loans in the secondary market, and the number of portfolio loan options has comparatively diminished.

Two of the main players in the secondary market are the **Federal National Mortgage Association (Fannie Mae)** and the **Federal Home Loan Mortgage Corporation (Freddie Mac)**. For a bank to sell to them, they must adhere to standards established by these major loan purchasers. In order to compare lenders, you have to know what items to evaluate. While there can be minor differences, here are the basic loan guidelines.

1. *Loan-to-value ratios.* Conventional lenders have retreated from those overly flexible loan options (e.g., 100 percent, 97 percent, 95 percent financing) and now limit loans to the 90 percent loan-to-value level.

    As a matter of evaluating risk, conventional lenders often lower their LTV ratios on two-to-four-unit residential properties, condos, nonowner-occupied, raw land, and cash out refinance loans.

2. *Type of property.* It can be said that there has been a "flight to quality" regarding property which lenders will finance. Appraisers have become increasingly critical and new rules have been introduced (to be detailed in Chapter 8) in an effort to reassure investors' reliance upon home values.

    Lenders also make decisions regarding the type of property they will accept as security for a loan. Property condition, minimum size requirements, zoning restrictions, multiple unit, and/or condo limitations are a few of the lenders' considerations. There is less variation between lender requirements following the excesses of a few years ago.

3. *Maximum loan amounts.* As the number of portfolio lenders continues to dwindle, most lenders have adopted the Fannie Mae/Freddie Mac loan maximums discussed in Chapter 7. These are called "conforming" loans, and allow participating lenders to sell their loans in the secondary market. These loan limits can change each year based upon government guidelines. Jumbo loan amounts, which exceed the Fannie Mae and Freddie Mac limits,

are available accompanied by higher interest rates. A new category of loan limits, called conforming "high balance" loans, has been developed in response to the rising home values in some areas.

4. *Interest rates.* Perhaps the one item most "shopped" by consumers is the interest rate. Interest rates reflect the risk level accompanying each loan, for instance, a higher loan-to-value ratio loan likely requiring a higher interest rate. With a greater desire to resell their loans to Fannie Mae, Freddie Mac, and the government entities (e.g., FHA, DVA) interest rates have become much more competitive and there is often little, if any, difference between lender quoted rates. Rates do frequently adjust, mostly as investors perceive market risk changes. When a rate change occurs, the adjustment is reflected simultaneously in all lenders' quotes. Lenders have adopted "risk based" pricing wherein there is a rate adjustment depending upon LTV, credit scores, and property type. It is not easy for a consumer to compare rates between lenders if the lender does not have an accurate profile of the borrower. This makes the consumers' opportunity to shop rates not what it used to be.

5. *Loan fees.* The loan fee is how the lender gets paid, and the amount is determined by each lender. For the most part, these have also become more competitive as the source lenders (those ultimately funding the loan) have limited the amount a loan originator can earn on any given loan. These rules were enacted in response to perceived past abuses in subprime loan charges. That said, consumers who mostly concentrate on interest rates (noted above) need to pay more attention to how loan fees are identified.

   Tiered pricing has become the norm, with loan fees (points) decreasing as the interest rate accepted by the borrower increases. In essence, the ultimate investor is willing to provide the lender with a "rebate" or fee for providing a higher yielding interest rate. Called, "rebate pricing" or the use of "yield spread premium," this will be discussed in greater detail in Chapter 7. Suffice it to say here that the enticing "no points" loan is a good example of the use of rebate pricing, wherein the borrower trades a higher interest rate for a lower loan fee. This is an acceptable strategy in some situations, but the borrower must recognize that the "no points" offer is not a lender giveaway, but is being compensated via a higher interest rate.

6. *Prepayment penalties.* Fannie Mae, Freddie Mac, and government loans are very unlikely to include prepayment penalties today. Portfolio-type loans are more likely to contain such provisions. This would include the popular "equity line" loans that were used so extensively to access homeowner's equity in the past few years.

When included, the typical prepayment penalty on a conventional loan is six months' interest on the amount prepaid that exceeds 20 percent of the original amount of the loan. However, penalties vary with each lender, and all terms are negotiable. The typical penalty for the early termination of an equity line loan is between a $300 and a $500 fee.

7. *Borrower qualifications.* There is now greater standardization among lenders in regards to how they qualify borrowers. Local lenders retain some flexibility in qualifying guidelines for loans they choose not to sell. Most conventional lenders adhere to the Fannie Mae/Freddie Mac guidelines outlined in Chapter 9. The emphasis on tougher and ever-changing qualifying guidelines, and the need to fully understand them, are reasons enough to seek out professional lender representation when seeking a loan.

8. *Types of loans.* During the height of the subprime frenzy, lenders seemed to be competing with each other in designing loan options to meet every borrower's situation. The number of new loan instruments seemed to expand daily. After the collapse of what turned out to be mostly unsafe loans, the number of loan options reduced significantly. Whereas different lenders used to emphasize different loan types, most lenders now offer the same fixed rate, ARM, and other loans. One difference may be those lenders' ability to offer FHA loans. Government financing and what is required to be an authorized FHA lender will be addressed in Chapter 6.

   Lenders regularly review their loan portfolios and revise lending policies based on economic changes, lending goals, and available funds. The examination of default ratios for various loans determines if a particular loan type will be continued or eliminated. For instance, many predicted that the option ARM would be modified when home appreciation rates began to decline and some of the loans went into default.

   The point is that policies and standards set by conventional lenders are not static. Conventional lenders change their property and borrower standards in order to accomplish certain goals. If a lender has a surplus of money, it has to find a way to make more loans. It may lower its property or borrower standards. Or it can lower the interest rate or change some other policy that will enable it to make more loans. If the conventional lender wants to reduce loan demand, it could tighten up on its standards and increase the interest rate and loan fees; however, its policies and standards cannot be discriminatory under fair housing laws.

5.2 KEEPING UP WITH LENDER POLICIES

Since conventional lender policies are subject to frequent changes, it can be a challenge to stay up-to-date. Professional real estate salespeople recognize the importance of financing to their success: if a property cannot be financed, it is less likely to be sold. As we have seen, the world of real estate financing has become increasingly complicated. So, what kind and how much information does a real estate licensee need to best represent his or her sellers and buyers? The most obvious information sought is the current interest rate. But how about property standard changes and the introduction of new lending programs? With each borrower and each property representing a unique situation, real estate licensees may find it advantageous to convey only basic finance information to clients and depend upon competent mortgage representatives to identify appropriate financing. This said, let's look at some of the ways to acquire information.

1. *Communication with lenders.* Recognizing that there may be less difference between lenders and their financing capacity, most salespeople determine a lender or two who they can call for up-to-date interest rate quotes. Since this is usually done when the licensee has a specific property in mind, they can discuss any potential property issues (e.g., condition of the home, excess land, well-water requirements). Some real estate offices survey lenders periodically, especially regarding interest rates, and this information is then distributed to all the salespeople within an office. With rate changes occurring so frequently, caution should be exercised before relying upon such surveys.

2. *Representatives* from lending institutions visit real estate offices and builders to solicit business and to inform them of their companies' current lending practices. Any changes in interest rate, loan programs, and so on can immediately be brought to the attention of the real estate agents and builders. Some offices, however, now restrict what they consider interruptions to real estate staff, and this option for obtaining information is not always available. With the increased use of e-mail marketing, many lenders use this avenue to "push" information out to agents. The result may be for agents to depend upon this information without doing their own "searching" for or verification of the information.

3. *Other salespeople* who have recently secured a loan are a good source of loan information. Since they have recently secured a loan, they know which lenders offered appropriate financing. Again, be cautious as each transaction can be unique; the loan that worked for one situation may not work for another and/or may not be the best option for the new transaction.

4. *Internet services.* A wide variety of Internet services are available for those seeking up-to-the-minute (or at least daily) rate quotes and other pertinent data for loans of all types. The difficulty with Web sources is that the information may be out-dated or, worse, may be "too good to be true." Additionally, comparisons with local rates can be difficult. Check with your favorite local lender to see if it has a website which you can consult.

5. *Newsletters and flyers* distributed by lenders show the current policy and rates. Other organizations such as title and escrow companies occasionally distribute reports on current financing. Again, e-mail has become more popular for this purpose.

6. *MLS meetings.* Almost every area in California has periodic Multiple Listing Service (MLS) meetings, during which lenders are permitted to quote their current programs and rates and may offer handouts/flyers.

Which Lender to Use?

Experienced real estate licensees usually put together a "team" that includes various consultants, and certainly includes several favorite lenders. When you are ready to obtain financing for or have questions about a specific property, you depend upon your team members for accurate answers. In many cases, the more savvy licensees will "shop" service and expertise rather than simply looking for the lowest interest rate. Since, as we've noted, many lenders offer the same loan programs, rates, and terms (i.e., so that the loan can be sold to Fannie Mae or Freddie Mac), competency, reliability, and quality of service become more important than just the rate.

While everyone talks about service, what does it really mean? Does a lender communicate with everyone in the transaction, regularly and honestly? Are the processing times promised reliable? Is the lender organized and detail oriented and capable of meeting the various timelines required in every loan transaction? Will the lender take time to help a potential buyer know what he or she must do to prepare for acquiring a loan? Finally, if the lender cannot offer the best loan option for your borrower, does he or she help find an appropriate lending source?

5.3 BUY-DOWN LOANS

The goal of every real estate transaction should be to create a "win–win" situation for both buyer and seller. At the same time, it seems that everyone wants a "good deal," too. An interest rate buy-down can often be the vehicle to accomplish this win–win arrangement.

On a **buy-down loan**, the interest rate reduction is financed "upfront" by placing funds into an account from which the lender subsidizes the monthly payments.

Sellers generally compensate the lender, but it can also be the borrower who pays the lender to reduce the rate.

Why the Seller Participates

There are typically three primary ways that a seller can profit by offering a buy-down to a buyer. It will "differentiate" the seller's property within the market place and thereby "create an interest" to attract buyers. The buy-down can also increase the buyer's "ability to "qualify" for a loan ... by qualifying at the lower "bought down" interest rate. Finally, a buy-down offer can often be less than a price reduction, the latter being too often the only method used to stimulate interest in the seller's property. The buy-down can actually "maximize the seller's profit" by eliminating the need for any price reductions.

Temporary Buy-Down Plans

From the buyer's perspective, a buy-down will assist in his or her qualifying to purchase and is usually of greater benefit than a price reduction. Buy-downs can be either "temporary" or "permanent." The most common form of a temporary buy-down is known as the 2/1 buy-down. The buyer's initial interest rate is reduced 2 percent below the normal start rate. For instance, if the current fixed rate is 6.5 percent, payments for the first year of the mortgage would be calculated at 4.5 percent, the second year payments at 5.5 percent, and the third and subsequent years would be at the full 6.5 percent rate. The buyer qualifies at the second year buy-down rate of 5.5 percent and, thus, qualifies for a larger loan amount and a higher purchase price. (Qualifying at the second year buy-down rate is a more recent program adjustment due to the changes in qualifying standards. The borrower used to qualify at the first year buy-down rate, which would have been the 4.5 percent in this scenario.)

Using the abovementioned scenario, if the loan is bought down from 6.5 percent to 4.5 percent for the first year and to 5.5 percent for the second year, let's calculate the amount necessary to affect the buy-down on a $100,000 loan. We must calculate the difference in the payments between the 6.5 percent loan and the payments at 4.5 percent and then at 5.5 percent.... This difference is the amount that must be deposited in an account at the close of escrow. In our example, the total amount would be approximately $2,276. In most cases, this is paid by the seller as an incentive for the buyer to purchase. (For an example, see the chart below.)

A temporary buy-down can benefit the buyer whose current income is a bit low, but who anticipates that it will increase during the next two years. The lower payments during the first two-year period can help the buyer qualify and be able to comfortably make the increased payments as his or her income grows. This can be a better alternative in meeting the initial low income problem than acquiring an adjustable rate mortgage, which is often negatively amortized.

BUY-DOWN ON A $100,000 LOAN AT 6.5 PERCENT INTEREST

Months	Interest Rate	Monthly Payment @6.5%	Borrower's Payments	Monthly Buy-Down Amount	Total Buy-Down Amount
1–12	4.5%	$632.06 –	$506.69 =	$125.38 × 12 =	$1,504.56
13–24	5.5%	$632.06 –	$567.79 =	$ 64.28 × 12 =	$ 771.36
25–360	6.5%	$632.06 –	$632.06 =	0 × 12 =	0
				Total	= $2,275.92

Depending upon the economic climate at the time, the seller may want to add this "subsidy" to the price of the house, which then must reflect the added cost in the appraised value. As the buy-down subsidy increases, trying to recapture it in the sales price can become problematic.

Permanent Buy-Down Plans

Another alternative is the permanent buy-down, in which the interest rate is reduced for the entire life of the loan; for instance, if the current rate is 6.5 percent, the rate might be reduced to 5.5 percent for the full 30-year period. While the seller's cost for each of these options is nearly the same, many buyers prefer the temporary buy-down. Under most circumstances, the buyer is unlikely to remain in the home for a 30-year period. Thus, the temporary buy-down is typically a better arrangement.

Obviously, in a brisk real estate market, sellers are not enthusiastic about providing this kind of incentive. With a more difficult-to-sell property, or during slower market conditions, buy-downs become more popular. Lenders and buyers may also pay the fee for a buy-down. The lender buy-down is infrequently used and, in many cases, the buyer does not have sufficient cash available to contemplate a buy-down.

5.4 LOW DOWN PAYMENT CONVENTIONAL LOANS

Both the Federal National Mortgage Association and the Federal Home Loan Mortgage Corporation recognize that accumulating a down payment, and the required closing costs, keeps many people from buying a home. To help this situation, both have created several **low down payment programs**. Although there are minor differences between Fannie Mae and Freddie Mac, the gist of the popular Fannie/Freddie 97 programs is as follows:

- A down payment of only 3.5 percent is required, meaning a 96.5 percent LTV loan is granted.
- The 3.5 percent down payment can be a "gift."
- Income qualifying ratios are easier.
- Borrowers can have a "less than perfect" credit history, but by December 2009, most lenders had increased the minimum score from a former low of 580 to a minimum of 620 with anticipation that the minimum score could increase to 640. Borrowers must attend a home buyer educational seminar.
- In some cases, there may be a maximum income level requirement for the borrower (based on the income of all family occupants—these limits are more generous in California than in most other states).
- The loan can be used to buy only principal residences, including single-family residences, condos, planned unit developments, one-to-four-unit residential income property, and manufactured homes attached to a permanent foundation.

Another popular Fannie Mae/Freddie Mac offering is called the **Community Home Buyer's Program**. This plan is designed especially to help low- and moderate-income home buyers and features what is called the 3/2 option. The 3/2 option provides for a low 5 percent down payment, but with a twist. It allows borrowers to put only 3 percent of their own money toward a down payment. The other 2 percent may be obtained from family gifts or by means of a grant or loan from the state, a local government agency, or a nonprofit organization.

Traditional credit standards are required, but other underwriting criteria are eased to qualify applicants, with greater emphasis on stable job history, steady rent and utility payments, and a ceiling on the qualifying income level, since the program is limited to those less affluent. Though creditworthiness is always important, a greater percentage of applicants' gross monthly income may be used to meet mortgage payments. Because of the high loan-to-value ratio, the 3/2 Option loans must be covered by private mortgage insurance, discussed later. But with what amounts to 97 percent financing, coupled with reduced closing costs and cash reserve requirements, more families may find the dream of homeownership affordable.

NOTE: These programs were temporarily phased out by many lenders during 2009 when the PMI companies scaled back coverage to 90 percent loan-to-value ratio loans. Despite criticism from the lending industry indicating that the PMI companies' reactions were counterproductive in an environment where housing required help, not impediments, these loans continued only at a much reduced level. The action resulted in a flight to government-backed loan options, especially FHA (to be discussed in Chapter 6).

Special Interest Topic
Bank Failures at Historic Levels

The lending landscape changed dramatically as a historic number of bank failures were registered in 2009. By December 2009, 140 banks had closed, compared with 25 in 2008 and only 3 in 2007. In spite of the record bank closures, consumers remained calm, recognizing that the Federal Deposit Insurance Corporation (FDIC) insured each regular account up to $250,000. This amount had been raised from $100,000 in 2008.

Initially, it was the larger banks that closed because of overly aggressive investment in what became known as the "toxic" loans of the subprime loan boom. The costliest failure, estimated at a 10.7 billion FDIC loss, was the 2008 seizure of IndyMac Bank, one of the largest California lenders.

As the economic crises unfolded, the term "too big to fail" was coined to refer to many of the huge institutions. In an effort to maintain consumer confidence in the economic systems, mergers (or one lender absorbing another) were encouraged. One of the larger such combinations was Bank of America's absorption of Countrywide. The latter corporation was referred to as the largest provider of subprime loans in the nation.

By mid-2009, smaller banks were being affected. Their problems were caused mostly by losses on ordinary loans, accompanied by a troubled economy, falling home values, and increasing unemployment. Their situation was exacerbated by their tendency toward too much rapid growth and aggressive lending in the subprime hot markets, including California. Toward the end of 2009, the number of "troubled" banks remained high, but there were hopes of avoiding many more actual closures.

Of greater concern was the solvency of the FDIC insurance fund. Expectations are that total bank failures will cost the fund nearly 70 billion dollars through 2013. Efforts will be devoted to replenishing the fund while it continues to protect consumers from unexpected losses via future bank failures.

5.5 CALIFORNIA FAIR LENDING REGULATIONS

The Housing Financial Discrimination Act (Anti-Redlining Law) applies to owner-occupied residential properties of one to four units. The act also includes nonowner-occupied loans up to four units if 50 percent or more of the loan proceeds are to be used to improve the property.

The act states that financial institutions cannot deny or discriminate in fixing the amount, interest rate, or length of the loan based upon:

1. Neighborhood considerations as listed below, unless the institution can prove that such considerations are necessary to avoid unsafe and unsound business practices.

    a. Age of other properties in the neighborhood.
    b. Location of the property in the neighborhood.
    c. Location of the property on or near land zoned industrial or commercial.
    d. Other conditions, characteristics, or trends in the neighborhood.

2. Race, color, religion, sex, marital status or registered domestic partnership, sexual orientation, national origin, handicap, ancestry, family size, or other characteristics of the borrower.

3. Racial, ethnic, religious, national origin, or income-level composition of a neighborhood or whether that composition is expected to change.

    The act also prohibits **discrimination by effect**. That means that the institution cannot engage in a lending practice that has a discriminatory effect against a protected group, unless that practice is required to achieve a legitimate business purpose. If it is clear that a practice could have a discriminatory effect, then the burden is on the institution to show that the practice is required. Called the "Effects Test," it is difficult to adequately define and confusing when attempting to implement it.

To avoid accusations of discrimination by effect, the lending industry has adopted practices like credit scoring models and qualification checklist/guidelines that presumably apply to all borrowers. The debate continues regarding whether high credit-score requirements, for instance, discriminate against the minority and lower-income groups; or whether this same group is disadvantaged when the rule for counting part-time income requires the part-time employment to be in the same field over a minimum two-year period.

The act has spelled out additional regulations in its attempt to clarify what loan terms an institution can enforce in its efforts to avoid *unsafe and unsound* business practices.

4. If the institution can document the factors in the neighborhood that are likely to cause the value of the property to decrease during the first five years, then it may make adjustments to the loan (reduce the loan amount, for example). As an example, during the economic housing downturn of 2006–2009, appraisers were required to address a neighborhood's "declining values" in determining the appraised value of the subject property.

5. The institution may consider natural or other hazardous conditions surrounding the property. A steep, unstable site would be an example of a hazardous condition and reason for rejection of the property. Requiring flood insurance for a property located near a potentially flooding water source is another acceptable way to mitigate a lender's risk.

6. A loan does not have to be made if it is clearly evident that the physical condition of the property would create an imminent threat to the health or safety of the occupant. Again, appraisers are relied upon to serve as the eyes for the lender and report any such threats.

7. Decisions on the loan security must be based solely on the value of the individual property, unless the institution can document specific neighborhood conditions that affect its present or short-range value (three to five years). Such conditions may include market trends based upon actual transactions involving comparable property and trends indicating increasing numbers of abandoned, vandalized, or foreclosed properties in the immediate vicinity of the property. A statement that there are abandoned, vandalized, or foreclosed properties in the neighborhood will not, by itself, support a conclusion that a neighborhood is declining. The evidence necessary to document a probable decline must be specific.

8. If pending or recent zoning would affect the short-term value of the property (three to five years), the loan may be denied or the

terms may be altered. However, the fact that a property is located on or near land zoned industrial or commercial will not, in itself, be an adequate basis for denying the loan. On the other hand, a trend of converting many homes in the area to commercial use could present a reason for a reduction in the loan amount or even for a loan denial, based on the changing use in the community. If the lender is reasonably sure that a building permit would not be issued in the event of casualty loss due to zoning, the lender may be justified in denying the loan.

9. Supplemental income such as overtime, bonuses, and part-time employment must be considered, *if stable*. Lenders consider such income stable when it can be verified as having occurred within the same employment field for a minimum of two years.

   Not to consider stable supplemental income could be discriminatory because minority and low- and moderate-income families often rely on this type of income.

10. The combined income of husband and wife must be considered.

11. The lender cannot favor applicants who have previously owned homes.

12. Payment-to-income ratios should be flexible. Inflexible ratios could discriminate against low- or moderate-income persons who often devote a greater percentage of their income to housing.

13. A lender may not deny a loan or require corrective work because of code violations or conditions of the property unless the cost of corrective work is more than 10 percent of the value before repairs or it is necessary to correct conditions that are a threat to the health and safety of the occupants. An example of this is the house having no heater (or a lack of gas), broken glass, chipped or peeling paint (that may contain lead), etc.

14. A lender cannot use a rigid list of onsite characteristics as an automatic basis for rejecting a loan, such as a minimum square footage requirement.

15. Each lender must have written loan standards available to the public.

16. Upon submission of a written loan application, the applicant must be given a fair lending notice (see Figure 5.1).

5.6 PRIVATE MORTGAGE INSURANCE (PMI)

Private Mortgage Insurance (PMI) is designed to protect a lender in the case of a loan default in the higher loan-to-value ratio loans. Typically required for any loan exceeding a loan-to-value

FIGURE 5.1 Fair lending notice.

THE HOUSING FINANCIAL DISCRIMINATION ACT OF 1977

FAIR LENDING NOTICE

DATE: COMPANY:

APPLICATION NO:

PROPERTY ADDRESS:

It is illegal to discriminate in the provisions of or in the availability of financial assistance because of the consideration of:

1. Trends, characteristics or conditions in the neighborhood or geographic area surrounding a housing accommodation, unless the financial institution can demonstrate in the particular case that such consideration is required to avoid an unsafe and unsound business practice; or

2. Race, color, religion, sex, marital status, national origin or ancestry.

It is illegal to consider the racial, ethnic, religious or national origin composition of a neighborhood or geographic area surrounding a housing accommodation or whether or not such composition is undergoing change, or is expected to undergo change, in appraising a housing accommodation or in determining whether or not, or under what terms and conditions, to provide financial assistance.

These provisions govern financial assistance for the purpose of the purchase, construction, rehabilitation or refinancing of a one-to-four unit family residence occupied by the owner and for the purpose of the home improvement of any one-to-four unit family residence.

If you have any questions about your rights, or if you wish to file a complaint, contact the management of this financial institution or the agency noted below:

I/we received a copy of this notice.

_____   _____
                              Date   *Date*

Calyx Form - fln.hp (2/99)

ratio of 80 percent, PMI guarantees the payment of the upper portion of a conventional loan in case the lender forecloses and suffers a loss.

A bit of history will help us understand the evolution of private mortgage insurance and the role it plays in allowing borrowers to acquire low down payment mortgages. The insurance for conventional loan coverage is sold by PMI companies. (FHA's Mortgage Insurance Premium [MIP] and Mutual Mortgage Insurance [MMI] and the VA's funding fee are discussed in Chapter 6.) Before the depression of 1929–1934, there were a number of PMI companies in operation. Most of them went into bankruptcy

FIGURE 5.2   Mortgage insurance.

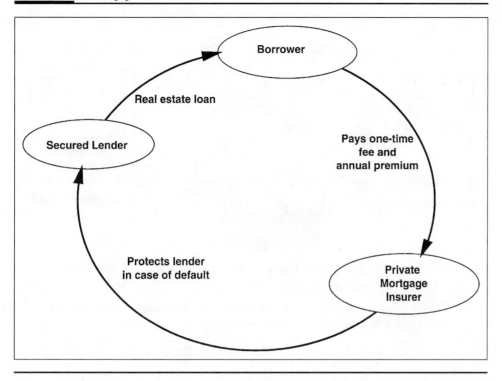

during the depression due to poor policies and inadequate regulations. The industry was dormant until the Mortgage Guarantee Insurance Corporation (MGIC) in Milwaukee began operations in 1957. Figure 5.2 shows the relationship between borrower, lender, and insurer.

The major growth of the PMI industry took place after 1970. One reason was that lenders and builders had become disenchanted with the FHA because of the red tape and the artificially low interest rate set by the government. Due to the low FHA interest rate, builders in those days had to pay high discounts (points) to sell their houses. To avoid these problems, builders and lenders turned to conventional mortgages insured by private mortgage insurance companies. As a result, they were able to eliminate high discounts and costly red tape. In addition, the mortgage insurance allowed lenders to continue making loans with low down payments.

Private mortgage insurance companies began to skyrocket in 1971 when lending institutions were given the authority to make 95 percent loan-to-value loans. In the same year, the Freddie Mac and Fannie Mae were given the authority to purchase high-ratio conventional loans. However, one of their requirements was that all loans above 80 percent must have mortgage insurance. When

FIGURE 5.3   The difference between private mortgage insurance and credit life insurance.

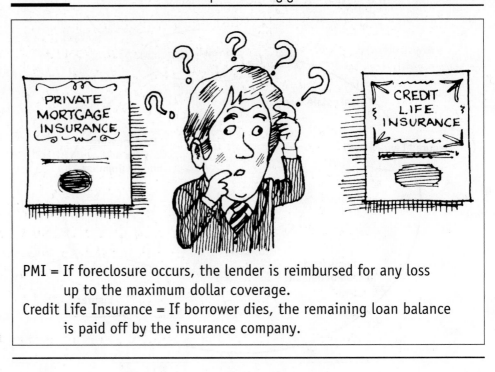

PMI = If foreclosure occurs, the lender is reimbursed for any loss
         up to the maximum dollar coverage.
Credit Life Insurance = If borrower dies, the remaining loan balance
         is paid off by the insurance company.

Freddie Mac and Fannie Mae began buying high-ratio conventional loans, they sparked the secondary market for conventional loans. Since these loans required mortgage insurance, this accelerated the growth of private mortgage insurance companies.

It should be noted that private mortgage insurance is not the same as **credit life insurance**. These two types of insurance are contrasted in Figure 5.3.

New Rules Emerge

Loan options introduced in recent years continued to make it possible for buyers to purchase with as little as three percent down or even with no down payment (100 percent financing). To avoid the mortgage insurance rule that any home loan with less than 20 percent down payment required PMI coverage, much of the 100 percent financing was creatively completed via two loans: a first trust deed for 80 percent of the purchase price (thereby eliminating the need for PMI), and a second trust deed for the remaining 20 percent of the purchase price. As loan options became increasingly risky, the rules were revised; today's lenders are required to provide better disclosure regarding PMI coverage and how it might be eliminated in the future.

The new rules (while continually revised) are contained in the Homeowner's Protection Act of 1998, which became effective July 29, 1999. The Act provides borrowers with certain rights when private mortgage insurance is required as a condition for obtaining certain residential mortgages. The new rules for conventional loans only include:

- PMI must be canceled upon the borrower's request under certain circumstances.
- PMI must be terminated automatically under certain circumstances.
- A borrower is entitled to receive notice of the right to cancel PMI, both at the consummation of the loan transaction and annually thereafter.
- Borrowers opting for *lender-paid mortgage insurance* programs must be provided with sufficient disclosures.

The general rule has been that PMI must continue for a minimum of two years, after which the equity in the home must have reached a minimum of 20 percent either via mortgage principal pay down, increased value due to home improvements (substantiated via a new appraisal), home appreciation, or a combination of these factors. Again, depending upon the investor, the combination of factors required to allow expunging the PMI could vary. In some cases, a borrower may be required to retain the PMI coverage for as long as five years, especially if the borrower is considered a high risk at the inception of the loan (see additional information below). Typically, a borrower signs a disclosure when signing loan documents that identifies the rules governing PMI coverage and its eventual elimination.

The rules indicate that a homeowner may cancel PMI when 20 percent equity is achieved. Automatic cancellation would occur when a 22 percent equity position is achieved. The only way a lender would "know" that the 22 percent equity position has been reached is via principal pay down, which could take many years. Thus, borrowers are advised to be aware of their equity position and petition their lender to have their PMI eliminated.

The rule applying to "lender-paid" mortgage insurance refers primarily to those cases where a 90 percent loan is acquired, supposedly without PMI. Most likely, the PMI premium was added as a part of the interest rate. This situation now requires greater disclosure at the time of acquiring the loan.

When the lender includes the PMI in its rate, the payments will never change, even when the loan-to-value reaches the level when it can generally be eliminated. At that point, the lender's yield increases by the amount of the premium the lender no longer pays for mortgage insurance coverage. PMI as a separate payment that can eventually be expunged, is more often the choice of buyers anticipating long-term ownership.

Special note: With regard to when PMI can be eliminated, both the California and federal laws cover only new insured loans granted from January 1998 for the state law, and January 1999 for the federal law. Loans already on record prior to those dates are not affected. In both cases, FHA mortgage insurance (MIP) cannot be cancelled.

When the time comes to seek elimination of the PMI coverage, homeowners have to be current on their payments and have no subordinate liens against the property. With the past proliferation of second trust deed and/or equity loan financing, some borrowers could find themselves ineligible for PMI cancellation. This applies also to those borrowers who acquired 100 percent financing using two loans (noted above). Requests to cancel mortgage insurance must be in writing. Jumbo loans (those loans that exceed the Fannie Mae/Freddie Mac conforming loan amount of $417,000) will be eligible for PMI cancellation at the 77 percent equity position. The availability in some "high cost" areas, where a high balance conforming loan limit exceeds the $417,000 loan amount, raises questions that can only be answered by contacting the lender.

With the advent of "credit scoring," borrowers are "risk rated" in relation to both their ability and willingness to pay back a mortgage. The lower the credit score, the higher the risk for the lender in making the loan. "High risk" mortgages, those made to borrowers with lower credit scores, may have additional conditions imposed for the elimination of mortgage insurance. Fannie Mae and Freddie Mac continually redefine industry guidelines that identify a "risky" borrower. For instance, in 2009, PMI companies reduced their risk exposure by refusing to cover loans in excess of 90 percent loan-to-value. The reason provided for the change was the concern over declining values in many housing areas, increasing the risk of exposure when there was less than 10 percent equity available. The conventional loan landscape was dramatically altered and the result was a flight to government-backed loans (discussed in Chapter 6) for any borrowers requiring a low down payment loan option.

How Is Mortgage Insurance Obtained?

Each PMI company sets its own policy regarding property and borrower standards. Generally, it follows the typical conventional lender standards set forth by FNMA/FHLMC. To obtain the insurance, an approved lender submits a loan package to the PMI company. After the package is received, the PMI company acts very quickly. The lender receives an answer by fax, e-mail, or telephone, usually the same day, and a written commitment follows later. This fast service is one of the main advantages of dealing with a PMI company. Some lenders are allowed to do in-house underwriting for PMI.

How Are Claims Handled?

If a foreclosure occurs on a property that is insured, the PMI company either:

1. Pays off the lender in full and takes title to the property, or
2. Pays the lender in accordance with the insurance, usually 20 to 25 percent of the principal balance plus certain expenses. The lender then keeps the property and is responsible for reselling it after foreclosure.

SUMMARY

Any loan that is not a government-backed loan is called a conventional loan. Some of the perceived advantages of a conventional loan are faster processing, higher loan amounts, and perhaps less red tape. In some cases, the disadvantages include higher down payments and occasional prepayment penalties.

There are many sources of conventional loans. The main sources are thrift institutions, commercial banks, and mortgage companies. Each lender that keeps its paper (called portfolio loans), sets its own policy regarding loan-to-value ratio, type of property, interest rates, loan fees, and borrower qualifications, as long as it is not discriminatory.

However, many lenders plan on reselling the loan in the secondary market to Fannie Mae or Freddie Mac. In doing so, the lender originating the loan loses flexibility and must abide by the Fannie Mae or Freddie Mac guidelines.

On a buy-down loan, the interest rate is reduced by paying the lender an up-front fee or discount. A standard buy-down loan allows the rate to be reduced no more than 2 percent. The California Housing Financial Discrimination Act forbids discrimination in residential loans based on neighborhood considerations or on race, color, religion, sex, marital status or registered domestic partnership, sexual orientation, handicap, national origin, family size, or ancestry of the borrower.

Mortgage insurance is used to guarantee the upper portion of conventional loans and is used primarily on loans whose loan-to-value ratio exceeds 80 percent.

IMPORTANT TERMS AND CONCEPTS

Buy-down loan

Community Home Buyer's Program

Conventional loan

Credit life insurance

Discrimination by effect (Effects Test)

Federal Home Loan Mortgage Corporation (Freddie Mac)

Federal National Mortgage Association (Fannie Mae)

Government-backed loans

Low down payment

Portfolio loan

Private mortgage insurance (PMI)

REVIEWING YOUR UNDERSTANDING

Questions for Discussion

1. List five items of comparison when shopping with conventional lenders for a real estate loan.

2. Describe how private mortgage insurance (PMI) works, including coverage and costs.

3. The Housing Financial Discrimination Act (Anti-Redlining Law) prohibits discrimination based upon a variety of considerations. List at least five of these.

Multiple-Choice Questions

1. A nongovernment-backed loan is best known as a
   a. portfolio loan.
   b. standard loan.
   c. conventional loan.
   d. normal loan.

2. Assume an application for a $450,000 loan is made and that the lender charges 1.5 points as a condition for granting the loan. The loan fee will be
   a. $6,750.
   b. $4,500.
   c. $67,500.
   d. none of the above.

3. Private mortgage insurance covers the
   a. upper portion of the loan amount.
   b. middle portion of the loan amount.
   c. lower portion of the loan amount.
   d. entire loan.

4. The most flexible loan terms (not necessarily the lowest interest rate) are usually obtainable on what type of loan?
   a. portfolio
   b. standard
   c. conforming
   d. FHA

5. Subsidized loans issued by the state of California and its counties and cities are usually funded by
   a. conventional sources.
   b. bond issues.
   c. stock issues.
   d. the Federal Reserve Bank.

6. In the event of foreclosure of a PMI-backed conventional loan, the insurer may
   a. pay off the lender in full and take back the property.
   b. pay the lender up to the amount of insurance.
   c. do either (a) or (b).
   d. do neither (a) nor (b).

7. When a seller or builder buys down the borrower's interest rate for the life of the loan, it is called
   a. a 3/2/1 buy-down.
   b. an adjustable buy-down.
   c. a fixed buy-down.
   d. a permanent buy-down.

8. Private mortgage insurance
   a. protects lenders in case of loan default.
   b. protects homebuyers in case they default on their loans.
   c. is required for any loan in excess of 20 percent loan-to-value.
   d. is required of all government-backed loans.

9. One might expect to find the shortest processing time in the case of
   a. government-backed loans.
   b. portfolio loans.
   c. loans that are to be sold in the secondary market.
   d. loans on which discount fees are charged.

10. Which of the following is often required for a Fannie Mae/Freddie Mac low down payment first-time home buyer loan?
    a. an educational seminar
    b. sufficient rental income
    c. a five-year work history
    d. tougher income qualifying ratios

11. Regulations affecting a lender's policy on qualifying borrowers would include
    a. supplemental income, such as overtime pay.
    b. part-time employment.
    c. combined income of both spouses.
    d. all of the above.

12. When might a buyer want to pay down the interest rate on a loan?
    a. when the seller needs to net more profit
    b. when the buyer plans to move within two years of the purchase
    c. when the buyer plans to own the property for a long time
    d. when the bank requires it

13. When lenders regularly review their loan portfolios and revise lending policies, they do not base their decisions on
    a. economic changes.
    b. available funds.
    c. racial considerations.
    d. lending goals.

14. Qualifying standards for borrowers using conventional loans that are to be sold to Fannie Mae/Freddie Mac
    a. differ widely, depending upon the particular lender.
    b. are usually the same throughout the range of lenders.
    c. are set by various government bodies.
    d. differ greatly, depending upon whether the lender is state or federally chartered.

15. An interest rate that is tied to an index that is subject to change is most commonly called
    a. fluctuating.
    b. adjustable.
    c. changeable.
    d. irregular.

16. California's Housing Financial Discrimination Act allows lenders to discriminate in residential lending only in the case of
    a. the loan applicant's low ratio of payment to income.
    b. the location of the property near industrial property.
    c. a situation that would lead to unsafe and unsound business practices.
    d. ethnic or racial mix.

17. Buy-down loans offer sellers an opportunity to
    a. profit at the buyer's expense.
    b. help a buyer qualify for a loan.
    c. attract primarily buyers of lower-priced homes.
    d. increase the asking price in exchange for the buy-down.

18. The erosion in the purchasing power of money, and for which lenders may adjust interest rates under ARM loans, is labeled
    a. deflation.
    b. inflation.
    c. devaluation.
    d. stagflation.

19. The type of insurance that pays off the mortgage balance in the event of the borrower's death is called

a. private mortgage insurance.

b. standard life insurance.

c. credit life insurance.

d. disability insurance.

20. Of the buy-down loan plans, the type that's usually best for the buyer is the

a. temporary buy-down for two years.

b. temporary buy-down for five years.

c. permanent buy-down plan.

d. plan with full amortization.

CASE & POINT

The Stimulus Bill and Accompanying Legislation

The Stimulus Bill of early 2008 was the first effort to provide assistance to distressed homeowners. This initial legislation *encouraged* banks/lenders to *voluntarily* modify loans, but failed to identify eligibility or enforcement guidelines. Borrowers remained bewildered as to what they needed to do to be eligible. The broad guidelines addressed first loans only, seemingly eliminating buyers who used what had been a popular 80 percent first loan and 20 percent second loan with past 100 percent loan programs. Investor loans were deemed ineligible for modification, and the most glaring omission was no meaningful solution to the equity loss suffered by many homeowners.

The Economic Recovery Act of 2008 was the immediate outgrowth of the Stimulus Bill effort. It was promoted as a way to provide housing relief to as many as 400,000 distressed homeowners. While it fell well short of that goal, it did spawn the "Make Home Affordable" program with loan modification and refinance guidelines to help save homes from foreclosure. This legislation was also compromised, as lenders did not fully embrace its lofty goals. Here is a quick overview of some of the bill's provisions.

The main thrust of the legislation was to help those homeowners in immediate risk of losing their homes to foreclosure by reducing their mortgage balances and interest rates to a more affordable level. There were, however, several limitations, that in retrospect, hampered success.

The plan relied upon the voluntary cooperation of the lenders and allowed each lender the latitude to determine the credit worthiness of the borrower and other aspects of each refinance/modification request. This lack of consistent guidelines resulted in long delays for borrowers who were then often deemed ineligible for assistance. Confusion reigned: some lenders required an eligible borrower to be delinquent in payments while others required the borrower to be current with payments. At the same time, lenders adopted a "net present value" calculation, that in translation meant that they would compare the cost of a loan modification with a foreclosure and would implement whichever option provided the lesser cost or loss to the lender. This net present value calculation was performed by the lender without notification to the borrower resulting in many borrowers being denied assistance without fully understanding why they didn't qualify for help.

The lack of clear guidelines for dealing with a loss of equity and the inability of borrowers to now "qualify" for refinanced or modified loans (remember the exaggeration of incomes with all of the "liar" loans) wherein they had to document their income eliminated many struggling borrowers. Borrowers found themselves waiting months only to find that their application for refinancing and/or loan modification had been denied. Foreclosure or a short sale (see the Case & Point following Chapter 11) soon followed.

During this same period of time, the FHA was being promoted as the agency that would allow many borrowers to refinance loans with more affordable rates and terms. The FHA's response was a reluctance to be the depositor of what it sensed was a lot of bad debt. The resulting FHA guidelines became so restrictive that far fewer borrowers could acquire relief than originally anticipated.

By march of 2010, FHA announced that nearly 30 % of the streamline refinances that they had funded during the past two years were "underwater" (had lost value) and were possible foreclosures.

While some borrowers did find relief, the well-meaning efforts of all the legislation may be deemed mostly ineffective in staving off an increasing number of foreclosures during 2009 and 2010. In its final analysis, the lack of a clear concept of how to really solve the needs of distressed borrowers accompanied by the desire to protect both borrowers and lenders resulted in mostly ineffective legislation.

Chapter

6

PREVIEW

This chapter covers four major sources of government-backed loans: the Federal Housing Administration (FHA), U.S. Department of Veterans Affairs (DVA), California Department of Veteran Affairs (Cal-Vet), and the California Housing Finance Agency (CalHFA).

After completing this chapter, you should be able to:

1. List the main advantages and disadvantages of FHA-insured loans.
2. Identify the guidelines governing FHA loans.
3. Explain the key features of DVA-guaranteed loans.
4. List the main characteristics of the Cal-Vet loan system.
5. Outline the CalHFA first-time home buyer program.

Government-Backed Financing

6.1 FEDERAL HOUSING ADMINISTRATION

In this section, we discuss what the Federal Housing Administration (FHA) does and some of the advantages and disadvantages of an **FHA-insured loan**. Commonly used FHA programs are explained here, with examples. Full details regarding the FHA can be found at www.hud.gov.

What Is the FHA?

The FHA, part of the Department of Housing and Urban Development, was established in 1934 to improve the construction and financing of housing. Since its creation, it has had a major influence on real estate financing. Some of today's loan features that are taken for granted were initiated by the FHA. For example, before the FHA, it was common practice to make real estate loans for short periods of time (one to five years). These loans were not fully amortized and every few years, borrowers had to renegotiate loans with their lender. This created problems, particularly during the Great Depression of the 1930s. During that time, when loans were due, many lenders were not willing or able to renew the loans and as a result there were massive foreclosures.

The need for reform spawned the FHA and its three major goals:

1. Provide affordable financing
2. Create increased homeownership
3. Upgrade property standards

To accomplish the stated goals, the following were introduced:

- Fully amortized loans
- Low down payment loans
- Low interest rates
- Mandatory collection of taxes and fire insurance premiums via the establishment of impound accounts
- Minimum property standards to promote an improved quality of construction and create some uniformity via a new appraisal process
- Standards for qualifying owner-occupant borrowers

What Does the FHA Do?

The FHA is not a lender—it does not make loans. Qualified mortgage companies, savings banks, and commercial banks make the loans. The FHA insures these lenders against loss in the event of foreclosure.

Authorized lenders, called correspondents, use FHA guidelines for approving the borrower and the property. They also fund the loan, which, in turn, is insured by the FHA. As of 2006, borrowers must pay two mortgage insurance premiums. In 2009, the FHA introduced a risk-based pricing model using credit scores, loan-to-value (LTV) ratio, and the term of the loan to determine the amount of these premiums. The first is identified by the initials "UFMIP." It is an upfront, nonrefundable fee that varied in 2009 from 1.25 to 2.0 percent of the loan amount. It may be paid in cash through escrow or it can be financed by adding it to the loan amount. If the borrower attends a qualified homeowner education class, the upfront fees can be lowered further.

The second, monthly MIP (mortgage insurance premium), is calculated at .50 or .55 (dependent upon the risk-based pricing model) times the base loan amount, which is the purchase price less the required 3.5 percent down payment. This amount is then divided by 12 and paid monthly. Here is an example of the calculations: A purchase price of $300,000 less the 3.5 percent down payment of $10,500 equals a base loan amount of $289,500. This amount times the .50 percent MMIP factor equals $1,447.50 divided by 12 months equals a monthly payment of MMIP of $120.63. For 15-year loans, the upfront fees are lower and monthly MMI drops to .25 percent. MMI premiums may be discontinued when the remaining loan balance is 78 percent LTV or less, provided the premium has been paid for at least five years. The 78 percent remaining balance is determined by principal pay down only and does not include property appreciation. Risk-based premiums are subject to change annually.

This insurance should not be confused with credit life insurance. The FHA's insurance does not insure the borrower's life. The FHA insurance premiums go into a "pool" to be used by the FHA to cover losses on foreclosed properties. If a lender forecloses on an FHA-insured property, the lender then transfers title to the FHA, which in turn reimburses the lender if there is a loss.

Advantages of FHA Loans

FHA financing was considered by many to have become too restrictive in its property requirements and had declined in popularity prior to 2007. In California, one of the biggest restrictions was the cap on purchase price. Competing alternative conventional loans were introduced that allowed 100 percent financing and contained more flexible guidelines regarding property conditions, pest control inspections, and borrower qualifying ratios. By 2008, following the real estate downturn, most of these 100 percent loan options and conventional FHA "look-alike" loans had disappeared and FHA loans were once again in vogue. In the meantime, the FHA had introduced some changes, making the loans more competitive and popular. The FHA is now one of the most utilized forms of financing for *owner-occupied* home loans. Some of the additional advantages of FHA financing include:

1. Low down payment. 3.5 percent is generally indicated as the necessary down payment for an FHA loan.
2. The maximum loan fee is 1 percent of the loan amount. The buyer normally pays this fee.
3. While seldom used, secondary financing is allowed with a new FHA loan provided the combined FHA loan and second loan do not exceed the FHA maximum.
4. The maximum loan term is 30 years or 75 percent of the remaining economic life of the property, whichever is less. The remaining economic life, identified in the appraisal must be at least 40 years to meet the 30-year requirement.
5. The FHA requires that monthly payments include principal and interest, taxes, fire insurance, and Monthly Mortgage Insurance (MMI). The monthly amounts paid toward taxes, insurance, and MMI are deposited in an impound account, also called an escrow account.
6. There is no maximum purchase price but maximum loan amounts. These are established regionally by the FHA and do

vary. While the buyer can pay more than the FHA appraisal, the loan will be based on the appraised value or the purchase price, whichever is lower.

7. The interest rates and discount points are negotiable between the lender and the borrower, making FHA loans competitive with conventional interest rates.

8. Loans are able to be assumed on a "subject to" basis, allowing a new "credit worthy," owner-occupant borrower to take over the loan without a change in the interest rate. During high-interest rate times, being able to take over a loan with a lower rate may assist a seller.

9. FHA appraisals (called "**conditional commitments**") are good for six months on existing property and one year on new construction. The FHA has used independent FHA-authorized fee appraisers until recently when after having declared that there would be no change to the FHA's appraisal process, the FHA announced in early 2010 that it was adopting a process similar to that used with conventional financing. A discussion of this new Home Valuation Code of Conduct (HVCC) can be found in chapter 8.

10. The FHA rules no longer automatically require pest control reports or clearances. These newly adopted rules rely upon appraisers to determine if a pest control and/or other inspections will be required. (Note: This flexibility regarding pest control requirements was widely interpreted as pest control reports and/or clearances were no longer required by the FHA. In actuality, the burden of determining the need for reports was simply shifted to appraisers. In turn, many appraisers resisted the added responsibility and liability. The result was that pest control requirements prevailed more frequently than originally anticipated.)

11. The FHA no longer prescribes what are "allowable" or "unallowable" closing costs, but any fees charged to the borrower must be "customary and reasonable" and necessary to close the loan. While sellers may pay up to 3 percent (reduced from 6% in early 2010) of all loan closing costs for the buyer, these more typically include the nonrecurring costs (one time fees), such as the loan origination fee, appraisal, inspections, home warranty, and title and escrow fees. Recurring costs such as prepaid interest and tax impounds are more frequently paid by the buyer rather than via seller contributions. There is a "lender pays fees" option but the borrower will pay for this privilege via a higher interest rate.

12. Direct endorsement. A previous disadvantage was the length of time it took to approve an FHA loan. However, many lenders now have "direct endorsement" approval, which means the

lender can underwrite the loans, complete the FHA processing in-house, and fund the loan. The loan is then insured by the FHA.

13. The 3.5 percent required "cash investment" (down payment) may be acquired via gift funds from appropriate sources. The gifting party (family, friend, etc.) is not required to be on the loan, much like a conventional loan. This amount also may be borrowed in some instances, as previously allowed through the CalHFA program.

14. FHA loans may be paid off at any time without a prepayment penalty.

15. Credit-challenged borrowers with lower credit scores (or with less than typical credit history, may still be able to acquire an FHA loan. By the end of 2009, 640 was the minimum credit score accepted by most lenders. FHA lenders can advise how nontraditional credit references can be used to "build" a borrower's credit history.

Calculating FHA Loan Amounts

Like conventional lenders, FHA-insured loan amounts are calculated using the lower of the property's sales price or appraised value. FHA loan-to-value ratios require the borrower to make a "cash investment" of at least 3.5 percent in the home. The allowable **nonrecurring closing costs** consist of items such as loan origination fee, appraisal fee, credit report, and title and escrow fees.

Calculating the final loan amount can be a bit complicated and should be left to mortgage lenders and their computer programs. This maximum mortgage amount, without any upfront mortgage insurance, cannot exceed the annually determined statutory limit for the county in which the property is located. These county limits vary, with some areas now designated as high-cost areas with loan limits as high as $729,750. These high balances were temporarily adopted and it is unknown if they will be renewed when their current identified expiration date occur in 2010.

To determine the maximum FHA-insured loan for your area, you will need to ask a local FHA-approved lender or go to the HUD website at www.hud.gov and search for maximum FHA loan amounts. Then input the state and county and the current maximum FHA-insured loan amount will appear.

FHA regulations originally stated that the required cash investment should come from the borrower's own funds. However, current FHA guidelines will allow the 3.5 percent cash investment to be a bona fide gift from a family member, or a loan from a government agency. While a gift can be obtained from a friend, the

FHA requires documentation of the friendship as the FHA will otherwise consider the funds as merely a disguised loan. If using a loan, this additional loan payment must be counted in the qualifying ratios to determine whether the borrower is qualified for the FHA-insured loan. In addition, the junior loan must not require a balloon payment within the first five years.

The 3.5 percent cash investment cannot come from loans from other sources, such as the seller, the builder, or an outside private source. If the seller or builder attempts to circumvent this rule by offering a "decorating allowance" or any other inducements, the maximum FHA-insured loan is decreased by said amounts.

FHA Programs

The National Housing Act of 1934 created the FHA. The act has eleven titles, or subdivisions, with further subdivisions called sections.

This chapter deals with only some of the sections under Title II of the act, since these are the most important to the average consumer or real estate agent. Title II authorizes the FHA to insure the financing on proposed or existing dwellings for one-to-four-family residences. The main sections are 203(b) and 245(a). Each of these programs is discussed below.

Section 203(b)

Under the 203(b) program:

1. Anyone 18 and over is eligible.
2. Loans are available on owner-occupied properties of from one to four units.
3. U.S. citizenship is not required; resident aliens are eligible.
4. As indicated before, the FHA establishes a range of maximum loan amounts for one-to-four-unit dwellings that vary according to state and county.

Non-occupant borrower. The FHA requires the borrower to occupy the property. The only exception is if an investor purchases a HUD repossession and provides a 25 percent down payment.

Houses less than one year old. You cannot obtain a standard maximum FHA loan on a house that is less than one year old which was not built under FHA or DVA inspections. This restriction also applies to houses that were moved onto the site less than one year earlier. The underlying reason for this requirement is that the FHA wants a property to have endured all four seasons. The FHA's maximum loan on these properties is reduced to 90 percent LTV of the sales price or appraised value, whichever is lower.

Section 245(a) FHA Adjustable Rate Loan

This loan is available on single-family dwellings. The maximum loan-to-value ratio is the same as for the 203(b) program. There are five adjustable rate options but one plan, number III, has remained the most popular. It has the lowest starting payment but also the steepest payment increases. The 7.5 percent annual payment increases (for five years) are predictable and allow borrowers to plan for each adjustment. The down payment for this 245 loan option is greater than the typical FHA mortgage in order to assure that the balance, including accrued negative amortization, would never exceed the beginning balance of a normal FHA loan.

As with any adjustable rate mortgage, a borrower must fully understand the index, margin, adjustment periods, and both the annual and lifetime cap rates (see Chapter 4) when selecting an ARM product.

Section 203k Rehabilitation Mortgage

Used for the acquisition of properties that need repairs or rehabilitation, the 203k is much like a construction/take-out type loan. The loan is sufficient to acquire the property, with the money for rehabilitation placed into an escrow account and disbursed in increments as the repairs occur. The loan amount is determined by taking the "as is" appraised value or purchase price (whichever is less) plus the rehabilitation cost (identified via submitted plans) plus a minimum 10 percent reserve.

Unlike most construction loans, the 203k loan is completely funded when the escrow closes. While the rehabilitation funds are held in an escrow account (noted above) the borrower begins payments on the entire loan amount at the close of escrow. If the home is uninhabitable, the borrower can finance up to six months PITI while rehabilitation work is completed.

What Is Ahead for the FHA?

The main thrust of the Economic Recovery Act of 2008 (discussed in the Case & Point in Chapter 5) was to help homeowners in immediate risk of losing their homes to foreclosure by reducing their mortgage balances and interest rates to a more affordable level. The FHA was perceived as the agency that would do much of the refinancing, but it indicated a reluctance to be the depositor of what it sensed was a lot of bad debt.

Among a host of newly created rules, the FHA imposed a maximum loan amount of 90 percent of the current market value of the property, not the value of the house when the original loan was funded. This change is insured through a new legislatively created fund. Along with a proposed 3 percent insurance fee for these risky loans (the fee is to be included in the refinance loan), the plan translated into fewer funds for the original lender than with an FHA-refinanced loan. A small window of opportunity was proposed wherein for qualification purposes a borrower had to demonstrate a lack of capacity to pay his or her current mortgage but to show sufficient income to qualify for the new (presumably smaller) fixed rate FHA loan.

If the above restrictions were not enough to discourage borrowers, a more onerous provision was an equity sharing agreement regarding future appreciation and equity gains from subsequent sale of the property. Time schedule limitations were proposed for future sales, and, after those time frames elapsed, FHA would be entitled to up to 50 percent of future appreciation identified from the date of refinancing to the date of sale. The FHA clearly did not intend for their "troubled loan" refinance program to be a free bailout. It was no surprise that the expected FHA refinance resurgence was a disappointment.

Nevertheless, after seeing its influence dramatically reduced during the subprime era, the FHA has been and is expected to play an increasingly important role in home loan financing in the future. As conventional lenders have become more conservative in their loan options, low down payment FHA loans, in spite of many qualifying restrictions, have grown in appeal to large numbers of potential home buyers. Real estate financing, however, remains an evolving process and the FHA will have to continue to adjust when we enter the next cycle of real estate loan offerings. (See Case & Point at the end of this chapter for proposed FHA changes for 2010 and beyond).

6.2 DEPARTMENT OF VETERANS AFFAIRS
What Is the Department of Veterans Affairs (DVA)?

The U.S. Veterans Bureau was founded in 1916 to assist needy veterans of the Civil War and Spanish American War. Its name changed to the Veterans Administration in 1930, then again in 1989, when it was elevated to cabinet level with the designation Department of Veterans Affairs. We use DVA throughout the text, but most lenders and agents continue to use the shorter, long-used "VA" whenever dealing with veterans loans. Full details regarding DVA-guaranteed loans can be found at www.homeloans.VA.gov.

Administration of DVA Home Loan Program

The Loan Guarantee Division of the DVA is responsible for the administration of its home program. Like the FHA, the DVA is a government program; however, there are some major differences.

1. The DVA guarantees a loan, whereas the FHA insures a loan.
2. The DVA guarantees only a part of the loan, whereas the FHA insures the entire loan.

The **DVA-guaranteed loan** amount is calculated as 25 percent of the current Freddie Mac conforming loan amount and can be paid to the lender in the case of foreclosure. Each year, if the Freddie Mac conforming loan amount increases, the DVA guarantee to an approved lender also increases. For example, as of December 2009, the maximum Freddie Mac conforming loan was $417,000, thus $25\% \times 417,000 = \$104,250$ maximum DVA lender guarantee.

DVA-approved lenders simply grant a no-money down payment loan to qualified veterans that is four times the DVA guarantee. Going into 2010, it will be $\$104,250 \times 4 = \$417,000$ as the maximum no down payment DVA-guaranteed loan. Bottom line, the maximum DVA no money down loan amount is the same as the maximum Freddie Mac conforming loan amount.

A high-balance loan amount of $729,750 was allowed for some identified counties with high-cost home values. The higher loan limit was designed to expire on December 31, 2009, but pressure was applied to extend the program. The same 25 percent guarantee calculation for determining the maximum DVA loan amount, when applied to this higher balance, was $182,430.

Whether a loan is insured or guaranteed is important only if a foreclosure occurs. If a foreclosure occurs, the DVA has two options:

1. It can pay the lender the principle balance and take back the property.
2. It can give the lender the property and pay it the amount of any deficiency, up to the maximum amount of the DVA guarantee.

DVA Loans
What You Need to Know

1. *No down payment.* It is often believed that a veteran needs absolutely no money to purchase a home. While a qualified veteran may purchase a home with 100 percent financing (i.e., no down payment) there are other costs that must be accommodated. Closing costs can, however, be paid for the veteran (see #2 below). In some

situations, a veteran may be required to have two months of principal, interest, taxes, and insurance payments in the bank as reserves at the close of escrow, but these funds can be gift funds. So, in essence, a veteran can purchase without any cash of his or her own.

2. *Other costs.* While there are typical closing costs required, in some situations a seller may be willing to pay these fees on behalf of the veteran in what is called a "no-no" loan … meaning that the veteran has no down payment and no closing costs. A gift could also come from a relative or friend (with sufficient documentation of the relationship), similar to the allowances of the FHA.

3. *Qualification requirements.* A VA loan is unusual in that a buyer qualifies via both a "ratio" calculation and a "residual" requirement.

    —Ratio: the total amount of monthly housing debt (principal, interest, taxes and homeowner's insurance), plus total monthly consumer debt should not exceed 41 percent of the buyer's gross monthly income. Compensating factors allow exceeding this ratio.

    —Residual: a required amount "left over" after subtracting from a buyer's gross monthly income all his or her estimated taxes, monthly consumer debt, as well as monthly housing debt. The amount of residual required is dependent upon the size of the family.

4. *Funding fee.* This fee is much like the private mortgage insurance premium assessed in conventional financing. Rather than requiring the fee to be paid in cash, VA allows the fee to be added to the loan amount, as long as the maximum loan limits are not exceeded. The amount added is 2.15 percent of the loan amount if the buyer is a first-time user of VA eligibility and 3.3 percent if he or she is a multiple user.

5. *Rating factor worksheet.* The DVA qualification process requires this worksheet to be completed, with satisfactory ratings on the following:
   • Job stability
   • Credit history
   • Debt ratio
   • Balance available for support (residual)
   • Liquid assets (reserves)

6. *Possible assumability.* DVA loans recorded before March 1, 1988, are fully assumable, and without a rate increase. These DVA loans do not have alienation clauses; therefore, they are fully assumable. These loans can be taken by new borrowers "subject to" the existing loan balance and no approval from the lender or DVA is necessary.

The lender can charge only a reasonable fee for changing the records. DVA loans recorded after February 29, 1988, can be assumed only if the new buyer meets DVA qualifications. However, the veteran who obtained the original loan remains personally liable to the DVA. If there is a foreclosure and subsequent loss to the DVA, the veteran can be charged for the amount of the loss. A veteran can be released from liability by obtaining a Release of Liability from the DVA. The new owner must be an owner-occupant and complete the specific procedure set up by the DVA to obtain the release.

7. *Certificate of Reasonable Value (CRV)*. DVA appraisals are made by independent licensed fee appraisers. The DVA then issues the CRV to the veteran buyer, identifying what it believes to be the reasonable value of the property. The buyer is allowed to pay more than that value but must do so by increasing down payment funds.

Dispelling Some Myths

As with all elements of home financing, the DVA continues to make changes, albeit sometimes slowly. Recent years have seen the DVA streamline many of its processes and many of the old criticisms have been resolved.

1. *Red tape and processing time*. The increase in local lenders' authorization to process DVA loans on an automatic basis has eliminated much of the frustration that used to accompany long time frames in closing a DVA loan. Much like the FHA, the loan is completed by the local lender, according to DVA requirements, and then sent for the guarantee.

2. *Excessive repairs*. This concern is a "holdover" from the past days when sellers were sometimes required to perform all kinds of repair work. The DVA has adopted a "habitability standard" and only items identified by the appraiser as "health and safety" factors need be done. Cosmetic repairs are no longer required.

3. *Accepting a DVA loan offer costs the seller too much*. While this may have been true several years ago, the additional costs for accepting a VA offer are fairly minimal today. The "extra" seller paid fees include the entire escrow fee, including the portion normally paid by the buyer (DVA prohibits a veteran from paying an escrow fee). There are items like tax service, flood certification, and document preparation that must be paid by the seller on behalf of the veteran. The additional cost to the seller on a full $417,000 DVA loan is likely to be about $1,200. This does not include a lender's processing fee, that could be another $500. Many DVA lenders

waive this fee in order to reduce the total seller costs. This relatively minor amount of extra cost can often be accommodated in the negotiated sales price. The increased ability for buyers to be qualified via the DVA's more flexible guidelines often far outweighs any adverse consequences of the additional seller costs.

4. *Discount points.* Many sellers still remember the days when the DVA required sellers to pay discount points on behalf of the veteran buyer, to allow a lower market interest rate. This is no longer the case.

Who Is Eligible for a DVA-Guaranteed Loan?

General Rules for Eligibility

Long unchanged, the general rules of eligibility state that a veteran is eligible for VA home loan benefits if he or she is currently serving or has served duty in the U.S. Army, Air Force, Marine Corps, or Coast Guard. If he or she has served in the past, the discharge must be for other than dishonorable reasons.

Specific time frames for having served during wartime and/or peacetime are available on the DVA website. Questions about eligibility for a DVA loan can be addressed with the agency directly.

Under all service time frames, if the veteran was discharged for a service-connected disability before meeting the service time requirement, he or she may still be eligible for a DVA-guaranteed home loan. There are other special rules for unmarried spouses of veterans who died in the service because of war or a service-connected accident, for spouses of veterans missing in action or prisoner of war, and for those who have served as a U.S. public health officer, as cadet in the U.S. Military academies, and so on.

Certificate of Eligibility

To establish eligibility for a DVA loan, a veteran must obtain a **Certificate of Eligibility**, which indicates the amount of the veteran's entitlement. The entitlement is the maximum number of dollars that the DVA will pay, up to the DVA's maximum guarantee amount (currently $104,250 in non-high-balance loan areas), if the lender suffers a loss.

Reinstatement of Full Entitlement

In the past, a veteran could have full entitlement restored only if an originally VA financed property was sold and the original loan paid in full. New rules allow full entitlement reinstatement and the veteran to purchase another home if the original property has been refinanced. This can be done only once. Entitlement may continue to be restored if an eligible veteran agrees to assume the loan and substitute his or her entitlement for that of the original veteran. The new veteran must also qualify for the loan.

If a veteran sells a home with the new buyer assuming the loan, the veteran may be released from liability by the DVA if the new buyer is qualified. The veteran remains personally liable for any deficiency if the release is not obtained. The veteran must obtain both the Reinstatement of Entitlement and Release of Liability.

Partial Entitlements

The entitlement amount has been increased several times since the DVA program began, so veterans who have previously used their entitlement may have an unused partial entitlement. A veteran may purchase another home with a partial entitlement even if the previous DVA loan has not been paid off. The veteran can keep the first home and purchase another using DVA financing. This is the only way in which a veteran can technically have two or more DVA loans at the same time. To determine partial entitlements and their maximum loan amounts, veterans should contact their nearest DVA regional office.

General Guidelines

In contrast to FHA loans, the DVA has only one program. It offers either fixed or adjustable interest rates and one set of guidelines that generally apply to all its loans.

1. *Type of property.* The DVA guarantees loans on properties from one to four units and units in approved planned unit developments and condominiums projects. The DVA approves new properties only if they were built under FHA or DVA inspections. If a property was not built with FHA or DVA inspections, you have to wait one year after the house has been completed before ordering the appraisal. While some exceptions to this one-year rule are identified in the guidelines, they are not easily obtained. The two more common exceptions are (a) property located in a remote area where obtaining FHA or DVA inspections would be inconvenient; and (b) property built by a small builder who does not normally use DVA loans to finance the sale of houses.

2. *Interest rate.* The interest rate and discount points are negotiable between the lender and veteran-borrower. Contrary to past practices, when the seller was required to pay all discount points,

the seller or the buyer may pay the discount points, the buyer and seller may split the payment, or these points can be paid by a third party.

3. *Loan origination and funding fees.* The loan fee cannot exceed 1 percent of the loan amount. This 1 percent loan fee goes to the lender. The veteran is charged a funding fee, originally designed as a way to reduce the cost of 100 percent DVA loans to taxpayers. The funding fee, in actuality, is used primarily for lender reimbursement up to the DVA guarantee amounts in case of loan defaults. Veterans who receive disability compensation for service-related medical issues, or who are entitled to get compensation while not drawing retirement pay, are exempt from the VA funding fee. The current funding fee schedule is anticipated to remain the same through September 30, 2011, but is always subject to change. The funding fee is calculated as a percentage of the loan amount, and the veteran has the option of paying the fee up front or financing it as part of the DVA-guaranteed loan as long as the amount to be financed does not exceed the maximum allowed loan amount (currently $417,000). The current funding fee schedule for a home purchase is given below:

Type of Veteran	Down Payment	First Time Use	Subsequent Use
Regular Military	None	2.15%	3.30%
	5%–9.99%	1.50%	1.50%
	10% or more	1.25%	1.25%
Reserves/National Guard	None	2.4%	3.30%
	5–9.99%	1.75%	1.75%
	10% or more	1.50%	1.50%

Note: There are different funding fees for a DVA-guaranteed refinance and for manufactured home loans and loan assumptions.

4. *Term of loan.* The term cannot exceed the remaining economic life of the property, with a maximum term of 30 years.

5. *Down payment.* The DVA does not require a down payment—the veteran is allowed to borrow the full amount of the purchase price up to the maximum allowed by the DVA-approved lender. What happens if the DVA appraises the property for less than the purchase price? While the veteran, for many years, was prohibited from paying more than the appraised value for a home, the DVA will now allow a veteran to pay more than the

appraisal, but the loan amount cannot exceed the appraisal. The difference between the purchase price and the appraisal has to be in cash.

6. *Maximum loan.* There is no maximum loan amount under DVA rules. This can be confusing because since the DVA guarantees only a portion of the loan, lenders do limit the amount they will lend on DVA loans.

   The main point to remember is that the DVA does not set the maximum loan amount; it is the lender that determines the amount. And that maximum loan amount is based upon the DVA's requirement to reimburse the lender only for the amount of entitlement, regardless of what the lender's loss may be upon foreclosure.

7. *Occupying the property.* The veteran must occupy the property. The DVA does not have a program for veterans who do not intend to occupy the property.

8. *Monthly installments.* Technically, the DVA requires only monthly principal and interest payments. It does not require property taxes and insurance to be included. However, the DVA recommends that these be included, and the deed of trust provides lender authority to collect them. As a practical matter, all lenders establish an impound account and collect the taxes and insurance in the monthly payment.

9. *Appraisal and* **Certificate of Reasonable Value (CRV)**. We have discussed previously that the issued CRV represents the DVA's opinion of reasonable or current market value.

   It is no coincidence that the CRV never exceeds the purchase price. In practice, the DVA never issues a certificate showing a value greater than the sales price. If a home sells for $400,000, but the appraisal comes in at $425,000, the CRV will be for the $400,000 sales price, not the $425,000 appraised value. However, if the sales price is $400,000, but the appraisal comes in a $375,000, the CRV will be for the $375,000 appraised value.

10. *Secondary financing.* It is commonly believed that a second loan on a DVA transaction is prohibited. This is not technically correct. Seconds are allowed but rarely used because they are not practical or not understood.

    Secondary financing can be approved on a case-by-case basis. The DVA Regional Office will determine on what basis it is acceptable. Generally, it is desirable that the second carry the same interest rate and terms as the first loan. The first and second loans added together cannot under any circumstances be more than the CRV. An example where a second can be used is as follows:

Sales price/CRV	$450,000
Maximum loan available from lender	−417,000
Down payment from buyer	−20,000
Second mortgage	$13,000

In this example, we need an additional $13,000 to complete the transaction. If the seller is willing to carry back a second loan at the same rate and terms as the first, the sale can be made.

11. *Pest inspections, reports, and clearances.* The DVA requires that a structural pest control report be obtained from a recognized inspection company. Required repairs indicated under both sections 1 and 2 (active infestation and that which might lead to infestation) of the report must be completed, and both the veteran and an inspector must certify that the work is done satisfactorily.

    The DVA requires inspection of all detached buildings (e.g., detached garages, cottages, potting sheds, or green houses). The veteran cannot waive this requirement.

    On older properties this can be a problem. A detached garage may cost more to repair than it is worth. If it is not economical to repair the garage, then it may be torn down and the value of the property adjusted accordingly. For example, assume that it costs $25,000 to repair a garage and the DVA has appraised it at only $23,000. You would be better off removing the garage and reducing the value by $23,000. Always consult with the DVA first in such situations.

12. *Closing costs.* As previously discussed, the DVA will not allow the veteran to pay for nonrecurring (one time) closing costs, such as termite reports, escrow fees, tax service fees, document preparation fees, notary fees, or a certificate of reasonable value that was ordered before the veteran agreed to purchase the property. While these may be considered "extra" seller expenses, it may be worth paying the costs, depending upon the purchase price offer.

    The DVA allows the seller to pay all of the closing costs, including prepaid expenses and **recurring closing costs** such as tax impounds, fire insurance, and so on. Most lenders require buyers to pay for prepaid items. A "seller pay all" is often referred to as a "VA no-no"—no down, no closing costs.

13. *Internet underwriting.* Today's lenders are "LAPP" (Lender Appraisal Processing Program) approved, and the processing time for approval is greatly reduced via this Web-based direct underwriting (DU) capacity.

Choosing a Lender for FHA and DVA Loans

Many lenders, such as commercial banks, savings banks, and mortgage companies, are authorized to process FHA and DVA loans. Because they have authorization does not automatically mean they do a good job. Processing FHA and DVA loans can be very complex, technical, and time consuming. Certain lenders specialize in processing government loans. They are experienced, they know what to do, and they keep up to date. Choose a lender that has this type of experience—otherwise, it can be very frustrating and costly.

6.3 CAL-VET LOANS

The **Cal-Vet loan** program is administered by the California Department of Veterans Affairs, Division of Farm and Home Purchases. Applicants can apply directly to Cal-Vet or apply through a Cal-Vet certified mortgage broker. The money that funds Cal-Vet loans is obtained from the sale of general obligation bonds and revenue bonds. For qualified veterans with wartime service, there is a program that uses designated unrestricted funds. This can be used only as funds are available. Full details regarding Cal-Vet loans can be found at www.cdva.ca.gov.

Who Is Eligible for Cal-Vet Loans?

Cal-Vet eligibility rules are more liberal than the federal DVA rules. A veteran is eligible with the required income and credit rating and the following service: currently on active duty, received an honorable discharge, and served for a minimum of 90 days—not counting basic training. It makes no difference if the service was during war or peacetime.

Veterans who served for fewer than 90 days may still be eligible under certain circumstances. Details can be found at the Cal-Vet Web page.

Current members of the U.S. Military Reserves and the California National Guard—who do not otherwise qualify under the aforementioned rules—become eligible after they serve a minimum of one year of a six-year obligation, provided they qualify as a first-time home buyer or purchase a home in certain targeted areas.

It should be noted that if the veteran is currently in the military, Cal-Vet requires that the veteran, or a member of the immediate family, must occupy the home until the Cal-Vet loan is paid off. Therefore, a change in active duty station would require a payoff of the Cal-Vet loan unless the veteran's family remains in the home. This required resale could result in a loss if a veteran is transferred after a short period of time, since any short-term appreciation may be insufficient to cover closing costs and the remaining loan balance.

General Information about Cal-Vet Loans

1. *Property.* Cal-Vet has basically the same property standards as the FHA and DVA. The property must be an owner-occupied, single-family dwelling or a unit in an approved condominium or planned unit development complex. Owner-occupied farms and mobile homes are also acceptable.

2. *Maximum loan.* The maximum Cal-Vet loan amounts can vary each year. There are separate maximums for single-family dwellings, farms, and mobile homes. As of March 2010, the current single-home maximum loan amount was $521,250. To find the current maximum for other loan options go to the Cal-Vet website, www.cdva.ca.gov.

3. *Down payment and loan fees.* A Cal-Vet loan can be submitted one of two ways—by adhering to regular VA guidelines or to Cal-Vet guidelines. Cal-Vet/VA loans are available for no money down up to the current maximum DVA-guaranteed loan amount. On straight Cal-Vet loans, without a DVA guarantee, the loan amount available is greater (noted above) but requires a down payment of 3 percent of the purchase price or appraised value, whichever is the lesser amount.

   Cal-Vet charges a 1 percent loan origination fee, plus a loan guarantee fee that ranges from 1.25 percent to 2 percent of the loan amount. Under certain circumstances, the loan guarantee fee may be financed, but the 1 percent loan origination fee is treated as a closing cost and must be paid in escrow. If a veteran puts 20 percent or more down, only the 1 percent loan-origination fee applies and the loan guarantee fee is waived.

4. *Term of loan.* Cal-Vet loans are set up as 30-year loans. A veteran is allowed to make additional principal payments to shorten the length of the loan and there is no prepayment penalty for paying off the loan early.

5. *Interest rate.* All Cal-Vet loans have a variable interest rate. The initial interest rate is set at the time of the loan based on the cost of bond funds and market conditions. Once set, the interest rate has a lifetime cap of only a half percent over the start rate.

6. *Secondary financing.* At the time of purchase, secondary financing is permitted. However, the two loans together cannot

exceed 98 percent of the Cal-Vet appraisal. In addition, some lenders are unwilling to make a loan behind a land contract of sale.

7. *Occupancy.* The veteran or an immediate member of the family who qualifies as a dependent must occupy the property.

8. *Insurance.* All properties are covered by Cal-Vet's Disaster Indemnity program, which provides protection against loss from floods and earthquakes (with limitations). All Cal-Vet contract holders under age 62 must carry basic life insurance. Based on health status at time of application, coverage provides payments of principal and interest for up to five years following the death of the insured. Buyers with "substandard health risks" will have payments made for only 36 months; those with "highly substandard health risks" for only 12 months. Under certain circumstances, optional life insurance, spouse life insurance, and disability insurance may be obtainable. Disability insurance terminates at age 62 and all life insurance coverage terminates at age 70.

9. *Monthly payments.* In addition to monthly mortgage payments of principal and interest, property taxes, fire, disability, and life insurance premiums are also collected and placed into an impound account.

10. *Title to property.* When a property is being financed with a Cal-Vet loan, the title is first conveyed to the Department of Veterans Affairs of the State of California by the seller. The department then sells the property to the veteran under a **land contract of sale**. The department continues to hold the legal title, while the veteran holds what is called "equitable" title. Only after the veteran has paid the loan in full, does he receive a grant deed. The department uses a standard CLTA joint protection title policy, rather than a "lender's" ALTA policy.

11. *Application fee.* A small application fee and appraisal fee is paid by the applicant.

12. *Construction loan.* All other qualifications remain the same. Cal-Vet usually uses a five-draw system, with the construction period ordinarily nine months, followed by 29-year/3-month amortization.

13. *Refinancing.* For the most part, no refinancing is available. However, if your old loan is paid off, a new Cal-Vet loan is available. Cal-Vet loans may be paid off without penalty and may be obtained multiple times.

For additional information about your area and qualifications, contact the California Department of Veterans Affairs website.

Advantages and Disadvantages of Cal-Vet Loans

The main advantages of the Cal-Vet loan are its relatively low interest rate; inexpensive life, fire, and disaster insurance (flood and quake); and low closing costs.

Disadvantages include lack of refinancing and occasional shortage of available funds for the program. For unmarried couples who are not registered as domestic partners, another disadvantage might be that Cal-Vet can refuse to allow assignment of the veteran's contract of sale to the couple as joint tenants.

6.4 CALIFORNIA HOUSING FINANCE AGENCY PROGRAM (CALHFA)

The **CalHFA** program is designed to help first-time home buyers acquire a home in California's expensive housing market by allowing a buyer to borrow the 3.5 percent down payment afforded through the FHA. This state agency sells mortgage revenue bonds to investors, and then uses the funds to buy loans from approved lenders who make loans under CalHFA guidelines. Thus, like the FHA, DVA, Fannie Mae, and Freddie Mac, CalHFA does not make loans directly to borrowers. Instead, this state agency purchases the loans made by approved lenders. CalHFA prides itself by not using state funds and taxpayer dollars to operate its program. Full details regarding CalHFA can be found at www.calhfa. ca.gov.

Two Main Programs

CalHFA offers a 30-year fixed rate conventional loan program and an "interest-only plus" plan.

30-Year Fixed Rate Conventional Loan Program

This program features a below-market fixed interest rate amortized loan for 30 years and a maximum loan-to-value ratio of 100 percent. In special circumstances, the loan can be as high as 107 percent loan-to-value ratio and the loan origination fee cannot exceed 1.5 percent of the loan amount. Mortgage insurance is required, and CalHFA provides this coverage at a very low fee.

Property eligibility. The property must meet all of the following requirements:

1. Sales price of the home cannot exceed CalHFA price limits. These limits vary by counties and can be found at its website.
2. Must be an owner-occupied single family, one-unit home, condo, or PUD.
3. Manufactured homes are allowed if they meet CalHFA construction standards.

The borrower must meet the following requirements:

1. Be a U.S. citizen, permanent resident alien, or qualified alien.
2. Be a first-time home buyer, unless the home is located in a federally designated targeted area that is deemed to need an infusion of investment. A first-time homebuyer is designated as one who has not owned real estate in the past three years.
3. Occupy the home as a primary residence; non-owner-occupied loans are not allowed.
4. Income cannot exceed CalHFA income limits established for the county where the home is located.
5. Meet CalHFA credit requirements.

There are certain special circumstances in which a home or borrower may still qualify even if it or he or she cannot quite meet all of the requirements listed. See CalHFA for additional details.

Interest-Only PLUS Program

Discontinued, at least temporarily in 2009, this CalHFA plan featured a conventional loan with (1) a below-market fixed interest rate, (2) a 35-year term, and (3) interest-only payments for the first five years. Then the payments switched to an amortized loan for the remaining 30 years. The interest rate remained fixed for the entire 35-year term. The loan-to-value ratio was 100 percent, increasing to 107 percent under special circumstances. Mortgage insurance was required and provided by CalHFA at very low rates. The property and borrower eligibility requirements are identical to the ones listed previously for the 30-year fixed rate program.

Whether the Interest-Only PLUS program is reinstated depends somewhat on the newer CAL30 loan option. Adopting the same first-time home buyer requirements, including income and sales price limits, the maximum loan-to-value is 95 percent. Qualified borrowers can combine this LTV limit with down payment and closing cost assistance programs. For more information about any first-time home buyer program, contact CalHFA at its website, www.calhfa.ca.gov.

TABLE 6.1   Comparison of government-backed loans (January 2006).

Feature	Federal Housing Administration	U.S. Department of Veterans Affairs (GI)	Cal-Vet
Purpose of loan	1–4 units	1–4 units	Single dwellings, condominiums
Eligibility	Any U.S. resident	U.S. veteran	Qualified veterans
Expiration of eligibility	Indefinite	Indefinite	Must apply within 30 years from date of discharge
Maximum purchase price	None	None	None
Maximum loan	Varies by counties	None by DVA; lenders limit loan amount	Varies for homes, farms, and mobile homes
Down payment	Section 203(b) Minimum 3.5%	None, but loan limited to CRV	0–3%
Maximum term	30 years	30 years	30 years
Secondary financing	Allowed with limitations	Allowed with limitations	Allowed with limitations
Interest rate	Fixed	Fixed	Floating (variable) rate
Prepayment penalty	None	None	None

SUMMARY

The FHA, DVA, and CalHFA are government agencies that do not make loans; they either insure, guarantee, or purchase loans made by approved lenders using their agency's guidelines. FHA-insured loans are made to any qualified borrower, whereas DVA-guaranteed loans are made to qualified veterans. CalHFA-backed loans focus on California first-time home buyers. Contrary to the FHA, DVA, and CalHFA programs, the Cal-Vet program is a direct loan made to qualified veterans. Table 6.1 compares the major features of the FHA, DVA, and Cal-Vet programs.

IMPORTANT TERMS AND CONCEPTS

CalHFA

Cal-Vet loan

Certificate of Eligibility

Certificate of Reasonable Value (CRV)

Conditional commitment

DVA-guaranteed loan

FHA-insured loan

Land contract of sale

Nonrecurring closing costs

Recurring closing costs

REVIEWING YOUR UNDERSTANDING

Questions for Discussion

1. List three advantages and three disadvantages of an FHA-insured loan.

2. Compare the borrower requirements for an FHA, DVA, Cal-Vet, and CalHFA loan. What are the down payment requirements for each?

3. What are the maximum loan fees a lender can charge for FHA, DVA, Cal-Vet, and CalHFA loans?

4. In your area, which of the four programs listed in Question #3 will allow the greatest loan amount?

Multiple-Choice Questions

1. The major goals of the Federal Housing Administration include
   a. upgrading property standards.
   b. financing homes priced over $417,000.
   c. promoting rental housing.
   d. all of the above.

2. The maximum entitlement under the DVA non-high-cost loan program can be as high as 50 percent of the loan balance, but not to exceed
   a. $22,500.
   b. $36,000.
   c. $60,000.
   d. $104,250.

3. A veteran purchased a home for $200,000 five years ago with DVA 100 percent financing. Three months ago the property went into foreclosure and there was a balance of $195,000 owing on the loan. The sale price at the time of foreclosure is $178,000. The maximum amount of liability, excluding costs of sale, is
   a. $50,750.
   b. $46,000.
   c. $17,000.
   d. none of these.

4. Cal-Vet financing
   a. requires no down payment.
   b. has no prepayment penalties.
   c. cannot be used for construction.
   d. uses a mortgage as security for the loan.

5. Which program is specifically designed for first-time home buyers?
   a. FHA.
   b. DVA.
   c. Cal-Vet.
   d. CalHFA.

6. To accomplish its goals, the FHA introduced
   a. partially amortized loans.
   b. high down payment loans.
   c. impound or escrow accounts.
   d. high interest rates.

7. The DVA differs from the FHA in that the
   a. DVA insures loans, while the FHA guarantees loans.
   b. DVA guarantees only part of the loan, whereas the FHA insures the entire loan.
   c. DVA loan limits exceed maximum FHA loan limits.
   d. down payments increase with higher loan amounts for both FHA and DVA loans.

8. Cal-Vet loans
   a. require a land contract of sale.
   b. are available only for owner-occupied properties.
   c. are subject to a 1 percent loan origination fee plus a loan guarantee fee.
   d. each of the foregoing is true.

9. The FHA
   a. makes most of the nation's single-family dwelling loans.
   b. insures loans made by approved lenders.
   c. does not require a down payment on approved loans.
   d. all of the above are correct.

10. Which statement regarding the FHA is correct?
    a. The down payment is generally 25 percent or more.
    b. The buyer normally pays the loan fee.
    c. The maximum loan fee is 10% of the loan amount.
    d. Secondary financing is not permitted.

11. Eligible for FHA loans are
    a. any U.S. residents.
    b. only naturalized citizens.
    c. qualified veterans.
    d. those meeting the 10 percent required down payment.

12. The Lender Appraisal Processing Program is associated with
    a. automatic underwriting standards.
    b. conventional appraisals.
    c. loan processing of DVA loans via the internet
    d. in-house appraisals.

13. The FHA requires a 3.5 percent cash investment that must come from the borrower's own funds, or from
    a. a bona fide gift.
    b. a loan from a family member.
    c. a governmental agency or instrumentality.
    d. any of the above sources.

14. The U.S. Department of Veterans Affairs
    a. guarantees loans made to qualified veterans by approved lenders.
    b. permits interest rates to be set by mutual agreement with the lender.
    c. operates its real estate loan program under the GI Bill of Rights, passed by Congress in 1944.
    d. does all of the above.

15. Another name for local FHA lenders is
    a. correspondents.
    b. model lenders.
    c. guideline lenders.
    d. risk-based lenders.

16. Which of the following is a recurring closing cost?
    a. Cal-Vet hazard insurance policy.
    b. FHA loan origination fee.
    c. DVA funding fee.
    d. CalHFA credit report.

17. The initials CRV refer to
    a. certified regional valuations.
    b. a DVA appraisal.
    c. a loan guaranteed by the Department of Veterans Affairs.
    d. a real estate agent who specializes in GI loans.

18. The following is used as the security instrument to finance a Cal-Vet loan
    a. deferred deed.
    b. land contract.
    c. mortgage.
    d. trust deed.

19. FHA-insured loans insure lenders against
    a. decline in real estate values.
    b. loss due to foreclosure.
    c. loss due to borrowers losing their jobs.
    d. late payments by borrowers.

20. The stated goal of all government home loan programs is to
    a. encourage speculation in housing.
    b. assist struggling real estate agents during down markets.
    c. offer subsidized interest rates to minority groups.
    d. foster homeownership.

CASE & POINT

New FHA Guidelines Will Affect the Lending Landscape

As the FHA has continued to adjust to the changing lending environment, it announced proposed changes to be initiated in 2010. While the industry is not expected to adopt all of the changes, the following is the list of proposals designed to improve the way in which the FHA intends to conduct future business.

1. *Appointment of a Chief Risk Officer.* Accompanying the appointment of the new FHA commissioner following the 2008 election, the appointment of a new FHA chief risk officer was considered to be the catalyst for all of the other proposed changes.

2. *Underwriting Changes.* Tightening underwriting standards is expected to be accompanied by the development of the FHA's own automated underwriting system. This will effectively replace the current method of manually underwriting loans. FHA underwriters will now function more like their conventional loan counterparts and be responsible for making sure that accurate documentation accompanies every "automatically approved" loan application.

3. *Risk Management.* The FHA had already adopted some risk management grids, not unlike conventional lenders. The agency intends to target a better loan review process for earlier discovery of poor product performance and/or policy problems.

4. *Lender Oversight.* Early default rates will be monitored, and lenders who do not meet agency standards will be precluded from continuing to offer FHA loans. Higher net worth requirements will be imposed upon approved direct endorsement (DE) lenders to a recommended one million dollars. These lenders, in turn, will determine the mortgage brokers/originators from whom they will accept FHA-originated loans. In other words, loan correspondents will no longer receive independent FHA approval for origination eligibility. The Direct Endorsement lenders will be responsible for the origination and oversight process of these lenders and loans, much like retail loans are currently treated in the conventional loan arena. While expected to be in place by early 2010, as of February 2010, FHA had yet to confirm this change. The change was still fully expected to be adopted.

5. *Relaxation of Loan Correspondent Eligibility.* The elimination of loan correspondent approval is perhaps the most significant change. Permitting FHA Direct Endorsement lenders to accept applications from any source that meets state and federal guidelines (e.g., RESPA) eliminates current lender approval requirements. Mortgage brokers, for instance, will no longer undergo even the cursory review and will not have to demonstrate a minimal $63,000 net worth. This rule alone will change the FHA landscape. The results of the approval relaxation rules could be mixed. The number of lenders offering FHA loans should increase, but the knowledge and expertise of many of the new lenders could easily be called into question.

6. *Appraisal Change.* After indicating that FHA would not change its appraisal process, it announced that it would institute its own Home Value Code of Conduct (HVCC) system by mid February 2010. Loan originators will no longer be allowed to order appraisals nor have any contact with the appraisers. Interestingly, the conventional market has been so negatively impacted by the HVCC appraisal process, that during this same period in 2010 consideration was still being given to its elimination. (More information on HVCC can be found in the Case & Point at the end of Chapter 8.)

7. *Streamline Refinances.* HUD will now require income, asset, and employment documentation as well as limit the amount of closing costs that can be rolled into the new loan. In the past, the streamline loan was easy to acquire, requiring only that the borrower had made previous payments on time and verification that the new payment would be lower than the one being refinanced. This move toward documentation is likely to substantially reduce the number of refinances.

8. *Reduced Reserves.* The reduced insurance reserves forced the FHA to explore plans for increasing its insurance funds. By February 2010 some changes were instituted while others remained possibilities that could very easily be adopted in the near future.

9. *Higher Down Payments.* Critics indicate that the current 3.5 percent down payment is too small an amount of "skin in the game." Some have suggested raising the required down payment to 10 percent, but critics argue that this fails to support the FHA's purpose of serving consumers of modest

means. It might make sense to raise the initial down payment to 5 percent, especially if most conventional lenders retain their current 10 percent down payment requirement.

10. *Higher Mortgage Insurance Premiums.* Some believed that the logical way to replenish insurance funds was to raise either one or both of the mortgage insurance premiums. The first step was the increase of the up-front MIP by .50 to 2.25%. If legislative authority is granted to increase the annual MIP, the FHA has indicated its intent to shift some of this up-front increase to the annual premium. The shift will be important as it will allow for less impact to the consumer because the annual MIP is paid over the life of the loan instead of at the time of closing of escrow. Industry officials have indicated that if the raising of the upfront premium can ultimately be set at 2 percent (from the current 1.75 percent) and the monthly MMI to 0.6 (from the current 5.5 percent) it would result in less than a $10 increase in the monthly payment on a $200,000 loan amount.

11. *Tougher Credit Standards.* While many FHA lenders have raised their minimum credit scores to 640 (from as low as 580 not long ago), the FHA remains a more lenient and flexible home lender in regards to evaluating credit worthiness. It is worth noting that the FHA guidelines still allow a 580 credit score. With more responsibility for loan quality being shifted to lenders, they have concluded that their risk is reduced by requiring the higher credit score. Previously suggested risk-based pricing models, in which riskier borrowers would pay a higher interest rate and/or increased fee, have been put on hold until at least the end of 2010. The FHA's adoption of an automated underwriting program to replace its current manual underwriting sometime in early 2010 will likely toughen the credit standards a little.

12. *Reducing Home-Seller "Concessions."* Home-sellers, up until February 2010 were able to pay up to 6 percent of the home's purchase price for the buyer's closing costs. Long time critics claimed this to be excessive and suggested that this allowance contributed to financially marginal buyers being encouraged to purchase homes beyond their qualifying capacity. These critics pointed out that the policy of allowing 6 percent in seller contributions made no sense when the current maximum down payment remained at 3.5 percent. A maximum 3 percent of the purchase price seller concession was adopted as of February 2010.

13. *There is no way to know how many, if any of the other above suggested changes will actually be adopted by the FHA.* What we do know is that the financial landscape is ever changing, and mortgage lenders and real estate practitioners will need to adapt.

Chapter

7

PREVIEW

This chapter explains points, discounts, and two other terms called price and yield. Although, some of these terms can be used in other context, this chapter solely looks at the secondary mortgage market, where existing loans are bought and sold. The main purpose of the secondary market is to re-circulate money by shifting funds from capital surplus areas to capital shortage areas. This is accomplished in part by lenders selling loans to each other. Capital is brought into the mortgage market by the operations of large corporations, including the Federal National Mortgage Association (Fannie Mae) and the Federal Home Loan Mortgage Corporation (Freddie Mac), and by the use of mortgage-backed securities.

After completing this chapter, you should be able to:

1. Explain the difference between the terms, points and discounts.
2. Define the term premium and contrast this to discount.
3. Differentiate between secondary financing and secondary mortgage market.
4. Describe the purpose of Fannie Mae and Freddie Mac.
5. Explain how a Ginnie Mae mortgage-backed security works.
6. Discuss the role of investment bankers in mortgage-backed securities and the secondary market.

Points, Discounts, and the Secondary Mortgage Market

7.1 SECONDARY MORTGAGE MARKET

When lenders speak about the secondary mortgage market, they are not referring to second mortgages or deeds of trust. They are talking about a market where existing loans are bought and sold. The difference between a secondary mortgage market and secondary financing is illustrated in Figure 7.1.

When a lender makes a loan directly to a borrower, that action takes place in the **primary mortgage market**. Later, that loan may be sold to a bank, pension fund, or some other investor. The sale of that loan takes place in the secondary market. For example, if a savings bank makes a loan directly to a borrower, it is involved in the primary market. If the loan is subsequently sold to the Federal Home Loan Mortgage Corporation, that sale takes place in the secondary market.

The secondary market consists of private and institutional lenders, investors, and government agencies that buy and sell mortgages to each other. In the secondary market, discounts are used constantly. Buyers and sellers of mortgages negotiate on the basis of yield. Discounts are used to adjust yields so agreements can be reached and sales made.

Purpose of the Secondary Market

Why do lenders need a secondary market? Why don't they just make loans and keep them? That would work well if every lender had a perfect balance between demand for loans and supply of money. However, such a perfect balance rarely exists. The main purpose of the secondary market is to shift money from areas where there is a surplus to areas where there is a shortage, thereby maintaining a steady supply of money for loans.

FIGURE 7.1   The difference between secondary financing and secondary mortgage market.

Secondary Financing

versus

Secondary Mortgage Market

Secondary Financing
A new loan secured by a *second* or *junior* mortgage or deed of trust—lender granting a loan to a borrower.

Secondary Mortgage Market
The purchasing and selling of *existing* mortgages and deeds of trust—lenders selling loans to other lenders and investors.

In the early 1970s, depository institutions sold only a small portion of the loans they originated. They were able to rely on their savings inflow to finance the loans they made. During this time, interest rates and the flow of deposits were relatively stable. As the 1970s progressed, the institutions were forced to sell more loans in the secondary market because loan volume had increased greatly. A slow rate of new deposits, typically referred to as "rate of savings inflow," was not sufficient to take care of the higher demand for loans.

In the 1980s, institutions found their cost of acquiring deposits increasing dramatically. They also experienced a major outflow of deposits due to higher rates offered by competing investments, such as mutual funds and certain bonds. Recall from Chapter 1 that this is labeled "disintermediation." With less money to support the demand for loans, the institutions have increasingly turned to the secondary market for funds.

One industry that has always operated in the secondary mortgage market is mortgage banking. Mortgage bankers do not have deposits to lend; therefore, they have to sell the loans they make to other investors. They operate as a conduit between the primary market and the secondary market. Today, almost all mortgage lenders operate in the secondary market to maintain liquidity and to stabilize the supply and demand for mortgage money.

Additional Sources for the Secondary Market

With consumer savings rates estimated at only 1 to 2 percent on a nationwide basis, deposits in institutions are not sufficient to meet the demand for mortgages. Therefore, to obtain additional funds for mortgages, lenders have had to revert to the capital market. The capital market is the market for long-term investments, which include government and corporate bonds as well as mortgage loans. Some of the investors in the capital market that buy long-term investments are insurance companies, trusts, pension funds, and individuals.

How Are Mortgage Funds Shifted?

There are a number of methods used in the marketplace to shift funds to where they are needed. One method is lenders selling loans to each other. For example, a savings bank in California may have more demand for loans than it can meet. A savings bank in Florida may have the opposite problem. The solution is to have the California savings bank sell loans to the Florida savings bank. The California savings bank would thereby obtain additional funds to use to make new loans, and the Florida savings bank would be investing surplus funds.

Another method to move funds from one source to another is called **participation**. Participation occurs when one institution sells a part interest in a block of loans to another institution. For example, assume the California savings bank wanted to sell $10,000,000 in loans to the Florida savings bank. Rather than sell the entire block of loans, it could sell a 90 percent interest, or $9,000,000. The other 10 percent share, $1,000,000, would be retained by the lender. The California bank would continue to service the loans and pass on 90 percent of the mortgage payments to the Florida bank. FNMA and FHLMC may also participate in 5 percent increments, purchasing 90 or 95 percent of a loan.

This enables the loan seller to leverage its funds. However, FNMA and FHLMC are more often involved in the sale of "whole" loans obtained from the primary market.

The Federal Government's Involvement

The federal government is greatly involved in these fund transfers as its *federal funds rate* determines the amount that banks charge each other for loans. Adjusting this rate is one way that the Federal Reserve influences the available supply of money. Raising the federal funds rate will dissuade banks from taking out such inter-bank loans, which in turn will make cash that much harder to procure. Conversely, dropping the interest rates will encourage banks to borrow money and therefore invest more freely. The Federal Reserve decision in 2009 to reduce the federal funds rate to near zero was designed to increase liquidity and encourage lending.

7.2 POINTS AND DISCOUNTS

While focusing primarily on the secondary market, it is important to understand the relationship of the yields in the primary market in preparation for their sale into the secondary arena.

Pricing in the primary market is typically done with "points." A **point** is 1 percent of the loan amount. It is used because it is more convenient to say one point than it is to say 1 percent of the loan amount. A point is *not* 1 percent of the sales price; it is always a percentage of the loan amount.

A **discount** is the amount of money a lender deducts from the loan amount when loan proceeds are funded.

Example:

Loan amount	$150,000
Less 2-point discount	−3,000
Net funds	$147,000 excluding appraisal and other fees

The size of a discount is expressed in points, often using the expression "discount points."

Points are also used to measure loan fees. Loan origination fees of 1 percent or 1.5 percent of the loan amount are referred to as 1 or 1.5 points respectively.

A **premium**, on the other hand, involves a loan sold for more than the face amount or balance of the loan. A $100,000 loan sold at a premium of 2 percent is sold for $102,000. Why would a loan sell for more than its face amount? Because of the higher interest rate and higher yield to the lender that the loan carries in the marketplace, this premium is referred to as a "service release premium" (SRP), yield spread premium (YSP) or "rebate pricing." YSP, when used appropriately, allows lenders to pass this savings along to the consumer-borrower in the form of zero-point loans or a reduction in the loan fee. On the other hand, rebate pricing has been abused, and the amount permitted to be earned by loan originators is now limited in many cases.

Loan premiums, although still popular, remain a concern to lenders for two reasons. First, carrying a higher-than-market-interest rate makes them more likely to be paid off early through refinancing at a lower rate. Second, there has been controversy over the proper disclosure to borrowers regarding the premiums paid.

This concern over the lack of appropriate disclosure and/or borrower understanding of YSP prompted the requirement of a new three-page Good Faith Estimate (GFE) form for all transactions beginning January 1, 2010. The expectation that the form will simplify the borrower's understanding of all of the costs accompanying his or her loan will need to be tested during future transactions. Critics have already suggested that the new form complicates the lender's ability to accurately disclose a rebate or yield spread premium and that borrowers are likely to be deprived of this option of paying for loan costs. This is yet another indication of the spate of rules being enacted as a result of past lending abuses. Time will determine if the form, as re-created, will perform as anticipated by its advocates.

Why Are Discounts Used?

Lenders use discount points to increase their actual return, which is called the **yield**. Also called the **effective interest rate**, this is generally the calculation used to determine the **annual percentage rate (APR)**. The APR is discussed in detail in Chapter 13.

Example: Assume you borrowed $100,000 for one year at a 10 percent interest rate. At the end of the year, you would repay the lender the $100,000 plus $10,000 in interest. The lender's yield would be calculated as follows:

$$\frac{\text{Interest}}{\text{Money Borrowed}} = \frac{\$10,000}{\$100,000} = 10\%$$

If the lender charged you a loan fee, the result would be different. If the fee were five points, or $5,000, you would receive only $95,000,

(continued)

because the lender subtracts the points from the loan amount and remits the difference. At the end of the year, you would pay the lender the $100,000 principal balance plus $10,000 in interest. In addition to the interest, the lender also collects the $5,000 in points. The effective interest rate that the lender has achieved is 15.8 percent, calculated as follows:

$$\frac{\text{Interest} + \text{Discount}}{\text{Money Disbursed}} = \frac{\$15,000}{\$95,000} = 15.8\%$$

To determine yields at various discounts, lenders can use a table such as the one shown in the following pages. The yield representations in Tables 7.1, 7.2, and 7.3 are more likely yield calculations used in what is called the "hard money lending" arena where loans are made to riskier borrowers.

Table 7.1 shows yields on an 11 percent, 30-year loans at fees ranging from 1 to 10 points. Yields are also determined by the date the loan is paid off. Even though the term is 30 years, the average life of a loan is considerably less. While past industry studies identified the average home ownership period to be seven to eight years, it is expected to lengthen in the future. The yield, and the discounts required on any given loan, however, is also dependent upon the initial interest rate, the term of the loan, and the payback rate.

Table 7.1 and the two that follow, 7.2 and 7.3, are for demonstration purposes only, to show that such tools exist. Real estate calculators have made yield and discount calculations much easier. The formulas and the calculator operations required for performing the computations are beyond the scope of this text, but readers may find the topic to be of at least marginal interest.

TABLE 7.1   Yields on an 11 percent, 30-year loan at various discounts prepaid in 12 years.

Discount (# of points)	Effective Yield (%)
0	11.00
1	11.16
2	11.31
3	11.48
4	11.64
5	11.81
6	11.97
7	12.14
8	12.00
9	12.49
10	12.67

Price and Yield

When real estate salespeople and borrowers deal with lenders, the terms used are typically points and loan fees. When lenders sell loans to other lenders or investors, they deal in terms of price and discount. Price + Discount = Face Value, or par.

Price is another way of quoting the discount. A lender selling a loan at a five-point discount would quote a price of 95. The lender is saying that it will sell the loan for 95 percent of the loan amount.

Therefore, an existing $100,000 loan would be sold to another lender for $95,000 (95 percent × $100,000). Price and discount added together always equal 100, which is called par (face value). To determine price, you deduct the discount from 100. For example, if the discount is three points, what is the price?

Par	100
Discount	−3
Price	97

If you know the price and you want to determine the discount, you reverse the process. If the price is 97, what is the discount?

Par	100
Price	−97
Discount	3

If you know the price, it is simple to determine the effective return, which lenders call yield. When a loan is sold with no discount, at par, the return on the loan and the yield are the same. With a discount, the yield will be higher than the interest rate on the loan.

At a price of 97, based on a 12-year payoff, the yield is 10.46 percent. Investors who purchase existing loans use such tables or financial calculators to determine the price they can pay to achieve a certain yield. They are usually comparing mortgage loans with other competing investments, such as corporate bonds; these are compared on the basis of yield. For example, if an investor wants to achieve a yield of 11.10 percent on the purchase of an existing $100,000 mortgage, what price should the investor pay? Looking at Table 7.2 and assuming the loan will be prepaid in 12 years, the investor would pay a price of 93, or $93,000 (93 percent of $100,000).

All lenders use computerized "pricing modules" to price their loan options on a daily basis. As previously indicated, for those skilled with the use of financial calculators, tables such as these can be constructed for virtually any interest rate, term, and prepayment period. Chapter 13 examines some calculator applications to real estate problems.

TABLE 7.2   Desired yield on a 10 percent, 30-year loan at various prices prepaid in 12 years.

Price	Effective Yield (percent)
90	11.61
91	11.43
92	11.26
93	11.10
94	10.93
95	10.77
96	10.61
97	10.46
98	10.30
99	10.15
100	10.00

Where Are Discounts Used?

A mortgage or deed of trust recorded after the first mortgage is called a **junior mortgage**. If the junior mortgage is recorded after the first mortgage, it is called a second mortgage (not to be confused with the secondary market). A mortgage recorded after the first and second mortgages is called a third mortgage. While there is no limit on how many liens can be placed on a property, the risk for the lien holder can increase depending upon its position. A detailed discussion of junior mortgages and deeds of trust is presented in Chapter 14.

Junior loans are also bought and sold by investors. For example, sellers of a property may need to carry back a second deed of trust to sell their house. After the sale, the sellers may want to sell the second to obtain cash. To sell, they probably have to offer the second deed of trust at a discount. Discounts on junior loans vary widely—sometimes from 10 to 50 percent depending on note rate, size of monthly payments (rate of payoff), due date, borrower payment history, amount of equity in the property, and prevailing yields in the marketplace. As the risk increases, the discount increases, resulting in a higher yield. Stated differently, the higher the discount, the higher the yield.

Yields at various discounts can be determined from published tables, as shown in Table 7.3, or by a financial calculator like those reviewed in Chapter 13.

Assume that in the real estate market, interest rates increase and seller-carried seconds at 15 percent interest become common.

TABLE 7.3 Discount required for various yields on a loan with a 15 percent interest rate with the balance due in five years.

Desired Yield (%)	Monthly Payoff Rate		
	1.25%	1.5%	2%
15	0.0	0.0	0.0
17	6.7	6.2	5.1
19	12.9	11.8	9.8
21	18.5	17.1	14.2
23	23.7	21.9	18.3
25	28.4	26.3	22.1
27	32.8	30.4	25.7

(Yes, even first mortgages were charging 18 percent and more in 1980 to 1982, with junior liens commanding more than 15 percent!) Table 7.3 indicates yields and discounts for mortgages at a 15 percent interest rate, with the entire remaining balance due in five years. Note that the rate of monthly payoff has an effect on the discount. To obtain a 21 percent yield, with a 1.25 percent per month payoff rate, you would need an 18.5 percent discount. If the loan pays off at a rate of 1.5 percent per month, the discount to obtain the same 21 percent yield reduces to 17.1 percent. At a payoff rate of 2 percent per month, only a 14.2 percent discount is required to obtain the 21 percent yield.

The monthly payoff rates are derived by dividing monthly payment by the principal balance. For example:

$$\text{Monthly payment} \div \text{Principal balance} = \text{Rate of payoff}$$
$$\$200 \div \$10,000 = 2\% \text{ per month}$$

Example: If a 15 percent second loan due in five years has a balance of $50,000, and monthly payments of $1,000, how much of a discount would be required to yield 25 percent?

Solution:

$$\frac{\text{Monthly payment}}{\text{Principal balance}} = \frac{\$1,000}{\$50,000} = 2\% \text{ rate of payoff}$$

(continued)

To achieve a 25 percent yield, the last column in the table shows that a discount of 22.1 percent will be required. The purchase price of the junior lien is calculated as follows:

Principal balance	$50,000
Less : 22.1% of 50,000	−11,050
Purchase price	$38,950

Mortgage-Backed Securities

Today, the most common method used to move funds is the use of mortgage-backed securities, which are backed by a pool of mortgages. Mortgage-backed securities were created to make investing in mortgages as simple as buying stocks or bonds. Before these securities, lending institutions sold and purchased loans among themselves. This was not an efficient method—it was time consuming and involved a lot of paperwork. In addition, each lender had its own property and borrower standards, which further complicated transactions. More importantly, there was no system to obtain money from the capital markets. Lenders had to depend on deposits, which had proven to be volatile. The invention of the mortgage-backed security revolutionized the operation of the secondary market.

As the number of home mortgages grew, fueled by the subprime, these securitized instruments morphed into what became known as "mortgage swaps." In retrospect, the swap was a "created mortgage instrument" and was so complicated that no one truly understood how it functioned. These swaps were sold worldwide with the anticipation that the Wall Street companies that sold them also insured and guaranteed them. When the mortgage collapse occurred, it was quickly discovered that these Wall Street sellers did not have the reserves to cover the mounting losses from the increasing number of mortgage defaults and that they were only presumed to have been guaranteed by the U.S. government. The ensuing monetary crises, the lack of liquidity, and the government's intervention to prop up not only the nation's economy but the world's is now well documented. We discuss the continuing impacts upon our real estate financial options in various sections of this book.

Three agencies play an important role in the secondary market: the **Government National Mortgage Association (GNMA)**, the **Federal Home Loan Mortgage Corporation (FHLMC)**, and the **Federal National Mortgage Association (FNMA)**. The GNMA is a government agency; the FHLMC was a quasi-government agency until recently; and the FNMA was a former government agency turned private corporation (in 1968) but has now, along with the FHLMC, been placed under conservatorship and is literally owned by consumers through this latest government intervention (see the Case & Point at the end of this chapter for further explanation). The function of these agencies is to support the secondary market through the purchase of loans or the guarantee of **mortgage-backed securities** issued by lenders. These agencies, along with other minor players—such as the Federal Agricultural Mortgage Corporation, or Farmer Mac; and the Student Loan Marketing Association, or Sallie Mae—are known as **government-sponsored enterprises (GSEs)**.

Government National Mortgage Association (GNMA)

The first mortgage-backed security was developed by the Government National Mortgage Association, commonly called Ginnie Mae. Ginnie Mae was established in 1968 as a government agency within the Department of Housing and Urban Development (HUD). Its basic mission was to create and operate a mortgage-backed security program for FHA and DVA mortgages. It took over the duties formerly performed by FNMA after it was given private status.

In 1970, Ginnie Mae issued the first security backed by a pool of FHA and DVA mortgages. It was called a **pass-through security** because the monthly principal and interest payments collected from the borrowers were passed through to the investor. Ginnie Mae does not purchase mortgages. Its function is to guarantee that principal and interest will be paid every month. Since it is a government agency, the guarantee is backed by the "full faith and credit" of the U.S. government. For this guarantee, Ginnie Mae receives a small fee from the lender, which is collected monthly. The minimum amount that can be placed in a pool is $1,000,000. The mortgages cannot be more than one year old and must have met predetermined average yields for the pool of loans. The pool can contain any combination of FHA and DVA mortgages. The lender can apply to Ginnie Mae for a commitment to issue a certificate at any time. When applying, it must indicate the size of the pool and the rate of interest on the mortgages. If Ginnie Mae approves the request, it issues a commitment that is good for one year.

Before the certificate is sold, Ginnie Mae requires that the mortgages be in the hands of a third party. This party acts as a trustee for Ginnie Mae and is called the custodian. The custodian is usually a bank, but it could be any federal or state financial institution acceptable to Ginnie Mae. The lender delivers the mortgage documents to the custodian, who checks the information carefully. Once the custodian is satisfied that it has all the documents, it notifies Ginnie Mae. The certificate is then issued to the lender.

With the certificate in hand, the lender is able to sell the mortgages to an investor. When the investor buys the mortgages, it receives the certificate. Typically, the securities are purchased by securities dealers who trade in Ginnie Mae securities. They in turn sell the securities to other investors, such as insurance companies, pension funds, other lenders who need mortgages, and individuals. The securities can be broken down into smaller denominations to satisfy the demands of the various investors (the smallest denomination is $25,000). The securities are traded on Wall Street just like stocks and bonds. There is an active market for the securities, which makes them a liquid investment.

Readers wishing more information on the GNMA can access its website at http://www.gnma.com.

Federal Home Loan Mortgage Corporation (FHLMC)

Because Ginnie Mae included only FHA and DVA mortgages in its securities, there was a great need to develop a mortgage-backed security for conventional loans. In 1971, the Federal Home Loan Mortgage Corporation, also known as Freddie Mac, introduced the first security backed by conventional loans. Freddie Mac was a subsidiary of the Office of Thrift Supervision (OTS), which supervised the federally chartered thrifts. As a government-chartered, stockholder-owned corporation, FHLMC bought mortgages and sold them in the secondary market.

Freddie Mac bought conventional loans from lenders such as savings banks, commercial banks, and mortgage companies. It then assembled a pool of mortgages and issued a security backed by the mortgages. The security is called a *Participating Certificate (PC)* or Guaranteed Mortgage Certificate. The agency guarantees the full payment of principal and the timely payment of interest. The security is later sold to investors in the capital markets. For the guarantee, Freddie Mac receives a monthly fee paid by the investors.

For more information on FHLMC, access its website through a link at www.fhlmc.com.

Federal National Mortgage Association (FNMA)

The Federal National Mortgage Association, known as Fannie Mae, was established by Congress in 1938 to provide a secondary market for mortgages. It remained a part of the federal government until 1968, when it became a private corporation. Even though it was private, the corporation had a public purpose and maintained strong government ties. It was subject to some regulations by the

Department of Housing and Urban Development (HUD). It also had the ability to tap the U.S. Treasury if necessary.

Fannie Mae issues a security backed by conventional loans and operates the issuance of its securities much like Freddie Mac. It buys mortgages from lenders, places them in a pool, and issues a security.

The security is sold to investors, who *receive a guarantee that principal and interest will be paid monthly, whether or not payments have been collected from the borrowers.* Fannie Mae charges a monthly fee for the guarantee.

Note: The italicized statements regarding "guarantees" led to problems in 2008 that could no longer be ignored. See the Case & Point at the end of the chapter.

Collateralized Mortgage Obligations

Fannie Mae issues mortgage-backed securities called **collateralized mortgage obligations (CMOs)**. They were designed to limit prepayment risk to investors. Prior to this time, mortgage-backed securities were pass-throughs, which means that all the principal and interest collected were passed on to the investor. The investor had no protection from the early prepayment of principal. If borrowers in the pool decided to pay their mortgages in full, the proceeds were passed on to the investors.

When investors calculate yield, they make assumptions regarding the repayment of principal. When mortgages are paid early, the investors' yield is reduced, since they collect less total interest. Therefore, investors are looking for a security that can provide some protection against early prepayment and loss of return on investment.

A CMO is divided into classes. For example, the first CMO had three classes. Each class paid interest on the outstanding balance. However, all collections of principal from the pool were first applied to class one. After that class had been paid in full, all principal collections went to class two. After class two had been paid in full, the remaining principal payments went to class three. The CMO gives investors opportunities to choose classes that offer different rates and maturities. The creation of the CMO attracted investors that were not normally mortgage investors and, in the end, not savvy enough to understand the process. Those notorious "swap" instruments created by Wall Street were not far behind in attractiveness for investors and equally misunderstood.

For readers wishing more information on the FNMA and on Fannie Mae Foundation, which offers information on finding and financing homes, access their websites through links at www.fnma.com.

FIGURE 7.2   Contribution of secondary markets to home loans.

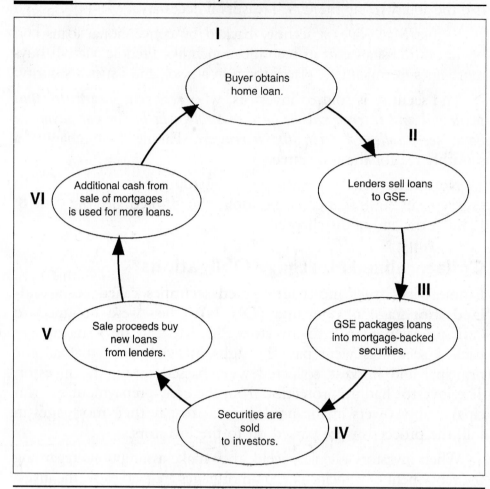

	Ginnie Mae	Freddie Mac	Fannie Mae	Bonds
Who Owns	Government agency	Government chartered Stockholder owned	Started as gov't Now private corp	State/local gov't issued
Buy What	FHA & DVA loans	Conventional	Conventional	Low income loans
How	Backed by U.S. gov't Pool loans into package Sell stock for funds Guarantee P/I for fee	Pool loans into package Sell stock for funds Guarantee P/I for fee	Pool loans into package Sell stock for funds Guarantee P/I for fee Can tap U.S. Treasury	Offers tax-exempt returns Offers less return to investor Offers less APR to buyers
When Pay	Through stock/ bond returns	Tiered at buyer payoff	In "classes" of CMO	Over long term/fixed amount
More Info	www.ginniemae. gov	www.freddiemac. com	www.fanniemae. com	www.treasurydirect.gov www.investinginbonds. com

Nonconforming Loans

The U.S. Congress sets the maximum loan amount on conventional loans purchased by Freddie Mac and Fannie Mae. The 2009 maximum for single-family loans was $417,000. The maximum loan amount changes based on economic conditions; it may be adjusted each year by FNMA and Freddie Mac—who bundle these loans to resell to investors—to reflect local price trends.

In early 2009, a new category of **conforming loan** was introduced called the "high balance" conforming loan, with loan amounts up to $729,750. Although they weren't available in all areas, these higher loan amounts were created to provide affordable financing for those areas that had experienced substantial home value appreciation. This led to some confusion, as some areas remained at the $417,000 conforming loan limit while other areas were eligible for the higher loan amount. While this new high-balance loan required a higher interest rate than the typical conforming loan, it was lower than jumbo or **nonconforming loan** rates.

Whereas in the past, **jumbo loan** interest rates were priced at approximately one-quarter percent higher than the normal conforming loan, by early 2009, jumbo financing had become not only largely unavailable but nearly unaffordable. To add to the confusion, in those areas designated as lower cost, a jumbo loan meant any loan over $417,000. In the higher cost areas, jumbo financing was above the new high-balance amount of $729,750. Jumbo loan financing during this time literally dried up, leaving many homeowners little recourse for new purchases or refinances.

The private corporations, often subsidiaries of large financial institutions, that had formed to issue mortgage-backed securities backed by jumbo loans, had become cautious and found little market for their securities. Their parent organizations were facing difficult times with bank failures and mergers seemingly occurring daily. It was only toward the end of 2009 that jumbo loans began to reappear as available financing. The future of the high-balance loan may be limited as it is currently approved only until the end of 2010.

Investment Bankers

Investment bankers made a market for both new and seasoned mortgage-backed securities. These Wall Street firms, called *securities dealers*, bought and sold securities from lenders and investors.

Defining themselves as "bankers," these investment firms were perceived by the public to function like a bank with required reserves, insurance for protection of clients' investments, and a relative safety for investment purposes. These companies developed the instrument now known as a "swap," a complicated and little understood method of reducing a subprime loan into pieces for sale, mostly abroad. Purchasers were led to believe that these swaps had not only the safety of a bank investment but enjoyed the full backing of the U.S. government, and these investments were sold at what turned out to be exorbitant prices.

Morgan Stanley, Lehman Brothers, and Merrill Lynch are three of the well-known entities that were exposed in 2008 as being a virtual house of cards. When the subprime market totally collapsed in 2008, the investment banks were found to have no reserves or insurance and were unable to cover the mounting losses. They turned instead to the government to pay their investors. (See the Case & Point at the end of Chapter 4 for a discussion of the government's role in helping borrowers.)

Mergers were encouraged with Merrill Lynch merging with Bank of America Corporation and Morgan Stanley with Goldman Sachs. The latter merger redefined Goldman Sachs as a traditional bank holding company rather than an investment firm. This brought an end, at least for the present, to the era of investment banking on Wall Street. By early 2010 Congress continued to grapple with how best to rein in some of Wall Street's practices and provide for more safety of investments.

Standardization

One major benefit brought about by the creation of mortgage-backed securities by Freddie Mac and Fannie Mae is the standardization of conventional loan forms and property and borrower standards. FHA and DVA loans have been readily sold in the secondary market for years. One of the reasons is that their forms are standardized. As an investor, you could buy an FHA or DVA loan anywhere in the United States and know the exact loan provisions. Previously this could not be done with a conventional loan.

To have a functional secondary market for conventional loans, you must also have *standardization*. Freddie Mac and Fannie Mae have accomplished this by using the same forms and by having basically the same property and borrower standards. Almost all lenders today use the standard forms, and many adhere to the property and borrower standards set forth by the agencies. This gives the lenders great flexibility in ensuring that their loans can be sold in the secondary market.

Mortgage Revenue Bonds

The State of California and local governments—cities and counties—have the authority to issue bonds. Interest paid on the bonds is tax exempt to the investors. Bonds sold by state and local governments and used to finance mortgages are called **mortgage revenue bonds**. Because the bonds are tax exempt, the interest rate is less than on a standard bond and, as a result, mortgage loans can be made at below-market rates. The government agencies do not guarantee the bonds. The bonds are backed by the mortgages created by the bond funds. The issuer of the bond merely acts as a conduit; local lenders process, close, and then service the loans for the government. These bond issues generally work the same way as other mortgage-backed securities, but the paperwork is much more complex. Local bond issues typically are used to promote lower-income or affordable housing ventures. Borrower requirements usually include income and/or price limits, length of time ownership requirements, and limitations on the amount of equity to be retained upon resale.

SUMMARY

A point, by definition, is 1 percent of the loan amount. Points are used to measure discounts, loan origination fees, and premiums. Lenders charge discounts to increase the effective yield they receive on a loan. When lenders sell loans to investors, they sell on the basis of price. Price is another way of quoting discount. A loan with a discount of three points would have a price of 97; price and discount added together equal 100, or **par**. When lenders buy or sell loans, they look at the yield, or effective interest rate. Yield on a loan can be adjusted by varying the discount. Lenders use discounts to increase their yield on any given loan. As the discount increases the yield increases. Discounts are also used on conventional loans, government loans, and junior mortgages and in the secondary mortgage market. Existing loans are bought or sold in the secondary market. The purpose of the secondary market is to shift funds from capital surplus areas to capital short areas. One method involves lenders selling loans to each other. Lenders also sell participating interests in blocks of loans to other lenders. Mortgage-backed securities are another tool used to obtain money from the capital market. There are securities backed by FHA and DVA loans and others backed by conventional loans. Since 1978, tax-exempt bonds have been widely used by state and local governments to finance housing.

IMPORTANT TERMS AND CONCEPTS

Annual percentage rate (APR)

Collateralized mortgage obligation (CMO)

Conforming loan

Discount

Effective interest rate

Federal Home Loan Mortgage Corporation (FHLMC)

Federal National Mortgage Association (FNMA)

Government National Mortgage Association (GNMA)

Government-sponsored enterprises (GSE)

Jumbo loan

Junior mortgage

Mortgage revenue bonds

Mortgage-backed securities

Nonconforming loan

Par

Participation

Pass-through security

Point

Premium

Price

Primary mortgage market

Secondary mortgage market

Yield

REVIEWING YOUR UNDERSTANDING

Questions for Discussion

1. Describe what price means when one lender sells existing real estate loans to another lender. How is yield computed?

2. Explain why borrowers pay loan origination fees when obtaining a loan.

3. What is the difference between secondary financing and the secondary mortgage market?

4. What is a mortgage-backed security?

Multiple-Choice Questions

1. Securities that are usually exempt from federal and state income taxation are popularly labeled
   a. conventional mortgage-backed securities.
   b. mortgage revenue bonds.
   c. private mortgage-backed certificates.
   d. participation loans.

2. Interest rates on FHA and DVA loans are set by
   a. HUD.
   b. the Department of Veterans Affairs.
   c. an agreement between the borrower and lender.
   d. the lender solely.

3. A lender selling a loan at a six-point discount would quote a price of
   a. 106.
   b. 94.
   c. 100.
   d. none of the above.

4. Which of the following parties would likely not sell mortgage loans to Freddie Mac?
   a. mortgage companies
   b. commercial banks
   c. individuals
   d. savings banks

5. The chief purpose of the secondary mortgage market is to
   a. shift funds from the capital shortage areas to capital surplus area.
   b. shift funds from the capital surplus areas to capital shortage areas.
   c. guarantee a market so money can be re-circulated.
   d. both (a) and (c) are correct.

6. Regarding points charged for a home loan
   a. one point is equal to 1 percent of the sales price.
   b. one point is equal to 1 percent of the loan amount.
   c. points are always paid by the buyer-borrower.
   d. points are always paid by the seller.

7. Which of the following is a major buyer and seller in the secondary mortgage market?
   a. FHA
   b. FNMA
   c. DVA
   d. Cal-Vet

8. Which of the following is also significantly involved in the secondary mortgage market?
   a. Federal Reserve Board
   b. Federal Housing Administration
   c. California Housing Finance Agency
   d. Federal Home Loan Mortgage Corporation

9. Fannie Mae is the popular name for
   a. Federal National Mortgage Association.
   b. Federal National Marketing Association.
   c. Federal Home Loan Mortgage Corporation.
   d. Federal Housing Administration.

10. The federal government is intimately involved in the transfer of mortgage funds through its federal funds rate, which
    a. determines what banks charge each other for overnight loans.
    b. influences the available supply of money.
    c. can drop to near zero in order to increase liquidity and encourage lending.
    d. all of the above.

11. When forwarding loan proceeds to the escrow holder, lenders generally
    a. forward the loan amount, and look to the escrow holder to disburse the discount and lender's fees.
    b. deduct the amount of the discount and its fees.
    c. insist on having a check for the amount of any discount or fee.
    d. none of the above.

12. When dealing in the secondary market, price and discount
    a. are synonymous with points and discounts.
    b. when added together, equal 100 percent, or par.
    c. actually describe "sales price" and "effective yield."
    d. none of the above.

13. Conforming loans are periodically adjusted by the
    a. U.S. Treasury.
    b. Federal Reserve Board.
    c. Real Estate Commissioner.
    d. Government-Sponsored Enterprises.

14. The term secondary market
    a. describes any junior lien, whether second or lower in priority.
    b. is where loans are actually made to the borrower.
    c. describes a market where existing loans are bought and sold.
    d. involves FNMA, GNMA, and FHLMC as the only participants.

15. "Mortgage "swaps"
    a. grew out of the subprime easy money mortgage market.
    b. were sold worldwide with the anticipation that the Wall Street firms selling them also insured and guaranteed them.
    c. led to the mortgage collapse of the mid-2000s.
    d. each of the above is connected to mortgage swaps.

16. Investment bankers
    a. make a market for both new and seasoned securities.
    b. buy and sell securities from lenders and investors.
    c. are very active in the secondary market.
    d. are involved in each of the foregoing activities.

17. If you were selling a loan at a two-point premium, you would quote a price of
    a. 2.
    b. 102.
    c. 98.
    d. 100.

18. The objectives and mechanics of the secondary mortgage market are many and varied, including
    a. making below-market interest rate loans to home buyers.
    b. buying and selling existing mortgages.
    c. providing funds for needy sellers.
    d. insuring loans for home buyers.

19. Which of the following is the popular name for the Federal Home Loan Mortgage Corporation?
    a. Fannie Mae
    b. Freddie Mac
    c. Ginnie Mae
    d. Fed Mae

20. You list a home for $220,000, and then the real estate market begins to decline. A young couple offers to purchase the home for $175,000, and after a series of counteroffers it sells for $180,000. The couple apply for a $150,000 loan, and the lender commits to a two-point fee. Ignoring other charges, the amount of proceeds to be disbursed will be
    a. $147,000.
    b. $176,000.
    c. $196,000.
    d. $150,000.

CASE & POINT

Fannie/Freddie … Going Forward?

As noted on pages 184 and 185, both Fannie Mae and Freddie Mac "guarantee" the payment of principal and interest for the securitized loans, known as mortgage-backed securities (MBS), that were sold to investors. Wall Street divided these securities into what would come to be known as "swaps" and sold them globally. In 2008, as mortgage defaults began to balloon, it became clear that the GSEs did not have sufficient insurance and/or reserves to cover the mounting losses. The U.S. Treasury Department determined that ambiguities in the GSEs congressional charters were perceived by global investors as proof that the government guaranteed the securities. In other words, investors believed their investments to be virtually risk-free, and, because the U.S. government created the ambiguities, it had the responsibility to avert the risk created by the failure of the GSEs.

The result was the government's decision to place Fannie and Freddie under conservatorship in an effort to avoid a complete collapse of the mortgage market. The initial infusion of $100 billion to each entity was promoted to the public as a temporary measure to provide liquidity and to quiet the concerns of the investment community. The federal government was authorized to acquire up to an 80 percent stake in the companies depending upon how much of the $200 billion of the total allotment of funds became necessary to guarantee liquidity. But much remained unclear and it was to be left to the new Administration to sort out the details in 2009.

By the end of 2009, questions still remained about the financial soundness of the entities, as well as their future structure and even their continuation. While many anticipate that a future reduction in the portfolio holdings of both Fannie Mae and Freddie Mac is inevitable, there are those who question whether any such reduction in the size of the GSEs is wise. The other piece of proposed reform is to adopt a market discipline that requires shareholders to bear both the risk and the reward of their investments. Others question whether we need a new entity, with new regulation and oversight, to assume the role of the GSEs. In other words, there is little agreement regarding how the GSEs can best fulfill their mission going forward.

The most reliable source of home loans today are those sold to Fannie or Freddie who together currently hold or securitize nearly half—roughly $5 trillion—of all mortgages in the U.S.

The talk of reducing the size and influence of the GSEs or privatization or nationalization of the agencies creates some anxiety. The fear is that the nation's housing markets cannot withstand the financial disruption that could occur if major changes to the GSEs were made without compensating conduits for future loans.

While we wait for history to be made, we do recognize that without an institutionalized mortgage-backed securities market, mortgage capital will likely become less predictable and more expensive. In the meantime, we have seen what some would call an overreaction to past lending excesses by adopting higher down payment and less flexible borrower qualifying requirements for 30-year, fixed rate mortgages. Let us hope government does not overreact and take a sledgehammer to a problem that may merely require a few taps to readjust.

Chapter

PREVIEW

This chapter describes the procedures lenders use in qualifying or appraising a property for loan purposes: The neighborhood is analyzed, the property is inspected, and a value is determined based upon market variables. This chapter also reviews the use of an appraisal form in depth and lists special considerations by lenders on planned unit developments and condominiums.

After completing this chapter, you should be able to:

1. Discuss the influence of Freddie Mac and Fannie Mae and the new Home Valuation Code of Conduct (HVCC) on a lender's property qualifying standards.
2. Describe what an appraiser looks for when analyzing a neighborhood.
3. Outline the steps used in the market data approach to estimating loan value.
4. Demonstrate why sales price is not the same as fair market value.
5. Differentiate the formal classifications of real estate appraisers in California.
6. Suggest possible ways to communicate with an appraiser within the rules of the new Home Valuation Code of Conduct.

Qualifying the Property

8.1 WHAT DOES QUALIFYING THE PROPERTY MEAN?

The expression "qualifying the property" often is used interchangeably with the term "appraising the property." When making a loan, one of the lender's early actions is to obtain an appraisal to determine whether the property is sufficient collateral for the requested loan amount.

Although state and federal laws prohibit a lender from "redlining" an area based on neighborhood, ethnic, racial, or other illegal reasons, a lender is allowed to require that the value of the property be high enough to justify the loan. A lender will base the loan amount on the market value of the property or the purchase price, *whichever is the lesser*. This, coupled with the borrower's income and credit profile, determines the maximum loan-to-value ratio the lender will allow as a condition for making the loan.

Note: Appraisers' prime responsibility is not necessarily to determine market value. Their major objective is to determine if the value is sufficient to serve as security (enough collateral) for the lender's projected loan amount which, in turn, we refer to as the market value.

Lenders' Property Standards

While Fannie Mae and Freddie Mac guidelines are widely accepted as property standards, lenders who do not intend to sell their loans to Fannie Mae or Freddie Mac can establish their own guidelines. Depending upon the economic climate, the availability of funds, and the strength of the borrower, some flexibility among lenders can exist. When exceptions to a lender's basic policy occur, the possibility of being accused of illegal discrimination must be addressed.

Changes in lenders' basic property standards are generally related to fluctuations in the availability of funds to loan out and/or market conditions. When funds are plentiful, the lender will be more likely to loosen its standards. Conversely, when there is less money available for the loans being requested, the lender will stiffen property standards. Market conditions also affect lenders' flexibility. When property values are increasing (much like the run-up in home values from 2000 to early 2006) appraised values and property standards became secondary to a borrower's credit score and creating easy-to-purchase guidelines. On the other hand, when home values adjust downward, property standards toughen and reliance upon appraised values increases. As noted in the next section, a lender's attitude will also be influenced by whether the loan will be sold in the secondary market or kept in its own portfolio.

Influence of Freddie Mac and Fannie Mae

Freddie Mac and Fannie Mae influence a conventional lender's property standards. A lender that intends to sell its loans to either agency must follow the particular agency's standards. Some lenders, such as mortgage companies, sell most of their loans to Fannie Mae. Thus a mortgage company will not approve a loan on a property unless the property is acceptable to Fannie Mae. If the property were not acceptable to Fannie Mae, the mortgage company would be stuck with the loan. There are other lenders, such as savings banks, that retain loans in their own portfolio. They may still want to use Freddie Mac or Fannie Mae property standards for all of their loans to ensure that their loans are saleable to these agencies; this gives the lender more flexibility in managing its funds. Therefore, most lenders adhere to the property requirements of both Fannie Mae and Freddie Mac.

FHA and DVA Property Standards

The Federal Housing Administration and the Department of Veterans Affairs do not operate like conventional lenders; they *insure* or *guarantee loans*. In the past, government loans often required extensive repairs and improvements to property prior to issuing a loan. More recently, they have adopted more flexible guidelines, known as habitability standards. Some of these standards include a working heater, water, and electricity and include any health issues, such as broken glass, peeling paint, etc. Both the FHA and the DVA rely heavily upon appraisers to determine if a home meets specific property requirements. They do not adjust the loan-to-value ratio because of the property—if the property meets the minimum standards, it will be entitled to the maximum loan amount under existing FHA and DVA guidelines. Likewise, the interest rate is not affected by the property.

Procedure for Qualifying a Property

How do lenders qualify or appraise a property? FHA and DVA requirements differ from most requirements for conventional loans. First let's discuss how the FHA and the DVA qualify property.

Qualifying for FHA and DVA

The primary responsibility of the FHA and the DVA is to ensure that a property meets their minimum property standards. The appraiser serves as the eyes of the bank. In addition, he or she must establish a market value for the property. An FHA appraisal must be ordered through an approved FHA lender (commercial banks, savings banks, and most mortgage companies can be approved lenders).

Prior to 2010, all FHA approved lenders were required to use state-certified appraisers for FHA-insured mortgages. Since the FHA no longer assigned appraisers, appropriate appraisers were found through the FHA Connection, a Web-based program for the use of approved originating lenders. A selected appraiser from the appraiser roster was designated as either certified residential or certified general. All eligible FHA appraisers are independently licensed and FHA-qualified fee appraisers. In 2010, the FHA adopted a Home Valuation Code of Conduct (HVCC) patterned after the process initiated in 2009 for conventional lenders. While this FHA appraisal program is new, an idea of what to expect may be acquired by reviewing the Case & Point at the end of this chapter for the HVCC process as it currently relates to conventional loans.

After the appraiser has inspected and appraised the property, a **conditional commitment** is issued. The "conditional" includes any other conditions that the FHA is requiring, such as termite work and repairs. A copy of the conditional commitment is sent back to the lender who ordered the appraisal. Whereas in the past, pest control reports were always required, FHA appraisers are now responsible for determining if a report should be acquired. Along with all other appraisal conditions, any pest work or repairs identified in a required report must be completed and a clearance provided before FHA insurance will be issued.

The DVA operates in much the same way as the FHA. A DVA appraisal is ordered by a DVA-qualified lender. The appraisal is sent by the DVA to a licensed independent fee appraiser who is

DVA qualified. The DVA uses fee appraisers for all of its field work. It does have full-time staff appraisers, but their function is to act as reviewers and supervisors. Once the fee appraiser has completed the appraisal, it is sent to the DVA office for review. If approved, a **Certificate of Reasonable Value (CRV)** is issued, which includes other conditions and repairs that the DVA requires on the property. A pest control report and clearance are still required on all DVA loans. A copy of the CRV is mailed to the person who ordered it and to the veteran-buyer.

Conventional Lenders and the New Appraisal Process

Conventional lenders have generally used a less complicated process than FHA or DVA in appraising the property. Typically, the borrower completes a loan application, which is reviewed by the lender or its loan correspondent. If the application and the accompanying required documentation are sufficient to proceed with a borrower's loan request, a credit report and appraisal are ordered.

In the past, local licensed staff or fee appraisers were contacted to conduct the appraisal. The newly enacted Home Valuation Code of Conduct (HVCC) establishes a much more complicated system whereby appraisals must be ordered via Appraisal Management Companies (AMCs). The new process can impact both the timeliness and the quality of the appraisal (see the Case & Point at the end of the chapter for details).

The process remains the same in that after an appraisal is completed, the lender reviews it for completeness as well as to determine whether the value of the property is sufficient for the loan request. While the appraisal is being done, the lender uses this time to acquire any additional information or lender "conditions" required to qualify the borrower.

The final loan amount is always based on the lesser of the purchase price or the appraised value. For instance, with a sales price of $580,000 and an appraised value of only $550,000, the lender will base the maximum loan on the lower $550,000 figure. If the appraisal were at a value of $600,000, then the lender would base the maximum loan on the lower sales price of $580,000.

Assuming that the appraisal issue is settled and the borrower is qualified, the entire loan package is submitted to a loan committee, or underwriter, who reviews the package and makes the final approval or rejection. If the loan committee or underwriter needs additional information prior to making a final decision, the request for additional information is sent back down the chain to the loan officer or correspondent.

New Rules Impact Appraisal Time Frames

New regulations (discussed in this chapter's Case & Point) continue to influence the entire appraisal process. Another new rule, the Mortgage Disclosure Improvement Act (MDIA) coupled with the HVCC rules, has seriously increased the time in which appraisals can be completed. Beginning July 30, 2009, the MDIA reemphasized that disclosures must be delivered to the customer within three days of receipt of an application. While several other mandates are included in the new legislation, the one affecting appraisals is that "no fee (except for a credit report fee) can be collected from the customer until delivery of the disclosures has occurred."

With few exceptions, lenders now require a "mini" loan package consisting of a loan application and credit report, among other items. Receipt of these items by the lender initiates the three-day notification period, after which an appraisal can be ordered. The other regulations contained in the legislation are beyond the scope of this book at this time.

Now, let's examine a likely time frame for acquiring an appraisal.

Day 1:   Loan application and supporting information sent to selected lender

Day 4:   Time frame elapses and appraisal can be ordered

Day 6:   Appraisal assigned through appraisal management company (AMC)

Day 8:   Appraiser views property, takes measurements and pictures

Day 11:   Appraiser completes report, including comparable information pictures

Day 12:   Lender receives completed appraisal from AMC and it is sent for review

Day 15:   Review process completed and appraisal deemed acceptable

With most lock periods now being 30 days, this optimum appraisal schedule takes up half of the timeline. If appraisal errors occur or conditions are imposed, the schedule may well have an impact on whether the loan is completed on time. How does this issue concern real estate licensees? When preparing purchase contracts, realtors must accommodate realistic time frames into their contracts.

8.2 APPRAISING A PROPERTY

Qualifying a property, via appraisal, is one of the most critical phases of the lending process. (Qualifying the borrower is another;

that is covered in the next chapter.) The lender relies on the appraisal report to determine the acceptability of the property as collateral. The main purpose of an appraisal is to estimate **fair market value (FMV)**, defined as "the most probable price in terms of money that a property should bring in a competitive and open market under all conditions requisite to a fair sale, the buyer and seller acting prudently, knowledgeably and assuming the price is not affected by undue stimulus." There are many reasons for appraisals—lending, insurance, income taxes, property taxation, probates to settle estates, divorce, bankruptcy, and other legal concerns. The reason for the appraisal will affect the appraiser's approach to the task. For example, insurance appraisals are done to estimate replacement value of the improvements and therefore are not concerned with land value.

In this chapter, we're concerned with appraisals only for loan purposes. In spite of new regulations affecting the appraisal process, the elements influencing value remain the same. Because what the appraiser does is so important, we need to know how the value of properties is determined.

Location

We've heard it said that "location, location, location" is essential in determining property value. It is logical, then, that the first thing the appraiser does when assigned an appraisal is to check out the location of the property. In analyzing the location, both city and neighborhood influences must be considered. But appraisers must not be influenced by lenders who may attempt to systematically exclude certain neighborhoods under a prohibited, discriminatory practice called **redlining**, discussed in Chapter 11.

Neighborhood Influence

Within a given city, there are many neighborhoods, each of which can vary greatly in quality and desirability. How do you check a neighborhood? In most cases, an appraiser looks at the same items a cautious buyer might evaluate. The main items that buyers and appraisers check when considering a neighborhood's influence are the following:

1. *Approach to the property.* This is the first thing of which a prospective buyer will be aware. To get to the property, do you drive through a pleasant neighborhood, or do you have to drive through a run-down area?

2. *Appeal of neighborhood.* Does the neighborhood have sales appeal? For example: Is it attractive? Does it have tree-lined streets? Is it

laid out in a grid pattern, or does it have winding streets with cul-de-sacs? Does it have overall "curb appeal"?

3. *Neighborhood homogeneity.* Are the properties all single-family dwellings, or is there a mixture of apartment houses and commercial buildings? Are the properties of about the same age and same price range? Homogeneous neighborhoods are considered more desirable by most buyers and therefore more desirable to lenders.

4. *Neighborhood condition.* Do the neighbors take care of their homes? Many appraisers identify this characteristic as "pride of ownership." You can easily determine pride of ownership by driving through the area and checking the landscaping and the exterior of the homes. Homes in well-maintained neighborhoods have greater value and marketability.

5. *Neighborhood trend.* An appraiser will carefully analyze the trend of the neighborhood. Is it stable, improving, or declining? Since the lender is concerned about the future of the property, this determination is very important. A neighborhood may be in a state of transition where single-family homes are being replaced by apartment houses. Have a lot of the homes been turned into rentals? These kinds of trends have an effect on the desirability of the neighborhood. Again, appraisers and lenders must guard against redlining.

6. *Adverse influences.* An example of an adverse influence would be property located next to a noisy freeway. Any adverse influence will affect the value of the property. Other identified adverse influences include airport flight patterns, slide and flood areas, climate (too foggy or windy), and obnoxious odors.

7. *Schools and shopping.* Buyers who have school-age children are interested in the proximity of schools. Proximity to shopping facilities is also important to a potential buyer.

8. *Other neighborhood amenities.* Appraisers also look for such items as curbs and gutters, libraries, and proximity to police and fire protection.

An experienced appraiser may already know the quality of the neighborhood since he or she usually works in a certain area. An appraiser who is not familiar with the neighborhood checks the area while driving to the property. Upon arriving at the property, the appraiser probably has a good idea of the quality of the neighborhood with his/her impression of driving through it.

There are other location features that the appraiser must check—see the sample appraisal form (Figure 8.1). Many appraisal forms are used, but they all contain the same basic information.

FIGURE 8.1   Residential appraisal report.

Uniform Residential Appraisal Report   File

The purpose of this summary appraisal report is to provide the lender/client with an accurate, and adequately supported, opinion of the market value of the subject property.

SUBJECT

Property Address		City	State	Zip Code

Borrower	Owner of Public Record	County

Legal Description

Assessor's Parcel #	Tax Year	R.E. Taxes $

Neighborhood Name	Map Reference	Census Tract

Occupant ☐ Owner ☐ Tenant ☐ Vacant   Special Assessments $ ☐ PUD   HOA $ ☐ per year ☐ per month

Property Rights Appraised ☐ Fee Simple ☐ Leasehold ☐ Other (describe)

Assignment Type ☐ Purchase Transaction ☐ Refinance Transaction ☐ Other (describe)

Lender/Client   Address

Is the subject property currently offered for sale or has it been offered for sale in the twelve months prior to the effective date of this appraisal? ☐ Yes ☐ No

Report data source(s) used, offering price(s), and date(s).

CONTRACT

I ☐ did ☐ did not analyze the contract for sale for the subject purchase transaction. Explain the results of the analysis of the contract for sale or why the analysis was not performed.

Contract Price $ Date of Contract   Is the property seller the owner of public record? ☐ Yes ☐ No Data Source(s)

Is there any financial assistance (loan charges, sale concessions, gift or downpayment assistance, etc.) to be paid by any party on behalf of the borrower? ☐ Yes ☐ No
If Yes, report the total dollar amount and describe the items to be paid.

NEIGHBORHOOD

Note: Race and the racial composition of the neighborhood are not appraisal factors.

Neighborhood Characteristics			One-Unit Housing Trends				One-Unit Housing		Present Land Use %	
Location ☐ Urban	☐ Suburban	☐ Rural	Property Values ☐ Increasing	☐ Stable	☐ Declining		PRICE	AGE	One-Unit	%
Built-Up ☐ Over 75%	☐ 25–75%	☐ Under 25%	Demand/Supply ☐ Shortage	☐ In Balance	☐ Over Supply		$ (000)	(yrs)	2-4 Unit	%
Growth ☐ Rapid	☐ Stable	☐ Slow	Marketing Time ☐ Under 3 mths	☐ 3–6 mths	☐ Over 6 mths		Low		Multi-Family	%
Neighborhood Boundaries							High		Commercial	%
							Pred.		Other	%

Neighborhood Description

Market Conditions (including support for the above conclusions)

SITE

Dimensions	Area	Shape	View

Specific Zoning Classification	Zoning Description

Zoning Compliance ☐ Legal ☐ Legal Nonconforming (Grandfathered Use) ☐ No Zoning ☐ Illegal (describe)

Is the highest and best use of the subject property as improved (or as proposed per plans and specifications) the present use? ☐ Yes ☐ No If No, describe

Utilities	Public	Other (describe)		Public	Other (describe)	Off-site Improvements—Type	Public	Private
Electricity	☐	☐	Water	☐	☐	Street	☐	☐
Gas	☐	☐	Sanitary Sewer	☐	☐	Alley	☐	☐

FEMA Special Flood Hazard Area ☐ Yes ☐ No FEMA Flood Zone   FEMA Map #   FEMA Map Date

Are the utilities and off-site improvements typical for the market area? ☐ Yes ☐ No If No, describe

Are there any adverse site conditions or external factors (easements, encroachments, environmental conditions, land uses, etc.)? ☐ Yes ☐ No If Yes, describe

IMPROVEMENTS

General Description		Foundation		Exterior Description	materials/condition	Interior	materials/condition
Units ☐ One	☐ One with Accessory Unit	☐ Concrete Slab	☐ Crawl Space	Foundation Walls		Floors	
# of Stories		☐ Full Basement	☐ Partial Basement	Exterior Walls		Walls	
Type ☐ Det. ☐ Att.	☐ S-Det./End Unit	Basement Area	sq. ft.	Roof Surface		Trim/Finish	
☐ Existing ☐ Proposed	☐ Under Const.	Basement Finish	%	Gutters & Downspouts		Bath Floor	
Design (Style)		☐ Outside Entry/Exit	☐ Sump Pump	Window Type		Bath Wainscot	
Year Built		Evidence of ☐ Infestation		Storm Sash/Insulated		Car Storage ☐ None	
Effective Age (Yrs)		☐ Dampness	☐ Settlement	Screens		☐ Driveway # of Cars	
Attic ☐ None		Heating ☐ FWA ☐ HWBB	☐ Radiant	Amenities	☐ Woodstove(s) #	Driveway Surface	
☐ Drop Stair ☐ Stairs		☐ Other	Fuel	☐ Fireplace(s) #	☐ Fence	☐ Garage # of Cars	
☐ Floor ☐ Scuttle		Cooling ☐ Central Air Conditioning		☐ Patio/Deck	☐ Porch	☐ Carport # of Cars	
☐ Finished ☐ Heated		☐ Individual	☐ Other	☐ Pool	☐ Other	☐ Att. ☐ Det. ☐ Built-in	

Appliances ☐ Refrigerator ☐ Range/Oven ☐ Dishwasher ☐ Disposal ☐ Microwave ☐ Washer/Dryer ☐ Other (describe)

Finished area **above** grade contains: Rooms   Bedrooms   Bath(s)   Square Feet of Gross Living Area Above Grade

Additional features (special energy efficient items, etc.)

Describe the condition of the property (including needed repairs, deterioration, renovations, remodeling, etc.)

Are there any physical deficiencies or adverse conditions that affect the livability, soundness, or structural integrity of the property? ☐ Yes ☐ No If Yes, describe

Does the property generally conform to the neighborhood (functional utility, style, condition, use, construction, etc.)? ☐ Yes ☐ No If No, describe

Freddie Mac Form 70 March 2005   Page 1 of 6   Fannie Mae Form 1004 March 2005

FIGURE 8.1   Residential appraisal report. *(continued)*

Uniform Residential Appraisal Report

File #

| There are | comparable properties currently offered for sale in the subject neighborhood ranging in price from $ | to $ |
| There are | comparable sales in the subject neighborhood within the past twelve months ranging in sale price from $ | to $ |

FEATURE	SUBJECT	COMPARABLE SALE # 1		COMPARABLE SALE # 2		COMPARABLE SALE # 3	
Address							
Proximity to Subject							
Sale Price	$		$		$		$
Sale Price/Gross Liv. Area	$ sq. ft.	$ sq. ft.		$ sq. ft.		$ sq. ft.	
Data Source(s)							
Verification Source(s)							
VALUE ADJUSTMENTS	DESCRIPTION	DESCRIPTION	+(-) $ Adjustment	DESCRIPTION	+(-) $ Adjustment	DESCRIPTION	+(-) $ Adjustment
Sale or Financing Concessions							
Date of Sale/Time							
Location							
Leasehold/Fee Simple							
Site							
View							
Design (Style)							
Quality of Construction							
Actual Age							
Condition							
Above Grade	Total Bdrms. Baths	Total Bdrms. Baths		Total Bdrms. Baths		Total Bdrms. Baths	
Room Count							
Gross Living Area	sq. ft.	sq. ft.		sq. ft.		sq. ft.	
Basement & Finished Rooms Below Grade							
Functional Utility							
Heating/Cooling							
Energy Efficient Items							
Garage/Carport							
Porch/Patio/Deck							
Net Adjustment (Total)		☐ + ☐ -	$	☐ + ☐ -	$	☐ + ☐ -	$
Adjusted Sale Price of Comparables		Net Adj. % Gross Adj. %	$	Net Adj. % Gross Adj. %	$	Net Adj. % Gross Adj. %	$

I ☐ did ☐ did not research the sale or transfer history of the subject property and comparable sales. If not, explain

My research ☐ did ☐ did not reveal any prior sales or transfers of the subject property for the three years prior to the effective date of this appraisal.
Data source(s)

My research ☐ did ☐ did not reveal any prior sales or transfers of the comparable sales for the year prior to the date of sale of the comparable sale.
Data source(s)

Report the results of the research and analysis of the prior sale or transfer history of the subject property and comparable sales (report additional prior sales on page 3).

ITEM	SUBJECT	COMPARABLE SALE # 1	COMPARABLE SALE # 2	COMPARABLE SALE # 3
Date of Prior Sale/Transfer				
Price of Prior Sale/Transfer				
Data Source(s)				
Effective Date of Data Source(s)				

Analysis of prior sale or transfer history of the subject property and comparable sales

Summary of Sales Comparison Approach

Indicated Value by Sales Comparison Approach $

Indicated Value by: Sales Comparison Approach $ Cost Approach (if developed) $ Income Approach (if developed) $

This appraisal is made ☐ "as is", ☐ subject to completion per plans and specifications on the basis of a hypothetical condition that the improvements have been completed, ☐ subject to the following repairs or alterations on the basis of a hypothetical condition that the repairs or alterations have been completed, or ☐ subject to the following required inspection based on the extraordinary assumption that the condition or deficiency does not require alteration or repair:

Based on a complete visual inspection of the interior and exterior areas of the subject property, defined scope of work, statement of assumptions and limiting conditions, and appraiser's certification, my (our) opinion of the market value, as defined, of the real property that is the subject of this report is $, as of   , which is the date of inspection and the effective date of this appraisal.

FIGURE 8.1   Residential appraisal report. *(continued)*

Uniform Residential Appraisal Report

File #

ADDITIONAL COMMENTS

COST APPROACH TO VALUE (not required by Fannie Mae)

Provide adequate information for the lender/client to replicate the below cost figures and calculations.

Support for the opinion of site value (summary of comparable land sales or other methods for estimating site value)

COST APPROACH

ESTIMATED ☐ REPRODUCTION OR ☐ REPLACEMENT COST NEW	OPINION OF SITE VALUE .... = $
Source of cost data	Dwelling Sq. Ft. @ $ .... = $
Quality rating from cost service Effective date of cost data	Sq. Ft. @ $ .... = $
Comments on Cost Approach (gross living area calculations, depreciation, etc.)	
	Garage/Carport Sq. Ft. @ $ .... = $
	Total Estimate of Cost-New .... = $
	Less Physical Functional External
	Depreciation = $( )
	Depreciated Cost of Improvements......................... = $
	"As-is" Value of Site Improvements.......................... = $
Estimated Remaining Economic Life (HUD and VA only) Years	Indicated Value By Cost Approach .... = $

INCOME APPROACH TO VALUE (not required by Fannie Mae)

INCOME

Estimated Monthly Market Rent $ X Gross Rent Multiplier   = $ Indicated Value by Income Approach

Summary of Income Approach (including support for market rent and GRM)

PROJECT INFORMATION FOR PUDs (if applicable)

PUD INFORMATION

Is the developer/builder in control of the Homeowners' Association (HOA)? ☐ Yes ☐ No   Unit type(s) ☐ Detached ☐ Attached

Provide the following information for PUDs ONLY if the developer/builder is in control of the HOA and the subject property is an attached dwelling unit.

Legal name of project

Total number of phases	Total number of units	Total number of units sold
Total number of units rented	Total number of units for sale	Data source(s)

Was the project created by the conversion of an existing building(s) into a PUD? ☐ Yes ☐ No If Yes, date of conversion

Does the project contain any multi-dwelling units? ☐ Yes ☐ No Data source(s)

Are the units, common elements, and recreation facilities complete? ☐ Yes ☐ No If No, describe the status of completion.

Are the common elements leased to or by the Homeowners' Association? ☐ Yes ☐ No If Yes, describe the rental terms and options.

Describe common elements and recreational facilities

FIGURE 8.1 Residential appraisal report. *(continued)*

Uniform Residential Appraisal Report   _{File #}

This report form is designed to report an appraisal of a one-unit property or a one-unit property with an accessory unit; including a unit in a planned unit development (PUD). This report form is not designed to report an appraisal of a manufactured home or a unit in a condominium or cooperative project.

This appraisal report is subject to the following scope of work, intended use, intended user, definition of market value, statement of assumptions and limiting conditions, and certifications. Modifications, additions, or deletions to the intended use, intended user, definition of market value, or assumptions and limiting conditions are not permitted. The appraiser may expand the scope of work to include any additional research or analysis necessary based on the complexity of this appraisal assignment. Modifications or deletions to the certifications are also not permitted. However, additional certifications that do not constitute material alterations to this appraisal report, such as those required by law or those related to the appraiser's continuing education or membership in an appraisal organization, are permitted.

SCOPE OF WORK: The scope of work for this appraisal is defined by the complexity of this appraisal assignment and the reporting requirements of this appraisal report form, including the following definition of market value, statement of assumptions and limiting conditions, and certifications. The appraiser must, at a minimum: (1) perform a complete visual inspection of the interior and exterior areas of the subject property, (2) inspect the neighborhood, (3) inspect each of the comparable sales from at least the street, (4) research, verify, and analyze data from reliable public and/or private sources, and (5) report his or her analysis, opinions, and conclusions in this appraisal report.

INTENDED USE: The intended use of this appraisal report is for the lender/client to evaluate the property that is the subject of this appraisal for a mortgage finance transaction.

INTENDED USER: The intended user of this appraisal report is the lender/client.

DEFINITION OF MARKET VALUE: The most probable price which a property should bring in a competitive and open market under all conditions requisite to a fair sale, the buyer and seller, each acting prudently, knowledgeably and assuming the price is not affected by undue stimulus. Implicit in this definition is the consummation of a sale as of a specified date and the passing of title from seller to buyer under conditions whereby: (1) buyer and seller are typically motivated; (2) both parties are well informed or well advised, and each acting in what he or she considers his or her own best interest; (3) a reasonable time is allowed for exposure in the open market; (4) payment is made in terms of cash in U. S. dollars or in terms of financial arrangements comparable thereto; and (5) the price represents the normal consideration for the property sold unaffected by special or creative financing or sales concessions* granted by anyone associated with the sale.

*Adjustments to the comparables must be made for special or creative financing or sales concessions. No adjustments are necessary for those costs which are normally paid by sellers as a result of tradition or law in a market area; these costs are readily identifiable since the seller pays these costs in virtually all sales transactions. Special or creative financing adjustments can be made to the comparable property by comparisons to financing terms offered by a third party institutional lender that is not already involved in the property or transaction. Any adjustment should not be calculated on a mechanical dollar for dollar cost of the financing or concession but the dollar amount of any adjustment should approximate the market's reaction to the financing or concessions based on the appraiser's judgment.

STATEMENT OF ASSUMPTIONS AND LIMITING CONDITIONS: The appraiser's certification in this report is subject to the following assumptions and limiting conditions:

1. The appraiser will not be responsible for matters of a legal nature that affect either the property being appraised or the title to it, except for information that he or she became aware of during the research involved in performing this appraisal. The appraiser assumes that the title is good and marketable and will not render any opinions about the title.

2. The appraiser has provided a sketch in this appraisal report to show the approximate dimensions of the improvements. The sketch is included only to assist the reader in visualizing the property and understanding the appraiser's determination of its size.

3. The appraiser has examined the available flood maps that are provided by the Federal Emergency Management Agency (or other data sources) and has noted in this appraisal report whether any portion of the subject site is located in an identified Special Flood Hazard Area. Because the appraiser is not a surveyor, he or she makes no guarantees, express or implied, regarding this determination.

4. The appraiser will not give testimony or appear in court because he or she made an appraisal of the property in question, unless specific arrangements to do so have been made beforehand, or as otherwise required by law.

5. The appraiser has noted in this appraisal report any adverse conditions (such as needed repairs, deterioration, the presence of hazardous wastes, toxic substances, etc.) observed during the inspection of the subject property or that he or she became aware of during the research involved in performing this appraisal. Unless otherwise stated in this appraisal report, the appraiser has no knowledge of any hidden or unapparent physical deficiencies or adverse conditions of the property (such as, but not limited to, needed repairs, deterioration, the presence of hazardous wastes, toxic substances, adverse environmental conditions, etc.) that would make the property less valuable, and has assumed that there are no such conditions and makes no guarantees or warranties, express or implied. The appraiser will not be responsible for any such conditions that do exist or for any engineering or testing that might be required to discover whether such conditions exist. Because the appraiser is not an expert in the field of environmental hazards, this appraisal report must not be considered as an environmental assessment of the property.

6. The appraiser has based his or her appraisal report and valuation conclusion for an appraisal that is subject to satisfactory completion, repairs, or alterations on the assumption that the completion, repairs, or alterations of the subject property will be performed in a professional manner.

FIGURE 8.1   Residential appraisal report. *(continued)*

Uniform Residential Appraisal Report   File

APPRAISER'S CERTIFICATION: The Appraiser certifies and agrees that:

1. I have, at a minimum, developed and reported this appraisal in accordance with the scope of work requirements stated in this appraisal report.

2. I performed a complete visual inspection of the interior and exterior areas of the subject property. I reported the condition of the improvements in factual, specific terms. I identified and reported the physical deficiencies that could affect the livability, soundness, or structural integrity of the property.

3. I performed this appraisal in accordance with the requirements of the Uniform Standards of Professional Appraisal Practice that were adopted and promulgated by the Appraisal Standards Board of The Appraisal Foundation and that were in place at the time this appraisal report was prepared.

4. I developed my opinion of the market value of the real property that is the subject of this report based on the sales comparison approach to value. I have adequate comparable market data to develop a reliable sales comparison approach for this appraisal assignment. I further certify that I considered the cost and income approaches to value but did not develop them, unless otherwise indicated in this report.

5. I researched, verified, analyzed, and reported on any current agreement for sale for the subject property, any offering for sale of the subject property in the twelve months prior to the effective date of this appraisal, and the prior sales of the subject property for a minimum of three years prior to the effective date of this appraisal, unless otherwise indicated in this report.

6. I researched, verified, analyzed, and reported on the prior sales of the comparable sales for a minimum of one year prior to the date of sale of the comparable sale, unless otherwise indicated in this report.

7. I selected and used comparable sales that are locationally, physically, and functionally the most similar to the subject property.

8. I have not used comparable sales that were the result of combining a land sale with the contract purchase price of a home that has been built or will be built on the land.

9. I have reported adjustments to the comparable sales that reflect the market's reaction to the differences between the subject property and the comparable sales.

10. I verified, from a disinterested source, all information in this report that was provided by parties who have a financial interest in the sale or financing of the subject property.

11. I have knowledge and experience in appraising this type of property in this market area.

12. I am aware of, and have access to, the necessary and appropriate public and private data sources, such as multiple listing services, tax assessment records, public land records and other such data sources for the area in which the property is located.

13. I obtained the information, estimates, and opinions furnished by other parties and expressed in this appraisal report from reliable sources that I believe to be true and correct.

14. I have taken into consideration the factors that have an impact on value with respect to the subject neighborhood, subject property, and the proximity of the subject property to adverse influences in the development of my opinion of market value. I have noted in this appraisal report any adverse conditions (such as, but not limited to, needed repairs, deterioration, the presence of hazardous wastes, toxic substances, adverse environmental conditions, etc.) observed during the inspection of the subject property or that I became aware of during the research involved in performing this appraisal. I have considered these adverse conditions in my analysis of the property value, and have reported on the effect of the conditions on the value and marketability of the subject property.

15. I have not knowingly withheld any significant information from this appraisal report and, to the best of my knowledge, all statements and information in this appraisal report are true and correct.

16. I stated in this appraisal report my own personal, unbiased, and professional analysis, opinions, and conclusions, which are subject only to the assumptions and limiting conditions in this appraisal report.

17. I have no present or prospective interest in the property that is the subject of this report, and I have no present or prospective personal interest or bias with respect to the participants in the transaction. I did not base, either partially or completely, my analysis and/or opinion of market value in this appraisal report on the race, color, religion, sex, age, marital status, handicap, familial status, or national origin of either the prospective owners or occupants of the subject property or of the present owners or occupants of the properties in the vicinity of the subject property or on any other basis prohibited by law.

18. My employment and/or compensation for performing this appraisal or any future or anticipated appraisals was not conditioned on any agreement or understanding, written or otherwise, that I would report (or present analysis supporting) a predetermined specific value, a predetermined minimum value, a range or direction in value, a value that favors the cause of any party, or the attainment of a specific result or occurrence of a specific subsequent event (such as approval of a pending mortgage loan application).

19. I personally prepared all conclusions and opinions about the real estate that were set forth in this appraisal report. If I relied on significant real property appraisal assistance from any individual or individuals in the performance of this appraisal or the preparation of this appraisal report, I have named such individual(s) and disclosed the specific tasks performed in this appraisal report. I certify that any individual so named is qualified to perform the tasks. I have not authorized anyone to make a change to any item in this appraisal report; therefore, any change made to this appraisal is unauthorized and I will take no responsibility for it.

20. I identified the lender/client in this appraisal report who is the individual, organization, or agent for the organization that ordered and will receive this appraisal report.

FIGURE 8.1 Residential appraisal report. *(continued)*

Uniform Residential Appraisal Report
File #

21. The lender/client may disclose or distribute this appraisal report to: the borrower; another lender at the request of the borrower; the mortgagee or its successors and assigns; mortgage insurers; government sponsored enterprises; other secondary market participants; data collection or reporting services; professional appraisal organizations; any department, agency, or instrumentality of the United States; and any state, the District of Columbia, or other jurisdictions; without having to obtain the appraiser's or supervisory appraiser's (if applicable) consent. Such consent must be obtained before this appraisal report may be disclosed or distributed to any other party (including, but not limited to, the public through advertising, public relations, news, sales, or other media).

22. I am aware that any disclosure or distribution of this appraisal report by me or the lender/client may be subject to certain laws and regulations. Further, I am also subject to the provisions of the Uniform Standards of Professional Appraisal Practice that pertain to disclosure or distribution by me.

23. The borrower, another lender at the request of the borrower, the mortgagee or its successors and assigns, mortgage insurers, government sponsored enterprises, and other secondary market participants may rely on this appraisal report as part of any mortgage finance transaction that involves any one or more of these parties.

24. If this appraisal report was transmitted as an "electronic record" containing my "electronic signature," as those terms are defined in applicable federal and/or state laws (excluding audio and video recordings), or a facsimile transmission of this appraisal report containing a copy or representation of my signature, the appraisal report shall be as effective, enforceable and valid as if a paper version of this appraisal report were delivered containing my original hand written signature.

25. Any intentional or negligent misrepresentation(s) contained in this appraisal report may result in civil liability and/or criminal penalties including, but not limited to, fine or imprisonment or both under the provisions of Title 18, United States Code, Section 1001, et seq., or similar state laws.

SUPERVISORY APPRAISER'S CERTIFICATION: The Supervisory Appraiser certifies and agrees that:

1. I directly supervised the appraiser for this appraisal assignment, have read the appraisal report, and agree with the appraiser's analysis, opinions, statements, conclusions, and the appraiser's certification.

2. I accept full responsibility for the contents of this appraisal report including, but not limited to, the appraiser's analysis, opinions, statements, conclusions, and the appraiser's certification.

3. The appraiser identified in this appraisal report is either a sub-contractor or an employee of the supervisory appraiser (or the appraisal firm), is qualified to perform this appraisal, and is acceptable to perform this appraisal under the applicable state law.

4. This appraisal report complies with the Uniform Standards of Professional Appraisal Practice that were adopted and promulgated by the Appraisal Standards Board of The Appraisal Foundation and that were in place at the time this appraisal report was prepared.

5. If this appraisal report was transmitted as an "electronic record" containing my "electronic signature," as those terms are defined in applicable federal and/or state laws (excluding audio and video recordings), or a facsimile transmission of this appraisal report containing a copy or representation of my signature, the appraisal report shall be as effective, enforceable and valid as if a paper version of this appraisal report were delivered containing my original hand written signature.

APPRAISER

Signature_____
Name _____
Company Name _____
Company Address_____

_____
Telephone Number _____
Email Address_____
Date of Signature and Report_____
Effective Date of Appraisal _____
State Certification #_____
or State License #_____
or Other (describe) _____ State #_____
State _____
Expiration Date of Certification or License _____

ADDRESS OF PROPERTY APPRAISED

_____
_____
APPRAISED VALUE OF SUBJECT PROPERTY $ _____
LENDER/CLIENT
Name _____
Company Name _____
Company Address_____
_____
Email Address_____

SUPERVISORY APPRAISER (ONLY IF REQUIRED)

Signature_____
Name _____
Company Name _____
Company Address_____

_____
Telephone Number _____
Email Address_____
Date of Signature _____
State Certification #_____
or State License #_____
State _____
Expiration Date of Certification or License _____

SUBJECT PROPERTY

☐ Did not inspect subject property
☐ Did inspect exterior of subject property from street
   Date of Inspection _____
☐ Did inspect interior and exterior of subject property
   Date of Inspection _____

COMPARABLE SALES

☐ Did not inspect exterior of comparable sales from street
☐ Did inspect exterior of comparable sales from street
   Date of Inspection _____

At the Property

At the property, the appraiser remains outside and asks, Does the house fit in with the rest of the neighborhood? Is it in about the same price range or is it overimproved or underimproved? What is the sales appeal of the house? Are the exterior and landscaping well maintained? The answers to these questions have a significant bearing on the value of the property and will be included in the appraiser's remarks in the neighborhood section of the appraisal form.

8.3 USING A STANDARD APPRAISAL FORM

A completed appraisal form is used by the lender to determine the acceptability of the property as security and to set the amount of the loan. The form shown in Figure 8.1 is the standard used by Fannie Mae and Freddie Mac. Since its adoption by the agencies, most lenders have come to use it as well. The following is a discussion of the three basic sections of the appraisal form (Figure 8.1) which include neighborhood characteristics and trends, property description and information, and valuation.

Neighborhood

Following the identification of the property at the top of the appraisal form is the neighborhood section. A **neighborhood** is a group of properties relatively similar in land use and value. It can be large or as small as a single block or street. Some of the items that are important when analyzing a neighborhood are listed on the form and are discussed below.

Supply and Demand

If supply and demand is not in balance, it can affect prices in the neighborhood. For example, if there were an oversupply of houses, a buyer's market could exist and forced sales could result, which would depress property values. The increase in foreclosures and short sales in 2009 severely affected home values in most California communities.

Price Range

The price range of properties in a neighborhood are important because, with that information, we can determine if the subject property is over- or underimproved. If the sales price of the property exceeded the upper price level, it would be an overimprovement. Overimprovements have less marketability, because they may not be acceptable to the average buyer. A property with a sales price below the lower price level (underimprovement) generally has good marketability because it provides buyers an opportunity to live in a neighborhood they want but could not otherwise afford. It also provides the new buyer an opportunity to improve the property and enjoy the ensuing increase in value.

Neighborhood Description

The appraiser will summarize the items in a neighborhood that buyers consider to be of importance. These are a few of the main items:

1. *Employment stability.* An area where employment is provided primarily by just one industry would not have good employment stability. Small towns built around a lumber mill or auto manufacturing plant or a community that depends primarily on the computer and software industry are all good examples. A severe depression of any one such industry can caused wide spread unemployment.

2. *Convenience to employment, shopping, and schools.* Buyers care about these convenience factors, in terms of both time and mileage. As the cost of operating an automobile increases, these factors become more important.

3. *Protection from detrimental conditions.* A detrimental condition in a neighborhood affects the marketability and, therefore, the value of the property. Examples of detrimental conditions the appraiser checks for are high vacancy rate, poorly maintained properties, abandoned properties (e.g., maybe caused by increased foreclosures), obnoxious odors, poor climate, and annoying airport flight patterns.

Property

After the neighborhood has been analyzed, the appraiser inspects the site and the physical property. This portion of the report is divided into various sections: site, improvements, room list, interior finish and equipment, and a property rating.

Site

As the appraiser checks the site, these are some of the items that are carefully analyzed:

1. *Zoning.* It is important to know if the improvements conform to the current zoning of the site. If they do not, there may be a problem, since nonconforming properties generally cannot be reconstructed if destroyed. If the lender is positive that a new building permit would not be issued, it may deny the loan enitrely. Note: Older properties may be "grandfathered in" regarding

their zoning. The city or county may provide what is called a "burn-down" letter, indicating that the property, in its current state, could be rebuilt if it were, for any reason, destroyed.

2. *The lot.* The topography and drainage on a lot could be very important. A home built on a steep hillside could be subject to earth slides, particularly if there are drainage problems. The appraiser may reduce the value of a large parcel as "excess land" or mostly unusable property. A lender, in turn, may allow value for only 10 acres of a 20-acre parcel.

3. *Flood area.* If the property is located in a HUD-identified flood area, the property must carry flood insurance if a loan is made. It is the responsibility of the lender to make sure flood insurance is obtained, if required. The Federal Emergency Management Agency (FEMA) maintains flood maps. Designations do change and any property located in a low-lying area or near a stream, lake, or other body of water should be checked against the appropriate map. Most sales also include a Natural Hazards Report, which also shows this possible issue.

Improvements, Room List, Interior Finish and Equipment, Property Rating

These sections of the report serve as a good checklist while the appraiser is inspecting the property. The appraiser starts by checking the exterior of the improvements. The number and type of rooms and the floor plan are the next items noted.

The appraiser carefully checks for poor structural designs or unusual floor plans that could affect marketability of the property. This is referred to as **functional obsolescence**, a loss in value from sources within the property that affect its usability. In contrast, **economic obsolescence** is a loss in value from forces outside of the property that cannot be changed, such as adverse zoning or a freeway behind the property.

Examples of functional obsolescence include houses with unusual floor plans. To illustrate, a house located in a prime San Francisco Bay area was well built, in excellent condition, and nearly 3,500 square feet in living space. The problem? The home had only one bedroom, which seriously affected its marketability.

Other examples of problem floor plans include five bedrooms with one bath; access to the bath through another bedroom; and a bathroom opening into the kitchen, as was common for homes built in the 1920s.

While inspecting the interior of the building, the appraiser notes the condition of the paint, floor, kitchen equipment, and garage. The appraiser looks for signs of problems; water stains or moisture could be evidence of a roof or plumbing leak. Structural problems are far more serious than cosmetic problems; sagging floors, sticky doors, and large cracks could be caused by a settling foundation or a shifting of the structure—all forms of **physical depreciation**.

Photographs and Square Footage Measurement

In addition to the appraisal, lenders require a photograph of the front of the property, the street it is located on, and the side and back yards. Appraisers are not allowed to submit photos of the property with people visible. Banks have to be careful not to discriminate, as mentioned above, and this is one way they avoid it. The appraiser must also obtain the square footage of the house, since this information is used in calculating the value.

To obtain the square footage, the appraiser measures the house from the outside and draws a sketch as shown in Figure 8.2. The photographs and the sketch are attached to the report when it is completed.

FIGURE 8.2   Computing square footage.

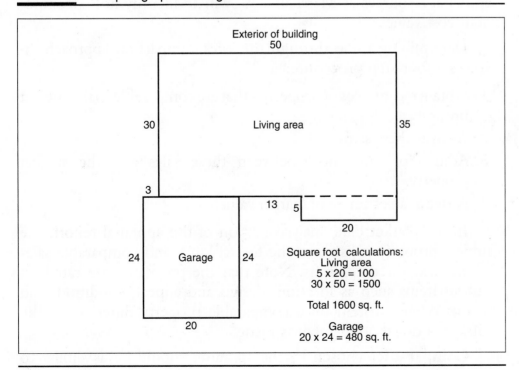

Valuation

The valuation section outlines market data, cost, and income approaches that will aid in determining market value.

Sales Comparison Approach

The basis of the **sales comparison approach** to value, also popularly called **market data approach**, is that a buyer will not pay more for a property than the cost of acquiring an equally desirable substitute property. This is what economists refer to as the "principle of substitution." For example, assume a property is for sale at $500,000. In the same neighborhood, there are two other properties with the same amenities that are for sale at $475,000. A buyer will not pay $500,000 when an equally desirable property is available at $475,000. Therefore, the first property is not worth $500,000, because knowledgeable buyers will not pay that much.

Buyers and real estate salespeople use a simplified market data approach when valuing property. To arrive at a value of a property, they seek answers to these questions: What properties have sold recently that are similar to the subject property? How did these properties compare with the subject? How much are those differences worth? After subtracting or adding for the differences, called **adjustments**, they arrive at a value for the subject property. Appraisers use the same procedure; however, they do it in a more systematic and precise manner, utilizing such specialized types of appraisal resources as Marshall and Swift to identify home component cost values.

Determining value through the sales comparison approach involves a four-step procedure:

1. Obtain recent sales of properties that are comparable to the subject property.
2. Analyze these sales.
3. Adjust for differences between these sales and the subject property.
4. Arrive at an estimate of market value.

In the market data analysis section of the appraisal report, the subject property is listed in the first column and comparable sales in the next three columns. Note that the properties are rated on various items such as location, design and appeal, condition, and so on. When an item on a comparable property differs from the subject, a dollar adjustment is made.

Comparables chosen by the appraiser should be as similar to the subject property as possible, because this minimizes the need for and size of dollar adjustments, which ordinarily should not exceed 15 percent. The appraiser attempts to obtain comparables that have sold recently and are in the same neighborhood. This reduces the need for time and location differences. Dollar adjustments should reflect the market reaction to the differences, not necessarily the cost of the differences. For example, swimming pools, intercom systems, and elaborate landscaping may not increase market value to the full extent of their cost.

Appraisers must pay particular attention to the "Sales or Financing Concessions" item. This item includes adjustments for different types of financing that can affect the sales price. Examples include the seller carrying back a loan at a lower rate than the market, the buyer assuming a loan at a low rate, and the seller paying points to enable the buyer to obtain an interest buy-down loan. When sellers pay points, they usually increase the price of the property to cover the cost of the points. The appraisal must then reflect the increased price. Examples of sales concessions are gifts of merchandise such as a new car with the purchase of a home.

Note: An appraiser must indicate whether a purchase contract has been reviewed. It is the purchase contract that will provide information about finance concessions, personal property, if any, included in the sales price, and whether the seller is paying all or part of the buyer's closing costs. When personal property (e.g., refrigerator, washing machine or dryer) is included in the contract, the appraiser often comments that they "do not affect" the appraised value or, in other words, they have been given no value.

Because choosing good comparables is so important, appraisers use many sources in obtaining information on comparable sales, including the following:

1. The appraiser's own files.
2. Multiple listing service of real estate boards.
3. Real estate agents.
4. Public records (county assessor and recorder via documentary transfer tax shown on deeds).
5. Web-based sites. These have proliferated in recent years; however, the data contained on them is viewed cautiously as they are often inaccurate and out dated.

Note how the adjustments are handled: If the item on the comparable property is superior to the subject property, a *minus* (–) adjustment is made. If *inferior*, a plus (+) adjustment is made. After the adjustments have been made for each comparable, they are totaled at the bottom of the column. This plus or minus total is applied to the sales price of the comparable to arrive at an indicated value of the subject property.

The appraiser's next task is to arrive at one figure, which represents the "indicated value by sales comparison approach." There is no formula that the appraiser can use. You cannot average the three results and come up with a figure. It is a matter of exercising good judgment. Typically, appraisers give the greatest weight to the comparable sale that required the least adjustments.

Declining Values Affected the Use of Comparables

By 2008, the economic downturn in housing was pronounced and declining home values were commonplace. Appraisers are required to include additional information to satisfy lenders that a given property is indeed sufficient collateral for the requested loan amount. The comparable section of the appraisal has to reflect several current listings as well as the most recent sales. Appraisers must now provide a market conditions report which identifies the number of properties currently on the market within the property's price range and the rate of sales (called the absorption rate). Recent short sales and foreclosure transactions have to be included. In spite of the fact that these sales are accompanied by the appraisers' comment that "as a distress sale, the value does not reflect a typical sale between a willing buyer and a willing seller," lenders sometimes allow these lower sales to affect their value decisions.

Cost Approach

Cost approach is based on the principle that property is worth what it would cost to duplicate. Adjustments to cost are made to allow for any loss in value due to economic age, condition, and other factors that reduce marketability.

Determining value through the cost approach involves a three-step procedure:

1. Estimate the total cost to reproduce the structure at current prices.
2. Subtract the estimated depreciation from all sources.
3. Add the estimated value of the land, based on the comparison or market data approach.

Note: The cost approach is the most reliable method of establishing value for a unique property (e.g., church, school).

Income Approach

The principle of the **income approach** is that there is relationship between the income the property can earn and the property's value. On owner-occupied homes, an appraiser may omit the income approach on the theory that an owner-occupied home will not be rented. But if an income approach is used on a home, the appraiser will usually use a **gross rent multiplier (GRM)**, instead of standard income approach to value.

Gross rent multipliers are ratios that state the relationship between gross rental income and sales price. They are typically used on an annual basis. GRMs provide a ballpark amount and not a precise figure of value.

The formula for the gross rent multiplier is:

$$\frac{\text{Sales Price}}{\text{Gross Annual Rent}} = \text{Gross Rent Multiplier (GRM) on an annual basis}$$

Example: A single family home sold for $500,000. The property could be rented for $2,500 per month. What is the GRM?

Solution:

$$\text{Annual basis}: \frac{\$500,000}{\$30,000(\$2,500 \text{ month} \times 12 \text{ months})} = 16.67 = \text{GRM}$$

To establish a valid market GRM, the appraiser must locate similar properties in comparable neighborhoods that were recently sold or rented at the time of the appraisal. Sometimes it may be difficult to establish a market GRM because of the lack of recent information. However, once a valid market GRM is established, the appraiser uses the following formula to arrive at indicated value.

$$\text{Subject Property's Annual Rent} \times \text{Market GRM} = \text{Indicated Value}$$

Example: On another property, an appraiser determines that the market rent should be $2,000 per month. What is the indicated value?

Solution: $24,000 annual rent ($2,000 × 12) × 16.67 GRM = $400,080 Indicated Value

---

On larger-income properties such as apartment buildings, office buildings, and shopping centers, the standard income approach—often called the **capitalization** method—is used. This approach determines the present value of a property based on the net operating income of the property (or property income less property expenses; this does *not* include any loan payments).

The standard income approach uses this procedure:

1. Calculate the annual gross scheduled income (GSI), which is income from all sources (including any parking or laundry income), assuming 100 percent occupancy.

2. From the GSI, deduct reasonable vacancy and collection losses to arrive at the **gross operating income**.

3. Estimate all expenses such as taxes, wages, utilities, insurance, repairs, and management, and deduct them from the gross operating income to determine the **net operating income (NOI)**. It is important to note that mortgage payments, called debt service, are not considered an operating expense.

4. The **capitalization rate** is the rate of return that an investor would seek as a reasonable return on an investment as if he was paying all cash for the property. Again, the cap rate does not include any debt service.

5. Divide the market capitalization rate into the subject property's net operating income.

$$\frac{\text{Subject Property's Net Operating Income}}{\text{Market Capitalization Rate}} = \text{Indicated value}$$

Example: Small Rental Property:

Annual Gross Scheduled Income	$100,000
Less : Vacancy and Collection Losses	−5,000
Equals : Gross Operating Income	$95,000
Less : Annual Operating Expenses	−35,000
Equals : Net Operating Income	$60,000

Assume Market Capitalization Rate (Cap Rate) @ 8 percent

$$\frac{\$60{,}000 \text{ Net Operating Income}}{8 \text{ percent Market Capitalization Rate}} = 750{,}000 \text{ Indicated Value}$$

Final Market Value

The appraiser's approach to determine value, called a final reconciliation, depends on the type of property being appraised. In the appraisal of single-family properties, more weight is given to the sales comparison or market approach because it is the most reliable. The cost approach is not as reliable, because it is difficult to estimate depreciation and to determine the value of land in a built-up neighborhood. The cost approach is best used for special-purpose properties such as churches, schools, government buildings, and anything unusual that does not sell routinely in the marketplace. The use of a gross rent multiplier may not be used in appraising a single-family owner-occupied property, because the majority of buyers do not buy them for income purposes.

Next, the appraiser analyzes the data used in the report for completeness and reliability. The final step is to arrive at market value. Again, this is not an averaging process, but one in which the appraiser evaluates each approach, then selects a single estimate of value.

Sales Price versus Fair Market Value

The sales price and the fair market value of a property are not always the same. Some reasons for the differences may be an unknowledgeable buyer or seller, financing concessions (seller paying fees or points or carrying a loan), personal property included in the sale, or a seller under pressure to sell.

Appraisers realize that appraising is not an exact science and that a lot of judgment is involved. Although the value of a property cannot be pinpointed, appraisers know that the sales price is one of the best indications of value. If the data in the appraisal report are adequate and reliable, then the lender should have no problem accepting the sales price as market value. If the figures are different, the lender bases the loan on the sales price or the appraised value, whichever is lower.

8.4 UNDERWRITING THE APPRAISAL

After the appraisal has been completed, it may also undergo a review process, either by an in-house appraiser or a review appraiser. Then, the appraisal is ready for underwriting by the lender. The purpose of underwriting is to determine if the property is acceptable by lender standards and if the market value supports the loan requested and meets the lender's requirements in other ways. The lender may alter the terms or conditions of a borrower's loan request based on the appraisal findings. For example, if the appraisal indicates that the roof leaks, the lender may add a condition to the loan approval that the roof be repaired.

Underwriting the appraisal is only one portion of the whole loan underwriting process wherein the borrower must also be approved as eligible for the requested loan. In an unpredictable economic market (as evidenced beginning in late 2007 through 2009) the appraisal can take on additional importance. The reviewer is useful, for instance, in helping the lender evaluate the future value of the property because, in case of foreclosure, there must be sufficient value to cover the loan. Lenders are very concerned about the early years of the mortgage. If the underwriter is certain, and able to document, that value will likely decrease during the first one to five years, then the terms of the loan may be adjusted (such as reducing the loan amount).

8.5 PLANNED UNIT DEVELOPMENTS AND CONDOMINIUMS

Many **planned unit developments (PUDs)** and **condominiums** have been built in the United States and it is important that you know what they are and how they are appraised. It is important because some lenders have different loan policies on PUDs and condominiums as opposed to single-family homes.

A PUD or condominium can be defined as a type of development, usually accompanied by a specific management process. A PUD refers to separate, individual fee ownership of a lot and dwelling. In addition, you own a proportionately undivided interest jointly with others in the development of the common areas and any recreational facilities. A typical PUD is illustrated in Figure 8.3. While sometimes called a townhouse development, the term *townhouse* refers to a type of architecture and not the type of ownership. A PUD could be a group of single-family homes if there were joint ownership of a common area. In a PUD, there is no one living in the "airspace" above anyone else. A de minimus PUD, a common development in California, is one in which the common areas are limited (e.g., greenbelts, parking areas, playground) and have minimal affect on value.

A condominium (see Figure 8.3) is a type of development in which a person owns a specified residential unit (three-dimensional airspace), together with an undivided interest in all the land including recreational facilities. A condominium may be part of a high rise, attached row house, or even a single-family detached development. In a legal sense, a condominium owner acquires a fee title interest in the airspace of the particular unit and an undivided interest (with the other condominium owners) in the land plus all other common areas such as hallways, elevators, utility rooms, carports, and recreational facilities.

Both PUDs and condominiums have homeowner association (HOA) groups that are responsible for the management of the development. These groups meet regularly and are governed by specific regulations. It is the association's responsibility to maintain the common areas. It also sets the dues that each owner must pay

FIGURE 8.3   (a) A typical PUD (b) A typical condominium.

(a)

(b)

in order to maintain the common areas and the exteriors of the individual structures. To be eligible for loans, occupancy ratios are reviewed, with lenders usually requiring a high owner-occupancy ratio compared to the number of rental units within the project. A review of the budget will reveal if owners are current on dues and if sufficient reserves are in place for anticipated future repairs. Finally, the officers will most likely have to be covered by errors and omissions Insurance. As a side note, FHA loans require a condo complex to be "approved," which fulfills the FHA's concerns above. PUDs, however, are not required to complete this process.

A lender appraising a PUD or condominium unit is interested in more than just that particular unit. The lender is interested in the overall project, because the value of one unit is affected by the quality and the operation of the entire project. For this reason, the lender will review, in addition to the budget mentioned above, the Articles of Incorporation, the Covenants, Conditions & Restrictions (CC&Rs) and the bylaws. When an appraiser appraises a PUD or condominium, these are some of the items checked:

1. General appearance of the project.
2. Recreational and other amenities that are adequate and well maintained.
3. Adequate parking for owners and guests.
4. Maintenance of common areas.

A unit in a PUD or condominium is appraised basically the same way as a single-family dwelling. The appraiser uses the three approaches to value and relies primarily on the market data approach in arriving at a final value.

Figure 8.4 is the uniform FNMA/FHLMC rider attached to condominium loans.

Figure 8.5 is the FNMA/FHLMC rider for PUD loans.

8.6 THE LICENSING OF REAL ESTATE APPRAISERS

Federal law has created the requirement that real estate appraisers must be licensed if the property transaction requires financing by a lender that is insured or backed by a federal agency, such as the Federal Deposit Insurance Corporation and similar such agencies. Under federal law, each state is charged with enforcing the law within their borders. In California, the Office of Real Estate Appraisers (OREA) is the enforcement agency.

As of 2009, there are four levels of real estate appraiser licensing. They are:

1. *Trainee License*. A trainee cannot do an appraisal on his/her own. He/she can only work under the technical supervision of a licensed appraiser.
2. *Residential License*. This license allows a person to appraise non-complex, one-to-four-unit residential property up to a transaction

FIGURE 8.4   FNMA/FHLMC condominium rider.

CONDOMINIUM RIDER

THIS CONDOMINIUM RIDER is made this   day of   ,   ,
and is incorporated into and shall be deemed to amend and supplement the Mortgage, Deed of Trust or Security Deed (the "Security Instrument") of the same date given by the undersigned (the "Borrower") to secure Borrower's Note to

(the "Lender")

of the same date and covering the Property described in the Security Instrument and located at:

[Property Address]

The Property includes a unit in, together with an undivided interest in the common elements of, a condominium project known as:

[Name of Condominium Project]

(the "Condominium Project"). If the owners association or other entity which acts for the Condominium Project (the "Owners Association") holds title to property for the benefit or use of its members or shareholders, the Property also includes Borrower's interest in the Owners Association and the uses, proceeds and benefits of Borrower's interest.

CONDOMINIUM COVENANTS. In addition to the covenants and agreements made in the Security Instrument, Borrower and Lender further covenant and agree as follows:

A. Condominium Obligations. Borrower shall perform all of Borrower's obligations under the Condominium Project's Constituent Documents. The "Constituent Documents" are the: (i) Declaration or any other document which creates the Condominium Project; (ii) by-laws; (iii) code of regulations; and (iv) other equivalent documents. Borrower shall promptly pay, when due, all dues and assessments imposed pursuant to the Constituent Documents.

B. Hazard Insurance. So long as the Owners Association maintains, with a generally accepted insurance carrier, a "master" or "blanket" policy on the Condominium Project which is satisfactory to Lender and which provides insurance coverage in the amounts, for the periods, and against the hazards Lender requires, including fire and hazards included within the term "extended coverage," then:

(i) Lender waives the provision in Uniform Covenant 2 for the monthly payment to Lender of one-twelfth of the yearly premium installments for hazard insurance on the Property; and

(ii) Borrower's obligation under Uniform Covenant 5 to maintain hazard insurance coverage on the Property is deemed satisfied to the extent that the required coverage is provided by the Owners Association policy.

Borrower shall give Lender prompt notice of any lapse in required hazard insurance coverage.

In the event of a distribution of hazard insurance proceeds in lieu of restoration or repair following a loss to the Property, whether to the unit or to common elements, any proceeds payable to Borrower are hereby assigned and shall be paid to Lender for application to the sums secured by the Security Instrument, with any excess paid to Borrower.

C. Public Liability Insurance. Borrower shall take such actions as may be reasonable to insure that the Owners Association maintains a public liability insurance policy acceptable in form, amount, and extent of coverage to Lender.

D. Condemnation. The proceeds of any award or claim for damages, direct or consequential, payable to Borrower in connection with any condemnation or other taking of all or any part of the Property, whether of the unit or of the common elements, or for any conveyance in lieu of condemnation, are hereby assigned and shall be paid to Lender. Such proceeds shall be applied by Lender to the sums secured by the Security Instrument as provided in Uniform Covenant 10.

E. Lender's Prior Consent. Borrower shall not, except after notice to Lender and with Lender's prior written consent, either partition or subdivide the Property or consent to:

(i) The abandonment or termination of the Condominium Project, except for abandonment or termination required by law in the case of substantial destruction by fire or other casualty or in the case of a taking by condemnation or eminent domain;

(ii) any amendment to any provision of the Constituent Documents if the provision is for the express benefit of Lender;

(iii) termination of professional management and assumption of self-management of the Owners Association; or

(iv) any action which would have the effect of rendering the public liability insurance coverage maintained by the Owners Association unacceptable to Lender.

F. Remedies. If Borrower does not pay condominium dues and assessments when due, then Lender may pay them. Any amounts disbursed by Lender under this paragraph F shall become additional debt of Borrower secured by the Security Instrument. Unless Borrower and Lender agree to other terms of payment, these amounts shall bear interest from the date of disbursement at the Note rate and shall be payable, with interest, upon notice from Lender to Borrower requesting payment.

BY SIGNING BELOW, Borrower accepts and agrees to the terms and provisions contained in this Condominium Rider.

_____ (Seal)   _____ (Seal)
                                      -Borrower   -Borrower

_____ (Seal)   _____ (Seal)
                                      -Borrower   -Borrower

MULTISTATE CONDOMINIUM RIDER -- Single Family -- **Fannie Mae/Freddie Mac UNIFORM INSTRUMENT**   **Form 3140 9/90**
ITEM 1623L0 (9102)   Great Lakes Business Forms, Inc. ■ To Order Call: 1-800-530-9393 ☐ FAX 616-791-1131

FIGURE 8.5   FNMA/FHLMC planned unit development rider.

PLANNED UNIT DEVELOPMENT RIDER

THIS PLANNED UNIT DEVELOPMENT ("PUD") RIDER is made this . . . . .day of
. . . ., 20 . . . ., and is incorporated into and shall be deemed to amend and supplement
a Mortgage, Deed of Trust or Deed to Secure Debt (herein "security instrument") dated of even date herewith, given by
the undersigned (herein "Borrower") to secure Borrower's Note to . . . .
. . . .(herein "Lender") and covering the Property described in the
security instrument and located at . . . .
                                                                       (Property Address)
. . . . The Property comprises a parcel of land improved with a dwelling, which, together with
other such parcels and certain common areas and facilities, all as described in . . . .
. . . .
. . . .
(herein "Declaration"), forms a planned unit development known as . . . .
. . . .
                                                        (Name of Planned Unit Development)
(herein "PUD").

PLANNED UNIT DEVELOPMENT COVENANTS. In addition to the covenants and agreements made in the security
instrument, Borrower and Lender further covenant and agree as follows:
   A. PUD Obligations. Borrower shall perform all of Borrower's obligations under the: (i) Declaration; (ii)
articles of incorporation, trust instrument or any equivalent document required to establish the homeowners
association or equivalent entity managing the common areas and facilities of the PUD (herein "Owners Association");
and (iii) by-laws, if any, or other rules or regulations of the Owners Association. Borrower shall promptly pay, when
due, all assessments imposed by the Owners Association.
   B. Hazard Insurance. In the event of a distribution of hazard insurance proceeds in lieu of restoration or repair
following a loss to the common areas and facilities of the PUD, any such proceeds payable to Borrower are hereby
assigned and shall be paid to Lender for application to the sums secured by the security instrument, with the excess,
if any, paid to Borrower.
   C. Condemnation. The proceeds of any award or claim for damages, direct or consequential, payable to
Borrower in connection with any condemnation or other taking of all or any part of the common areas and facilities
of the PUD, or for any conveyance in lieu of condemnation, are hereby assigned and shall be paid to Lender. Such
proceeds shall be applied by Lender to the sums secured by the security instrument in the manner provided under
Uniform Covenant 9.
   D. Lender's Prior Consent. Borrower shall not, except after notice to Lender and with Lender's prior written
consent, consent to:
   (i) the abandonment or termination of the PUD;
   (ii) any material amendment to the Declaration, trust instrument, articles of incorporation, by-laws of the
Owners Association, or any equivalent constituent document of the PUD, including, but not limited to, any
amendment which would change the percentage interests of the unit owners in the common areas and facilities of
the PUD;
   (iii) the effectuation of any decision by the Owners Association to terminate professional management and
assume self-management of the PUD; or
   (iv) the transfer, release, encumbrance, partition or subdivision of all or any part of the PUD's common areas
and facilities, except as to the Owners Association's right to grant easements for utilities and similar or related purposes.
   **E. Remedies. If Borrower breaches Borrower's covenants and agreements hereunder, including the covenant
to pay when due planned unit development assessments, then Lender may invoke any remedies provided under the
security instrument, including, but not limited to, those provided under Uniform Covenant 7.**

   IN WITNESS WHEREOF, Borrower has executed this PUD Rider.

value of $1 million, and nonresidential property up to a transaction
value of $250,000.

3. *Certified Residential License.* This license allows a person to appraise all one-to-four-unit residential property without regard to complexity or value, and nonresidential property up to a transaction value of $250,000.

4. *Certified General License.* This license allows a person to appraise all types of property without any value or complexity restrictions. Certified General is currently the highest level of licensed appraiser.

There are various educational and experience requirements for each license level, and these requirements are subject to change. For the latest requirements, contact the Office of Real Estate Appraisers website at www.orea.ca.gov.

It is important to note that a real estate licensee may provide what is called a **comparative market analysis (CMA)** outlining what other similar properties have sold for, but under no circumstance can the real estate licensee call this a certified appraisal, unless the real estate licensee also holds an appropriate, separate appraisal license. A **certified appraisal report** is any written communication of an analysis, opinion, or conclusion relating to the value that is termed certified. For property containing one to four residential units, almost all appraisers use the standard FNMA/FHLMC appraisal form, illustrated in Figure 8.1. The details go beyond the scope of this text but are thoroughly covered in any appraisal course.

8.7 WORKING WITH APPRAISERS: THE DO'S AND DON'TS

People in the real estate business who are involved in buying or selling will come into contact with appraisers. The new rules have redefined how we can relate to appraisers. In an attempt to avoid undue influence or coercion of an appraiser, real estate licensees and mortgage lenders are now prohibited from contacting an appraiser directly. All contact is to be made from the mortgage originator to the lender to the **appraisal management company (AMC)** and to the appraiser, and all via e-mail or the AMCs electronic system. The process can be lengthy and unsatisfactory, especially when trying to resolve a problem and/or error in an appraisal. In reality, licensees will likely have some contact with the appraiser during scheduling and inspections. It pays to know the current "do's and don'ts" in dealing with appraisers.

1. *Access to property.* Upon ordering the appraisal, instructions about whom to contact and how to access the property are conveyed. The real estate licensee is often identified as the contact person and is the one with whom the appraiser makes arrangements for access. This appraiser relationship has not changed: Make it easy for the appraiser to see the property. Be on time for the appointment. If the appraiser is to meet the owner, be certain that the owner will be there. Nothing irritates an appraiser more than to be told to go directly to the property because "the owner is always home." Then, when the appraiser arrives, no one is there. Be considerate of his or her time, and make it convenient to see the property.

2. *At the property.* Whether the owner or salesperson is at the property when the appraiser arrives, do not follow the appraiser around the property. Some people do this while talking constantly about all the good features of the property. Do not distract the appraiser; however, most appraisers welcome any information on the property that would be helpful to them. Be available, but not pushy. It might be helpful, for instance, to give the appraiser a printed list of those special amenities that may not be obvious in an initial observation. Prepare the owner in advance regarding what to expect. Homeowners are often concerned because the appraiser seemed to "be in and out" so quickly.

3. *Comparable sales.* If you have information on comparable houses that have sold, ask the appraiser if he or she would like to have it. Most appraisers still appreciate any data that will help them in their appraisal. If you prepare such information, make it as complete as possible. On comparable sales the appraiser needs to know such things as the date of sale, number of bedrooms and baths, square footage, age of property, sale price, and so on. Most likely, the appraiser has this information, so use it to be helpful and never assume your information will affect their valuation.

4. *Influencing the appraiser.* Don't try to influence appraisers by giving them a sales talk. Most appraisers are experienced and knowledgeable. They are not influenced by a sales pitch—in fact, it may backfire on you. Appraisers try to be objective; however, if they are irritated while at the property by an overaggressive individual, it may affect their outlook on the property. And finally, it can be tempting to ask an appraiser to overlook or minimize a condition in the property (e.g. uncompleted repair work). To do so could be viewed as a request for an appraiser to violate his or her standards of practice or ethics. On the other hand, it is acceptable to ask "will this uncompleted repair work affect the appraised value?"

SUMMARY

It is the future, not the past, that will determine whether a loan is good or bad. That is why conventional lenders emphasize the future resale potential of a property. Lenders want to make sure that if they must foreclose, they can resell the property quickly and recover the loan amount. Conventional lenders set up specific property standard policies. These standards vary with each lender, are flexible, and vary with market conditions. But, if the loan is to be resold to Fannie Mae or Freddie Mac, the lender must follow their appraisal standards and forms.

The ordering and monitoring of the appraisal process changed with the introduction of new rules under the Home Valuation Code of Conduct. Transaction time frames have been impacted by an increase in the time required for the new appraisal process. With the economic downturn, market conditions have taken on greater importance and appraisers are required to provide information and comment accordingly.

Real estate appraisers evaluate a neighborhood with great care because location has a great influence on the value of a property. Appraisers also pay particular attention to the condition and quality of the property. It is important to note, however, that redlining is illegal.

In determining market value, the appraiser can use three approaches: the cost, sales comparison, and income approaches. On one-to-four-unit properties, the sales comparison approach is the most reliable. Even when using the income approach, comparable properties must be used for the evaluation.

PUDs and condominiums present special appraising and lending problems. Lenders are concerned about the entire project as well as the value of a single unit within the project.

IMPORTANT TERMS AND CONCEPTS

Adjustments

Appraisal management company (AMC)

Capitalization

Capitalization rate

Certificate of Reasonable Value (CRV)

Certified appraisal report

Comparables

Comparative market analysis (CMA)

Conditional commitment

Condominiums

Cost approach

Economic obsolescence

Fair market value (FMV)

Functional obsolescence

Gross rent multiplier (GRM)

Gross operating income

Income approach

Market data approach

Neighborhood Data

Net operating income (NOI)

Physical depreciation

Planned unit development (PUD)

Redlining

Sales comparison approach

REVIEWING YOUR UNDERSTANDING

Questions for Discussion

1. "The sales price and the fair market value of a property are not always the same." Explain this statement.

2. Discuss how property standards for local lenders are influenced by Freddie Mac and Fannie Mae.

3. List five characteristics an appraiser looks for when checking a neighborhood.

4. What are the basic steps in the cost approach to value?

5. Explain the sales comparison (market data) approach to value.

6. When appraising single-family homes and large apartments, do appraisers use the same income approach techniques? Explain the techniques used.

7. How does a planned unit development (PUD) differ from a condominium?

8. List some "do's and don'ts" for establishing a good working relationship with a real estate appraiser.

Multiple-Choice Questions

1. Adverse influences that tend to reduce property values include
   a. gentle curving in street pattern.
   b. noisy freeways.
   c. acceptable school system.
   d. presence of recreational facilities.

2. The loss in value due to negative neighborhood influences is called
   a. physical deterioration.
   b. economic obsolescence.
   c. functional obsolescence.
   d. structural obsolescence.

3. To arrive at total square footage of a structure, appraisers measure the
   a. exterior of the structure.
   b. interior dimensions of the house, plus the garage.
   c. interior dimensions of the house, excluding the garage.
   d. length, width, and height of the building.

4. Loss in value from poor structural design is referred to by appraisers as
   a. physical deterioration.
   b. economic obsolescence.
   c. functional obsolescence.
   d. structural obsolescence.

5. Buyers will not pay more for a property than the cost of acquiring an equally desirable substitute property. Economists refer to this as the principle of
   a. conformity.
   b. desirability.
   c. acquisition.
   d. substitution.

6. The cost per square foot would usually be the least for
   a. garages.
   b. homes.
   c. PUD buildings.
   d. condo buildings.

7. The most reliable approach to establishing values of single-family dwellings is the
   a. cost approach.
   b. income approach.
   c. gross multiplier.
   d. sales comparison approach.

8. When comparing properties with one that is being appraised, certain adjustments are made for differences in construction, quality, and other characteristics. In the event a comparable house is exactly the same as the subject house, except that the comparable or "comp" is in better condition, the appraiser will
   a. deduct from the "comp."
   b. deduct from the subject property.
   c. make no adjustments.
   d. find that insufficient information is given to accurately determine the kind of adjustments required, if any.

9. The organization that publishes periodic summaries of sales in a designated area and available to real estate agents is
   a. Multiple Listing Service.
   b. County Recorder.
   c. County Assessor.
   d. Institute of Continuing Education.

10. Under the Mortgage Disclosure Improvement Act (MDIA), disclosures must be delivered to loan applicants, with some exceptions, within
    a. 3 days of receipt of an application.
    b. 30 days of applying for a loan.
    c. 5 days of application.
    d. none of the above.

11. A dollar amount, subtracted from depreciation to arrive at the present value of the improvements, is used in the _____ approach to value.
    a. cost
    b. income
    c. market
    d. GRM

12. The location of a particular property is
    a. no longer considered a determinant of value as a result of anti-redlining legislation.
    b. of considerable importance in determining the value of property.
    c. relevant only on commercial properties.
    d. relevant on all properties except owner-occupied SFDs.

13. When using the FHLMC/FNMA appraisal report form for single-family dwellings appraisers
    a. normally use at least three comparable sales.
    b. make note of off-site improvements.
    c. consult available sources like Marshall & Swift to arrive at a cost per square foot.
    d. do all of the above.

14. FHA property standards
    a. are similar to conventional standards.
    b. require extensive repairs and improvements prior to issuing a loan.
    c. include suitability to meet specific needs of buyers.
    d. rely heavily upon appraisers to determine if a home meets property requirements.

15. Assume a property sells for $800,000 but is appraised for $650,000. Under HVCC, the final loan will be based
    a. midway between $650,000 and $800,000.
    b. on a maximum of $1,000,000 for joint borrowers.
    c. on $650,000.
    d. on $800,000.

16. Under the Home Valuation Code of Conduct (HVCC)
    a. appraisers are hired to determine precise property values.
    b. the major objective is to determine if the value of the property is sufficient to serve as collateral for a given loan.
    c. the credit score of the borrower is secondary to the property value.
    d. a lender's property standards have no bearing on how much it will finance.

17. Regarding pest control reports
    a. any pest repairs work may be waived by an FHA loan applicant.
    b. they are required for every FHA appraisal.
    c. FHA appraisers are responsible for determining if a report should be ordered.
    d. compared to the FHA, DVA loans do not require pest control clearance.

18. When a lender hires an appraiser, the lender is usually looking for the property's
    a. book value.
    b. market value.
    c. adjusted cost value.
    d. depreciated value.

19. Given an annual gross multiplier of 8 for a given rental market where the gross rents are $80,000 and the net operating income is $50,000, the indicated value of the property is
    a. $640,000.
    b. $400,000.
    c. $1,000,000.
    d. none of the above.

20. Which of the following regarding the income approach to value is true?

a. The lower the capitalization rate, the lower the property value.

b. The lower the gross rent multiplier, the higher the property value.

c. The lower the capitalization rate, the higher the property value.

d. The lower the net operating income, the higher the property value.

CASE & POINT

Appraisals and the New HVCC Rules

The appraisal process for conventional financing was, for many years, less complicated than that for FHA or DVA loans. In May 2009, that process was severely impacted with the adoption of the *Home Valuation Code of Conduct (HVCC)*. Lenders (including mortgage brokers and other loan originators) were no longer able to order an appraisal from a selected local appraiser. Instead, a system of Appraisal Management Companies (AMCs) was established from which appraisal assignments would occur.

The motivation for these changes was to establish regulations to "enhance the quality and independence of the appraisal process." In other words, it was to "protect" the appraiser from coercive interference from lenders or real estate licensees, who were thought to have contributed to an invalid valuation process by "running up" home values during the heyday of subprime lending.

Critics immediately countered that the new process was a way to deflect attention away from the fact that the agencies did not provide sufficient oversight in the housing debacle. Plus, critics indicated that local appraisers did not create the market, but were most often caught in a spiral in which they were "chasing" home values as properties kept selling for ever increasing amounts. Ironically, the fraudulent case that spawned this "regulation" was conducted via an appraisal management company, the very same entity that is now proposed to protect consumers from appraisal fraud.

Concerns that the new rules would impact how local appraisers, mortgage lenders, and realtors did business began to manifest themselves immediately as the new process was initiated. But worse still were the perceived negative impacts for the borrower/consumer. The increase in the cost of appraisals, while most noticeable, was the least of the impacts. More critical was that a lender had to be identified immediately in order to initiate the appraisal process. Previously, the borrower's application and documentation could be acquired along with the appraisal before selecting a lender. This allowed the loan originator to search for the best loan option, avoid guideline changes that could affect the borrower, and "discuss" any concerns with an appraiser before incurring a cost for an appraisal that might prove ineffective.

Lenders were also affected. They incurred additional costs as they had to establish procedures and commit staff to monitoring the process and developing quality controls with the AMCs. Most costly was devoting time to working out appraisal errors and valuation problems through a convoluted communication process that did not allow for direct contact with the appraiser. Complaints about errors, inappropriate comparison properties, inaccurately identified additions (requiring nonexistent building permits) and just plain bad appraisals mounted, especially during the first months of the new process. The mortgage originators had little access to the appraisal in order to identify valuation irregularities. Acquiring an appraisal copy only after it had been completed and delivered to the lender coupled with the prohibition to contact the appraiser directly eliminated any timely or easy way to correct problems.

As feared, many local appraisers, who best knew the market, were taken out of the process. It seemed that too many appraisers who were assigned were not only new and/or inexperienced, but seemed extremely conservative in their valuations. Complaints of receiving undervalued appraisals, compromising home sales, seemed numerous. Because the AMCs represented a third party that must be paid, appraisers received less money per appraisal. The result in some situations was a reduction of service (e.g., acquiring building permits when required). Advocates of the new process indicated that the complaints were exaggerated. Whether accurate or not, the "perception" that something was very wrong can and did often replace reality. The process was likely neither as bad as its critics suggested, nor did it perform as well as its advocates anticipated.

What many loan originators, lenders, and appraisers believe is that appraisers were made the scapegoats. It was suggested that they were responsible for the skyrocketing home value spiral, when in fact it was the unregulated "easy" credit with its lack of any buyer qualification that spawned the subprime debacle. Whether the HVCC process will reduce the perceived fraud within the valuation procedure is problematic, given the fact that the fraudulent case that spawned this "regulation" (as noted above) was conducted via an appraisal management company. We do know that the timeliness of the appraisal process has been expanded, the potential for errors seems to have increased, and any local loan originator expertise and assistance in guiding borrowers' appraisal experience has disappeared. The success of continuing efforts to revise and/or eliminate the HVCC process are yet to be known.

Chapter 9

PREVIEW

The process of qualifying borrowers for real estate loans continues to change as does our marketplace. With the collapse of the subprime programs, we have gone from virtually no qualifying guidelines back to the standards of old, where lenders have traditionally looked at prospective borrowers and determined the 3 Cs of lending: Credit/Stability, Capacity/Ability, and Collateral—in other words, a credit file that indicates the likelihood of continued loan payments (using credit history as a guide), the ability and willingness to pay the loan (with income and reserve documentation), and a property with sufficient equity to protect the lender in the event of default.

In order to understand the qualifying guideline changes that have occurred we need only review the relaxed standards that prevailed during the mid-2000s. Although the 3 Cs still applied, in many situations the focus had shifted primarily to addressing the issue, "How can we qualify the buyer?" As home values increased, lenders relaxed qualifying standards, resulting in a plethora of "alternative" loan instruments such as interest-only, stated income loans and "negatively amortized" option ARM loans. At the same time, lenders came to rely almost exclusively upon borrower credit scores as the primary measure of the likelihood of loan repayment.

While lenders likely recognized the risks involved in these alternative loan options, everyone wanted to believe that a borrower's good credit at least provided a good chance that the loan would be repaid, and that appreciation rates would protect them should the borrower have to foreclose. Although it is unlikely that lenders deliberately made loans that might result in foreclosure, their dependence on the then rapid appreciation rates to protect them in case of default proved to be very wrong.

Qualifying the Borrower

Despite the flight to the alternative mortgage instruments, many loans were still qualified under the more normal guidelines or the tried-and-true methods of evaluating a borrower's ability and willingness to pay a loan. As we move forward, these are the guidelines we will use to evaluate a borrower's ability to purchase. In fact, some say that the pendulum has swung too far and today's qualifying guidelines have adjusted too much. As we said above, change is always occurring, and we can expect that the borrower qualifying process will continue to evolve.

After completing this chapter, you should be able to:

1. Discuss income requirements to qualify for different types of loans.
2. Explain what effect debts have on a prospective borrower's qualifications.
3. Describe how lenders analyze stability of income.
4. Explain why lenders are concerned about borrowers' credit history and credit score.
5. Draw up a list of things that real estate agents can do to help clients obtain financing.

9.1 HOW LENDERS QUALIFY PROSPECTIVE BORROWERS

Using the typical methods for qualifying a borrower, the lender attempts to answer the question, "Do we expect the borrower to make timely payments on the mortgage?" To answer this question, the lender analyzes two general areas: the borrower's capacity and willingness to pay.

1. *Ability or Capacity to Pay.* To determine ability or capacity to repay loans, lenders seek answers to these questions: Do the borrowers earn enough to make the required payments? If so, is it a steady source of income? Do the borrowers have enough cash to buy the property? What other assets do they have?

2. *Desire or Willingness to Pay.* A person may have the ability to pay but lack the desire or willingness to do so. The desire to pay is just as important, but more difficult to measure. Lenders typically measure this with a credit score, but can also use a number of additional methods to determine a person's desire (as discussed later in the chapter).

It should be emphasized that qualifying a borrower is not a strict, precise operation. It is a process in which flexibility and judgment are very important. There are rules that are used to qualify borrowers, but they are merely guidelines and are meant to be flexible depending on the availability of money and the type of property under consideration. Each borrower is qualified on a case-by-case basis. All aspects of the loan must be weighed before a final decision can be made. Having said all this, it should be noted that some flexibility and what we used to call "make sense underwriting" have been lost since the economic downturn.

The automated qualifying systems (e.g., Fannie Mae's Desktop Underwriting and Freddie Mac's Loan Prospector) have made the qualifying process more objective and faster. Often forgotten in the ease of using the automated systems is that supporting documentation must be acquired and ultimately "signed off" on by an underwriter. More importantly, it is not as easy to "explain" any unusual aspects of a borrower's profile (e.g., recent credit difficulties, reduced savings record, the impact of recent health issues), as the computer is unsympathetic and underwriters are reluctant to override the computer result.

9.2 ABILITY OR CAPACITY TO PAY: A CASE HISTORY

A young mother contacted a loan officer in a local savings bank. Their conversation revealed the facts that her husband had recently died, and she wanted to buy a home to provide more permanent housing than a rental unit would furnish for herself and her three children, ages 6, 9, and 12.

The discussion further indicated that she had just returned to work for the first time in a dozen years, at age 38. The woman had a bachelor's degree in liberal arts and had been an executive secretary before having children. For the past 12 years, her husband had been the sole provider, but she had just been hired as an executive secretary with a take-home salary of $3,400 per month.

She had found a small, but suitable home listed at $245,000. Her intent to put a 20 percent down payment would result in a loan of $196,000. A 30-year loan at 5.25 percent per annum would require monthly payments of $1,082.31 principal and interest, plus taxes and insurance of $308.80, for a total monthly payment of $1,391.11.

A quick computation demonstrates that her "top" payment ratio was 40.9 percent. Her long-term debt was approximately $275 per month, producing a "bottom" ratio of 49.0 percent. Both ratios were near the maximum allowed, even under the more relaxed FNMA/FHLMC guidelines permitting a maximum 50 percent bottom ratio. Note: Late 2009, the maximum bottom ratio was reduced to 45 percent (at least temporarily) as Fannie Mae and Freddie Mac focused on strengthening their loan portfolios).

As the interview continued, the loan officer discovers that her credit was mostly combined with her deceased husband's. Her debt consisted of two credit card accounts in her own name plus a $150 auto payment that would continue for four years. Her mid-credit score was 742. Other disclosures indicated that she had received $150,000 in life insurance policy proceeds. The couple had also accumulated $40,000 in the form of savings deposits, stock, and CD investments during their 14-year marriage.

This additional information allowed the loan officer to strengthen the loan file by using the concept of "compensating factors." These involved consideration of the fact that the woman's employer indicated that her likelihood of continued employment was excellent. Her low credit debt demonstrated a commitment to retaining a low debt total. Her money in the bank represented more than the normally required amount of reserves, a financial cushion that would protect the lender from a threat of future loan default. And the substantial 20 percent down payment was viewed as protection for the lender.

The application was taken, and a fixed rate loan was approved.

What Does This Case Illustrate?

Lenders typically have general guidelines upon which to base their lending decisions. Although expanded guidelines, as indicated in the Preview, have been used in the past, more recently, lenders have returned to more typical loan-qualifying guidelines. Thus, real estate licensees are urged to suggest to prospective buyers that lenders require stable income, sufficient assets, and acceptable credit. The days of easy-qualifying loans are over, at least for now.

Although compensating factors can be used under some circumstances, recognize that lenders mostly use these expanded guidelines to help an otherwise "marginal" buyer qualify by strengthening the buyer's file. No amount of compensating factors can overcome major deficiencies in a file (e.g., very low credit scores, lack of stable income).

Why Qualify Borrowers?

Some people ask, Why bother to qualify borrowers? If the borrower doesn't make the payment, the lender can just take back the property! There are several reasons why a lender qualifies a borrower.

First, lenders are not in the business of foreclosing and taking back properties. That is the last thing a lender wants to do. Lenders are in the money business, not the real estate business. In most cases, when lenders foreclose they suffer a loss in both time and money.

In earlier years, when a much larger down payment was required, qualifying the borrower was not as important as it is today. With large down payments there was less need to worry about the borrower's qualifications. Few borrowers were willing to allow a loan to default and lose a large amount of equity. With large equity, borrowers in financial trouble could simply sell the property, pay the lender, and salvage what they could or refinance the loan to lower the interest payments or rate. Today, the situation is different—lenders are still making reasonably high-ratio conventional loans up to 90 percent LTV or government-backed loans that require little, if any, down payment. With these loans, lenders must rely heavily on borrower qualifications because there is little, if any, equity in the property. The criteria remains: the greater the equity, the greater the incentive to make mortgage payments. The less the equity, the less the incentive. In falling markets, values can actually drop below remaining loan balances. Known as being "upside down" on the mortgage, historic numbers of borrowers found themselves in this predicament by mid-2009. Short sales have become more commonplace as borrowers are unable to sell their properties for what they owe in loans. (Short sales are more fully discussed in Chapter 11).

While lenders had for many years subscribed to the notion that it was a disservice to approve a loan beyond the borrower's financial capabilities, the subprime loan frenzy caused them to lose sight of that lending principle. We've previously discussed the difficulties that were created by excessively relaxing lending guidelines. Suffice it to say, we have returned to the belief that by turning down an unqualified buyer, the lender is actually doing the buyer a favor. It is axiomatic that *if a loan is not sound for the borrower, it is not sound for the lender, and vice versa.* In this regard, the creative financing options mentioned earlier have created great hardships for some buyers and subsequently for lenders who have been forced to either foreclose or accept a short sale. The term "abusive lending practices" has entered the lexicon, and oversight agencies now indicate that penalties may be imposed in cases in which lenders arranged financing for borrowers who were unable to comply with the loan's requirements, including excessive negative amortization and fast-rising mortgage payments, to name a few. The low- or no-documentation loans are under particular scrutiny as charges of fraud mount. This is a perfect example of how lending practices change and evolve as lenders determine not only what lending instruments the market may need but what actually works.

9.3 CAPACITY TO PAY

Whether the borrower earns enough to make the monthly payments on a loan is the first consideration in determining the applicant's ability or capacity to repay the loan. There is no one answer, because various lenders use different formulas depending upon the type of loan. Conventional lenders, the FHA, the DVA, and Cal-Vet each have their own distinctive method of qualifying a borrower. To compare the qualifying methods used, we'll look at one set of borrowers. Figure 9.1 provides hypothetical information on the borrowers, a couple whom we'll use as applicants for a conventional loan. We will then compare this type to FHA and DVA requirements.

Income Ratios

Lenders use the **monthly payment** on a property to determine a borrower's qualifications. The payment includes principal, interest, property taxes, and insurance—commonly referred to as **PITI**. Even if the borrowers are paying their own taxes and insurance (not impounded), the lender adds them all together for qualifying purposes. Private mortgage insurance (PMI) and/or Home Owner Association (HOA) dues must also be included in the calculation when applicable. For the FHA, both an Up Front Mortgage Insurance Premium (UFMIP) and Monthly Mortgage Insurance (MMI) are also included.

FIGURE 9.1   Basic information about sample borrowers.

Name	John and Janet Smith	
Dependents	Two, aged 4 and 6	
Employment		
John Smith		
Employer	Self-employed	
Position	Consultant	
Years on job	6 years	
Income	$3,200 per month	
Janet Smith		
Employer	County Assessor's Office	
Position	Administrative assistant	
Years on job	3 years	
Income	$2,100 per month	
Cash in bank	$60,000	
Debts:	Payment	Balance
Car	$300	$5,000
Furniture	75	1,000
Dept. Store	20	100
Loan Information:		
Purchase price of home	$300,000	
Loan amount	$250,000	
Interest rate	5.25%	
Term	30 years	
Monthly Payment:		
Principal and interest	$1,288	
Taxes	312	
Insurance	66	
Private Mortgage Insurance	104	
Total PITI	$1,770	

Lenders use ratios in qualifying borrower income. The "housing ratio" is quoted as the total monthly payment divided by the borrower's gross monthly income. The overall **qualifying ratio** is calculated by adding the housing expense plus all other credit debt divided by the borrower's gross monthly income.

The long-time accepted qualifying housing ratio used by the agencies is 33 percent, indicating that a borrower's monthly housing payments should not exceed 33 percent of his or her gross monthly income. Expressing it as a multiplier, we would say that the borrower should earn approximately three times the monthly payment. Qualifying ratios used by the agencies change depending upon various circumstances: as the cost of housing increases, borrowers must allocate more of their income to housing; compensating factors may allow an expansion of the ratios; and high credit score buyers are granted greater flexibility in their ratios. Thus, although the 33/42 ratios are identified in "policy" manuals, the agencies accommodate some flexibility. That flexibility reached unprecedented ratios accompanied by minimum documentation during the subprime loan era. Borrowers today, depending upon their down payment, credit scores, amount of consumer debt and compensating factors, can be qualified up to 45 percent and, under some loan programs to nearly 50 percent of their gross monthly income. As indicated, the qualifying ratios are merely a guide; many loans are approved with higher ratios, especially when "compensating factors" exist that serve as potential protection for the lender in case the borrowers have trouble making payments. The following are some examples of when a lender might feel justified in approving a higher loan ratio.

- Borrowers have a substantial cushion/reserve. If the net worth is liquid, it can be used to make the mortgage payments, if necessary.
- Borrowers have a credit-worthy co-borrower with additional income. Co-borrower rules apply. Remember also that a co-borrower, regardless of how qualified, will not compensate for the bad credit rating of the main borrower.
- Borrowers have excellent potential for higher earnings due to education or training, and current income is stable. Recent graduates fall into this category as they begin their careers, as do nurses and police officers.
- Borrowers are making a large down payment.
- Borrowers have no "payment shock," meaning that they have been making the change to their mortgage or rent payments at about the same level as the new loan payment.

Let's look at our sample borrowers, the Smiths from Figure 9.1, to determine how they qualify. Their monthly PITI payment is $1,770, and their monthly income is $5,300.

$$\frac{\text{Mortgage payment}}{\text{Gross income}} = \frac{\$1,770}{\$5,300} = 33.4\%$$

This ratio is frequently referred to as the housing ratio, top ratio, or front-end ratio. The Smiths would qualify based on current income guides.

FIGURE 9.2   Summary of qualifying procedure for conventional lenders.

Income
    Allowable gross income $5,300

Housing Payment and Expenses
    Principal and interest   1,288
    Property taxes   312
    Homeowner's Insurance   66
    Private Mortgage Insurance   104
    Total mortgage payment $1,770
    Long-term debts   375
    Total monthly expenses $2,145

Qualifying Guidelines:

1. $\dfrac{\text{Mortgage payment}}{\text{Gross income}} = \dfrac{\$1,770}{\$5,300} = 33.4\%$ (front-end ratio)

This ratio should not exceed 33% (under "perfect" ratio requirements)

2. $\dfrac{\text{Total monthly expense}}{\text{Gross income}} = \dfrac{\$2,145}{\$5,300} = 40.5\%$ (back-end ratio)

This ratio should not exceed 41% (under "perfect" ratio requirements)

Debts

So far, we have discussed only a borrower's housing ratio. Lenders must also take into account the borrower's debts. Lenders break debts down into two categories, short term and long term. The short-term debts are generally ignored, and only long-term debts are considered in qualifying a borrower. How are **long-term debts** defined? Conventional lenders follow the standards of Fannie Mae, Freddie Mac, the FHA, and PMI companies, which define a long-term debt as a debt that will take 10 months or longer to pay off (Some lenders use six months for long-term debt definition). Child support payments are also considered long-term debts if they will continue for more than 10 months. Caveat: Because a significant monthly payment (e.g., a $650 car payment) could compromise the borrower during the first six months of new loan payments, such high monthly payments may be calculated into qualifying ratios even though only six months of payments remain.

Once long-term debts have been determined, the lender adds the total to the monthly payment. The two, added together, are called **total monthly expenses**. The total monthly expenses are divided by the borrower's gross monthly income, which results in another ratio, called the over-all ratio, bottom ratio, or **back-end ratio**. Conventional lenders use Fannie Mae and Freddie Mac most recent standards, which state that this ratio should not exceed 41 percent, including PMI. Our borrowers, the Smiths, have three debts. Their car and furniture payments will take more than one year to pay off. Therefore, these are long-term debts. The department store debt is a short-term debt. Long-term debts total $375 per month, which, added to the mortgage payment of $1,770, gives us a total monthly expense of $2,145.

$$\frac{\text{Total monthly expense}}{\text{Gross income}} = \frac{\$2,145}{\$5,300} = 40.5\%$$

On the basis of this back-end ratio, the Smiths also qualify, since their total monthly expenses are less than 41 percent. Borrowers must qualify on both tests. Some qualify on the first test but not on the second test because they have excessive debts. The second ratio is almost always the more important of the two. In fact, lenders will allow borrowers to exceed the typical housing ratio if their credit history demonstrates minimal consumer debt service. Figure 9.2 summarizes the qualifying procedure for conventional loans.

9.4 QUALIFYING UNDER GOVERNMENT-BACKED LOANS

Federal Housing Administration (FHA)

The FHA uses the same qualifying procedure as conventional lenders, except that the FHA states that the front-end ratio should not exceed 29 percent, while the back-end ratio—the more important of the two qualifying tests—should not exceed 41 percent, including MMI. The 29/41 ratios are considered "just right" but, as in conventional financing, there is some flexibility allowed—especially when compensating factors are present.

Department of Veterans Affairs (DVA)

The DVA uses a two-phase qualifying procedure: (1) the **residual income** method and (2) the application of qualifying income ratio.

Figure 9.3 outlines the DVA's procedure. The DVA starts with **gross income** and subtracts federal and state income tax and Social Security or retirement payments to arrive at net take-home pay.

FIGURE 9.3   Summary of DVA qualifying procedure.

Allowable gross income	$5,300
Less: Federal income tax	677
State income tax	172
Social Security or retirement	382
Net take-home pay	$4,069
Housing payment and fixed obligations	
Principal and interest	$1,288
Property taxes	312
Homeowner's insurance	66
Total mortgage payment	$1,666
Maintenance/utilities	
(@14 cents/sq. ft.)	140
Total housing expense	$1,806
Alimony and child support	0
Long-term debts	$ 375
Job-related expense	0
Total housing and fixed obligations	$2,181
Analysis	
Net take-home pay	$4,069
Less: Housing and fixed expenses	2,181
Residual income	$1,888

Phase 1: Residual Income Method

Housing expense consists of principal and interest, taxes, home-owner's insurance, maintenance, and utilities. The DVA uses a maintenance fee calculation of 14 cents per square foot.

To the housing expense, the DVA adds alimony, child support payments, and long-term debts. The DVA defines a long-term debt as any debt that will take six months or more to pay off. Once again, this is not a hard and fast rule; the DVA tries to be realistic. For example, if an applicant has a car payment of $400 a month with a balance of $1,500 and little cash reserve, it would probably count this debt, even though there are less than six months remaining on that loan. The DVA considers the first few months of the loan critical. A large payment of $400 a month, lasting for five months, could naturally affect a buyer's ability to make loan payments during the first few months, and therefore the DVA would count it in qualifying the borrower.

Another item that the DVA includes is called a job-related expense. This mainly refers to babysitting expenses when both husband and wife work and have small children; travel and/or living expenses when employment requires commuting; or those jobs in which additional expenses are likely to occur for uniforms, tools, etc. Policemen, firemen, and construction workers, among others, fall into this category. There is no specific rule as to how much can be subtracted for job-related expenses. Schedule A of the 1040 tax returns generally identifies the amount of "unreimbursed business expenses" a borrower has incurred. This is the amount most often shown in the qualifying formula. The babysitting expenses can be mitigated if one parent works at home or if a relative is available for child care. Commuting expenses can be reduced if an individual living away from home stays with a relative or if housing is paid for by the employer. In our example, because the husband is self-employed at home, we have not identified any babysitting costs.

Now that we have determined net take-home pay for the Smiths, along with their total expenses, we're ready to qualify them. The DVA subtracts the total expenses of $2,181 from the net take-home pay of $4,069, leaving $1,888 as residual income. The next question we must answer is, "Is this residual income enough money to buy food and clothes, and provide for the other needs of the family?" To answer this, we must look at several significant factors:

1. *Family size.* It is obvious that one needs more money to feed and clothe six children than two children.
2. *Geographic area.* Cost of living varies according to area.
3. *Price of home and neighborhood.* The more expensive the house and neighborhood, the more it costs a family to live there.
4. *Borrowers' living pattern.* Not all borrowers are created equal. All have their own lifestyle. When considering the question, "Is this enough to live on?," we must consider how the particular family lives. An older couple with no children will likely require less income than a large family. To do a proper job of qualifying, we must consider these factors. It is easy to think about, but in practice difficult to apply, because it is not so simple to obtain the facts. However, there are clues that help. Looking at previous housing expenses and how much the borrowers were able to save is a good clue as to how they live. The number of debts and size of each also give a good indication of their lifestyle.

A number of factors affect how much money is needed to support a family. We have listed some basic ones and you can probably think of more. The DVA considers each case to determine how much a prospective home buyer will need. The Department of Labor provides statistics regarding cost of living for various family sizes.

Going back to our sample case, the Smiths have $1,888 left over to support their family. Based on the geographic area, we use guides provided by DVA residual income tables, which vary by region. In California (for 2009), for example, we have:

Family Size	Amount Needed
1	$491
2	823
3	990
4	1,117
5	1,158
6+	Add $80 for each additional family member up to 7

Using the guide, Mr. and Mrs. Smith with their two children need $1,117 a month to qualify. The "amount needed" is of course subject to periodic increases as cost of living increases. They actually have $1,888; therefore they would qualify under the residual income method.

Phase 2: DVA Income Ratio Application

The income ratio is determined by taking the monthly housing expenses—principal, interest, property taxes, insurance, and long-term debts—and dividing this by the gross monthly income. If this ratio is 41 percent or less (considered the "perfect" ratio), the borrowers qualify. If the ratio is above 41 percent, then the DVA underwriter, in order to justify the loan, must look at any compensating factors (see below for what constitutes compensating factors). The DVA allows 41 percent ratios because it includes items other than those used by conventional lenders.

In the case of the Smith family, we show:

$$\frac{\text{Housing Payment and Long-Term Debt}}{\text{Gross Monthly Income}} = \frac{\$2,181}{\$5,300} = 41.2\%$$

Based on the general guideline of 41 percent or less, the Smiths would qualify, especially with compensating factors. On the other hand, if we were to add $250 a month for babysitting, this ratio would increase to 45.9 percent; which may be pushing the envelope for approval, even with compensating factors.

DVA administrators stress that DVA underwriting standards are guidelines and that they are willing to review individual veteran borrowers who do not automatically qualify, similar to the **compensating factors** considered by the FHA. Examples of compensating factors include larger-than-normal down payment, insignificant use of credit cards, no vehicle payments, substantial net worth, and stable work experience and history and more than the minimum required residual income, as in this case with the Smiths. The DVA uses the tightest qualifying standards in lending due to the lack of initial equity.

Cal-Vet

The qualifying procedure used by Cal-Vet is as follows: From gross income, subtract federal and state income taxes and Social Security to arrive at **adjusted gross income**. Housing expense is arrived at by adding principal, interest, taxes, property and disability insurance, maintenance, and utilities. Next, long-term debts, which are any debts that will take longer than one year to pay off, are totaled and subtracted. The remaining income is then divided by the adjusted gross income to determine the relationship between that and the amount of money left over. This residual should be at least 50 percent of adjusted gross, though under some circumstances it can be less. This is merely a guide, since Cal-Vet looks closely at the balance of funds left over to determine if they are sufficient to support the family.

9.5 WHAT IS INCOME?

We have learned how a lender determines if a borrower earns enough to qualify for a loan. The next consideration is what income lenders include. There is no question that income from regular employment is included, but do lenders count income from overtime, part-time work, or sales commissions? To be counted as stable, income must normally be earned in the same or similar occupation for at least two years. This section covers how lenders look at a variety of income sources.

FNMA and FHLMC

The Federal National Mortgage Association (FNMA) and Federal Home Loan Mortgage Corporation (FHLMC) greatly influence the qualification process. First, they affect the sale and purchase of qualifying loans. While borrowers do not deal directly with either FNMA or FHLMC, these two agencies purchase, via the secondary market (discussed in Chapter 7), the bulk of conventional, conforming loan limit loans. The phrase among many lenders is that "if the loan cannot be sold to FNMA or FHLMC, we can't do the loan."

Second, they foster uniformity. Loans sold to either FNMA or FHLMC must comply with the qualifying ratios of the purchasing agency. Consequently there is greater standardization and uniformity in the lenders' qualifying process with the expectation of selling loans to either of the "big players." Any conventional loan sold to these agencies, in 2009, could not exceed the then conforming loan limit of $417,000 for a one-unit dwelling, fixed rate loan. Hence many lenders limited their loans secured by houses to this "conforming" loan amount of $417,000. Of course this figure is subject to periodic changes, usually upward as house prices go up.

Commissioned People and Tradespeople

Commissioned people do not earn a set figure each month. Since their income varies over the year, they must be judged on the basis of annualized earnings. Lenders usually look at the earnings over the last two to three years (documented by tax returns). Some commissioned people incur expenses that are not reimbursed by the employer. These expenses, shown on Schedule A of the 1040 tax returns, must be subtracted from income to arrive at a true income figure. Lenders require income tax returns from commissioned people to verify incomes.

Tradespeople, such as carpenters and painters, are treated basically the same as commissioned salespeople. The lender determines the stability of income over the previous two years' by means of W-2 forms and/or tax returns. If considerable variance in income occurred, the lender will often average the income over the past two years. Hourly rates are not used because employment may not have been regular and full time during the year.

Overtime and Bonus

Lenders are reluctant to include overtime because, in most cases, it is not consistent and dependable. If borrowers can prove that they will continue to work overtime in the future, lenders will consider overtime pay. In other words, the borrower must have had consistent overtime in the past two years and must have a job that demands overtime. A good example would be a police officer working as a detective, since the nature of the job consistently requires overtime. Other examples include firefighters, grocery clerks, truck drivers, and phone company and other utility employees.

Bonus income counts only if the lender believes it will continue in the future. A past record of consistent bonuses is the main way to prove it will continue and can be documented with past tax returns. How many years are required to show that a bonus is consistent? This is a matter of lender policy, though most lenders require at least two years of bonus pay before they include it as income.

Part-Time Work

At one time, earnings from part-time work were not counted by lenders. The Federal Equal Credit Opportunity Act specifically prohibits lenders from discounting income solely because it is part time. For example, if a borrower works only 20 hours a week, the income must be counted if the job is stable. Many people work multiple jobs, some being part time. In order to provide the benefit of this income, lenders will average part-time employment income over the past two years.

Spousal/Alimony and Child Support

Income from alimony and child support must be counted by the lender if the borrower can provide a court order and a history of consistent payments. However, as will be demonstrated in Chapter 10, under the Equal Credit Opportunity Act borrowers need not reveal such income, and lenders cannot ask about receipt of income from either child support or alimony. However, a lender can ask about payment of child support or alimony for long-term debt purposes.

Pensions and Social Security

Income from pensions and Social Security are counted if such sources are expected to continue on a steady basis. Copies of pension plans are required. Because this income may not always be fully taxable, lenders allow the amount to be "grossed up" using a 1.15 to 1.25 percent factor.

Military Personnel

Military personnel receive extra pay for quarters, clothing, and rations in addition to their base pay. When qualifying someone in the military, all of these extras are added to arrive at the true income. In addition, lenders take into account that military personnel receive free medical and other services.

Income from Real Estate

Lenders consider positive cash flow, or spendable income, from real estate as income. Lenders use the 75 percent rule in calculating cash flow for lending purposes. They take 75 percent of the gross income less principal and interest payments, taxes, insurance, and any other operating expenses. The cash flow generated by an investment in a single-family dwelling depends largely on the amount of down payment used in the purchase. Without a sizeable down payment, an investment in a single-family dwelling will most likely show a negative cash flow. Negative cash flow is regarded as a long-term debt rather than a reduction of income.

When a person wishes to buy and occupy a unit in a two-, three-, or four-unit building, the question that pops up is, "Does the income from the other units count?" The answer will vary by lender. The typical lender will count the income after subtracting a realistic figure for expenses and vacancy factor. The DVA includes the same income except for one condition: the veteran must have enough cash reserve to be able to absorb from three to six months' payments to cover the likelihood of vacant units. The reason for this is that the DVA has found that most foreclosures on two-to-four-unit buildings occur in the first year.

Self-Employment

A self-employed borrower can present a bit of a challenge for qualifying purposes. While balance sheets and profit and loss statements used to be required, lenders now rely upon tax returns to determine a borrower's capacity to buy. Lenders will review two or three years of returns, examining the Schedule C of said returns for net income after all business expenses have been deducted. A business should show a growth pattern over the examined years, whereas a decline in income from year to year would represent a concern for a lender. Under review, depreciation identified in the Schedule C as well as all depreciation on real estate (usually reported on Schedule E) is not considered a cash expense and therefore is usually added back to net income.

9.6 CO-BORROWING

What effect do multiple borrowers—more than one borrower on a loan—have on an application for a real estate loan? The technical name lenders give a sole borrower is mortgagor. If there is more than one borrower, we have **co-mortgagors** (often husband and wife), sometimes called co-borrowers. Co-mortgagors sign the note and deed of trust and their names go on the title together. It should be noted that **co-signers** are not the same as co-mortgagors: Co-signers sign the note as guarantors but are not on the title, do not sign the trust deed, and therefore are rarely acceptable to real estate lenders. Co-mortgagors help with income qualifying but, contrary to common belief, will not help cure bad credit.

Lenders include all income and all debts from all parties to qualify for the loan. If one or more of the co-mortgagors is not to occupy the home, then things can get complicated. Some lenders insist that all co-mortgagors occupy the home or they will deny the loan. Other lenders will try to work with the parties by counting some of the nonoccupying co-mortgagor's income after deducting the co-mortgagor's own housing expenses and other monthly debts. Some lenders require the nonoccupying co-mortgagor to be a close relative. Fannie Mae and Freddie Mac, however, have dropped the close relative requirement, but insist that the co-mortgagor not be the seller, builder, real estate broker, or any party who has an interest in the sales transaction. In short, the issue of nonoccupying co-mortgagor is fluid and constantly changing and it is difficult to give any definitive guidelines.

All co-mortgagors, but particularly those who participate to strengthen the loan qualification of a primary borrower, need be aware of the credit ramifications that accompany co-borrowing.

9.7 AFTER INCOME, WHAT THEN?
Stability of Income

After a lender has determined whether a borrower earns enough money, the next step is to analyze the stability of that income. To accomplish this, lenders look at such things as:

1. *Length of time on the job.* Lenders apply flexibility and common sense in determining what represents sufficient time on the job. The generally accepted criterion is a minimum of two years in the same job or line of work. College graduates with a degree and a new job in their field of study are considered to have had two years of experience and the new position will be acceptable for qualifying purposes.

   Another exception would be an engineer who has been on the job for one month, with prior work in another company for five years, also as an engineer. The new job was an advancement and it pays a higher salary. A lender would qualify this engineer because both jobs are in the same line of work and the new job is an advancement. In this case, the borrower may be required to provide a letter from the employer that the "likelihood of continued employment is good."

2. *Type of job.* The type of work a person does also determines the stability of income. In the past, highly skilled individuals whose skills have been in demand, such as a physician, nurse, civil service position, or teacher typically did not have to worry about a job. As job losses mounted and unemployment levels increased during 2008 and 2009, lenders had to take a more cautious view of all employment. While not considered "unstable," these traditionally safe jobs were being lost along with traditionally nonstable jobs, like construction work.

Self-employed borrowers are also carefully scrutinized to determine their stability of income. Lenders look at the length of time they have been in business, the net income, the financial condition of the business, and the general prospects for the particular type of business.

3. *Age of the borrower.* Many borrowers ask, "I'm over 50 years old. Do you think I could get a 30-year loan?" Years ago the answer would have been no. Lenders used to have a rule that said the age of the borrower plus the term of the loan could not exceed age 65, the normal retirement age. Lenders were understandably concerned about how the borrower was going to make the payments after retirement. Now, lenders are concerned only if the borrower is going to retire in the next few years. If the borrower is going to retire one year from now, for example, the lender wants to know what the borrower's income will be after retirement. If there is sufficient income to make the payments, lenders will approve such loans. It makes no difference if applicants are 55 or 95; if they make enough money to meet loan repayments, they will be approved. Age is no longer a factor.

Borrower's Assets

When analyzing a borrower's capacity to pay, it should be apparent why lenders want to know how much money the borrower earns and the stability of those earnings. What is not so apparent is why lenders analyze borrower assets: because they want to be sure the borrower has enough cash for the down payment and closing costs. In addition to verifying sufficient funds, lenders want to know their source: savings, sale of personal property, or liquidation of other assets (e.g., stocks or bonds). Lenders refer to this as "sourcing the funds" to assure that there is no undisclosed debt for having borrowed money.

Young couples often receive money for a down payment from their parents. If it is a gift and not a loan, no lender objects to it. However, like all funds, it must be verified, usually by a **"gift letter."** The gift letter must contain certain information, perhaps the most important being the phrase "this is a gift and need not be repaid." In most cases, the borrower must document the gift with a cancelled check or other evidence showing that the funds came from the parents' account and were not borrowed.

The amount and type of assets a borrower has will influence lenders. If the borrower has substantial liquid assets, lenders feel more secure, realizing that, with ample assets, a borrower will continue making the loan payments even if some problems arise. Lenders also give some leeway in qualifying if borrowers have reserves to fall back on. Borrowers with good bank accounts or other assets also demonstrate that they live within their means, are conservative in financial affairs, and have the ability to accumulate and manage money.

9.8 DESIRE TO PAY

It was stated earlier that there are two major considerations in qualifying. One is the ability or capacity of the borrower to pay, which has been discussed. The other is the **desire** (or willingness) **to pay** of the borrower. Does the borrower really have a sincere desire to continue making payments once the loan has been granted? It is difficult to answer that question. When they apply for a loan, borrowers automatically imply that they will repay the loan. But the lender has to have something more tangible than the borrower's *intent*. How does a lender determine a *borrower's desire*? Let's look at some indicators.

Past Payment Record

How a borrower has paid debts in the past is a good indication of what can be expected in the future. If borrowers have paid debts on time in the past, they will likely continue paying on time. On the other hand, if they had problems paying debts in the past, chances are that they will have problems in the future. People develop specific credit patterns. Reliance upon automated credit evaluation systems has virtually eliminated a borrower's ability to "explain" credit blemishes. Loan underwriters, in the past, could ignore the occasional blemish, focusing instead on the overall credit history of the borrower. Credit scoring has mostly replaced this common sense method of credit evaluation.

If the borrower has owned a home before, the lender is particularly interested in the previous payment record. The reasoning has always been that when a borrower is applying for another home loan, past payment records on a previous mortgage loan are the best indication of what can be expected in the future. This may no longer be true. Historic levels of foreclosures resulting from numerous causes including, among others, an inability to meet rising loan payments coupled with the inability to sell because of the loss of home equity or the loss of employment have caused loan defaults in otherwise very responsible borrowers.

Will this kind of poor credit history automatically eliminate a future buyer from any type of real estate loan? The rules about how long one must wait following a foreclosure before being eligible for another loan are pretty clear. The question is whether the rules will be relaxed in the future, due to foreclosures often being beyond the control of the borrower. The industry remains aware that people get into financial difficulties for other reasons beyond their control. Unemployment and medical problems are the most common reasons. While divorce is often cited, lenders do not consider it beyond one's control. If a borrower had a credit problem in the past because of unemployment or illness, it does not mean the borrower lacks the desire to pay, it just means there was a temporary problem.

People who have had bankruptcies are a special problem. They have had "credit failures." It is possible for them to get another loan, but it is much more difficult because bankruptcy is usually regarded as an inability to accumulate and manage money.

In considering those who have had a bankruptcy, lenders want to know the type of bankruptcy. Was it a liquidation (Chapter 7) bankruptcy or a Chapter 13 bankruptcy? Under a Chapter 13 bankruptcy, also called the wage-earner's bankruptcy, the individual pays off all creditors in full under a schedule approved by the bankruptcy court. The debtor makes payments to a court-appointed trustee, who, in turn, makes the payments to the creditors over a two- to three-year period. Lenders look at someone who opted for a Chapter 13 bankruptcy with more leniency, and a borrower can acquire a loan while making payments on said bankruptcy as long as he or she can otherwise qualify.

Unfortunately, the credit scoring system no longer differentiates the reason for the bankruptcy. It makes no difference to the computer scoring whether it was due to circumstances beyond the borrower's control or due to poor financial management. While the answer used to be weighed in the lender's loan decision, that is no longer the case. Lenders also insist that a certain time period elapse since the discharge of the bankruptcy, with most conforming lenders requiring a minimum of three to four years. Another requirement is that borrowers have established good credit since the bankruptcy.

Lenders want evidence that the buyer is paying existing debts on a timely basis. Missed payments on a credit obligation following a bankruptcy is often sufficient cause for a loan denial. Under a Chapter 13 bankruptcy, payments to the trustee would serve as a credit reference.

Credit Scoring—FICO

Credit scoring has become the accepted method of evaluating an applicant's credit history for the purpose of determining the probability of repayment of debts. The process is ordinarily identified as FICO, from Fair Isaac Corporation. This type of credit analysis has been in use for many years by users of credit information for purposes other than real estate loans, such as automobile credit purchases.

Scoring ranges from about 300 to about 900, with the lower scores indicating a greater likelihood of default. Since 2009, an applicant-borrower with a score less than 620 has become ineligible for a loan even should compensating factors be present.

The three major reporting agencies/repositories are *Equifax*, *Experian*, and *TransUnion*—and different scores can be disclosed by each of them, indicating differences in attitudes by the reporting companies. Also, various firms that extend credit to consumers may not report to all companies. The lender's copy of the report includes the scores from all three repositories. The borrower's middle score is used in determining loan eligibility. Borrowers now have the right to see their scores. Under the *Federal Fair and Accurate Credit Transaction (FACT) Act*, everyone is entitled to a free copy of their credit report once a year, thus helping to keep tabs on credit scores and guard against identity theft.

More than 30 underwriting factors are taken into consideration in arriving at a FICO score. The number of credit accounts are observed. Having either too many accounts, especially if opened in the past 12 months, or too few accounts is not considered "good"—the lender wants to know the ability of the borrower to manage credit payments.

If late payments turn up, such as 30, 60, or 90 days late within the preceding two years, if there are current delinquencies, or if credit has been used to its maximum allowance, scores drop. How long the credit has been established is important, since the lender must be in a position to evaluate its use.

If there are collections, judgments, or write-offs, they must be considered. Of definite concern is bankruptcy, as well as the type of bankruptcy (Chapter 7 or Chapter 13) and how much time has lapsed since the filing. An older bankruptcy with clean credit for the past several years is acceptable as long as credit scores have sufficiently improved.

The number of credit inquiries, particularly recently, are taken into consideration in the ratings. Too many unused accounts with zero balances (called "available credit") provide opportunities for use, which could be detrimental to the borrower's score.

The adoption of risk-based pricing models are now designed to benefit the higher-scoring borrowers. Whereas a 680 credit score used to be considered quite good, by 2009 a 720 score was required to acquire the best loan terms and rates. As lenders have become more adept at understanding what affects the computer scoring system, they can provide better guidance to prospective borrowers who want to improve low scores.

Motivation

When examining a borrower's desire to pay, we must also consider the borrower's motivation. Sometimes a strong desire on the part of the borrower to make the payments is one of the most important reasons for approving a loan. Among the things a lender considers when trying to determine motivation are the following:

1. *Down payment.* The amount of down payment heavily influences the borrower's desire to keep up loan payments. If you purchased a house for $300,000 and made a down payment of $100,000, you would do everything possible to maintain the payments. If it became impossible to keep up the payments, you would sell the house. One way or another, you would not let the lender take your house by foreclosure: you would protect your $100,000 investment.

   On the other hand, if you had purchased the same property with little or no down payment, you would not be as motivated to maintain the payments. If you ran into financial problems, it might be easy to talk yourself into letting the lender take back the property. If you have no money invested in the property, you really have nothing to lose except your credit rating. You could easily decide to let the lender foreclose.

   Lenders recognize the importance of the size of the down payment. As the down payment increases, the lender's risk decreases. The size of the down payment is one of the most important factors in determining whether a loan will be approved.

2. *Reason for buying.* When trying to determine the borrower's motivation, lenders also examine the reason for buying. Is the borrower

buying the home for personal use or is the purchase an *investment* that is going to be rented? If the purchase is for personal use, the borrower is more likely to keep up the payments. If the purchase is an investment, the borrower may not have the same motivation.

Note: The more recently adopted risk-based pricing models include incentives based on credit scores (noted above), loan-to-value, and property use (e.g., personal residence or investment).

9.9 WORKING WITH LENDERS

By now, you have learned that qualifying a borrower is not a precise mechanical function. A lender does not decide to say yes or no by looking at any one factor. The borrower's income, the stability of that income, and the credit record are all analyzed, and the decision is based on an overall impression of the borrower. While there are no hard and fast rules when it comes to qualifying, the inconsistencies among lenders' approval processes have been reduced considerably. Nevertheless, more than one person looking at the same loan and using the same qualifying standards can come up with different opinions. The human element cannot be fully eliminated—one must be able to recognize and learn how to work with it. Learn the idiosyncrasies of the various lenders. While general guidelines are the same, some are more lenient than others, in the amount and type of documentation required. This is the main reason that loan originators use different lenders.

Every lender, if at all possible, would approve every loan submitted because it is not only more pleasant to approve loans than to reject them, but they make money only by making loans. Lenders prefer to say yes, but borrowers and real estate agents must make it easy for them to say yes.

What are some of the things that can make it easier to obtain a loan?

1. *Possibility.* Don't insult the lender with a loan that can't possibly be approved. For example, if the borrower declared bankruptcy a few months ago, don't try to force the loan through. You know what the answer will be. The lender will be irritated because you are wasting valuable time.
2. *Honesty.* Always be honest with the lender. If the borrower has had credit problems, he or she should level with the lender. If the borrower has a good reason, lenders will listen and try to help. If the borrower tries to hide credit problems, lenders will find out anyway after the credit report comes in.

3. *Cooperation.* Lenders ask for items that are necessary, so cooperate with them. Arguing with a lender as to why documents are needed does not get the loan approved. Different lenders may very well require different documentation.

4. *Lender input.* Do not be insulted if the lender says the borrower is not qualified for the loan. Ask the loan officer what you can do to make the borrower qualified. A good lender may have some helpful suggestions. For example, the loan officer may suggest a co-mortgagor, a larger down payment, or a reduction of long-term debt and may explore other ways of making the loan acceptable.

5. *Government-backed loans.* Most lenders today are FHA "direct endorsement" and DVA "automatic" lenders that speed up the process as compared to when, in the past, loan packages had to be submitted directly to the agencies. It is rare today to have a loan submitted directly to the FHA or the DVA. Sometimes the loan can be approved or disapproved depending on how well the information is presented. Be sure the lender you are working with has had experience processing FHA and DVA loans.

6. *Exceptions and cover letters.* As with all loan submissions, a loan can sometimes be approved or denied depending upon how well the information is presented. If the borrower has loan weaknesses, loan officers must emphasize the borrower's strengths and be prepared to prove to the lender that the loan is a good risk. If one can present a convincing argument, backed up with written documentation, the borrower's chances of a loan approval may be enhanced.

Loan officers usually include a "cover letter" with the loan submission, in which the positives and the negatives and the reasons for loan approval are identified for the underwriter. A good cover letter, with accompanying documentation, can be persuasive when an underwriter begins the loan review. Rather than attempting to conceal loan weaknesses the loan officer can tackle them head on while explaining why they are not so important and/or why other aspects improve the quality of the loan submission.

Finally, if you are in doubt as to how to proceed with a particular loan, ask yourself this question: "If I were going to use my own money to make this loan, what would my attitude be?" You will be surprised at some of the answers. It will help you deal with lenders and understand them.

For additional information on how lenders view credit and what goes into a credit score, access the website of Fair, Isaac through the link at http://www.myfico.com.

SUMMARY

When qualifying a borrower, lenders try to answer the question "Will the borrower repay the loan on a timely basis?" Lenders qualify borrowers by analyzing their ability or capacity and their desire to pay.

An analysis of the ability to pay includes the amount and stability of income; the borrower's income is probably the most important factor in qualifying. Conventional lenders and the FHA use front- and back-end (top and bottom) ratios when they qualify the borrower's income, while the DVA uses an income ratio and residual methods. Cal-Vet looks for a residual or remaining income—after deducting for all housing debt, non-housing, long-term debt and disability insurance—that is at least 50 percent or more of adjusted income. The stability of income must also be considered. It is influenced by the length of time on the job and by the type of job.

Lenders measure a borrower's desire to pay partly by past credit performance. They also examine the borrower's motivation to continue making payments; the amount of down payment and credit score are the main measuring sticks.

One rule of thumb that applies to all lenders is that qualifying a borrower is a matter of applying guidelines with a great deal of judgment.

IMPORTANT TERMS AND CONCEPTS

Adjusted gross income

Back-end ratio (bottom ratio)

Co-mortgagor

Compensating factors

Co-signer

Credit scoring

Desire to pay

Gift letter

Gross income

Long-term debt

Monthly payments

PITI

Qualifying ratio

Residual income

Total monthly expense

REVIEWING YOUR UNDERSTANDING

Questions for Discussion

1. What is the difference between "ability to pay" and "desire to pay"?

2. When trying to anticipate whether a borrower can be expected to make timely payments, what two questions must be answered for lenders?

3. Name the "compensating factors" lenders are most likely to consider

when evaluating a borrower's risk level.

4. List four reasons why a borrower might have the income to qualify for a real estate loan but still be turned down by a lender.

5. How do real estate lenders count commissions? Part-time jobs?

Multiple-Choice Questions

1. A monthly loan payment is called PITI. This stands for
   a. principal, interest, taxes, indebtedness.
   b. payments, including timed interest.
   c. past due, insurance, taxes, interest.
   d. principal, interest, taxes, insurance.

2. To arrive at adjusted gross income under Cal-Vet financing, the agency takes the gross income and subtracts
   a. long-term debts, including total housing expense.
   b. long-term debts, excluding housing expense.
   c. all voluntary payroll deductions.
   d. payroll taxes, including Social Security.

3. Given a gross income of $5,000, mortgage payments (PITI) of $1,400, and long-term monthly debts of $350, the monthly payment or front-end ratio is
   a. 15 percent.
   b. 28 percent.
   c. 35 percent.
   d. 41 percent.

Alimony? Income from real estate investments?

6. Why are lenders concerned with a borrower's credit score? Will a past bankruptcy automatically disqualify a borrower from a real estate loan?

4. Referring to Question 3, the back-end ratio is
   a. 35 percent.
   b. 28 percent.
   c. 7 percent.
   d. none of these.

5. Which of the following is considered a negative for credit-scoring purposes?
   a. a score of 800
   b. at least three current lines of credit
   c. no bankruptcy
   d. a former collection account paid in full

6. In qualifying a VA loan, the Department of Veterans Affairs deducts income taxes, Social Security, and retirement contributions from allowable gross income. The balance is called
   a. gross effective income.
   b. net effective income.
   c. net take-home pay.
   d. gross spendable income.

7. Which of these is likely to be the most important factor in qualifying a buyer for a loan?
   a. amount of savings
   b. type of job
   c. number of dependents
   d. adequacy and stability of income

8. You are applying for an FHA loan. Your gross income is $3,200 per month. The total monthly payment is $800. Another $600 is paid out monthly for long-term debts. The ratio of total mortgage payment to gross income is
   a. 32.8 percent.
   b. 25 percent.
   c. 43.8 percent.
   d. none of these.

9. Using the data from Question 8, the total back-end ratio to gross income is
   a. 43.8 percent.
   b. 50 percent.
   c. 53.8 percent.
   d. none of these.

10. In the process of making a loan, the loan officer will correlate the characteristics of the borrower, characteristics of the loan, and the characteristics of the property in making a decision to grant a loan. The most important consideration is
    a. property rental value.
    b. degree of risk.
    c. location of property.
    d. neighborhood.

11. The rules used by conventional lenders to qualify borrower-applicants
    a. are rigid and uniform throughout the industry.
    b. are all different with no two lenders being the same
    c. can be similar, with each lender setting its own flexible policies.
    d. are strictly governed by regulatory bodies.

12. In qualifying borrowers, conventional real estate lenders generally
    a. use ratios that relate monthly payments to income.
    b. will always make loans if the circumstances appear reasonable.
    c. state that a loan is available to borrowers whose monthly payment does not exceed 50 percent of gross income.
    d. apply a "20 percent standard."

13. Income from overtime in regular occupations
    a. will not be considered by most lenders.
    b. is counted if it is stable and consistent.
    c. will be considered by a lender only to offset an equal amount of long-term debt.
    d. must be earned for at least three years before lenders will count it.

14. Income is considered stable by most lenders if
    a. it has been earned regularly for two years.
    b. the applicant has been in the same line of work for several years, even if he or she has been on a new job for one month.
    c. the type of occupation would normally warrant it.
    d. all of the above apply.

15. Regarding alternative loan options during the global crisis that had begun by 2005
    a. lenders were assured that loans granted to borrowers with good credit would be repaid.
    b. it was thought that escalating appreciation rates would protect lenders against foreclosure.
    c. most lenders deliberately made loans that might result in foreclosure.
    d. none of the above.

16. FNMA and FHLMC influence the borrower qualification process by
    a. buying qualifying loans.
    b. applying uniform qualifying ratios for all lenders.
    c. both (a) and (b).
    d. neither (a) nor (b).

17. For condominiums, the initials PITIA designate
    a. principal, interest, time, insurance, assessments.
    b. points, inflation, trustor, impounds, assurances.
    c. profits, income, transfers, installments, acceleration.
    d. principal, interest, taxes, insurance, home owner association fees.

18. Each of the following is considered income except
    a. continuing spousal support.
    b. gifts from family members.
    c. positive cash flows from rentals.
    d. self-employment income.

19. Due to the subprime loan debacle, by 2009
    a. many borrowers were "upside down" or "under water," owing more than their homes were worth.
    b. short sales became commonplace.
    c. both (a) and (b) are correct.
    d. neither (a) nor (b) is correct.

20. Regarding loan qualification, risk-based pricing models include incentives predicated on
    a. loan-to-value ratio.
    b. whether property is to be used as a residence or investment.
    c. credit score.
    d. all of the above.

CASE & POINT

The New Good Faith Estimate (GFE)

New regulations require all loan originators, beginning January 2010, to use a newly revised GFE. The primary purpose of the new form is to eliminate last minute surprises regarding the interest rate and/or the fees accompanying a loan transaction. Specific emphasis has been placed on how the Yield Spread Premium (YSP) is disclosed (See the Case and Point in chapter 3 for a full discussion of YSP).

The GFE must be delivered to the borrower within three (3) business days of the acquisition of a loan application. What represents an actual loan application is defined with the new regulations. The two critical elements to be contained in an application which, in turn will trigger the 3 day notice period, is denoting an address of the subject property along with an anticipated loan amount.

Yield Spread Premium in the past was too often abused when loan originators would promote a higher than necessary interest rate in order to receive additional compensation, often undisclosed or hidden. Advocates of the new GFE feel that it better alerts borrowers to the total costs related to obtaining financing. YSP must now be disclosed only as a credit to buyer costs and the GFE attempts to more clearly alert borrowers to the relationship of YSP to the acceptance of a higher interest rate. Additionally, the form is designed to promote borrower shopping for a loan, comparing bottom line costs and interest rate quotes.

Critics complain that the new GFE, lumping all closing costs into one figure without a clear breakdown of the fees, allows the borrower to be easily misinformed about the true costs of financing. Plus, the new stipulation provides no margin of error by making the loan originator fully responsible to pay for any fees under-quoted on the GFE. The result is that that loan originators over-quote on the proposed fees to avoid what they consider a punitive penalty for even a genuine mistake that could be perceived as under-quoting.

One large number identifying all fees, especially when over-quoting of those fees is the recommended procedure, is seen by critics as an over-simplification of the process that actually precludes a borrower from comparing costs. To remedy the lack cost breakdown, loan originators have mostly adopted forms much like the original Good Faith Estimate forms, wherein each fee is itemized. These cost estimates are usually provided upon initial borrower consultation and before a new GFE form is required to be provided. Regulators have expressed concern that these cost estimates, so resembling the old GFE documentation, not be used to compromise the new GFE disclosure format. The loan originators, on the other hand, can't comprehend how borrowers can make good comparisons of loan terms and costs without a clear delineation of those fees.

While the new GFE, in spite of its critics, may ultimately be recognized as the best way to inform borrowers of fees, there are two other portions of the form that require additional understanding.

A GFE must be issued upon receipt of a loan application and must quote an interest rate and proposed fees even though the rate may not be "locked in" and some terms might change. When the loan rate is finally determined and "locked", a new GFE must be issued identifying the new rate. Disturbingly, the initial quoted loan costs, with rare exception, can not be modified. This is another reason for the initial over-quoting of expected costs (noted above) as protection against an unexpected increase in fees resulting in the loan originator having to literally pay to place the loan.

Although the new procedures were installed to protect the borrower, there are some unintended consequences of the new regulations. All mortgage lenders remain obligated to the 3 day disclosure rules mandated by the Mortgage Disclosure Improvement Act or MDIA (see Case and Point in chapter 10). This regulation requires that three days elapse from the original disclosure (via the estimate of costs above) before any cost can be incurred on behalf of the borrower, including ordering an appraisal.

The new rules provide for a change in the GFE only upon a bonafide **Change of Circumstance** defined as a change in the loan amount (either an increase or decrease), a change in appraisal requirements (e.g. request for inspections or repairs) or a specific request from the borrower. Any such change will need to be documented, provided to the lender and accompanied by a new GFE.

Lenders are understandably reluctant to proceed with the processing of a loan until they are assured that the borrower has ceased any "shopping" promoted by the GFE form. Thus a borrower must make a formal declaration of his/her *Intent to*

Proceed" accompanied by a ***Certification of Receipt of the GFE*** before any loan processing will begin. These and all subsequent GFE's (prompted by interest rate changes or an acceptable change of circumstances) must accompany a loan's final submission.

Like many new rules, regulations or documentation, the new GFE has encountered considerable criticism. Whether it results in more clarity for borrowers or merely creates more unnecessary paperwork remains to be determined. What is clear is that we have entered a lending phase that will continue to be impacted by additional regulation. It is laudable that that authorities wish to promote better disclosure within the industry. The question is whether they will actually enforce the rules they hae or continue to rely mostly upon the introduction of new forms in their efforts to mold industry behavior?

Chapter

10

PREVIEW

This chapter describes how lenders process real estate loans using the loan application form and proceeding through a typical loan package. The loan approval process and the steps required to close the loan are discussed in detail. Finally, loan servicing, which occurs after the escrow closes, completes the discussion.

After completing this chapter, you should be able to:

1. List the items that make up a loan package.
2. Describe the process by which conventional, FHA, and DVA loans are approved.
3. List and explain borrowers' closing costs.
4. Describe the difference between "assuming" a loan and taking the property "subject to" the loan.
5. List rights that prospective borrowers have under the Fair Credit Reporting Act in the event that errors are shown in their credit reports.
6. Cite the chief provisions of the Truth-in-Lending Law.

Processing, Closing, and Servicing Real Estate Loans

10.1 PROCESSING THE LOAN

Loan processing starts with the **loan application**. Most lenders use the FNMA/FHLMC standard application form shown as Figure 10.1.

After receiving the application and other requested documents, the lender can make a preliminary determination of the borrower's likelihood of qualifying for a loan. In many cases, the information is either forwarded to an underwriter or submitted to an automated qualifying program to acquire a preapproval. The preapproval identifies the "conditions" required from the borrower before final loan approval.

Armed with the preapproval, the lender starts the loan processing, which includes getting needed information to meet the lender's conditions, acquiring title and escrow information, and initiating the appraisal process (see the new Home Valuation Code of Conduct information in Chapter 8).

Qualifying the borrower continues as the lender receives the various required exhibits. Chapter 9 discussed the standards used to qualify a borrower. In this chapter, we will go step by step into how real estate lenders process and close loans.

Even though applications may vary in format and length, they generally ask the same basic questions regarding: (1) employment, (2) income, (3) assets, (4) debts, and (5) credit history. Many lenders use the FNMA 1003 form even if the loans are not intended to be sold in the secondary market.

FIGURE 10.1 FNMA/FHLMC residential loan application.

Uniform Residential Loan Application

This application is designed to be completed by the applicant(s) with the Lender's assistance. Applicants should complete this form as "Borrower" or "Co-Borrower," as applicable. Co-Borrower information must also be provided (and the appropriate box checked) when ☐ the income or assets of a person other than the Borrower (including the Borrower's spouse) will be used as a basis for loan qualification or ☐ the income or assets of the Borrower's spouse or other person who has community property rights pursuant to state law will not be used as a basis for loan qualification, but his or her liabilities must be considered because the spouse or other person has community property rights pursuant to applicable law and Borrower resides in a community property state, the security property is located in a community property state, or the Borrower is relying on other property located in a community property state as a basis for repayment of the loan.

If this is an application for joint credit, Borrower and Co-Borrower each agree that we intend to apply for joint credit (sign below):

Borrower _____ Co-Borrower _____

I. TYPE OF MORTGAGE AND TERMS OF LOAN				
Mortgage Applied for: ☐ VA ☐ FHA	☐ Conventional ☐ USDA/Rural Housing Service	☐ Other (explain):	Agency Case Number	Lender Case Number
Amount $	**Interest Rate** %	**No. of Months**	**Amortization Type:** ☐ Fixed Rate ☐ GPM	☐ Other (explain): ☐ ARM (type):

II. PROPERTY INFORMATION AND PURPOSE OF LOAN	
Subject Property Address (street, city, state & ZIP)	No. of Units
Legal Description of Subject Property (attach description if necessary)	Year Built

| Purpose of Loan | ☐ Purchase ☐ Construction ☐ Other (explain): ☐ Refinance ☐ Construction-Permanent | Property will be: ☐ Primary Residence ☐ Secondary Residence ☐ Investment |

Complete this line if construction or construction-permanent loan.

Year Lot Acquired	Original Cost $	Amount Existing Liens $	(a) Present Value of Lot $	(b) Cost of Improvements $	Total (a + b) $

Complete this line if this is a refinance loan.

Year Acquired	Original Cost $	Amount Existing Liens $	Purpose of Refinance	Describe Improvements ☐ made ☐ to be made Cost: $

Title will be held in what Name(s)	Manner in which Title will be held	Estate will be held in: ☐ Fee Simple ☐ Leasehold (show expiration date)

Source of Down Payment, Settlement Charges, and/or Subordinate Financing (explain)

Borrower	III. BORROWER INFORMATION	Co-Borrower
Borrower's Name (include Jr. or Sr. if applicable)		Co-Borrower's Name (include Jr. or Sr. if applicable)

Social Security Number	Home Phone (incl. area code)	DOB (mm/dd/yyyy)	Yrs. School	Social Security Number	Home Phone (incl. area code)	DOB (mm/dd/yyyy)	Yrs. School

☐ Married ☐ Unmarried (include ☐ Separated single, divorced, widowed)	Dependents (not listed by Co-Borrower) no. ages	☐ Married ☐ Unmarried (include ☐ Separated single, divorced, widowed)	Dependents (not listed by Borrower) no. ages
Present Address (street, city, state, ZIP) ☐ Own ☐ Rent ____No. Yrs.		Present Address (street, city, state, ZIP) ☐ Own ☐ Rent ____No. Yrs.	
Mailing Address, if different from Present Address		Mailing Address, if different from Present Address	

If residing at present address for less than two years, complete the following:

Former Address (street, city, state, ZIP) ☐ Own ☐ Rent ____No. Yrs.		Former Address (street, city, state, ZIP) ☐ Own ☐ Rent ____No. Yrs.	

Borrower	IV. EMPLOYMENT INFORMATION	Co-Borrower
Name & Address of Employer ☐ Self Employed	Yrs. on this job Yrs. employed in this line of work/profession	Name & Address of Employer ☐ Self Employed	Yrs. on this job Yrs. employed in this line of work/profession
Position/Title/Type of Business	Business Phone (incl. area code)	Position/Title/Type of Business	Business Phone (incl. area code)

If employed in current position for less than two years or if currently employed in more than one position, complete the following:

Uniform Residential Loan Application
Freddie Mac Form 65   7/05 (rev.6/09)   Page 1 of 5   Fannie Mae Form 1003   7/05 (rev.6/09)

FIGURE 10.1 FNMA/FHLMC residential loan application. (*continued*)

Borrower		IV. EMPLOYMENT INFORMATION (cont'd)		Co-Borrower	
Name & Address of Employer	☐ Self Employed	Dates (from – to)	Name & Address of Employer	☐ Self Employed	Dates (from – to)
		Monthly Income $			Monthly Income $
Position/Title/Type of Business	Business Phone (incl. area code)		Position/Title/Type of Business	Business Phone (incl. area code)	
Name & Address of Employer	☐ Self Employed	Dates (from – to)	Name & Address of Employer	☐ Self Employed	Dates (from – to)
		Monthly Income $			Monthly Income $
Position/Title/Type of Business	Business Phone (incl. area code)		Position/Title/Type of Business	Business Phone (incl. area code)	

V. MONTHLY INCOME AND COMBINED HOUSING EXPENSE INFORMATION

Gross Monthly Income	Borrower	Co-Borrower	Total	Combined Monthly Housing Expense	Present	Proposed
Base Empl. Income*	$	$	$	Rent	$	
Overtime				First Mortgage (P&I)		$
Bonuses				Other Financing (P&I)		
Commissions				Hazard Insurance		
Dividends/Interest				Real Estate Taxes		
Net Rental Income				Mortgage Insurance		
Other (before completing, see the notice in "describe other income," below)				Homeowner Assn. Dues		
				Other:		
Total	$	$	$	Total	$	$

* Self Employed Borrower(s) may be required to provide additional documentation such as tax returns and financial statements.

Describe Other Income   *Notice:* **Alimony, child support, or separate maintenance income need not be revealed if the Borrower (B) or Co-Borrower (C) does not choose to have it considered for repaying this loan.**

B/C		Monthly Amount
		$

VI. ASSETS AND LIABILITIES

This Statement and any applicable supporting schedules may be completed jointly by both married and unmarried Co-Borrowers if their assets and liabilities are sufficiently joined so that the Statement can be meaningfully and fairly presented on a combined basis; otherwise, separate Statements and Schedules are required. If the Co-Borrower section was completed about a non-applicant spouse or other person, this Statement and supporting schedules must be completed about that spouse or other person also.   Completed ☐ Jointly ☐ Not Jointly

ASSETS Description	Cash or Market Value	Liabilities and Pledged Assets. List the creditor's name, address, and account number for all outstanding debts, including automobile loans, revolving charge accounts, real estate loans, alimony, child support, stock pledges, etc. Use continuation sheet, if necessary. Indicate by (*) those liabilities, which will be satisfied upon sale of real estate owned or upon refinancing of the subject property.		
Cash deposit toward purchase held by:	$			
List checking and savings accounts below		LIABILITIES	Monthly Payment & Months Left to Pay	Unpaid Balance
Name and address of Bank, S&L, or Credit Union		Name and address of Company	$ Payment/Months	$
Acct. no.	$	Acct. no.		
Name and address of Bank, S&L, or Credit Union		Name and address of Company	$ Payment/Months	$
Acct. no.	$	Acct. no.		
Name and address of Bank, S&L, or Credit Union		Name and address of Company	$ Payment/Months	$
Acct. no.	$	Acct. no.		

Uniform Residential Loan Application
Freddie Mac Form 65   7/05 (rev. 6/09)

Page 2 of 5

Fannie Mae Form 1003   7/05 (rev.6/09)

FIGURE 10.1   FNMA/FHLMC residential loan application. (*continued*)

VI. ASSETS AND LIABILITIES (cont'd)			
Name and address of Bank, S&L, or Credit Union		Name and address of Company	$ Payment/Months	$
Acct. no.	$	Acct. no.		
Stocks & Bonds (Company name/ number & description)	$	Name and address of Company	$ Payment/Months	$
		Acct. no.		
Life insurance net cash value	$	Name and address of Company	$ Payment/Months	$
Face amount: $				
Subtotal Liquid Assets	$			
Real estate owned (enter market value from schedule of real estate owned)	$			
Vested interest in retirement fund	$			
Net worth of business(es) owned (attach financial statement)	$	Acct. no.		
Automobiles owned (make and year)	$	Alimony/Child Support/Separate Maintenance Payments Owed to:	$	
Other Assets (itemize)	$	Job-Related Expense (child care, union dues, etc.)	$	
		Total Monthly Payments	$	
Total Assets a. $		Net Worth (a minus b) ▶ $	**Total Liabilities b.**	$

Schedule of Real Estate Owned (If additional properties are owned, use continuation sheet.)

Property Address (enter S if sold, PS if pending sale or R if rental being held for income) ▼	Type of Property	Present Market Value	Amount of Mortgages & Liens	Gross Rental Income	Mortgage Payments	Insurance, Maintenance, Taxes & Misc.	Net Rental Income
		$	$	$	$	$	$
Totals		$	$	$	$	$	$

List any additional names under which credit has previously been received and indicate appropriate creditor name(s) and account number(s):

Alternate Name	Creditor Name	Account Number

VII. DETAILS OF TRANSACTION		VIII. DECLARATIONS					
		If you answer "Yes" to any questions a through i, please use continuation sheet for explanation.		**Borrower**		**Co-Borrower**	
				Yes	No	Yes	No
a.	Purchase price	$	a. Are there any outstanding judgments against you?	☐	☐	☐	☐
b.	Alterations, improvements, repairs		b. Have you been declared bankrupt within the past 7 years?	☐	☐	☐	☐
c.	Land (if acquired separately)		c. Have you had property foreclosed upon or given title or deed in lieu thereof in the last 7 years?	☐	☐	☐	☐
d.	Refinance (incl. debts to be paid off)		d. Are you a party to a lawsuit?	☐	☐	☐	☐
e.	Estimated prepaid items		e. Have you directly or indirectly been obligated on any loan which resulted in foreclosure, transfer of title in lieu of foreclosure, or judgment?	☐	☐	☐	☐
f.	Estimated closing costs		(This would include such loans as home mortgage loans, SBA loans, home improvement loans, educational loans, manufactured (mobile) home loans, any mortgage, financial obligation, bond, or loan guarantee. If "Yes," provide details, including date, name, and address of Lender, FHA or VA case number, if any, and reasons for the action.)				
g.	PMI, MIP, Funding Fee						
h.	Discount (if Borrower will pay)						
i.	Total costs (add items a through h)						

Uniform Residential Loan Application
Freddie Mac Form 65   7/05 (rev.6/09)

Page 3 of 5

Fannie Mae Form 1003   7/05 (rev.6/09)

FIGURE 10.1   FNMA/FHLMC residential loan application. (*continued*)

VII. DETAILS OF TRANSACTION		VIII. DECLARATIONS				
			Borrower		Co-Borrower	
		If you answer "Yes" to any questions a through i, please use continuation sheet for explanation.	Yes	No	Yes	No
j.	Subordinate financing	f. Are you presently delinquent or in default on any Federal debt or any other loan, mortgage, financial obligation, bond, or loan guarantee?	☐	☐	☐	☐
k.	Borrower's closing costs paid by Seller	g. Are you obligated to pay alimony, child support, or separate maintenance?	☐	☐	☐	☐
l.	Other Credits (explain)	h. Is any part of the down payment borrowed?	☐	☐	☐	☐
		i. Are you a co-maker or endorser on a note?	☐	☐	☐	☐
m.	Loan amount (exclude PMI, MIP, Funding Fee financed)	j. Are you a U.S. citizen?	☐	☐	☐	☐
n.	PMI, MIP, Funding Fee financed	k. Are you a permanent resident alien?	☐	☐	☐	☐
o.	Loan amount (add m & n)	l. Do you intend to occupy the property as your primary residence? If Yes," complete question m below.	☐	☐	☐	☐
p.	Cash from/to Borrower (subtract j, k, l & o from i)	m. Have you had an ownership interest in a property in the last three years?	☐	☐	☐	☐
		(1) What type of property did you own—principal residence (PR), second home (SH), or investment property (IP)?	___		___	
		(2) How did you hold title to the home— by yourself (S), jointly with your spouse (SP), or jointly with another person (O)?	___		___	

IX. ACKNOWLEDGEMENT AND AGREEMENT

Each of the undersigned specifically represents to Lender and to Lender's actual or potential agents, brokers, processors, attorneys, insurers, servicers, successors and assigns and agrees and acknowledges that: (1) the information provided in this application is true and correct as of the date set forth opposite my signature and that any intentional or negligent misrepresentation of this information contained in this application may result in civil liability, including monetary damages, to any person who may suffer any loss due to reliance upon any misrepresentation that I have made on this application, and/or in criminal penalties including, but not limited to, fine or imprisonment or both under the provisions of Title 18, United States Code, Sec. 1001, et seq.; (2) the loan requested pursuant to this application (the "Loan") will be secured by a mortgage or deed of trust on the property described in this application; (3) the property will not be used for any illegal or prohibited purpose or use; (4) all statements made in this application are made for the purpose of obtaining a residential mortgage loan; (5) the property will be occupied as indicated in this application; (6) the Lender, its servicers, successors or assigns may retain the original and/or an electronic record of this application, whether or not the Loan is approved; (7) the Lender and its agents, brokers, insurers, servicers, successors, and assigns may continuously rely on the information contained in the application, and I am obligated to amend and/or supplement the information provided in this application if any of the material facts that I have represented herein should change prior to closing of the Loan; (8) in the event that my payments on the Loan become delinquent, the Lender, its servicers, successors or assigns may, in addition to any other rights and remedies that it may have relating to such delinquency, report my name and account information to one or more consumer reporting agencies; (9) ownership of the Loan and/or administration of the Loan account may be transferred with such notice as may be required by law; (10) neither Lender nor its agents, brokers, insurers, servicers, successors or assigns has made any representation or warranty, express or implied, to me regarding the property or the condition or value of the property; and (11) my transmission of this application as an "electronic record" containing my "electronic signature," as those terms are defined in applicable federal and/or state laws (excluding audio and video recordings), or my facsimile transmission of this application containing a facsimile of my signature, shall be as effective, enforceable and valid as if a paper version of this application were delivered containing my original written signature.

Acknowledgement. Each of the undersigned hereby acknowledges that any owner of the Loan, its servicers, successors and assigns, may verify or reverify any information contained in this application or obtain any information or data relating to the Loan, for any legitimate business purpose through any source, including a source named in this application or a consumer reporting agency.

Borrower's Signature	Date	Co-Borrower's Signature	Date
X		X	

X. INFORMATION FOR GOVERNMENT MONITORING PURPOSES

The following information is requested by the Federal Government for certain types of loans related to a dwelling in order to monitor the lender's compliance with equal credit opportunity, fair housing and home mortgage disclosure laws. You are not required to furnish this information, but are encouraged to do so. The law provides that a lender may not discriminate either on the basis of this information, or on whether you choose to furnish it. If you furnish the information, please provide both ethnicity and race. For race, you may check more than one designation. If you do not furnish ethnicity, race, or sex, under Federal regulations, this lender is required to note the information on the basis of visual observation and surname if you have made this application in person. If you do not wish to furnish the information, please check the box below. (Lender must review the above material to assure that the disclosures satisfy all requirements to which the lender is subject under applicable state law for the particular type of loan applied for.)

BORROWER ☐ I do not wish to furnish this information	**CO-BORROWER** ☐ I do not wish to furnish this information
Ethnicity: ☐ Hispanic or Latino ☐ Not Hispanic or Latino	**Ethnicity:** ☐ Hispanic or Latino ☐ Not Hispanic or Latino
Race: ☐ American Indian or Alaska Native ☐ Asian ☐ Black or African American ☐ Native Hawaiian or Other Pacific Islander ☐ White	**Race:** ☐ American Indian or Alaska Native ☐ Asian ☐ Black or African American ☐ Native Hawaiian or Other Pacific Islander ☐ White
Sex: ☐ Female ☐ Male	**Sex:** ☐ Female ☐ Male

To be Completed by Loan Originator:
This information was provided:
☐ In a face-to-face interview
☐ In a telephone interview
☐ By the applicant and submitted by fax or mail
☐ By the applicant and submitted via e-mail or the Internet

Loan Originator's Signature X		Date
Loan Originator's Name (print or type)	Loan Originator Identifier	Loan Originator's Phone Number (including area code)
Loan Origination Company's Name	Loan Origination Company Identifier	Loan Origination Company's Address

Uniform Residential Loan Application
Freddie Mac Form 65   7/05 (rev.6/09)   Page 4 of 5   Fannie Mae Form 1003   7/05 (rev.6/09)

FIGURE 10.1 FNMA/FHLMC residential loan application. (*continued*)

CONTINUATION SHEET/RESIDENTIAL LOAN APPLICATION		
Use this continuation sheet if you need more space to complete the Residential Loan Application. Mark **B** f or Borrower or **C** for Co-Borrower.	Borrower:	Agency Case Number:
	Co-Borrower:	Lender Case Number:

I/We fully understand that it is a Federal crime punishable by fine or imprisonment, or both, to knowingly make any false statements concerning any of the above facts as applicable under the provisions of Title 18, United States Code, Section 1001, et seq.

Borrower's Signature	Date	Co-Borrower's Signature	Date
X		X	

Uniform Residential Loan Application
Freddie Mac Form 65   7/05 (rev.6/09)   Page 5 of 5   Fannie Mae Form 1003   7/05 (rev.6/09)

Completing Loan Application Forms

The application form provides the lender with the borrower's financial and other information with which to make a loan decision. The completeness and accuracy of the information can affect whether a loan request is approved or rejected.

The buyer's loan package that gets submitted to underwriting typically contains two applications, a handwritten one provided by the borrower and a typed application that often includes an expansion of the information originally supplied by the borrower. The typed application is the result of a personal interview and allows the lender and/or mortgage broker to fill in any gaps left by the handwritten application.

With the increase in financial fraud, the importance of the loan application, in the borrower's own handwriting, has taken on greater significance. In the Acknowledgement and Agreement section of the loan application (Figure 10.1, Section IX), the borrower confirms that the information provided is accurate and is warned that deliberate misrepresentation can result in severe punishment.

If the loan officer or mortgage correspondent's workload allows, there is a number of good reasons why it may be beneficial to have him or her present as a guide when the borrower completes the loan application.

- This gives the loan person an opportunity to further interview the borrower and perhaps acquire additional information not asked for in the application. This information may be helpful to the borrower's package.

    For example, the borrower may be receiving a promotion or an increase in salary in the immediate future. When the loan officer recognizes that this information will help in qualifying the borrower, it can be added to the application.

- Many borrowers are applying for a real estate loan for the first time. They are not sure what to expect and have questions regarding the whole process. The loan officer can answer their questions and explain the process to them. If they understand what is involved, the entire transaction will go much more smoothly.

- If during the interview, the borrower seems unable to qualify, the loan officer or correspondent may be able to offer alternative loan options for which the borrower may be able to qualify. In some cases, the loan person merely creates a "roadmap" by providing the prospective borrower with a list of what they must do regarding, income, assets, etc., to qualify for a loan.

A prospective borrower usually is provided with a basic list of items that the lender will need when the borrower applies for a loan. The list is a reminder of the information a lender will need to make a final loan decision. The list usually includes pay stubs, bank statements, tax returns, W-2 forms, etc. In the past, many borrowers were "guided" to the "stated income" or "no documentation" type of loan simply because the documentation requirements were much fewer.

Equal Credit Opportunity Act (ECOA)

The federal **ECOA** prohibits discrimination on the basis of race, color, religion, national origin, age, sex, or marital status, or on the grounds of receipt of income from a public assistance program. Since the act includes any person who regularly extends or arranges credit, it clearly applies to real estate lenders.

Some of the basic provisions of the act that affect real estate lenders are these:

1. Lenders cannot ask if the borrower is divorced or widowed. They may ask if the borrower is married, unmarried, or separated. For purposes of the law, unmarried means single, divorced, or widowed.

2. Lenders cannot ask about receiving alimony or child support unless the borrower is first notified that it need not be revealed. However, lenders may ask about obligations to pay alimony or child support.

3. Lenders cannot ask about birth control practices or childbearing intentions or capabilities.

4. Lenders must notify applicants in writing within 30 days as to what action has been taken on their applications. In case of disapproval, the reason must be given.

5. While borrowers may still provide information explaining blemishes, with the reliance upon automated credit scoring explanation, such letters have largely lost their persuasive ability. Divorce remains a major reason for blemished credit history on joint accounts. It should be noted, however, that many lenders do not consider divorce as "beyond the control" of the borrower (unlike a job loss or medical complications), and this often does impact a loan decision.

Real Estate Settlement Procedures Act (RESPA)

Known as **RESPA**, this law applies only to first loans on one-to-four-unit residential properties. The main provisions of the act are as follows:

1. A lender must give the borrower a written estimate of the settlement or closing costs. This estimate is called a GFE, or good faith estimate (see the Case and Point in Chapter 9). The estimate includes reserves collected for taxes, insurance, or prorations, if the loan is to be impounded. The estimate must be given or mailed to the borrower within three business days of the date of the loan application. One day before settlement, the borrower has the right to inspect an itemized list of the closing costs. (See the Case & Point at the end of this chapter regarding the expansion of this rule with the 2009 enactment of the Mortgage Disclosure Improvement Act, known as the MDIA.)

2. Within the same three business days, the borrower must be given the Department of Housing and Urban Development's booklet that explains and gives information on closing costs.

3. Escrow and/or title companies must use a HUD-1 Settlement Sheet.

4. An anti-kickback provision prohibits real estate agents from generating unearned referral fees.

Verifying the Information on the Application

What happens after the loan application is completed? Fully documented loans as well as many other loan options require written verification of employment and checking and savings account data. A credit report is ordered, which itemizes current debt balances and monthly payments. Each of these debts is then rated. Credit reports also disclose recorded information, such as judgments, divorces, and other liens against the borrower. Then, the borrower's credit history is given as a credit score. See Chapter 9, Qualifying the Borrower, for more details.

Because conventional lenders depend more and more on credit scores for their approval decisions, to stay competitive, Fannie Mae, Freddie Mac, the FHA, the DVA, and Cal-Vet have adopted an "alternative documentation" process for their loan-verification requirements. The most recent three months of bank statements and pay stubs plus the last two years of W-2 forms often are used as sufficient verification, especially for salaried borrowers with high credit scores. Tax returns are still required for self-employed borrowers or those who own rental real estate.

Loan Package

The loan officer or correspondent's next job is to assemble the **loan package**, which consists of all the forms, documents, and reports the lender needs to make a decision on the loan. If the loan officer does not have the authority to make the loan, the package is then given to a loan committee or to an underwriter who represents a lender.

A typical loan package might include: (1) borrower's loan application, (2) appraisal of the property, (3) verification of employment, (4) verification of banks statements, (5) credit report, (6) purchase contracts, (7) escrow instructions and preliminary title report, (8) documentation showing where the funds for the down payment and closing cost are coming from, which is often called "source of the funds," and (9) other supporting documents, such as tax returns, W-2 forms, and so on.

Experienced loan officers realize the importance of a loan package. They know that a complete and neat package is more likely to be approved. They also anticipate the questions or objections that a committee or underwriter may have and answer them in advance. For example, if the borrower has had a bankruptcy, the loan officer knows that there will be questions such as: Why did the borrower have a bankruptcy? When was it discharged? Has the borrower reestablished credit? Depending upon the severity of the information, the loan officer includes an explanation, usually in the cover letter submitted with the loan package.

With today's market conditions, it is much more likely that the loan officer will help a borrower do the things necessary to improve a credit score prior to submission.

10.2 HOW IS A LOAN APPROVED?

The loan approval process varies depending upon the lender. Conventional loans made by banks and thrift institutions are approved by authorized individuals or by a loan committee. If the approval is to be made by an individual, he or she will have the authority to approve loans up to a specific dollar amount. Any loan greater than the said dollar amount must be approved by a supervisor or a loan committee. Large banks and thrift institutions may have layers of committees with loan amount limitations at each level.

Technical advances now allow loan officers to submit a borrower's information directly to a Fannie Mae or Freddie Mac authorized automated loan analysis program. The complete loan file, including all supporting documentation, is then submitted for final approval by authorized underwriters. These underwriters, in turn, determine if any other documentation is required. These "conditions" must be satisfied before the loan can be completed. The automated systems have eliminated what used to be called personal or handwritten underwriting. As long as underwriters do not override the automated system with any personal decisions, they are protected from any responsibility in the case of the borrower's default.

Federal Housing Administration (FHA) and Department of Veterans Affairs (DVA)

Criticism of the former practice of submitting all FHA- and DVA-backed loan packages directly to these agencies led to the adoption of the FHA Direct Endorsement System and the DVA Automatic System. Lenders approved to underwrite loans under these systems are labeled as either *supervised* or *nonsupervised lenders*, with nonsupervised lenders having the most latitude. Today, the majority of FHA- and DVA-backed loans are approved by nonsupervised lenders, such as mortgage companies.

To be approved as a nonsupervised lender, companies must meet the guidelines set forth by FHA and DVA. For example, a nonsupervised mortgage company may be sponsored by an approved direct endorsement lender, to whom the mortgage company submits the FHA-backed loan for final approval. In this case, FHA requires both the direct endorsement lender and the mortgage company to meet certain net worth requirements and to submit to an annual audit procedure. Note: See the case and Point in Chapter 6 wherein it is noted that FHA has recommended a significant change to this lender authorization and endorsement procedure.

Once the mortgage company submits the FHA or DVA package to its sponsoring direct endorsement lender, and said lender approves the package, the loan is also automatically approved by the FHA or DVA and sent to be insured or guaranteed by the appropriate agency. This "in-house" form of underwriting dramatically reduces the time required for FHA or DVA loan approval and closing.

Fair Credit Reporting Act

The federal **Fair Credit Reporting Act** affects credit reporting agencies and users of credit information. If a loan is rejected because of information in a credit report, the borrower must be notified and given the name and address of the credit agency. The borrower then has the right to obtain from the agency the following:

1. All the information it has in its file on the borrower.
2. Sources of the information.
3. All the creditors to whom the agency has furnished reports within the last six months.

If an error is found, the credit agency must make the correction. If there is a dispute over any reported credit information, the borrower has the right to submit a Consumer Statement, which is generally limited to 100 words or less, explaining his or her side of the story. The credit agency must include this consumer statement in all subsequent credit inquires.

The reliance upon credit scoring has spawned a process by which, for a fee, consumers can accelerate a positive change in their credit scores by correcting inaccurate information quickly and then having the credit agency recalculate their new credit score to take advantage of a more favorable interest rate on their loan. Normally, a correction and recalculation of a credit score could take 60 days or longer. Called "rapid rescoring," this fee-based, special fast-track system might be able to reduce that time to just a day or two. But the cost can be substantial and may be a deterrent for some situations.

10.3 CLOSING THE LOAN

Once a loan has been approved, the next phase is called closing. Loan closings are usually handled by independent third parties, such as title and escrow companies. All the parties involved in the real estate transaction (buyer, seller, and lender) deliver their instructions, documents, and money to the escrow company. While a broker may deliver "instructions" to the escrow holder, it should be noted that the broker is not a party and does not directly control the closing. Exceptions arise, of course, when brokers act as principals.

In southern California, it is customary for escrows to be handled by independent escrow companies or the escrow departments of banks and title companies. In northern California, it is more common for escrow departments of title companies to handle the escrow. Some real estate companies, particularly the larger ones, have their own escrow departments. These companies close their own transactions, if approved by the lender to do so, and use the title company only for the title insurance. With the demand for more transparency and arm's length transactions, these in-house services are dwindling.

When all the instructions have been complied with, the escrow company instructs the title company to record the applicable deeds and notes. Escrow also prepares closing statements, and disburses the money after recording has been confirmed. This final step of recording is when ownership changes hands.

Loan Documents for Escrow

The main loan documents prepared by the lender are:

1. Promissory note (Figure 10.2).
2. Deed of trust (Figure 10.3).
3. Truth-in-lending disclosure statement (Figure 10.4).

The promissory note outlines the financial terms of the loan: amount of loan, interest rate, monthly payments, date of first

FIGURE 10.2 Promissory note (partial).

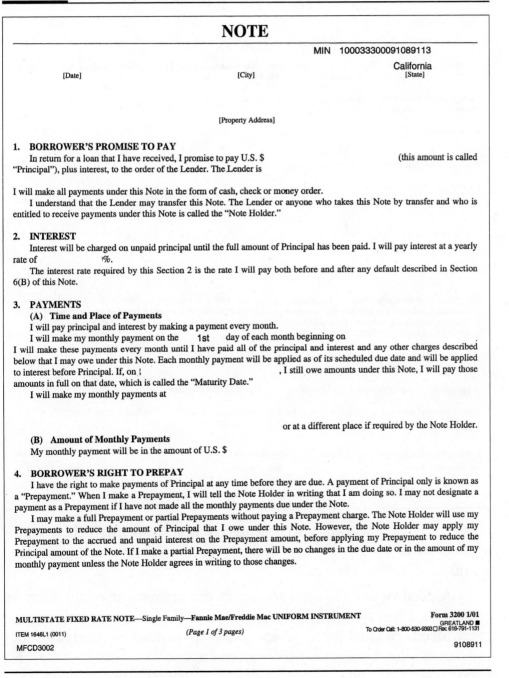

NOTE

MIN 100033300091089113

California
[State]

[Date]   [City]

[Property Address]

1. BORROWER'S PROMISE TO PAY

In return for a loan that I have received, I promise to pay U.S. $ (this amount is called "Principal"), plus interest, to the order of the Lender. The Lender is

I will make all payments under this Note in the form of cash, check or money order.

I understand that the Lender may transfer this Note. The Lender or anyone who takes this Note by transfer and who is entitled to receive payments under this Note is called the "Note Holder."

2. INTEREST

Interest will be charged on unpaid principal until the full amount of Principal has been paid. I will pay interest at a yearly rate of   '%.

The interest rate required by this Section 2 is the rate I will pay both before and after any default described in Section 6(B) of this Note.

3. PAYMENTS

(A) Time and Place of Payments

I will pay principal and interest by making a payment every month.

I will make my monthly payment on the   1st   day of each month beginning on   . I will make these payments every month until I have paid all of the principal and interest and any other charges described below that I may owe under this Note. Each monthly payment will be applied as of its scheduled due date and will be applied to interest before Principal. If, on   , I still owe amounts under this Note, I will pay those amounts in full on that date, which is called the "Maturity Date."

I will make my monthly payments at

or at a different place if required by the Note Holder.

(B) Amount of Monthly Payments

My monthly payment will be in the amount of U.S. $

4. BORROWER'S RIGHT TO PREPAY

I have the right to make payments of Principal at any time before they are due. A payment of Principal only is known as a "Prepayment." When I make a Prepayment, I will tell the Note Holder in writing that I am doing so. I may not designate a payment as a Prepayment if I have not made all the monthly payments due under the Note.

I may make a full Prepayment or partial Prepayments without paying a Prepayment charge. The Note Holder will use my Prepayments to reduce the amount of Principal that I owe under this Note. However, the Note Holder may apply my Prepayment to the accrued and unpaid interest on the Prepayment amount, before applying my Prepayment to reduce the Principal amount of the Note. If I make a partial Prepayment, there will be no changes in the due date or in the amount of my monthly payment unless the Note Holder agrees in writing to those changes.

MULTISTATE FIXED RATE NOTE—Single Family—Fannie Mae/Freddie Mac UNIFORM INSTRUMENT   Form 3200 1/01
                                                                            GREATLAND ■
ITEM 1646L1 (0011)   *(Page 1 of 3 pages)*   To Order Call: 1-800-530-9393 □ Fax 616-791-1131

MFCD3002   9108911

FIGURE 10.3 Deed of trust (partial).

RECORDING REQUESTED BY

AND WHEN RECORDED MAIL TO

─────────────────────────[Space Above This Line For Recording Data]─────────────────────────

DEED OF TRUST

MIN: 100033300091089113

DEFINITIONS

Words used in multiple sections of this document are defined below and other words are defined in Sections 3, 11, 13, 18, 20 and 21. Certain rules regarding the usage of words used in this document are also provided in Section 16.

(A) "Security Instrument" means this document, which is dated   , together with all Riders to this document.

(B) "Borrower" is

Borrower is the trustor under this Security Instrument.

(C) "Lender" is
Lender is a   organized and existing under
the laws of   . Lender's address is

(D) "Trustee" is

(E) "MERS" is Mortgage Electronic Registration Systems, Inc. MERS is a separate corporation that is acting solely as a nominee for Lender and Lender's successors and assigns. **MERS is the beneficiary under this Security Instrument.** MERS is organized and existing under the laws of Delaware, and has an address and telephone number of P.O. Box 2026, Flint, MI 48501-2026, tel. (888) 679-MERS.

(F) "Note" means the promissory note signed by Borrower and dated   The Note states that Borrower owes Lender
                                    Dollars (U.S. $) plus interest. Borrower has promised to pay this debt in regular Periodic Payments and to pay the debt in full not later than

(G) "Property" means the property that is described below under the heading "Transfer of Rights in the Property."

CALIFORNIA—Single Family—Fannie Mae/Freddie Mac UNIFORM INSTRUMENT   **Form 3005 1/01**
ITEM 9926L1 (0011)—MERS   *(Page 1 of 12 pages)*   GREATLAND ■
                                                                                To Order Call: 1-800-530-9393 □ Fax 616-791-1131
MFCA3114   _9108911

payment, and so on. The promissory note also lists other conditions such as late charges, prepayment privileges and penalties, and acceleration clauses.

A deed of trust is used to secure the repayment of the loan by creating a lien against the property. As explained in an earlier chapter, deeds of trust are used in California instead of mortgages because of the ease with which a lender can foreclose in case of a borrower's default.

FIGURE 10.4 Sample truth-in-lending disclosure statement.

TRUTH-IN-LENDING DISCLOSURE STATEMENT
(THIS IS NEITHER A CONTRACT NOR A COMMITMENT TO LEND)

Applicants: Prepared By:

Property Address:

Application No: Date Prepared:

ANNUAL PERCENTAGE RATE	FINANCE CHARGE	AMOUNT FINANCED	TOTAL OF PAYMENTS
The cost of your credit as a yearly rate	The dollar amount the credit will cost you	The amount of credit provided to you or on your behalf	The amount you will have paid after making all payments as scheduled
%	$	$	$

☐ REQUIRED DEPOSIT: The annual percentage rate does not take into account your required deposit

PAYMENTS: Your payment schedule will be:

No. of Pmts	Amount of Payments **	Payments Due	No. of Pmts	Amount of Payments **	Payments Due	No. of Pmts	Amount of Payments **	Payments Due	No. of Pmts	Amount of Payments **	Payments Due

☐ DEMAND FEATURE: This obligation has a demand feature.

☐ VARIABLE RATE FEATURE: This loan contains a variable rate feature. A variable rate disclosure has been provided earlier.

CREDIT LIFE/CREDIT DISABILITY: Credit life insurance and credit disability insurance are not required to obtain credit, and will not be provided unless you sign and agree to pay the additional cost.

Type	Premium	Signature	
Credit Life		I want credit life insurance.	Signature:
Credit Disability		I want credit disability insurance.	Signature:
Credit Life and Disability		I want credit life and disability insurance.	Signature:

INSURANCE: The following insurance is required to obtain credit:

☐ Credit life insurance ☐ Credit disability ☐ Property insurance ☐ Flood insurance

You may obtain the insurance from anyone you want that is acceptable to creditor.

☐ If you purchase ☐ property ☐ flood insurance from creditor you will pay $ for a one year term.

SECURITY: You are giving a security interest in:

☐ The goods or property being purchased ☐ Real property you already own.

FILING FEES: $

LATE CHARGE: If a payment is more than   days late, you will be charged   %

PREPAYMENT: If you pay off early, you ☐ may ☐ will not have to pay a penalty.

                      ☐ may ☐ will not be entitled to a refund of part of the finance charge.

ASSUMPTION: Someone buying your property

☐ may ☐ may, subject to conditions ☐ may not assume the remainder of your loan on the original terms.

See your contract documents for any additional information about nonpayment, default, any required repayment in full before the scheduled date and prepayment refunds and penalties ☐ * means an estimate ☐ all dates and numerical disclosures except the late payment disclosures are estimates.

You are not required to complete this agreement merely because you have received these disclosures or signed a loan application.

* * NOTE: The Payments shown above include reserve deposits for Mortgage Insurance (if applicable), but exclude Property Taxes and Insurance.

THE UNDERSIGNED ACKNOWLEDGES RECEIVING A COMPLETED COPY OF THIS DISCLOSURE.

Applicant   Date   Applicant   Date

Applicant   Date   Applicant   Date

Lender   Date

As shown in Figure 10.3, a deed of trust does not outline specific financial terms like the promissory note. A deed of trust shows only the loan amount, not the interest rate, monthly payments, or other information. The deed of trust shows that, if the debt it secures is not paid, the property may be sold to satisfy the debt. The deed of trust is recorded, while the promissory note is not. Thus, to maintain confidentiality between the lender and borrower, the deed of trust shows only the amount of the loan, not the repayment terms. In addition, the deed of trust contains many other detailed agreements between the borrower and lender.

Truth-in-Lending Law (Regulation Z)

In 1968, Congress passed the **Truth-in-Lending Law**, known as TIL, in an effort to create a way for borrowers to compare loan costs from one lender to another as they shop for the best terms. A key feature of TIL is the requirement for lenders to calculate and present to the borrower a statement showing the annual percentage rate (APR). In addition to the interest rate on the loan, the APR takes into account the "total cost" of the loan, which includes certain fees and other costs incurred to acquire the loan.

The TIL applies whether the loan is for real estate or personal property. For example, when you borrow to purchase a car, the lender must disclose the APR. Today's use of computers and financial calculators has eliminated the use of old-fashioned charts and tables to arrive at the APR.

There continues to be confusion about the definition of APR is and how it is calculated. The APR is usually greater than the interest rate on the promissory note, as it includes additional costs. To understand the APR, let's start with some definitions. A **prepaid finance charge** is a fee paid separately to a lender or a fee withheld from the loan proceeds. These prepaid finance charges typically include loan origination fees, prepaid interest, tax service fee, and mortgage insurance, to name a few. The amount financed is the loan amount minus the prepaid finance charges. The amount financed is the figure used to calculate the APR. Here is a simple example:

If a borrower applies for a $50,000 loan and the prepaid finance charges total $2,000, the amount financed is $48,000 ($50,000 − $2,000). The interest rate for the $50,000 loan is 7 percent amortized for 10 years; this results in a monthly payment of $580.54.

The calculations are as follows:

Total Payments	$69,665	[$580.54×120 months (10 yrs×12) = $69,664.80 round to $69,665]
Less: Loan Amount	−50,000	
Total Interest	$19,665	(total interest to be paid over the life of the loan)
Plus: Prepaid Finance Charge	+2,000	
Total Finance Charge	$21,665	

Having calculated the amount financed, total payments, and the finance charge, we turn to the APR. Using a computer program or a programmed financial calculator, the APR would be determined to be 7.928 percent. Here is one way to think about APR: The monthly payment for borrowing $50,000 for 10 years at 7 percent is $580.54. If one borrowed only $48,000 ($50,000 minus the $2,000 fees), and retained the 10-year term and the same payment, the rate would be 7.928 percent. It stands to reason that if one borrows less money for the same term and payment, the rate will increase. Thus, the APR rate is higher than the note rate.

The APR does not determine the note interest rate but is a way of informing the borrower of the "effective" rate of interest when comparing loan costs. The bottom line is that, when shopping a loan, interest rate quotes can be deceiving when closing costs vary from lender to lender, so the APR is meant to serve as a guide as to which loan offer might be best. This percentage could also be used when comparing what type of loan to get versus using a credit card, or getting a personal line of credit; it is a way to compare "apples to apples." Since there is so much confusion about how the APR is calculated, borrowers are often advised to compare the loan costs identified on a good faith estimate (GFE).

In addition to disclosing the APR, TIL requires the lender to disclose other information about the loan, such as the prepayment penalty, if any; late charge fees; and, if applicable, the three-day right to cancel on any refinance loan. TIL is regulated by the Federal Reserve under its Regulation Z.

Closing Costs

Calculating closing costs for a borrower is not a simple task. Real estate agents frequently estimate closing costs by using simple rules of thumb. Lenders must be more precise: they itemize each cost and then give a good faith estimate of the total.

Figure 10.5 lists the typical closing costs for the sale of a $250,000 home financed with a $200,000 loan at 7 percent interest, amortized for 30 years. Closing costs may vary by location.

Nonrecurring Closing Costs

Nonrecurring closing costs are one-time charges that the buyer-borrower usually pays at close of escrow. However, it must be stressed that the payment of closing costs is negotiable between the buyer and seller. Nonrecurring closing costs would include:

1. *Loan origination fee.* This fee compensates the lender for some of its expenses in originating the loan, preparing documents, and

FIGURE 10.5 Sample closing cost.

Sales Price	$250,000
Loan Amount	$200,000
Loan Origination	$3,000
CLTA Title Policy	1,122
ALTA Title Policy	475
Escrow Fee	450
Credit Report	20
Appraisal Fee	400
Tax Service	75
Notary and Misc. Fees	140
Recording Fees	80
Pest Control Inspection	125
Total Nonrecurring Closing Costs	$5,887
Tax Proration	$275
Hazard Insurance Premium	475
Prepaid Interest	690
Total Recurring Closing Costs	$1,440
Combined Closing Costs	$7,327

related work. The fee is usually a percentage of the loan, typically around 1 percent. It is common today for the originating lender to charge an additional processing fee.

2. *Title policy.* Title policies are issued by title insurance companies, insuring buyers' and lenders' interests in the property against defects of title. There are two basic types of coverage in California—the California Land Title Association, or CLTA, and the American Land Title Association, or ALTA (sometimes referred to as the buyer's policy). Most lenders require the ALTA policy because it provides additional coverage for the lender and is usually paid for by the buyer. The CLTA is often referred to as the seller's policy, as it assures the lender and borrower that the seller has a "good title" to convey. Who pays for the CLTA or standard title policy varies in California. For example, in southern California it is customary for the seller to pay; in central California it is often customary for the buyer to pay. There are other counties where the cost is split between the buyer and seller. However, it must be stressed that regardless of custom, the issue of who pays can always be negotiated. In our example, the buyer is paying for the policy.

3. *Escrow fee.* The escrow fee is charged for handling and supervising the escrow. As with title policies, custom also tends to dictate who

pays the escrow fee. The buyer is paying the entire fee in our example, although in reality, escrow fees are often split in some fashion between buyer and seller. Remember that the veteran in a DVA loan cannot pay an escrow fee.

4. *Credit report.* The lender obtains a credit report in qualifying a buyer. The cost of the report is usually charged to the buyer.

5. *Appraisal.* The cost of the appraisal varies with the type of loan and property and is usually paid "at the time of service" instead of at the close of escrow.

6. *Tax service.* This fee is paid to a tax service agency that, for the life of the loan, each year reviews the records of the taxing agencies. If a borrower fails to pay the property taxes, the agency reports this to the lender. If the lender is paying the taxes for the borrower, the agency also obtains the tax bill for the lender.

7. *Recording fees.* These cover the cost of recording the grant deed and deed of trust reconveyance.

8. *Notary fees.* Signatures on documents to be recorded, such as the grant deed, deed of trust, and reconveyances must be notarized. Be aware that new fees surface from time to time.

9. *Pest control inspection fee.* The buyer or seller may pay this charge, depending on local custom. The charge varies from area to area but is always negotiable. It has become the custom in many areas to sell "as is" in an effort to avoid pest control inspections and any subsequent work required. Caution should be exercised when selling a property in an "as is" condition. One cannot escape the responsibility for disclosure via an "as is" sale.

Recurring Closing Costs

The buyer also pays **recurring closing costs**, which are the expenses that continue during the ownership of the property. In our example in Figure 10.5, the buyer will be paying property tax prorations, hazard insurance premium, and prepaid interest. In other transactions, these recurring closing costs could include additional items beyond our example.

1. *Tax proration.* Most sales agreements provide for property tax prorations between the buyer and seller. This is calculated based upon the seller's current taxes and includes any prepaid or past due property taxes the seller may have paid or still owes. It is wise to remember that new taxes will be assessed based upon the sales price of a new purchase. Often the purchase price is substantially higher than the seller's current tax base and the buyer's taxes will be higher than the seller's previous taxes. In a market where

foreclosure and short sales occur with regularity, the buyer's new taxes could be lower than the seller's current assessment. This new "supplemental tax" consequence, especially if it represents an increase, is not prorated at the close of escrow. The new buyer receives a supplemental tax bill typically between 60 to 120 days following the close of escrow.

2. *Hazard insurance premiums.* Lenders require that the property be covered by insurance. In special flood zones, flood insurance is also required. Borrowers select their own insurance carriers and determine their coverage and premium cost. The buyer pays for the first-year premium at the close of escrow.

3. *Prepaid interest.* Depending upon which day escrow closes, the first loan payment may not be due on the first day of the next month, but rather the following month. However, the lender is entitled to interest from the day of funding, which is usually the close of escrow. The escrow company collects interest from the buyer on behalf of the lender from the day escrow closes until the day the buyer's loan payments begin to cover the interest. This is called prepaid interest. Note: Whereas rent is paid in advance, interest is paid in arrears. In other words, when a borrower pays the mortgage payment, he or she is paying for the use of the funds for the previous month.

10.4 AFTER THE LOAN: RIGHTS AND RESPONSIBILITIES

Loan Payments

Loan payments are usually due on the first of each month. After the loan is closed, the borrower is notified as to how to make payments. There are basically three methods lenders use to collect payments. One is the *monthly billing system.* Before the first of each month, lenders mail a notice of payment due. Borrowers mail payments with the notice. The second method is the use of *coupons.* Each month, borrowers send in the monthly payment and enclose a coupon furnished by the lender. The third is the automatic monthly withdrawal from the borrower's checking account. Most lenders now also allow such payment methods as ACH automatic withdrawal, pay by phone, and online payments.

After the first of the year, most lenders give borrowers a yearly statement for the previous year. California law requires this accounting to be provided no later than January 31 of the new year. The statement shows the principal, interest, and taxes and insurance (if included in the payments) that were paid during the year. If taxes and insurance are included in the payment, a reserve analysis is also included. The analysis calculates the amount of tax and insurance reserve that should be in the reserve account.

If there is a shortage in the impound (reserve) account due to a tax or insurance increase, the lender may ask that the shortage be made up immediately. A more common practice is to spread the shortage over the next 12 months along with the required increase for the future. For example, assume a borrower had a shortage of $180 in the reserve account. Rather than demand the entire $180 immediately, the lender would increase the monthly payment by $15, which would make up the shortage in one year. In addition, an adjusted amount would be collected for any shortages expected in the following year. If there is a surplus in the account, the borrower may apply it to a future mortgage payment, ask for it in cash, or apply it against the principal. Some banks simply send a check to the borrower after this evaluation is done.

In addition to checking the reserve balances, the lender also analyzes the monthly payment. The payment may be increased or decreased if there has been a change in taxes or insurance premiums.

Late Charges

When borrowers fail to make payments on time, lenders may collect late charges. The amount of the late charge and when it is collected is stated in the promissory note or deed of trust and on the payment coupon. Late charges by type of loan are as follows:

1. *FHA and DVA.* Four percent of the monthly payment, if not paid within 15 days of the due date. If the payment, including taxes and insurance, were $1,000 per month, the late charge would be $40.
2. *Cal-Vet.* Payments are late if made after the 10th of the month. The late charge is a flat $4.
3. *Conventional Loans.* Late charges on conventional loans vary. The State of California has a civil code provision that limits late charges on single-family, owner-occupied dwellings to 6 percent of the principal and interest payment, with a $5 minimum. The borrower must be given a minimum of 10 days to make payment, but conventional lenders usually charge 5 percent of the monthly payment if it is not paid within 15 days of the due date.

Prepayment Privileges and Penalties

Most lenders allow borrowers to make extra payments on the principal balance without penalty. This is called a prepayment privilege. When a prepayment penalty does exist, typical conventional loans allow 20 percent of the original loan amount as a prepayment privilege per year as set forth in civil code. This 20 percent includes any amounts paid toward principal reduction. For example, if the original loan amount were $100,000, the borrower could make an extra $20,000 payment, that is, 20 percent of $100,000, in any one year without penalty. If the borrower exceeds the privilege, a prepayment penalty of six months' interest on the then remaining balance may be charged. FHA and DVA loans do not permit **prepayment penalties**. However, the FHA requires that the interest on a loan be paid for the full month in which it is paid off. Thus, if a loan is paid off on the 5th of the month, the interest must be paid through the end of the month. For this reason, when FHA-insured loans are to be paid off, especially via a new refinance loan, the refinance is generally scheduled to close near the end of the month.

Cal-Vet does not charge penalties for early repayment. There is no standard prepayment penalty on conventional loans. Effective January 1, 2006, California law (Chap. 531; Financial Code Section 497) prohibits a prepayment penalty on certain owner-occupied dwellings after 36 months. However, recall from Chapter 3 that the time stretches to seven years for loans that come under the Real Property Loan Law. Because of this array of rules and laws, a borrower should check the promissory note and deed of trust to find out what a prepayment penalty, if any, might be.

Finally, in recent times prepayment penalties have virtually disappeared on most conventional loans. However, during times of high turnover due to frequent refinancing, lenders may reinstate prepayment penalties to reduce this "churning."

10.5 HANDLING LOAN TAKEOVERS

Loan Assumptions/Subject to Transfers

Enforceable due-on-transfer (sale) clauses are included in most promissory notes in an effort to prevent the takeover of existing loans by another new owner without the lender's prior permission. Transferring property on a "subject to" basis is typically done without the lender's permission. There can be serious ramifications to both buyer and seller in either type of transfer but these are beyond the scope of this text at this time. A short discussion on both forms of transfers is given below.

A real estate loan is assumed when the new borrower is approved by the lender and a formal assumption agreement is executed. When a loan is assumed, the original borrower—the seller—can be relieved of responsibility, provided release of liability is given.

In other words, if the original borrower wants to be relieved of liability, the new borrower must formally assume the loan and the original borrower must obtain a release of liability. This usually requires the new borrower to qualify for the loan. Unless there is a complete novation, both parties could be liable on a formal assumption. Loans can be formally assumed by applying to the lender.

Subject To's

Where property is purchased "**subject to**" the existing loan of record, the buyer does not agree to assume primary liability for the debt. Instead, the seller continues on the obligation; that is, although the buyer makes the payments directly to the lender, the seller remains responsible for any deficiency if a judgment is obtained.

As a practical matter, however, even though the buyer is not obligated to make the payments, the buyer will naturally continue the payments in order to keep the property. This is because the debt is secured by the property and the lender's security is held intact regardless of who makes the payments. Thus, if the buyer fails to make the payments, the lender proceeds against the property through foreclosure. The only time that the distinction between "assumption" and "subject to" becomes important is when the foreclosure results in a deficiency. If a deficiency judgment is obtained, the lender could proceed only against the maker of the note, the seller, if the buyer purchased subject to the existing loan. Had the buyer assumed primary liability for the debt, the buyer could be held liable for the deficiency. As for when a lender may or may not be able to obtain a deficiency judgment, see Chapter 11.

SUMMARY

Loan processing starts with receipt of the loan application, which includes basic information regarding the borrower's employment, income, assets, and debts. The lender usually confirms the information by obtaining verifications of employment and bank deposits, and checks the borrower's credit. During this time an appraisal is ordered. Automated approval programs are now used extensively to determine if other documentation may be required. After a loan package is assembled, the loan is submitted to appropriate individuals, underwriters, or committees for approval. This function is now largely to assure that the required documentation has been acquired and that it is congruent with the original loan application submission.

Beginning in 2009, following the economic downturn of the previous years, sufficient disclosure, including truth-in-lending and good faith estimates, has taken on added importance. The Mortgage Loan Improvement Act outlines the time table for such disclosures.

After the loan is approved, loan documents are prepared by the lender and sent to the escrow agent. Loan documents include a promissory note, deed of trust, and truth-in-lending disclosure statement.

The closing costs paid by the borrower are broken down into nonrecurring and recurring costs. Payments on loans are usually due on the first of the month. If the payments are late, the borrower owes a late charge. If the loan is paid off early, there may be a prepayment penalty. FHA, DVA, and Cal-Vet loans do not have a prepayment penalty, while some conventional loans do. With the lender's permission, some loans may be formally assumed or they may be taken subject to an existing loan.

IMPORTANT TERMS AND CONCEPTS

Equal Credit Opportunity Act (ECOA)

Fair Credit Reporting Act

FHA Direct Endorsement System

Loan application

Loan package

Nonrecurring closing costs

Nonsupervised lender

Prepaid finance charge

Prepayment penalty

Real Estate Settlement Procedures Act (RESPA)

Recurring closing costs

"Subject to"

Supervised lender

Truth-in-Lending Law (Regulation Z)

REVIEWING YOUR UNDERSTANDING

Questions for Discussion

1. Explain why many real estate lenders might qualify the buyer before appraising the property.

2. Briefly explain the purpose of the (a) Equal Credit Opportunity Act, (b) Real Estate Settlement Procedures Act (RESPA), (c) Fair Credit Reporting Act, and (d) Truth-in-Lending Law (Regulation Z).

3. List five forms, documents, or reports that are contained in a typical loan package.

4. Discuss how the procedures for approving a conventional real estate loan may differ from the procedures for approving an FHA-insured loan.

5. Define annual percentage rate (APR), prepaid finance charge, and loan origination fee.

6. Indicate who in your area customarily pays for the following closing costs: title insurance policy, escrow fee, pest control work, broker's commission, loan origination fee,

discount points on an FHA or DVA loan, pest control inspection fee, credit report, appraisal fee, and tax service.

7. What is the difference between recurring and nonrecurring closing costs? Give four examples of each.

Multiple-Choice Questions

1. Which of the following would be the most important information sought by lenders about a potential borrower?
   a. sex of the borrower
   b. need for a loan
   c. credit history of the applicant
   d. racial makeup of the area in which the property is located

2. Under the Equal Credit Opportunity Act, lenders are required to notify loan applicants on what action has been taken within a reasonable time period not exceeding
   a. two weeks.
   b. 30 days.
   c. three months.
   d. any time mutually agreed to between borrower and lender.

3. Processing an application for a real estate loan may include verification of
   a. employment.
   b. bank deposits.
   c. debts.
   d. all of the above.

8. What is the difference between assuming a seller's existing loan and purchasing subject to a seller's existing loan?

4. Under the Fair Credit Reporting Act, an applicant who has been denied credit is entitled to receive which of the following information from the credit reporting agency?
   a. sources of the information
   b. the financial standing of the reporting agency
   c. all of the debtors to whom the agency has furnished reports
   d. only the data that the agency provided the lender that rejected the loan

5. APR as used under Regulation Z stands for
   a. annuity percentage rate.
   b. annual percentage rate.
   c. annual property return.
   d. amortized property return.

6. The last step in originating and processing loans is
   a. a formal closing.
   b. qualifying the buyer.
   c. completing the application.
   d. qualifying the property.

7. A federal law that prohibits discrimination in lending solely on the basis of sex or marital status is the
   a. Equality in Sex and Marital Status Act.
   b. Equal Credit Opportunity Act.
   c. Truth-in-Lending Law.
   d. Fair Credit Reporting Act.

8. Property taxes for the fiscal year, July 1 to June 30, are $3,600 and they have not been paid. Escrow closes August 1. The tax proration will be:
   a. credit the seller $300.
   b. debit the seller $3,300.
   c. debit the buyer $3,300.
   d. credit the buyer $300.

9. For a typical home loan, the final approval or rejection rests with the
   a. real estate broker.
   b. mortgage broker.
   c. underwriter.
   d. escrow officer.

10. Recurring closing costs include
    a. title fee.
    b. property taxes.
    c. appraisal fee.
    d. credit report.

11. Under the Real Estate Settlement Procedures Act, lenders
    a. must comply with all requirements for income properties.
    b. must provide the applicant with a booklet on closing costs.
    c. are required to provide exact closing costs.
    d. may not use their own escrow firms.

12. The loan committee of a conventional home lender
    a. contains at least three members.
    b. might be one individual with authority limited to a specific dollar amount.
    c. typically meets only three days per week.
    d. has only limited authority to approve loans, since final authority for loan approval always rests with the chief managing officer of the lender.

13. In California, once a person has an owner-occupied home, any refinances or junior loans secured by a junior lien
    a. are illegal.
    b. are made only by private lenders.
    c. involve a three-day right of rescission.
    d. are not made by institutional lenders.

14. Nonrecurring closing costs include which of the following items: I. Loan origination fees, II. Escrow fees, III. Hazard insurance fees, IV. Tax reserves, V. Recording fees
    a. I, II, and III only.
    b. II, III, and IV only.
    c. I, II, and IV only.
    d. I, II, and V only.

15. Loan payments, whether required on the first of the month or another date
    a. may include reserves for taxes and insurance.
    b. are billed by either the monthly billing system, the coupon method, or by automatic deduction from a checking account.
    c. may involve charges for a late payment.
    d. involve all of the above.

16. The APR for a $100,000 loan at 7 percent amortized for 30 years, with no loan fees or financing charges of any sort is:
    a. 8.1 percent.
    b. 7.4 percent.
    c. 7.12 percent.
    d. 7 percent.

17. Under the Truth-in-Lending Law, Annual Percentage Rate refers to the
    a. nominal interest rate.
    b. effective interest rate.
    c. stated interest rate.
    d. any of the foregoing.

18. Loan escrows may not close without full compliance with the written instructions of
    a. the lender and borrower.
    b. the escrow company and borrower.
    c. the escrow company and lender.
    d. the broker and borrower.

19. RESPA is specifically designed to
    a. reduce settlement costs.
    b. standardize settlement costs.
    c. accomplish both (a) and (b).
    d. accomplish neither (a) nor (b).

20. Assumption of a loan is best illustrated when a
    a. property is sold subject to the loan.
    b. new owner of the property makes payments on a timely basis.
    c. takeover buyer signs a formal assumption and is approved by the lender.
    d. seller agrees to let buyer assume the loan, subject to approval by buyer's agent.

CASE & POINT

The Mortgage Disclosure Improvement Act (MDIA)

As a continuation of legislation designed to curb abusive lending practices, the MDIA rules went into effect on July 31, 2009. The new rules reemphasized the requirement that the original disclosures (the Mortgage Loan Disclosure Statement, the good faith estimate, and the truth-in-lending form) must be delivered to a prospective borrower within three days of receipt of the loan application. While the three-day rule has always been a lender requirement, the new legislation contained other important requirements.

Borrowers were relieved of the obligation to pay any fee (except a credit report fee) until the delivery of the disclosures. What represents "delivery" of the disclosures was clarified in the legislation. Only after the delivery period has elapsed are borrowers allowed to pay for the appraisal and other fees. The result of this section of the rules was to delay the initiation of the appraisal portion of any conventional loan file by at least three to six days.

A loan lock period can also be impacted by this delay in ordering the appraisal. Locking a loan and then having to wait 6 days before ordering the appraisal and another 10 days before receiving the completed appraisal can use up 16 days of a 30-day lock period, increasing the difficulty in closing the loan within the lock period.

Coupled with the Home Valuation Code of Conduct (HVCC), conventional appraisals must be ordered by the lender (originators are prohibited from ordering appraisals). Prior to ordering, a minimum broker's loan package detailing the estimated fees and costs must be received; only then can the lender send its disclosures and initiate the opening timeframe. Brokers complain that this process—requiring the immediate selection of a lender—prohibits them from later choosing a lender that may have a better interest rate or program for their borrower.

Following the original disclosure, if the annual percentage rate (APR) increases by more than 0.125 percent, a re-disclosed truth-in-lending form must be provided to the consumer. Loan documents cannot be signed until three business days have elapsed from this newly disclosed TIL. Again, brokers point out that they are unable to change rates and terms, even those that are advantageous for their borrowers, because last-minute delays in the disclosure process result in the loss of rate lock-ins or cause unacceptable delays in escrow closing periods.

While critics of the MDIA legislation point out that the inherent delays in the loan process negatively impact borrowers, advocates compliment the legislations as protecting consumers from abusive loan practices.

Chapter

11

PREVIEW

The basic responsibilities of the parties to a real estate loan appear very simple. In exchange for money loaned, borrowers agree to repay the loan according to the terms and conditions stipulated in the promissory note and deed of trust. However, in actual practice, there is much more to real estate loans than merely repaying principal and interest.

After completing this chapter, you should be able to:

1. Explain the major provisions outlined in a typical promissory note and deed of trust.
2. Outline the steps in a foreclosure procedure.
3. Demonstrate why lenders in California prefer trust deeds over mortgages as security for their loans.
4. List five ways a borrower and lender can minimize the possibility of a default and foreclosure.
5. Discuss how private and government mortgage insurance has reduced the lender's risk in granting real estate loans.
6. Calculate the mechanics of insurance coverage under PMI for 90 percent loans.
7. Describe the controversial practice known as redlining.
8. Explain the role of the Community Reinvestment Act (CRA).

Foreclosures and Other Lending Problems

11.1 COLLATERAL PROVISIONS OF DEEDS OF TRUST

Figure 11.1a is an example of the front page of a typical deed of trust, while Figure 11.1b is a list of major items in the complete document, which can run many pages, and contains several provisions designed to reduce the chance of default and foreclosure. The deed of trust defines the rights and duties of the three parties to the loan—the trustor or borrower, trustee or title holder, and the beneficiary or lender. Even if the trustor is current with payments on the promissory note, the beneficiary can still foreclose should the trustor default in the performance of any of the other requirements—the collateral provisions of the trust deed—including the following:

1. *Maintenance of the property.* The typical trust deed requires the trustor to keep the property in good condition, to pay for labor and materials whenever improvements are made, not to lay waste to the property and to comply with local building ordinances and other laws affecting the property—in short, to preserve the value of the property as security for the repayment of the loan.

2. *Hazard insurance.* To protect the security, the trustor agrees to maintain basic fire and windstorm insurance, with a "loss payee" clause in favor of the beneficiary. Under a loss payee provision, the lender may use any insurance proceeds to reduce the loan indebtedness, or turn over the funds to the owner to rebuild. When the trustor fails to maintain insurance satisfactory to the beneficiary, the latter may obtain a policy and charge the cost to the trustor. The cost of lender-acquired insurance is very high and is paid by an increase to the monthly impound account payment or, for

FIGURE 11.1a Partial deed of trust form.

Order No.

Escrow or Loan No.

RECORDING REQUESTED BY

When Recorded Mail To:

_____

SPACE ABOVE THIS LINE FOR RECORDER'S USE

DEED OF TRUST WITH ASSIGNMENT OF RENTS
(With Acceleration Clause)

This DEED OF TRUST, made _____, between _____ herein called TRUSTOR, whose address is _____, Placer Title Company, a California corporation, herein called TRUSTEE, and _____, herein called BENEFICIARY, WITNESSETH: That Trustor grants to Trustee in Trust, with Power of Sale, that property in the _____ County of _____, State of California, described as:

Together with the rents, issues and profits thereof, subject, however, to the right, power and authority hereinafter given to and conferred upon Beneficiary to collect and apply such rents, issues and profits.

For the Purpose of Securing (1) Payment of the sum of _____ with interest thereon according to the terms of a promissory note or notes of even date herewith made by Trustor, payable to order of Beneficiary and extensions or renewals thereof, and (2) the performance of each agreement of Trustor incorporated by reference or contained herein (3) Payment of additional sums and interest thereon which may hereafter be loaned to Trustor, or his successors or assigns, when evidenced by a promissory note or notes reciting that they are secured by this Deed of Trust.

If the Trustor shall convey or alienate said property or any part thereof or any interest therein or shall be divested of his title in any manner or way, whether voluntary or involuntary any indebtedness or obligation secured hereby, irrespective of the maturity date expressed in any note evidencing the same, at the option of the holder hereof and without demand or notice shall become due and payable immediately.

Signature of Trustor

BY _____   BY _____

BY _____   BY _____

BY _____   BY _____

Dated:

STATE OF CALIFORNIA   )

COUNTY OF _____)

On _____ before me, the undersigned Notary Public in and for said County and State, personally appeared

_____

_____

_____

personally known to me (or proved to me on the basis of satisfactory evidence) to be the person(s) whose name(s) is/are subscribed to the within instrument and acknowledged to me that he/she/they executed the same in his/her/their authorized capacity(ies), and that by his/her/their signature(s) on the instrument the person(s), or the entity upon behalf of which the person(s) acted, executed the instrument.

Witness my hand and official seal.

_____

Notary Public in and for said County and State   (Space above for official notarial area.)

FIGURE 11.1b   Partial deed of trust form. (*continued*)

1.   *Document number:* This is assigned to the document by the County Recorder's office. The book and page of the County Recorder's index books where the document is entered are shown adjacent to the document number.

2.   *County recorder stamps:* The large stamp reflects the time and date of recording of the document as well as reference to the fee paid for recording. These stamps are placed on the document by the clerk in the Recorder's Office.

3.   *Recording requested by:* This identifies the party requesting that the document be recorded and often shows the names of title companies when they submit groups of documents to the county for recording.

4.   *When recorded mail to:* After recording, the document will be mailed by the county to the addressee shown in this section. This would be the lender who issued the loan.

5.   *Title order no. and escrow no.:* On this line the title company order number will appear along with the customer escrow number if the document was recorded as part of a title order that culminated in the closing of an escrow.

6.   *Date of execution:* This should be the date of the signing of the deed of trust by the trustor (borrower) and also can be the date the document is prepared.

7.   *Trustor:* The name of the borrower, who is the record owner and identified as the trustor, is shown, as well as the borrower's status of record.

8.   *Trustee:* The name of the entity that is being granted the property with legal title to exercise a power of sale if necessary is shown and is referred to as the trustee.

9.   *Beneficiary:* The name of the lender is shown and is referred to as the beneficiary. This is the creditor to whom the debt is owing.

10.   *Words of conveyance:* These are the words used by which legal title to the property is transferred from the trustor to the trustee with power of sale. On the sample the wording "grants, transfers, and assigns to trustee, in trust, with power of sale" satisfies this need.

11.   *Legal description:* This identifies the property in question, which is usually by lot, block, and tract, by metes and bounds, or by government survey.

12.   *Amount of indebtedness:* The amount shown in the promissory note.

13.   *Signature of the trustor:* The signature of the trustor (borrower) will appear on the line in this section, and the name should be printed or typed beneath the signature.

14.   *Acknowledgment:* In this area a formal declaration is personally made before a notary public by the borrower who has executed (signed) the document, that such execution is borrower's act and deed. (This is a requirement before the instrument can be accepted for recording.) The borrower signs before the notary public, who then completes the acknowledgment.

15.   *Venue:* This identifies the state and county where the acknowledgment is taken.

16.   *Notary seal or stamp:* In this section the official seal of the notary public must be affixed or stamped.

those not impounded, via a bill sent for payment to the borrower. The lender could choose to add the premium cost to the principal, constituting an advance to the trustor, which could result in a default. Finally, if a borrower fails to maintain adequate insurance, the lender may accelerate the loan—that is, call the total principal balance immediately due and payable.

3. *Property taxes and other liens.* The trustor agrees to pay for property taxes, assessments, and all prior liens. Unless this is done, the beneficiary's interest can be eliminated by a tax sale, in which the state, after five continuous years of unpaid taxes, may sell the property. To help guard against this, the beneficiary may pay for these tax liens and then be reimbursed by the borrower. Depending on the lender, such advances may be billed to the trustor directly, with possible foreclosure action in the event of failure to repay, or the beneficiary may simply add the advances to the principal indebtedness. The loan is considered in default until the lender is reimbursed.

4. *Assignment of rents.* This clause is found in almost every trust deed. It provides that upon default by the trustor, the beneficiary may take possession of the property through a court-appointed trustee or receiver and collect the rents, applying them to the loan and to costs and expenses incurred. When there are sufficient sums collected from tenants in a property, it is possible that by applying them to the delinquent payments during the reinstatement period, default may be avoided. This is unlikely, however, because if the income from the property paid all the debts, there probably wouldn't be issues in the first place.

11.2 DEFAULT AND FORECLOSURE

Borrowers default on repayment of loans for a variety of reasons, some because of events beyond their control. Medical expenses, disability, death, and financial reversals such as loss of a job or business probably head the list. Other circumstances include the dissolution of marriage, bankruptcy, the excessive use of credit, and poor budgeting, although these circumstances are not considered beyond the control of the individual. Unless arrangements can be made with the lender to work out a satisfactory schedule for repayment following default, foreclosure is the ultimate price that the delinquent borrower must pay. However, most lenders try to avoid foreclosure wherever possible and use it only as a last resort, since most lenders are in the business of lending money and do not want to become involved in owning and managing real estate.

As foreclosures continued to mount, in early 2009, new legislation was introduced to encourage lenders to take steps to help borrowers retain their homes. (See the Case & Point at the end of this chapter for details.)

As noted earlier, a borrower may be in default not only through delinquency on payments of principal and interest, but also when there is a violation of other terms of the trust deed agreement to maintain the property and pay other liens in a timely manner. Regardless of the violation, lenders in California must follow a prescribed procedure in removing the delinquent debtor. Foreclosure may be accomplished through either trustee's sale or judicial sale.

Trustee's Sale

Virtually all trust deeds contain a power of sale clause, which empowers the trustee, in the event of default by the trustor, to sell the property at public auction. While the provisions of the power of sale are a matter of contract and may vary from instrument to instrument, there are statutes that specifically regulate foreclosures through a **trustee's sale**, found in California's Civil Code. The statutory requirements are as follows:

1. *Notice of default.* After notification and sufficient time for the trustor to satisfy any delinquent payments, the beneficiary will reach a point of being reasonably certain that a trustor is unable to make good on delinquent installment payments. The beneficiary then delivers the note and trust deed to the trustee. The trustee is instructed to record a **Notice of Default** in the county where the property is located and this filing starts the foreclosure clock. It must be recorded at least three months before a notice of sale can be advertised. An example of such notice is given in Figure 11.2. The notice must contain a correct legal description of the property, name of trustor, nature of the breach, and a statement to the effect that the party executing the notice of default has elected to sell the property in order to satisfy the obligation. While a trustor requests a Notice of Default through the Deed of Trust, under California law anyone may request a copy of the notice.

    Within 10 days after filing the Notice of Default, a copy must be sent by registered or certified mail to anyone whose request for notice appears on record. These are typically second trust deed holders who filed a Request for Notice, but there may be others with a recorded interest who may be affected, for whom the time is extended to 30 days. This notice must be sent by the trustee.

    During the three-month period preceding the advertising for sale, the trustor may reinstate the loan by paying all delinquent

FIGURE 11.2 Sample notice of default.

RECORDING REQUESTED BY
Serrano Reconveyance Company

AND WHEN RECORDED MAIL TO
NAME Serrano Reconveyance Company
STREET ADDRESS 13640 Roscoe Boulevard
CITY STATE ZIP Panorama City, CA 90051

———— SPACE ABOVE THIS LINE FOR RECORDER'S USE ————

NOTICE OF DEFAULT AND ELECTION TO SELL
UNDER DEED OF TRUST

NOTICE IS HEREBY GIVEN:
SERRANO RECONVEYANCE COMPANY , a corporation, is Trustee under a Deed of Trust
dated November 1, 200X
executed by Mr. & Mrs. John Foresight
                                                              as Trustor, to secure obligations
in favor of Serrano Mortgage Company
              (Loan # 277529)   as beneficiary
recorded November 10, 200X   as document no. 77-281295
in book T10686   page 822   of Official Records in the office of the
Recorder of Los Angeles   County, California, describing land therein as:

Lot 11 of Tract 5852 as per map recorded in Book 61, page 69 of Maps; and that
portion of Montevista, in the City of Los Angeles, County of Los Angeles, as per
Map recorded in Book 6, Page 324 of Miscellaneous Records, all known as 10522
Fernglen Ave, Tujunga
                                                              said obligations
including   one   note   for the sum of $ 23,000

That the beneficial interest under such deed and the obligations secured thereby are owned by the undersigned;
That a breach of, and default in, the obligations for which such deed is security has occurred in that payment has
not been made of:

The November 15, 200X and all subsequent installments are now in default
with interest paid to October 10, 200X .

That by reason thereof, the undersigned, present beneficiary under such deed, has executed and delivered to said
Trustee a written Declaration of Default and Demand for Sale, and has deposited with said Trustee such deed and
all documents evidencing obligations secured thereby, and has declared and does hereby declare all sums secured
thereby immediately due and payable and has elected and does hereby elect to cause the trust property to be sold
to satisfy the obligations secured thereby.

NOTICE
You may have the right to cure the default described herein and reinstate the mortgage or deed of trust. Section 2924c of the Civil Code permits certain defaults to be cured upon the payment of the amounts required by that section without requiring payment of that portion of principal and interest which would not be due had no default occurred. Where reinstatement is possible, if the default is not cured within three months following the recording of this notice, the right of reinstatement will terminate and the property may be sold. To determine if reinstatement is possible and the amount, if any, necessary to cure the default, contact the beneficiary or mortgagee or their successors in interest, whose name and address as of the date of this notice is

Name   Serrano Mortgage Company

Address 3731 Wilshire Blvd, Los Angeles

Dated   March 8, 200X

Serrano Mortgage Company

Penny Pincher, President

Title Order No. _____ T.S. No. 47739

TS-1 A&p(o.s.)

installments, costs, and trustee's fees. This **right of reinstatement**, or period of reinstatement, continues until five business days before the scheduled sale.

2. *Notice of sale.* After expiration of the reinstatement period, which includes three weeks for advertising the time and place of the trustee's sale, the beneficiary is entitled to the entire unpaid balance of the note, plus costs and trustee's fees. But the trustee must first record a **Notice of Sale**, similar to the sample shown in Figure 11.3. The Notice of Trustee's Sale must be recorded at least two weeks before the sale.

FIGURE 11.3 Sample notice of trustee's sale.

Foreclosures

Notice of Trustee's Sale
Under Deed of Trust
TF 47739
Loan No. 277529
57831
BT

Notice is hereby given that SERRANO RECONVEYANCE COMPANY, A California corporation as trustee, or successor trustee, or substituted trustee pursuant to the deed of trust recorded November 10, 20XX in book T10686 page 822 of Official Records in the office of the County Recorder of Los Angeles County, California, and pursuant to the Notice of Default and Election to Sell thereunder recorded March 21, 20XX Instrument No. 77-281295 of said Official Records, will sell on August 16, 20XX at 11:00 A.M., at the Oxford Street entrance to the building located at 3731 Wilshire Boulevard, City of Los Angeles, County of Los Angeles, State of California, at public auction, to the highest bidder for cash (payable at the time of sale in lawful money of the United States) all right, title, and interest conveyed to and now held by it under said deed in the property situated in said County and State described as follows:

PARCEL 1:

    Lot 11 of Tract 5852, in the City of Los Angeles, County of Los Angeles, State of California, as per map recorded in Book 61, Page 67 of Maps, in the office of the County Recorder of said County.

PARCEL 2:

    That portion of Montevista, in the City of Los Angeles, County of Los Angeles, State of California, as per map recorded in Book 6, Page 324, of Miscellaneous Records, described as follows:

    Beginning at Southeasterly corner of Lot 11 of Tract 5852, in the City of Los Angeles, as per map recorded in Book 61 Page 67 of Maps; thence along the Easterly line of said Lot 11, North 0 degrees 01' 40" West 40 feet to the Northeasterly corner of said Lot 11; thence Easterly along the Easterly prolongation of the Northerly line of said Lot 11 to a line that is parallel with and distant 10 feet Easterly, measured at right angles, from the Easterly line of said Tract 5852; thence South 11 degrees 16' 40" East to the Intersection with the Easterly prolongation of the Southerly line of said Lot 11; thence Westerly along the Easterly prolongation of said Southerly line to the point of beginning.

Property Address purportedly known as: 10522 Frengien Av., Tujunga, CA 91042.

Said sale will be made, but without covenant or warranty, express or implied, regarding title, possession or encumbrances, to satisfy the indebtedness secured by said Deed, including the fee and expense of the trustee and of the trusts created by said deed, advances thereunder, with interest as provided therein, and the unpaid principal of the note secured by said deed; to wit: $23,000.00 with interest thereon from November 15, 20XX as provided in said note.

Dated: July 8, 20XX

SERRANO RECONVEYANCE
COMPANY,
as such Trustee
(213) 385-3321
By J.E. Cornwall,
President
Authorized officer

(J85505 Tues. Jul 19, 26, Aug 2)

The notice must contain a correct identification of the property, such as the street address or legal description. It also must be published in a newspaper of general circulation in the county or jurisdiction in which the property is located. The publication must appear at least once a week for three weeks, not more than seven days apart. The notice must also be posted in a public place, such as a courthouse, and in some conspicuous place on the property, such as an attachment to a front door. Notice must be posted on the property no later than 20 days prior to sale. The sale must be held in a public place, during business hours, on a weekday, Monday through Friday. A copy of the Notice of Sale must also be mailed to those who had requested a copy of the notice of default.

3. *Final sale.* Any person, including the trustor and beneficiary, but not the trustee, may bid on the property through auction. The holder of the debt may offset the amount owed, up to the amount of the debt. Others must pay cash or its equivalent. A trustee's deed, similar to the one illustrated in Figure 11.4, is issued to the highest bidder. Any surplus funds—that is, funds remaining after paying off all costs, fees, and expenses, along with all junior liens in order of their priority—are given to the trustor.

   While no right of redemption exists after a trustee's sale, remember that the right of reinstatement, or period of reinstatement, continues until five days before the scheduled sale. Then, at the time of sale, the purchaser acquires all rights held by the former owner, becoming the successor in interest, and is entitled to immediate possession, subject to those having rights prior to the time when the trust deed was recorded (e.g., tenants' rights under a bona fide lease agreement). Lenders in California prefer the use of the Trustee's Sale under a Deed of Trust due to the fact that the procedures involved and the time required, which is approximately four months, are relatively easy to determine, whereas foreclosures under the judicial method and foreclosures involving mortgages entail court actions, with consequent uncertainty as to time. (See Figure 11.5.) If a trustee's sale is used instead of a judicial foreclosure, the lender cannot sue for a deficiency should one exist.

Judicial Sale

Instead of a trustee's sale, a trust deed may also be foreclosed as a mortgage, that is, through court action. Court foreclosures of trust deeds are not common and usually occur only when the lender seeks a deficiency judgment.

1. *Procedure.* After serving a complaint upon the defaulting debtor, trial is held and a judgment is entered through a decree of

FIGURE 11.4 Sample trustee's deed for a foreclosure resale.

RECORDING REQUESTED BY

SERRANO RECONVEYANCE COMPANY

AND WHEN RECORDED MAIL TO

NAME Lone Successor
ADDRESS 5800 Felton Avenue
CITY & STATE Van Nuys, CA 19401

If Required Affix Documentary Stamps Here

SPACE ABOVE THIS LINE FOR RECORDER'S USE

Documentary transfer tax $ 31.35
☒ Computed on full value of property conveyed, or
☐ Computed on full value less liens & encumbrances remaining thereon at time of sale.
Safeco Title Insurance Company
Signature of declarant or agent determining tax - firm name
☐ Unincorporated area City of Tujunga

TRUSTEE'S DEED

Executed by Serrano Reconveyance Company, a corporation, as Trustee under the deed of Trust referred to below and herein called "Trustee." to **Lone Successor, a single person**

herein called "Grantee".

The Deed of Trust herein referred to was executed by John Foresight & Mary Foresight and recorded on **November 10, 20XX** in book **T10686** page **822** , of Official Records in the office of the Recorder of **Los Angeles** County, California (herein referred to as "said Official Records", "said Recorder" and "said County and State", respectively) and was made for the purpose of securing obligations stated therein and other obligations thereunder.

Default under said Deed of Trust occurred as set forth in a notice of default and election to sell which was recorded in book **162** page **4** of said Official Records, and such default existed at the time of sale. After the lapse of at least 3 months after the recording of said notice of default and election to sell, Trustee gave notice of sale of the property described below, stating the time and place thereof, in the manner and for a time as required by law and by the provisions of said Deed of Trust. All requirements of said Deed of Trust for sale thereunder, all requirements of law regarding the mailing, publication, posting or personal delivery of copies of notice of default or notice of sale, and all other requirements of law relating to the making of said sale and this Deed were complied with.

Trustee, in the exercise of its powers under said Deed of Trust, offered said property for sale at public auction on **August 16, 20XX** at **11:00** A.M. o'clock, the time stated in said notice and at the place stated in said notice in **the Oxfords St entrance to the building at 3731 Wilshire Blvd. Los Angeles,** in said county and state, and sold said property to grantee for $ **28,500** , subject to all prior liens and encumbrances, said grantee being the highest bidder.

Trustee, in the exercise of its powers under said Deed of Trust, hereby grants to grantee, without any covenant or warranty whatsoever, the property referred to herein, which is located in said County and State and described as follows:

Lot 11 of Tract 5852 as per map recorded in Book 61, page 69 of Maps; and that portion of Montevista, in the City of Los Angeles, County of Los Angeles, as per Map recorded in Book 6, Page 324 of Miscellaneous Records, all known as 10522 Fernglen Ave, Tujunga.

Dated August 16, 20XX

STATE OF CALIFORNIA
COUNTY OF_____ } SS.

On_____ before me, the undersigned, a Notary Public in and for said County and State, personally appeared _____ known to me to be the _____President, and _____ _____ known to me to be _____Secretary of the corporation that executed the within Instrument, known to me to be the persons who executed the within Instrument on behalf of the corporation therein named, and acknowledged to me that such corporation executed the within instrument pursuant to its by-laws or a resolution of its board of directors.

_____
Signature of Notary

_____
Name (Typed or Printed) of Notary

MAIL TAX STATEMENTS TO:_____

Title Order No. _____ T. S. No._____
TS-23 (G.S.)

SECURITY TITLE INSURANCE COMPANY

By Joe E. Lewis
Joe E. Lewis Vice President
By Minica M Bond
Minica M Bond Assistant Secretary

FOR NOTARY SEAL OR STAMP

Name Address, City & State Zip

FIGURE II.5 Deeds of trust versus mortgages.

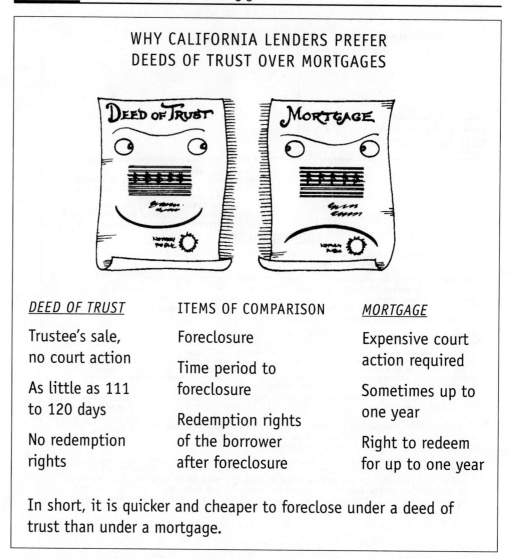

WHY CALIFORNIA LENDERS PREFER DEEDS OF TRUST OVER MORTGAGES

DEED OF TRUST	ITEMS OF COMPARISON	_MORTGAGE_
Trustee's sale, no court action	Foreclosure	Expensive court action required
As little as 111 to 120 days	Time period to foreclosure	Sometimes up to one year
No redemption rights	Redemption rights of the borrower after foreclosure	Right to redeem for up to one year

In short, it is quicker and cheaper to foreclose under a deed of trust than under a mortgage.

foreclosure and order of sale by an officer of the court, such as a sheriff or marshall. Meanwhile, the debtor has the right to reinstate by paying all delinquent installments plus costs and attorney's fees.

2. *Sale.* A notice of the time, place, and purpose of the sale is posted and publicized. The court thereafter conducts a public auction sale. The highest bidder receives a Certificate of Sale.

This conveys title to the property, subject to the debtor's right of redemption for a period of one year after the sale if there is a deficiency. If there is no deficiency, the deed is issued after three months. In addition to payment of the debt, the debtor is ordinarily also required to pay legal interest. If no redemption is made within this time, a deed is issued to the successful bidder.

Note that there is a right of "reinstatement" when a trustee's sale is undertaken. This allows the trustor to pay all delinquencies, including late charges, plus all costs of foreclosure, including trustee's fees, recording charges, publishing costs, etc. The trustor is then in a position to resume scheduled payments under the loan. When a judicial foreclosure is undertaken, there is a right of "redemption." This involves repayment of the debt.

3. *Deficiency judgments.* In the event that the sale does not bring enough funds to satisfy the debt, the creditor may obtain a **deficiency judgment**. However, certain types of loans are not subject to deficiency judgments under California's "Anti-deficiency Law." Purchase money loans on owner-occupied dwellings up to four units are the exceptions. Thus, when a person borrows money to purchase a home and thereafter loses it through foreclosure action, no deficiency judgment is permitted, except for FHA- and DVA-guaranteed loans. In the case of FHA and DVA loans, federal law supersedes state law, and the FHA and the DVA can and do seek deficiency judgments.

Deed in Lieu of Foreclosure

To avoid the costly and time-consuming process of foreclosure, the lender may accept a voluntary conveyance from the defaulting borrower. Usually this is accomplished by a **Deed in Lieu of Foreclosure**, though it could be by grant or **quitclaim deed** which should be simultaneously recorded with a deed of reconveyance. One advantage of such a transaction for the borrower is that there won't be a deficiency judgment, with a judicial foreclosure. The downside is that lenders will not accept such a deed if there are other liens, such as unpaid real estate taxes, because lenders want to take property free and clear of any other claims.

A Deed in Lieu requires cancellation of debt and reconveyance, while a quitclaim deed does not necessarily require this. Moreover, some future creditor may still view a Deed in Lieu of Foreclosure as a repossession and the borrower as a poor credit risk. The stigma and subsequent reduction in credit scores is much the same whether the loss of property is through a Deed in Lieu of Foreclosure or by foreclosure itself. There is also a serious question regarding liens not eliminated by a quitclaim deed, but this is better left to an attorney.

11.3 MINIMIZING LOAN DEFAULTS

It has been said that a loan that is not good for the lender is not good for the borrower. If the loan is marginal, as when the credit rating is poor, the borrower is more likely to default on payments, with the result that the lender will end up with a sour loan followed by foreclosure and, usually, the lender will take over the property. This section outlines a variety of ways to minimize or mitigate the chance of loss for both borrower and lender.

Impound Accounts

One way to reduce the possibility of default is through the establishment of an **impound account**. Under this concept, the borrower is required to pay, as a condition for receiving the loan, a pro rata portion of the annual property taxes and insurance each month. This effectively forces the debtor to budget each month amounts that would fall due in large sums if paid only once or twice a year. Requiring such payments 12 times a year by having borrowers add one-twelfth of the tax bill and insurance premiums to monthly payments of principal and interest reduces the chance of default. After all, even if the debtor is current on loan payments, the property may go into foreclosure because of default in payments on other property-related debts, in accordance with the terms of the trust deed.

In some areas an impound account is referred to as an **escrow account** or loan trust fund. Whatever its designation, it means the same. The lender deposits the tax and insurance portions of the installment payments into an escrow or impound account, remitting payments to the tax collector and insurance company as they fall due. The lender is assured that these bills are paid, while the debtor is relieved of a large obligation falling due in one or two lump sums at a time when it may be inconvenient to pay. Borrowers may establish these accounts and bear the responsibility for proper payments themselves.

Forbearance

By far, the most common default on real estate loans is for delinquent payments. When borrowers have legitimate reasons for their inability to pay, lenders will often make special arrangements to help such debtors retain their properties. Any arrangement that effectively delays or forestalls foreclosure action is referred to as **forbearance**. There are various ways in which lenders (through their loan administration efforts) can assist borrowers. These include a variety of moratorium schemes and recastings. (See the Case & Point at end of this chapter for information regarding 2008–2009 government intervention to assist struggling home buyers.)

Moratorium

A **moratorium** is a temporary suspension or **waiver** of payments. It acts to delay or defer action for collection of a debt. Four types of moratoria are explained below.

1. *Waiver of principal payments.* One form of moratorium is the suspension of principal payments, allowing delinquent borrowers to regain their financial balance. Only interest is paid in such cases. Since the principal portion of the monthly payment is the smaller amount, especially during the early years of a mortgage, this option is often of little assistance to a struggling borrower.

    A variation of this moratorium is skipping the entire monthly payment of Principal and Interest. For instance, if P&I ran $1,200 per month, and the lender permitted up to 10 months suspension, then $12,000 (10 × $1,200) would be added to the principal, which would result in higher payments once resumed.

2. *Deferring of interest.* Another form of moratorium is the suspension of interest payments. Interest is not forgiven but is added to the principal indebtedness, much like loans with negative amortizations. This can offer significant relief to the debtor whose installments are almost all interest—either because it is a relatively high-interest loan or because it is not a seasoned loan, or both.

    In the case of DVA loans, interest that accrues during a period of forbearance becomes a part of the guaranteed indebtedness.

    Consequently, holders of DVA mortgages can assist veterans through forbearance without incurring loss.

3. *Partial payments.* Lenders may also agree to accept partial payments. Indeed, the DVA encourages holders of GI loans to extend such privileges so that veterans may be given every opportunity to retain their homes while awaiting financial recovery. This may result in negative amortization, but it's a way to preserve one's property from foreclosure. If by contrast payments were made because of special circumstances, such as temporary unemployment or disability, lenders may be persuaded to stop foreclosure proceedings if assurances can be made that an extra, say, $100 per month will be paid to repay the delinquent installments.

4. *Prepayments.* Prepayments credited to principal in the past may be reapplied for the purpose of curing a default or preventing a subsequent default. Similarly, some loans may have been credited with lump-sum payments derived from proceeds of a partial sale of property to highway departments, local municipalities, or private parties.

Note: A potential problem with all options is that borrowers may never recover financially and be able to restart full payments.

Recasting

Another form of borrower assistance is through **recasting** or loan modification. It actually involves a change in loan terms. In order to assist a delinquent borrower, the lender may agree to rearrange the loan in some fashion. This can be done at the outset, when the debtor first defaults, or it may be done after a moratorium, in order to minimize the impact of having to repay both current and past installments.

The Department of Housing and Urban Development (HUD) adopted special forbearance regulations aimed at helping financially troubled homeowners save their houses. Under the relaxed rules, forbearance may be granted under any circumstances contributing to a default beyond the homeowner's control. For example, as the recession continued, by 2009 monthly income was being regularly affected by required pay reductions, imposed partial furloughs resulting in fewer hours worked, and other cost reduction measures taken by employers. Here are four methods of recasting:

1. *Extended term.* If permitted by law or regulations, one way to re-cast a loan is to extend the original period of repayment, sometimes called reamortization. Extending to 30 years an existing loan that has, say, 15 years remaining of an original 25-year term will result in lower monthly payments. Some lenders may extract a higher interest rate for this privilege, but the alternative might be foreclosure. Regulations may, however, prohibit institutional lenders from extending the term while a default exists.

2. *Increase of debt.* Though it's unlikely in situations where borrowers are going under, some lenders may increase the debt when they are satisfied that the debtor's dilemma will be solved, tiding over the debtor whose financial reversals are apparently temporary in nature. Again, the lender may exact a higher interest rate, but the new note can be extended for a longer term that may more than offset the increase in payments due to the higher rate. The proceeds of the new loan might be put in an "assigned" savings account for the borrower, which is then used to make the payments on both the old and new loans.

   Under DVA-backed loans, advances may be made from the assigned account for maintenance, protective repairs, taxes, assessments, and hazard insurance. GI debtors may well save their homes when such funds are advanced.

3. *Reduction of interest.* Still another form of recasting a loan is a reduction of the interest rate, even if the reduction is only temporary. While most uncommon, a lender may be amenable to reducing the interest rate when the market warrants it. For example, an existing 8.75 percent rate might be reduced to 8 percent when the market is at, say, 7.5 percent.

4. *Reduction of principal amount owed.* The 2008–2009 negative equity dilemma introduced, in some instances, loan modifications involving a reduction in principal loan amounts. It was a last resort solution for a lender and, although encouraged by government-introduced guidelines, was seldom used.

Recasting options in this time were made more difficult for three reasons:

1. Home values declined substantially in many areas, resulting in mortgage amounts far in excess of home values.

2. Recasting generally required the approval of the secondary market investors. With mortgages having been packaged and sold globally, this approval was difficult and, in some cases, impossible to acquire.

3. HUD counseling centers, established to specifically assist homeowners determine their options to avoid foreclosure, were swamped with requests and many borrowers found it difficult to get help.

Mortgage Guaranty Insurance

Insurance against loss through foreclosure is likely the best means of protecting the financial interests of lenders. This is accomplished through public and private mortgage insurance plans.

Government-Insured and Guaranteed Loans

With the introduction of Cal-Vet in 1923, the FHA program in 1934, and the DVA program in 1944, many more buyers have been able to enter the housing market. This is because of the willingness on the part of lenders to extend loans with high loan-to-value ratios that are backed by insurance or a government guarantee.

Federal Housing Administration Options

As noted in an earlier chapter, risks to lenders can be eliminated through a federal insurance plan. The FHA is not the lender, but rather the insurer of the loan made by a qualified lender. Both private mortgage insurance (PMI) and mutual mortgage insurance (MMI) are now automatically discontinued when the loan-to-value reaches 78 percent of the original loan amount via principal paydown. On most FHA loans the typical length of time to reach this percentage is seven to eight years. Under the plan, the lender is assured that in case of foreclosure, the FHA will pay any loss in either cash or government debentures. Or the lender may, with prior FHA approval, assign the defaulted loan directly to the FHA before final foreclosure action in exchange for insurance benefits. Whichever way it acquires the property, the FHA sometimes repairs, refurbishes, and resells the property in order to minimize the losses to the FHA. In most cases, however, the FHA simply sells the property in an "as is" condition.

The cost of the insurance is borne by the borrower. Either the Mortgage Insurance Premium (MIP) is paid upfront in cash or, more often, it is financed as part of the loan and paid monthly. The MMI is paid with the monthly payments.

The FHA also offers a loan assignment program. For loans more than three months in default, and when the cause is not the fault of the borrower, the loan is assigned to HUD, which will pay off the lender. The homeowners, thereafter, make payments directly to HUD under a flexible schedule designed to meet their needs. Contact your local FHA office for additional information on this, the location of HUD counseling centers, and HUD's pre-foreclosure program.

Department of Veterans Affairs Options

For qualified veterans, the DVA guarantees lenders that, if the veteran defaults, the DVA will satisfy at least part of the debt. Suppose, for example, that a 100 percent loan is made for the purchase price of $200,000. Assume the property thereafter goes on the auction block under foreclosure action and sells for $170,000. Finally, assume that there is $180,000 owing at the time of the foreclosure. How much will the DVA be liable for? Recall from Chapter 6 that loans in excess of $144,000 have a maximum guarantee of 25 percent of the loan balance. Multiplying the $180,000 loan balance by 25 percent equals $45,000. Next we compare this figure with the actual loss (ignoring costs), which is $180,000 less $170,000, or $10,000. Hence, the DVA's liability to the lender will be limited to $10,000.

Veterans are charged an up-front funding fee for this guarantee. However, should a deficiency arise, the veteran is liable for any claim paid by the DVA, which is said to have the right of **subrogation** for the amount paid. Suppose a veteran homeowner sells a property secured by a GI loan. How can the veteran be released from liability for any default caused by the new owner? There are two ways to do this: (1) pay off the existing loan in full from the proceeds of the purchaser's new loan, or (2) secure a written release from the Department of Veterans Affairs. Even though a buyer offers to assume the veteran seller's personal liability for the repayment of the loan, the veteran must still obtain written release from liability on the loan from the DVA. Under most circumstances, a loan is assumed only if the rate is lower than what can be acquired via the current marketplace. To qualify for a release, four tests must be met:

1. A new purchaser must have requisite entitlement remaining.
2. The loan must not be delinquent.
3. The purchaser transferee must be acceptable to the DVA from an income and credit standpoint.
4. The purchaser assumes the loan and the indemnity obligation signed by the veteran at the time the loan was originally made.

Like the FHA, the DVA offers forbearance for vets in foreclosure. Once the veteran has missed three payments, the lender must notify the DVA and provide a description of what it has done to remedy the default. The DVA provides counseling and mediation services between lender and borrower.

Under the Soldiers and Sailors Civil Relief Act, various forms of relief are provided to active military members who get behind with their mortgage payments. Applicants are encouraged to double check with military lawyers to determine eligibility.

Federal Home Loan Mortgage Corporation (FHLMC)

Guidelines on alternatives to foreclosure give mortgage lenders wide discretion to extend relief to borrowers who encounter hardships, are cooperative, and have proper regard for fulfilling their obligations. Among recommended remedies, Freddie Mac encourages temporary indulgences, allowing borrowers up to three months to cure any delinquency.

California Veterans Farm and Home Purchase Act Assistance

The Cal-Vet plan, as this program is called, contains a life insurance feature that only indirectly benefits the lender, the Department of Veterans Affairs of the State of California, which holds legal title to the security. The veteran debtor is the party who benefits most from the insurance feature.

Qualified veterans under Cal-Vet financing must purchase life and disability insurance through its home protection plan. The plan insures the debtor's life for the amount of the unpaid loan balance at the time of death. A double indemnity clause is also included, until age 70, up to a maximum of $75,000. The monthly premiums for the home protection plan, including the optional benefits, are based on the age of the insured, varying from $.50 to $.55 per $1,000 of unpaid balance, in addition to a flat monthly charge for a disability benefit. The portion of the life insurance policy covering the remaining loan balance is paid to the California Department of Veterans Affairs.

Permanent and total disability benefits are included for veterans under age 65 and employed full-time, including full-time homemakers. Under the plan, the veteran's full loan payment is paid after the first three months of total disability and payments continue until the contract is paid off or for a maximum of three years, whichever occurs first.

Private Mortgage Insurance

As we discussed in Chapter 5, in addition to public insurance, private companies have devised insurance plans to reduce, if not eliminate, the risk of loss on conventional mortgages. Lenders protect themselves by generally requiring PMI coverage on loans in excess of 80 percent loan-to-value (LTV). Prior to mid-2009, PMI-insured loans could be made up to 97 percent LTV. Reacting to the broadening foreclosure numbers accompanied by severe home value declines, PMI companies sought to reduce their risk by limiting their coverage to a maximum 90 percent loan-to-value and to borrowers with a minimum 720 FICO score. Whether PMI companies will again take a more aggressive stance on coverage in the future is a wait-and-see proposition. Private mortgage insurance does not insure the entire loan amount, only the top portion of the loan. Regulations governing how PMI coverage can be discontinued when the lender's equity is no longer endangered did not change.

Although residential properties make up the bulk of private mortgage insurance, coverage was extended to commercial and industrial loans and into lease guarantee insurance. Special policies were written for five years, with a renewal fee charged at the end of the period if the insurance was extended. There is no reason to believe that this shared-risk concept, under which both an insured lender and a private mortgage insurer assume part of the risk, could not be extended to virtually any type of property and any kind of financing transaction. In the short term, however, commercial properties were also impacted by the recession and we will see what occurs as the economy improves.

Automatic Payment Plans

Another way to reduce the chance of default is through an **automatic mortgage pay plan** offered by many lenders. Under the plan, a system of preauthorized monthly mortgage payments is established. It relieves the homeowner of the chore of paying each month and protects the debtor against forgetting to make a payment. Borrowers simply authorize their banks to make an automatic monthly deduction from their checking accounts and to forward this amount to the real estate lender. This option is typically made available when signing loan documents.

Consumer Protection Laws and Regulations

Still another way to mitigate or reduce the chance of default is through consumer protection laws and regulations.

Public Regulations

A wide variety of laws and regulations protect real estate buyers in one way or another. Among these is the Truth-in-Lending Law (see Chapter 10). Also called the Consumer Credit Protection Act, this federal law prescribes full disclosure of all borrowing charges. This calculation of the total cost of borrowing and the effective interest is called the APR. The federal government's anticipation is that borrowers can compare APR calculations to obtain the best loan terms when shopping for home financing. With certain kinds of loans, such as junior loans and refinancing, the borrower may rescind or cancel the credit arrangement within three business days without declaring any reason for doing so. This right does not apply in the case of a first trust deed created or assumed for the purpose of financing the purchase of a dwelling in which the borrower expects to reside (See a more complete explanation of APR in Chapter 13). On the state level, an important law designed to protect consumers is the right to cancel home-improvement contracts within three days of the time of their solicitation by a door-to-door salesperson. Even when such a contract is initiated by the homeowner, the truth-in-lending provisions allow cancellation within three business days if financing is involved. Thus, homeowners who change their minds for any reason may cancel during the first three days after signing any contract.

Home Warranties

Buyers of new or existing homes can encounter problems with major components of the home, resulting in financial hardship and difficulty in making their mortgage payments. Private industry over the years has offered a variety of home-warranty programs in an effort to mitigate financial burdens at a time when borrowers can least afford such repairs. Most programs protect the new buyer for a specified time period, usually one year after close of escrow. Although warranties can differ, most cover the major home components, including plumbing, electrical system, heating and/or air conditioning, walls, roof, and foundation. Special elements, like swimming pools, can be protected via the payment of additional policy fees. Sellers and real estate licensees most often provide and pay for a home warranty as a way to provide a benefit to the new buyer but also to protect themselves from being negatively impacted by unknown component difficulties after the close of escrow. Buyers may also purchase home warranties, but must do so before the close of escrow. During the warranty coverage period, homeowners pay an approximate $50 per service call fee as a "deductable."

11.4 OTHER LENDING PROBLEMS
Usury

The cost of money is always related to the anticipated risk to the lender providing the financing. One way in which lenders may be compensated for any increase in potential loss is to charge higher interest rates. Those borrowers most susceptible to high interest rate loans are those who, for various reasons, have proven to be unable to acquire more conventional financing and/or are potential credit risks. However, there are state limitations on the amount of interest that can, regardless of the reason, be charged a borrower. The maximum rate that may be charged on loans made by nonexempt individuals, whether or not secured by real estate, is 10 percent, or 5 percent above the Federal Reserve discount rate, whichever is greater. Remember from Chapter 1 that the Federal Funds rate is the rate of interest one bank charges another for the overnight use of excess reserves.

Regulated institutional lenders in California are not limited in the rate of interest they may charge. The marketplace generally dictates their rates. Effective yields are increased through the use of points or discounts, as illustrated in Chapter 7.

Borrowers who deal with noninstitutional lenders are protected against usurious transactions. These lenders consist of private parties making hard money loans. This protection is reinforced with the disclosure requirements under Regulation Z of the Truth-in-Lending Act. As pointed out in Chapter 10, this federal law requires that borrowers receive a written statement of the total costs involved in any financial transaction. Truth-in-Lending does not prescribe limits on interest rates. But by requiring that the pre-paid costs and expenses be translated into an annual percentage rate, it provides one way for borrowers to compare loan costs when shopping for their best loan terms.

Lenders making loans secured by junior trust deeds usually charge the maximum interest rate allowed in an effort to secure the highest yield permitted by law, in order to offset the increased risks associated with their secondary positions.

What does usury have to do with foreclosures and other lending problems? When sellers are dissatisfied with their rate of return dictated by the maximum rate allowed by law, they may seek ways to circumvent the law. One commonly used method is to increase the sales price of the property, which effectively increases the amount to be repaid. This, in turn, could result in a borrower's financial overextension and ultimate default.

Assume, for example, that an owner is selling property for $185,000, and that the buyer is to make a small down payment and take over the existing first trust deed. The seller is to carry back a second mortgage for the difference. The seller could raise the sales price to, say, $188,000, with the extra $3,000 being added to the second lien. Even though the second trust deed is drawn at the maximum interest rate negotiated, the yield has been effectively raised by the additional amount of money included in the junior lien. Sellers carrying back loans—so-called carrybacks—are exempt from usury laws, as are real estate brokers.

The impact of usury statutes on money markets is a controversial subject. Proponents insist that borrowers need protection from unscrupulous lenders. Critics suggest that such limitations can reduce the money supply. Their argument is that by keeping interest rates down, at whatever levels, lenders naturally gravitate to those places where money can be put to more productive use. Thus, a lender from an eastern state with a usury rate of, say, 9 percent, may pour money into California, where there might be a higher usury limit. If California were to lower its usury rate, the flow of funds from other states would decline. The net effect on potential home buyers would be a decrease in mortgage funds and a postponement of purchases.

Redlining

A problem that occasionally resurfaces in real estate lending is redlining, the practice of systematic refusal to lend mortgage money in high-risk areas. These are usually older urban areas containing high minority concentrations, around which lenders in the past placed red lines delineating such neighborhoods as off-limits to mortgage credit. Little, if any, consideration is given to the creditworthiness of the individual borrower.

By limiting or refusing credit, the lender hopes to reduce its exposure to delinquencies and foreclosures. However, in the process, it has been demonstrated that the withholding of real estate financing has hastened the decay of these neighborhoods. The so-called closed neighborhoods fall prey to speculators and absentee landlords, dubbed "slumlords" in some areas, who, some claim, drain the community, leaving deterioration and destruction in their paths. The few homes that are financed often end up abandoned and foreclosed—thus compounding the problem of redlining. Meanwhile, buyers in these neighborhoods find the money spigots turned off, with no place to turn for help. These buyers may be the very ones who place their savings into local financial institutions and then find themselves unable to borrow from these institutions while their deposits may be used to finance homes outside the redlined areas.

Both the federal and state governments have tried to resolve this dilemma. All federally regulated mortgage lenders are required to disclose publicly just where they make their mortgage loans. Also, the State of California has imposed guidelines relating to fair lending practices that prohibit denying credit or altering the terms of a loan solely because of neighborhood factors. When a person is denied a loan, the lender must notify the applicant, in writing, of the reasons for denial within 30 days of the application.

To help guard against the continued practice of redlining, state-chartered savings banks are required to file periodic reports with the California Department of Financial Institutions. Written details of how and where loans are being made are submitted so lending patterns can be determined. Many items must be included in the report: county and census tract; purpose of the loan and outcome—made, denied, purchased, or sold; amount of loan requested and amount issued; type of property, appraised value, year built, square footage; sales price; interest rate, and whether fixed or variable, discounts, fees charged; existing balance on loans refinanced and how the proceeds were used, such as for repairs or improvements; borrower's and total family income; race or ethnic makeup of the applicant, sex and age of borrower; data on co-borrowers and co-applicants; and information on whether neighborhood factors were considered in underwriting the loan.

Community Reinvestment Act (CRA)

To stop discriminatory practices, including redlining, Congress passed the **Community Reinvestment Act (CRA)**, which requires federally supervised financial institutions to disclose lending data in their lobbies and elsewhere. The Financial Institutions Reform, Recovery and Enforcement Act (FIRREA) requires lenders to report data on the race, gender, income, and census tract of people to whom they make loans. Its stated purpose is "to assist in identifying discriminatory practices and enforcing antidiscrimination statutes." CRA and FIRREA encourage lenders to offer mortgages for low- and moderately priced housing and meet other credit needs for low- and moderate-income families. Lenders are required to make positive efforts to provide loans in areas from which savings are received. FIRREA requires evaluation reports and CRA ratings of lender practices to be made public for all institutions. In cooperation with other government agencies, it grades each institution on how well it:

- Knows the credit needs of its community.
- Informs the community about its credit services.
- Involves its directors in setting up and monitoring CRA programs.
- Participates in government-insured, guaranteed, or subsidized loans.
- Distributes credit applications, approvals, and rejections across geographic areas.
- Offers a range of residential mortgages, housing rehabilitation loans, and small business loans.

All of these criteria are designed to protect consumers against unlawful discrimination. A positive CRA rating is a prerequisite for institutions to open new branches and to engage in expansions, acquisitions, and mergers, since outside third parties can petition agencies to deny these activities to institutions with poor CRA grades.

Home Mortgage Disclosure Act (HMDA)

Mortgage lenders are required to provide an annual report regarding the borrowers who both applied for and acquired loans. Referred to as the HMDA report, the information is obtained via section X of the loan application. This section, entitled Information for Government Monitoring Purposes, seeks voluntary information from borrowers including ethnicity, race, and sex. Although the information is voluntary, borrowers are informed that "if you do not furnish ethnicity, race or sex, under federal regulations, this lender is required to note the information on the basis of visual observation and surname." Combating discrimination is critical in every aspect of the lending industry.

Short Sales

As property values continued to decline during the 2007–2009 period, more and more sellers were unable to sell their homes for prices sufficient to cover the outstanding loan balances and costs of selling (this is known as being "upside down" on their mortgage). Lenders were faced with either accepting less than what they were owed or foreclosing on the property. **Short sales** became an often used method of disposing of property under these circumstances.

Prior to 2007, short sales were not as popular because of the income tax consequences of such a sale. Called the "phantom tax" consequence, the loan relief or forgiveness portion of the lender's current mortgage amount was taxable. For example, if a borrower owed $200,000 but the short sale garnered only $150,000, the $50,000 of "forgiven" debt became taxable as income, even though the borrower had acquired no cash. It is easy to see that short sales were not popular, with many defaulting borrowers opting for foreclosure or deeds in lieu of foreclosure. The Mortgage Debt Forgiveness Act of 2007 was a welcome relief and made debt forgiveness retroactive for sales from January 2007. Greatly easing the problem on debt forgiveness for up to $2 million for a personal residence, it allowed the use of short sales to proliferate. (The act is effective through 2012, unless it is extended.)

While the seller remained in possession of his or her home during the short sale process, the lender was the entity who had to agree to any terms of sale. Any offer to purchase was referred to the lender, who either accepted or countered the offer. As more and more of these transactions began to occur, the time frames for the conclusion of a short sale grew longer, sometimes stretching into months. The growing number of borrowers seeking short sales not only overwhelmed a system unprepared for such volume but lenders became wary of the steadily mounting losses.

While sellers and potential buyers became more and more frustrated with the lengthening time frames, lenders were beginning to lean toward foreclosure as a better remedy for them than the short sale route. The government made efforts to promote lenders' participation in helping borrowers with their declining home values. (See the Case & Point at the end of this chapter.)

The obvious result of the foreclosure and short sale explosion has been changes in both the loan instruments available (e.g., the elimination of 100 percent financing and other high LTV loan options, the reduction in PMI promoted LTVs) and a tightening of underwriting standards.

Web Help and Its Reliability

It is easy to turn to the Web for information about practically any subject, including all things financial. Borrowers seeking foreclosure, short sale, and other assistance seek information on the Web, as do those deciding to enter the real estate purchase market.

The reliability of the information must always be considered. Many of the websites that discuss this information are actually sales sites. Others simply have wrong data. Outdated and/or inaccurate information is not always easy to detect. Calculator sites are a good example. Unless one knows the "internal formulas" used to calculate estimated taxes or homeowners' insurance, the information is unlikely to be useful in every situation.

While you might use the Web to seek general information and to initiate your education in real estate finance, it is advised that you seek professional assistance when you are ready to proceed with any kind of real estate financing. With the ever-changing nature of the financial community, a "do it yourself" education via the Web may not be the best choice.

However, there are some sites that are kept updated and provide accurate information. www.hud.gov (The official site for FHA mortgage information includes home buying tips, information on how to avoid foreclosure, and abusive lending warnings.) www.fanniemae.com (The Federal National Mortgage Association provides information on their "Home Affordable" program, tips on loan modification and refinance options, and a host of information for new and experienced homeowners.) www.freddiemac.com (The Federal Home Loan Mortgage Corporation site addresses relevant buying and homeowning issues.) www.ftc.gov (The Federal Trade Commission site offers general information about current finance frauds, etc. The Consumer Protection section has considerable lending information, including credit guidelines.) www.mbaa.org (The Mortgage Bankers Association of America site features a Home Loan Learning Center along with up-to-date economic news and forecasts.) www.mortgagemag.com (A magazine-like format offers information on all aspects of mortgage lending. Ignore the ads and focus on the information.)

SUMMARY

A deed of trust securing a promissory note requires more than simply repaying a loan. A default and possible foreclosure may result not only from delinquencies and nonpayment of the loan but also from noncompliance with many other provisions of the trust deed. These include proper maintenance of the property, carrying adequate hazard insurance, paying property taxes and other liens when due, and complying with all local building and safety ordinances.

A foreclosure action through a trustee's sale begins with the filing of a Notice of Default, followed by the publication of a Notice of Sale, and then the actual sale through auction. Liens are paid off in their order of priority, with remaining proceeds, if any, paid to the defaulting trustor. No redemptive rights exist thereafter. Foreclosure through judicial action is much more complicated and time consuming. Up to a one-year redemption period exists in favor of the defaulted trustor following final sale. Lenders therefore mostly resort to a trustee's sale, unless a deficiency judgment is sought, in which case court action is the only remedy.

Defaults can be largely minimized through establishment of an impound account; forbearance proceedings, including moratoriums and modifications or recasting; mortgage insurance, both public and private; automatic payment plans; repayment workouts; temporary indulgences; and an assortment of consumer protection laws and regulations.

IMPORTANT TERMS AND CONCEPTS

Automatic mortgage
  pay plan
Community Reinvestment
  Act (CRA)
Deed in Lieu of
  Foreclosure
Deficiency judgment
Escrow account

Forbearance
Impound account
Moratorium
Notice of Default
Notice of Sale
Quitclaim deed
Recasting

Right of
  reinstatement
Short sales
Subrogation
Trustee's sale
Waiver

REVIEWING YOUR UNDERSTANDING

Questions for Discussion

1. List four ways in which a borrower can default under the terms of a trust deed.

2. How does an assignment-of-rents clause operate to protect a lender?

3. What is meant by power of sale? Which party benefits from it, the beneficiary or trustor?

4. Contrast a Notice of Default to a Notice of Sale.

5. How does an impound account mitigate against risk of loss?

6. List six ways that a lender's procedures can assist delinquent borrowers.

7. What is redlining? How does it affect lenders? Borrowers? Neighborhoods?

Multiple-Choice Questions

1. Reasons for defaulting on the repayment of a real estate debt are many and varied, including which one of the following?
   a. marriage
   b. increased earnings
   c. judicious budgeting
   d. disability

2. Following a foreclosure sale, surplus funds remaining after paying off all costs, fees, expenses, and liens are given to the
   a. successful bidder.
   b. trustee.
   c. beneficiary.
   d. trustor.

3. The successful bidder at a judicial sale of real estate property receives a
   a. Trustee's Deed.
   b. Certificate of Sale.
   c. Judicial Deed.
   d. Deed in Lieu of Foreclosure.

4. A temporary suspension or waiver of payments on a debt is termed
   a. forbearance.
   b. forestallment.
   c. wavering.
   d. recasting.

5. The MIP premium on FHA-insured loans
   a. must be paid at the end of the loan.
   b. can be added to the loan.
   c. is optional.
   d. is usually paid by the seller.

6. In the event of nonpayment of property taxes, the beneficiary may pay for the obligation directly, and thereafter
   a. bill the trustor directly.
   b. add the advances to the principal indebtedness.
   c. do either (a) or (b).
   d. do neither (a) nor (b).

7. Which of the following parties is not generally permitted to bid on a property offered at a foreclosure auction?
   a. trustor
   b. outside party
   c. beneficiary
   d. trustee

8. The right of redemption following a trustee's sale is good for
   a. one year.
   b. 90 days.
   c. three months.
   d. none of the above.

9. Assume that in a declining market, a small condo with an existing $119,000 GI loan sells for only $110,000 at a foreclosure sale. Ignoring foreclosure costs, the DVA will reimburse the foreclosing lender
   a. $9,000.
   b. $21,000.
   c. $27,500.
   d. $30,250.

10. The trustor under a deed of trust became delinquent in his monthly payments, thereafter abandoning the premises and moving to another city. Which of the following actions is not part of the foreclosure procedure?
    a. Notify trustor of default
    b. Issue reconveyance deed
    c. Publish Notice of Sale
    d. Record Notice of Sale

11. If a borrower does not provide a real estate lender with proof of hazard insurance when required, the lender may
    a. purchase insurance coverage and add it to the principal balance of the loan.
    b. purchase insurance coverage and proceed with foreclosure if the borrower does not pay for it.
    c. institute foreclosure proceedings.
    d. do any of the above.

12. A trustee in a deed of trust may issue a trustee's deed upon a foreclosure sale as a result of
    a. violation of the due-on-sale clause.
    b. the power of sale contained in the deed of trust itself.
    c. provisions of the Business and Professions Code.
    d. the applicable sections of the Civil Code.

13. Proper foreclosure procedures include
    a. advertising in a newspaper of general circulation at least once a week for three months.
    b. posting a copy of the Notice of Sale on the property and in a public place.
    c. recording a copy of the newspaper advertisement.
    d. mailing a copy of the notice to the trustee by certified mail.

14. After the issuance of a Trustee's Deed at a foreclosure sale,
    a. all rights formerly held by the trustor are extinguished.
    b. the trustor has a one-year right of redemption.
    c. a successful bidder gets the full fee title, free of restrictions and with priority over the deed of trust foreclosed.
    d. the trustor has a three-month right of reinstatement.

15. Mortgage guaranty insurance, whether undertaken through government-backed or private sources,
    a. is designed to pay off the mortgage balance in the event of the death of a borrower.
    b. protects the lender against loss in the event of foreclosure.
    c. is paid for by the lender, since it is the lender that is protected.
    d. is a one-time charge paid for by borrowers.

16. The Community Reinvestment Act (CRA)
    a. prohibits redlining practices.
    b. requires posting of lending data for federally chartered lenders.
    c. may inhibit lender expansions and mergers.
    d. is involved in each of the above.

17. Recasting a loan may be accomplished by
    I. extending the term of the loan.
    II. increasing the debt.
    III. reducing the interest rate.
    IV. giving a Deed in Lieu of Foreclosure.
    a. I only.
    b. I and II only.
    c. I, II, and III only.
    d. I, II, III, and IV.

18. A homeowner fails to pay her special bond assessment due to loss of her job. The lender may
    a. pay the overdue tax and bill the homeowner.
    b. pay the overdue tax and add the amount to the loan.
    c. do either (a) or (b).
    d. do neither (a) nor (b).

19. A home with an existing $140,000 DVA loan nets $120,000 at a foreclosure sale. The amount owing at time of sale was $110,000. The borrower-trustor is entitled to
    a. $10,000.
    b. $20,000.
    c. $30,000.
    d. none of the above.

20. Should a borrower fail to maintain satisfactory property insurance, the lender's best cause of action would be to
    a. foreclose without any notice to the borrower.
    b. evict the borrower.
    c. sue the borrower for breach of contract.
    d. purchase a policy and add the premium to the loan.

CASE & POINT

Foreclosure and Short Sales: Government Intervention Falls Short!

Very early in the subprime meltdown, it was recognized that ARM financing accounted for a disproportionate number of the growing foreclosures. Only later would it be identified that nearly 60 percent of the borrowers facing foreclosure had been eligible for a more stable loan option. Instead, they had opted for, or as some complained, had "been sold" an ARM product. The "option arm" with its very low start rate was very popular, in spite of its negatively amortized aspect. The rationale of the lenders was that they were helping buyers maximize their purchasing power. Buyers seemed eager to accept lower payments that allowed them to qualify for more loan amount and hence a more expensive home. As it turned out, buyers were "betting" that continued double digit appreciation would not only protect them from equity erosion from negative amortization but that there were huge profits to be gained as home values seemed to continue to explode. How wrong everyone was!

By January 2008, the rate of foreclosures was alarming. Borrowers who acquired loans starting in 2005 through June 30, 2007, were experiencing significant rate changes and projections were that millions more would soon be facing foreclosure. The Administration quickly announced plans aimed at borrowers currently making on-time payments on loans still at their introductory rates but who were identified as unable to afford the soon-to-be-adjusted rates and accompanying payments. The information was unfortunately vague as to the procedure for determining those who would not be able to afford payment adjustments. Plus, it seemed that those who had already missed payments, thereby signaling that they were unable to make their adjusted payments, were not eligible for this remedy. Ironically, many of the borrowers who were now ineligible for assistance had been advised by these same institutions that the only way to receive any help was to actually go into default and possible foreclosure. Having taken that advice, they now found that having missed payments made them ineligible under the new guidelines.

Government plans remained unclear while proposals were tweaked and revised in an effort to find relief for a growing number of distressed homeowners. The process was complicated, as the very institutions that had perpetrated the loan excesses were now being asked to "voluntarily" work to resolve the burgeoning foreclosure situation.

As is too often the case with new government plans, an overemphasis was placed on making sure that ineligible borrowers could not abuse the programs. Plus, the lenders charged with voluntarily implementing the plans continued to demonstrate a reluctance to really make them work. The result was constant revisions to eligibility and relatively few borrowers ultimately acquiring assistance. The original anticipation that millions of homeowners would be helped proved to be overly optimistic.

As the eligibility criteria continued to develop, it became clear that the number of borrowers who were likely to meet the increasingly complicated requirements would decline. New predictions estimated that no more than 100,000 to 600,000 borrowers would ultimately be assisted nationwide, far fewer than the millions projected when the proposals were first introduced.

During the first quarter of 2008, Washington legislators announced that they were planning to help all borrowers who were struggling with home payments—not just those facing potential foreclosure. No details were provided and, again, many believed that to be an empty promise. By the third quarter of 2009 the programs had been revised several times but still with little real assistance to the increasing growing number of struggling borrowers. Many began to see these efforts as merely bailout plans serving the banks and other investors, to the detriment of the consumer, who desperately required help. By the end of 2009 the housing market continued to struggle and it was reported that 24 percent of mortgages nationally were either under water or in foreclosure. While some economists indicated that the worst of the recession was behind us, other pundits were predicting that by 2011 nearly 50 percent of mortgages would be under water or in foreclosure. It is safe to say that the housing difficulties are not over yet!

Chapter 12

PREVIEW

This chapter covers the broad field of financing construction projects. Topics in this chapter include sources and types of construction loans, loan costs, the construction loan process, and mechanic's liens.

After completing this chapter, you should be able to:

1. List five types of construction lenders.
2. List and define at least six technical words and terms that are common to the field of construction lending.
3. Explain borrowers' costs under a construction loan.
4. List the stages followed in processing a construction loan.
5. Discuss the supporting documentation used in connection with construction financing.
6. Outline the steps to take in filing mechanic's liens.
7. Cite three California laws that deal with assessments for the cost of construction of public improvements.

Construction Loans

12.1 NATURE OF CONSTRUCTION LOANS

Construction financing is the provision of funds to pay for labor and materials that go into the construction of a new or existing property. The funds may come from two sources: (1) a general line of personal credit that a borrower has with financial institutions, materials suppliers, or subcontractors, and/or (2) a construction loan that is evidenced by a promissory note and secured by a trust deed. The first involves the use of bank and commercial unsecured credit and is not classified as real estate credit. The second, the construction loan, is the subject of this chapter.

A *construction loan* is a short-term, interim, or temporary loan for building purposes, as contrasted to permanent or long-term financing on already existing property. A typical construction loan for a single-family residence is usually for a term of 9 to 12 months and for a major project, such as an apartment house, a term of 18 months to two years may be normal. Apartment house construction loans generally allow sufficient time for completion and partial rental before full loan payments begin. Permanent loans on existing structures are written for longer terms, typically 15 to 30 years. When used in conjunction with a construction loan, a permanent loan is called a **take-out loan**. It is not unusual for a borrower to obtain a short-term construction loan from one lender, then, when the project is completed, obtain a permanent or take-out loan from another lender to pay off the amount owed on the construction loan. Commercial banks favor interim construction loans (particularly where take-outs have been provided), while savings banks prefer combination loans.

A construction loan is made for a specific dollar amount agreed upon before work begins. Construction funds are not paid to the borrower in a lump sum, but advanced in stages via a predetermined number of "draws" as the construction process progresses. The permanent loan, in contrast, is placed after construction is completed and is paid over the loan term.

The construction loan is usually evidenced by a promissory note and secured by a deed of trust on the property under construction. The principal sum of the construction loan is nonamortized, though interest payments are periodically required from the borrower only on the money advanced.

Sources of Funds

Construction loans are made primarily by local financial institutions, mainly banks and credit unions.

The extent to which lenders are active in the construction loan market in a given area depends on several factors. Some lenders as a matter of policy do not make construction loans, whereas others may be in and out of the market as economic conditions change. Still others may make construction loans on a regular basis.

Kinds of Loans

There are two basic kinds of construction loans. The first is one that combines a construction loan with a permanent take-out mortgage, called a **combination loan** (sometimes mistakenly called a package). These construction-to-permanent combination loans involve only one loan closing. The second type is the interim, short-term, straight construction loan, which is independent of the permanent loan, though the lender does anticipate that the proceeds of a permanent loan from some source will pay off the construction loan. Some banks will even allow a purchase loan-to-construction-to-permanent loan. This can be used for properties in disrepair or for a homeowner needing to remodel at the offset of ownership. When using any of these options, the borrower must qualify for the payments of the final loan and any property will have to appraise for the future value, after work is complete.

Construction-to-Permanent Combination

Both the construction loan and the permanent loan originate in advance of construction and are secured under one instrument. The permanent loan begins according to the terms on the note at a predetermined time, designed to coincide with completion of construction. Two variations are common. In the first one, the lender approves the ultimate borrower on the permanent mortgage, has the borrower sign the loan instruments, and makes advances as construction proceeds. Interest-only payments are made on money as it is advanced during construction. This is frequently done in the financing of single-family homes built for an owner under contract with a builder for a custom home.

The second variation is also used in cases of single-family dwellings. Here, the lender commits itself in advance of construction to make both the construction loan and permanent loan, but retains the right to approve the ultimate borrower, who is perhaps not yet known. The legal instruments are prepared so that the permanent loan can be assumed by the ultimate borrower. This kind of arrangement is in contrast with large-scale projects where lenders provide builders with construction money, perhaps a conventional blanket construction mortgage on an entire tract of land or subdivision, and the builders refer home buyers to the lender for permanent financing. The buyers, however, have no obligation to place their loan through that particular lender.

The combination loan has potential advantages for both builder and ultimate buyer. Presumably there will be fewer expenses for the lender and these reductions or savings benefit the builder and buyer.

Short-Term Construction Loans

The interim, short-term, straight construction loan and the take-out loan often involve two lenders and two sets of loan instruments compared with the single lender and instrument under the combination loan. The **short-term construction loan** can be made by a lender other than the lender making the permanent loan. The construction lender may require a commitment from the permanent take-out lender, or the construction loan may be made to the builder without any commitment from a final take-out lender. The loan is for a short term—say, one year—at which time it is due and payable. It is up to the borrower-builder to provide a take-out buyer or to obtain permanent financing.

Loan Costs

The costs of a construction loan to the borrower consist of several items. Lenders may charge a flat fee, usually a percentage of the amount of the loan (such as 1, 2, or 3 percent) at the time the loan originates. These fees increase the effective rate of return on the loan to the lender, though a portion of the fee is used to cover the cost of originating the loan.

Charges may be made to cover the necessary items of expense in the origination and underwriting of the loan. Typical borrower's items would be charges for the appraisal report, credit report, survey, title insurance, legal fees, accrued interest, escrows, and premiums for hazard insurance and performance bond if required. Recall that these are similar to the nonrecurring costs discussed in Chapter 10 under closing costs for home loans. Lenders charge a flat fee, expressed in points (typically two to three), to cover all these items, or charge them in addition to their required points.

Construction loans, including combination loans, almost always involve higher fees than purchase money loans. This is due to higher overhead costs to the lender, such as onsite inspections, progress payments, and checking for mechanic's liens, and because of the higher risks involved. This is especially true if the home or project is being built "on spec" meaning that there is no predetermined buyer or tenant.

12.2 EVALUATION AND LENDING PROCESS

Lender Considerations for a Construction Loan

Before committing themselves to financing a construction project, construction lenders consider several factors.

Plans and Specifications

The construction lender will require a set of plans sufficiently detailed to determine room or space size, appropriateness of design features, proper use of lot topography, layout, and competitive amenities. The materials used in the project—and listed in the specifications (specs)—are viewed as to their durability, soundness, and appeal. A soil report is also required in some cases.

Cost Breakdown

On improvement projects, the bank usually likes to see at least two competitive bids. Evaluation of costs is of great concern to both construction lenders and title insurers who underwrite policies insuring the lender's priority position. This is especially true when construction costs are surging. Cost breakdowns list the cost to the builder of each component of construction.

Construction lenders differentiate between hard costs and soft costs. **Hard costs** are those used for the construction of the property (materials, labor, etc.), while **soft costs** include nonconstruction items (permits, engineering, plan copies, etc.). Some commercial lenders limit their construction loan offerings to the amount of the hard cost.

Construction Contract

The contract between the builder and owner should spell out in detail the segments of construction and performance standards for which the contractor will be responsible, the costs for such construction, the method of funding and disbursement schedule, and other provisions. The contract usually identifies an estimated completion date and may include a monetary penalty if said completion date is exceeded.

Source of Repayment

Loan repayment may take on many forms. The developer may request a combination loan, where the construction loan is combined with the permanent loan, using only one lender.

When government-insured or -guaranteed loans are used, commitments from the applicable agency are required in addition to a commitment to finance the ultimate purchaser's loan by an approved permanent lender. In the case of income property, the permanent loan, to be funded in the future, is obtained prior to arrangement for construction financing. A definite commitment for future permanent financing is termed a take-out commitment.

Financial Data

Supporting data will be required from the builder, owner, commercial tenants, and others who may have a financial interest in the project. Depending on the type and scope of construction, a lender might also require a narrative history of the builder's past experience, as well as a credit report furnished by a local Industry Credit Bureau (ICB). Other important aspects of the project—such as tract and condominium private deed restrictions, data from an economic and environmental point of view, rental and expense trends, lease provisions for income-producing properties, projected resale prices, and so on—would also have to be analyzed.

A financial analysis of the borrower is essential in order to assess his capacity to repay the loan. How much does the borrower now have available to put into the project? How much income will the borrower have from other sources in the future, if there are problems? This is important because history suggests that project costs often exceed original estimates and borrowers must be able to carry the financial load ahead of draws. Note: Owner-builders are required to either have a contractor's license or they must hire a general contractor. The lender requires assurance that the construction will be overseen by someone with a valid license and who can be held accountable for the final product. Most construction loans will not allow an owner to do his or her own construction because of this liability. While most cities allow for an "owner-builder", when paying someone more than $500 to do any work on your property, that worker must have a contractor's license.

Lending and Disbursement Procedures

There are many variables in financing, and no two lenders have the same standards for making construction loans. There are, however, certain basic steps in the construction lending process that apply to most real estate lenders. These include:

1. Loan application with necessary accompanying data and documents, including plans and specifications, estimated costs for the proposed project, construction contract, credit data, and a financial statement of the borrower and builder.

2. Appraisal of the site and proposed construction, with an estimate of value upon completion determined from plans and specs and based on current market conditions.

3. Title examination, preparation of documents and legal instruments needed to secure the loan, and issuance of the commitment to make the loan.

4. Disbursement system for releasing money as construction progresses according to a predetermined schedule. The payout of loan funds as construction progresses is one of the major distinguishing characteristics of a construction loan. This requires the establishment of a "loans-in-progress" account from which the lender pays the periodic construction expenses. Such an account is more easily monitored to assure that there will be sufficient funds to complete the project and make all required payments. An anticipated payout schedule is ordinarily incorporated into a **building loan agreement** between lender and borrower, an example of which is found in Figure 12.1.

   A building loan agreement is a very important document (the heart of a construction loan) that distinguishes a construction loan from other loans. It embodies the whole agreement between lender and borrower, and, if appropriate, a builder.

5. Escrow and settlement procedure.

6. Loan servicing system to assure loan repayment during the life of the loan.

FIGURE 12.1   Sample building loan agreement (partial).

Building Loan Agreement and Assignment of Account

This Agreement is executed for the purpose of obtaining a building loan from EASTERN NATIONAL
BANK, and as a part of the loan transaction, which loan is evidenced by a Note of the undersigned for $ 500,000
of even date herewith, in favor of Bank, and is secured, among other things, by a Trust Deed affecting real property
in the County of __Los Angeles_____, State of California, described as:

Portion of Lot 10, Tract 10907, as shown on map recorded in Book 195, pages 1 and 2
of Maps, in the office of the county recorder.

Otherwise known as 13515 Addison Street, Sherman Oaks, California.

Upon recordation of the Trust Deed, the proceeds of the loan are to be placed by the Bank, together with the sum of
$ 100,000 deposited by the undersigned, in special non-interest bearing Accounts with the Bank. Such deposit
of the loan proceeds shall be deemed full consideration for the Note. Each of the undersigned hereby irrevocably assigns
to the Bank as security for the obligations secured by the Trust Deed, all right, title and interest of the undersigned in
said Accounts and all moneys to be placed therein. It is agreed that any funds deposited by the undersigned shall be disbursed in accordance with the terms of this Agreement prior to disbursement of the proceeds of the loan. By its acceptance of this Agreement the Bank agrees to use the moneys in said Accounts in accordance with the terms hereof.

The undersigned, jointly and severally, further agree as follows :

1.   To commence construction of the improvements to be constructed on the property within 15 days after written
notice has been given the undersigned by the Bank that it has received a satisfactory Policy of Title Insurance insuring that the Trust Deed is a first lien on the property. Should work of any character be commenced on, or any materials
be delivered upon or to the real property or in connection with said improvement prior to receipt of said written notice
from the Bank, the Bank at its sole option, may apply the funds in said Accounts to the indebtedness secured by the Trust
Deed and to pay expenses incurred in connection with the transaction.

2.   Construction shall be in accordance with plans and specifications approved by the Bank, and without change or alteration, except with the written consent of the Bank, and said construction shall be completed within __six__ months
from date hereof. All of the materials, equipment and every part of the improvement shall be paid for in full and become
a part of the real property.

3.   The terms of the Note notwithstanding, to pay to Bank on the first day of each calendar month interest at the rate
of 10.00 % per annum on loan funds advanced, from the date of the respective advances to __December 21,__ 20XX ,
20____; thereafter, interest on the entire principal amount of the Note shall be payable at the rate, at the time and in accordance with the terms stated in said Note. If such interest is not paid, the Bank may, at its option, pay the same to itself
from the Accounts.

4.   Subject to the provisions of this Agreement the proceeds of said Accounts are to be disbursed by the Bank as follows :
A.   To pay all costs and demands in connection with the closing of the loan transaction.
B.   To pay the sum of $ 500,000 in the proportions set out below to provide funds for the construction of the
improvements, to any of the undersigned, or at the option of the Bank, to contractors, material-men and laborers,
or any of them, and at such time as the construction, in accordance with the plans and specifications, has reached
the following stages :

    1.   22% ($110,000) when foundation is complete, all ground mechanical systems
                                       are in place, sub floor installed, and all rough lumber is
                                       on the site.
    2.   21% ($105,000) when framing is complete, roof on, and all mechanical systems
                                       are roughed-in complete.
    3.   12% ($ 60,000) when interior drywall is complete, two coats on exterior
                                       and/or wood siding on and primed, including priming of all
                                       wood sash, door frames, etc., which contact drywall.
    4.   15% ($ 75,000) when sash and doors, cabinets and finish lumber are installed,
                                       flooring set (except hardwood finish, linoleum, or carpet).
    5.   20% ($100,000) when all improvements are complete (including flat concrete
                                       work, driveway and grading, plus removal of all debris), Bank
                                       has approved final inspection and a valid Notice of Completion
                                       has been recorded.
    6.   10% ($ 50,000) when the title company which issued the title policy insuring
                                       the lien of the Trust Deed will issue an endorsement or policy
                                       of title insurance with mechanics' lien coverage; and gives
                                       its written permission to release funds retained pursuant to
                                       an indemnity agreement, if any.

As mentioned above, the loan's payout schedule, proceeding as construction progresses rather than in a lump sum, is a major distinguishing feature of a construction loan. These payments are referred to by a variety of names: vouchers, **disbursements**, pay-outs, draws, **progress payments**, and advances. There are many types of payment systems but, regardless of the method used, the objective is to protect the lender in four matters:

1. The value of the work in place and materials delivered, plus the lot, will equal or exceed the total amount paid out.
2. Waivers of liens (debts owed to subcontractors, laborers, and material suppliers) will be obtained for each item of material work covered by the draw so as to avoid mechanic's liens.
3. The borrower and the lender will jointly authorize all draws.
4. There will always be sufficient funds in the possession of the lender to complete construction of the property.

With subdivision projects, a lot advance—an amount included in construction funds—may be made, so that a builder-borrower has funds sufficient to pay off any remaining balance on the vacant land being improved. Disbursement of funds can be made by a variety of methods: **draw system**, with payments made in stages as construction progresses; percentage of progress, involving incremental disbursement of construction completed based on 90 percent of work in place or delivered to the job on a monthly basis, with the remaining 10 percent retained for completion at the expiration of the mechanic's lien period; a **voucher system**, when money is disbursed on presentation of receipted bills by licensed building contractors, subcontractors, and material suppliers with appropriate lien waivers and releases; and through the use of a so-called **builder's control service**, an outside third party that acts as an intermediary in the control and disbursement of funds.

A typical example of how the draw system operates is illustrated in Figure 12.2.

There are many variations in the amount and number of **advances** based on the percentage of construction completed at any given time. The five-draw plan shown in Figure 12.2, for instance, could be rearranged into three advances, or seven advances, and so on. Whatever system is used, the lender inspects the work at regular intervals before, during, and upon completion of construction. The purpose of these compliance or progress inspections is to make certain that the builder has followed the terms of the construction loan agreement and other documents; that construction is proceeding according to the plans, specifications, time schedules, and estimated costs; that a

FIGURE 12.2   Example of a draw system for a construction loan.

Five-Draw Release Payments for a Construction Loan

Draw One—20% of loan amount upon completion of foundation, rough plumbing, and subfloor.

Draw Two—30% of loan amount upon completion of framing, roof, windows, and doors.

Draw Three—20% of loan amount upon completion of exterior and interior walls. Includes plumbing, wiring, and ducting.

Draw Four—20% of loan amount upon completion of finished floors, cabinets, trim, and all remaining aspects of construction. Notice of completion is recorded.

Draw Five—Final 10% of loan amount is released after the filing period for mechanic's lien has expired, or after issuance of a lien-free endorsement to the lender's ALTA title insurance policy. This is referred to as **holdback**.

claimed stage of construction is actually in place; that there will be no disbursement of funds ahead of actual construction; and that the receipted bills for construction are verified.

Regardless of number of advances, the final draw is normally issued jointly to borrower and builder, so that the check cannot be cashed until the parties have all endorsed it and differences, if any, have been ironed out.

12.3 TAKE-OUT OR PERMANENT LOANS

As noted earlier, some construction lenders, as a prerequisite to making a construction loan, insist that the borrower have a firm take-out commitment from an approved permanent lender.

A take-out commitment is an agreement between the borrower and the permanent lender. It is essentially a promise by the permanent lender that, under stipulated conditions, it will issue a permanent loan upon satisfactory completion of the construction.

Take-out commitments vary depending on the credentials of the borrower, market conditions, property types, and policies of the lender. Certain provisions, however, are found in many take-out or permanent loan commitments, and they are an integral part of the terminology and practice of residential, commercial, and industrial construction financing.

As the move to construction/permanent loans continued, Fannie Mae (FNMA) introduced its HomeStyle Construction-to-Permanent Mortgage (HCPM), under which borrowers could finance the construction and permanent mortgage under one package, from qualified lenders. While not used very much during the subprime financing years, it is another way to eliminate a second closing after the construction is complete and, thereby, reduce paperwork and expense. Borrowers receive an "as completed" appraisal on which the loan will be determined. HCPM loans are thereafter sold to FNMA. Interest rates can be locked in for both the construction and postconstruction phases, with interest paid monthly on the amount drawn during the construction phase, based on a series of draws similar to those shown in Figure 12.2. Fannie Mae also made this financing available for use in renovating and/or making energy-efficient improvements to existing homes, whether it be a new purchase or refinance loan.

Subordination Clauses

A **subordination clause** is an agreement to reduce the priority of an existing loan to a new loan to be recorded in the future. For example, a developer purchases vacant land by putting some money down and the seller carries the rest of the purchase price as first deed of trust. The developer then locates construction funds to develop the property but construction lenders usually insist they be the first deed of trust. Under a subordination clause, the seller who was originally the first trust deed holder agrees to voluntarily accept a second position to a newly recorded first trust deed. Upon recordation, the subordination deed is recorded followed by the new first trust deed.

The provisions of sections 2953.1 through 2953.5 of the Civil Code require that deeds of trust containing subordination clauses, and separate subordination agreements, contain specified warning language. State judicial decisions require that a subordination clause or agreement be certain in its terms, and unless the maximum amount, maximum rate of interest, and terms of repayment of the loan secured by the future deed of trust are specified, the subordination clause or agreement will not be enforceable. Moreover, recent decisions clearly indicate that a subordination clause or agreement will not be enforceable unless it is fair and equitable to the beneficiary. An example of a subordination agreement is given in Figure 12.3.

Partial Release Clauses

Also common to construction lending, is the **partial release clause**. This provision is used with a trust deed placed on more than one parcel of property, termed a **blanket trust deed**, such as in the development of a subdivision. As each individual lot is sold and the funds delivered to the beneficiary, the lot is released from the blanket loan, the balance of which is correspondingly, but not necessarily proportionately, reduced. The release is accomplished when the lender issues a **partial reconveyance deed** on the individual lot being sold. Without a partial release clause, the trustor has no automatic right to receive a partial release.

The beneficiary (lender) requests that the trustee execute and record a partial reconveyance deed describing the portion of the property released from the blanket trust deed. The promissory note is usually endorsed to show that a partial release was given. When a series of such partial releases is contemplated, the deed of trust will usually provide that the trustee may receive the released proceeds for the beneficiary and give the partial reconveyance deeds without further demand or request from the beneficiary.

A partial release clause must be carefully examined with respect to such matters as these:

- Whether or not a trustor in default is entitled to partial releases.
- Restrictions on the selection of portions of the property to be released.
- The precise amount of the **lot release provision** and the method of computing the release price; payments for each release must be provided for in the agreement.
- Whether the release prices merely reduce the amount of the secured obligation or apply to past, current, and future installments due on the obligation.

FIGURE 12.3 Sample subordination agreement (partial).

RECORDING REQUESTED BY

AND WHEN RECORDED MAIL TO

NAME

ADDRESS

CITY
STATE & ZIP

SUBORDINATION AGREEMENT

NOTICE: THIS SUBORDINATION AGREEMENT RESULTS IN YOUR SECURITY INTEREST IN THE PROPERTY BECOMING SUBJECT TO AND OF LOWER PRIORITY THAN THE LIEN OF SOME OTHER OR LATER SECURITY INSTRUMENT.

THIS AGREEMENT, made this _____15th_____ day of _____November_____ ,20XX, by _____John Doe

and Mary Doe _____, owner of the land hereinafter described and hereinafter referred to as "Owner," and _____John Smith

and Mary Smith _____, present owner and holder of the deed of trust hereinafter described and hereinafter referred to as "Beneficiary":

WITNESSETH

THAT WHEREAS, _____John Doe and Mary Doe_____ did execute

a deed of trust, dated_____August 15, 20XX, to____ABC Title Insurance Company_____, as trustee, covering:

(FULL LEGAL TITLE INSERTED)

to secure a note in the sum of $_____$250,000_____, dated _____August 14, 20XX_____ in favor

of _____John Smith and Mary Smith_____ ,

which deed of trust was recorded _____August 16, 20XX_____, as instrument number _____1763_____

Official Records of said county; and

WHEREAS, Owner has executed, or is about to execute, a deed of trust and note in the sum of $_____$250,000_____

dated ____August 14, 20XX_____, in favor of _____ LAST SAVINGS AND LOAN _____

_____, hereinafter referred to as "Lender, " payable with interest and upon the terms and conditions

described therein, which deed of trust is to be recorded concurrently herewith; and

WHEREAS, it is a condition precedent to obtaining said loan that said deed of trust last above mentioned shall unconditionally be and remain at all times a lien or charge upon the land hereinbefore described, prior and superior to the lien or charge of the security instrument first above mentioned; and

WHEREAS, Lender is willing to make said loan provided the deed of trust securing the same is a lien or charge upon the above described property prior and superior to the lien or charge of the security instrument first above mentioned and provided that Beneficiary will specifically and unconditionally subordinate the lien or charge of the security instrument first above mentioned to the lien or charge of the deed of trust in favor of Lender ; and

WHEREAS, it is to the mutual benefit of the parties hereto that Lender make such loan to Owner; and Beneficiary is willing that the deed of trust securing the same shall, when recorded, constitute a lien or charge upon said land which is unconditionally prior and superior to the lien or charge of the deed of trust first above mentioned.

NOW, THEREFORE, in consideration of the mutual benefits accruing to the parties hereto and other valuable consideration, the receipt and sufficiency of which consideration is hereby acknowledged, and in order to induce Lender to make the loan above referred to, it is hereby declared, understood and agreed as follows:

(1) That said deed of trust securing said note in favor of Lender, and any renewals or extensions thereof, shall unconditionally be and remain at all times a lien or charge on the property therein described, prior and superior to the lien or charge of the security instrument first above mentioned.

(2) That Lender would not make its loan above described without this subordination agreement.

(3) That this agreement shall be the whole and only agreement between the parties hereto with regard to the subordination of the lien or charge of the security instrument first above mentioned to the lien or charge of the deed of trust in favor of Lender above referred to and shall supersede and cancel any prior agreements as to such, or any, subordination including, but not limited to, those provisions, if any, contained in the deed of trust first above mentioned, which provide for the subordination of the lien or charge thereof to a deed or deeds of trust or to a mortgage or mortgages to be thereafter executed.

FIGURE 12.3   Sample subordination agreement (partial). (*continued*)

Beneficiary declares, agrees and acknowledges that

(a)   He consents to and approves (i) all provisions of the note and deed of trust in favor of Lender above referred to, and (ii) all agreements, including but not limited to any loan or escrow agreements, between Owner and Lender for the disbursement of the proceeds of Lender's loan;

(b)   Lender in making disbursements pursuant to any such agreement is under no obligation or duty to, nor has Lender represented that it will, see to the application of such proceeds by the person or persons to whom Lender disburses such proceeds and any application or use of such proceeds for purposes other than those provided for in such agreement or agreements shall not defeat the subordination herein made in whole or in party;

(c)   he intentionally and unconditionally waives, relinquishes and subordinates the lien or charge of the security instrument first above mentioned in favor of the lien or charge upon said land of the deed of trust in favor of Lender above referred to and understands that in reliance upon, and in consideration of, this waiver, relinquishment and subordination specific loans and advances are being and will be made and, as part and parcel thereof, specific monetary and other obligations are being and will be entered into which would not be made or entered into but for said reliance upon this waiver, relinquishment and subordination; and

NOTICE: THIS SUBORDINATION AGREEMENT CONTAINS A PROVISION WHICH ALLOWS THE PERSON OBLIGATED ON YOUR REAL PROPERTY SECURITY TO OBTAIN A LOAN A PORTION OF WHICH MAY BE EXPENDED FOR OTHER PURPOSES THAN IMPROVEMENT OF THE LAND.

_____   _____

_____   _____
                Beneficiary   Owner

STATE OF CALIFORNIA
COUNTY OF _____ } SS.

On _____ before me, _____,
personally appeared _____
personally known to me (or proved to me on the basis of satisfactory evidence) to be the person(s) whose name(s) is/are subscribed to the within instrument and acknowledged to me that he/she/they executed the same in his/her/their authorized capacity(ies), and that by his/her/their signature(s) on the instrument the person(s), or the entity upon behalf of which the person(s) acted, executed the instrument.

WITNESS my hand and official seal.

Signature_____   (This area for official notarial seal)

STATE OF CALIFORNIA
COUNTY OF _____ } SS.

On _____ before me, _____,
personally appeared _____
personally known to me (or proved to me on the basis of satisfactory evidence) to be the person(s) whose name(s) is/are subscribed to the within instrument and acknowledged to me that he/she/they executed the same in his/her/their authorized capacity(ies), and that by his/her/their signature(s) on the instrument the person(s), or the entity upon behalf of which the person(s) acted, executed the instrument.

WITNESS my hand and official seal.

Signature_____   (This area for official notarial seal)
                          (ALL SIGNATURES MUST BE ACKNOWLEDGED)

IT IS RECOMMENDED THAT, PRIOR TO THE EXECUTION OF THIS SUBORDINATION AGREEMENT, THE PARTIES CONSULT WITH THEIR ATTORNEYS WITH RESPECT THERETO

(CLTA SUBORDINATION FORM "A")
                          SUBAGMTA.DOC

Rental Achievement Clauses

When the construction of commercial (and sometimes industrial) property is being financed, a **rental achievement clause** is common.

The granting of a construction loan for rental properties is usually contingent on the developer-borrower's ability to prelease a stated amount of space in the building. The developer usually provides a certified rent roll indicating who the tenants will be, the space to be leased, length of the leases, and the annual rents to be paid. The loan servicing agents then recertify that the developer's certified statements have been verified.

The rental achievement condition in the commitment for commercial property is of prime concern to construction lenders. Lenders do not want to finance construction projects and then discover that tenants are lacking for the rental space. Consequently, lenders are hesitant to advance any construction loan until the rental requirements of the take-out or permanent lender have been satisfied. It is typical for the permanent lender, in deference to the construction lender's concern, to provide that a certain portion of the loan be disbursed without any rental requirement and the balance, when rentals reach a stipulated level. The amount of the construction loan may be set at the lower amount, called the floor loan, at least until the necessary rentals have been achieved. Additional sums are then disbursed later as the rental schedule submitted with the loan application is met; however, this must be done within a specified time, usually one or two years after the closing of the floor loan.

There can be a gap between the higher amount and the floor amount, to which the permanent lender will commit if all rentals are achieved. The gap is usually 15 to 20 percent of the larger amount. The developer would like to obtain the full amount of the loan, that is, the full rental achievement commitment, in order to generate as much leverage as possible. Yet, the construction lender will usually commit itself only for the floor amount.

The construction lender may be willing, however, to commit for the full or larger amount if another lender will "stand by" or commit itself to provide the gap financing. The **gap commitment** guarantees that the borrower will have the difference between the floor loan and the upper level of the permanent loan if the rental achievement for the larger amount is not reached. A fee is charged for the gap commitment and the interest rate is often higher because the loan, if made, would be a second mortgage. The developer, however, does not expect to actually have to draw the funds from the gap commitment (and the gap lender does not expect it either).

Mechanic's Liens and Their Impact on Construction Loans

All construction lenders are wary about the possibility of mechanic's liens, that is, creation of liens against real estate by those improving it. Mechanic's liens can arise if a builder does not complete the project or if the job is completed and the builder fails to pay material suppliers, subcontractors, and workers. The probability of a lien by one or more subcontractors and material suppliers is ever present, possibly jeopardizing the construction lender's priority position. This applies to all forms of real estate construction, including home improvement loans. An example of a mechanic's lien is given in Figure 12.4.

Mechanic's lien rights are protected by the state constitution and are granted to contractors, subcontractors, laborers, and material suppliers who have contributed to or worked on the property and have not been paid for their services. The law requires that in addition to a contract to do the work, a pre-lien notice in the form of a notice of intent to lien, if provider is not paid, must be filed with the owner and construction lender's office within 20 days of commencement of each particular segment of work. The period for filing a lien varies from as few as 30 days to not more than 90 days after completion of a building or other work of improvement.

Notice of Completion

If a **Notice of Completion** (see Figure 12.5) is filed by the owner (not the contractor) within 10 days after the job is substantially completed, the original contractor has 60 days in which to file a lien, while all other parties have 30 days. If no notice of completion is recorded, or if a notice of completion is faulty in any respect, all parties have 90 days from the date of **substantial completion**. To protect themselves, as well as the builder and lender, against mechanic's liens, owners can purchase **completion bonds**—extremely rare with home construction loans, but required for Cal-Vet construction loans, and always required for government construction jobs—usually costing 1.5 percent of hard costs.

Should a job not be completed due to acts of God, strikes, impossibility of performance, disagreements, work stoppage, or for any other reason, then a **Notice of Cessation of Labor** or **Notice of Abandonment** may be filed. These have time limits similar to those of a completion notice.

If any work of improvement started prior to recording the construction loan, a mechanic's lien may take priority over other

FIGURE 12.4 Sample mechanic's lien.

MECHANIC'S LIEN

③ RECORDING REQUESTED BY
CHARLES L. LOAFER
WHEN RECORDED MAIL TO

r ⌐ Charles L. Loafer
Name 2432 Mountain Ave
Street
Address Willow Springs, Calif.
City &
State ⌐

① 1436

② Recorded in Official
Records of Oakdale
County, Calif.

May 23, 20xx at 1:00p.m.

GEORGE L. FISH, County
Recorder

FEE
$3.00
A

(SPACE ABOVE THIS LINE FOR RECORDER'S USE)

MECHANIC'S LIEN

NOTICE IS HEREBY GIVEN that: Pursuant to the provisions of the California Civil Code,
⑤ Charles L. Loafer

hereafter referred to as "Claimant" (whether singular or plural), claims a lien upon the real property and buildings, improvements or structures thereon, described in Paragraph Five (5) below, and states the following:

⑥ (1) That demand of Claimant after deducting all just credits and offsets, is _$3,800_
together with interest thereon at the rate of _5_ % per annum from _April 1_ _20xx_

⑦ (2) That the name of the owner(s) or reputed owner(s) of said property, is (are) _____
James M. Broke and Joanne S. Broke
(name, or state "unknown")

⑧ (3) That Claimant did from_March 25_ _20xx_, until _March 28_ ,20xx
perform labor and/or supply materials as follows: _Replacement of front main line, meter to_
(general statement of kind of work done or materials furnished, or both)
house. Replaced all valves and reconnected to sprinkler system
with all valves up by porch, on a time and material basis.
Material $800, sales tax $70, labor $2,900. Permit $30.

for the construction, alteration or repair of said buildings, improvements or structures, which labor, or materials, or both of them, were in fact used in the construction, alteration or repair of said buildings, improvements or structures, the location of which is set forth in Paragraph Five (5) below.

(4) Claimant furnished work and materials under contract with, or at the request of,
⑨ James M. Broke and Joanne S. Broke

(5) That the property upon which said lien is sought to be charged is situated in the City of _Harrisport_ ,
County of _Oakdale_ . State of California, commonly known as _____
⑩ _20436 S. Grand, Harrisport, California_
(street address)
and more particularly described as _Lot 306, tract 1415 as per map recorded in book_
563 pages 21 to 25 inclusive of maps, in the office of the county
recorder of said county.
(legal description)

⑪ DATED: This _22nd_ day of _May_ _20xx_

⑫ Firm Name _Loafer Plumbing Service_
By _Charles L. Loafer_

(Verification for Individual Claim)

STATE OF CALIFORNIA,
⑭ County of_Oakdale_ } ss.

⑮ _Charles L. Loafer_ ,
being first duly sworn, deposes and says: That_____ he is the
_____ Claimant
named in the foregoing claim of lien, that___ he has read the
same and knows the contents thereof, and that the statements therein
contained are true; and that it contains, among other things, ⑬
correct statement of _his_ demand, after deducting all just
credits and offsets. May
Dated: this_22nd_day of 20xx, at _Willow Springs_,
(City & State) Calif.
Charles L. Loafer
(Signature of affiant)
Subscribed and sworn to before me

May 22 _20xx_
John Fairchild
Notary Public in and for said State.

OFFICIAL SEAL
JOHN FAIRCHILD
NOTARY PUBLIC — CALIFORNIA
PRINCIPAL OFFICE IN
LOS ANGELES COUNTY
My Commission Expires Nov. 9,

(Verification for other than Individual Claim)

STATE OF CALIFORNIA,
County of_____ } ss.

being first duly sworn, deposes and says: That_____
the Claimant herein, is a ¹_____
that affiant is ²_____

and for that reason he makes his affidavit on behalf of said ³
that he has read the same and knows the contents thereof, and that
the statements therein contained are true; and that it contains,
among other things, a correct statement of the demand of Claimant,
after deducting all just credits and offsets.
Dated: this_____ day of 20____, at_____
(City & State)

_____
(Signature of affiant)
Subscribed and sworn to before me

_____19__

_____
Notary Public in and for said State.

MECHANIC'S LIEN—1024

8 pt. type or larger

FIGURE 12.5 Sample notice of completion.

RECORDING REQUESTED BY

SAFECO TITLE INSURANCE COMPANY

AND WHEN RECORDED MAIL TO

NAME Alfred S. Busybody
ADDRESS 14602 Victory Blvd.
CITY & STATE Van Nuys, CA 91401

SPACE ABOVE THIS LINE FOR RECORDER'S USE

Notice of Completion
Individual
Before using this form, refer to recommended procedure stated on reverse side of this form

NOTICE IS HEREBY GIVEN THAT:

1. The undersigned is owner of the interest or estate stated below in the property hereinafter described.
2. The full name of the undersigned is Alfred S. Busybody
3. The full address of the undersigned is 14602 Victory Blvd, Van Nuys, CA 91401
4. The nature of the title of the undersigned is: In fee "Lessee"
   (If other than fee, strike "In fee" and insert, for example, "purchaser under contract of purchase," or "lessee".)
5. The full names and full addresses of all persons, if any, who hold title with the undersigned as joint tenants or as tenants in common are:

NAMES	ADDRESSES
Alfred S. Busybody	14602 Victory Blvd., Van Nuys, CA

6. A work of improvement on the property hereinafter described was completed on May 1, 20XX
7. The name of the original contractor, if any, for such work of improvement was
   Cave-in Construction Company, Inc.
   (If no contractor for work of improvement as a whole, insert "none".)
8. The full name(s) and address(es) of the transferor(s) of the undersigned is (are):

NAME(S)	ADDRESS(ES)
N O N E	

   (Complete where undersigned is successor to owner who caused improvement to be constructed)
9. The property on which said work of improvement was completed is in the city of Van Nuys
   , county of Los Angeles , state of California, and is described as follows:

   Lot 7, Tract 13075, as per map recorded in Book 326, pages 10 to 15 inclusive of maps, in the office of the county recorder of said county.

10. The street address of said property is 14602 Victory Blvd, Van Nuys, CA

   (If no street address has been officially assigned, insert "none".)

Dated June 2, 20XX

Signature of owner named in paragraph 2 } *Alfred S. Busybody*
Alfred S. Busybody

Verification for individual owners

STATE OF CALIFORNIA,
County of Los Angeles } SS.

The undersigned, being duly sworn, says: That he is the owner of the aforesaid interest or estate in the property described in the foregoing notice; that he has read the same, and knows the contents thereof, and that the facts stated therein are true.
Signature of owner named in paragraph 2

SUBSCRIBED AND SWORN TO before me on June 2, 20XX
Robert J. Bond
Robert J. Bond

FOR NOTARY SEAL OR STAMP

OFFICIAL SEAL
ROBERT J. BOND
NOTARY PUBLIC · CALIFORNIA
LOS ANGELES COUNTY
My comm. expires JAN 31, 20XX

Title Order No. 7062351   Escrow No. 1616-22   6511 Van Nuys Blvd., #12, Van Nuys, CA 91401 liens that were placed on the property after the job was started. This is referred to as the **doctrine of relation back**. The financial interests of all others furnishing labor or materials are perceived to have begun from this initial date, even though they came on the scene subsequent to the creation of the trust deed. For this reason, lenders, and others making construction loans, carefully check to determine that no construction work has been started prior to the recordation of a loan; or lenders may require indemnity of an ALTA title policy protecting them against loss from mechanic's liens.

What constitutes "start of construction"? It could be delivering material, clearing the lot, setting grade stakes, grading, ditching, placing chemical toilets on the lot, setting power poles, setting location markers, marking chalk lines, clearing trees, and so on. In other words, start of construction is when the first action of the job starts, even if it's only the first shovel touching the dirt.

Anyone filing a mechanic's lien must institute a suit to foreclose the lien within 90 days after recording the lien. The suit is similar to a mortgage foreclosure, resulting in a court-ordered sale in order to satisfy the claims. In the event of insufficient funds following the sale, the court may award a deficiency judgment against the debtor for the balance. If no suit is filed, a mechanic's lien expires after 90 days.

Notice of Non-responsibility

Sometimes a lien is filed against property whose owner did not contract for the improvement, as when a tenant negotiates a contract for major repairs or alterations to a leasehold interest. To protect themselves, the owners may repudiate responsibility and liability by recording a Notice of Non-responsibility within 10 days of the time they acquired knowledge. A sample is shown in Figure 12.6. A copy of the notice must be posted on the property. The contractor would then have to look to the contract for remedy—that is, sue the contracting party for collection of money due. Most contractors check the ownership of property and will not contract with tenants to avoid this very issue.

Release of Mechanic's Liens

A mechanic's lien may be discharged by the running of the statute of limitations, after 90 days, if no foreclosure action is commenced:

- by written release, through the recording of a **Release of Mechanic's Lien** (illustrated in Figure 12.7);

FIGURE 12.6   Sample notice of non-responsibility.

RECORDING REQUESTED BY

ALBERT E. CAUTIOUS

WHEN RECORDED MAIL TO

21536

Recorded in Official Records
of Oakdale County, Calif.

January 17, 20XX at 10:00a.m.

GEORGE L. FISH, County
Recorder

FEE
$3.00
D

Name Albert E. Cautious
Street 7503 S. Juniper Street
Address Hawthorne, Calif.
City &
State

———— (SPACE ABOVE THIS LINE FOR RECORDER'S USE) ————

NOTICE
NON-RESPONSIBILITY

TO ALL WHOM IT MAY CONCERN: NOTICE IS HEREBY GIVEN:

(1) That __I__ to wit, __Albert E. Cautious__
(I—we)   (Insert name or names)
                                                        (am—are)

the __Fee Owner__
              (Insert herein the nature of title or interest)

of certain property located in the City of __Hawthorne__
County of __Oakdale__, State of California, and more particularly described as:
Lot __11__, in Block __--__, of Tract No. __27735__
                                                            as

per map recorded in Book __6317__, Page __33__ of
Records of __Oakdale__ County, State of California.

(2) That __I__ have obtained knowledge that __Construction of a Swimming__
(I—we)   (Insert brief description of improvement, alteration or repair)
__Pool__
                                                            is
                                                          (is—are)
__Being Done__ on said property.
        (in the course of construction—are being made)

(3) That ten (10) days have not elapsed since __I__ obtained this knowledge.
                                          (I—we)

(4) That __I__ will not be responsible for the __Construction__
(I—we)   (erection, alteration or repair)
of said __Swimming Pool__,
              (building—improvement)
or for the material or labor used or to be used thereon, or which has been performed, furnished or used in
any manner or way upon said land, or upon the __Swimming Pool__
                                                  (building—improvement)
thereon, or addition thereto, or which may hereafter be
performed, furnished, or used upon said land, or upon the __Swimming Pool__
                                                        (building—improvement)
thereon, or addition thereto, or for the services of any architect.

(5) That ____
                  (Insert name or names)   (is—are)
the purchaser of said property under a contract of purchase.7503 S. Juniper St   City of
(6) That the street address of said property is
Hawthorne California, and that Peter I. Sneak
                                    (Insert name or names)
__is__ the lessee of said property.
(is—are)

Dated __January 13, 20XX__

Albert E. Cautious

STATE OF CALIFORNIA,
                              } ss.
County of __Oakdale__
Albert E. Cautious
, being first duly sworn, deposes and says: That the above and within
notice is a true and correct copy of a notice posted in a conspicuous place on Lot __11__ in Block __--__
of Tract No __27735__, in the City of __Hawthorne__
County of __Oakdale__ State of California on the __13th__ day of __January__
20XX by __Albert E. Cautious__ and that the facts stated therein are true of __his__ own knowledge,
and that he is making this affidavit for and on behalf of the person for whose protection said notice was given.

Subscribed and sworn to before me this __16th__ day of __January__ 20XX

OFFICIAL SEAL
ARNOLD T. CHECKER
NOTARY PUBLIC — CALIFORNIA
PRINCIPAL OFFICE IN
LOS ANGELES COUNTY
My Commission Expires Nov. 9, 20XX

Title Order No

Notary Public in and for said County and State.

Escrow or Loan No

NOTICE—NON-RESPONSIBILITY
WOLCOTTS FORM 1186—REVISED

FIGURE 12.7   Sample release of a mechanic's lien.

RECORDING REQUESTED BY

JAMES M. BROKE & JAONNE S. BROKE

AND WHEN RECORDED MAIL TO

NAME James M & Jaonne S Broke
ADDRESS 20536 S Grand Ave.
CITY & STATE Harrisport, California

———— SPACE ABOVE THIS LINE FOR RECORDER'S USE ————

Release of Mechanic's Lien

That Notice of Mechanics Lien executed by   Charles L. Loafer

————————————————, naming as obligors (including the owners or reputed owners) ————

James M Broke and Jaonne S Broke

Recorded   May 23, 20XX   , as Instrument No. 1436

in Book 5883   , Page 25   , Official Records of the County of   Oakdale

State of California, upon that Real Property in said County and State described as:

Lot 306, Tract 1415 as per map recorded in Book 563, pages 21 to 25 inclusive of maps, in the office of the county recorder of said county.

Is hereby released, the claim having been fully paid and discharged.

Dated August 14, 20XX

STATE OF CALIFORNIA
COUNTY OF   } SS.

On   August 14, 20XX
before me, the undersigned, a Notary Public in and for
said County and State, personally appeared

Charles L. Loafer

known to me to be the person(s) whose name(s) is (are)
subscribed to the within instrument and acknowledged that
he   executed the same.

Robert J. Bond

Loafer Plumbing Service

By: Charles L. Loafer

FOR NOTARY SEAL OR STAMP

OFFICIAL SEAL
ROBERT J. BOND
NOTARY PUBLIC - CALIFORNIA
LOS ANGELES COUNTY
My comm. expires JAN 31.
6511 Van Nuys Blvd., #12, Van Nuys, CA 91401

Title Order No.   Escrow No.

- by the issuance of a bond to release the lien;
- by satisfaction of the judgment lien against the debtor;
- or by dismissal of the action when the court is convinced that a valid claim is not sustainable.

12.4 PUBLIC CONSTRUCTION

Often property owners are assessed for public construction projects that are proposed to improve the general health and welfare of the community. At the same time such public projects increase the value of properties of the affected owners in theory if not also in practice.

Assessment liens are imposed upon properties benefiting from capital projects that are classified as off-site improvements, such as street widening and installation of curbs, gutters, sidewalks, storm drains, sewers, and street lights. A number of state laws allow for the imposition of an assessment tax on the benefited properties, which share in the costs on a proportioned basis. The property owners may either pay the assessment in full within 30 days after completion—defined as final inspection and approval of the job by the applicable local regulatory agency—or pay the lien in installments over a period not to exceed 15 years through an assessment bond.

There are four significant state laws or improvement acts, as they are called, that provide for the construction and financing of capital improvements for which the property owner is assessed in whole or in part:

1. *Vrooman Street Act.* This law confers authority on city councils to grade and finish streets, construct sewers, and perform other improvements within municipalities or counties and to issue bonds secured and redeemed by tax levies. It also provides for the acquisition of public utilities by the local governing body.

2. *Street Improvement Act of 1911.* This law, with its amendments, provides that bonds may be issued by the municipality ordering the improvements and that the assessments may be paid in equal installments during the term of the bonds. The installments may be paid with property taxes over a 15-year period, but can be paid off at any time. The assessee must pay a share of the project within 30 days of its completion or bonds will be issued at an interest rate determined by the issuing local legislative body. The bonds will remain as liens against the property until paid in full.

3. *Improvement Bond Act of 1915.* This law, also as amended, provides for the issuance of series bonds for subdivision street improvements, including the construction of sewers. The cost of

the redemption of the bonds issued and the interest thereon, usually 6 percent, is assessed in a proportioned manner against the owners of property directly affected.

4. *Mello-Roos Community Facilities Act.* This law arose as a result of Proposition 13, which restricts taxing districts from raising taxes upon the sale or transfer of property. The Mello-Roos CFA established another method whereby almost every municipal subdivision of the state may form a special, separate tax district to finance a long list of public improvements/facilities by the sale of bonds and finance certain public services on a pay-as-you-go basis. Initially developed to provide for new schools in newly constructed subdivisions, the program was expanded to encompass practically all necessary public services. Formed by local governments, the developer of a new project may impose the bonds and then market the properties, subject to individual lot assessments. For example, each purchaser of a home in such districts, is assessed a pro rata share of the costs to put in the public facilities that can include freeway access routes and build and maintain roads, sewers, community centers, and even schools that serve the housing project.

SUMMARY

Construction loans are short-term or interim loans. Combination loans combine the short-term interim loan with the permanent or take-out loan. Some banks even allow a purchase-construction-take out loan combination. The Federal Housing Administration (FHA) has a similar "rehab" loan called 203-k.

Construction lenders look for many things before finally committing themselves to fund a construction project. These include evaluation of the plans and specifications, detailed breakdown of the costs involved, analysis of the building contract, source of repayment, and supporting financial data required on the owner, builder, and others who may have a financial interest in the project. A construction loan contract may contain a variety of provisions that protect the lender and borrower, including a subordination clause, partial release clause, rental achievement clause, and others. **Mechanic's liens** protect those who improve real property by means of their labor, skills, services, and materials furnished for the job. Construction lenders must be on guard to see that their security is not impaired because of faulty construction, noncompliance with the building loan agreement, start of work before the construction trust deed is recorded, and other construction problems.

IMPORTANT TERMS AND CONCEPTS

Advances

Assessment lien

Blanket trust deed

Builder's control service

Building loan agreement

Combination loan

Completion bond

Disbursements

Doctrine of relation back

Gap commitment

Hard costs

Hold back

Lot release provision

Mechanic's liens

Notice of Abandonment

Notice of Cessation of Labor

Notice of Completion

Partial reconveyance deed

Partial release clause

Progress payments

Release of Mechanic's Lien

Rental achievement clause

Short-term construction loan

Soft costs

Subordination clause

Substantial completion

Take-out loan

Voucher system

REVIEWING YOUR UNDERSTANDING

Questions for Discussion

1. How do construction loans differ from take-out loans?

2. What is meant by progress payments?

3. List several methods of disbursing funds for construction projects.

4. What is a subordination clause? How does such a clause protect the construction lender?

5. Differentiate between a partial release clause and a rental achievement clause. For whose benefit are these provisions set up?

Multiple-Choice Questions

1. A lien filed by contractors due to the failure of an obligated party to pay for work of improvement is a
   a. contractor's lien.
   b. subordination lien.
   c. mechanic's lien.
   d. superior lien.

2. The payoff of a construction loan is normally accomplished through
   a. a take-out loan.
   b. cash flow generated from an income property.
   c. sale of the completed project.
   d. bonded indebtedness.

3. In a five-draw construction loan payment schedule, mechanic's liens are considered in (hint: see Figure 12.2)
   a. draw 4.
   b. draw 5.
   c. draw 1.
   d. draw 2.

4. The system of disbursements of construction funds upon presentation of receipted bills by contractors is called a
   a. percentage of progress.
   b. voucher.
   c. stage of completion.
   d. proof of billings.

5. An agreement between borrower and permanent lender relative to future delivery of a take-out loan upon completion is called a
   a. construction contract.
   b. building loan agreement.
   c. take-out commitment.
   d. tri-party agreement.

6. A contract between borrower, contractor, and lender establishing the obligations and duties of each party during the period of construction is a
   a. construction contract.
   b. building loan agreement.
   c. take-out commitment.
   d. bilateral agreement.

7. A construction loan may lose first-lien position to mechanic's lien claimants by
   a. commencement of work prior to recording of a construction loan.
   b. commencement of work prior to recording of a combination loan.
   c. either (a) or (b).
   d. neither (a) nor (b).

8. The largest number and volume of interim construction loans are generally made by
   a. local institutions.
   b. credit unions.
   c. real estate investment trusts.
   d. casualty insurance companies.

9. The document that is filed by the owner after a project is substantially completed is a
   a. Notice of Cessation of Labor.
   b. Mechanic's Lien.
   c. Notice of Non-responsibility.
   d. Notice of Completion.

10. When a mechanic's lien is filed against a property, the threat of loss of title rests with the
    a. lender.
    b. contractor.
    c. owner.
    d. subcontractor.

11. The costs of a construction loan to a borrower are greater than a regular purchase money loan because
    a. costs and interest rates are increasing daily.
    b. the lender knows that construction costs are constantly going up.
    c. the lender knows that values will have risen by the time the project is completed.
    d. the lender has more overhead and greater risks.

12. In California, construction loans cannot be made
    a. unless a take-out loan has been committed by a responsible lender.
    b. for less than one year.
    c. except on an owner-occupied basis.
    d. none of the above is correct.

13. The amount of a construction loan
    a. is paid out in a lump sum upon completion of construction.
    b. normally is paid out in various stages.
    c. must be disbursed in no fewer than five draws.
    d. generally begins to be amortized as soon as the first disbursement is made.

14. A subordination clause in a deed of trust is most likely to be found in the case of
    a. a package deed of trust.
    b. a combination loan.
    c. a regular deed of trust.
    d. land loans.

15. If a developer has signed a deed of trust covering all the lots in a subdivision, he or she will find that partial releases
    a. cannot be required unless provided for specifically in the deed of trust.
    b. can always be obtained, even if not specifically provided for, upon payment of a pro rata amount of the principal balance due.
    c. can be obtained only if a subordination agreement is incorporated in the deed of trust.
    d. cannot be obtained until at least 50 percent of the lots in a subdivision are sold.

16. Which document separates a regular real estate loan from a construction loan?
    a. building loan agreement
    b. promissory note
    c. appraisal report
    d. credit report

17. Which of the following is a direct result of Proposition 13?
    a. Mechanic's Lien Law
    b. Improvement Bond Act of 1915
    c. Street Improvement Act of 1911
    d. Mello-Roos Community Facilities Act

18. A partial release clause is usually used in connection with a
    a. combination loan.
    b. blanket loan.
    c. floor loan.
    d. standby loan.

19. Major alterations to a rental house were contracted for by the tenants. To disavow themselves from possible mechanic's liens against their property, the owners should file and post a
    a. Rental Achievement Clause.
    b. Notice of Completion.
    c. Notice of Non-responsibility.
    d. Release of Mechanic's Lien.

20. Another name for an interim loan is
    a. nonamortized loan.
    b. progress loan.
    c. take-out loan.
    d. short-term loan.

Chapter 13

PREVIEW

A basic understanding of the mathematics of real estate finance is vital to the agent, consumer, and investor. Words are hardly enough. A buyer will ask how much his payment will be. A seller will ask how much she will net from the sale. Understanding numbers—figures—is essential to close any real estate transaction.

After completing this chapter, you should be able to:

1. Differentiate between a straight note (interest-only) and an amortized note.

2. Explain how financial calculators and computers are used to determine monthly payments, principal and interest allocation, balloon payments, price and yields on notes, plus a variety of other real estate calculations.

3. Discuss how biweekly loan payments differ from traditional monthly payments.

4. Understand what inputs are used to calculate the annual percentage rate (APR) for a real estate loan.

Basic Mathematics of Real Estate Finance

13.1 REVIEW OF THE BASIC COMPONENTS OF A REAL ESTATE LOAN

1. *Interest is the charge or price, expressed as dollars, paid for the use of money.* Much like a tenant pays rent for the use of living space, a borrower pays interest for the use of money. A borrower can be viewed as a tenant, renting money for an agreed period of time, returning the rented funds with an additional charge for their use. The "interest rent" may be paid either at the end of the period—the maturity date—or, more commonly, at periodic intervals, such as monthly payments.

2. *Principal is the amount of money borrowed.* It is the initial amount that appears on the promissory note.

3. *Rate is the percentage of interest charged on the principal and is usually expressed* as an annual rate.

4. *Time (or term) denotes the length of the loan and the frequency of payments.* The term is usually expressed as years, with the payment due monthly. Payments are rarely due annually, semiannually, or quarterly.

Review of Promissory Notes

Straight Note (Interest-Only Payments)

The **straight note** usually calls for "interest-only" payments, with the entire principal due in a lump sum at a future date. The interest is usually paid monthly, but some notes may call for other payment intervals such as quarterly or annually.

Example: Assume a $100,000 straight note at 8 percent interest per annum, payable monthly, all due in five years. What is the monthly interest payment?

Solution: $100,000 principal × .08 = $8,000 interest for the year ÷ 12 months = $666.67 per month, with the entire $100,000 principal due and payable at the end of five years.

Amortized Loan

An **amortized loan** calls for installment payments that include both principal and interest. Two main types are:

1. *Installment Note—Fully Amortized.* This is the most common note found in real estate financing transactions. Each payment remains constant, with interest computed on the unpaid balance of the note, which is defined as simple interest. Hence, each payment decreases the principle owed and, therefore, decreases the amount of interest due. Since the installments continue in equal amounts until the entire obligation is repaid, this type is referred to as a fully amortized note.

2. *Installment Note—Partially Amortized with a Balloon Payment.* This note calls for payments of interest and principal, but not enough principal to completely pay off the loan by the due date. The payments remain constant until a stated date, at which time the outstanding balance, called a balloon payment, is due. As described in Chapter 1, a *balloon payment* is defined as any payment at least twice the size of the normal payment.

Why Amortized Loans Are Used

Prior to the Great Depression of the 1930s, many real estate loans made no provision for the reduction of the principal through periodic payments. In those days, if a person borrowed $10,000 at, say, 8 percent interest, the buyer was expected to pay only the annual interest of $800, in monthly installments, without reducing the principal. Then at some time in the future, the entire principal of $10,000 would become due and payable. During the Great Depression, people lost their jobs and could not make the monthly interest payments or pay the principal loan amount when it came due. This resulted in massive foreclosures and the weakness of this "interest-only" payment plan became evident. Then lending reforms, led by several government agencies, resulted in the current practice of monthly payments that include principal reduction.

How to Compute Amortized Loan Payments

To determine the required payments on a loan, one can use an amortization table, a financial calculator or an online calculator. The **amortization table** contains tables that show the amounts needed to pay off (a) varying amounts of loans, (b) at specified rates of interest, and (c) for specified periods (or terms). A sample page from an amortization table is shown in Table 13.1.

To use Table 13.1 to find monthly payments at 12 percent interest, merely locate the amount of the loan, then the term or number of years of the loan. At the point of intersection the monthly payment is given. For example, an $80,000 loan at 12 percent for 30 years will require an $822.90 monthly payment. What will be the payments for a $100,000 loan at 12 percent payable for 20 years?

Another type of amortization table is shown in Table 13.2. This table shows the amount of payment per $1,000 of loan amount at

TABLE 13.1 Monthly loan amortization payments at 12 percent.

| | TERM (YEARS) | | | | | | | |
Amount	3	5	10	15	20	25	30	40
80,000	2657.17	1779.56	1147.85	960.18	880.90	842.60	822.90	806.80
81,000	2690.38	1801.80	1162.19	972.18	891.91	853.13	833.19	816.89
82,000	2723.61	1824.04	1176.54	984.18	902.92	863.66	843.47	826.97
83,000	2756.82	1846.29	1190.89	996.19	913.93	874.19	853.76	827.06
84,000	2790.05	1868.53	1205.24	1008.19	924.94	884.73	864.05	847.14
85,000	2823.22	1890.78	1219.59	1020.19	935.95	895.26	874.33	857.23
86,000	2856.44	1913.02	1233.94	1032.19	946.96	905.79	884.62	867.31
87,000	2889.65	1935.27	1248.28	1044.20	957.98	916.32	894.90	877.40
88,000	2922.88	1957.51	1262.63	1056.20	968.99	926.86	905.19	887.48
89,000	2956.10	1979.76	1276.98	1068.20	980.00	937.39	915.48	897.57
90,000	2989.29	2002.00	1291.33	1080.20	991.01	947.92	925.76	907.65
91,000	3022.42	2024.24	1305.68	1092.20	1002.02	958.45	936.05	917.74
92,000	3055.69	2046.49	1320.02	1104.21	1013.03	968.99	946.34	927.82
93,000	3088.89	2068.73	1334.37	1116.21	1024.04	979.52	956.62	937.91
94,000	3122.09	2090.98	1348.72	1128.21	1035.05	990.05	966.91	947.99
95,000	3155.36	2113.22	1363.07	1140.21	1046.06	1000.58	977.19	958.08
96,000	3188.55	2135.47	1377.42	1152.22	1057.08	1011.12	987.48	968.16
97,000	3221.75	2157.71	1391.76	1164.22	1068.09	1021.65	997.77	978.25
98,000	3255.00	2179.96	1406.11	1176.22	1079.10	1032.18	1008.05	988.33
99,000	3288.22	2202.20	1420.46	1188.22	1090.11	1042.71	1018.34	998.42
100,000	3321.43	2224.44	1434.81	1200.22	1101.12	1053.25	1028.62	1008.50

TABLE 13.2 Monthly payments needed to amortize a $1,000 loan at various interest rates.

Term (Years)	RATE OF INTEREST (%)									
	6	7	8	9	10	11	12	14	15	20
3	30.42	30.88	31.34	31.80	32.27	32.74	33.22	34.18	34.67	37.17
5	19.34	19.81	20.28	20.76	21.25	21.75	22.25	22.76	23.79	26.50
6	16.58	17.05	17.54	18.03	18.53	19.04	19.56	20.08	21.15	23.96
7	14.61	15.10	15.59	16.09	16.61	17.13	17.66	18.75	19.30	22.21
8	13.15	13.64	14.14	14.66	15.18	15.71	16.26	17.38	17.95	20.96
9	12.01	12.51	13.02	13.55	14.08	14.63	15.19	16.34	16.93	20.03
10	11.11	11.62	12.14	12.67	13.22	13.78	14.35	15.53	16.14	19.33
15	8.44	8.99	9.56	10.15	10.75	11.37	12.01	13.32	14.00	17.57
20	7.17	7.76	8.37	9.00	9.66	10.33	11.02	12.44	13.17	16.99
25	6.45	7.07	7.72	8.40	9.09	9.81	10.54	12.04	12.81	16.79
30	6.00	6.66	7.34	8.05	8.78	9.53	10.29	11.07	12.65	16.72
35	5.71	6.39	7.11	7.84	8.60	9.37	10.16	11.76	12.57	16.69
40	5.51	6.22	6.96	7.72	8.50	9.29	10.09	11.72	12.54	16.68

interest rates from 6 percent to 20 percent, and repayment terms from 3 to 40 years.

To use Table 13.2, assume a $100,000 loan to be repaid in 30 years, in equal monthly installments, including interest of 8 percent per annum. What is the monthly payment?

First, locate 30 in the number of years column in Table 13.2. Then look across, to the entry under the column headed 8 percent. Here we find the number 7.34. This means that the monthly payment, including principal and interest, is $7.34 for each $1,000 of loan amount. Multi-plying 7.34 by 100, since we are looking for a monthly payment for a $100,000 loan, results in $734 (rounded to the nearest dollar). It should be understood that this table shows the payments based on so much per thousand, though realistically the figures would typically be rounded to the nearest penny only after carrying them out to at least six places. The actual payment, using a financial calculator, is $733.76 per month.

13.2 THE REAL WORLD OF FINANCIAL CALCULATORS AND COMPUTERS

The computation of loan payments, interest rates, principal and interest allocations, discount yields, remaining balances, balloon payments, and many other mathematical real estate problems are no longer solved by using complicated tables. Instead, professionals use **financial calculators** and computers. Although surrounded by a world of computers, a real estate professional in the field frequently still needs the convenience of a financial calculator. The ability to use a financial calculator and quickly compute loan payments, qualifying ratios, and other numbers is essential in today's competitive real estate market. With the growth of technology, many cell phones also have downloadable applications to assist with these calculations.

Financial calculators should not be confused with the simple four-function calculators sold at variety stores. Nor should they be confused with scientific calculators. Financial calculators are pre-programmed to handle the time value of money, and can therefore compute most real estate finance and investment problems without the need for amortization tables. In addition, there is no need to memorize complicated formulas, as financial calculators are programmed to handle all the mathematics internally.

Several calculators have been popular over the years. The Hewlett Packard 12C has been in use for the longest period of time—over 25 years. Texas Instruments BA-II Plus is also a useful tool and a little less costly. A newer addition to the industry, and now being promoted by the California Association of Realtors, is Calculated Industries' Qualifier Plus IIIx. There is no "right" calculator to use. You can buy any of these or others on the market to serve the same purpose.

It would be impractical to discuss and illustrate applications for each of these models, so there is a summary of typical calculations in the last section using the Calculated Industries' Qualifier Plus IIIx. The Case & Point at the end of the chapter illustrates the key strokes using the Hewlett Packard Model 12C.

13.3 ILLUSTRATED USE OF CALCULATED INDUSTRIES QUALIFIER PLUS IIIX REAL ESTATE CALCULATOR

All financial calculators have five special keys that deal with the time value of money (TVM). On the Qualifier Plus IIIx real estate calculator, the five financial keys are as follows:

Term   This refers to the length of time. The period could be years, months or days.

Int   This refers to the interest rate. Here you enter the interest per period, be it annual, monthly, or daily interest.

[Loan Amt]   Here is where you enter the loan amount.

[Pmt]   This is the key you push to solve for payment, be it an annual, monthly, or daily payment.

[Shift]   **[Loan Amt]** (FV)

This stands for future value. This combination of keys is used when you wish to find a financial answer that lies in the future, such as a future balloon payment. For all real estate loan problems you are given three elements to enter into three of these keys, then you push a fourth key to obtain your answer. Usually one key—the fifth—is not needed. Your job is to figure the three elements you know and enter them, then from the two remaining keys, select the one that will calculate the information you seek. For example, a real estate loan payment has four elements: the term (number of payments), interest rate, loan amount, and payment.

If you enter any three elements, the Qualifier Plus IIIx solves for the fourth unknown element. The order in which you enter the known information does not matter.

Loan Payments

The Qualifier Plus IIIx can compute any type of loan payment. It does not matter if the payment is annual, semiannual, quarterly, monthly, biweekly, weekly, or daily. The thing to remember is that all of the financial keys must be in the same time frame!

Example: On a $100,000 loan at 10 percent for 30 years, what is the monthly payment?

Description	Keystrokes	Display
Clear Calculator	**[On/C] [On/C]**	0.00
Enter loan amount	**① ⓪ ⓪ ⓪⓪⓪ [Loan Amt]**	LA 100,000.00
Enter Term	**③ ⓪ [Term]**	ANN TERM 30.00
Enter Interest	**① ⓪ [Int]**	ANN INT 10.00 %
Find monthly P & I payment	**[Pmt]**	P+I 877.57 PMT

You can enter any element in any order. You do not need to enter the loan amount first, then the interest, then the payments. Any order is acceptable to all financial calculators.

Caution: Clear the calculator between each calculation to assure that no leftover numbers remain in the financial keys that could distort the correct answer in your next calculation. Make sure that FV (future value) is always shown as 0.00 (zero) when entering computations.

Making Larger Loan Payments

How fast will a loan be paid off if larger monthly payments are made?

Example: Using the same figures as above:

Description	Keystrokes	Display
Clear Calculator	On/C On/C	0.00
Enter loan amount	1 0 0 0 0 0 [Loan Amt]	LA 100,000.00
Enter Term	3 0 [Term]	ANN TERM 30.00
Enter Interest	1 0 [Int]	ANN INT 10.00 %
Find monthly P & I payment	[Pmt]	P+I 877.57 PMT

If the borrower paid $900 per month, how long would it take to pay off his loan?

Enter new payment amount	9 0 0 [Pmt]	P+I 900.00 PMT
Solve for new Term	[Term]	ANN TERM 26.14

If the borrower paid $1,000 per month, how long would it take to pay off this loan?

Enter new payment amount	1 0 0 0 [Pmt]	P+I 1000.00 PMT
Solve for new Term	[Term]	ANN TERM 17.99

The lesson here is that a borrower can make larger payments and greatly reduce the total amount of interest paid and the length of time it takes to pay off a loan.

Interest and Principal Allocation

People often want to know how much of a payment is interest and how much is principal. Or after borrowers have made a series of payments, they may want to know the breakdown of each payment into interest and principal, and what the remaining balance is.

The Qualifier Plus IIIx easily does this using the **Amort** key (amortization).

Example: Assume a $100,000 loan at 10 percent for 30 years. What is the monthly payment? What is the remaining loan balance? How much of the first payment is principal? Interest?

Description	Keystrokes	Display
Clear Calculator	**On/C** **On/C**	0.00
Enter loan amount	**1** **0** **0** **0** **0** **0** **Loan Amt**	LA 100,000.00
Enter Term	**3** **0** **Term**	ANN TERM 30.00
Enter Interest	**1** **0** **Int**	ANN INT 10.00 %
Find monthly P & I payment	**Pmt**	P+I 877.57 PMT
Enter number of payments	**1** **Shift** **←** **Amort**	AMRT 1 – 1 PER
Find Interest of first payment	**Amort**	AMRT 833.33 TTL INT
Find total principle of first payment	**Amort**	AMRT 44.24 TTL PRIN
Find remaining balance	**Amort** **Amort**	BAL 99,955.76

Principal and Interest Allocation for 12 Months

Example: Using the Qualifier Plus IIIx, assume a $100,000 loan at 10 percent for 30 years. What is the monthly payment? What is the remaining loan balance after 12 payments? What is the principal paid for 12 months? What is the interest paid after making 12 monthly payments?

Description	Keystrokes	Display
Clear Calculator	**On/C** **On/C**	0.00
Enter loan amount	**1** **0** **0** **0** **0** **0** **Loan Amt**	LA 100,000.00
Enter Term	**3** **0** **Term**	ANN TERM 30.00

Description	Keystrokes	Display
Enter Interest	① ⓪ **Int**	ANN INT 10.00 %
Find monthly P & I payment	**Pmt**	P+I 877.57 PMT
Enter Year 1	① **Amort**	AMRT 1 – 12 PER
Find total interest in year 1	**Amort**	AMRT 9,974.98 TTL INT
Find total principle in year 1	**Amort**	AMRT 555.88 TTL PRIN
Find remaining balance	**Amort** **Amort**	BAL 99,444.12

This calculation is handy for estimating interest for annual income tax deductions.

Balloon Payments

Balloon payments are also called remaining loan balance and outstanding loan balance. To solve for the balance on a loan after a series of payments, all four parts of a loan must be in the calculator:

Term, **Int**, **Loan Amt** and the payment in the **Pmt** key

If the payment is missing, you first must solve for payment; then the balloon payment can be found by correctly using the future value function.

Example: Use the Qualifier Plus IIIx for a $100,000 loan at 10 percent amortized for 30 years, but due in five years. What will be the balance after five years?

Description	Keystrokes	Display
Clear Calculator	**On/C** **On/C**	0.00
Enter loan amount	① ⓪ ⓪ ⓪ ⓪ ⓪ **Loan Amt**	LA 100,000.00
Enter Term	③ ⓪ **Term**	ANN TERM 30.00
Enter Interest	① ⓪ **Int**	ANN INT 10.00 %

(continued)

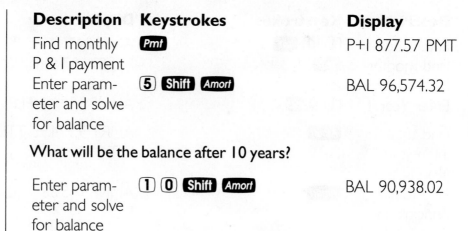

Description	Keystrokes	Display
Find monthly P & I payment	**Pmt**	P+I 877.57 PMT
Enter parameter and solve for balance	**5** **Shift** **Amort**	BAL 96,574.32

What will be the balance after 10 years?

Description	Keystrokes	Display
Enter parameter and solve for balance	**1** **0** **Shift** **Amort**	BAL 90,938.02

More Complicated Calculations

(Note to readers: This section is optional and can be skipped by moving to the biweekly payment section.) The preceding examples are typical real estate calculations that can be done with most financial calculators. In addition, a few financial calculators with special real estate keys can also do the following.

Calculating Loan Payments That Include PITI (Principal, Interest, Taxes, and Insurance)

Example: A buyer is interested in a home that is listed for $500,000. An 80 percent loan of $400,000 at 7.5 percent for 30 years is available to qualified buyers. What would be the monthly PITI required to buy this home?

Solution: First, key in the typical property tax and insurance percentage for the area. Let's say property taxes in a high-cost area run 1.5 percent of the purchase price and high-quality personal liability and homeowner's insurance is .5 percent of the purchase price.

The keystrokes using the Qualifier Plus IIIx real estate model are:

Description	Keystrokes	Display
Clear Calculator	**On/C** **On/C**	0.00
Enter property tax	**1** **.** **5** **Tax**	ANN TAX 1.50 %
Enter property insurance rate	**.** **5** **Ins**	ANN INS 0.50 %
Enter sale price	**5** **0** **0** **0** **0** **0** **Price**	PR 500,000.00

Description	Keystrokes	Display
Enter Term	③ ⓪ **Term**	ANN TERM 30.00
Enter annual interest	⑦ ⊙ ⑤ **Int**	ANN INT 7.50 %
Enter down payment	② ⓪ **Dn Pmt**	DN PMT 20.00 %
Find P & I payment	**Pmt**	P&I 2,796.86 PMT
Find PITI payment	**Pmt**	PITI 3,630.19 PMT

Calculating Monthly Income Needed to Qualify for a Loan

Example: A buyer is interested in a home that is listed for $500,000. An 80 percent loan at 7.5 percent for 30 years is available if the buyers have a 20 percent down payment. The buyers have monthly long-term debts of $500. What would be the monthly income required to buy this home?

Description	Keystrokes	Display
Clear Calculator	**On/C** **On/C**	0.00
Enter annual interest	⑦ ⊙ ⑤ **Int**	ANN INT 7.50 %
Enter term in years	③ ⓪ **Term**	ANN TERM 30.00
Enter tax rate	① ⊙ ② ⑤ **Tax**	ANN TAX 1.25 %
Enter insurance rate	⊙ ③ **Ins**	ANN INS 0.30 %
Enter sale price	⑤ ⓪ ⓪ ⓪ ⓪ ⓪ **Price**	PR 500,000.00
Enter down payment %	② ⓪ **Dn Pmt**	DNPMT 20.00
Enter monthly debt	⑤ ⓪ ⓪ **Debt**	MO DEBT 500.00
Find loan amount	**Loan Amt**	LA 400,000.00
Find P&I payment	**Pmt**	P&I 2,796.86
Find PITI payment	**Pmt**	PITI 3,442.69

(continued)

Then key in typical loan qualifying ratios used by lenders, such as 28 percent for total monthly housing expense and 36 percent for total monthly housing and debt expense. Qualifier Plus IIIx **Qual 1** default stored value is 28%:36% ratio.

Display qualifying ratios	**Qual 1**	ENT 28.00 − 36.00
Find annual income required	**Qual 1**	REQ 147,543.92
Find monthly income required	**÷** **1** **2** **=**	12,295.33

Note: These standards are flexible.

Calculating What a Buyer Can Afford to Borrow and the Price Range of Homes

Rather than looking at a home and then computing what income is needed to qualify as in the previous example, here we know the buyers' income and debts and we are trying to figure out what price range of homes, given current loan terms, the buyers are qualified to purchase.

Example: The buyers have combined monthly income of $8,000 and monthly debts of $400. Assume an 80 percent loan at 7.5 percent for 30 years is available if the buyers have a 20 percent down payment. What loan amount and price range of homes do the buyers appear to qualify for?

Description	Keystrokes	Display
Clear calculator	**On/C** **On/C**	0.00
Enter term in years	**3** **0** **Term**	ANN TERM 30.00
Enter annual interest	**7** **•** **5** **Int**	ANN INT 7.5 %
Enter tax rate	**1** **•** **2** **5** **Tax**	ANN TAX 1.25 %
Enter insurance rate	**•** **3** **Ins**	ANN INS 0.30 %
Enter monthly income	**8** **0** **0** **0** **Shift** **Inc**	INC MO 8,000.00
Enter monthly debt	**4** **0** **0** **Debt**	MO DEBT 400.00
Enter down payment %	**2** **0** **Dn Pmt**	DMPMT 20.00 %

Description	Keystrokes	Display
Display quali-fying ratio	[Qual 1]	ENT 28.00 − 36.00 %
Find qualifying loan amount	[Qual 1]	MAX LA 260,261.49
Find price	[Price]	PR 325,326.87
Find monthly P&I payment	[Pmt]	P&I 1,819.79
Find down payment required	[Dn Pmt] [Dn Pmt]	DNPMT 65,065.37

This is a handy series of keystrokes to estimate what price range of homes to show buyers, and what will be the loan amount, monthly payment, and down payment requirements.

Finding Price or Yields When Buying Existing Notes and Deeds of Trust

Some people prefer to invest in notes and deeds of trust secured by real estate rather than purchase the real estate itself. They are attracted by the rates of return and do not wish to deal with the problems of being a landlord. Financial calculators make it easy to compute price and **yields** when negotiating for the purchase of notes and deeds of trust.

Finding the Price of a Note When You Know the Desired Yield

Example: A $79,000 note at 8.5 percent is amortized for 30 years, but due in 7 years. An investor wishes buy this note at a price that will yield 18 percent. What price should the investor pay?

Description	Keystrokes	Display
Clear calculator	[On/C] [On/C]	0.00
Enter loan amount	[7] [9] [0] [0] [0] [Loan Amt]	LA 79,000.00
Enter term	[3] [0] [Term]	ANN TERM 30.00
Enter annual interest	[8] [•] [5] [Int]	ANN INT 8.50 %
Find P&I payment	[Pmt]	P+I 607.44 PMT

(continued)

Description	Keystrokes	Display
Find balloon payment	(7) **Term** **Shift** **Loan Amt**	73,532.45 FV
Enter desired yield	(1) (8) **Int**	ANN INT 18.00 %
Find purchase price	**Loan Amt**	LA 49,955.09
Enter desired yield	(1) (8) **Int**	ANN INT 18.00 %
Find purchase price	**Loan Amt**	LA 49,955.09

Calculating the Yield When You Know the Discount Price of the Note

Example: A $79,000 note at 8.5 percent is amortized for 30 years, but due in seven 7 years. An investor can buy this note for $49,955.09. What will be the investor's yield?

Description	Keystrokes	Display
Clear calculator	**On/C** **On/C**	0.00
Enter loan amount	(7) (9) (0) (0) (0) **Loan Amt**	LA 79,000.00
Enter term	(3) (0) **Term**	ANN TERM 30.00
Enter annual interest	(8) (•) (5) **Int**	ANN INT 8.50 %
Find P&I payment	**Pmt**	P+I 607.44 PMT
Find balloon payment	(7) **Term** **Shift** **Loan Amt**	73,532.45 FV
Enter purchase price	(4) (9) (9) (5) (5) (•) (0) (9) **Loan Amt**	LA 49,955.09
Find desired yield	**Int**	ANN INT 18.00 %

Biweekly Loan Payments

Occasionally, some real estate borrowers are given the option of making biweekly instead of monthly loan payments. **Biweekly loan payments** are made every two weeks (26 payments per year), instead of once a month (12 payments per year). Many times this better matches the borrower's paycheck (paid on the job every two weeks). In short, a biweekly program takes a monthly payment then divides it in half, and this amount is paid 26 times per year.

A payment every two weeks is equal to approximately 13 monthly payments per year instead of the usual 12 monthly payments. Making biweekly loan payments can save on interest paid and reduce the time it takes to pay off a loan. The Qualifier Plus IIIx and some other financial calculators are pre-set to easily compute biweekly payments.

Example: Using the Qualifier Plus IIIx, for a $100,000 loan at 10 percent for 30 years, what are the biweekly payments?

Description	Keystrokes	Display
Clear calculator	On/C On/C	0.00
Enter loan amount	1 0 0 0 0 0 Loan Amt	LA 100,000.00
Enter Interest	1 0 Int	ANN INT 10.00%
Enter term	3 0 Term	ANN TERM 30.00
Find Bi-Weekly term	Shift Term	BI ANN TERM 20.96
Find Bi-Weekly P & I	Pmt	P&I BI PMT 438.79
Find the interest saved	Term Term	SVG BI TTL INT 76,816.82

This illustrates the savings under a biweekly payment system as compared with the normal monthly payment program.

13.4 ANNUAL PERCENTAGE RATES

Under the federal Truth-in-Lending Law, most commercial lenders must disclose the total cost of real estate financing. The disclosure includes the total interest paid, the estimated costs of acquiring the financing, and the annual percentage rate (APR). The impetus for the mandated Truth-in-Lending (TIL) form is to provide consumer protection by requiring lenders to disclose the "cost" of borrowing with this standardized form. It was intended to make it easy for borrowers to compare lenders, loan options, and the "effective" rate of interest or true cost of borrowing. With this form from multiple lenders, a borrower can compare "apples to apples" to see the best cost. (We discuss the TIL and the APR in detail in Chapter 10.)

Disclosure of Total Interest Paid

Assume a $100,000 loan at 8 percent interest for 30 years with a monthly payment of $733.76. The total interest on the actual loan, excluding any financing fees, can easily be calculated with a financial calculator:

Total scheduled to be paid over 30 years ($733.76 × 360 months)	$264,155.25
Less : Original loan amount	−100,000.00
Total interest paid over scheduled life of the loan	$164,155.25

Disclosure of Annual Percentage Rate

When there are charges other than interest, some of these charges must be considered in determining the annual percentage rate (APR). The additional financial charges on real estate loans, other than interest, include loan fees and certain other miscellaneous finance fees. The APR calculation must take into consideration loan fees and these other miscellaneous finance fees, as well as the note's interest rate. A detailed calculation is shown in the last section.

Example: Assume a $100,000 loan at 8 percent interest for 30 years, and the lender charges 1.5 points, plus $1,000 in other financing fees covered by the Truth-In-Lending Law. What is the APR?

Description	Keystrokes	Display
Clear calculator	On/C On/C	0.00
Enter loan amount	1 0 0 0 0 0 Loan Amt	LA 100,000.00
Enter term	3 0 Term	ANN TERM 30.00
Enter interest	8 Int	ANN INT 8.00 %
Find monthly P & I payment	Pmt	P+I Pmt 733.76
Recall loan amount	Rcl Loan Amt	LA 100,000.00
Find point cost	✕ 1 • 5 % =	1,500.00
Add fees and find total	+ 1 0 0 0 =	2,500.00
Find APR	Shift Int	"run" APR 8.27 %

SUMMARY

Real estate mathematics is used to clearly communicate the cost of a loan. Real estate promissory notes come in a variety of forms, and the interest and principal calculations depend on the specific type of note used. The two basic types are: (1) the straight note, which is payable interest-only with the principle entirely due on the due date, and (2) the amortized loan, which contains payments of both principal and interest. The amortized loan can be either fully or partially amortized. If partially amortized, a balloon payment will be owed on the due date. Financial calculators and computers have simplified all real estate lending arithmetic. In addition to calculating loan payments, principal and interest allocation and balloon payments, financial calculators and computers can calculate price and yields on notes, biweekly payments, annual percentage rates (APR), and much more.

Finally, most financial calculations in a real estate transaction are for the buyer. A lender will be doing most of these for the loan, but it is always helpful for an agent to know the basics as well. Monthly payment calculations, balloon payment balances, and loan qualifying calculations are a few of the examples demonstrated. When a buyer asks what his payment will be, an agent will appear more professional if he or she can say, "It will be approximately $1,800" rather than, "I don't know." For the most part, a seller is concerned with how much he or she will have after the sale closes. This calculation doesn't necessarily require a financial calculator, as an agent will typically provide an Estimated Net Sheet.

IMPORTANT TERMS AND CONCEPTS

Amortization table

Amortized loan

Balloon payment

Biweekly loan payment

Financial calculator

Straight (or interest-only) note

Yield

REVIEWING YOUR UNDERSTANDING

Questions for Discussion

1. If a borrower consistently makes larger payments than required, what impact will this have on a real estate loan?

2. Explain how a biweekly loan payment differs from a traditional monthly payment. What impact will a biweekly payment have on the length of the loan?

Multiple-Choice Questions

1. A partially amortized note will always contain
   a. an adjustable interest rate.
   b. a balloon payment.
   c. a level payment for the entire life of the loan.
   d. an alienation clause.

2. A $200,000 straight note at 8 percent interest, payable monthly, will have what size payment?
   a. $1,333.33.
   b. $1,467.53.
   c. $1,274.17.
   d. $1,194.86.

3. You borrow $40,000 secured by a second loan against your home and pay $322 per month. If the interest is 9 percent per annum, the first month's interest will be
   a. $322.00.
   b. $300.00.
   c. $36.00.
   d. $289.80.

4. Using the data from Question 3, the unpaid balance remaining at the end of the first month's payment is (in round numbers)
   a. $39,678.
   b. $39,710.
   c. $39,964.
   d. $39,978.

5. What is another word used for the duration of time of a loan?
   a. Total interest paid
   b. Term
   c. Loan length
   d. Future Value

6. What allows the lender to compare costs "apples to apples"?
   a. Total interest paid
   b. Interest rate
   c. APR
   d. Origination fee

7. The FV key on a financial calculator stands for
   a. forbearance value.
   b. future value.
   c. financial value.
   d. frequence variable.

8. In financial terms, TVM stands for
   a. time variable math.
   b. twice valued multiple.
   c. time value of money.
   d. tomorrow's value of money.

9. On a fixed-rate amortized loan, if a borrower makes larger than required payments,
   a. the total interest paid will increase.
   b. the nominal interest rate will decline.
   c. the balloon payment will increase.
   d. the term of the loan will be reduced.

10. On a fixed-rate amortized loan, if a borrower makes larger than required payments,
    a. the total interest paid will decline.
    b. the income tax deductions for interest will increase.
    c. the owner's equity will decrease.
    d. the lender will foreclose.

11. Under an amortized loan, a balloon payment is defined as any payment
    a. more than twice the size of a regular payment.
    b. under a fully amortized loan.
    c. paid in advance of the due date.
    d. past due.

12. A PITI loan payment includes
    a. prepayment, interest, taxes, and insurance.
    b. principal, interest, taxes, and insurance.
    c. partial amortization, interest, taxes, and insurance.
    d. principal, interest, and taxable income.

13. When a fixed-rate loan is fully amortized, the amount allocated each month to principal
    a. slowly decreases.
    b. slowly increases.
    c. stays constant.
    d. decreases in the early years and increases in the later years.

14. In many ways, interest is to principal as
    a. rent is to property.
    b. capital is to money.
    c. profit is to risk.
    d. yield is to rate of return.

15. When notes and deeds of trust are sold, they are most often purchased at a
    a. discount.
    b. face amount.
    c. par amount.
    d. usury value.

16. The number of biweekly payments in one year is
    a. 26.
    b. 52.
    c. 24.
    d. 13.

17. Biweekly loan payments
    a. increase the amount of interest paid.
    b. are monthly payments divided in half and paid every two weeks.
    c. are illegal in California.
    d. are commonly used on FHA-backed loans.

18. APR stands for
    a. annual percentage rate.
    b. annual prime rate.
    c. amortized packaged rate.
    d. amortized percentage rate.

19. The purpose for requiring lenders to quote their financing terms using APR is to
    a. confuse the general public.
    b. allow borrowers to compare the true cost of money.
    c. increase the lender's yield.
    d. generate fees to support government housing programs.

20. Which of the following is true?
    a. APR and the interest rate on the note are always the same.
    b. The higher the loan fee, the lower the APR.
    c. APR is designed to discover the financial impact of certain specific fees.
    d. APR must be quoted as a dollar amount instead of as a percentage.

CASE & POINT

Using the HP-12C to Simplify Real Estate Math

Functions of the Keys

Notice that the plural is used: since most of the 39 keys in the HP-12C have more than one use, let's briefly acquaint ourselves with the functions most often encountered in real estate problems. We'll expand on their meanings through a series of notes located throughout the manual.

|ON| This is both the on and off key. The calculator has built-in memory, so it will retain information for as long as you wish. If you enter the number 12, that number reappears on your screen even if you don't turn it back to ON until next year (or next century, if your battery doesn't sour).

|ENTER| Enters numbers into the calculator, which automatically appear on the display screen, for doing calculations.

The Financial Keys

In the top row of your HP-12C, there are five financial keys that we will be using most of the time: |n| |i| |PV| |PMT| |FV|. A brief description of what the letters generally mean is as follows:

|n|	|i|	|PV|	|PMT|	|FV|
(number of payments)	(rate per period)	(amount of loan)	(amount of payments)	(remaining balance)

$\longleftarrow$ DATA keys and QUESTION keys $\longrightarrow$

The arrows indicate that these five keys in essence are data and questions keys. Why? Because we enter given data (the known) into four of the keys and compute for the fifth key (or cell), the unknown. So if you know how long a loan is to run (n), its interest rate (i), the amount of loan (PV), and the amortization provision (FV)—balloon vs. no balloon—you push the |PMT| button to determine the amount of payments. The |n| may represent the number of monthly payments, quarterly payments, semiannual payments, annual payments, or any other periods. The |i| is always the rate of interest or yield per period. The

Adapted with permission from "The HP=12C in Action!" by Robert J. Bond, Financial Publishing House, Williamsburg, VA, 1997.

three remaining keys, |PV|, |PMT|, and |FV| are always expressed in monetary terms, although the monetary symbols, such as the $ or pound sign, never show up on the screen.

To summarize the financial keys:

|n|	Registers the number of periods, or term.
|i|	Registers the interest rate per period.
|V|	Registers the Present Value, or initial cash flow, of a loan or amount of investment.
|PMT|	Registers payments for money paid out or received.
|FV|	Registers the Future Value, or final cash flow, of a loan or investment.

Let's now examine some less frequently used but equally important keys to help round out our knowledge of the keyboard:

|f|	Gold-colored key to the right of |ON|, used to answer questions for the 16 keys where the gold appears at the top.
|g|	Blue-colored key to the right of |f|, used to answer questions for the 30 keys where the blue appears at the bottom.
|CHS|	Changes a number from positive to negative (Change Sign) or from negative to positive.
|%|	Computes the ratio, or percentage (%).
|R/S|	Runs and Stops programs, similar to a full-fledged computer.
|SST|	Single step in a series of steps used when the calculator is in the program mode.
|R↓|	Rolls down data stored within the calculator.
|X≷Y|	Exchanges stored data, in its so-called X and Y registers.
|CLX|	Clears the data displayed in the X register.
|1/x|	Reciprocal key, used to change whole or mixed numbers to fractions, or fractions to whole numbers.
|Δ%|	Calculates % of difference between two numbers (stored in the calculator's X and Y registers).
|%T|	Calculates % that one number represents of the total.
|STO|	Stores numbers in each of the cells labeled 1 through 9 for later use through recall (RCL).

|RCL| Recalls stored numbers by pressing RCL and the numerical cell (0 through 9) into which the data was stored.

0, 1, 2, 3, 4, 5, 6, 7, 8, 9

+ − × ÷   Keys on right side of calculator. Used for calculating the numerical or arithmetic functions: addition, subtraction, multiplication, division. When |STO| key is pressed at the same time as one of the cells, data can be stored in that cell.

Lesson I: How Do I Calculate Trust Deed or Mortgage Payments?

Data

1st Trust Deed	$100,000
Interest Rate	10%
Term	30 years
Balloon Payments	none

Question

How much are the monthly payments?

Solution

Key	Screen
1. 30 |g| |12		360
2. 10 |g| |12÷|	0.83
3. 100000 |PV|	100,000
4. 0 |FV|	0.00
5. |PMT|	?

Notes

In step 1, we enter the number of years, 30, followed by the blue-colored |g| key that converts 30 years into months. (The blue key is described in the footnote at the end of this exercise on the next page.) In step 2, the annual interest rate of 10 percent is automatically converted into the monthly rate by using the blue key. Enter the loan amount into the PV cell for step 3. The number 0 is entered for step 4 to reflect that there is no balloon payment, which means that the loan is fully amortized with equal monthly installments for the full term. In step 5, the negative figure showing on your screen reflects money paid out. You would read the monthly payments as shown in the answer below.

Answer
$877.57

Self-Help
To help you master certain financial calculations, we offer a series of test questions throughout this Case & Point. See how well you understand the calculation of mortgage payments by doing the self-test questions that follow. After you finish, compare your answers with the correct ones given at the end of the test.

TEST YOURSELF
Self-Test 1

    Trust deed: $200,000

    Interest rate: 10 percent

    Term: 30 years

    Question: How much are the yearly payments?

Self-Test 2

    Trust deed: $200,000

    Interest rate: 10 percent

    Term: 15 years

    Question: How much are the monthly payments?

Note: Concerning the gold and blue keys:

To the right of the |ON| button at the lowest rung of keys are the prefix keys, which are secondary to the primary keys that you have been dealing with up to this point.

The |f| key is colored gold and the |g| key is colored blue. These have no meanings per se, but they offer a second and third level of calculations, so that each of the keys in the top three rows to the left of the |ENTER| key, including the enter key itself, can perform three separate functions. Thus if you wanted to calculate the amortization of a mortgage loan, you would press the gold |f| key before pressing the |AMORT| that shows up above the |n| key. This will be demonstrated in a later lesson, so don't be concerned at this stage. All you need to know now is that the HP-12C is a very versatile instrument, allowing you to perform zillions of calculations, combinations, and permutations, offering added meanings when the two specially colored keys are used in conjunction with most of the other keys.

|f|, the gold key, is used for solving problems above the key.

Example. The |AMORT| above the |n| key computes loan payments attributable to principal reduction, called amortization, as well as remaining balances.

|g|, the blue key, is used for solving problems below the key.

Example. The |12 ×| below the |n| key is used to convert the number of years into months.

Self-Test 3

Trust deed: $100,000

Interest rate: 5 percent

Term: 30 years

Question: How much are the monthly payments?

Self-Test 4

Trust deed: $100,000

Interest rate: 10 percent

Term: 30 years

Question: How much are the yearly payments?

Note: When calculating annually, do not convert years into months, and do not convert annual interest into monthly interest.

Answers

Self-Test 1: $1,755.14

Self-Test 2: $2,149.21

Self-Test 3: $536.82

Self-Test 4: $10,607.93

Lesson 2: How Do I Calculate Mortgage Interest Rates?

Data

1st Trust Deed	$100,000
Monthly Payments	$877.57
Term	30 years

Question

What is the interest rate?

Solution

Key	Screen
1. 30 |g| |12×|	360
2. 100000 |PV|	100,000
3. 0 |FV|	0.00
4. 877.57 |CHS| |PMT|	−877.57
5. |i|	?
6. 12 |×|	?

Notes

In step 6, we are converting the monthly interest rate to an annual rate by simply multiplying the step 5 result by 12, the number of months in a year. There is another way to calculate step 6. In our model we entered the digits 12 followed by the multiplier sign, ×. You could instead simply take the answer to step 5 and enter the blue key |g|, then press the |12 ×| key.

Answer

0.83% monthly interest rate (step 5), or annual rate of 10.00% (step 6)

TEST YOURSELF

Self-Test 1

    Trust deed: $200,000

    Term: 30 years

    Monthly payments: $1,755.14

    Questions: Monthly interest rate? Annual rate?

Self-Test 2

    Trust deed: $200,000

    Term: 15 years

    Monthly payments: $2,149.21

    Questions: Monthly interest rate? Annual rate?

Self-Test 3

    Trust deed: $100,000

    Term: 30 years

    Monthly payments: $536.82

    Questions: Monthly interest rate? Annual rate?

Self-Test 4

    Trust deed: $100,000

    Term: 30 years

    Annual payments: $10,607.93 Question: Interest rate?

    Careful: This asks you for *annual* interest rate, so do not convert annual payments to monthly payments. Thus you'll have the annual rate instantly calculated when you hit the |I| button.

Answers

    Self-Test 1: 0.83 percent monthly interest rate, or 10 percent annual rate

Self-Test 2: 0.83 percent monthly interest rate, or 10 percent annual rate

Self-Test 3: 0.42 percent monthly interest rate, or 5 percent annual rate

Self-Test 4: 10 percent annual rate. (The loan is paid once annually, so no need to convert to monthly.)

Lesson 3: How Do I Calculate Annual Percentage Rates (APR), Adjusted for a One-Time Loan Fee?

The calculation for APR is very similar to deriving the nominal, or stated, rate that was performed in the previous lesson. What is the difference? In computing an APR, loan costs, including "prepaid interest," must be deducted from the face amount of the loan.

What constitutes prepaid interest? It includes the familiar "points" paid by the borrower; origination fee; pro rata interest, since there usually are interest charges accumulated from COE to date of the initial mortgage payment; first year's mortgage insurance premium (MIP); and a few smaller items. Prepaid interest does not include one-time fees paid for an appraisal, credit report, title insurance, and other forms of insurance and costs that are independent of the loan, such as a homeowner's policy or homeowner's association (HOA) fees. In the comprehensive example, we'll assume the same facts as before, except that the borrowers are charged $5,000 loan costs.

Data

1st Trust Deed	$100,000
Prepaid Interest/Loan Costs	$5,000
Nominal Interest Rate	10%
Term	30 years

Question

What is the annual percentage rate (APR)?

Solution

Key	Screen
1. 30 |g| |12×|	360
2. 10 |g| |12÷|	0.83
3. 100000 |PV|	100,000
4. 0 |FV|	0.00

5.	PMT		−877.57
6. |RCL| |PV| 5000 |−| |PV|	95,000
7.	i		?
8. 12 |×| {or |g| |12×|}	?

Note

In step 8, we convert the monthly rate to an annual rate by multiplying step 7 result by 12, the number of months in a year. Step 8 could also be computed by pressing the blue |g| button followed by |12×|.

Answer

0.89 percent monthly rate (step 7), or 10.62 percent annual (step 8)

Bottom Line: With interest prepayments the effective rate, or APR, increased by .62 percent when compared to the nominal rate. This is equivalent to an increase of 62 "basis points," with each basis point the same as $\frac{1}{100}$th of a percent.

TEST YOURSELF
Data

1st Trust Deed	$150,000
Prepaid Interest/Loan Costs	$7,000
Nominal Interest Rate	10%
Term	30 years

Question

What is the annual percentage rate (APR)?

Answer

0.88 percent monthly, or 10.58 percent APR

Lesson 4: How Do I Calculate Annual Percentage Rates (APR), Adjusted for Points, Fees, and Balloon Payment?

The calculation for APR after adjusting for points and fees is very similar to that of the APR adjusted for a flat charge, with one variation. In the problem that follows we add in a balloon payment.

In the comprehensive example, we'll assume the same facts as before, except that the borrowers are charged two points plus $500 to obtain the loan, and assume a five-year due date with a balloon payment for the remaining balance at the end of five years.

Data

1st Trust Deed	$100,000
Prepaid Interest/Loan Costs	2 points + $500
Nominal Interest Rate	10%
Amortization Term, Due in Five Years	30 years
Monthly Payment	$877.57

Question

What is the annual percentage rate (APR)?

Solution

Key	Screen
1. 10 |g| |12÷|	0.83
2. 100000 |PV|	100,000
3. 877.57 |CHS| |PMT|	−877.57
4. 5 |g| |n|	60
5. |FV|	−96,574.44
6. |RCL| |PV| 2 |%| |−| 500 |−|	97,500
7. |PV|	97,500
8. |i|	0.89
9. 12 |×|	10.66

Notes

Step 5 represents the balloon payment. Step 6 represents the net amount that the borrower actually received after deducting the points (2) plus dollar amount ($500). In step 9, we are converting the monthly rate to an annual rate by multiplying step 8 result by 12.

Answer

0.89 percent monthly (step 8), or 10.656 annually (step 9), rounded to 10.66 percent

Bottom Line: With interest prepayments of two points plus $500, the effective rate, or APR, increased by .66 percent when compared to the nominal rate. This is equivalent to an increase of 66 "basis points," with each basis point the same as $\frac{1}{100}$th of a percent.

TEST YOURSELF
Data

1st Trust Deed	$120,000
Prepaid Interest/Loan Costs	1 point + $750
Nominal Interest Rate	10%
Amortization Term, Due in 5 years	30 years
Monthly Payment	$1,053.09

Question
What is the APR?

Answer
0.87 percent monthly interest rate, or 10.42 percent annual rate, is the APR

Lesson 5: How Do I Calculate Which Loan Is Better Based upon Costs and Holding Period?

Data

	Option A	Option B
Original 1st Trust Deed	$100,000	$100,000
Interest Rate	11%	10%
Term	360 months	360 months
Loan Fees	None	3 points + $300
Expected Holding Period	30 years	3 years

Question
Which is better, Option A, the "no-cost loan," or Option B, which costs three points plus $300 in loan fees, based upon the holding period or occupancy?

Solution for Option A

Key	Screen
1. 30 |g| |12×|	360
2. 11 |g| |12÷|	0.92
3. 100000 |PV|	100,000
4. 0 |FV|	0.00
5. |PMT|	−952.32
6. |i|	0.92
7. 12 |×|	11.00

Answer

0.92 percent per month (step 6), or 11 percent per annum (step 7)

Note

The 11 percent APR is the same as the nominal rate given in the data. This is because there are no loan costs. Let's see how this compares to Option B.

Solution for Option B

Key	Screen
1. 30 |g| |12×|	360
2. 10 |g| |12÷|	0.83
3. 100000 |PV|	100,000
4. 0 |FV|	0.00
5. |PMT|	−877.57
6. |RCL| |PV|	100,000
7. 3 |%| |−| 300 |−|	96,700
8. |PV|	96,700
9. |i|	0.87
10. 12 |×|	10.40

Answer

0.87 percent per month (step 9), or 10.40 percent APR annually (step 10)

Notes

The 10.40 percent APR is higher than the nominal rate of 10 percent because there is $3,300 in loan costs, calculated in step 7, and this results in only $96,700 in net loan proceeds to the borrower. Step 8 is necessary in order to lock the $96,700 into the calculator's memory.

On the surface, it appears as if Option B is the better choice because its APR is 10.40 percent, in contrast to the 11 percent APR in Option A. But remember, we need to deal with the holding period, which will have an impact on the real cost of the loan to us, beyond the required APR disclosure. So let's continue with additional steps needed to compute the APR adjusted for the holding period, when the loan is to be paid off.

Key	Screen
11. 100000 |PV|	100,000
12. 10 |g| |12÷|	0.83
13. 36 |n|	36

14. |FV|	−98,151.65
15. |RCL| |PV| 3 |%| |−| 300 |−|	96,700
16. |PV|	96,700
17. |i|	0.94
18. 12 |×|	11.31

Note

It is necessary to reenter the original loan amount, $100,000, in step 11 because that's the amount the borrowers will repay to the lender, and not the $96,700 that they actually received after discounting by the loan fees of $3,300. For the same reason we restore the nominal interest rate, 10 percent, in step 12. In step 13, we enter the period that the borrowers expect to stay with the loan, three years or 36 months. Step 14 displays the loan balance at the end of the three-year period. Step 15 calculates the net proceeds, while step 16 locks the figure into the memory. Step 17 recomputes the true rate based upon the three-year holding period, and not the original 30 years.

Bottom Line

Though the APR in Option B, the 10 percent loan, was still lower (10.4 percent) than the 11 percent loan in Option A, it is higher when adjusted for the holding period. The APR for Option B rises to 11.31 percent in three years because of the much shorter period for recovery of the one-time upfront fees. (Recall the time value of money concept.)

Lesson 6: How Do I Calculate Blended Interest Rates?

Data

1st Trust Deed	$100,000
Interest Rate on 1st TD	10%
Second Trust Deed	$25,000
Interest Rate on 2nd TD	12%
Term of Each Loan, Payable Monthly	30 years

Question

What is the blended or composite interest rate?

Solution

Key	Screen
1. 100000 |STO| |0|	100,000
2. 10 |%|	10,000
3. 25000 |STO| |+| |0| 12 |%|	3,000
4. |x≷y| |R↓| |+|	13,000
5. |RCL| |0|	125,000
6. |÷|	?

Answer

0.10, or 10 percent (If you want to expand the rate to three decimal places, enter \|f\| 3, and your screen will show 0.104, or 10.4 percent.)

Notes

Step 1 stores the existing first loan balance for later recall. Step 2 shows the first year's interest on that loan, and step 3 stores the $25,000 second loan, then adds this amount to the stored first loan and computes the first year's interest on the second loan. Step 4 combines total interest, adding up steps 2 and 3. Step 5 recalls the total amount of loans ($125,000) and divides this into the total interest of $13,000 (step 4) to answer the question asked in step 6 (10%).

TEST YOURSELF
Self-Test 1
Data

1st Trust Deed	$100,000
Interest Rate on 1st TD	8%
Second Trust Deed	$20,000
Interest Rate on 2nd TD	10%
Term of Each Loan	30 years

Question

What is the blended or composite interest rate?

Answer

0.0833, or 8⅓ percent

Self-Test 2
Data

1st Trust Deed	$150,000
Interest Rate on 1st TD	9%
Second Trust Deed	$50,000
Interest Rate on 2nd TD	10%
Term of Each Loan	30 years

Question
What is the blended or composite interest rate?

Answer
0.0925, or 9.25 percent

Lesson 7: How Do I Calculate the Remaining Term of a Loan?

Data

Original 1st Trust Deed	$100,000
Current Balance	$90,000
Interest Rate	10%
Monthly Payments	$877.57

Question
How many monthly payments are required to pay off the loan if it is fully amortized, that is, if there is no balloon payment?

Solution

Key	Screen
1. 10 |g| |12÷|	0.83
2. 90000 |PV|	90,000
3. 877.57 |CHS| |PMT|	−877.57
4. 0 |FV|	0.00
5. |n|	?
6. |12| |÷|	?

Answer
233 months, computed in step 5 (step 6 converts this to number of years, 19.42, to pay off the loan)

Notes
The calculator will round up to the next whole number. For example, if the exact number of monthly payments was 232.8, the

HP-12C will show 233. Thus the final payment will be slightly lower. To compute the exact amount of the last installment, press the following keys:

|RCL| |PMT| |+|

This displays $858.15 as the final payment.

TEST YOURSELF
Self-Test 1
    Trust deed: $200,000
    Interest rate: 10 percent
    Monthly payments: $1,755.14
    Question: What is the term of the loan?

Self-Test 2
    Trust deed: $200,000
    Interest rate: 10 percent
    Monthly payments: $2,149.21
    Question: What is the term of the loan?

Self-Test 3
    Trust deed: $100,000
    Interest rate: 5 percent
    Monthly payments: $536.82
    Question: What is the term of the loan?

Self-Test 4
    Trust deed: $100,000
    Interest rate: 10 percent
    Annual payments: $10,607.92
    Question: What is the term of the loan?

Answers
    Self-Test 1: 360 months, or 30 years
    Self-Test 2: 180 months, or 15 years
    Self-Test 3: 360 months, or 30 years
    Self-Test 4: 30 years

(Note: Since payments are made only once a year, and not monthly, Self-Test 4 asks us to compute number of years only.)

Lesson 8: How Do I Calculate the Original Amount of a Trust Deed Loan?

Data

Interest Rate	10%
Term	30 years
Monthly Payment	$877.57
Age of Loan	10 years

Questions
1. What was the original loan amount?
2. What will be its value 10 years from now?

Solution

Key	Screen
1. 30 |g| |12×|	360
2. 10 |g| |12÷|	0.83
3. 877.57 |CHS| |PMT|	−877.57
4. 0 |FV|	0
5. |PV|	?
6. 240 |n|	?
7. |PV|	?

Answer for Step 5
$100,000.00

Answer for Step 7
$90,938.00

Notes

Step 5 calculated the original loan amount. In step 6, simply change the number entered in step 1 (360 months) to reflect that the loan has been in existence for 10 years, or 120 months, so there are 240 months remaining. Enter 240 into |n|, then press |PV|. The identical answer can be derived by taking the 120 months for which the loan has been paid, and entering that number into |n|, then pressing |FV|.

Deleting Pennies: To delete the pennies column, just press the gold key |f|, then enter |0| to the right of the ENTER button. Your answers then would be rounded to 100,000 without the decimal point and two zeros that follow the decimal symbol in step 5, and 90,938 without the 2 cents that follow in step 6. Incidentally, the $877.57 monthly payment from the DATA is already rounded to the nearest penny, so we do not need to press |g| |RND|.

TEST YOURSELF

Self-Test 1

> Interest rate: 10 percent
>
> Term: 30 years
>
> Monthly payments: $1,755.14
>
> Question: What was the original loan amount?

Self-Test 2

> Interest rate: 10 percent
>
> Term: 15 years
>
> Monthly payments: $2,149.21
>
> Question: What was the original loan amount?

Self-Test 3

> Interest rate: 5 percent
>
> Term: 30 years
>
> Monthly payments: $536.82
>
> Question: What was the original loan amount?

Self-Test 4

> Interest rate: 10 percent
>
> Term: 30 years
>
> Annual payments: $10,607.92
>
> Question: What was the original loan amount?

Answers

(Note: Enter |f| |0| to delete the pennies.)

> Self-Test 1: 200,000
>
> Self-Test 2: 200,000
>
> Self-Test 3: 100,000
>
> Self-Test 4: 100,000

(Note: For Self-Test 4, you don't need to convert to monthly payments as required in the first three tests, since the loan is being repaid on an annual, not monthly, basis.)

Lesson 9: How Do I Determine the Unpaid Balance on a Loan?

Data

1st Trust Deed	$100,000
Interest Rate	10%
Term	30 years

Question

What is the unpaid balance after five years?

Solution

Key	Screen
1. 30 |g| |12×|	360
2. 10 |g| |12÷|	0.83
3. 100000 |PV|	100,000
4. 0 |FV|	0.00
5. |PMT|	−877.57
6. |F| |RND| |PMT|	−877.57
7. 5 |g| |12×|	60.00
8. |FV|	?

Answer

$96,574.44

Notes

Step 6 is not absolutely necessary. It simply rounds off the monthly payments to the nearest penny. Remember, the calculator has a continuous memory, hence it carries the theoretical payment to fractions of a cent. But since the lowest currency in the U.S. dollar is a penny, it is impossible to pay in smaller denominations (i.e., $877.5715701 if carried to the seventh decimal place). All the digits following $877.57 are adjusted up or down (depending on the precise language in the promissory note) in the final monthly installment. Since there are digits that follow the .57, you'd have a larger final installment 360 months from now. If, on the other hand, the note called for monthly payments of $877.58, your final payment would be less than $877.58.

For those of you who appreciate precision, without step 6 the unpaid balance at the end of five years would amount to $96,574.32, or a decrease of 12 cents.

TEST YOURSELF
Self-Test 1
Data

1st Trust Deed	$120,000
Interest Rate	10%
Term, Payable Monthly	30 years

Questions
1. What is the unpaid balance after three years?
2. What is the unpaid balance after five years?

Answers
1. $117,781.98 after three years ($117,781.80 if payments of $1053.09 are rounded via |f| |RND|)
2. $115,888.18 after five years ($115,888.87 if payments are rounded)

Self-Test 2
Data

1st Trust Deed	$150,000
Interest Rate	10%
Term, Payable Monthly	30 years

Questions
1. What is the unpaid balance after three years?
2. What is the unpaid balance after five years?

Answers
1. $147,227.47 after three years ($147,227.36 if payments of $1316.36 are rounded via |f| |RND|)
2. $144,861.48 after five years ($144,861.28 if payments are rounded)

Lesson 10: How Do I Calculate the Number of Payments under a Balloon Loan?

Data

Original 1st Trust Deed	$100,000
Current Balance	$90,000
Interest Rate	10%
Monthly Payments	$877.57
Term	360 months
Balloon, End of Term	$10,000

Question

How many payments are required to pay off the loan if, in addition to periodic monthly payments, there is a balloon payment of $10,000 at the end of the term, payable with the final installment?

Solution

Key	Screen
1. 10 |g| |12÷|	0.83
2. 90000 |PV|	90,000
3. 877.75 |CHS| |PMT|	−877.57
4. 10000 |CHS| |FV|	−10,000
5. |n|	?
6. |12| |÷|	?

Answer

221 months (step 5), or 18.42 years (step 6)

Note

The calculator will round off to the next whole number. For example, if the exact number of monthly payments was 220.8, the HP-12C will show 221. Thus the final payment will be slightly lower. To compute the exact last installment, press the following three keys: \|RCL\| \|PMT\| \|+\|

This will display $859.15 as the final payment.

TEST YOURSELF
Self-Test 1
   Trust deed: $200,000
   Interest rate: 10 percent
   Monthly payments: $1,755.14
   Balloon: $50,000
   Question: What is the term of the loan?

Self-Test 2
   Trust deed: $200,000
   Interest rate: 10 percent
   Monthly payments: $2,149.21
   Balloon: $25,000
   Question: What is the term of the loan?

Self-Test 3
   Trust deed: $100,000
   Interest rate: 5 percent

Monthly payments: $536.82

Balloon: $10,000

Question: What is the term of the loan?

Self-Test 4

Trust deed: $100,000

Interest rate: 10 percent

Annual payments: $10,607.92

Balloon, end of term: $20,000

Question: What is the term of the loan?

Answers

Self-Test 1: 328 months, or 27⅓ years

Self-Test 2: 168 months, or 14 years

Self-Test 3: 341 months, or 28.42 years

Self-Test 4: 28 years

(Note: Self-Test 4 asks us to compute number of years, since payments are made only once a year, not monthly.)

Lesson 11: How Do I Calculate Interest and Principal Components of a Loan?

Data

Trust Deed Loan	$100,000
Interest Rate	10%
Term, Payable Monthly, Fully Amortized	30 years

Questions

1. How much are the monthly payments at 10 percent?
2. Of the monthly payments, how much represents interest and how much represents principal during each of the first five years?

Solution

Key		Screen
1a.	30 |g| |12×|	360
1b.	10 |g| |12÷|	0.83
1c.	100000 |PV|	100,000
1d.	0 |FV|	0.00
1e.	|PMT|	−877.57

2a.	12 |f| |AMORT|	−9,974.98
2b.	|x≷y|	−555.86
3a.	12 |f| |AMORT|	−9,916.77
3b.	|x≷y|	−614.07
4a.	12 |f| |AMORT|	−9,852.46
4b.	|x≷y|	−678.38
5a.	12 |f| |AMORT|	−9,781.44
5b.	|x≷y|	−749.40
6a.	12 |f| |AMORT|	−9,702.96
6b.	|x≷y|	−827.88

Answer 1

$877.57 monthly payments (from step 1e)

Notes

Steps 1a through 1e calculate the monthly payments for the 30-year loan. Steps 2a and 2b compute the (decreasing) interest and (increasing) principal portions of the first year's payments. Steps 3a and 3b compute the interest and principal portions of the second year's payments. Steps 4a and 4b compute the interest and principal portions of the third year's payments. Steps 5a and 5b compute the interest and principal portions of the fourth year's payments. Steps 6a and 6b compute the interest and principal portions of the fifth year's payments. We can summarize these in simpler tabular form as follows:

Answer 2

Year	Interest	Principal
1	$9,974.98	$555.86
2	9,916.77	614.07
3	9,852.46	678.38
4	9,781.44	749.40
5	9,702.96	827.88

TEST YOURSELF
Data

Trust Deed Loan	$100,000
Interest Rate	12%
Term, Payable Monthly, Fully Amortized	30 years

Questions
1. How much are the monthly payments at 12 percent?
2. Of the monthly payments, how much represents interest and how much represents principal during each of the first two years?

Answer
1. $1,028.61

2.

Year	Interest	Principal
1	$11,980.47	$362.85
2	11,934.45	408.87

Lesson 12: How Do I Calculate Negative Amortization?

Data

1st Trust Deed	$100,000
Interest Rate	9% the first year, 10% thereafter
Term, Payable Monthly	30 years

Question
What will the loan balance be at the end of the first year?

Solution

Key	Screen
1. 30 |g| |12×|	360
2. 9 |g| |12÷|	0.75
3. 100000 |PV|	100,000
4. 0 |FV|	0.00
5. |PMT|	−804.62
6. 10 |g| |12÷|	0.83
7. 12 |n|	12.00
8. |FV|	?

Answer
$100,360.77

Notes
Step 6 shows the new interest rate, 10 percent, converted into a monthly rate. Observe also that the $100,361 (enter \|f\| \|0\| to get rid of the pennies) balance is larger than the loan originally secured, $100,000. That's because you paid less than the 10 percent

contract interest rate during the first year, resulting in negative amortization.

TEST YOURSELF
Self-Test 1
Data

1st Trust Deed	$120,000
Interest Rate:	9%, but at only 8% the first year
Term, Payable Monthly	30 years

Question
What will be the loan balance at the end of the first year?

Answer
$120,243.68

Self-Test 2
Data

1st Trust Deed	$150,000
Interest Rate	5% the first year, 10% thereafter
Term, Payable Monthly	30 years

Question
What will be the remaining balance at the end of the first year?

Answer
$155,588.76

Lesson 13: How Do I Calculate How Much Price and Loan Buyers Can Afford?

Data

Interest Rate	10%
Term, Payable Monthly	30 years
Down Payment	$25,000
Monthly Payments, including PITI (Principal, Interest, Taxes, Insurance)	$1,000
Percentage Attributable to Taxes & Insurance	4%

Questions
1. How much loan can buyer-borrower afford?
2. How much property can buyer-borrower afford?

Solution

Key	Screen
1. 30 |g| |12×|	360
2. 10 |g| |12÷|	0.83
3. 1000 |CHS| |ENTER|	−1,000
4. 4 |%| |−| |PMT|	−960
5. |PV|	?
6. 25000 |+|	?

Answer to Question 1
Buyer can afford a loan of $109,392.79 (step 5), rounded to $109,400

Answer to Question 2
Buyer can afford a property for $134,392.79 (step 6), rounded to $134,400

Notes
Step 3 shows the monthly PITI of $1,000, but in step 4 we deduct the 4 percent attributable to property taxes and insurance, which shows the net amount going for debt service (principal and interest) of $960. Step 5 calculates amount of loan ($109,400) which buyer-borrower can support for the $960 that goes for the monthly payment of P&I. Step 6 adds the down payment ($25,000) to the loan amount to arrive at the maximum purchase price ($134,400).

TEST YOURSELF
Data

Interest Rate	10%
Term, Payable Monthly for	30 years
Down Payment	$40,000
Monthly Payments, including PITI (Principal, Interest, Taxes, Insurance)	$2,000
Percentage Attributable to Taxes & Insurance	4%

Questions
1. How much loan can borrowers afford?
2. How much property can borrowers afford?

Answers
1. $218,785.57, rounded to $218,800
2. $258,785.57, rounded to $258,800

Lesson 14: How Do I Calculate Payments for Adjustable Rate Mortgages (ARM)?

The calculation for adjustable rate mortgage payments, or ARMs for short, differs from fixed rate mortgages (FRMs) due to the fluctuations in payments whenever rates go up or down under an ARM loan. Thus we must adjust the payments as interest rates on the loan are adjusted under the terms of the mortgage instrument.

In the example that follows, we'll assume that the borrower starts out with a 7 percent ARM rate, and that the rate can go up or down as much as 1 percent per year, called an annual cap, subject further to a five-point lifetime cap.

Data

1st Trust Deed	$100,000
Beginning ARM Interest Rate	7%
Assumed 2nd Year Interest Rate	8%
Assumed 3rd Year Interest Rate	7.5%
Amortization Term	30 years

Questions

1. What are the monthly payments during the first year at 7?
2. What are the monthly payments during the second year at 8?
3. What are the monthly payments during the third year at 7.5?

Solution

Key	Screen
1. 30 |g| |n|	360.00
2. 7 |g| |12÷|	0.58
3. 100000 |P|	100,000
4. 0 |FV|	0
5. |PMT|	−665.30
6. 12 |f| |AMORT|	−6,967.81
7. |RCL| |n| 24 |−| |n|	348
8. 8 |g| |12÷|	0.67
9. |PMT|	−732.43
10. 12 |f| |AMORT|	−7,886.06
11. |RCL| |n| 24 |−| |n|	336
12. 7.5 |g| |12÷|	0.63
13. |PMT|	−699.19

Answers

Year 1 monthly payments (step 5)	$665.30
Year 2 monthly payments (step 9)	$732.43
Year 3 monthly payments (step 13)	$699.19

Notes

Steps 1 through 5 represent the monthly payments during the first year. Step 6 computes the amount of first-year payments that apply to principal reduction. Step 7 gives us the number of months remaining after one year. Step 8 calculates monthly interest rate for the second year. Step 9 reflects monthly payments for the second year. Step 10 computes the amount of second-year payments that apply to interest. Step 11 calculates the number of months remaining after two years. Step 12 calculates monthly interest rate for the third year. Step 13 shows monthly payments for the third year.

TEST YOURSELF
Data

1st Trust Deed	$120,000
Beginning ARM Interest Rate	6%
Assumed 2nd Year Interest Rate	7%
Assumed 3rd Year Interest Rate	8%
Amortization Term	30 years

Questions
1. What are the monthly payments during the first year at 6?
2. What are the monthly payments during the second year at 7?
3. What are the monthly payments during the third year at 8?

Answers
1. $719.46
2. $796.65
3. $875.37

Chapter

14

The term "creative financing" has been coined to designate approaches to financing real property in ways that are not normally found through traditional sources. Many of these involve people-to-people financing, for seller carrybacks, some of which are explained here. The various techniques are limited only by one's imagination and knowledge.

In this chapter, we examine some creative methods used to solve both the difficult and not so difficult situations in which borrowers find themselves when they seek a real estate loan in a tight money market. These are not to be confused with the alternative mortgage instruments, or AMIs, discussed in Chapter 4. While AMIs are potentially very creative, they are variations on the basic fixed rate, fixed term, level payment, fully amortized loan that has been part of the permanent financing scene since 1934.

After completing this chapter, you should be able to:

1. Differentiate between traditional and creative financing techniques.
2. Identify at least five ways in which real estate can be financed through ways other than the traditional methods.
3. Contrast the all-inclusive trust deed to the installment Contract of Sale, citing at least three differences.
4. Apply the formula to calculate blended interest rates.
5. Name the instruments required to close a sale using the creative techniques presented in this chapter.
6. List at least six items that must be disclosed under the Creative Financing Disclosure Act.

Creative Financing Approaches

14.1 SECONDARY FINANCING TECHNIQUES

Second Trust Deeds Carried by the Seller

Second trust deeds are sometimes referred to as "gap loans" carried back by sellers, who in effect help finance a portion of the selling price. The amount financed represents a part of the seller's equity. The difference between the down payment plus loan amount and the sale price leaves a gap that is filled by the seller carrying back paper—the note secured by the second trust deed. The loan amount may be either a new loan commitment or an existing loan that the purchaser agrees to take over, whether under an assumption agreement or a "subject to" clause. Like first mortgages and trust deeds, seller carrybacks are referred to as **purchase money mortgages** because the seller's loan helps in the purchase.

Example: Assume that a property sells for $300,000 with a $30,000 down payment, and that an institutional lender has made a first trust deed commitment of $240,000 for 30 years at 6.5 percent interest per annum. The seller agrees to carry back the $30,000 balance in the form of a purchase money note with a second deed of trust. Terms of the second loan call for a straight, interest-only note with 7 percent interest per annum, all due and payable in four years. Ignoring closing costs, the buyer's position will appear as follows:

Sale price	$300,000
Cash down payment	−30,000
Balance needed to finance	$270,000

(continued)

First trust deed	−240,000
Purchase money second (gap loan)	$ 30,000
Monthly interest-only payments	$ 175
Lump sum payment, end of 4 years	$ 30,000

The balance due at the end of four years, referred to as a lump sum payment, is $30,000 on a $30,000 second loan. In the event the buyer-borrower is unable to meet the lump sum payment, there are several options. He or she may: (1) renegotiate the note, if the beneficiary is willing to extend the term of the note; (2) secure a new loan from outside sources in order to pay off the debt; and (3) refinance the entire loan. The last alternative assumes, however, that enough equity has been built up during the four years to allow this. The new loan would pay off the balance on the existing first—$228,143—plus the $30,000 due on the second. Thus, a net of $258,143 is needed, before points and other charges are paid from the loan proceeds.

There are risks involved in carrying back junior trust deeds. Figure 14.1 suggests ways in which sellers can minimize risks to themselves.

Note: The preceding information is for example purposes only. Second trust deeds, whether seller carried or an accompanying loan provided by the first TD lender, became popular for avoiding PMI. In our example, the borrower with a 10 percent down payment and a 10 percent seller carry second required only an 80 percent first TD and thereby avoided PMI coverage.

In mid-2009, institutional lenders eliminated second TD financing, at least temporarily, from the Fannie Mae and Freddie Mac loan programs. Prior to this ban on second TD financing, lenders developed secondary loan guidelines including: (a) a five-year minimum term, (b) minimum interest-only payments, and (c) a requirement that the borrower qualify with the identified second TD payments.

Collateralizing Junior Loans

Using the previous example, what if the seller does not wish to carry a second trust deed? One solution to this problem is to obtain a collateralized loan using a seller-carried note and second deed of trust as an asset. **Collateralization** is a process by which a note and deed of trust are pledged as collateral for a loan, usually through private parties, mortgage brokers, and commercial banks,

FIGURE 14.1   Protection devices for sellers.

PROTECTION DEVICES FOR SELLERS WHO CARRY BACK SECOND DEEDS OF TRUST

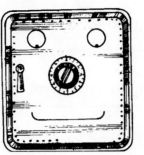

1. Insert an alienation (due-on-sale) clause in the promissory note and deed of trust as a condition for granting the extension of credit.

2. File a request for copy of notice of default and sale on the existing first deed of trust.

3. Add the name of the beneficiary (seller) on the new buyers' fire insurance policy as second loss payee.

4. At the time of the sale ask the title company to issue a joint protection title insurance policy coinsuring both the new buyer and the beneficial interest of the seller.

for a percentage of the face value of said note, at a discounted value.

To illustrate its application, assume the same data as under the credit extension loan above.

Assume also that in order for the note to be accepted as collateral, it might be reduced to half its face value and a fee of ten discount points charged by the lender. With interest payable at 7 percent per annum on the note carried back by the seller and 10 percent payable on the collateralized note the selling beneficiary's position will appear as follows:

Second loan carried by seller	$30,000
Collateral loan (50% from another lender)	−15,000
Deferred portion	$15,000

Interest seller is to receive on $30,000 second deed of trust at 7% for 4 years		$ 8,400
Less: Interest paid on $15,000 collateral loan at 10% for 4 years	$6,000	
Less: Discount fee of 10 points (fee to lender for granting collateral loan)	1,500	7,500
Net interest income over interest expense		$ 900
Final installment (lump sum) receivable at end of 4 years		$30,000
Final installment (lump sum) repayable at end of 4 years		15,000
Net payable to seller-borrower		$15,000

This technique is an alternative for the seller who wishes to retain an interest in the second trust deed but who also needs cash. In this example, the seller received use of $15,000 from the investor.

Collateralizing an existing note and second trust deed may or may not be advantageous, depending on the relationship between the terms and payout on the second loan owned by the seller and the terms and payout on the collateral loan. Collateralizing the note and deed of trust provides a means by which the borrower can obtain immediate cash of $13,500 ($15,000 loan less $1,500 discount fee) and still keep control over an investment yielding 7 percent per year. The seller-borrower will receive interest income of $8,400 over the four-year period, or $2,100 annually, against a yearly payment of $1,500 in interest charges, netting $600 per year (plus the $1,500 discount fee). Then, at maturity, the seller-borrower will receive a lump sum of $30,000 from the purchaser of the property and pay out $15,000 on the collateralized note for net cash proceeds of $15,000.

Advantages of collateralizing to the seller-borrower include retention of the benefits of the original note; avoidance of loss through discounting of the note; and avoidance of additional debt—that is, the cash flow from seller's carryback note may more than offset the payments on the collateral note, as is true in the example above. (Offsetting these would be the interest plus points paid and the time value of money.)

As mentioned, such loans usually are obtainable through mortgage brokers, commercial banks, newspaper ads, and private parties. To save extra title insurance and escrow expenses, it would be more practical to arrange such a transaction during the sale escrow.

Seller Sells the Second Loan

Another solution is for the seller or real estate agent to arrange to sell the note and second trust deed that was carried back as part of the purchase price—in other words, to sell the junior lien. This will generate instant cash for the seller. However, selling junior liens almost always involves selling at a discount. This is particularly true in the case of a newly issued note, since there is no history of payments to establish any past record. Other factors that determine the amount of discount include interest rate, location and appraised value of the property, loan-to-value ratio, type and terms of the note, and the desired yield of the investor.

The amount of discount on the sale of a second note and trust deed depends on many variables (as explained in Chapter 3). Assuming the discount to be 25 percent and given the same facts outlined earlier, the application of discounting would appear as follows:

Face value, second trust deed note	$30,000
Less: 25% discount	7,500
Cash proceeds to seller	$22,500

The primary motivation for most **seller carrybacks** is to get the transaction done. The seller of the deed generally accepts a discount and sells at a loss only when there is no better option available (e.g., another offer with a larger down payment). The sale of notes secured by trust deeds is accomplished through the simple act of an assignment executed by the selling beneficiary, called the assignor, in favor of the purchaser, called the assignee. To protect the interest of the new holder of the note, the assignment form should be recorded. An illustration of a completed assignment of deed of trust form is shown in Figure 14.2. **Special note:** If the note is to be discounted and sold in the same escrow in which it is created, it must first be offered to the buyer-borrower on the same terms. If the buyer-borrower refuses the offer, written evidence should be maintained in the escrow files and the broker's files, since the California Department of Real Estate may investigate and the broker may be subject to license revocation for not making the offer to the buyer-borrower.

If the note is sold after the escrow closes, this offer does not have to be made to the buyer-borrower.

Investors—buyers of seconds—can be found through escrow companies, loan brokers, holders of maturing junior trust deed loans, as disclosed by reconveyance deeds recorded at the County Hall of Records, classified ads, and, in the case of licensees, their own client files, particularly those disclosing previous sellers who carried back paper for part or all of the purchase price. Sellers are

FIGURE 14.2 Sample assignment of deed of trust.

LTIC-CAL T-400
RECORDING REQUESTED BY

SAFETY TITLE INSURANCE CO.

AND WHEN RECORDED MAIL TO

NAME ⌐ U. R. Gogetter

ADDRESS 5800 Think St.
Moon City, CA 90020
CITY & STATE ⌐

Title Order No. 3691215 Escrow No.

SPACE ABOVE THIS LINE FOR RECORDER'S USE

Assignment of Deed of Trust
THIS FORM WAS FURNISHED BY LAWYERS TITLE INSURANCE CORPORATION

FOR VALUE RECEIVED, the undersigned hereby grants, assigns and transfers to   U.R. Gogetter,
an unmarried man

all beneficial interest under that certain Deed of Trust dated   June 2, 20XX   ,

executed by   I. M. Tyred, a widower   , Trustor,

to   Docurich Escrow Company   , Trustee,

and recorded as Instrument No.   3691215   on   June 22, 20XX   in book   1850   ,

page   9   , of Official Records in the County Recorder's office of   Lost Angels   County,

California, describing land therein as: Lot 16, Blueview Tract, as per map recorded in
Book 66, page 99, of Maps in the office of the County Recorder of said County.

TOGETHER with the note or notes therein described or referred to, the money due and to become due thereon
with interest, and all rights accrued or to accrue under said Deed of Trust.

Dated   August 14, 20XX

STATE OF CALIFORNIA
COUNTY OF   Lost Angels   ⎰ ss.
On   August 14, 20XX   before me,
the undersigned. a Notary Public in and for said County and
State, personally appeared   Igot Stuck

known to me to be the person(s) whose name(s) is (are)
subscribed to the within instrument and acknowledged that
   he   executed the same.

Knote Airy
Knote Airy

Name (Typed or Printed)
Notary Public in and for said County and State.

(This area for official notarial seal)

cautioned, of course, to look into a variety of criteria, and not just the amount of discount offered, before entering any transaction with any investor or investor entity.

Broker Participation

Another creative approach to solving real estate finance problems is to have the broker become a lender for part of the equity. Whatever the scheme, the broker effectively becomes a partner with the seller in the secondary loan by breaking down the note into two component parts. The seller is named the beneficiary but assigns part or all of the note to the broker as commission through a collateral agreement such as shown in Figure 14.3. As with the previous secondary loan variations, this plan is utilized when the seller of property needs more cash than is generated through a down payment that is less than the seller's equity, after allowance for the senior security. Under the plan, the note and second trust deed are assigned to the real estate agent. Caveat: Since you are taking on a partner, that person's attitudes must be considered in any action taken regarding the collateral.

Example: Assume the sale of a home for $300,000 with a $240,000 first loan commitment. Assume further that the buyer has limited resources, say, a 10 percent down payment, or $30,000.

The commission rate is 6 percent, and the seller agrees to carry back a second loan, if enough cash can be generated so that the seller can in turn purchase another home. Suppose that the seller needs the cash and cannot afford to carry back the four-year note to maturity, yet the seller does not like the idea of collateralizing or selling at discount. The real estate agent can provide the solution by participating in the second trust deed loan, as follows:

Sales price		$300,000
Cash down payment		−30,000
Balance needed to finance		$270,000
First trust deed loan		−240,000
Junior financing for the balance	$30,000	
Broker's share at 6% of sales price	−18,000	
Seller's share for balance	$12,000	
Combined purchase money second trust deed		$ 30,000

FIGURE 14.3   Sample installment note.

INSTALLMENT NOTE--COLLATERAL SECURITY

$ __18,000__   __Utopia__ , California, ____ __July 6__ ____, 20__xx__

In installments as herein stated, for value received, _____

__Igot Stuck, Sellers__ _____ promise____ to pay to

_____ __Mrs. Broker and Mr. Salesman__ _____

_____ , or order, at

__Utopia, California__ _____

the principal sum of ___ Eighteen thousand ($18,000) and no/100 _____ DOLLARS,

with interest from __date endorsed hereon__ _____ on unpaid principal at the

rate of __Twelve (12%)__ _____ per cent per annum; principal and interest payable in installments of

____ Two hundred seventy ($270) and no/100 _____ Dollars

or more on the __same__ _____ day of each __calendar__ _____ month, beginning

on the __first (1st)__ ____ day of __September__ _____, 20__xx__ , __and continuing__

__until August 1, 20xx , at which time the entire unpaid balance of__

__principal and interest shall become due and payable.__

and continuing until said principal and interest have been paid.
Should any installment of principal or interest not be so paid, then the whole sum of principal and interest shall immediately become due and payable at the option of the holder hereof; principal and interest payable only in lawful money of the United States.
Should this note not be paid according to the terms hereof and suit be filed or an attorney employed or expenses incurred to compel payment of this note, or any portion hereof, I agree to pay a reasonable sum in in addition to attorney's fees.
The makers and endorsers of this note hereby waive diligence, demand, presentment for payment, notice of non-payment, protest and notice of protest.

/s/ Mr. Igot Stuck

/s/ Mrs. Igot Stuck

As collateral security for the payment of this note and interest as stated therein and expenses which may accrue thereon __we__ _____ have deposited with __Mrs. Broker__ _____ , the

following personal property of which __we are__ _____ sole owner__s__ , to-wit: _____

1. Note executed by Mr. & Mrs. Buyer, dated July 4, 20xx
2. Deed of Trust securing said Note, recorded July 5, 20xx
3. Duly executed Assignment of Trust Deed and Note by Mr. & Mrs. Stuck, recorded August 19, 20xx

And should the said note or any part thereof, or the interest, or the interest that may grow thereon, remain due and unpaid _____ according to the tenor of said note, ____ __we__ ____ hereby irrevocably authorize and empower said

__Mrs. Broker and Mr. Salesman__ _____ , their heirs, executors, administrators or assigns,

to sell and dispose of the above mentioned personal property, or any part thereof, at public or private sale, without any previous

notice to __us__ _____ of any such sale, and from the proceeds arising therefrom to pay the

principal and interest and all charges that shall then be due, and the costs of sale, and the balance, if any, to pay over to

____ __our__ _____ or_____ representatives upon demand.   In case of

deterioration of any of the above securities, or fall in the market value of the same ____ __we__ _____
hereby promise____ and agree____ on demand to reduce the amount of said debt, or to increase the security in proportion to
such deterioration or decrease of value, in default of which this note is to be considered due under the above stipulation.   On
the payment of this note and interest according to the terms of the same, and all charges, this agreement is to be void, and the

above named securities to be returned to __us.__ _____

Presentment, protest and notice of protest are hereby waived.

Dated ____ __August 19,__ _____ , 20__xx__

/s/ Mr. Igot Stuck

/s/ Mrs. Igot Stuck

NOTE—COLLATERAL SECURITY—INSTALLMENT—WOLCOTTS FORM 1426

The mechanics of this transaction are as follows: (1) A promissory note and trust deed are executed by the buyer of the property in favor of the seller for the full amount of the second deed of trust, $30,000. (2) Then an instrument similar to the installment note, the collateral security form in Figure 14.3, is executed by the sellers to the broker for the amount of commission, $18,000 in this case. The collateral agreement is, in effect, an assignment of the seller's note and trust deed for the portion representing the broker's interest. It states in so many words that for value received, the seller promises to pay to the broker the agreed amount at so much per month, including interest at so much per annum. In case of default, the broker would have a right to foreclose through either public or private sale of the collateral, the secured promissory note. When more than one licensee is taking part or all of the commission through this mechanism, like a selling salesperson and employing broker, both may be shown under the payee provision of the collateral note for the amount or percentage representing their respective commission interests. It is advisable to check with the lender and your broker to determine the acceptability of carrying one's commission.

Combination or "Split" Junior Liens

As a compromise to carrying back paper that the seller is unwilling to sell or collateralize, and when the broker is not willing to take a junior lien for all or part of the commission, the seller might be amenable to taking back a concurrent second and third trust deed, both carrying a 12 percent yield. The purchase money loan is "split." Instead of one large second, the seller might agree to two smaller junior liens. Using the sales price and terms outlined in the original example, with a 10 percent down payment and assumed 70/30 split junior lien, the position of the junior trust deeds would appear as follows:

Sales price	$300,000
Cash down payment	−30,000
Balance needed to finance	$270,000
First trust deed	−240,000
Junior financing	$ 30,000
Second trust deed carried by seller	−21,000
Third trust deed carried by seller	$ 9,000

While both loans contain exactly the same terms, the advantage of such an arrangement is that it is easier to market a second of a smaller size, thus providing the seller with some immediate cash relief. Yet the seller is able to retain a relatively safe interest in the property at an attractive rate of return. The $30,000 junior financing may be divided into any portions that will allow the greatest flexibility to the seller. It may be a $21,000 second and $9,000 third as just illustrated, or a $15,000 second and $15,000 third, and so on. The buyer's costs are not substantially increased, since split loans require only two extra documents, one extra recording fee, and one extra reconveyance fee. Payoff terms can be adjusted to increase yield on the second or third that is to be sold.

14.2 ALL-INCLUSIVE TRUST DEED (AITD)

Definition

An AITD, for reasons that will soon become clear, is also referred to as a **wrap-around trust deed** or overriding trust deed. It may also be mistakenly referred to as a *blanket trust deed*, since it includes more than one trust deed loan within the framework of the instrument. A blanket trust deed encumbers more than one property (e.g., new developments), while an AITD usually covers just one property. An *all-inclusive trust* deed is always a *junior* deed of trust, often a purchase money deed of trust loan, given back to the seller that includes in its scope the amount of the first encumbrance as well as any secondary liens. It normally contains a provision that the seller will pay off the senior loan or loans from monies the seller is to receive from the buyer. It is subject to, yet includes, encumbrances to which it is subordinate.

Since the concept essentially involves the seller as lender, it is most often used when money is tight or unavailable. Care and discretion must be exercised in its adoption, particularly when a real estate agent recommends its use.

An example of an all-inclusive deed of trust is shown in Figure 14.4. The instrument could be used on virtually any type of property where circumstances are appropriate. Brokers should not attempt to draft such trust deeds but should have them prepared by the parties' legal counsel and approved by the title company that is to insure them.

FIGURE 14.4   Sample all-inclusive deed of trust.

**ALL INCLUSIVE PURCHASE MONEY PROMISSORY NOTE SECURED BY
ALL-INCLUSIVE PURCHASE MONEY DEED OF TRUST**
(INSTALLMENT NOTE, INTEREST INCLUDED)

$ __500,000__   __Van Nuys__ , California,   __April 15__ 20__XX__

In installments as herein stated, for value received, I / We ("Maker") promise to pay to __James W. Johnson__

("Payee") or order, at __6515-6517 Van Nuys Blvd, Van Nuys, CA__

the principal sum of __Five hundred thousand and no/100__ _____ DOLLARS, with interest

from __date hereof__ _____ on unpaid principal at the rate of

__twelve (12%)__ per cent per annum; principal and interest payable in installments of __$5143.00__

or more on the __first (1st)__ day of each __calendar__ _____ month, beginning

on the __first (1st)__ day of __June__ 20__XX__ , and continuing until said p̶r̶i̶n̶c̶i̶p̶a̶l̶ a̶n̶d̶

i̶n̶t̶e̶r̶e̶s̶t̶ h̶a̶v̶e̶ b̶e̶e̶n̶ p̶a̶i̶d̶ June 1, 20**XX**, when the unpaid balance shall be due and payable.

Each installment shall be applied first on the interest then due and the remainder on principal; and interest shall thereupon cease upon the principal so credited.

The total principal amount of this Note includes the unpaid principal balance of the promissory note(s) ("Underlying Note(s)") secured by Deed(s) of Trust, more particularly described as follows:

1.   (A) PROMISSORY NOTE:
    Maker: __Newstate S & L and Allstate Mortgage Ltd.__
    Payee: _____
    Original Amount: __$300,000__
    Date: _____

    (B) DEED OF TRUST:
    Beneficiary: _____
    Original Amount: _____
    Recordation Date: _____
    Document No. _____ Book _____ Page _____
    Place of Recordation: _____ , County, California

2.   (A) PROMISSORY NOTE:
    Maker: _____
    Payee: _____
    Original Amount: _____
    Date: _____

    (B) DEED OF TRUST:
    Beneficiary: _____
    Original Amount: _____
    Recordation Date: _____
    Document No. _____ Book _____ Page _____
    Place of Recordation: _____ , County, California

By Payee's acceptance of this Note, Payee covenants and agrees that, provided Maker is not delinquent or in default under the terms of this Note, Payee shall pay all installments of principal and interest which shall hereafter become due pursuant to the provisions of the Underlying Note(s) as and when the same become due and payable. In the event Maker shall be delinquent or in default under the terms of this Note, Payee shall not be obligated to make any payments required by the terms of the Underlying Note(s) until such delinquency or default is cured. In the event Payee fails to timely pay any installment of principal or interest on the Underlying Note(s) at the time when Maker is not delinquent or in default hereunder, Maker may, at Maker's option, make such payments directly to the holder of such Underlying Note(s), in which event Maker shall be entitled to a credit against the next installment(s) of principal and interest due under the terms of this Note equal to the amount so paid and including, without limitation, any penalty, charges and expenses paid by Maker to the holder of the Underlying Note(s) on account of Payee failing to make such payment. The obligations of Payee hereunder shall terminate upon the earliest of (i) foreclosure of the lien of the All-Inclusive Purchase Money Deed of Trust securing this Note, or (ii) cancellation of this Note and reconveyance of the All-Inclusive Purchase Money Deed of Trust securing same.

Should Maker be delinquent or in default under the terms of this Note, and Payee consequently incurs any penalties, charges or other expenses on account of the Underlying Note(s) during the period of such delinquency or default, the amount of such penalties, charges and expenses shall be immediately added to the principal amount of this Note and shall be immediately payable by Maker to Payee.

Notwithstanding anything to the contrary herein contained, the right of Maker to prepay all or any portion of the principal of this Note is limited to the same extent as any limitation exists in the right to prepay the principal of the Underlying Note(s). If any prepayments of principal of this Note shall, by reason of the application of any portion thereof by Payee to the prepayment of principal of the Underlying Note(s), constitute such prepayment for which the holders of the Underlying Note(s) are entitled to receive a prepayment penalty or consideration, the amount of such prepayment penalty or consideration shall be paid by Maker to Payee upon demand, and any such amount shall not reduce the unpaid balance of principal or interest hereunder.

At any time when the total of the unpaid principal balance of this Note, accrued interest thereon, all other sums due pursuant to the terms hereof, and all sums advanced by Payee pursuant to the terms of the All-Inclusive Purchase Money Deed of Trust securing this Note, is equal to or less than the unpaid balance of principal and interest then due under the terms of the Underlying Note(s), Payee, at his option, shall cancel this Note and deliver same to Maker and execute a request for full reconveyance of the Deed of Trust securing this Note.

Should default be made by Maker in payment of any installments of principal, interest, or any other sums due hereunder, the whole sum of principal, interest and all other sums due from Maker hereunder, after first deducting therefrom all sums then due under the terms of the Underlying Note(s), shall become immediately due at the option of the holder of this Note. Principal, interest and all other sums due hereunder payable in lawful money of the United States. If action be instituted on this Note, I/we promise to pay such sums as the Court may fix as attorney's fees. This Note is secured by an ALL-INCLUSIVE PURCHASE MONEY DEED OF TRUST to Lawyers Title Insurance Corporation, a Virginia corporation, as Trustee.

_____   _Jack B. Quick_   Jack B. Quick
     (Maker)   (Maker)

The undersigned hereby accept(s) the foregoing All-Inclusive Purchase Money Promissory Note and agree(s) to perform each and all of the terms thereof on the part of Payee to be performed.

Executed as of the date and place first above written.

_____   _____
     (Payee)   (Payee)

(THIS NOTE IS FOR USE ONLY IN PURCHASE MONEY TRANSACTIONS. IT IS RECOMMENDED THAT, PRIOR TO THE EXECUTION OF THIS NOTE, THE PARTIES CONSULT WITH THEIR ATTORNEYS WITH RESPECT THERETO.)

061-4-284-0000
FORM T204   THIS FORM FURNISHED BY LAWYERS TITLE INSURANCE CORPORATION

Uses for All-Inclusive Trust Deeds

The **all-inclusive trust deed** is used under a variety of circumstances. Some sellers will use it in lieu of an installment sales contract, the so-called land contract. It may also be used where there exists a loan with a lock-in clause (not to be confused with "lock-in-rate") that provides that the existing loan cannot be paid off before a certain date. A third use is when an owner is anxious to sell and a prospective purchaser will buy only under an all-inclusive device that incorporates features favorable to the buyer such as income tax benefits. Sellers may also offer this type of instrument when they have overpriced the property and creative financing may make the transaction attractive to a buyer. Low down payments may also tempt owners to sell this way.

Another type of transaction calling for a wrap-around is when there is a low-interest loan that the seller would prefer to keep, particularly when a buyer's credit is marginal, so that in the event of foreclosure by the selling beneficiary, the underlying low-cost loan is retained. When the seller is firm on price but not on terms, again its use may be justified.

Another circumstance is when a prospective buyer cannot qualify for required financing under a normal sale. When a seller would need to carry back a substantial junior loan, the all-inclusive may be more satisfactory. In cases involving heavy and burdensome prepayment penalties, buyers and sellers may resort to the AITD. In still another situation, an owner may need cash but the beneficiary under the existing trust deed will not commit itself to additional advances, forcing the seller to retain the prior lien or liens using an all-inclusive. Finally, when a severe money crunch hits the mortgage market, this device takes on added significance. After all, it is especially during periods of tight money that most creative financing techniques appear on the market.

Although we have advanced a dozen reasons for using the all inclusive deed of trust, sellers and buyers may, of course, be motivated by a combination of two or more of these. Remember, an AITD cannot be used to get around an otherwise enforceable **due-on-sale clause** the loan must be assumable. Lenders can discover a concealed AITD when the homeowner's insurance policy is endorsed.

Comprehensive Application of AITD

As an example of an AITD, assume that a property is to sell for $600,000 and that it has an existing first trust deed loan of $236,000 payable at $2,360 per month, including interest at

8 percent per annum; and a second loan of $64,000 payable at $640 per month, including 10 percent annual interest. Deducting the $300,000 in loans from the $600,000 sale price leaves an equity of $300,000. Suppose the parties agree to a one-sixth down payment, or $100,000. The balance of the purchase price, $200,000 is the remaining seller's equity that could be financed by carrying back either a third trust deed or an AITD. Since a substantial third would be involved—representing one-third of the sales price—such a step may not be advised. A better resolution may lie, therefore, with the wrap-around, if the existing loan(s) is assumable and/or the lenders agree to waive their due-on-sale rights. Schematically, the transaction would appear as follows:

SALE PRICE: $600,000			
$100,000	$500,000 All-inclusive trust deed, $5,143 per month at 12%		
Down payment (Buyer's equity) interest	$236,000 First loan payable $2,360 per month at 8% annual interest	$64,000 Second loan payable $640 per month at 10% annual interest	$200,000 Seller's remaining equity

In the illustration, the seller's remaining equity is $200,000 and it is added to the existing liens under the banner of an AITD, payable at $5,143 per month including interest of 12 percent per annum.

Characteristics and Limitations

The AITD is characterized by a number of features. First, it can increase the seller's rate of return above what the rate would be under a traditional carryback loan. Second, it is a purchase money transaction, subject to, but still including encumbrances, to which it is subordinate. The buyer becomes a trustor-grantee, while the seller becomes a beneficiary-grantor. By virtue of its purchase money character, the transaction is subject to California's antideficiency statutes if it is a one-to-four-unit, owner-occupied residential property, so that the buyer-trustor is held harmless in the event of a deficiency on the promissory note should foreclosure occur.

Legal title is actually conveyed, usually by grant deed, and may be insured by a policy of title insurance. Finally, in the event of default and foreclosure, the seller-beneficiary follows the same procedures that would apply in the foreclosure of any trust deed. However, the action is filed only against the seller's equity, representing the difference between the underlying liens and the overriding obligation—$200,000 in the preceding illustration. Again, the AITD is useful only if existing loans are assumable, or if the due-on-sale clause is waived by the prior lender.

Types of AITDs

The AITD may be one of two types:

1. *Equity payoff.* This takes place when the buyer, who is the trustor on the AITD, with the permission of the lender, takes over the prior loans after the seller's equity has been paid off. A deed of reconveyance is issued by the seller-beneficiary of the AITD. In the preceding example, once the buyer has paid off the difference between the $500,000 AITD and the $236,000 first trust deed plus the remaining due under the $64,000 second, the buyer steps into the shoes of the seller and makes payments on the prior notes directly to the beneficiaries of these senior liens.

2. *Full payoff.* Here the buyer-trustor is obligated to the seller until the entire balance of the AITD is paid off. Thus the seller-beneficiary continues to pick up the override, the difference between the 12 percent paid the seller and the lower rates due on the underlying notes (8 percent on the first, 10 percent on the second).

Benefits to Seller

There are a number of advantages to the seller in using the all-inclusive to solve financing problems. It may be the only practical way to dispose of a property when there is a lock-in clause. Furthermore, a broader market is created for the property when a seller is willing to carry back substantially all of the paper. A carryback by a seller does not incur loan fees and a variety of other financing charges. This attracts buyers and thereby increases the demand for the seller's property.

Moreover, the all-inclusive device affords flexibility so that the seller may be able to obtain a higher price due to the built-in financing terms. In effect, the seller has manufactured money by deferring the recapture of the seller's equity through this method. The seller retains the favorable terms of the existing loans in the event the seller is forced to repossess the property through foreclosure. During the holding period, the seller is able to increase the net yield on the overall trust deed. Recall that sellers' carryback purchase money mortgages and trust deeds are not subject to any interest rate limitations. Using the data from our previous example, if a simple interest rate were applied to each of the loans, the yield to the investor on the AITD would be almost 17.4 percent, computed as follows:

Interest income:	12% of $500,000 on AITD		$60,000
Interest expense:	8% of $236,000 on existing first deed	$18,880	
	10% of $64,000 on existing second deed	6,400	25,280
Net interest income over interest expense:			$34,720

$$\text{Yield} = \frac{\text{Seller's net interest income}}{\text{Seller's equity}} = \frac{\$34,720}{\$200,000} = 17.4\%$$

The effective yield is significantly greater than the 12 percent stated on the AITD note because the seller will collect 12 percent while paying out only 8 percent and 10 percent on the existing notes, thereby earning an additional 4 percent on the first, and 2 percent on the second trust deed. The extra $34,720 interest received is equivalent to another 5.4 percent return on the $200,000 remaining equity. That is,

$$\frac{(4\% \times \$236,000 + (2\% \times \$64,000)}{\$200,000} = 5.4\%$$

Adding this to the 12 percent buyer's contract rate produces a 17.4 percent effective rate to the seller. It should be noted that calculations using the foregoing formula are only approximations. They show the yield on a first-year basis only and not over the life of the loan. Furthermore, they do not take into account other variables, including special features of the note, such as term, balloon payments, or variable rates; nor do they take into account income tax consequences and time value of money. Use the formula judiciously.

Another benefit might ensue in the event the seller-beneficiary had to cash out the all-inclusive note secured by a trust deed. A lower discount is commanded when a high effective yield is obtained. Even without a discount, when the purchaser could assume the underlying liens, in the previous example, the yield would be 17.4 percent.

A significant advantage to the seller is that this device makes the seller aware immediately of any buyer's default, in contrast to taking back a junior deed of trust accompanied by the recording of a request for notice: months may pass before a senior lienholder files a notice of default should the trustor-buyer default in a prior loan, so that if the junior lienholder's own loan payments are current, such default would be unnoticed. When compared to a land contract of sale, the AITD may again be superior, because in case of foreclosure, a trustee's sale is speedier, surer, and absolute, while foreclosure under a land contract requires court action to become effective.

Finally, income tax advantages to the seller may be enhanced. For example, in a straight sale with conventional forms of financing, the entire gain is recognized in the year of sale. In contrast, in the AITD, the seller may declare only the actual receipts received each year, on a prorated basis over the term of the AITD note. This is because an AITD, since it is payable over more than one calendar year, is by its very nature an installment sale, as defined in the Internal Revenue Code, Section 453.

Benefits to Buyer

The AITD also offers many advantages to buyers. They may be able to acquire properties for which they may not otherwise qualify (for example, the purchaser who is retired and, although having substantial resources, has relatively little if any dependable income). When financing can be obtained, the buyer may acquire a larger property for the same low down payment, utilizing the principle of leverage. Moreover, one monthly payment will be required instead of a series of payments that comes when the buyer assumes the prior liens and executes another junior secured note in favor of the seller. Costs are reduced on appraisal fees, loan points, loan escrow fee, and other charges.

Greater flexibility may also be offered in the structure of the loan. When the seller is cooperative, the purchaser might be able to tailor the spendable income to his or her particular needs, such as through a lower debt service stretched over a longer period of time, and thus afford to pay more for the property by bargaining for better terms. There are no restrictions on lending, unlike institutional financing. Thus extra-long terms can be negotiated, with no points and no prepayment penalties as part of the bargain. And if the purchaser should pay more for the property, the basis will be thereby increased, with a subsequent lower capital gain (or larger write-off in the event of a qualified sale at a loss).

Finally, when contrasted with a purchase under a land contract, the buyer gets a grant deed, or ownership in fee, up front, as opposed to a land contract, which gives legal title at the end of the contract, though it is also an insurable title.

Another advantage to both buyer and seller is that since the buyer will not ordinarily incur loan fees and a variety of financing charges, properly structured, this feature should attract more buyers and increase the demand for the seller's property.

Some Pitfalls of AITDs

Just as there are benefits to both buyers and sellers who structure the AITD correctly, precautions must be taken since this vehicle is not a cure-all for most housing transactions.

Precautions for Sellers

Of course, both parties should take steps to guard against certain pitfalls that may arise in connection with the use of the wrap-around trust deed. For example, an impound account might be set up to cover taxes, insurance, and balloon payments on the prior liens. The seller might also have the installment payments on the wrap-around loan fall due at least a week before payments on the senior loan are due. This way, the seller will be using the buyer's money to make the payments on any senior loan.

A limit, if not an outright prohibition, might be imposed on further use of another AITD upon resale by inserting a due-on-sale clause in the AITD. Similarly, the seller should reserve the right to have the buyer refinance the property. The seller may wish to have the buyer refinance when the money market is more favorable, or when the lock-in period has expired, or when balloon payments are due on the senior debt. The seller should also make provision for the time when the purchaser may need to assume the existing loans (as discussed above, under Types of AITDs), should such loans outlive the AITD.

Finally, when income-producing property is involved, the seller should reserve the right to approve all leases that might impair the value of the AITD. A shrewd buyer might, for example, lease the premises with substantial prepaid rents paid to the buyer, intending to "milk" the property, then walk away from it, leaving the seller stuck with the legal problems of dealing with the prepaid rents for each of the lessees, in addition to having to deal with the remaining lease terms, which may be economically unfavorable to the seller who must now step in to protect remaining interests. By reserving the right to prescreen all leases, the seller is protected against such problems in the AITD, since all subsequent leases are to be subordinated to the seller's superior interest as the beneficiary under the AITD. (It should be noted that leases with priority over the underlying deed of trust are extremely rare.)

Precautions for Buyers

Precautions should also be taken by the buyer, of course. The all-inclusive agreement should provide protections for the buyer in case the seller defaults on the loan being wrapped.

The buyer might, for example, insert the right to make payments on the seller's underlying liens, and credit such payments toward the AITD. Payments might be made to a bank collection department, escrow, trust, or directly to the holder of the included encumbrances, stipulating that they be used in turn to reduce existing liens. The costs of setting up such machinery should be stipulated. If payments on the AITD are not sufficient to cover existing liens, provision should be made for seller's payment of any differences, such as through a bond. Further, the buyer might reserve the right to pay off part or all of the senior debts, assuming or retiring some or all of them.

All buyers should record a request for notice of default and notice of sale on the seller's senior liens to make sure they keep abreast of the status of these loans. If a notice of default is recorded, buyers will automatically receive notice.

Procedures in Setting Up an AITD

The procedures required in negotiating for and creating an AITD might follow these broad steps:

1. Examine existing trust deeds to determine whether there is an enforceable due-on-sale, alienation, or acceleration clause. If any exist, provision should be made either to pay off the loans or renegotiate them.

2. Outstanding balances, periodic payments, and balloon provisions should be ascertained so that a realistic payment schedule can be set up on the all-inclusive. For example, the new loan schedule may call for a longer or shorter period for payment, depending on the particular requirements of the respective parties. The AITD is of course recorded as a junior lien, subject to the existing liens. The purchaser may later, with the lender's permission, take over the senior loans, whereupon the seller

would need to obtain a reconveyance of the AITD as a fully discharged instrument.

A realistic payment schedule should be constructed to cover (a) periodic installments; (b) outstanding balances; (c) partial balloons on existing loans; and (d) any variations in payments, such as for adjustable or variable rates.

3. Decide who is to collect and disburse payments on the AITD and who is to pay the cost of setting up and administering the collection process. If the payments under the AITD are not sufficient to cover the senior loans, a system should be set up to see that the additional amounts are paid. Similarly, if there is an impound account for taxes, insurance, or other matters in the underlying note, it would be prudent to incorporate an impound account in the AITD note as well.

4. Spell out the conditions giving rise to default and what foreclosure procedure is to be followed. These are similar to those found in the standard trust deed, except that only the seller's remaining equity is affected.

5. Have the necessary agreements and documents drawn up, using essential phraseology to gain acceptance by title companies for insurance purposes. A joint protection policy of title insurance, insuring both the interests of the buyer as owner and the interests of the seller as lender and as to priority of lien, should be obtained.

6. Determine property insurance coverage so all parties are amply protected.

14.3 INSTALLMENT SALES CONTRACT

The **installment sales contract**, more popularly called a conditional sales contract, or land contract of sale is another vehicle that can be used to solve real estate financing problems. Unlike the all-inclusive deed of trust, however, the fee title remains with the seller-vendor until the terms and conditions of the contract are fulfilled. This is an important distinction for a number of reasons, among which is that the use of the all-inclusive deed of trust permits a private sale of the property by the trustee in the event of default, eliminating the problems of a time-consuming and cumbersome judicial foreclosure. In contrast, the usual land contract may not contain a power of sale provision, so that a lawsuit is necessary for an effective foreclosure by the vendor. However, it may be noted that almost all title companies have produced contract forms that incorporate a power of sale provision. Figure 14.5 is an example of one furnished by an early pioneer in this field, Stewart-West Coast Title Company.

FIGURE 14.5 Sample land contract (partial).

RECORDING REQUESTED BY

AND WHEN RECORDED MAIL TO

Name   James Oliva

Street
Address

City &
State

————SPACE ABOVE THIS LINE FOR RECORDER'S USE————

FORM 1

LONG FORM SECURITY (INSTALLMENT) LAND CONTRACT WITH POWER OF SALE

THIS AGREEMENT, made and entered into this   20th   day of   May   , 20XX , by and
between   JAMES OLIVA, a married man and MICHAEL OLIVA, a married man,   (Vendor's name),
           each as to an undivided one-half interest
whose address is

(hereinafter sometimes referred to as "Vendor"), and   WILLIAM FERRELL and SHARON FERRELL
husband and wife, and RONALD SACHS and
CAROL SACHS, husband and wife, all as joint tenants(hereinafter sometimes referred to as "Vendee"); and
STEWART-WEST COAST TITLE CO. (hereinafter sometimes referred to as "Trustee.")
                    W I T N E S S E T H :
WHEREAS, Vendor is now the owner of certain real property situated in the County of
State of California, commonly known as   8527 Sunshine Ln, Panorama City, CA
                                    (property street address), and described as follows:

Lot 62 of Tract No. 15479, as per map recorded in Book 336, Pages 44,45, and 46
in the office of the County Recorder of said County.

WHEREAS, Vendor has agreed to sell, and Vendee has agreed to buy said real property on the terms and conditions hereinafter set
forth;
WHEREAS, Vendor shall retain legal title as a security interest in said real property until the payment of the balance of the purchase
price has been paid by Vendee to Vendor as set forth below.
NOW, THEREFORE, THE PARTIES HERETO DO HEREBY AGREE AS FOLLOWS:
PURCHASE PRICE
1. Vendor agrees to sell, and Vendee agrees to buy all of the aforedescribed real property for the sum of
                                            (Total purchase price) ($_____),
lawful money of the United States, as hereinafter more fully set forth.

REQUEST FOR NOTICE OF DEFAULT
2. In accordance with Section 2924b, Civil Code, request is hereby made by the undersigned Vendor and
Vendee that a copy of any Notice of Default and a copy of any Notice of Sale under Deed of Trust re-
corded_____in Book_____, Page_____, Official Records of
_____ County, California, as affecting above described property, executed by
_____as Trustor in which_____
is named as beneficiary, and_____as Trustee, be mailed to Vendor
and Vendee at address in paragraph 3 below.
NOTICES AND REQUEST FOR NOTICE
3. Notices required or permitted under this agreement shall be binding if delivered personally to party
sought to be served or if mailed by registered or certified mail, postage prepaid in the United States mail
to the following:
Vendor: _____

Vendee: _____   Trustee: Stewart-West Coast Title Co.
                                                           2675 West Olympic Boulevard
                                                           Los Angeles, California 90006

Vendor and Vendee hereby request that notice of default and notice of sale hereunder be mailed to them at the above address.

PAYMENT OF PURCHASE PRICE
4. Vendee shall pay said purchase price of $_____as follows:
  (a) Vendee shall pay to Vendor the sum of $_____(Down Payment) as and for a down payment.
  (b) Vendee shall take subject to and pay the balance due on that certain note secured by a first trust deed on the above mentioned real property, the principal balance of which is $_____, together with interest thereon at the rate of
percent per annum, payable in installments of
$. _____, (monthly payments amount; add "or more" if applicable) per month on the   day of each and
every month with the whole of the then outstanding balance thereof due on the   day of
19   . Each such payment includes payment of the following items under the terms of said note and trust deed:
      (1) Principal and interest;
      (2) Impounds for taxes;   (Strike out
      (3) Impounds for fire insurance; inapplicable
      (4) Impounds for   items.)
Payments shall be made by Vendee directly to beneficiary of said first trust deed at the following address:

                    (If a second trust deed exists, complete (c) below)
  (c) Vendee shall take subject to and pay the balance due on that certain note secured by a second trust deed on the above
mentioned real property, principal balance of which is $. _____ together with interest thereon at the rate of
percent per annum, payable in installments of $. _____ _____ _____(monthly payment amount; add "or more"

> **Example:** To illustrate the math involved in the sale of real property through a land contract, suppose a vacant lot sold for $100,000 and has an existing assumable 10 percent first trust deed loan of $60,000. The buyer is to make a down payment of 10 percent, or $10,000, and has agreed to execute an installment contract secured by the property for the balance of the purchase price. The contract is to be repaid at $966, rounded to the next dollar, per month, based on a 30-year amortization schedule including interest of 13 percent per annum, all due and payable in 15 years. Note that under such schedule the payments are reduced from the $1,138.72 that would be payable under 15-year amortization.
>
> | | |
> |---|---:|
> | Sales price | $100,000 |
> | Down payment at 10% | −10,000 |
> | Balance payable $996 monthly at 13% | $ 90,000 |

The seller continues to make payments on the $60,000 first trust deed, at the more favorable 10 percent interest rate. Instead of a second trust deed of $30,000 ($90,000 less $60,000) at, say, 10 percent, the seller will receive more on a 13 percent loan on the entire unpaid balance of $90,000—meanwhile continuing with a 10 percent interest rate on the existing $60,000, yielding a differential of 3 percent on the full $60,000.

Like any seller carryback, including the AITD, the installment contract of sale offers a significant income tax benefit to sellers, the ability to prorate capital gains over the life of the note. Check with a tax consultant for further details. Incidentally, a land contract can be used for any type of real estate, including vacant land.

14.4 LENDER PARTICIPATIONS

A **participation** is the sharing of an interest in the property by a lender. When money is tight, or available only at high interest rates or both, the lender will insist on a higher yield to itself to compensate for the greater risk involved. Without this, the lender may not be motivated to commit funds. This is especially true of large projects, for which an equity participation provides a means by which substantial investment capital could be raised.

Participation can be created in a variety of ways and may be classified according to the following categories:

1. *Lender participation in the revenue of the project.* For example, if a project costs $1 million to develop, in order to maximize leverage

and yield on return, the developer will want to obtain the largest possible loan. But lenders may not be content with a fixed rate of return. One alternative would be to offer a "piece of the action" through a participation in the income. This may be either a percentage of gross revenue or a percentage of net revenue. Since there may be a minimum amount, or floor, the excess income is referred to as overage. For instance, an institutional lender might finance 75 percent of the project at 10 percent interest per annum, payable over 25 years, with the provision that the lender is to also receive 20 percent of the net income, before depreciation and income taxes. If net income amounted to $50,000, the lender would receive $10,000 in addition to the 10 percent on the $750,000 loan—an effective yield of approximately 11.33 percent. Of course, to make the venture attractive to the developer, the overall yield will need to equal or exceed 11.33 percent per annum return.

2. *Equity participation.* In the previous example, instead of a percentage of profits, the lender may insist on a certain percentage of ownership. If 20 percent were agreed upon, the lender would have a direct title interest in 20 percent of the equity in the real property (or stock or other ownership interest) as a condition for making the loan. Assuming again a $250,000 equity in the development, after a $750,000 commitment on a $1 million project, the lender would thus have a $50,000 ownership interest (20 percent × $250,000), or 5 percent of the entire property. The lender would thus be entitled to 5 percent of all income, in addition to all of the other benefits of ownership, such as depreciation write off and capital gain. Of course, the lender would also be burdened by 5 percent of all expenses and costs of operation, just as with any real property ownership.

3. *Fees and discounts.* The lender could also increase the loan yield by charging a fixed interest rate but, in addition, requiring a one-time fee or points as a condition of making the loan. In effect, the loan is discounted by the amount of points charged at the front, much as government-backed loans are when the buyer or seller is charged a loan commitment fee.

4. *Profit participation.* Instead of sharing in the income, the lender may opt for a participation in the profits of a venture. Thus, when a lender believes that a project is expected to increase in value, it may prefer to share in capital gains at time of sale or exchange, rather than in the income during the holding period. For example, if the parties agreed to a 25 percent participation, and the $1 million development were subsequently sold for a net of $1.4 million, the lender would be entitled to 25 percent of the $400,000 gain, or $100,000.

5. *Multiple lenders.* This involves the purchase of a portion of loans made by other lenders. It is similar to the concept of reinsurance, when two or more insurance companies participate in a high-risk project. Similarly, in mortgage lending, large loans may be underwritten by more than one lender. Such schemes are common in corporate loans for large capital projects.

14.5 SALE-LEASEBACK

The **sale-leaseback** is also referred to as a purchase and lease-back, a purchase-lease, a sale-lease, a lease-purchase, and so on. But whatever its designation, it is characterized by a sale of one's property to another party, usually a large financial institution, which, in turn, leases it back to the seller. The property could consist of land only (ground lease), improvements only, or both land and improvements. This technique is a popular financing vehicle among strongly rated companies with excellent credit. Although it can be used with the sale and purchase of homes, our primary focus in this section is on nonresidential transactions.

Procedure

The mechanics of a sale-leaseback encompass four essential steps:

(1) Investors buy property that they desire. This may be improved or unimproved. (2) If unimproved, the investor develops the land to its specifications. A large grocery chain, for example, may wish to build a 50,000-square-foot grocery store on a parcel of land it now owns. (3) The owner sells the land or improvements to a major investor, such as a life insurance company, pension fund, trust, or even a nonprofit organization. (4) The investor-purchaser leases the property back to the seller at an agreed rent under a long-term lease.

The seller becomes the lessee, and the buyer becomes the lessor. No specific form is used. An offer to purchase is a contract that describes the terms and conditions; after acceptance, it is followed by a mutually acceptable lease agreement between the parties to the transaction.

Advantages to Seller

Among the possible advantages and benefits to the seller-lessee are the following:

- Lease payments are fully tax deductible for business and investment properties. This includes rents paid on both land and improvements, which in most instances will result in a greater write-off than interest payments on a loan or depreciation on just the value of the improvements.

- Rent may be lower than loan payments. During an inflationary period, a fixed rental schedule favors the lessee. Furthermore, the lease term can be made longer than the loan term—leases may run for as long as 99 years in some cases.
- Improvements made by the lessee can be deducted through depreciation write-off.
- When only the land is sold and leased back, not only are the ground rent payments deductible but depreciation on the improvements is deductible as well.
- Capital that would otherwise be tied up in equity is freed for other uses. To the extent that funds are raised through outright sale, maximum financing is achieved. More capital can normally be raised in this way than by borrowing.
- Since long-term leases are not ordinarily shown as a long-term liability, the balance sheet of the seller-lessee will appear stronger, thereby enhancing the credit position of the lessee.
- By selling the development at a profit, the lessee is able to obtain cash today but repay with constantly inflating dollars. Additionally, the time value of money, due to the return on invested capital, works to the lessee's advantage.
- The owner may structure the sale so as to provide a buy-back privilege through a repurchase option.

Disadvantages to Seller

Obviously the seller may find some drawbacks to a sale and lease-back arrangement, including the following:

- The seller-lessee is committed to a lease contract that may run for a considerable length of time.
- Any increase in the value of the property will not accrue to the lessee's benefit.
- Fixed rental schedules may prove cumbersome, if not fatal, in times of economic distress. Even in normal times, the rents may be higher than payments on a fully amortizing loan.
- The expiration of the lease period may come at an inopportune time, with either no provision for renewal, or renewal only at excessively high rents. This might occur, for example, after the seller-lessee, who is using the property, has developed the business to a very successful level that may be due in large measure to the specific location of the property.

- When land only is sold and leased back, the costs to the seller-lessee of constructing improvements may absorb the bulk of the capital generated from the sale of the land.

Advantages to Buyer

Among the possible benefits or advantages to the buyer-lessor are the following:

- The sale-leaseback may return a higher yield than is available through a trust deed investment. Furthermore, there are none of the risks of a premature payoff that are associated with early retirement of a secured debt either through sale or refinancing of property. Hence, the investor-lessor will not need to be concerned with seeking alternative good-quality investments when suddenly confronted with a large amount of cash. (This is one of the reasons that lenders charge prepayment penalties on premature loan payoffs.) Also, the lessor has better control of the property through ownership than is gained through a security interest in a deed of trust.
- Any increase in value through appreciation will accrue to the lessor-owner.
- In the event of the lessee's default, the lessor may proceed against other assets of the lessee. When the lessee has a high credit rating, these assets may be substantial.
- Lease payments may be sufficiently large to recover the original investment several times over, in the case of long-term leases, and still leave the lessor with the fee title to the property. Moreover, by continued leasing, regardless of how long the leasehold period may extend, a capital gains tax is avoided.
- Depending on the arrangement, the lease could specify that the lessee is to pay for all repairs, maintenance, insurance, utilities, taxes, and operating expenses, so that the lessor is left with a carefree investment (such an arrangement is termed a **triple net lease**, or net-net-net.)
- A buyer in a poor cash position may be able to resell yet retain the same lessor interests through a second sale-leaseback arrangement.

Disadvantages to Buyer

- Lease payments to the lessor, including the first month's payment, and perhaps the last two months' payments, are fully taxable as ordinary income, after deducting lessor-incurred operating expenses.

- Unless carefully structured, the leasehold term may, in a time of inflation, favor the lessee, whose contractual rents in time may be less than the economic rent. A shrewd lessor will guard against such a prospect by inserting a clause that would tie the rents to an index, such as the Consumer Price Index (CPI) or the Producer's Price Index (PPI), a wholesale price index.

- If the lessee defaults, the buyer will have to operate the property. This may occur at an economically depressed time and could lead to disastrous consequences for the buyer.

- When only a ground lease is involved, the buyer-lessor will not be entitled to the benefits of depreciation deductions when the land is subsequently improved by the lessee.

- Capital that could otherwise be used in the buyer-lessor's business is tied up in equity.

- In the event of insolvency of the seller-lessee, the buyer-lessor's rights are restricted to those of a lessor only, and not to those of a secured creditor, for the balance owed on account of the purchase price.

- Though the lessee may be strong at the execution of the lease, the lessee may turn sour at a later date. If the lessee improves the property in a special way and then files for bankruptcy, the lessor may be left with a special-purpose development that is unsaleable and unleaseable.

- In times of inflation, the lessor is paid rents with constantly deteriorating dollars.

- When a repurchase option (which can be tied to an index) is inserted in the contract, the lessee may be allowed to profit at the expense of the lessor should the agreed repurchase price be significantly less than the value existing at the time the repurchase option is exercised.

14.6 OPEN-END TRUST DEED

In some deeds of trust, no provision is made for the borrower to secure additional funds. Thus, in order to obtain additional money to finance repairs or improvements, a borrower would need to refinance the property or seek other sources of funds. This could prove very expensive, not only because of the prepayment penalties and other costs incurred in such a transaction, but because of the added burden incurred when market rates are higher than the interest rate currently being paid on the note. Homeowners are particularly vulnerable, since dwellings cannot generate revenue as is the case with income-producing properties. Secondary financing may not be the answer because it is unavailable or very expensive.

The solution is to find a loan at the very outset that will include an open-end clause, permitting a borrower, at the lender's option, to add to the loan amount at periodic intervals. In addition to re-borrowing the amount repaid through amortization, the debtor could, in some cases, arrange to have the loan increased to reflect the appreciated value of the property. Such arrangements are more readily realized during times when demand for funds is sluggish, while the supply is abundant.

Under the open-end mortgage or trust deed, the new loan is added to the old one. Monthly payments can be increased to absorb the differential, or the term for repayment can be extended so that the combined loan will be amortized through monthly installments. Such clauses are permitted in government-backed as well as conventional loans. The procedure is to fill out an application, sign a new note, and record a notice of additional advance. The new note is still secured by the original deed of trust. The original note continues to carry the original interest rate and terms, while the new note can carry any interest rate and terms agreed by the parties. These do not merge into one debt. Moreover, the notice of additional advance does not have to be recorded to be valid, but it should be recorded to avoid possible situations where priority could be disturbed. This procedure dates back to the days when institutional lenders could not legally make loans secured by second deeds of trust unless they also held the first. It should be noted that since most lenders can now legally make second mortgages, the need for an open-end clause is less frequent.

14.7 COMMERCIAL LOAN

A nonmortgage way of financing real estate is through a loan from a commercial bank. Since these are unsecured, a **commercial loan** is usually of short duration, seldom extending beyond three years, and are ordinarily limited to borrowers of substance. And because there will be no real property collateral, reliance is placed on the credit of the borrower or other security. The amount and terms of the loan are based on the income and credit standing of the borrower, along with the condition of the money market. However, proceeds from a straight bank loan of this type can be used to purchase real estate or to finance home improvements.

If the prospective borrower is interested only in financing home improvements, a home improvement loan or installment purchase contract may be more advisable. This is ordinarily a secured transaction, in the nature of a secondary loan at relatively high interest, and repayable in periodic installments, usually monthly.

A third use for commercial loans is in the area of equity buying. Investors who specialize in purchasing at foreclosure and other forms of involuntary sales are required to pay all cash. After the property has been successfully acquired, repaired, and marketed, proceeds from the resale can in turn be used to pay off the commercial loan.

14.8 STOCK EQUITY/PLEDGED ASSET LOANS

A **stock equity** loan, another type of personal loan, is obtainable most commonly through a securities brokerage firm or commercial bank. Securities owned by the borrower, including those bought on margin—that is, with funds borrowed from the brokerage firm—are pledged as collateral. These include common and preferred stock, bonds, and debentures. One Wall Street firm did about half of its $10 billion in annual client home loans with pledged asset mortgages. Like the straight bank loan, the proceeds from the note can be used to purchase real estate, to finance desired improvements, or for further investment. Like the commercial loan, after the property's value is enhanced as a consequence of installing improvements, the appreciated value of the property will likely justify a significantly larger mortgage thereafter—in time to pay off the short-term note at maturity.

14.9 BLENDED-RATE LOANS

As an alternative to all-inclusive or other forms of seller carryback, the buyer-borrower may consider approaching a lender for a **blended-rate loan**, also called blended-yield. Under this plan the buyer would not take over an existing low-interest-rate loan, because it may have too low a balance. Instead, a new loan for a higher amount is negotiated with the existing lender, providing an interest rate that is based upon a weighted average of the relatively low existing rate and the relatively high rate charged on the added funds needed to complete the purchase of a property.

The central idea is to combine the low existing contract rate and the high new market rate into a blended rate that accomplishes two objectives: (1) increases the loan amount and (2) blends the two interest rates into one single rate that is higher than the existing rate but lower than the market rate. Such an approach is especially important if the existing loan is callable, that is, if the alienation clause is enforceable.

The method for determining the blended yield, or weighted average between the old and new interest rates, is as follows:

$$\text{Blended yield} = \frac{(\text{Existing rate} \times \text{Existing loan balance}) + (\text{Market rate} \times \text{Net new money})}{\text{Total financing}}$$

In the numerator we have essentially the total annualized interest cost. In the denominator, total financing consists of both the old loan and the amount added thereto, so we could call this combined figure the new loan amount. An example will help clarify.

Example: Assume that interest rates skyrocket during a credit crunch and you are buying a $225,000 property that has an existing loan of $80,000 at 10 percent. You need a total of $180,000, however, after the 20 percent ($45,000) down payment. Assume that the existing lender is charging 15 percent for new loans. What will be the probable charge under a blended rate?

$$\text{Blended yield} = \frac{(10\% \times \$80,000 + (15\% \times \$100,000)}{\$180,000}$$

$$\text{Blended yield} = \frac{\$8,000 + \$15,000}{\$180,000}$$

$$\text{Blended yield} = 12.78\%$$

The 12.78 percent rate, which may be rounded up to 12 7/8 (12.875) percent by the lender, is higher than the 10 percent on the existing loan, but lower than the 15 percent market rate.

Benefits of the Blended Rate

- Buyers receive a below-market rate.
- The borrower qualifies more easily, since the loan is based upon a lower rate.
- Cash proceeds are greater, so that the seller is not required to carry back as much paper.
- The lender has an opportunity to increase its effective yield on old low-rate loan balances. Indeed, the blended rate need not necessarily be a fixed rate but can be a variable or adjustable blended rate.

TABLE 14.1 Blended yield with seller carryback of junior trust deed.

	Loan Amount	×	Interest Rate	=	Annualized Interest Cost
Existing loan balance	$80,000		10%		$ 8,000
Net new money	70,000		15		10,500
Second trust deed	30,000		12		3,600
Totals	$180,000				$22,100

$$\text{Blended yield} = \frac{\$\ 22,100}{\$180,000} = 12.28\%$$

- The blended-yield loan can be made even more creative through seller participation when financing is tight. Referring to the previous example, suppose the existing lender is willing to offer total financing of only $150,000, and not $180,000, and that the seller is willing to accept a note secured by a second trust deed for the balance of $30,000 at 12 percent per annum. What is the effective or blended rate? Table 14.1 summarizes the data and provides the answer. The blended rate for the three separate rates is 12.28 percent, or 0.5 percent less than the blended rate of 12.78 percent in the previous case, where the seller did not participate in the financing.

14.10 CREATIVE FINANCING DISCLOSURE ACT

For the protection of both sellers and buyers when sellers are to carry back loans in the sale of properties of from one to four dwelling units, certain disclosures must be made. These usually involve small investors or individuals dealing with private homes, who are less likely to understand the obligations and difficulties involved with creative financing. The law requires that arrangers of credit, usually real estate brokers involved in the sale of the property, must disclose the following items for the benefit of the buyer-borrower:

1. Description of the terms of the loan taken back by the seller.
2. Description of any other financing on the property.
3. A warning that if refinancing of the seller's existing loan is required because of negative amortization, such financing might be difficult or impossible to obtain.

4. If an AITD is involved, information about who is responsible for potential problems with senior trust deeds.

5. Terms of any balloon payments involved in the transaction.

The law also requires disclosures by agents for the seller's benefit, including:

6. Credit information about the buyer, including occupation, employment, income, debts, and the like. In the alternative, a written statement may be made that no representation as to the creditworthiness of the buyer is being made by the credit arranger.

7. Warnings to the seller about antideficiency limitations available to the seller in case of the buyer's default, if applicable.

Additional provisions of the law include requirements for balloon payments. Holders of such loans on one-to-four-unit dwellings must give written notices to the debtor not less than 90 days, nor more than 150 days, before the balloon payment is due, with date due, amount, and a description of the rights of the borrower to refinance the balloon. Failure to provide the notice does not excuse the liability, but the holder cannot collect the payment until 90 days after proper notice is made. See Figure 14.6 for the creative financing disclosure form most commonly used in California.

14.11 IMPUTED INTEREST

The **imputed interest** rule was included as part of the 1984 tax act in order to stop tax avoidance by people making loans at artificially low interest rates. The IRS requires that an **applicable federal rate (AFR)** be applied to all loans of six or more months in duration, with the specific minimum rate determined by the term of the mortgage instrument. The AFR that applies is the published rate for the month in which any applicable loan is created. The old rule of thumb was that the seller had to carry at 9 percent interest or the AFR, whichever was lower. In recent years, the AFR has been in the 5 percent or less range and has had less effect on seller-carry financing than in the past.

Why is the IRS concerned with the interest rate on these seller carry loans? The IRS is afraid that a seller who carries at a very low interest rate will be able to increase the sales price. The increase in sales price would be taxed at a low capital gain tax rate, rather than the higher ordinary rate that applies to interest income. This imputed interest rule is complicated and, if necessary, counsel should be sought from a CPA or directly from the IRS at www.irs.gov.

FIGURE 14.6 Sample seller financing disclosure statement.

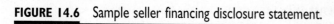

CALIFORNIA
ASSOCIATION
OF REALTORS®

SELLER FINANCING ADDENDUM AND DISCLOSURE
(California Civil Code §§2956-2967)

(C.A.R. Form SFA, Revised 10/02)

This is an addendum to the ☐ Residential Purchase Agreement, ☐ Counter Offer, or ☐ Other _____
_____, ("Agreement"), dated _____,
On property known as _____ ("Property"),
between _____ ("Buyer"),
and _____ ("Seller").
Seller agrees to extend credit to Buyer as follows:
1. **PRINCIPAL; INTEREST; PAYMENT; MATURITY TERMS:** ☐ Principal amount $ _____, interest at _____%
    per annum, payable at approximately $ _____ per ☐ month, ☐ year, or ☐ other _____,
    remaining principal balance due in _____ years.
2. **LOAN APPLICATION; CREDIT REPORT:** Within **5 (or ☐ _____) Days** After Acceptance: **(a)** Buyer shall provide Seller a completed
    loan application on a form acceptable to Seller (such as a FNMA/FHLMC Uniform Residential Loan Application for residential one to four
    unit properties); and **(b)** Buyer authorizes Seller and/or Agent to obtain, at Buyer's expense, a copy of Buyer's credit report. Buyer shall
    provide any supporting documentation reasonably requested by Seller. Seller, after first giving Buyer a Notice to Buyer to Perform, may
    cancel this Agreement in writing and authorize return of Buyer's deposit if Buyer fails to provide such documents within that time, or if
    Seller disapproves any above item within **5 (or ☐ _____) Days** After receipt of each item.
3. **CREDIT DOCUMENTS:** This extension of credit by Seller will be evidenced by: ☐ Note and deed of trust; ☐ All-inclusive
    note and deed of trust; ☐ Installment land sale contract; ☐ Lease/option (when parties intend transfer of equitable title);
    OR ☐ Other (specify) _____
    **THE FOLLOWING TERMS APPLY ONLY IF CHECKED. SELLER IS ADVISED TO READ ALL TERMS, EVEN THOSE NOT
    CHECKED, TO UNDERSTAND WHAT IS OR IS NOT INCLUDED, AND, IF NOT INCLUDED, THE CONSEQUENCES THEREOF.**
4. ☐ **LATE CHARGE:** If any payment is not made within _____ **Days** After it is due, a late charge of either $ _____,
    or _____% of the installment due, may be charged to Buyer. **NOTE:** On single family residences that Buyer intends to occupy,
    California Civil Code §2954.4(a) limits the late charge to no more than 6% of the total installment payment due and requires a
    grace period of no less than 10 days.
5. ☐ **BALLOON PAYMENT:** The extension of credit will provide for a balloon payment, in the amount of $ _____,
    plus any accrued interest, which is due on _____ (date).
6. ☐ **PREPAYMENT:** If all or part of this extension of credit is paid early, Seller may charge a prepayment penalty as follows (if
    applicable): _____. Caution: California Civil Code
    §2954.9 contains limitations on prepayment penalties for residential one-to-four unit properties.
7. ☐ **DUE ON SALE:** If any interest in the Property is sold or otherwise transferred, Seller has the option to require immediate
    payment of the entire unpaid principal balance, plus any accrued interest.
8.* ☐ **REQUEST FOR COPY OF NOTICE OF DEFAULT:** A request for a copy of Notice of Default as defined in California Civil
    Code §2924b will be recorded. **If Not**, Seller is advised to consider recording a Request for Notice of Default.
9.* ☐ **REQUEST FOR NOTICE OF DELINQUENCY:** A request for Notice of Delinquency, as defined in California Civil Code §2924e,
    to be signed and paid for by Buyer, will be made to senior lienholders. **If not**, Seller is advised to consider making a Request for
    Notice of Delinquency. Seller is advised to check with senior lienholders to verify whether they will honor this request.
10.* ☐ **TAX SERVICE:**
    A. If property taxes on the Property become delinquent, tax service will be arranged to report to Seller. **If not**, Seller is
    advised to consider retaining a tax service, or to otherwise determine that property taxes are paid.
    B. ☐ Buyer, ☐ Seller, shall be responsible for the initial and continued retention of, and payment for, such tax service.
11. ☐ **TITLE INSURANCE:** Title insurance coverage will be provided to **both** Seller and Buyer, insuring their respective interests
    in the Property. **If not**, Buyer and Seller are advised to consider securing such title insurance coverage.
12. ☐ **HAZARD INSURANCE:**
    A. The parties' escrow holder or insurance carrier will be directed to include a loss payee endorsement, adding Seller to
    the Property insurance policy. **If not**, Seller is advised to secure such an endorsement, or acquire a separate
    insurance policy.
    B. Property insurance **does not** include earthquake or flood insurance coverage, unless checked:
    ☐ Earthquake insurance will be obtained; ☐ Flood insurance will be obtained.
13. ☐ **PROCEEDS TO BUYER:** Buyer will receive cash proceeds at the close of the sale transaction. The amount received will be
    approximately $ _____, from _____ (indicate source of
    proceeds). Buyer represents that the purpose of such disbursement is as follows: _____
14. ☐ **NEGATIVE AMORTIZATION; DEFERRED INTEREST:** Negative amortization results when Buyer's periodic payments are
    less than the amount of interest earned on the obligation. Deferred interest also results when the obligation does not
    require periodic payments for a period of time. In either case, interest is not payable as it accrues. This accrued interest
    will have to be paid by Buyer at a later time, and may result in Buyer owing more on the obligation than at its origination.
    The credit being extended to Buyer by Seller will provide for negative amortization or deferred interest as indicated below.
    (Check A, B, or C. CHECK ONE ONLY.)
    ☐ **A.** All negative amortization or deferred interest shall be added to the principal _____
    (e.g., annually, monthly, etc.), and thereafter shall bear interest at the rate specified in the credit documents (compound interest);
    OR ☐ **B.** All deferred interest shall be due and payable, along with principal, at maturity;
    OR ☐ **C.** Other _____.

*(For Paragraphs 8-10) In order to receive timely and continued notification, Seller is advised to record appropriate notices and/or to
notify appropriate parties of any change in Seller's address.

SFA REVISED 10/02 (PAGE 1 OF 3) Print Date

Buyer's Initials (_____)(_____)
Seller's Initials (_____)(_____)

Reviewed by _____ Date _____

EQUAL HOUSING
OPPORTUNITY

SELLER FINANCING ADDENDUM AND DISCLOSURE (SFA PAGE 1 OF 3)

FIGURE 14.6   Sample seller financing disclosure statement. (*continued*)

Property Address: _____   Date: _____

15. ☐ **ALL-INCLUSIVE DEED OF TRUST; INSTALLMENT LAND SALE CONTRACT:** This transaction involves the use of an all-inclusive (or wraparound) deed of trust or an installment land sale contract. That deed of trust or contract shall provide as follows:
     A. In the event of an acceleration of any senior encumbrance, the responsibility for payment, or for legal defense is: _____
     _____ ; OR ☐ **Is not** specified in the credit or security documents.
     B. In the event of the prepayment of a senior encumbrance, the responsibilities and rights of Buyer and Seller regarding refinancing, prepayment penalties, and any prepayment discounts are: _____ ;
     OR ☐ **Are not** specified in the documents evidencing credit.
     C. Buyer will make periodic payments to _____ (Seller, collection agent, or any neutral third party), who will be responsible for disbursing payments to the payee(s) on the senior encumbrance(s) and to Seller. **NOTE:** The Parties are advised to designate a neutral third party for these purposes.

16. ☐ **TAX IDENTIFICATION NUMBERS:** Buyer and Seller shall each provide to each other their Social Security Numbers or Taxpayer Identification Numbers.

17. ☐ **OTHER CREDIT TERMS** _____

18. ☐ **RECORDING:** The documents evidencing credit (paragraph 3) will be recorded with the county recorder where the Property is located. **If not**, Buyer and Seller are advised that their respective interests in the Property may be jeopardized by intervening liens, judgments, encumbrances, or subsequent transfers.

19. ☐ **JUNIOR FINANCING:** There will be additional financing, secured by the Property, junior to this Seller financing. Explain: _____

20. **SENIOR LOANS AND ENCUMBRANCES:** The following information is provided on loans and/or encumbrances that will be **senior** to Seller financing. **NOTE:** The following are estimates, unless otherwise marked with an asterisk (*). If checked: ☐ A separate sheet with information on additional senior loans/encumbrances is attached

		1st	2nd
A.	Original Balance	$ _____	$ _____
B.	Current Balance	$ _____	$ _____
C.	Periodic Payment (e.g. $100/month):	$ _____	$ _____ / _____
	Including Impounds of:	$ _____	$ _____ / _____
D.	Interest Rate (per annum)	_____ %	_____ %
E.	Fixed or Variable Rate:	_____	_____
	If Variable Rate: Lifetime Cap (Ceiling)	_____	_____
	Indicator (Underlying Index)	_____	_____
	Margins	_____	_____
F.	Maturity Date	_____	_____
G.	Amount of Balloon Payment	$ _____	$ _____
H.	Date Balloon Payment Due	_____	_____
I.	Potential for Negative Amortization? (Yes, No, or Unknown)	_____	_____
J.	Due on Sale? (Yes, No, or Unknown)	_____	_____
K.	Pre-payment penalty? (Yes, No, or Unknown)	_____	_____
L.	Are payments current? (Yes, No, or Unknown)	_____	_____

21. **BUYER'S CREDITWORTHINESS:** (CHECK EITHER A OR B. Do not check both.) In addition to the loan application, credit report and other information requested under paragraph 2:
     A. ☐ No other disclosure concerning Buyer's creditworthiness has been made to Seller;
OR B. ☐ The following representations concerning Buyer's creditworthiness are made by Buyer(s) to Seller:

Borrower _____	Co-Borrower _____
1. Occupation _____	1. Occupation _____
2. Employer _____	2. Employer _____
3. Length of Employment _____	3. Length of Employment _____
4. Monthly Gross Income _____	4. Monthly Gross Income _____
5. Other _____	5. Other _____

22. **ADDED, DELETED OR SUBSTITUTED BUYERS:** The addition, deletion or substitution of any person or entity under this Agreement or to title prior to close of escrow shall require Seller's written consent. Seller may grant or withhold consent in Seller's sole discretion. Any additional or substituted person or entity shall, if requested by Seller, submit to Seller the same documentation as required for the original named Buyer. Seller and/or Brokers may obtain a credit report, at Buyer's expense, on any such person or entity.

Buyer's Initials (_____)(_____)
Seller's Initials (_____)(_____)

SFA REVISED 10/02 (PAGE 2 OF 3)

Reviewed by _____ Date _____

EQUAL HOUSING OPPORTUNITY

SELLER FINANCING ADDENDUM AND DISCLOSURE (SFA PAGE 2 OF 3)

FIGURE 14.6   Sample seller financing disclosure statement. (*continued*)

Property Address: _____   Date: _____

23. CAUTION:

    A. If the Seller financing requires a balloon payment, Seller shall give Buyer written notice, according to the terms of Civil Code §2966, at least 90 and not more than 150 days before the balloon payment is due if the transaction is for the purchase of a dwelling for not more than four families.

    B. If **any** obligation secured by the Property calls for a balloon payment, Seller and Buyer are aware that refinancing of the balloon payment at maturity may be difficult or impossible, depending on conditions in the conventional mortgage marketplace at that time. There are no assurances that new financing or a loan extension will be available when the balloon prepayment, or any prepayment, is due.

    C. If **any** of the existing or proposed loans or extensions of credit would require refinancing as a result of a lack of full amortization, such refinancing might be difficult or impossible in the conventional mortgage marketplace.

    D. In the event of default by Buyer: (1) Seller may have to reinstate and/or make monthly payments on any and all senior encumbrances (including real property taxes) in order to protect Seller's secured interest; (2) Seller's rights are generally limited to foreclosure on the Property, pursuant to California Code of Civil Procedure §580b; and (3) the Property may lack sufficient equity to protect Seller's interests if the Property decreases in value.

If this three-page Addendum and Disclosure is used in a transaction for the purchase of a dwelling for not more than four families, it shall be prepared by an Arranger of Credit as defined in California Civil Code §2957(a). (The Arranger of Credit is usually the agent who obtained the offer.)

Arranger of Credit - (Print Firm Name) _____   By _____   Date _____

Address _____   City _____   State _____   Zip _____

Phone _____   Fax _____

BUYER AND SELLER ACKNOWLEDGE AND AGREE THAT BROKERS: (A) WILL NOT PROVIDE LEGAL OR TAX ADVICE; (B) WILL NOT PROVIDE OTHER ADVICE OR INFORMATION THAT EXCEEDS THE KNOWLEDGE, EDUCATION AND EXPERIENCE REQUIRED TO OBTAIN A REAL ESTATE LICENSE; OR (C) HAVE NOT AND WILL NOT VERIFY ANY INFORMATION PROVIDED BY EITHER BUYER OR SELLER. BUYER AND SELLER AGREE THAT THEY WILL SEEK LEGAL, TAX AND OTHER DESIRED ASSISTANCE FROM APPROPRIATE PROFESSIONALS. BUYER AND SELLER ACKNOWLEDGE THAT THE INFORMATION EACH HAS PROVIDED TO THE ARRANGER OF CREDIT FOR INCLUSION IN THIS DISCLOSURE FORM IS ACCURATE. BUYER AND SELLER FURTHER ACKNOWLEDGE THAT EACH HAS RECEIVED A COMPLETED COPY OF THIS DISCLOSURE FORM.

Buyer _____   Date _____
    (signature)

Address _____   City _____   State _____   Zip _____

Phone _____   Fax _____   E-mail _____

Buyer _____   Date _____
    (signature)

Address _____   City _____   State _____   Zip _____

Phone _____   Fax _____   E-mail _____

Seller _____   Date _____
    (signature)

Address _____   City _____   State _____   Zip _____

Phone _____   Fax _____   E-mail _____

Seller _____   Date _____
    (signature)

Address _____   City _____   State _____   Zip _____

Phone _____   Fax _____   E-mail _____

THIS FORM HAS BEEN APPROVED BY THE CALIFORNIA ASSOCIATION OF REALTORS® (C.A.R.). NO REPRESENTATION IS MADE AS TO THE LEGAL VALIDITY OR ADEQUACY OF ANY PROVISION IN ANY SPECIFIC TRANSACTION. A REAL ESTATE BROKER IS THE PERSON QUALIFIED TO ADVISE ON REAL ESTATE TRANSACTIONS. IF YOU DESIRE LEGAL OR TAX ADVICE, CONSULT AN APPROPRIATE PROFESSIONAL.

This form is available for use by the entire real estate industry. It is not intended to identify the user as a REALTOR®. REALTOR® is a registered collective membership mark which may be used only by members of the NATIONAL ASSOCIATION OF REALTORS® who subscribe to its Code of Ethics.

SURE TRAC
The System for Success®

Published and Distributed by:
REAL ESTATE BUSINESS SERVICES, INC.
a subsidiary of the California Association of REALTORS®
525 South Virgil Avenue, Los Angeles, California 90020

SFA REVISED 10/02 (PAGE 3 OF 3)

| Reviewed by _____ Date _____ |

EQUAL HOUSING OPPORTUNITY

SELLER FINANCING ADDENDUM AND DISCLOSURE (SFA PAGE 3 OF 3)

Source: Reprinted with permission of California Association of REALTORS®.

Special note: This imputed interest provision does not apply to seller carryback loans in which buyers use the property as their principal residence.

The whole idea of imputed interest rates is to prevent sellers from converting interest income on deferred payments from ordinary income tax rates to the lower capital gains tax rate by making interest a part of the purchase price without specifying it as interest. Thus, if a seller carryback fails to specify any interest, or provides for an unreasonably low rate, the IRS may step in and read into the agreement its own interpretation of what it should be, thereby restructuring the transaction in a way that converts some of the capital gain into ordinary income.

SUMMARY

Secondary financing techniques include notes secured by second trust deeds carried back by sellers, representing the gap between sales price and liens now on the property or to be placed thereon. Collateralizing junior loans is a method by which existing loans are pledged as security for a loan without giving up legal title to the junior trust deed. Brokers may resort to a variety of techniques to put together transactions when the money market is tight.

All-inclusive deeds of trust are used in a variety of ways. They may be used in lieu of land contracts or when a lock-in clause is enforceable by a beneficiary. Low down payments, especially with an overpriced listing, make the AITD a mutually attractive vehicle. Care must be exercised to structure the AITD properly, including minimum interest rates that must be charged under the imputed interest rules, so as to protect both seller and buyer.

Lenders may increase their yields through participations or "equity kickers." They can participate in the revenue of a project, take a percentage of the equity, charge fees or discounts, or participate in the profit.

Sale-leaseback, open-end trust deeds, stock equity, and commercial loans are further examples of financing that can be effected through other-than-traditional approaches. Indeed, financing schemes are limited only by the knowledge, creativity, and ingenuity of the people involved. It should be noted that with the 2009 changes in home financing enacted by Fannie Mae and Freddie Mac, these lending techniques are more suited to larger loan transactions which often involve corporate borrowers.

IMPORTANT TERMS AND CONCEPTS

All-inclusive trust deed (AITD)

Applicable federal rate (AFR)

Blended-rate loan

Collateralization

Commercial loan

Creative Financing Disclosure Act

Due-on-sale clause

Imputed interest

Installment sales contract

Participation

Purchase money mortgages

Sale-leaseback

Seller carryback

Stock equity

Triple net lease

Wrap-around Trust Deed

REVIEWING YOUR UNDERSTANDING

Questions for Discussion

1. How does collateralization of a junior loan provide for retention of the legal title by the junior holder?

2. In what ways may a broker use junior liens to put together a real estate transaction when money is "tight"?

3. Describe five ways in which an all-inclusive trust deed can be more effectively used instead of the traditional junior trust deed transaction.

4. List three ways in which lenders may increase their yields through participations.

5. State the basic purpose of the Creative Financing Disclosure Act. Do you think this law is accomplishing what it was intended to accomplish?

Multiple-Choice Questions

1. Jayne Buyer is unable to meet a balloon payment on a junior lien now that it came due. Among her remedies might be to
   a. renegotiate the junior loan.
   b. secure a new loan from outside sources.
   c. refinance the entire loan.
   d. seek out any of the foregoing remedies.

2. A purchase money junior lien, given back to a seller, that includes the amount of the first encumbrance as well as any secondary liens, is called
   a. a hold-harmful lien.
   b. a wrap-around loan.
   c. a due-on-encumbrance lien.
   d. an overextension loan.

3. Retention of legal title by the seller in the financing of property is accomplished through the use of which one of the following instruments?
   a. all-inclusive trust deed.
   b. mortgage instrument.
   c. installment land contract.
   d. exchange agreement.

4. Assume a property is to sell for $160,000. It has an existing first loan of $78,000 and a second lien of $20,000. If a purchaser pays 15 percent as a down payment and an all-inclusive deed of trust is to be used to finance the transaction, the seller's remaining equity at close of escrow will amount to
   a. $38,000.
   b. $58,000.
   c. $62,000.
   d. $116,000.

5. A lender holding a junior trust deed, who wants to be informed when defaults and foreclosures occur on senior liens, should record:
   a. Assignment of Note and Trust Deed.
   b. Request for Notice of Default and Notice of Sale.
   c. Disclosure Statement.
   d. Collateral Security Agreement.

6. A variation of the secondary financing approach to solving real estate finance problems, wherein a junior trust deed is assigned to the licensee for part or all of his commission, is referred to as
   a. a broker participation loan.
   b. an assignment loan.
   c. a split junior lien.
   d. an open-end trust lien.

7. An all-inclusive trust deed is characterized by which one of the following statements?
   a. The seller-trustor under the existing liens becomes the beneficiary under the all-inclusive deed of trust.
   b. It is a senior encumbrance that includes all of the underlying liens.
   c. Legal title is retained until the terms and conditions of the lien are satisfied.
   d. Title insurance is not issued at the time of the sale.

8. Under the Creative Financing Disclosure Act, the written disclosure is prepared by the
   a. buyer.
   b. seller.
   c. insurer.
   d. agent.

9. Lenders may take participation interests in a property on which they are making a loan in a variety of ways. Which of the following would be the least likely method of participating in a lending transaction?
   a. a one-time initial points charge.
   b. open-end provisions.
   c. participation in the equity.
   d. revenue sharing.

10. Creative financing refers to techniques that are
    a. insured or guaranteed.
    b. used by institutional lenders to avoid banking regulations.
    c. legally used to finance a property in a nontraditional manner.
    d. commonly used on most home loans.

11. If you collateralize a note secured by a second deed of trust, it means that
    a. the note and deed of trust is sold at a discount.
    b. a third party lends money using the note and second deed of trust as security.
    c. the beneficiary's interest therein has been fully transferred.
    d. an additional junior lien has been created on the secured property.

12. An all-inclusive trust deed cannot be used to
    a. increase the seller's yield.
    b. lower the buyer's closing costs.
    c. help generate a higher sales price.
    d. avoid an enforceable due-on-sale clause.

13. A disadvantage found in a sale-leaseback transaction is that
    a. the seller-lessee can take full tax deduction for lease payments.
    b. the buyer-lessor gets a steady tenant.
    c. the seller-lessee can write off depreciation on improvements he or she adds.
    d. payments to buyer-lessor are taxed as ordinary income.

14. A $100,000 loan at 10 percent interest with payments of $800 per month appears to be
    a. fully amortized.
    b. partially amortized.
    c. negatively amortized.
    d. fundamentally sound.

15. Assume a new loan amount of $180,000 under a blended-rate arrangement. The existing loan has an $80,000 balance at 10 percent interest per annum. The rate the lender seeks for new loans is 15 percent. The blended rate will compute at
    a. 10.722 percent.
    b. 13.33 percent.
    c. 12.5 percent.
    d. 12.778 percent.

16. Legal title is transferred to the buyer by a deed when the property is financed by using
    a. an installment sales contract.
    b. an all-inclusive trust deed.
    c. a land contract.
    d. an agreement of sale contract.

17. You sold your home for $300,000. The buyers pay 15 percent down and secure a first trust deed for 80 percent of the purchase price. The amount needed to fill in the gap will be
    a. $30,000.
    b. $45,000.
    c. $22,500.
    d. $15,000.

18. Under the Creative Financing Disclosure Act, the agent must disclose the drawbacks of creative financing to
    a. all subagents to a transaction.
    b. buyers only.
    c. sellers only.
    d. both buyers and sellers.

19. The imputed interest rules found in the Internal Revenue Code apply to
    a. certain seller carryback loans.
    b. assumptions of existing loans.
    c. loans at 10 percent or greater interest rate.
    d. new loans granted by institutional lenders.

20. A creative financing scheme is best illustrated by
    a. seller carrying back a first trust deed loan for 25 percent of the sale price.
    b. seller carrying back under an all-inclusive trust deed.
    c. buyer paying 10 percent down, obtaining the balance through a PMI loan.
    d. buyer paying 50 percent down and getting a private hard-money loan for the balance.

CASE & POINT

Fraud Enforcement and Recovery Act (FERA)

The Fraud Enforcement and Recovery Act became law in May of 2009. Its focus was on mortgage fraud; it was based upon a congressional perception that rampant mortgage fraud was a major cause of the mortgage crises. Additionally, the perception was that mortgage brokers and nonfederally regulated lenders purposefully participated in predatory lending practices to misguide borrowers and that all parties intentionally encouraged borrowers to acquire loans that they could not afford and that later could not refinance.

The law addressed primarily two areas of loan origination:

1. Blatant falsification of mortgage application and documentation information.
2. The use and abuse of reduced-documentation loan programs mostly introduced in the subprime market and referred to as stated-income or no-income documented loans.

Anticipation was that the legislation would have little impact upon most lenders who had performed honestly and without participation in predatory lending practices. The legislation failed to recognize that the offending loan instruments were introduced to mortgage brokers by major lender representatives. These "loan reps" promoted these easy-to-acquire loan options and, in many cases, instructed brokers in how to submit their loans for easy underwriting approval. Most of these methods included exaggerating borrowers' income or not reporting it at all.

This emphasis on what became known as "liar loans" were accompanied by several of-used mantras at the time:

- It is the new wave of lending and everyone is doing it.
- I am helping borrowers acquire the American dream of homeownership.
- There is no way to lose, with home values escalating. If the borrower cannot make future adjusted payments, they can always sell the home for a big profit.

None of the rationalizations can excuse the fact that some brokers willingly took part in fraudulent practices, knowing that they were putting borrowers into untenable loan options. Perhaps the most egregious rationale was "if I don't give the buyer this loan, someone else will": in other words, tacitly acknowledging that it was not a good loan but being willing to do it anyway.

Misrepresentation and falsification of borrower information and documentation have always been a federal offense. While seemingly focused on mortgage brokers and nonfederally regulated entities, the legislation, in addition to mentioning fraud and tougher regulation, specifically addressed monetary policy, accounting practices, capital requirements, the concept of too-big-to-fail institutions, compensation structures, and other Wall Street excess that have been recently exposed.

While not majorly impacting mortgage brokers, particularly those who did not participate in any of the offending lending practices, FERA did pave the way for the adoption of the Home Value Code of Conduct (HVCC) that did affect the lending business (see the HVCC Case & Point at the end of Chapter 8).

The message for all lenders, including mortgage brokers, who want to protect themselves against unintended complications related to this new oversight is to concentrate on the basics of loan file documentation. In other words, return to the old-fashioned method of verifying everything. In addition to guarding against consumer fraud, it is important to develop a zero tolerance policy for originator and processor shortcuts. The result will be to reinstill consumer confidence in the loan process as well as to protect the licenses of loan originators and avoid any and all inferences of fraud or other criminal allegations. If this is accomplished, FERA will have been successful.

Chapter

15

PREVIEW

"What you owe today you are worth tomorrow!" This statement was made some years ago by a prominent Chicago real estate economist who advocated the purchase of investment real estate with as little cash down payment as possible and with maximum financing. The buyer could then either exchange upward or refinance and buy other properties with maximum financing until the buyer owed the amount of money he or she eventually wanted to be worth. At that point the buyer could halt buying and simply continue managing the existing property until the loans were paid off. The buyer would then be worth what he or she owed, and probably a lot more as inflation raised the real estate prices.

In this chapter we examine the financing characteristics of different residential investment properties—single-family dwellings, two-to-four-unit dwellings, and large apartment houses—and stress the advantages and disadvantages of each type of investment. Finally, we introduce the financing of commercial and industrial properties.

After completing this chapter, you should be able to:

1. Describe financing alternatives for residential income, commercial, and industrial properties.
2. List and briefly explain advantages and disadvantages to investing in each of the categories of investment property.
3. Calculate and apply "break-even analysis" to income-producing properties.
4. Discuss how financing conditions affect prices of income-producing properties.
5. Compute debt-coverage ratios.

Financing Small Investment Properties

15.1 THE SINGLE-FAMILY HOUSE AS INCOME PROPERTY

Key Characteristics

There is usually a large supply of single-family properties on the market from which to make a selection and management is usually easier than practically any other type of residential property. A single-family residence (SFR) generally has an active resale market, thus offering a higher degree of liquidity for investors, since it can sell faster than other types of property. Using what is known as a 1031 Tax Deferred Exchange, real estate can be sold outright or exchanged, with taxes deferred, for other *like-kind* property. Another way to describe eligible exchange property is "real for real," meaning that real property must be exchanged for other qualified real property and cannot be exchanged for personal property. Under this definition, a rental home can be exchanged for another rental home, multiple units, apartment complex, commercial property, or unimproved property (land).

Kinds of Financing Available for Nonowner-Occupied Single-Family Dwellings

A nonowner-occupied conventional loan of 75 percent of the lower of appraised value or the purchase price is the most often available loan from the majority of lending institutions, down from the 90 percent LTV loans that were routinely made prior to 2009. Fannie Mae and Freddie Mac will make financing available up to the 80 percent loan-to-value level, but the cost for this extra 5 percent loan balance is considerable. Plus, few borrowers can meet the qualifying criteria to borrow at this level because the result is nearly always a considerable negative cash flow. FNMA/FHLMC now require a borrower to have at least one year's experience as a landlord to be eligible for nonowner financing or the borrower must have a minimum of six months PITI reserve at the close of escrow. Lenders usually factor in no more than 75 percent of existing rents to help the borrower qualify for the note payments.

Complete seller financing is also possible, though unlikely. Many owners have had homes for years and own them free and clear. Rather than sell for cash, some may sell on an installment sale plan, charging the buyer an interest rate that generates a monthly cash flow. To accomplish this cash flow, a seller could also rent out the property. For most sellers, their goal is to cash out or exchange.

Interest Rate and Other Loan Terms for Rental Houses

Conventional lenders generally ask for 0.25 to 0.5 percent more interest on a rental home than if the same home were owner occupied. Of all residential rental properties, the single-family home commands the lowest interest rate and the best overall terms.

Conventional lenders may ask for the same loan fee or points from buyers as in the case of an owner-occupied home, but depending on their perceived risk they may ask for a higher loan fee.

Term of loan, late charges, and other provisions are generally the same as on owner-occupied, single-family homes. While adjustable rate loans were popular, as the economy worsened in 2007, fixed rate financing became the loan of choice for both lenders and investors.

Generally there are no prepayment penalties with fixed rate loans. California law limits prepayment penalties for owner-occupied, single-family homes to the first three years (seven years for loans covered under the Mortgage Loan Broker Law). The majority of nonowner-occupied loans follow this same rule. The prepayment requirements can differ, though, if the rental property loan is made by a niche lender.

Note: As the real estate market is cyclical and there are times when home values escalate, a term has been introduced to the lending world: "flipping." Investors purchase a home with the express purpose of holding it for a short period of time during escalating prices and selling it for an immediate profit. This was particularly true in 2006 and 2007 when savvy investors would enter long escrow periods, during which the property would appreciate, and then would often sell the property prior to having closed their original escrow. When the market suddenly changed and home values declined, investors found themselves holding homes which they could no longer sell, let alone sell for a profit. The result in 2008 and 2009 was that many investors simply "walked away" from these home investments. Is it any wonder that lenders have become reluctant to make non-owner occupied home loans? This helps us understand why the underwriting guidelines have toughened for these loans. Even in a flat market, with little or no escalation, some investors look for underpriced property or foreclosures to flip. Although less frequent in these times, these investors primarily use all-cash purchases and may not even do any repairs on the property.

Advantages of the Single-Family Home as an Investment Vehicle

1. A large selection of properties is usually available.
2. Management is easier than on other types of income properties.
3. The investment is more liquid than other forms of real property.
4. Tenants usually pay for all utilities and do the gardening and minor repairs, in contrast to larger properties where these services are furnished by outside employees or a property manager.
5. The ratio of improvements to overall investment may be high, giving a greater **depreciation** write-off, generally from 70 percent to 80 percent. This gives a greater tax shelter to the investor, since improvements are depreciable while investments in raw land are nondepreciable.
6. Tenants usually remain longer in single-family homes than in apartments. These tenants are often families, who may also be more financially stable.
7. Passive loss rules apply to rental houses, allowing investors to deduct up to $25,000 of losses against certain other taxable income, such as wages, salary, interest, dividends, etc.
8. Few people build single-family homes for investment, so there is little danger of glutting the market with competitive rentals. Thus vacancy factors in single-family homes are lower than in any other type of residential investment.
9. Home prices tend to rise more quickly and at a greater rate in inflationary years than for any other class of investment property, thereby giving investors a good hedge against inflation.
10. Investors were able to **leverage** (e.g., purchase with minimal down payment) single-family homes during the inflationary periods. However, when *home values sometimes decline, resulting in*

mortgages that exceeded home values, some investors choose to "walk away" from their home investment.

11. A single-family dwelling that is rented can be exchanged for other rental property or raw land of equal or greater value under section 1031 of the Internal Revenue Code.

Disadvantages of the Single-Family Home as an Investment Vehicle

1. *Cash flow.* Even with lower home prices, increasing rents, and possibly lower interest rates, it is difficult to leverage a home investment that will not generate a **negative cash flow**, that is, where the income is less than the outgo, even after an allowance for a tax shelter. The lender will require the investor to have the economic resources with which to meet the qualifying ratios and accommodate the negative cash flow. If a renter moves out, the bank wants to insure the loan will continue to be paid.

2. *Square footage.* Homes tend to have more square footage than apartments; the larger the unit, the less the rent per square foot in comparison.

3. *Vacancy.* When a home is vacant, 100 percent of the rent is lost until it is re-rented. Stated differently, since only one tenant is living in the house at any given time, the vacancy factor will be either 0 percent or 100 percent.

4. *Management.* In many cases the investor must personally manage the property because there is no resident manager, but professional management firms will now more often agree to take on single family homes for management. The fee for such management can be substantial (often equaling 10 percent of the monthly rent). In order to maximize the rental income acquired, owners may prefer to find their own tenants, show property and perform other landlord responsibilities. Performing such tasks will likely reduce time available for personal activities. Some owners are not temperamentally fit to handle calls from tenants, especially when complaints are made in the middle of the night (the sewer has stopped up) or just as the owner sits down for dinner.

5. *Repairs.* If the owner cannot do minor repair work himself, the cost of hiring plumbing, electrical, mechanical, and other contractors is becoming greater. One repair can represent a substantial proportion of the monthly rent.

6. *Economy of operations.* As an investor acquires more houses, in scattered locations, more money and time are required for travel

and other expenses than if the units were all under one roof, as in an apartment building.

7. *Tax deductions.* Tax benefits are increasingly subject to the whims of Congress, as demonstrated by the severity of the 1986 Tax Reform Act, especially in the passive loss rules. The U.S. government continues to use the tax code, especially as it relates to housing, for the purpose of social engineering.

15.2 THE TWO-TO-FOUR-UNIT RESIDENTIAL INCOME PROPERTY

Key Characteristics

An alternative to an SFR rental is the two- to four-unit residential income property. Management of this size property by new or inexperienced investors is still relatively simple. This type of property is in great demand by investors and will usually resell quickly, but not as quickly as an SFR. As demonstrated throughout the text, many laws that apply to protect investors in residential buildings of up to four units don't apply to five or more units. These include such items as prepayment privileges and penalties, provision for late charges, disclosures, and other consumer protection laws.

Kinds of Financing Available on Two-to-Four-Unit Dwellings

Conventional loans of up to 75 percent of value are usually available from most lenders. Some may allow 15 percent down and permit the borrower to obtain a second loan for the balance. However, fewer institutional lenders will accept seller carry financing, especially if there is a large negative cash flow. As with a single dwelling converted to a rental, lenders are likely to count a large percentage of the actual rents to offset monthly payments.

Seller financing for the first loan is generally not possible, since few have free and clear properties. However, some sellers may carry second loans behind new first loans, if lenders allow such financing.

Some buyers may choose to buy a two-to-four-unit building and live in one unit. It is possible to get owner-occupied financing on this size of property and there are even programs in FHA that will allow the purchase with the standard 3.5 percent down!

Interest Rates and Other Terms on Two-to-Four-Unit Properties

Much like an SFR, a two-to-four-unit lender first looks at the buyer and how much he/she can afford to purchase. Then, the lender qualifies the property, including its income and expenses. Conventional lenders generally ask from 0.5 percent to 1 percent higher interest than on owner-occupied single-unit dwellings. Borrower loan fees sometimes run higher than on owner-occupied houses. If the loan contains a prepayment penalty it will most likely call for six months' unearned interest, with a 20 percent payoff allowable in any one calendar year without penalty.

Advantages of Two-to-Four-Unit Dwellings as Investment Vehicles

Two-to-four-unit properties can be found in most communities. The owner can manage the property without the need for a resident manager. Tenants often pay their own utilities, maintain the garden, and do minor repairs. Units can be rented without furnishings. If the owner desires to delegate some of the management duties, such as gardening, sweeping, and laundry room cleanup, one of the tenants may often do such work for a nominal fee, saving the owner time and expense. This party may also show vacant units to prospective tenants.

For tenants, two-to-four-unit properties are very popular and will often rent while large multiunit apartment complexes remain vacant. Two-to-four-unit properties offer more privacy, with fewer people above or below a tenant's own apartment. These units can obtain good loan-to-value ratios from conventional lenders, offering greater leverage and requiring less cash. Generally there is a high ratio of improvements to overall investment, ranging from 70 percent to 80 percent of building to total value, offering a maximum depreciation basis and tax shelter.

Disadvantages of Two-to-Four-Unit Dwellings as Investment Vehicles

Because of the added income, compared to an SFR and the lower amount of required down payment (compared to 5+ units), two-to-four-unit properties are desirable and may demand higher prices because of the greater competition between potential buyers. As prices climb, the yield to the investor will not always be sufficient to meet operating costs and debt service, requiring owners to "feed the property" because of negative cash flow.

With a higher purchase price, a lender may have added liability. Because of this, a buyer will have to be more qualified with more reserves or possibly higher credit scores.

With any investment property the possibility of surprise repairs and unit turnovers requires that reserves should be put aside. An owner who fails to set aside reserves could end up short of funds for needed repairs at inconvenient times. The owner may need to pay for utilities, such as water, outside lights, and laundry room utilities, thereby creating more expense than in single-unit investments where the tenant pays all. Generally, repair costs are higher than for single-unit homes, but the per unit cost is lower. For example, to replace carpet in a home might cost $1,000. But, in a four-unit apartment building, it is not likely to cost four times as much. At certain times, when there is a high vacancy factor or a rise in uncollectible rents, owners are forced to keep rents lower than the break-even point, in order to compete with other units on the market. In some areas, rental income has lagged behind the inflation of operating costs, resulting in a smaller net cash flow to the owner. Owners should keep rents advancing at the same rate of increase as their taxes and other operating costs, but are constantly affected by the market costs of units in the area.

15.3 THE FIVE-PLUS UNIT RESIDENTIAL INCOME PROPERTY

Depending on local market conditions, a well-located apartment building is usually a "better buy" than the two-to-four-unit property. Since financing on these larger buildings requires a larger down payment, fewer investors can afford them. Therefore, demand is lower, which keeps prices down. As banks become more willing to lend and the overall market becomes stronger, five-plus unit properties will increase in price—usually less drastically than SFRs, though.

These larger properties are also more likely to sell at a price relative to their income, as opposed to a reliance on being in a nice area. This being said, if two identical properties with identical income were in contrasting areas, the property in the nicer area will sell for more because of the demand from buyers. With this higher price, the property will generate less income; however, some buyers believe a nicer area will have better tenants, less vacancies, and/or higher future income.

In most areas of California, there is not much vacant land available for building. In addition, most cities have established specific planning guidelines that require a certain amount of parking and open space area in new construction. Since there are not new rental units continually becoming available, tenants must seek out the best rental location at a cost they can afford. With any influx in population, vacancy rates begin to decline and rents may increase.

With a struggling economy, families tend to tighten their budgets and may try to squeeze more family members into fewer units. This causes an increase in vacancies and a decrease in rents. With less income from the property, these times can be challenging and may result in increased short sales, foreclosures, and REO sales.

Environmental factors and the lack of affordable funding are making apartments more difficult to build. New energy and insulation requirements, along with reduced land density in new city and county general plans have resulted in higher prices for new apartment construction. However, when it makes financial sense to build, newer construction coupled with higher rents (from nicer units) will usually bring a higher-than-market sales price.

Financing Options for Five-Plus Units

To purchase a 5+ unit building, unlike a two-to-four-unit building, a bank first looks at the property and the income it generates. If the property is qualified, the buyer must then be approved. Usually the minimum down is 30 percent, but if the property makes less money, the buyer will have to invest a larger down payment. If the property makes more, the buyer will have to bring in a smaller down payment. No matter the percentage down, there are fewer banks that will lend on larger apartment buildings. In the final analysis, LTV (loan-to-value) ratios are governed by the property's cash flow and the income "break-even" point, or debt coverage ratio (discussed in detail on pages 455 and 464 of this chapter).

Interest rates range from 0.5 to 2 percent higher, and loan fees are higher than for single units. Loan programs usually have 30-year terms, but have a shorter term fixed rate. For example, your loan may have a 1, 3, 5, 7 or 10-year fixed rate. After this rate expires, you have the choice to pay off the loan, refinance or allow the rate to convert to its preestablished variable amount. You agree to these terms, rates, index, and margin when you sign the loan docs during the purchase.

Lenders are also concerned about credit requirements. Borrowers must have good financial statements and stable income independent of the property, although the latter is used in evaluating the merits of the loan. In addition, a lender wants to know you will manage the property correctly. If you have never owned an apartment before, a lender might not allow you to borrow on a 5-plus unit building.

Regardless of the sales price of the building, lenders make their own evaluation of properties and base their loan-to-value ratios on their appraisal and the amount of debt that the projected income can support. For example, if present rents from the apartment are abnormally high, lenders may use the average market rents for similar units in the area as being a realistic long-term trend. If the property is furnished (which is rare), lenders deduct all of the rental income attributable to furniture and use the **capitalized income stream** from the unfurnished unit to determine the loan value. Thus, a $5 million furnished building may be valued at $4,500,000 on an unfurnished basis, resulting in a smaller overall loan and a greater down payment.

When money becomes tight, lenders often make apartment loans only to exceptionally qualified borrowers. Even those who do qualify may have to pay excessive interest rates, and perhaps even points, to obtain any type of loan. When conventional loans are unavailable, many of the creative financing techniques discussed in Chapter 14 can be used, either on an interim basis until conventional financing is again available or on a permanent basis.

Advantages of Investing in Five-Plus Units

Since housing is a basic need, there is a constant demand for housing, regardless of the ups and downs of the business cycle. Therefore, apartment investments tend to be safer than other real estate investments, like commercial property, retail centers, etc.

Management is concentrated in one location rather than diffused over a wide area for the same number of small units. A relatively inexperienced investor can acquire an apartment building and, with some personal effort, learn the business of apartment management. The owner can also hire a resident manager to handle the day-to-day work of managing the property, such as showing units, maintaining grounds, and collecting rent. This resident manager usually will have a reduction in rent for these services. The owner can then supervise the property overall and set up management policies. In California, apartment complexes of 16 units or more must have a resident manager, unless the owner resides on the premises.

There is also the option of hiring a professional management company to handle all the aspects of management. This company collects rent, schedules repairs, screens tenants, organizes evictions, and prints monthly accounting statements. For this service, an owner usually pays 5 to 7 percent of the gross income. As you own more property or negotiate fewer services, this fee can stay closer to 5 percent. In contrast, a management company will charge closer to 10 percent for the management of an SFR.

With five-plus units, the cost of operation is usually less per unit than in scattered properties. For instance, the cost of a new, inexpensive roof on a 1,200-square-foot SFR might run up to $5,000. This is the cost per unit, as there is only one unit. The cost of reroofing a three-story apartment house containing 24 units might be $24,000, so the cost per unit is only $1,000, because the one roof covers three stories.

Large apartment buildings can provide an excellent tax shelter, since typically 80 percent of the value is in improvements that can be depreciated. The cost of personal property (such as carpets, drapes, appliances, or furnishings) may be written off (deducted) on a 200 percent declining balance basis, typically ranging from five to seven years. An existing residential building can be fully depreciated using a 27.5 years straight line formula (an equal amount of depreciation each year for 27.5 years). Depreciation formulas, of course, are subject to change as tax laws change.

While there has been reduced inflation in recent years, the shortage of new apartment construction has tended to build some equity through appreciation, similar to other types of residential real estate. In addition, the rent paid by tenants goes toward reducing the principal balance (loan), which also helps acquire more equity.

Disadvantages of Investing in Five-Plus Units

Inexperienced investors often do not realize the true expenses of owning an apartment house, gloss over maintenance costs, do not set aside reserves for carpet and appliance replacements, and can wind up with a negative cash flow. Unless investor capital can be added to meet the cash outflow, the investor can wind up having to sell the building at a sacrifice price, especially at times when financing has become more difficult. As noted above, this is exactly why lenders are more selective when qualifying a buyer of the properties.

Changing neighborhood patterns and encroachments of heavy business or industrial buildings may cause building values to decrease. There are high-crime areas where apartment buildings are selling for less than they did 10 years before, despite the inflation factor, because tenants either pay lower rents or are completely unwilling to rent in these areas. Decreasing rents, high vacancies, bad debts, and difficulty of financing may make a sale of the building almost impossible. Though, at the right price, there is sure to be a buyer somewhere.

New consumer laws pertaining to owner-tenant relationships can lead to rent-collection problems and increasing legal fees. The cost of evicting tenants for nonpayment of rent, when they exercise their legal rights to defend against such an action, can run as high as $1,000 or more, including attorney fees, legal papers, and other eviction costs. This is in addition to lost rent and any refurbishing costs if a tenant has damaged an apartment.

As apartment vacancy rates go down and there is an insufficient supply of housing for the people of this state, some local jurisdictions have considered **rent control** laws that limit the amount of rental increases. Such laws tend to decrease the yield from an apartment, since allowable rental increases might lag behind operating costs. Investment capital would flow to other uncontrolled types of investments or to cities with no rent control, making it difficult to sell an apartment building.

Many owners do not have the temperament to deal with problems of management or with the multiplicity of tenant requests for services. Patience, tolerance, and the ability to deal with people tactfully are absolutely vital to operate apartment buildings successfully. This is a business! Finally, since tenants might not have the pride of ownership or the stability of a long-term lease, damage to the property is far more likely than for single dwellings.

15.4 BREAK-EVEN ANALYSIS

Both lenders and investors are interested in the viability of investments based upon financing considerations. One tool to help assess cash flow and the profitability of an investment property is a **break-even analysis**. Figure 15.1 shows the number of apartment units (though the process can apply to any property, both real and personal) that would need to be rented in an apartment project to break even—that is, the point at which the revenue exactly equals the outgo.

In the example below, let's assume a 30-unit apartment building, at $600 monthly rent per unit. Fixed outlays for taxes, insurance, debt service, licenses, and so on equal $8,000 per month. Variable costs, including management, maintenance, repairs, and utilities, are estimated at $100 per month per unit. We must then ask ourselves, given the amount of rent per unit, the fixed expenses that continue regardless of the number of units rented, and the variable expenses that are tied to the number of units actually rented, at what point does income equal the costs and expenses?

FIGURE 15.1   Monthly break-even analysis.

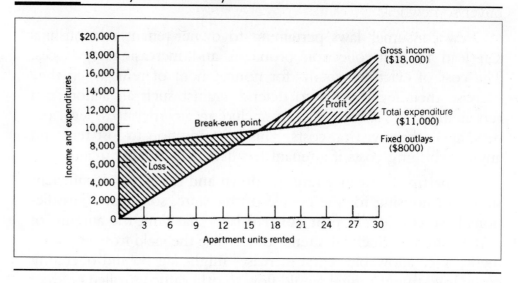

The vertical bar represents the dollar amount of income and expenses. The horizontal bar represents the number of units rented. Since the fixed expenses are $8,000, a straight horizontal line is drawn at the $8,000 level to represent fixed outlay. Then, as each unit is rented, $100 of variable expenses is added, thus adding to the $8,000 figure. We simultaneously plot the income figures at increments of $600 for each unit rented. Finally, where the total expenses equal gross income, we arrive at the break-even point. In the example, this point is at 16 units. Here, the income totals $9,600 and the expenses, including debt service (loan payments), equal $9,600. This is arrived at by charting the fixed expenses at $8,000, and superimposing thereon $100 per unit, cumulatively, for each rented unit. Since we know that each rented unit is $600 per month, we simply add $600 for each additional unit, cumulatively for all 30 units as if each were occupied. Where the two lines intersect, presto!—our break-even point.

Why such a fuss over break-even analysis? It is simply because as a condition for prudent lending and investing, both sides (the lender and investor) need to know exactly what the risks (and rewards) are, and at which point. The prudent lender is cognizant of the level below which the property is not carrying itself, and therefore increasing the risk of delinquency and foreclosure; the prudent investor is aware of the level above which the property is profitable, or above which he or she need not feed the property from outside income. As shown in Figure 15.1, the area below the break-even point is labeled the loss zone, where there is a negative cash flow; that is, expenses exceed revenues. In contrast, the area above the break-even point is labeled the profit zone, where there is **positive cash flow**; that is, revenues exceed expenses.

The number of units rented and plotted on the horizontal axis could, just as conveniently, be labeled occupancy-vacancy ratio, expressed as percentages. Thus, the break-even point would be 16/30, or 53.3 percent. So, 16 of the 30 units, or just over 53 percent of the total number of available units, would need to be rented to break even.

It should be emphasized that the analysis shown here for apartments also holds true for any type of occupancy-vacancy ratios. Thus, the analyses have equal application to commercial properties as well. It is not uncommon for lenders on commercial properties, for instance, to hold back a portion of the projected loan until a minimum percentage of occupancy, agreed upon by lender and borrower, is reached in the rentals. The minimum is called the floor amount, and could be 70 percent of the total loan amount.

15.5 FINANCING STARTS WITH THE LISTING

Why Sell Your Apartment Building?

Reasons for selling one's apartment building are many and varied. The two main reasons we will look at here are to cash out if the owner does not plan to purchase another property, and to exchange the building for a different type of property or different size apartment building. The reasons given by the owner for selling may not be the real reasons, but it is important to help your client reach their objectives. It is important to ask your client about any bad liens, code issues, vacancies, possible foreclosure, etc.

An owner may wish to sell to avoid spending money to comply with the requirements of city building inspections or code enforcement. Or the owner may want to sell because the area's property values may be decreasing and the owner wants to sell now before the property value shrinks more. Or the owner may be is in an area that has just passed a rent control ordinance or is considering controls (see Figure 15.2). Frequently, the amounts allowed for rental increases bear little resemblance to the actual costs of operating the apartment building; the potential inability to increase rents due to rent control ordinances tends to discourage development, ownership, and operation of apartment investments. However, if located in a highly desirable area, they might still sell for a premium.

FIGURE 15.2   The argument against rent controls.

RENT CONTROLS—DO THEY MAKE SENSE?

RENT CONTROLS—DO THEY MAKE SENSE?

LANDLORD   TENANT

Rent control is a controversial topic, with emotions and misconceptions running rampant on both sides of the issue.

From a purely economic point of view, rent controls make little sense. The issue has been repeatedly studied by both liberal and conservative economists, and most agree that rent controls do not solve housing problems. Rents are high because demand for apartment housing is high and supply is inadequate. The solution is to either decrease demand for rental units, increase the supply, or a combination of both.

Rent controls do neither. Rent controls artificially depress rent levels, which in turn stimulates rather than reducing demand. Rent controls reduce returns and yields on apartment investments, thereby discouraging the construction of new units or the conversion of large homes into apartments.

In the long term, rent controls can actually cause landlords to defer needed maintenance resulting in a property's deterioration. An often overlooked result of long-term rent control is the departure of investors in rental property altogether. If investors are unable to make a reasonable return on any specific type of investment, they will abandon it as an investment vehicle. The result over time is likely to be an ever decreasing number of available rental opportunities for tenants. Finally, never fully explored or understood is the psychological hostage-like situation that is established for tenants unwilling to move from their rent controlled apartments. Artificially maintained low rents can cause tenants to defer moving to areas where market rents prevail even when such a move may be to their overall economic benefit. In short, rent controls tend to perpetuate the ill they are supposed to cure!

An owner might also desire to sell their apartments to "exchange up." This can mean something different for each seller. It could mean that he/she wants to own more units, own fewer units that are easier to manage, own in a better area or just "closer to home," or maybe, after 28 years of ownership, there is no more depreciation benefit. There are specific tax laws that govern this exchange benefit. More information can be found at: www.irs.gov.

Obtain Financing Information on the Building

When you take a listing, it is important to know what financing is available for potential buyers. Knowing this information at the start of your market can assist qualified investors, and limit your wasted time on unqualified buyers. Obtaining a financial statement from the seller can also assist in knowing what the current balance is, what the interest rate is, and if the current lender will allow an assumption.

If there is more than one loan, the agent should find out similar information for each.

In the event of a short sale (see Chapter 11), having this information from your seller early on can help the process go more smoothly. If need be, and with signed approval from your seller, you can contact the bank directly to assist with the required paperwork and contracts.

Plan for Probable Financing of Sale

If an assumption is allowed by the lending institution, it is helpful to know what they are looking for; a minimum credit score, amount of down payment, fees, etc. If not assumable, will the existing bank create a new loan for the buyer? This can sometimes reduce fees or allow a smoother or faster sale, since the existing bank is already familiar with the property.

Most buyers do prefer to get their own financing, even if a loan is assumable. Determine what special terms the new loan will contain with respect to the interest rate, term of the loan, prepayment penalty, acceleration clause, loan fee, and other requirements. What down payment will be required? Will the lender allow a second loan? Will the new lender require an impound account for taxes or will this be waived? If a new first loan can be obtained for a higher amount than the present one, ascertain how much the holder of the second loan will require for a complete payoff. Will the second loan holder take some payoff and leave a portion of the loan on the property, to follow the lien of the new first loan? If you enter the field of investment property as a lender, these questions are of the utmost importance. As an agent, it might be best to allow your buyer to discuss these points of interest directly with his lender.

If the current financing market is poor, and both buyer and seller are willing to be creative, perhaps the owner can carry back a first loan or an all-inclusive loan with a provision that whenever the finance market improves, the owner can present the buyer with new financing at rates not in excess of the current rate being paid. The buyer may then be obligated to take out such new loan and pay off to the owner all or a portion of the seller carryback loan. This gives the buyer time to obtain conventional financing when the market is stronger and allows the seller to sell the building at a time when poor financing is available to the buyers.

How Market Financing Conditions Affect Property Prices

When interest rates go up, the net income after interest expenses decreases unless the rents can be raised or the expenses lowered. Since rents and expenses cannot always be easily changed, the net result of an increase in interest rates may be to decrease yields. Since apartment investments are competing in the marketplace with other investments, an increase in the interest rate results in a lower market value for the apartment building. Conversely, when interest rates decrease, yields are increased, which tend to raise the value of a property.

When purchasing an income property, the higher the property's capitalization rate (cap rate) the better. A property's cap rate is computed by dividing the net operating income by the sale price. As the interest rate on a loan goes up, the net income goes down and the cap rate decreases. This means that the owner will make less money from the property.

In difficult financing markets, existing low-interest assumable loans should be preserved if at all possible. There may be such loans, including insurance company loans, private loans, and so on. The balances on these loans may be low if they have been in existence for many years, so the sellers may have a large amount of equity. If the buyers put down only 15 or 20 percent, the sellers may have to carry an excessively large second loan, and if they need cash, over and above the down payment, they cannot sell such a loan because of its size. In this event, the agent can structure the sale so that the sellers' remaining equity could be split. For example, if the equity were $150,000, it could be split into a $50,000 second loan and $100,000 third loan. The sellers could then sell the second loan at the prevailing discount, receive some cash, and hold a $100,000 third loan until its due date or until the refinance clause can be invoked. This solution is similar to the creative options seen in Chapter 14.

Economic Principles versus Tax Shelter

A property should be priced so that it is a good investment for the buyers based upon economic principles and not just on tax shelter. If the property shows a return on investment, based only upon its

tax shelter, it may not be a good investment for the buyer because tax laws may change to eliminate certain tax shelter items; the depreciation shrinks each year so that the tax shelter decreases; and if the buyer later sells the property, there will invariably be recapture of some of the depreciation as taxable gain.

The agent must explain to the sellers that investors expect a realistic rate of yield and since an apartment requires more management and work than other types of investment, this additional work and risk must be taken into account in the form of a greater yield on the investment.

If a property is listed at an acceptable price, and if the owner has been informed of prevailing market conditions and will assist with some kind of financing to help the sale, the agent will have a highly marketable apartment complex. The buyer will then have a reasonable chance to have a successful investment. This can create good will for all and will build the reputation of the agent for integrity and honesty, without which no one can really succeed in the real estate brokerage business.

15.6 INTRODUCTION TO COMMERCIAL AND INDUSTRIAL PROPERTIES

Financing requirements for commercial and industrial properties are more strict than for residential property, unless the tenant is a major corporation with good credit standing. Again, similar to five-plus unit apartment buildings, lenders look at the property as an entity and factor in how much that property makes or loses. In shopping centers, a new freeway may alter travel patterns, encouraging the construction of competing centers, with resultant losses to older centers. Before illustrating the financing of a commercial property, it may be of interest to observe that many lenders prefer multipurpose office buildings and multipurpose retail buildings as security for loans. Special purpose facilities, such as bowling alleys, theaters, gyms, restaurants, and so on generally are not considered attractive security for real estate loans.

Commercial Properties

Commercial properties consist of the following:

- Neighborhood stores, including "strip malls," that is, stores running parallel to and fronting the street—"along the strip"
- Free-standing commercial buildings, either single purpose or multipurpose

- Neighborhood convenience centers, including clusters of stores around a minimarket, usually with some off-street parking
- Community shopping centers, consisting of a larger group of stores surrounding a major supermarket
- Department stores
- Service stations
- Garage buildings
- Franchise outlets
- Fast-food chain stores, either in a free-standing building or as part of a center, including automotive franchise buildings
- Motels, hotels, mobile-home parks
- Office buildings, including ground floor and multi-story, such as medical-dental buildings
- Rest homes and convalescent hospitals
- Special-purpose buildings, such as built-to-order drive-in banks

Industrial Properties

Industrial properties can be classified into three categories:

1. *Small industrial properties.* These are free-standing single buildings in industrially zoned areas of a city. Such buildings may be from 10,000 to 100,000 square feet, often divided into many small individual units that can be rented to many different tenants. They may or may not have rail facilities.
2. *Larger industrial properties.* These are large industrial buildings leased to one tenant on a long-term lease.
3. *Industrial parks.* These are planned parks where developers can buy land and develop individual buildings to the specifications of the master plan. They usually have landscaped areas surrounding the buildings.

Office Parks

An **office park** is an area for which a master plan of development is adopted and in which all buildings are designed for office occupancy. There are off-street parking areas and often landscaping to give a park-like setting. In many areas, the master plan of such a park allows restaurants and shops to be located in certain areas to serve the persons working in the office park. Hotels and motels may also be situated within the area to allow conferences. Examples of this type of development can frequently be found around airports and freeway interchanges.

Advantages of Investing in a Commercial or Industrial Property

If the property has a long-term lease with a strong tenant, there is a high likelihood of steady income. When compared with residential income properties, commercial and industrial ownership offers the advantage of greater stability of lessees as well as potentially low vacancy factors, in some markets. Sometimes the lessee will need to make major capital improvements to the property to make it suitable for its business.

Most commercial leases contain either a cost-of-living increase clause or a **percentage lease** in the case of retail establishments. This allows an owner to realize increased rents as operating costs increase. If the property is in a prime commercial location, the successful operation of the business tenant will result in a high percentage of the gross income, thereby providing overall rent of more than just minimum base rent.

The growth of the city creates greater demand for commercial properties, giving the owner increased rents. For the commercial investor, there is little risk of rent control, as rules are seldom approved by city government officials for commercial properties. Additionally, some investors prefer to deal with what is presumed to be a more professional approach from business tenants. Finally, lease insurance is available to protect both landlord and tenant in case of business interruption due to specified hazards outlined in the insurance policy; such as the destruction of part or all of the premises through fire, windstorm, earthquake, and the like.

Disadvantages of Investing in a Commercial or Industrial Property

A leased commercial or industrial property with a strong tenant can be a good investment. If this type of property becomes available to purchase, it often sells at a high price, which results in a lower yield than the interest required on the purchase loan. In periods of overbuilding, the market is flooded with unused commercial space. This results in lower rents and poor investment returns. During the accelerated market downturn in 2008 and 2009, owners of commercial property suffered increased vacancies due to poor business climate and loss of revenue.

Investments in older types of commercial buildings, such as older "Main Street" stores, can be a greater risk, because tenants may move to newer centers, and as they are created the resulting vacancies may take a long time to fill. Succeeding businesses may be of lower quality and not able to pay as high a rent. Changing neighborhood patterns may result in an entire commercial area becoming less desirable, with entire blocks of stores remaining vacant and subject to vandalism.

Some tenants may have long-term leases with fixed rental rates, thereby freezing the owners into fixed income while taxes and other expenses rise.

City requirements often force owners to add expensive improvements to safeguard the safety of occupants and the public. For instance, a hotel may have to install new fire doors, outside fire escapes, or different elevators to conform to fire, safety, and disability requirements. This can require owners to spend a substantial amount of capital.

15.7 DEBT COVERAGE RATIO

After carefully analyzing the borrower's qualifications, income property appraisal, and cash flow forecast, the loan underwriter frequently does a debt coverage ratio analysis. The property's annual **net operating income (NOI)** is divided by the property's annual debt service to compute the **debt coverage ratio (DCR)**.

$$\text{Debt coverage ratio} = \frac{\text{Annual net operating income}}{\text{Annual debt service}}$$

Annual net operating income is the annual estimated rents, less vacancies, and operating expenses; annual debt service is the required monthly loan payments ×12 months, which is labeled "loan constant."

Example: On a small income property, the figures might be as follows:

Gross rent estimate	$100,000
Less vacancy (10%)	−10,000
Gross operating income	$ 90,000
Less operating expenses (taxes, insurance, repairs, management, etc.)	−30,000
Net operating income	$ 60,000

The potential borrower has applied for a $500,000 loan at 9 percent amortized for 30 years with payments of $4,023 per month; multiplied by 12 this equals $48,276 annual debt service.

$$\text{Debt coverage ratio} = \frac{\$60,000}{\$48,276} = 1.24$$

The loan underwriter would then compare this DCR with the company policy guidelines to determine if the property's net income justifies the loan. If the DCR is acceptable and the borrower's qualifications and the appraisal are cleared, then the income property loan is approved. If the DCR is too low, the loan may be denied until either the net operating income is increased or the annual debt service is reduced (or both) to bring the DCR into line.

A lender's debt coverage ratio requirements will vary by property types, market conditions, and portfolio requirements. A call to your local loan representative can give you the current requirements. In today's real estate market, most lenders want a DCR of 1.1 or better.

Few, if any, lenders will accept a debt coverage ratio that breaks even or is negative, where income will not cover loan payments. Here, the bank will require more down payment to off-set the loan amount and lower the DCR. The main line of defense for an income property lender is the amount of net operating income (gross annual rents, less vacancies, and operating expenses). Income property lenders know that the money for the loan payments comes from the net income of the property. If the property has a negative cash flow, net income will not cover the loan payments. From this discussion, you can see why income property lenders place such importance on a property's net operating income and debt coverage ratios. However, it must be understood that an excellent net operating income and debt coverage ratio will not guarantee an approved loan if the borrower has questionable qualifications and the property appraisal is too low! Income property lenders insist upon good borrowers and adequate appraisals, but tremendous emphasis is placed on the property's net operating income.

SUMMARY

Houses that are used as rentals are not financed under the same terms as owner-occupied property. Some speculators simply buy property for short-term gain, renting out the house until an opportunity for a favorable resale arises. In cases where they believe that a house is being purchased by a speculator, lenders have been known to

(1) reduce the loan-to-value ratio, (2) increase the interest rate, (3) adjust loan fees (points) upward, or, in extreme cases, (4) refuse the loan altogether. Apartment buildings are generally financed from 60 percent to 75 percent of the lender's appraised value. For "oversold" properties, where the rental income does not cover all expenses and loan payments, often the lender's estimate of value will be below the actual sales price. This is because lenders reason that a project must be economically sound. Negative cash flows invite problems that may lead to subsequent delinquencies and defaults. Interest rates for apartments are higher than single-family homes because of the higher risk involved. More favorable terms can be negotiated if the property and the borrower's credit are both sound. Financing of commercial and industrial properties requires specialized knowledge of market conditions, management, quality of property and tenants, and other factors. There is no uniform lending pattern, though institutional lenders tend to shy away from loan-to-value ratios exceeding 70 percent. The key for commercial and industrial properties is an adequate debt coverage ratio (DCR). If a property's income does not cover the debt, more down payment will be required to offset the risk.

IMPORTANT TERMS AND CONCEPTS

Break-even analysis

Capitalized income
   stream

Debt coverage ratio
   (DCR)

Depreciation

Leverage

Negative cash flow

Net operating income
   (NOI)

Office park

Percentage lease

Positive cash flow

Rent control

Tax shelter

REVIEWING YOUR UNDERSTANDING

Questions for Discussion

1. List two advantages and two disadvantages of investing in
   a. apartment houses.
   b. commercial properties.
   c. industrial properties.

2. Discuss the risks involved in overfinancing or overleveraging, that is, too much borrowing against a property.

3. From a marketing viewpoint, why is it important to determine the motivation of owners who desire to sell their properties?

4. What is meant by the expression "feeding the property"?

Multiple-Choice Questions

1. The main advantage of a single-family rental, as compared to other real estate investments, is its
   a. liquidity.
   b. higher interest rates.
   c. fewer choices.
   d. difficulty of management.

2. Which of the following statements concerning the financing of large apartment projects is correct?
   a. The larger the size of a building, the lower the loan-to-value ratio.
   b. Loan fees for large complexes are usually lower than for single dwellings.
   c. Loan terms seldom exceed 15 years.
   d. Lenders ignore debt service in assessing the loan collateral.

3. If an owner is required to "feed the property" to meet operating costs and debt service, it is always due to
   a. positive cash flow.
   b. negative cash flow.
   c. excellent management.
   d. excess depreciation write-off.

4. Most apartment properties are financed by
   a. private loans.
   b. government loans.
   c. conventional loans.
   d. foreign loans.

5. The ability to assume an existing loan is determined by the
   a. method of taking title to the property.
   b. existence of a due-on-sale clause.
   c. amount of taxes.
   d. title insurance required by the lender.

6. Buying real estate with little down payment and with maximum financing is called
   a. equity buying.
   b. leverage.
   c. progression.
   d. regression.

7. The California Civil Code limits prepayment penalties on certain types of real estate loans to the first three years. Which of the following transactions qualifies for the limitation?
   a. owner-occupied single-family residence.
   b. a house purchased for rental.
   c. houses purchased on speculation.
   d. a vacant lot.

8. "Break-even analysis" refers to
   a. debt coverage ratio.
   b. use of very low leverage.
   c. positive cash flow.
   d. the point at which income equals outgo.

9. If the yield on a property is 9 percent, but the buyer must pay 11 percent interest, the net effect is termed
   a. negative leverage.
   b. positive leverage.
   c. neutral leverage.
   d. trading on the equity.

10. Which of the following properties are most likely to be subject to rent control ordinances?
    a. commercial.
    b. industrial.
    c. parking lots.
    d. apartments.

11. Buyers of nonowner-occupied single-family rentals
    a. are generally charged more interest than for owner-occupied homes.
    b. will never pay a higher loan origination fee than on an owner-occupied home.
    c. cannot be required to pay a prepayment penalty for an early payoff.
    d. are considered safer than equally qualified owners who occupy the premises.

12. The financing of a nonowner-occupied duplex generally means that
    a. lenders will never loan more than 70 percent of value.
    b. interest rates are higher than on owner-occupied single family dwellings.
    c. new loans are not available.
    d. rental management is not required.

13. With respect to apartment complexes, the experienced investor knows that
    a. a resident manager or owner is required by California law for 16 or more units.
    b. management of apartment units is scattered, rather than concentrated.
    c. the cost of operation per unit is greater for apartment units than in scattered properties.
    d. none of the above are true.

14. While the issue of rent controls is a controversial one, we find that
    a. the imposition of rent controls actually enhances rental income.
    b. yields on apartment houses increase under rent controls.
    c. rent controls discourage construction of apartment houses, leading to diminished supply and greater demand.
    d. rent controls tend to increase the capitalized value of apartment houses.

15. Special-purpose properties (restaurants, franchise fast-food outlets, and the like)
    a. are usually considered the best security by most lenders.
    b. are considered too risky by most lenders as security for loans.
    c. normally command lower interest rates than most other commercial properties because of their history of financial success.
    d. are favored by lenders because of their relatively easy conversion to other uses.

16. Which of the following statements concerning the financing of large apartment projects is true?
    a. Lenders usually don't bother with the borrower's credit for income-producing properties.
    b. In general, the larger the size of the project, the lower the loan-to-value ratio.
    c. Lenders usually ignore debt service in qualifying the loan.
    d. Loan fees are lower than for smaller properties.

17. Operating expenses for an apartment complex include
    a. interest payments.
    b. principal payments.
    c. depreciation write-offs.
    d. management fees.

18. Investors in two-to-four-rental units find that
    a. lenders qualify both the borrower and the property.
    b. loan assumptions are commonplace.
    c. no secondary financing is permitted if there is negative cash flow.
    d. government-backed financing is in abundance.

19. From a real estate agent's perspective, thoughts about financing should always begin with the
    a. offer.
    b. acceptance.
    c. listing.
    d. appraisal.

20. Investing in commercial property
    a. requires less down payment than apartment projects.
    b. requires a debt coverage ratio of less than 1.
    c. may involve the use of percentage leases.
    d. is less sophisticated than investing in rental homes.

CASE & POINT

Being Your Best!

Just as important as understanding the "nuts and bolts" of qualifying buyers/borrowers is recognizing the obligations that accompany our representation. Functioning from one's best self requires us to examine what some would call "ethics." Ethics can't be taught or regulated. But how we behave and function with our customers/clients will ultimately affect our success and the ability to develop that critically important relationship called "trust."

Trust is that intangible factor upon which every personal or business relationship relies to guarantee its continuation. It requires a lot of effort to develop, but can be undone in an instant. Trust means that one always functions from one's best self and with high regard for the interests of the other person(s) in the relationship. Relationships fail when there is a lack of trust.

Take, for instance, the 2009 congressional hearing with Wall Street CEOs, in which each of the company leaders claimed that they didn't see the financial problems coming, relied upon inaccurate computer models, and pledged "to do everything necessary to regain the trust of our investors and the American public." Who among us believed that they did not function out of greed and did not know exactly what they were doing? The incongruity and deceit in their statements don't bode well for the development of future trust.

Relating this to real estate, consider the question: "Does this need to be disclosed?" The answer is to DISCLOSE! One person exclaimed that when he is faced with a decision, one that may cause him to step over a self-imposed ethical line, he asks himself, "When I go home today, do I want my wife and sons to know what I did?" If the answer is no, he shouldn't do it. Each person must find his or her own evaluation method.

Developing trust relationships and always functioning from one's best self are very personal actions. But here are a few thoughts as you determine how you intend to stand out as one of the best in the industry.

Clients First Attitude: Always function from the position of doing what is best for the client. That doesn't mean that you can't have different opinions, or that the client is always right. But it does mean that everything you say to a client and every action you take is motivated genuinely in the best interests of the client. People will "get it," trust you, and tell everyone about you.

Own Your Mistakes: We all forget to dot an i or cross a t on occasion. Own up to your errors—the sooner the better. Once something starts to unravel, it seldom gets better. Don't blame others. Let your client know that there has been a glitch, but that "we are working hard to fix it." Your client doesn't care whose fault it was; he or she just wants to know everything will work out.

Your Word Is Your Bond: People used to make agreements by a handshake. Their word was their bond, and they didn't need an eight-page contract to make sure that they met their obligations. Times have changed. It would be foolish in these litigious times not to have agreements in writing; however, people need to be able to rely upon our word. If you say you'll do something, do it. Make no excuses!

Don't Be Afraid of Evaluation: We grow and improve by constant evaluation of what we've done. Live by the adage that "I don't have to be bad to get better." Be open to criticism (as long as it isn't mean spirited) and adopt those suggestions that make sense.

Bottom line: Ethical behavior is pretty simple. Always behave in a way that will never cause you to be embarrassed by what you've done. Behave as if the customer were going to take out a full-page ad in the newspaper describing the experiences he or she has had with you. If you are at ease with that, it is likely that you are doing pretty well, and that your trust relationships are in good shape.

Answers to Multiple-Choice Questions

Chapter 1

1. b	5. d	9. d	13. b	17. d
2. c	6. d	10. d	14. a	18. b
3. a	7. b	11. c	15. c	19. d
4. c	8. a	12. a	16. b	20. d

Chapter 2

1. a	5. b	9. a	13. b	17. d
2. d	6. d	10. c	14. b	18. a
3. b	7. d	11. a	15. c	19. d
4. c	8. c	12. c	16. a	20. d

Chapter 3

1. b	5. d	9. b	13. d	17. a
2. d	6. b	10. b	14. a	18. a
3. c	7. a	11. d	15. c	19. b
4. b	8. c	12. b	16. a	20. b

Chapter 4

1. d	5. c	9. b	13. c	17. c
2. d	6. c	10. d	14. b	18. d
3. a	7. d	11. c	15. a	19. b
4. b	8. c	12. d	16. a	20. a

Chapter 5

1. c	5. b	9. b	13. c	17. b
2. a	6. c	10. a	14. b	18. b
3. a	7. d	11. d	15. b	19. c
4. a	8. a	12. c	16. c	20. c

Chapter 6

1. a	5. d	9. b	13. d	17. b
2. d	6. c	10. b	14. d	18. b
3. c	7. b	11. a	15. a	19. b
4. b	8. d	12. c	16. a	20. d

Chapter 7

1. b	5. b	9. a	13. d	17. b
2. c	6. b	10. d	14. c	18. b
3. b	7. b	11. b	15. d	19. b
4. c	8. d	12. b	16. d	20. a

Chapter 8

1. b	5. d	9. a	13. d	17. c
2. b	6. a	10. a	14. d	18. b
3. a	7. d	11. a	15. c	19. a
4. c	8. a	12. b	16. b	20. c

Chapter 9

1. d	5. d	9. a	13. b	17. d
2. d	6. c	10. b	14. d	18. b
3. b	7. d	11. c	15. b	19. c
4. a	8. b	12. a	16. c	20. d

Chapter 10

1. c	5. b	9. c	13. c	17. b
2. b	6. a	10. b	14. d	18. a
3. d	7. b	11. b	15. d	19. d
4. a	8. d	12. b	16. d	20. c

Chapter 11

1. d	5. b	9. a	13. b	17. c
2. d	6. c	10. b	14. a	18. c
3. b	7. d	11. d	15. b	19. a
4. a	8. d	12. b	16. d	20. d

Chapter 12

1. c	5. c	9. d	13. b	17. d
2. a	6. b	10. c	14. d	18. b
3. b	7. c	11. d	15. a	19. c
4. b	8. a	12. d	16. a	20. d

Chapter 13

1. b	5. b	9. d	13. b	17. b
2. a	6. c	10. a	14. a	18. a
3. b	7. b	11. a	15. a	19. b
4. d	8. c	12. b	16. a	20. c

Chapter 14

1. d	5. b	9. b	13. d	17. d
2. b	6. a	10. c	14. c	18. d
3. c	7. a	11. b	15. d	19. a
4. a	8. d	12. d	16. b	20. b

Chapter 15

1. a	5. b	9. a	13. a	17. d
2. a	6. b	10. d	14. c	18. a
3. b	7. a	11. a	15. b	19. c
4. c	8. d	12. b	16. b	20. c

Appendix A

THE INTERNET INFLUENCE

Our reliance upon the Internet as a source of information continues to grow. We can check credit scores, search property values, apply for a home mortgage, calculate loan qualifying ratios, and find up-to-date information on nearly every subject, including home loan financing. However, there are some limitations to the Internet, and users are cautioned to remain skeptical of its credibility.

Acquiring a Loan Using the Internet

Just a few years ago, it was predicted that the Internet would revolutionize the financial arena. It was thought that one would be able to "shop" for the lowest interest rate and/or loan costs very quickly—saving money.

Internet lenders (deservedly) soon acquired the reputation that they only accommodate trouble-free transactions. Those borrowers who exhibit a need for credit counseling, or who may be short of cash, require a co-borrower, or need help with the vast number of other aspects of home loan financing often find themselves out of luck with Internet lenders. Recognizing the growing complexities of real estate financing, there may be compelling reasons for *not* acquiring a loan via the Internet.

With the disappearance of the subprime loans, fixed rate financing is back in vogue. Fixed rate loans today are "priced" to meet the requirements of the investor who will ultimately purchase the loan from the originating lender. In most cases, that investor is either Fannie Mae (Federal National Mortgage Association) or Freddie Mac (Federal Home Loan Mortgage Corporation). All lenders (including those who function on the Internet) typically quote a daily rate related to these investors' requirements for purchase. Thus, during any specific period, a borrower should receive the same (or nearly so) quote of rate and fees from every lender polled. If one lender is quoting a rate significantly better than all other lenders, a borrower should be suspicious: some lenders, even on the Internet, employ bait-and-switch quotes.

The lender must gather sufficient borrower documentation before providing any reliable rate quotes. Credit scores, the loan-to-value amount based on the down payment available, and the type of property being purchased or refinanced are all factored into any quoted interest rate. Quoted rates on the Internet and in most publications represent what may be available to the most qualified or "perfect" borrower—they seldom reflect rates that might be offered to the more "challenged" borrower.

It is also important for borrowers to become "educated" in regards to the loan process and procedures. Many borrowers require assistance in acquiring a loan, clearing credit items, developing a strategy for acquiring the necessary funds, or acquiring a co-borrower—the kind of guidance that is only available through a local lender source. Lenders on the Internet are basically unaccountable, whereas a local lender is more likely to feel that it must deliver on its promises, whether they involve quoted rates, costs, or a time period for closing the loan.

It would be unfair to suggest that one cannot acquire a loan via the Internet. However, given that it is unlikely that the loan interest rate and costs acquired via the Internet will be any better (and too often they are worse) than what can be acquired locally, most borrowers will be better served doing business with a lender whom they know. As the borrower is more likely to receive personal attention throughout the loan process, it may make sense for borrowers to function locally. This is the best way for a borrower to remain "in charge" of the process, knowing that it is proceeding in a timely fashion, and having the assurance that there will be no "surprises" at the last minute.

MORTGAGE CALCULATORS . . .
ARE THEY RELIABLE?

Web-based mortgage calculators that allow borrowers to test various financial scenarios are now available. While they are fun to experiment with, borrowers need to be cautious about relying upon their results. Few mortgage calculators are accompanied by an explanation of what assumptions are used in their calculations. Most calculator programs identify the "typical" qualifying ratios that prospective borrowers "should" meet to be eligible for a loan.

There are numerous variables that must accompany any calculation. For instance, does the calculation to determine a borrower's home buying qualification include mortgage insurance, or the tax and insurance calculation for an impound account when required? The more questions that the borrower is asked before clicking "calculate," the more reliable the outcome is likely to be (assuming the accuracy of the information entered).

With the advent of automated qualifying systems accompanied by the continued reliance upon "risk-based" scoring (i.e., taking into consideration the borrower's credit score, the amount of down payment, the type of property, etc.), the "normal" qualifying ratios often do not apply. Add to this the varying private mortgage insurance (PMI) requirements and the continuing changes in conventional, FHA, and VA loan qualifications, and it is clear that there is no way for a "programmed" calculator to account for all the possible variables existing in today's qualification matrix.

Borrowers using a real estate Web calculator may erroneously believe that they qualify for a real estate loan—or they may erroneously believe that they do not qualify. The best that some calculators can do is to identify a worst-case scenario. While useful up to a point, the reliability of the results depends upon the calculator's internal assumptions and formulas coupled with the accuracy of the user-entered information. It is easy to see that dependable results are unlikely.

With few exceptions, potential buyers will be better served by a face-to-face consultation with a competent loan officer who can assess the best loan option for their particular situation and determine their ability to qualify for a loan.

Credit and the Internet

The Fair Isaac Credit Bureau scores (known as FICO scoring) were introduced to mortgage lending over a decade ago. To arrive at the score, a borrower's credit history is examined to determine the likelihood of timely future payments on a new mortgage. This analysis has proven remarkably accurate: the system not only assesses how likely a borrower is to pay back a loan, but also measures the degree of risk a borrower represents to the lender. Scores range from 300 to 900, the higher score indicating better credit quality.

Consumers can check their credit profiles using the Internet, and it seems logical that they would do so in preparation for home loan financing. Although many sites indicate that one can acquire a "free" credit report, this can be somewhat misleading. In addition to checking if the information contained in one's credit report is accurate, the credit score is important when acquiring a home loan. When visiting most Web sites, one is urged to "upgrade" the report, at a cost, in order to acquire the credit score. Thirty-day free trials are popular, but usually unnecessary.

All three credit repositories (listed at the end of this Appendix) have Web sites through which borrowers can obtain good credit information and a score at a cost of $8.50–$14 per report. When applying for a home loan, the lender requires a report from all three repositories. Acquiring the reports individually costs more money, and the reports are not usable by an eventual lending source. Nevertheless, it may be useful for a borrower to "get an idea" of what his or her credit looks like by accessing one of the repositories. Equifax is recommended as the most user-friendly.

There is yet another possible complication in acquiring credit information over the Internet. Consumers may find it difficult to interpret the information. There are 33 variable criteria that influence a credit score. A borrower may get a clue as to what affects his or her score by reviewing the four "most significant reasons" given by the credit provider. These are generally the four most important factors affecting the score and perhaps keeping it from being higher. Lenders are schooled in interpreting the credit report results and in recommending actions required to improve the scores. It usually costs $15–$20 for a three-merged report (combining data from all three major credit reporting repositories)—this could be a good investment.

Using the Internet as a Tool

It is always tempting to acquire information from the Internet. However, be aware of some cautions. Many sources are mostly promotional rather than focused on consumer information. With rapid changes occurring in the financial arena, sites can be out-of-date and their information inaccurate.

With this in mind, we offer some sites (grouped by interest and/or specific information) that may prove helpful. In most cases, we have listed the sites alphabetically. Inclusion on the list should not be construed as a recommendation.

Government Sites (consumer information and specific loan data)

www.cdva.ca.gov (California VA loan information)
www.hud.com (FHA loans)
www.fanniemae.com (conventional loans)
www.freddiemac.com (conventional loans)

Loan rates via the Internet (mostly promotional)

www.ditech.com
www.eloan.com
www.lendingtree.com
www.loansdirect.com
www.mortgage.com

Consumer Education

www.aarp.org (senior information, especially reverse mortgages)

www.inman.com (well-known commentator's site)

www.hrblock.com (tax tips)

www.mbaa.org (Mortgage Bankers Association)

www.mortgageinfocenter.com (mortgage strategies and fact lists)

www.nolo.com (legal information)

www.responsiblelending.org (abusive lending alerts)

Credit Score Information (credit information and credit reports, usually for a fee)

www.equifax.com

www.experian.com

www.transunion.com

"Free" Credit Report Information (usually selling upgraded credit reports for credit scores)

www.creditkarma.com

www.credit.com

www.myfico.com

www.quizzle.com

Media Sites (financial news and articles)

www.bloomberg.com

www.kiplinger.com

www.thinkglink.com

Specific Service Sites

www.firstamres.com (promotes title services)

www.imoneynet.com (some investment information, but mostly promotional)

www.recyber.com (real estate software assistance)

www.seniorsites.com (nonprofit housing options for seniors)

Real Estate Calculators (see information in Appendix about Internet calculator sites)

www.aarp.com

www.kiplinger.com

www.mortgagecalc.com

www.mortgageprofessor.com

Home Valuation (relying upon Internet home valuations can be dangerous, as the information can be outdated)

www.homegain.com

www.willow.com

Finally, national bank sites (e.g., Bank of America, Chase, Wells Fargo) and real estate companies (e.g., Century 21, Coldwell Banker, RE/MAX) offer a plethora of information. Recognize that the information may be outdated and that the sites are often mostly promotional in their focus.

Glossary

A

Ability/Capacity to Pay The position of a borrower relative to repaying a loan, based on income and other assets.

Acceleration Clause Clause in trust deed or mortgage giving a lender the right to all sums owing to be immediately due and payable upon the happening of a certain event, such as a loan default.

Accrued Depreciation The difference between the cost of replacement of building new, as of the date of the appraisal, and the present appraised value. Depreciation that has accumulated over a period of time.

Adjustable Rate Mortgage (ARM) A loan pegged to an index; as the index goes up or down, the borrower's interest rate follows according to contractual limits, spelled out in the note and trust deed.

Adjusted Cost Basis The income tax cost basis of property with certain additions, such as the cost of improvements, and certain subtractions, such as depreciation in value.

Adjusted Gross Income Gross income less federal and state income taxes and Social Security.

Adjustment Interval The time between changes in the interest rate or monthly payments for an ARM, typically six months to one year.

Adjustments As part of an appraisal, the subtractions from the replacement cost of a property to allow for any loss in value due to age, condition, and other factors; also the additions to and subtractions from the values of comparable properties.

Advances Money advanced by the beneficiary under a trust deed to pay real estate taxes or other items to protect the lender's interest under the trust deed. Also refers to additional funds loaned under an open-end trust deed or mortgage. Also, periodic payments to the builder as construction progresses.

Alienation Clause A special type of acceleration clause that gives the lender the right to demand payment of the entire loan balance upon a sale or transfer of title. Also known as a due-on-sale clause.

All-Inclusive Trust Deed (AITD) A deed of trust that includes the amount due under a senior trust deed or deeds on the same property. Also known as a wrap-around.

Amortization Tables A table that shows amounts needed to pay off different loan amounts at specified interest rates for specified terms.

Amortization Book A book with information for determining monthly payment amounts, loan yields, and other financial calculations now more readily acquired via the use of a financial calculator.

Amortized Loan A loan that is completely paid off, interest and principal, by a series of regular payments that are equal or nearly equal. Also called *level-payment loan.*

Annual Percentage Rate (APR) Under the Truth-in-Lending Law, the APR is used to disclose the total cost of a loan to a borrower and is converted to the so-called effective rate.

Annuity A series of equal or nearly equal payments to be made over a period of time. The installment payments due to a landlord under a lease or installment payments due to a lender are examples of annuities.

Antideficiency Legislation Legislation that prohibits a lender from obtaining a judgment for money against a defaulting borrower under a note and deed of trust when the value of property foreclosed upon is not adequate to satisfy the debt. See *Deficiency Judgment.*

Applicable Federal Rate The rate used for imputed interest in a seller-financed transaction, equal to the rate on federal securities with a similar term.

Appraisal An estimate or opinion of value.

Appraisal Management Company (AMC) An organization through which all conventional appraisals must now be ordered.

Assessment Lien A lien against property for public construction projects that benefit the property, such as street improvements or sewers.

Assignment of Deed of Trust An instrument that transfers the security interest under a deed of trust from one lender to another.

Assignment of Rents Clause A clause in a trust deed that gives the beneficiary the right under limited circumstances to collect rents of the property if the borrower defaults.

Assumption Fee A lender's charge for changing and processing records for a new owner who is assuming an existing loan.

Assumption of Deed of Trust or Mortgage Taking over responsibility and liability for the payment of the existing deed of trust loan from the seller.

Automatic Payment Plan A plan whereby the borrower authorizes deduction of monthly payments from a checking account rather than sending payments.

B

Back-End Ratio (Bottom Ratio) A ratio representing the sum of the borrower's mortgage payment and long-term debts, divided by gross income.

Balloon Payment One installment payment on an amortized note that is at least double the amount of a regular installment. This is frequently a final payment on the due date.

Basis Property owner's ""book value" for income tax purposes. Original cost plus capital improvements less depreciation.

Beneficiary A lender under a note secured by a deed of trust.

Biweekly Loan Payments Real estate loan payments made every two weeks. A monthly payment is divided by two and paid 26 times per year.

Blanket Trust Deed A single trust deed covering more than one parcel of real estate.

Blended-Rate Loan An interest rate that is less than market rate, but greater than the existing contract rate. Sometimes offered as an alternative to a new buyer who wishes to assume an existing loan and needs additional funds.

Break-Even Analysis Calculation of the point where the income and expenses for a proposed project would be equal.

Bridge Loan A loan that bridges the gap between two other loans, usually for a short term. See *Swing Loan*.

Broker Participation A plan in which part of a seller's interest in a trust deed is assigned to the real estate broker to pay the commission on the sale, making the broker a partner with the seller on the loan.

Broker's Loan Statement A statement signed and received by the borrower at the time of a loan transaction, indicating the costs and deductions, including commissions, of a loan negotiated by a real estate licensee.

Builder's Control Service An outside third party that acts as an intermediary in the control and disbursement of funds to the builder in a building project.

Building Loan Agreement A document that contains the agreement between the lender, builder, and borrower concerning a construction project, including the schedule of disbursements to the builder.

Buy-Down Loan The purchase of a reduced interest rate, usually by home builders, allowing the borrower to qualify at a lower income level.

C

CalHFA Loans provided via the California Housing Finance Agency.

Cal-Vet Loans Loans made to eligible veterans by the Department of Veterans Affairs of the State of California for the purchase of real estate, utilizing a contract of sale.

Cap Upper limit on adjustable or variable interest rate loans on a periodic basis during life of loan.

Capital Gains Gains on the sale of property, as qualified by statute.

Capitalization In appraising, a method used to determine value of a property by dividing annual net operating income by a desirable capitalization rate.

Capitalization Rate The rate that is believed to represent the proper relationship between the value of the real property and the net operating income generated from the property.

Capitalized Income Stream Valuation approach to income-producing property measured by converting the income into a single present value.

Cash Equivalency Price in terms of cash versus other assets, such as trust deed, stocks, and bonds that may be worth less than their face amount.

Cash Flow The pattern of income and expenditures, which affects investment properties.

Certificate of Eligibility A certificate issued by the Department of Veterans Affairs that shows the amount of the veteran's entitlement.

Certificate of Reasonable Value (CRV) A document issued by the Department of Veterans Affairs that shows the appraised value of the property.

Certified Appraisal Report A written communication of an analysis, opinion, or conclusion relating to the value of real property certified according to state and federal requirements.

Closing Costs Costs paid by the borrower when borrowing for the purchase of a property. Costs paid by buyers and sellers on the sale of a property.

Cost of Funds Index (COFI) Adjustable-rate mortgage with rate that adjusts based on cost of funds index, after the 11th District Cost of Funds.

Collateralization The hypothecating of property, as security for a loan.

Collateralized Mortgage Obligation (CMO) A security issued by FNMA that is designed to limit the investor's risk that borrowers will prepay the loans early.

Combination Loan One loan combining a construction loan and permanent take-out loan after construction is completed.

Commercial Bank A financial institution chartered by a state or the federal government to receive, lend, and safeguard money and other items of value.

Commercial Loan Nonmortgage method of financing real estate through a personal loan from a commercial bank.

Commitment Agreement by a lender to lend mortgage money at a future date, subject to compliance with stated conditions.

Community Home Buyer's Program An FNMA/FHLMC program for purchasers with lower incomes that features 97 percent financing, with reduced closing costs and cash reserve requirements.

Community Reinvestment Act Federal law requiring financial institutions to lend in communities served, including low- and moderate-income areas, consistent with considerations of safety and soundness.

Co-Mortgagor A person who signs a note and deed of trust in addition to the primary borrower to give extra security to the loan. The co-mortgagor is jointly liable for the repayment of the loan, and is in title to the real estate.

Comparables Recently sold properties near the property being appraised and similar to it.

Comparative Market Analysis An opinion on a property's value prepared by a real estate licensee rather than a certified appraiser.

Compensating Factors Positive factors that are considered by lenders to approve loans to otherwise marginal borrowers.

Completion Bond A bond that the owners of a project can purchase to protect themselves, builders, and lenders from mechanic's liens.

Computerized Loan Originations (CLO) Accessing lender loan programs via computer.

Conditional Commitment The FHA appraisal, issued by an independent fee appraiser on the property, that includes any conditions such as repairs the FHA will require before insuring a loan.

Conditional Sale Contract A contract for the sale and purchase of property stating that delivery and possession is to be given to the buyer-vendee, but that legal title is to remain with the seller-vendor until the conditions of the contract have been fulfilled.

Condominium A form of ownership in which separate units of three-dimensional air-space are owned by individual owners. The individual owners also jointly own an undivided interest in the common areas such as hallways, swimming pools, and land. Sometimes referred to as a vertical subdivision.

Conduit Purchase of loans from mortgage bankers and commercial banks, then collateralizing them with mortgage-backed securities.

Conforming Loan Maximum loan amount purchased by FNMA and FHLMC.

Constant Debt service payments as a percentage of the original loan amount.

Construction Loan Loan made for the construction of improvements. Usually funds are disbursed at periodic intervals as the work progresses.

Contract of Sale See *Conditional Sale Contract.*

Conventional Loan Any loan that is not insured or guaranteed or made by a government agency.

Co-Op Similar to a long-term lease, but with right to sole and exclusive possession of the unit for an indefinite period.

Correspondent An abbreviated term meaning mortgage loan correspondent. Applies when a mortgage company originates a loan for an investor.

Co-Signer One who signs a note as guarantor but whose name is not on the title to the property.

Cost Approach A method in which the value of a property is derived by estimating the replacement cost of the improvements, then deducting the estimated depreciation, then adding the market value of the land.

Cost of Funds Costs incurred by lenders to obtain capital.

Creative Financing Any financing out of the ordinary, such as seller carrybacks wrap-arounds and sub prime loans.

Creative Financing Disclosure Act California law that requires disclosure of specified terms to the buyer-borrower in a seller carryback financing situation covering one to four dwelling units.

Credit History Summary of applicant's credit accounts that includes repayments, past due accounts, judgments and foreclosures.

Credit Life Insurance A form of declining term life insurance that will pay all or part of the mortgage if the borrower dies.

Credit Report Credit history of a person or business issued by a company in the credit reporting business, used to help determine creditworthiness.

Credit Scoring A method of evaluating an applicant's credit history for the purpose of determining the probability of repayment of debts. Also called *FICO score.*

Credit Union Cooperative organization of members of a particular group who agree to save money and make loans to its members.

D

Debenture Bonds issued without security, backed only by the credit standing and earning capacity of the issuer.

Debt Coverage Ratio (DCR) Net operating income divided by annual debt service. Used by lenders when analyzing income property loans.

Debt Service Another term for the principal and interest payments on a loan. Widely used for commercial and industrial properties.

Debt-to-Income Ratio Borrowers' monthly payment obligations as a percentage of their income.

Deed in Lieu of Foreclosure A voluntary conveyance to the lender from the defaulting borrower that avoids the foreclosure process.

Deed of Reconveyance Upon the repayment of a promissory note secured by a trust deed, trustee transfers legal title back to the trustor (borrower), thereby releasing the lien.

Deed of Trust Instrument by which title to real estate is transferred to a third-party trustee as security for repayment of a real estate loan. Used in California instead of a mortgage.

Default Failure to fulfill a duty or promise. Failure to make the payments on a real estate loan.

Deferred Interest See *Negative Amortization.*

Deficiency Judgment A judgment given when the security pledged for a loan does not satisfy the debt upon foreclosure. Certain conditions must be met.

Delinquency Failure to make timely payments on loans.

Demand Deposit Checking account or transaction deposit withdrawable upon demand, as opposed to time deposit.

Department of Veterans Affairs (DVA) Federal government agency that guarantees approved lenders against foreclosure loss on loans made to eligible veterans.

Deposit Receipt A form used to accept earnest money to bind an offer for the purchase of real property. When accepted by the seller, it creates a sale contract.

Depreciation A loss of value in real property brought about by age, physical deterioration, or functional or economic obsolescence. Broadly, a loss in value from any cause. Also called *write-off.*

Desire to Pay The predisposition of a borrower to repay a loan, suggested by prior credit history, size of down payment, and reason for buying.

Desktop Originator (FNMA) A program of the Federal National Mortgage Association that allows loan agents to take applications and prequalify borrowers immediately.

Development Loans Loans that finance the acquisition of land and the installation, prior to building, of utilities, sewage systems, roads, and so on. Sometimes called *land loan.*

Direct Private Lender Individual who invests directly in loans without going through an intermediary and expects to receive higher interest rate yields.

Disbursements Periodic payments as construction progresses.

Discount An amount deducted in advance from the loan before the borrower is given the money. Also referred to as Points. In secondary market sales, a discount is the difference between the sale price and the principal balance on the note. Contrast *Premium.*

Discount Rate The interest rate that the Federal Reserve Bank charges local member banks for funds they borrow.

Discount Tables Tables used by lenders and investors to show how much a given value is, called the discounted value, based upon various interest rates and terms of maturity.

Discrimination by Effect Lending practices that have a discriminatory effect against protected groups. Prohibited unless shown to be required to achieve a legitimate business purpose.

Disintermediation Relatively sudden outflow of funds from a financial intermediary when depositors can obtain higher returns elsewhere.

Doctrine of Relation Back The principle that if work on a project begins before the trust deed is recorded, all who furnish labor or materials there-after may file mechanics' liens that have precedence over the trust deed.

Down Payment The difference between the sale price of the property and the loan amount.

Draw System An arrangement by which a builder receives periodic payments as construction proceeds.

Due-on-Sale Clause Clause in a trust deed that allows lenders to demand immediate payment of the loan balance if borrower sells or transfers an interest in the property.

DVA Department of Veterans Affairs, a federal agency (not Cal-Vet). Formerly VA.

DVA Automatics Approvals of DVA loans by certain lenders qualified to use in-house underwriters.

DVA-Guaranteed Loan A loan for veterans under which the Department of Veterans Affairs guarantees to reimburse the lender a specified maximum amount in case of foreclosure.

E

Earnest Money Money paid with an offer to purchase, given to bind a sale.

Easy Money Loose money policy of the Federal Reserve Board, indicating increased availability of money in circulation.

Economic Life The period during which an improvement on a parcel of land can be used for any beneficial purpose.

Economic Obsolescence A loss in property value caused by forces outside the property, such as adverse zoning or neighborhood nuisances.

Effective Age The age assigned to the improvements by the appraiser, not necessarily the chronological age.

Effective Interest Rate The percentage of interest actually being paid by the borrower for the use of the money, including certain expenses for obtaining the loan. See *Annual Percentage Rate (APR)*.

Endowment Funds The invested funds that are received as gifts by institutions such as colleges and charities.

Entitlement The maximum amount that the DVA will pay if the lender suffers a loss on a DVA loan.

Equal Credit Opportunity Act (ECOA) Federal law prohibiting discrimination in the extension of credit.

Equifax One of three major credit reporting repositories, along with Experian and TransUnion.

Equity The interest or value that an owner has in real estate over and above liens against the property. The difference between market value and the existing indebtedness.

Equity Financing Lender finances high-ratio loan in exchange for a percentage of ownership and the right to share in the property's cash flow.

Equity Participation When a lender receives partial ownership interest in the project in order to increase its return on the loan.

Escalation Clause Refers to rent increases or decreases tied to an appropriate index.

Escrow A neutral depository, where a third party carries out instructions for the lender, buyer, and seller and is responsible for handling the paperwork and disbursing funds needed to transfer the property.

Escrow Account See *Impound Account*.

Experian One of three major credit reporting repositories, along with Equifax and TransUnion.

Extended Term Recasting of a loan by extending the remaining term, thereby lowering monthly payments.

F

Fair Credit Reporting Act Federal law that gives a rejected borrower the right to inspect and correct his or her credit agency file.

Fair Market Value (FMV) The price in terms of money that a parcel of property will bring on the open market when neither buyer nor seller is under any compulsion to act.

Federal Deposit Insurance Corporation (FDIC) Insures accounts at member banks up to $100,000.

Federal Fair & Accurate Credit Transaction Act (FACT) A seven-provision act wherein the two most important provisions are the establishment of procedures to help protect against identity fraud and allowing consumers to request a free credit report every 12 months from each of the three major credit repositories.

Federal Funds Rate The rate one bank charges another bank for overnight use of excess reserves.

Federal Home Loan Bank (FHLB) Provides credit reserves systems for member state and federal savings banks.

Federal Home Loan Mortgage Corporation (FHLMC) An agency known as Freddie Mac, which provides a secondary market for savings banks and other institutions.

Federal Housing Administration (FHA) Division of the U.S. Department of Housing and Urban Development that insures residential mortgage loans made by approved lenders against loss through foreclosure.

Federal Housing Finance Board (FHFB) Federal agency that regulates the 12 Federal Home Loan Banks.

Federal National Mortgage Association (FNMA) Popularly known as Fannie Mae, a private corporation whose primary function is to buy and sell mortgages in the secondary mortgage market.

Federal Reserve Bank Board (FRBB) An agency that oversees the Federal Reserve System, regulates commercial banks, and regulates the flow of money and credit.

Federal Reserve System Central banking system of the United States consisting of 12 Federal Reserve Banks and the Federal Reserve Board, which sets monetary policy.

FHA Direct Endorsement An automatic approval system that allows FHA loan approvals by an in-house underwriter.

FHA-Insured Loan A loan made by a bank or mortgage company with insurance from the FHA against loss to the lender in the event the loan must be foreclosed.

FHA 203(b) Program Loans insured by the FHA for one- to four dwelling units. Often referred to as a rehabilitation loan.

FICO Score See *Credit Scoring.*

Finance Charge Charges paid separately or withheld from the proceeds of the loan, such as loan origination fees or mortgage insurance premiums.

Finance Company A firm involved in lending usually to high-risk borrowers at high interest rates. Identified as an industrial bank.

Financial Calculator An electronic calculator that is designed to compute loan payments, interest rates, and other calculations used in real estate financing.

Financial Institutions Reform, Recovery, and Enforcement Act (FIRREA) Federal law that restructured deposit insurance funds and regulatory system for thrifts.

Financial Intermediary A depository that pools funds of clients and depositors and invests them into real estate loans.

Finder's Fee A fee paid by a lender or broker for referring a borrower to a certain lending institution or real estate office, often paid to a nonlicensee.

First Deed of Trust or Mortgage The first recorded loan; it takes precedence over junior loans and encumbrances. Also called *senior lien* or *primary lien.*

Fiscal Policy Programs by the federal government that are intended to influence economic activity by making changes in government expenditures and taxation, implemented by the U.S. Treasury.

Five-Step Financing Process The process of borrowing money that includes making application, qualifying the borrower and property, processing documents, closing, and servicing the loan.

Fixed Rate Loans Loans with constant fixed rates that will not change over the life of the loan.

Flipping Usually a predatory practice involving appraisal of run-down houses, much higher than FMV, and resold at inflated prices, usually to low-income buyers who end up in foreclosure.

Floor Loan A minimum amount that a permanent lender will provide for construction until the developer can secure all the planned tenants for the project.

Forbearance An arrangement that delays foreclosure action by restructuring and/or temporary postponement of monthly payments.

Foreclosure Process whereby property pledged as security for a real estate loan is sold to satisfy the debt if the borrower defaults.

Fractional Reserve Banking Money "created" by the banking system through monetary policy.

Front Money The money required to get a real estate project started.

Front-End Ratio (Top Ratio) A ratio representing the borrower's mortgage payment divided by gross income.

Functional Obsolescence Poor structural design or unusual floor plans that could affect marketability and value of a property.

G

Gap Commitment A lender's commitment to provide the difference between the floor amount that a developer will receive for a project and the full amount to be received when all rentals are achieved.

GI Loans Common term for loans guaranteed by the Department of Veterans Affairs for qualified veterans. Also known as DVA loans.

Gift Deed Deed for which no consideration is given except love and affection.

Gift Letter Verification that a gift to a borrower for a down payment is not an undisclosed a loan.

Government Mortgage Insurance Government programs that eliminate risk of loss to lenders from default on loans, thereby making the loans more attractive.

Government National Mortgage Association (GNMA) A federal corporation popularly known as Ginnie Mae. It is mainly involved in the administration of the mortgage-backed securities program and other federal programs.

Government-Backed Loans Loans obtained with the help of government agencies such as

FHA, Department of Veterans Affairs, Cal-Vet, or other programs.

Government-Sponsored Enterprise (GSE) Collective title for the secondary market entities consisting of the FNMA, FHLMC, GNMA.

Graduated-Payment Mortgage (GPM) Fixed interest rate loan on which the scheduled monthly payments start low, but rise later, then level off. Produces negative amortization.

Gross Income Total stable income before deductions.

Gross Operating Income (GOI) Gross scheduled income less a reasonable vacancy factor and rent collection losses.

Gross Rent Multiplier (GRM) A rule of thumb method of appraising income property that provides a "ballpark" figure only. It is an appropriate factor, usually determined by an appraiser, which, when multiplied by monthly or annual rents, indicates property value.

Gross Scheduled Income Total income from property before deducting any expenses.

Growth Equity Mortgage (GEM) Loan with fixed interest rate and scheduled annual increases in monthly payments, resulting in shorter maturity.

H

Hard Costs Costs for which the builder must pay out money.

Hard Money Loan Loan usually from a private lender. Actual money loaned and secured by a deed of trust as opposed to a loan carried back by a seller, in which no money passes.

Hazard Insurance Covers dwelling and contents for fire, wind, and water damage, theft, and other specified losses.

Holdback Final percentage of construction loan amount released after the filing period for mechanic's liens has expired.

Housing Economic Recovery Act Legislation whereby banks were encouraged to voluntarily assist struggling homeowners via established guidelines for modifying home loans. The Act also led to the establishment of minimum standards for all residential mortgage brokers and lenders, leading to the initiation of new disclosure rules.

Home Valuation Code of Conduct (HVCC) Legislation that established regulations to ensure the quality and independence of the appraisal process by protecting the appraiser from coercive interference from lenders or real estate licensees.

Home Warranty A protection policy to repair and/or replace major home components should such occur after the close of escrow.

HUD An abbreviation for the U.S. Department of Housing and Urban Development.

Hypothecate To give a thing as security without the necessity of giving up possession; for example, when real estate is used as security for a loan.

I

Impound Account Funds retained in a special account by a lender to cover property taxes and hazard insurance. Also called *trust fund account* or *loan trust fund*.

Improvement Bond Act of 1915 California law that provides for issuance of bonds for subdivision street improvements, to be paid from proportional assessments against affected property owners.

Imputed Interest A minimum interest rate that is applied to all seller-financed transactions to prevent sellers from treating interest income as capital gains in order to pay less in federal tax.

Income Approach One of three methods in the appraisal process, which analyzes income and expenses, then uses a capitalization rate to arrive at value.

Income Ratio The monthly payment on a loan (including principal and interest, taxes, and insurance) divided by the borrower's monthly gross income.

Indirect Lender Individual who invests in loans through a mortgage broker in order to benefit from the broker's expertise.

Inflation Sharp increase in prices for goods and services resulting from too much money in circulation and/or rising costs of materials and labor.

Installment Note A loan providing for payment of the principal in two or more installments.

Installment Sales Contract A sale in which legal title to the property remains with the seller until terms agreed upon have been satisfied.

Institutional Lender A savings bank, commercial bank, or insurance company that deals in real estate loans.

Interest Change Clause Provision in an adjustable rate mortgage that the interest rate can change at specified intervals according to changes in a specified index.

Interest Rate The charge made for a loan of money expressed as a percentage of the principal.

Interest-Only Note A straight nonamortizing loan, in which only interest is paid. Interest can be paid periodically or at maturity, when principal is paid in a lump sum. Also called *straight note.*

Interim Loan Any short-term financing, such as a Swing Loan, or a loan used to finance construction, due at the completion of the construction, which is usually paid off with the proceeds of a Take-Out Loan.

Intermediate-Term Loans Temporary short-term loans—ordinarily 3 to 10 years—that include home improvement loans, consumer loans, or loans for the purpose of permitting a developer to delay longer-term financing until more favorable loan terms become available.

Intermediation When a financial institution acts as go-between for saver-depositors and borrowers.

J

Joint Note A note signed by two or more persons who have equal liability for payment. Usually expressed as "joint and several," which includes individual liability.

Judicial Sale A sale of property by court proceedings to satisfy a lien.

Jumbo Loan Loan exceeding the maximum amount purchased by FNMA and FHLMC. Also called *nonconforming loan.*

Junior Mortgage A subordinate or inferior lien.

L

Land Contract of Sale See *Conditional Sale Contract.*

Late Charge An additional charge a borrower is required to pay as a penalty for failure to pay a regular installment when due, after the grace period expires.

Lease A contract between an owner and tenant, setting forth conditions upon which tenant may occupy and use the property.

Letter of Credit Letter from a bank asking that the holder be allowed to withdraw money from the recipient bank or agency that will be charged back to the first bank.

Leverage The relationship between an owner's equity and total debt on a property. The higher the leverage, the higher the debt in relation to the value of the property.

Lien A form of encumbrance that makes the property security for the payment of a debt. Examples include deeds of trust, mortgages, judgments, and mechanic's liens.

Life Insurance Company A business that collects a person's savings by selling contracts (policies) paid for through periodic premiums and providing cash payment upon death.

Lifetime Cap Ceiling for rate increases over the life of an ARM, expressed either as a particular percentage rate or as so many points over or under the initial rate.

Like-Kind A phrase used to identify an appropriate property for an exchange in a 1031 Tax Deferred Exchange transaction.

Liquidity of Investment The ease with which investments can be readily converted into cash.

Loan Application The written form submitted by the borrower, usually the standard form of FNMA/FHLMC.

Loan Assumption The lender's approval of a new borrower who takes over an existing loan.

Loan Closing When all conditions of the loan have been met, the lender authorizes the recording of documents.

Loan Commitment Agreement by a lender to make a loan subject to certain conditions being met, covering a specific period of time.

Loan Committee A committee or one individual in a lending institution that reviews loan packages and either approves or disapproves.

Loan Correspondent See *Correspondent.*

Loan Origination Steps involved in the loan application process prior to close of escrow.

Loan Origination Fee A charge, usually measured by points, made by a lender for originating the loan. Included in nonrecurring closing costs.

Loan Package Documentation consisting of all the forms, documents, and reports the lender needs in order to make a decision on the loan.

Loan Underwriting The process of approving or disapproving loan applications.

Loan-to-Value Ratio The amount of loan, expressed as a percentage of a property's value or sales price, whichever is lower.

Lock-in Clause A provision that prohibits paying off a loan before a specified date.

Lock-in Loan Lender's written guarantee that the rate quoted will be good for a specific period of time.

Long-Term Debt How long a term outstanding debt is to last, the precise term varying by lenders and agencies.

Lot Release Provision The release of an individual lot from the blanket trust deed covering a subdivision. Provides for a deed of partial reconveyance.

Low Down Payment Conventional Loans Loans offered through programs of FNMA and FHLMC that relax the usual down payment requirements for purchasers with lower incomes and excellent credit.

Lump Sum Payment of the entire principal amount due at maturity on a straight note.

M

Market Data Approach An appraisal method in which the value of a property is estimated by means of comparing it with similar properties recently sold.

Market Price Amount paid for property, regardless of motives, knowledge, and so on.

Market Value See *Fair Market Value*.

Maturity Date The date upon which a real estate note or other negotiable instrument becomes due and payable.

Mechanic's Lien A claim against the property by contractors, laborers, or material suppliers who have not been paid for their contributions to a building project. A summary right.

Mello-Roos Community Facilities Act California law that authorizes setting up a taxing district that can issue bonds to pay for a housing development's improvements, such as roads, sewers, and community center.

MIS Mortgage Information System.

Monetary Policy Policies of the Federal Reserve System that increase or decrease the supply of money in an effort to achieve designated economic goals.

Monthly Payments These always include principal and interest, and may also, depending upon lender or loan, include taxes and insurance.

Moratorium A temporary waiver or suspension of payments on a loan.

Mortgage A two-party instrument in which the borrower-mortgagor retains legal title during loan term while the real estate acts as collateral for the loan.

Mortgage Banker The packaging of real estate loans to be sold to a permanent investor often with servicing retained for a fee. Mortgage bankers act as correspondents for investors.

Mortgage Brokers Differ from mortgage bankers in that they invest no capital: their prime function is to bring together borrowers and lenders, and for this they are paid a fee.

Mortgage Company A firm that may represent other investors in arranging and servicing real estate loans. May also invest its own funds.

Mortgage Correspondent See *Correspondent*.

Mortgage Loan Disclosure Statement A legally required written statement to the borrower concerning estimated costs of a loan and the net amount to be received.

Mortgage Revenue Bonds Tax exempt bonds issued by units of government to finance mortgages at rates below market rate.

Mortgage-Backed Securities Investment securities similar to bonds, representing an interest in a pool of mortgages.

Mutual Savings Bank A savings bank originated in the New England states in which the depositors place their savings with the right to borrow money for home loans. There are no mutual savings banks in California.

N

Negative Amortized Loans Loans in which the required payment relative to the interest rate charged is insufficient to pay all of the interest due each month, resulting in negative amortization.

Negative Cash Flow The situation where income from investment property is less than outgo, so that money must be added to make the venture solvent.

Negotiable Instrument A promissory note or other instrument that meets certain legal requirements, allowing it to circulate freely in commerce.

Neighborhood A group of properties relatively similar in land use and value. It can be large or as small as a single block or street.

Net Operating Income (NOI) Gross annual income less vacancies, uncollectible rents, and other operating expenses.

Net Spendable Income Net operating income less debt service and income taxes on the property's taxable income.

Nominal Interest Rate The interest rate that appears on the real estate promissory note. Also called *note rate*.

Nonconforming Loan See *Jumbo Loan.*

Noninstitutional Lender Lenders on real estate loans other than commercial banks, insurance companies, and savings banks.

Nonrecurring Closing Costs Costs that are one-time charges paid at the close of escrow.

Nonsupervised Lender Mortgage company that must be approved in advance by DVA to make automatic approvals of borrowers.

Note A signed instrument acknowledging a debt and a promise to repay per the terms outlined.

Notice of Abandonment A notice filed in case a construction project is abandoned before completion.

Notice of Cessation of Labor A notice filed in case construction is not completed due to various reasons.

Notice of Completion A notice filed by the owner of a new construction project within 10 days after the job is completed, starting a period during which liens may be filed by con-tractors and other parties.

Notice of Default Recorded notice that a default has occurred under a deed of trust and that the beneficiary intends to proceed with a trustee's sale.

Notice of Sale Notice that property in default will be sold to pay off the loan. It must be advertised in a newspaper and posted at the property and in a public place.

NOW Accounts Stands for Negotiable Order of Withdrawal, a checking account permitted for savings banks.

O

Obligatory Advances Disbursements of money that the lender is required to make under the terms of a construction loan.

Office of Thrift Supervision (OTS) A branch of the U.S. Treasury that regulates all federally insured savings banks.

Office Park Planned development for office buildings and related services.

Online Loan Refers to ability to apply for a real estate loan through the Internet.

Open-End Deed of Trust A deed of trust containing a clause that permits the borrower to obtain additional advances of money secured by the same deed of trust, if the lender permits, but not necessarily under the same terms.

Open-Market Operations Federal Reserve actions to influence the money supply by selling or buying government securities.

Operating Costs The owner's expenses in operating investment property, such as utilities, repairs, and replacement of furnishings.

"Or More" Clause A clause in a note that permits extra payments on principal of the loan without penalty.

Origination Fee A charge for arranging and processing a real estate loan. See *Loan Origination Fee.*

P

Package Loan Loan secured by both real and personal property, often appliances and other fixtures.

Paper Term used by real estate agents, investors, and others to designate promissory notes, usually secured by deeds of trust.

Par The face amount of a loan with no premium or discount.

Partial Amortization A repayment schedule that does not pay back enough principal to completely pay off a loan by the due date, leaving a balloon payment.

Partial Entitlement The amount of additional entitlement allowed to a veteran who had previously used an entitlement when maximum amounts were lower.

Partial Reconveyance Deed A deed used to reconvey a portion of the land encumbered by a deed of trust.

Partial Release Clause A clause in a deed of trust that provides for release of part of the property from the deed of trust upon payment of a specific portion of the debt.

Participation When a lending institution sells a part interest in a block of loans to another institution or agency. Also, when a lender receives part of the income from a property to increase its return on the loan. Also see *Equity Participation*.

Pass-Through Securities Securities backed by a pool of FHA and DVA mortgages, issued by the Government National Mortgage Association.

Passive Loss Rules that apply to rental properties, especially houses, which allow investors to take a tax deduction for losses against certain other taxable income, such as wages, salary, interest, dividends, etc.

Payout Schedule The predetermined system of releasing money to the builder as construction progresses.

Pension Funds Public and private retirement savings funds held in trust, which can be invested in real estate loans, stocks, or government securities.

Percentage Lease A commercial lease in which the owner gets a percentage of the tenant's gross receipts.

Performance Bond A bond furnished to guarantee that a builder will perform in accordance with the contract terms and that the property at completion will be free of mechanic's liens.

Permanent Financing See *Take-Out Loan.*

Physical Depreciation Deterioration of property caused by wear and structural problems.

PITI An abbreviation for principal, interest, taxes, and insurance, commonly used when referring to the monthly loan obligation.

Planned Unit Development (PUD) A land-use design that combines private fee ownership of a parcel and joint undivided ownership of common facilities such as grounds, parking, and recreational facilities.

Plans and Specifications Architectural and engineering drawings and specifications for construction of a building, including description of materials and manner in which they are to be applied.

Points Amount paid by the borrower or the seller, which increases the effective yield for a lender. Each point equals 1 percent of the loan.

Portfolio Loan Any loan retained by the lender, as contrasted with selling it in the secondary market.

Positive Cash Flow The situation where income from investment property is greater than outgo, so that a profit is made.

Predatory Lending Term applying to all acts construed as having taken advantage of a borrower's naiveté related to the charging of excessive fees or interest rate.

Premium An amount, usually measured in points, in excess of the loan balance owing, paid for the purchase of a note and deed of trust.

Prepaid Finance Charge Charges paid separately or withheld from the proceeds of the loan, such as loan origination fees or mortgage insurance premiums.

Prepaid Items Expenses paid by buyer-borrower at closing, such as taxes, insurance, and interest. Used by FHA. See *Recurring Closing Costs.*

Prepayment Penalty A charge for the payment of a mortgage or deed of trust note before maturity.

Prepayment Privilege Allows borrowers to make certain extra payments on the principal balance without penalty.

Price The amount for which a lender will sell a loan to an investor, equal to the face value of the loan minus the discount or plus a premium.

Primary Mortgage Market The market in which loans are made directly to the borrowers.

Prime Rate Interest rate individual banks charge their most creditworthy preferred corporate customers.

Principal The face amount on a real estate loan, the amount upon which interest is calculated.

Private Lender Individual who invests his/her own funds into real estate loans, directly or through mortgage brokers.

Private Mortgage Insurance (PMI) Insurance written by a private company, protecting the mortgage lender against specified loss in case of foreclosure.

Processing Preparation of loan application and supporting documents for consideration by a lender or insurer; all procedures up to close of escrow.

Progress Payments Periodic payments to the builders as construction proceeds.

Promissory Note See *Note.*

Purchase Money Deed of Trust A trust deed securing a note given as part or all of the purchase price. Examples: carryback by a seller or a new loan from a lender.

Purchase Money Mortgages The term applied to loans, particularly those carried by sellers, in assisting in a purchase transaction.

Q

Qualified Mortgage Bond Program Use of low interest rate revenue bonds for targeted first-time home buyers under the Cal-Vet program.

Qualifying Ratio A lender's policy on how much income a borrower should have in order to make the payments of principal, interest, taxes, and insurance on the desired loan; for example, payments not exceeding 28 percent of gross income.

Quitclaim Deed A simple conveyance of rights in property without warranty.

R

Rate Lock See *Lock-In Loan.*

Real Estate Investment Trust (REIT) A corporation, trust, or association in which investors pool funds for investments in real estate but avoid double taxation as a corporation.

Real Estate Settlement Procedures Act (RESPA) A federal law that requires lenders to provide borrowers with certain information on settlement (closing) costs.

Real Property Land and buildings as opposed to personal property.

Real Property (Mortgage) Loan Law A California statute that governs real estate loan brokers, limiting commissions, requiring disclosure to the borrower, and regulating balloon payments and insurance requirements.

Recasting A change in loan terms to assist the borrower, such as by extending the term or reducing the interest rate.

Reconveyance See *Deed of Reconveyance.*

Recurring Closing Costs Repeating expenses paid by the borrower at close of escrow, such as tax reserves, hazard insurance, and prepaid interest. See *Prepaid Items.*

Redlining The illegal practice of refusing to lend mortgage money in certain areas without regard to the creditworthiness of the individual borrower.

Refinance To renew or replace the existing loan with additional financing, or to secure a loan on a free and clear property already owned by the borrower.

Regulation Z See *Truth-in-Lending Law/ Regulation Z.*

Reinstate To cure a default under a note secured by a deed of trust.

Reintermediation Return of savings to thrift institutions from previously higher-paying investment outlets.

Release of Liability An agreement by the lender to terminate the personal obligation of the borrower.

Release of Mechanic's Lien The lifting of a mechanic's lien, for example by written release, issuance of a bond, or satisfaction of a judgment.

Rent Control Local laws that limit the amount of increase in residential rents.

Rental Achievement Clause The provision in a loan agreement that the developer will secure tenants in advance for a new commercial or industrial project.

Replacement Cost Amount required to replace improvements of comparable quality, at today's prices. An appraiser's estimate of amount needed to rebuild an existing property at today's prices using cost approach.

Request for Notice of Default and Notice of Sale A recorded notice made by anyone requesting that he or she be notified in the event that foreclosure proceedings are instituted or that time and place for the sale has been set.

Reserve Requirement The amount of reserve funds that banks and thrift institutions must set aside in order to protect depositors; it may be raised or lowered by the Federal Reserve.

Residual Income DVA's calculation that from gross income subtracts taxes, housing payment, and fixed expenses such as child support and long-term debts. Also used by Cal-Vet.

Reverse Annuity Mortgage Stream of monthly payments provided to senior homeowners through an annuity purchased by a loan against the owners' accumulated equity in their home.

Right of Reinstatement The trustor's right to reinstate a loan by paying all delinquent payments, late charges, and foreclosure fees. Starts with recording of notice of default and lasts up to five business days before scheduled sale.

Risk Rating A process used by lenders to determine the soundness of offering a loan.

Rollover Loan that may extend beyond certain intermediate maturities.

S

Sale-Leaseback Land and/or buildings may be sold at 100 percent of value and then leased back by the seller. This is an alternative form of financing.

Sales Comparison Approach See *Market Data Approach to Value.*

Savings and Loan Association Deposit-type savings institution that lends in the residential field. The name/title has been virtually replaced by "Savings Bank."

Savings Association Insurance Fund (SAIF) Administered by the FDIC to insure deposits at savings banks and federal savings banks.

Savings Bank Savings and loan association using newly permitted designations.

Secondary Financing A loan secured by a junior trust deed.

Secondary Mortgage Market The purchasing and selling of existing notes secured by deeds of trust which promotes a constant flow of funds allowing lenders to continue to provide new loans to ready borrowers.

Securitization Debt issuance backed by mortgage portfolios or other types of assets.

Seller Carryback The seller's agreement to take payments on a note secured by a trust deed to help the buyer finance all or a portion of the purchase price.

Servicing Supervising and administering a loan after it has been made. This involves such things as collecting payments, keeping records, property inspections, and foreclosing on defaulted loans, and any process after close of escrow.

Short Sale Lender agreement to compromise a debt when the value of the security property is less than the debt owed.

Short-Term Construction Loan An interim loan that covers the construction of a building and can be paid off by a take-out loan.

Sight Deposit See *Demand Deposit.*

Soft Costs Costs to a builder for such noncash items as profit, overhead, and supervision.

Split Junior Loan (or Lien) Seller financing divided into second and third trust deeds, which may be easier to resell than one larger second lien.

Stability of Income The stability of the borrower's income, based on such things as length of time on the job and type of job.

Standardization Refers to the use of the same borrower and property standards accompanied by the same forms for loans acquired by investors in the secondary mortgage market.

Standby Commitment A contract—usually between FNMA/ FHLMC and a lender—to buy a pool of loans in the future from a lender at a specified yield.

Stock Equity Pledge of stock as collateral for the purchase of real estate, usually nonresidential.

Straight Note See *Interest-Only Note.*

Street Improvement Act of 1911 California law that allows assessments for street improvements to be paid off during the term of the bonds that are issued for them.

"Subject To" The taking of real property "subject to" an existing loan is done without being personally liable to the existing lender. This is in contrast to assuming a loan, when the buyer assumes responsibility and liability for the loan.

Subordination Clause An agreement under which a senior trust deed is made subordinate to an otherwise junior lien. Often used when a land loan subordinates to a new construction loan.

Subrogation Assignment of rights.

Substantial Completion The point from which a period for filing liens on a completed construction project is counted if a proper Notice of Completion is filed or not filed.

Supervised Lender Institution such as a commercial bank or savings bank that is supervised by an agency of the state or federal government and can approve DVA borrowers automatically, if qualified.

Swing Loan Used to assist in purchase of replacement house before sale of original house is completed. See *Bridge Loan.*

Syndication Investors pooling their resources to purchase real estate, usually through a limited partnership.

T

Take-Out Commitment The terms involved when lenders agree to lend on a specified property to a specified borrower for a certain length of time at a certain interest rate.

Take-Out Loan A permanent loan that pays off the existing construction loan.

Tax Service A fee paid to a tax service agency that each year reviews the records of taxing bodies and reports any delinquencies to the lender and borrower. The fee is usually paid by the borrower.

Tax Shelter A strategy for investment that should result in reduced tax liability.

Tax-Deferred Exchange A method of deferring capital gains taxes by exchanging one or more properties for other like property.

Terms Refers to all conditions involved in a loan. The word term often also refers to the number of years over which the loan is repaid.

Thrift Institution Savings bank and other institutions that invest principally in real estate trust deeds.

Tight Money A situation in which the demand for money exceeds the supply, causing interest rates to increase and borrower qualifications to be tightened.

Time Deposit Savings account with a fixed maturity, as opposed to demand deposit.

Title Insurance Insurance written by a legal reserve title insurance company to protect property owners and lenders against loss due to certain title defects.

Total Monthly Expense In qualifying for a loan, this is the addition of mortgage payments plus nonmortgage long-term debts. Used by FHA, DVA, and Cal-Vet.

Townhouse A residential unit connected to other similar units. Often a two-story structure. A style of architecture.

Trade Association Group that promotes the interests of the firms in their memberships and provide them with research and information.

Transaction Accounts Accounts used to make payments or transfers to others, such as checking accounts.

TransUnion One of three major credit reporting repositories, along with Equifax and Experian.

Triple Net Lease A lease arrangement in which the lessee pays for all repairs, maintenance, taxes, and operating expenses.

Trust Deed Deed from a borrower to a trustee who holds title for security purposes until loan terms are satisfied. See a *Deed of Trust.*

Trustee's Deed A deed given to the successful bidder at a trustee's sale (foreclosure).

Trustee's Sale Sale of property in foreclosure by the trustee, rather than through a judicial sale.

Trustor A borrower under a trust deed, who deeds property to trustee as security for the repayment of the debt.

Truth-in-Lending Law (Regulation Z) A federal law designed to show a borrower the total cost of a loan. The annual percentage rate (APR) is the term used to disclose the effective rate of interest.

U

Underwriting Evaluation by lenders of loan applicant's ability to repay a real estate loan.

Unrestricted Funds A Cal-Vet program for qualified veterans with wartime service.

Unsecured A loan that is not secured by a deed of trust, mortgage, or other property.

U.S. Treasury Cabinet-level agency that manages the federal government's spending and taxing policy.

Usury The charging of interest in excess of that permitted by law.

Usury Law Unlawful rate of interest. In California, the greater of 10 percent or 5 percent over the Federal Reserve Board's discount rate at any given time; however, regulated lenders, such as banks, savings banks, and life insurance companies, are exempt from the usury law. Also exempt are loans arranged by licensed real estate brokers and sellers who carry back.

V

VA (Veterans' Administration) See *Department of Veterans Affairs (DVA)*.

Variable Interest Rate An interest rate that can go up or down according to an independent index, as contrasted with a fixed interest rate that stays the same over the life of the loan.

Verification of Deposit (VOD) Form sent to a loan applicant's bank to verify funds for down payment and closing costs.

Verification of Employment (VOE) Checking on the accuracy of the applicant's information, usually by mailing forms directly to the employer, or by original pay stubs and W-2s.

Vesting The names of owners of real estate and the method or manner in which title is held.

Voucher System A plan to pay for construction costs upon presentation of receipted bills and lien waivers by licensed building contractors, subcontractors, and material suppliers.

VRM Variable Rate Mortgage See *Adjustable Rate Mortgage (ARM)*.

Vrooman Street Act California law that authorizes city councils to issue bonds secured by tax levies for street construction.

W

Waiver Suspension of principal payments on a loan in order to help debtors.

Warehousing Temporary storage of loans pending sale to investors.

Wrap-Around Trust Deed See *All-Inclusive Trust Deed (AITD)*.

Y

Yield The actual interest earned by the lender on the money loaned. Also called *rate of return*, it is usually expressed as a percentage.

Index

M